IELTS EXAMINER'S TIPS

An Academic Guide
to IELTS Speaking and Writing

Karolina Achirri

Chopstick Press
Ann Arbor, MI, USA

IELTS EXAMINER'S TIPS

An Academic Guide
to IELTS Speaking and Writing

KAROLINA ACHIRRI

ISBN-13: 978-1517126056
ISBN-10: 1517126053

CONTENTS

HOW TO USE THIS BOOK

IELTS Examiner's Tips: An Academic Guide to IELTS Speaking and Writing is the outcome of countless hours spent testing as well as assisting students in their preparation for IELTS testing.

This textbook provides you with a comprehensive understanding of the test (specifically its Academic Speaking and Writing components). It affords you with all the tools you will need to succeed in your test. The textbook is made extremely useful by real life examples. If you have already achieved a Band 6 and you're struggling to jump to Bands 7,8 & 9, this book is exactly what you need.

The textbook contains of seven chapters and two handy appendices. You don't have to read them in order. I suggest that you pick the information that is most helpful to your study and apply it.

The first chapter answers over 60 of the most frequently asked questions by test takers regarding IELTS in general and its Writing and Speaking parts. It is exclusive as it presents an experienced examiner's point of view.

The second chapter depicts specific dos and don'ts in IELTS Speaking Room. It also suggests most examiners' biggest pet peeves. There are over 25 examples of things candidates do wrong during their interviews. All of them are explained in a comprehensive way.

Chapter 3 tells you how you'll be assessed. It explains all Bands in a very approachable way.

Chapter 4 focuses on vocabulary. It offers you 100 words that candidates tend to overuse or misuse at IELTS. I have also created a list of more than 2000 substitutes for such words. All my suggestions aim at Band 7 or higher and include phonetic transcription for correct pronunciation. Last but not least, this chapter includes some native expressions for situational English. The hope is to help you sound more natural during the spoken part of your exam.

Next, Chapter 5 occupies the biggest part of this textbook. It focuses on IELTS Speaking. This chapter contains 114 topics for PART 1 with over 1000 questions examiners might ask you. Later, it specifies over 150 topics for Part 2. What's more important, I provide you with over 3200 native level words and phrases that will definitely boost your score. Finally, I list over 3600 real questions for Part 3 your examiner is likely to ask.

Chapter 6 deals with IELTS Writing test. It exhibits and analyzes all possible writing tasks and guides you how to write well. You will find a multitude of tips as to what to write and what not to write in both tasks. I explicate appropriate grammatical structures, punctuation, style and quoting way. You will see visual examples and necessary vocabulary for each question type here. I have also included three exemplar reports and essays for each writing task that would surely receive Bands 8 and 9. This chapter boosts your writing preparation and building skills, and delivers numerous vocabulary pieces for your dream score. Because students often face difficulties with the lack of ideas I have added a bank of 100 most common topics and key ideas that can be directly copied and used where relevant.

The last chapter of this book (Chapter 7) offers discourse markers (e.g. linking words for cohesion) for both IELTS Speaking and Writing. You will find here over 20 conversation fillers native speakers use and lots of discourse markers to express your opinion, compare and contrast, quote, agree, ask for clarification, give examples, etc.

Finally, the two Appendices at the end of this textbook accommodate your need for quotations (especially welcome in your essays) and your knowledge of tenses, explained in a rare and palpable manner.

Why is this textbook unique? Well… An examiner's perspective and authentic vocabulary bank make it simply the most practical guide on the market.

Feel free to use this textbook as your personal source of all you may need to obtain the top-notch score at your IELTS test. Keep calm and study for your IELTS exam!

CHAPTER 1

IELTS FEARS = Q&A section

Ad astra per aspera
(To the stars through difficulty)

GENERAL

1. *Can I use my IELTS score to apply to American universities?*
   Absolutely. IELTS score is currently accepted by most universities in the world. Particular university's website should supply more detailed information.

2. *What's the main difference between IELTS and TOEFL?*
   Both tests are constructed in a completely different way. In practice, TOEFL requires students to be able to understand future lectures and seminars at the university. It does not focus on communication as much as IELTS. The latter checks whether you will be able to easily convey your meaning to professors and classmates abroad. Also, IELTS emphasises language accuracy by paying close attention to grammar and lexis.

3. *If my IELTS score is 5.5, what is its TOEFL equivalent?*

Score Comparisons

IELTS Score	TOEFL Score
9	118-120
8.5	115-117
8	110-114
7.5	102-109
7	94-101
6.5	79-93
6	60-78
5.5	46-59
5	35-45
4.5	32-34
0-4	0-31

SPEAKING

1. *What criteria are used to assess my speaking?*
    There are 4 main categories examiners refer to when giving a score, namely <u>Fluency and Coherence</u>, <u>Lexical Resource</u>, <u>Grammatical Range</u> and <u>Pronunciation</u>.
    <u>Fluency</u> indicates how fluid your speech is, how many pauses you make. It is not about your speed but rather about hesitation, searching for words. The more you pause the lower your fluency score.
    <u>Coherence</u> means you speak logically and all the facts match. Your speech has content that makes sense to the listener. The more 'Why/what do you mean?' you hear from the examiner, the lower your coherence is.
    <u>Lexical Resource</u> represents vocabulary you use throughout your test. If you are targeting scores from 6 to 9, you need to make sure that your answers contain idioms and correct collocations. The more the better but be careful not to sound too artificial.
    <u>Grammatical Range</u> focuses on your sentence structures and grammar mistakes. Be sure to use a variety of structures, from simple sentences to complex ones. The number of mistakes matters as well if you want to cross over band 6. The fewer mistakes the better.
    <u>Pronunciation</u> is not only your accent but also particular sounds. Is your speech easy to understand? Do you use correct intonation and chunking in phrases? Many students worry that American accent is treated unfairly, as IELTS is a British test. I can assure you this is not the case. Generally speaking, examiners listen for elements of native accents, be it American, British, Australian or Canadian.

2. *What shall I focus on for Band 6 and higher?*
    That's a big issue. There seems to be a significant gap between Bands 6 and 7. Your coherence needs to be intact at all times and you need to be able to speak at length easily with a good number of linking words. You need to have enough vocabulary for a variety of topics, which means you should not be looking for words. The examiner needs to hear idiomatic expressions and parts of language, which are not common for day-to-day conversations. After all, IELTS is an academic test. What's more, your grammar should be correct with only a few basic mistakes from time to time. Plus your speech needs to be understood effortlessly by the examiner.

3. *How long is the Speaking test?*
    Part 1 = 4 to 5 minutes
    Part 2 = 3 to 4 minutes
    Part 3 = 4 to 5 minutes
    Which adds it up to between 11 and 14 minutes. Examiners target a 15-minute interview most of the time.

4. *How to speak better and with native (British/American) accent?*
    The only effective way to improve your accent is to not only listen to authentic materials (such as CNN or BBC) but also mimic pronunciation. Try to shape your lips as native speakers do. Observe their body language. Listen to English songs as it is also a grand way to make progress.

5. *Why don't examiners show any emotions?*

IELTS examiners are trained to remain unemotional and inexpressive. Don't take it personally. Their smile or the lack of it will not affect your score.

6. *What shall I do if I have no idea about the topic?*

Well, that seems to be a problem for many test takers. As the age to speak but actually having nothing to say. Not all answers must be your own ideas or opinions. What's important is that you keep going. Use your parents' conversations and TV news to broaden your general knowledge.

7. *How to extend my answers?*

Don't answer in the form of monosyllabic responses, such as 'Yes, no, I agree etc.' If you are using an adjective to describe your favourite book, explain what it means it's 'fascinating' and why you think so. Try to go on until the examiner stops you.

8. *I've taken the test thrice and keep getting 6.5. Why am I not improving?*

Probably because you don't know what your problems are. Ask your teachers to assess your English based on IELTS Speaking Test criteria. It's always better to know where our shortcomings are. This way we can focus on fixing them.

9. *I've practised with Cambridge books (4 to 9). What other materials could I use to prepare well?*

You have certainly made the first step into the right direction by getting this book. Past papers can help you master the test itself but they will not be helpful with skills and general English comprehension. Also, make sure you're using authentic materials prepared by professionals, not books written in your native language.

10. *What shall I do if my examiner interrupts me? Is it good or bad?*

Don't let it worry you. Examiners need to control the time of the interview, so if he or she interrupts you it is most probably because your answer isn't clear enough. Interruptions and additional questions (like 'Why?') are used to clarify your meaning. However, you should be aware that if an examiner needs to make sure they understand what your idea is, your Coherence score will most certainly be affected.

11. *What shall I say if the examiner speaks too fast and I can't catch the question?*

Ask her or him to repeat the question or slow down. It's better to make sure you understood clearly than start answering a completely different question. You will be off-topic then. In normal natural conversation speakers ask for clarification all the time.

12. *How can I overcome my grammar mistakes?*

First, make sure you know the correct grammar. Oftentimes candidates realize they have just made a mistake but they are afraid to correct it, thinking it will affect their score. Self-correction is a very crucial skill in any language. It shows you have awareness of grammar and your mistakes become errors. (For tenses reference see Appendices section of this book.)

13. *Why do I need sophisticated vocabulary for the Speaking test? It seems pretentious.*
You don't need it but it helps if your dream is Band 7 or higher. Remember that IELTS tests whether you can survive in an academic environment when you go abroad. Professors at universities use sophisticated vocabulary. You need it, too.

14. *How to classify and learn vocabulary in a clear way?*
There is an abundance of methods to learn vocabulary in a productive way. But first and foremost you should check what type of a learner you are. There are three main kinds: a visual, auditory and kinaesthetic learner. The first one learns through seeing while the auditory one needs to hear to remember. The last one wants to feel and experience to know. It's important to know which category you fall into.
Personally, I have always liked the concept from psychology called <u>SCREAMS</u>.
• <u>S</u>ay key vocabulary words
• Use <u>C</u>oncept mapping or word webs
• <u>R</u>ead words in context
• <u>E</u>xtract personal meaning
• <u>A</u>ctively learn through using the new word frequently
• <u>M</u>emory formation (sense-making) based on usefulness of the word
• <u>S</u>elf-monitoring for new opportunities to use the newly learned word
Always learn vocabulary in thematic groups (books, food, sounds etc.). A randomly heard word is not going to stay in your long-term memory if your brain cannot connect it with something you already know.

15. *How can I practise Speaking by myself?*
Yes, you can, but… Feedback will be missing. Having a study buddy is always a good idea. You can correct each other and benefit from each other's strengths and weaknesses. It is also a good idea to record your practice sessions and then hand them in to your teacher. A professional linguist will be able to locate problematic areas faster and more effectively.

16. *Do I need to jot anything down in Speaking Part 2?*
It is not a must. Paper and pencil are provided to candidates for the purpose of organizing their long-turn. A lot of test takers take notes but never use them during Part 2. If you decide to write something down, be certain to make use of it.

17. *I know quite a good number of high-level vocabulary but when it comes to my Speaking test my mind goes blank and I can't use any of them. What shall I do?*
It's one thing to understand the words you see in a text or hear around you, but a completely different thing to be able to apply them by yourself. Before coming to your IELTS Speaking Test, try to place 5 'good words' in one complex sentence. The more you'll practise the easier it will get.

18. *How to speak coherently?*
Firstly, listen to the question carefully. If it starts with 'when', talk about the time and not a place where something happened. Then, expand your answer as much as you can but still focus

on the main topic you decided to use. Making mind maps helps with coherence. Remember to ask the examiner to clarify or repeat the question if you are not sure what it refers to.

19. *What shall I do a week before my test?*
Relax. I know it sounds like a cliché, but you have studied hard and prepared for the past month or so. Now is the time for your brain to absorb all the knowledge and organize it. Do not memorize any answers! Think in English! Watch some good English films, read gripping books, talk to native speakers. Keep your stress levels tamed.

20. *How to sound more natural?*
Expose yourself to authentic listening and visual material put together by native speakers of English. BBC and CNN websites yield plenty of functional language material. Mimic chosen pronunciation by speaking out loud and shaping your lips properly. Copy, copy, copy!

21. *Shall I memorize the best answer?*
Never should you do that! Examiners hate memorized answers and believe me when I say it is extremely easy to discern them. A lot of candidates tend to lose logic once they forget one word in a sequence. This will take your score down drastically.

22. *Shall I look at the examiner while speaking?*
Yes. Normally, eye contact is a weighty part of a conversation. If you are too shy to look into your examiner's eyes, pick a spot right behind their head on the wall. Focus on it. To the examiner it will seem like you are still maintaining eye contact. Psychology claims that people who avoid eye contact are potential liars.

23. *Can I sing a song if the topic is related to music?*
Well, it depends on how relaxed you feel your Test is. I know of instances of candidates singing but mostly because they couldn't keep on talking for 2 minutes. It's always better to keep it professional and academic.

24. *Shall I correct my grammar or pronunciation mistakes when I realize I made them?*
Yes, but right after you've made them. Don't say: 'By the way, that sentence I used three questions ago was wrong.' Correct instantly and you will seem as a student with language awareness, which is a highly valued attribute.

25. *Can I ask the examiner to explain words I don't know? Is it going to affect my score?*
Examiners can basically explain words only in Parts 2 and 3. So don't ask: 'Could you rephrase the question?' in Part 1. They simply cannot do that. Only repeating a question once is allowed in Part 1. Asking for vocabulary simplification will affect your Lexical Resource score.

26. *I only covered one point in Part 2. Is that a problem?*
The points provided on a card in Part 2 are only there to help you organize your answer. You do not need to stick to them strictly. Just make sure you cover your topic and you will be fine. Answers like: 'Moving on to the second point…' are not examiners' favourite.

27. *The examiner stopped me. Will this affect my score?*

Usually when an examiner stops a candidate it means candidate's answer was clear and comprehensive. It simply means you were still talking when the time earmarked for your answer came to an end. Nothing to worry about.

28. *Can I ask the examiner to change my topic in Part 2?*

Unfortunately no, you can't. The topics are chosen for you before you enter the exam room. One part of being a capable English speaker entails the ability to talk about any topic.

29. *How can I come across as more confident during my test?*

Try to maintain eye contact. Sit up and react to questions with appropriate body language. As I always tell my students: 'Don't be a robot!'

30. *Can I give short answers?*

You can, but it will affect the Grammatical Range criterion. Follow one simple rule: ABS, which stands for ALWAYS BE SPEAKING! And you'll be fine. Beyond everything, you have come to the test to exhibit your English at its best.

31. *Does being fluent mean I need to speak fast?*

No, it does not. This concept is often mistaken. Being fluent means you do not need to pause too often to search for language to express yourself. Your speech pace has nothing to do with it.

32. *Will the examiner give me a higher score if I dress well and look pretty?*

Your attire is not a subject of assessment. Dress smart but comfortably. Also, contrary to what many female candidates believe, putting on heavy make-up to impress the examiner is not the most tenable notion.

WRITING

1. *On what factors is my Writing assessed?*

There are four criteria used for writing evaluation. Three of them are identical for Task 1 and 2 (Coherence and Cohesion, Lexical Resource and Grammatical Range and Accuracy), whereas one differs. In Task 1 it is called Task Achievement and in Task 2 Task Response.

Coherence represents logic of your writing and cohesion stands for linking words and the way you connect your ideas with each other. Lexical Resource means vocabulary you use, including collocations and idioms, but also spelling errors you make. Grammatical Range and Accuracy conveys the meaning of grammar errors as well as punctuation. The more error-free sentences you can write the higher your score will be.

As for Task Achievement in Task 1, it focuses on covering all requirements of the task, presenting a clear overview, categorizing information well and developing response in a clear way. Similarly, in Task 2, a candidate should not only present the main ideas but also extend and support them without overgeneralizing. Ideas need to be shown in a detailed way and supported with relevant examples.

2. *What shall I focus on for Band 6 and higher?*
In the Writing test, presenting a clear overview is extremely pivotal. Make sure you cover all major features. You may skip the details but the bullet points need to be present. In Task 2, your position should be obvious as well. The information needs to be organized logically and with a progressive trend, which basically means it needs to go somewhere. For Band 7 and higher, the number of grammar mistakes matters as well as your awareness of style and usage of idioms and collocations. The essay should present a wide range of sentence structures including a good number of complex sentences. Your writing does not need to be error free but only some slips should occur. Basically, the examiner needs to feel like nothing could be added to your answer.

3. *Which part of my writing test is more important? Task 1 or Task 2?*
Task 2 carries 60% of your final score for writing whereas Task 1 holds 40%.

4. *How many words shall I write in both parts of my writing test? Will I be penalized if I write fewer/more than required?*
There is a very clear word count for both parts of your Writing test. Task 1 should ideally have 150 words whereas Task 2 250. It is ok to exceed by 10%, but remember that the more you write the more mistakes you will most likely make. When it comes to writing too few words, your Task Achievement/Response criterion will be affected. The breakdown of penalties is as follows:
Task 1: 101-140 minus 1 in Task Achievement or Task Response, 51-100 minus 2 in TA/TR and below 51 words will cost you minus 3 in TA/TR category.

5. *How much time do I have for each Task?*
It is suggested that you spend 20 minutes on Task 1 and 40 minutes on Task 2. But of course it is up to you. Totally you will have 60 min for your Writing Test. I suggest you start with the task that you find more troublesome.

6. *What can I do if I don't understand the topic for Task 2 or simply have nothing to say on the topic?*
It's always important to show general knowledge on your IELTS test. However, if you really don't know anything about the topic and can't come up with any examples, write anyway. Change a topic slightly and write the essay. You will be penalised for the lack of logic, but the examiner will still assess your grammar and vocabulary. It is still possible to get a Band 3 or 4 even if your essay is completely off-topic.

7. *How to make the essay shorter and more to the point?*
Start with a plan. Many IELTS takers underestimate the power of a well-thought plan. It takes a minute but helps enormously with writing logically and providing pertinent ideas. Your plan can be in a form of a mind map, spider diagram or just rudimentary annotations. The form does not matter as long as you use it as the basis for your essay.

8. *How can I overcome my grammar mistakes?*
It may come to you as a surprise, but if only you read or scanned your essay before handing it in, you would be able to spot 50% of your mistakes. From my experience, the lion's share

of candidates does not bother to self-correct their writings. There is definitely enough time to do it, as it only takes a minute. Remember to correct what you can before your essay gets to examiners' hands.

9. *How to be logical in Writing?*

Follow the draft! I cannot emphasize this enough. The only way to start logically and stay cogent is to abide by your own strategy. Also, you would want to make sure that you use linking words properly, as for example 'and' and 'but' express two completely different concepts in one sentence.

10. *How can I practise my Writing more efficiently?*

Read more. By reading academic sources you will be able to not only broaden your vocabulary but also get accustomed to an assortment of phrases and sentences. Showing your writings to your teacher or classmate is a marvellous inkling too. They will be able to see what you might fail to catch.

11. *Can I use a model for my Writing?*

I do not advise it. It might work for TOEFL writing, but when it comes to IELTS models are just not inclusive enough. Besides, using a model for your introduction and conclusion could uncover your shortcomings. Any examiner is surely qualified to notice the difference between your language and the language used in the model. This will most definitely take your score down.

12. *How to make sure my essay is not boring?*

There is no good answer to this question. What I usually tell my students is to make sure they provide examples stemming from societal current events rather than their own circle of family and friends. Instead of using your uncle or your cousin to illustrate your point, say it is a trend in your society. This will make your paragraphs stronger and more gripping to read.

13. *Shall I use social news and events in my Writing?*

Yes, you should. This way your answers will be better rounded and you will come across as a young person who cares about the events in the world. Personalizing your essay isn't advised as it is against the idea of an academic form of writing.

14. *Is there enough time to write a draft?*

Yes, because you do not need to write it per se. All you need to do is jot down some ideas and organize them in a logical way, that is in a way which would make sense to you in your further writing process.

15. *Can I write in capital letters?*

Yes, it is not forbidden, so you are allowed to do so.

16. *What is a well-developed paragraph?*

Each paragraph should ideally consist of a topic sentence, which tells the reader what the paragraph is about; three to five supporting sentences (providing details, examples) and a concluding sentence, where you wrap up your ideas.

So if I were to give you a formula, it would look like this:

Topic Sentence = 1 sentence

Supporting Sentences = 3 to 5 sentences

Concluding Sentence = 1 sentence

17. *Can I use personal pronouns in Task 2?*

As mentioned before, IELTS writing is an academic type of writing, so personal pronouns should not occur. Only when expressing your opinion or conviction can you use 'I'. In order to avoid 'I' use group nouns, such as people or society; or refer to a particular part of your essay, e.g. 'This part of the essay will focus on…'. Definitely steer clear from using 'I' in Task 1. Your opinion is also not needed as you are to comment on facts and interpret data given.

12

CHAPTER 2

DOs and DON'Ts in IELTS Speaking Room
Examiners' pet peeves

Ipsa scientia potestas est
(Knowledge itself is power)

- Don't make mistakes in simple English, especially when it comes to grammar. That will stop you from getting Band 6.
  Examples: he/she, people is, she don't know etc.

- Don't use words you're not sure how to pronounce! It's better to change a word you have in mind into one you are more confident with. Don't show your limitations! Focus on your strengths!

- Lie, but show off☺! Not everything you are saying needs to be 100% true. It's okay to use other people's ideas. What matters most is to show the best language you have during your 15-minute interview. The examiner will not know whether your story is true, anyway.

- Don't be afraid to correct yourself or ask for a clarification if you're not certain about your question. Many candidates are afraid to ask to have their questions repeated and then start answering completely different ones. This situation affects their coherence. Always make sure you understand the question correctly. It is okay to ask for explanation, repetition or an unfamiliar word explanation. No one will penalize you for it.

- Pronounce clearly. If the examiner has problems understanding you due to your frequent mispronunciations, your score will go down to a 4. Here, not only particular sounds matter but also your intonation and chunking. Enunciate with exaggeration if you have to, but assure being understood.

- If you want to use idioms, use them correctly and regularly. Saying 'it's raining cats and dogs' once in a blue moon is not going to improve your score. Candidates dreaming of Band 7 must show the ability to utilize idiomatic expressions throughout the entire test.

- Don't be thrown off by examiners' poker faces. That's how they are trained. It is not personal so don't try to read into it. If they don't smile it's because they are focusing on giving you the most equitable score, not because they hate you.

- Record yourself and listen to it! This is very important before you come to your interview. Recording your own speech not only helps you spot pronunciation problems but also allows you to sound more natural and relaxed. Pay special attention to your intonation as it needs to be clear for Band 6 and higher.

- Speak until you are stopped. I can't emphasise this part enough. As I mentioned in Chapter 1, ABS is extremely handy to bear in mind during your Speaking Test. Always be Speaking! It shows your examiner that you are capable of conducting a longer conversation and that you can discuss topics at length and in depth.

- Display your best English! Exhibit your assets and conceal your flaws. Do not use a word if you are not sure how to. Use a different piece of vocabulary if you can't pronounce the word you have in mind. Do not say: 'I don't know anything about it', but rather go with 'I'm not so sure about this particular point, but I'd still say…'. You only have around 15 minutes to convince your examiner that you deserve a 7☺.

- Don't chop phrases according to intonation patterns in your native language. Make sure your sentences convey the same meaning by making your voice modulation more musical. Listening to lots of English songs is strongly advised here. You can copy the pitch and later on use it in your own answers.

- Listen carefully to the question! Questions are often similar but start with different question words: why, when, who, what, where, how. Be aware of the wh- words. It's a common mistake to focus only on key words in a question and ignore its full sense.

- Use the minute for preparation in Part 2 to organize your thoughts or simply calm yourself down. You are about to speak continuously for 2 minutes, so you need composure. Candidates who don't use paper and pencil provided tend to jump erratically from thought to thought making their examiner confused or dizzy. It's not a race. What you say is more important than how fast you utter it.

- Hesitation and pausing. A lot of test takers suffer from these two problems. It takes them many seconds to formulate an answer and even if they do, they pause lengthy after almost every sentence. This will keep their Fluency at 5. Speak more slowly but more persistently.

- Wrong tenses. Especially in Part 2, where many questions refer to past experiences, candidates forget about Past Simple and everything they say is in the Present. Since there is no free standing Grammar part on IELTS, this is how the test checks your grammar. If you always forget about it, write it down in the notebook provided. Also, make sure you know what tense a specific question should keep to. For this, read your prompt card carefully!

- Breathe & smile!!! In order to create a natural conversation with an examiner you need to become friends with your breathing and your smile. Sometimes my candidates look like they are going to lose consciousness with their faces looking pale and drawn. You do not need to say everything you want to say on one breath. You shouldn't. It's not natural. Smile even if your examiner doesn't, to imprint an impression of a friendly and easy-going person you are.

- Know the differences between Parts 1, 2 and 3. A lot of candidates do not know that Part 1 checks your personal experiences, so you are supposed to use 'I' in most of your answers. Part 2 likes to ask a candidate to describe, be it a person, a place or a situation. For this reason, it requires some descriptive vocabulary. Conversely, Part's 3 central point is the society. It would most likely refer to the media, culture and future predictions, all based on general knowledge, hence more universal answers are expected here. Despite the fact that by Part 3 your examiner already has a pretty good idea of what your level is, your score is always validated by your replies in Part 3.

- Don't try to be so American! There are some students of English who want to come across as very Westernized, so they would throw 'OMG' in between every two words they say. Don't pretend to be someone you are not. Be yourself.

- Don't spend too much time on memorizing and rote learning, but concentrate on developing skills (esp. for speaking and listening). This test checks your general English abilities, which means it is easy to see the gap between your real answers and the ones you have memorized. Trying to remember 50 words a day is also a bad idea. You won't know how to use them. Always use context related to your own life to study vocabulary and write down whole collocations, not just single words.

- Always answer the questions first! Don't give me the context of the whole story. Don't beat about the bush! Get to the point first and then extend it by providing extra information.

- Don't be a 'YES man'! You are not expected to agree with everything the examiner says. You must show your own opinions and views. Don't be afraid to say: 'I completely disagree with this statement'. If you don't like nature, say it!

- Be different! Don't use Kobe and basketball as your answer to every single question. If you are asked what's your favourite animal, say it's a 'gecko' instead of 'dog'. Originality will be rewarded.

- Use signposts! Linking words add to your cohesion and also help the examiner follow your logical thinking. You will find a complete list of signpost expressions in Chapter 7 of this book.

- Paraphrase! It doesn't matter how many years you have been studying English. There will always be words you simply don't know as a non-native speaker. Nobody is a walking dictionary☺. Not knowing the word for something you wish to express happens often in a test when you are feeling nervous. So, this is where the skill of paraphrasing comes in. It basically means you are able to describe a word using other words, such as synonyms, parallel expressions or descriptive adjectives.

CHAPTER 3

HOW WILL YOU BE ASSESSED?
ASSESSMENT CRITERIA

Aut viam inveniam aut faciam
(I'll either find a way or make one)

The information below will give you a sense of what competence is required for each band score.

Band 9: Expert User
Has a full command of the language: appropriate, accurate, fluent and effortless with complete understanding.

Band 8: Very good user
Has a full command of the language with occasional unsystematic errors. Confusion may occur in atypical or unfamiliar situations. Is able to formulate advanced and detailed arguments.

Band 7: Good user
Has advanced command of the language, though with a few occasional errors in some situations. Generally uses sophisticated vocabulary and complex syntax well. Comprehends detailed reasoning.

Band 6: Competent user
Has capable command of the language despite some errors and misunderstandings. Can use and comprehend moderately complex language, but mainly in familiar and typical situations.

Band 5: Modest user
Has limited command of the language. Is able to understand overall meaning in routine and typical situations. Makes numerous errors and has difficulty with the general meaning of conversations. Should be able to handle basic communication in own field.

Band 4: Limited user
Has limited basic competence restricted to routine and typical situations only. Has frequent problems with understanding and expression. Uses only simplistic vocabulary and syntax. Isn't able to use complex language.

Ban 3: Extremely limited user
Cannot follow a quite simple and common conversation even with the most simplistic vocabulary and syntax. Conveys and comprehends only general meaning in very familiar situations. Breakdowns in communication occur frequently.

Band 2: Intermittent user
No real communication is possible. Can only use isolated words and syntax to express basic needs. Has great difficulty understanding spoken and written English.

Band 1: Non user
Has basically no ability to use the language. Knows only a small number of random words. Has no understanding of English at all.

Band 0: Did not attempt the test

SPEAKING

Band	Fluency and coherence	Lexical resource	Grammatical range and accuracy	Pronunciation
9	• speaks fluently with only rare repetition or self-correction; any hesitation is content-related rather than to find words or grammar • speaks coherently with fully appropriate cohesive features • develops topics fully and appropriately	• uses vocabulary with full flexibility and precision in all topics • uses idiomatic language naturally and accurately	• uses a full range of structures naturally and appropriately • produces consistently accurate structures apart from 'slips' characteristic of native speaker speech	• uses a full range of pronunciation features with precision and subtlety • sustains flexible use of features throughout • is effortless to understand
8	• speaks fluently with only occasional repetition or self-correction; hesitation is usually content-related and only rarely to search for language • develops topics coherently and appropriately	• uses a wide vocabulary resource readily and flexibly to convey precise meaning • uses less common and idiomatic vocabulary skilfully, with occasional inaccuracies • uses paraphrase effectively as required	• uses a wide range of structures flexibly • produces a majority of error-free sentences with only very occasional inappropriacies or basic/non-systematic errors	• uses a wide range of pronunciation features • sustains flexible use of features, with only occasional lapses • is easy to understand throughout; L1 accent has minimal effect on intelligibility
7	• speaks at length without noticeable effort or loss of coherence • may demonstrate language-related hesitation at times, or some repetition and/or self-correction • uses a range of connectives and discourse markers with some flexibility	• uses vocabulary resource flexibly to discuss a variety of topics • uses some less common and idiomatic vocabulary and shows some awareness of style and collocation, with some inappropriate choices • uses paraphrase effectively	• uses a range of complex structures with some flexibility • frequently produces error-free sentences, though some grammatical mistakes persist	• shows all the positive features of Band 6 and some, but not all, of the positive features of Band 8
6	• is willing to speak at length, though may lose coherence at times due to occasional repetition, self-correction or hesitation • uses a range of connectives and discourse markers but not always appropriately	• has a wide enough vocabulary to discuss topics at length and make meaning clear in spite of inappropriacies • generally paraphrases successfully	• uses a mix of simple and complex structures, but with limited flexibility • may make frequent mistakes with complex structures, though these rarely cause comprehension problems	• uses a range of pronunciation features with mixed control • shows some effective use of features but this is not sustained • can generally be understood throughout, though mispronunciation of individual words or sounds reduces clarity at times
5	• usually maintains flow of speech but uses repetition, self-correction and/or slow speech to keep going • may over-use certain connectives and discourse markers • produces simple speech fluently, but more complex communication causes fluency problems	• manages to talk about familiar and unfamiliar topics but uses vocabulary with limited flexibility • attempts to use paraphrase but with mixed success	• produces basic sentence forms with reasonable accuracy • uses a limited range of more complex structures, but these usually contain errors and may cause some comprehension problems	• shows all the positive features of Band 4 and some, but not all, of the positive features of Band 6
4	• cannot respond without noticeable pauses and may speak slowly, with frequent repetition and self-correction • links basic sentences but with repetitious use of simple connectives and some breakdowns in coherence	• is able to talk about familiar topics but can only convey basic meaning on unfamiliar topics and makes frequent errors in word choice • rarely attempts paraphrase	• produces basic sentence forms and some correct simple sentences but subordinate structures are rare • errors are frequent and may lead to misunderstanding	• uses a limited range of pronunciation features • attempts to control features but lapses are frequent • mispronunciations are frequent and cause some difficulty for the listener
3	• speaks with long pauses • has limited ability to link simple sentences • gives only simple responses and is frequently unable to convey basic message	• uses simple vocabulary to convey personal information • has insufficient vocabulary for less familiar topics	• attempts basic sentence forms but with limited success, or relies on apparently memorised utterances • makes numerous errors except in memorised expressions	• shows some of the features of Band 2 and some, but not all, of the positive features of Band 4
2	• pauses lengthily before most words • little communication possible	• only produces isolated words or memorised utterances	• cannot produce basic sentence forms	• speech is often unintelligible
1	• no communication possible			
0	• does not attend			

22

Band	Task Achievement	Coherence and Cohesion	Lexical Resource	Grammatical Range and Accuracy
9	- fully satisfies all the requirements of the task - clearly presents a fully developed response	- uses cohesion in such a way that it attracts no attention - skilfully manages paragraphing	- uses a wide range of vocabulary with very natural and sophisticated control of lexical features; rare minor errors occur only as 'slips'	- uses a wide range of structures with full flexibility and accuracy; rare minor errors occur only as 'slips'
8	- covers all requirements of the task sufficiently - presents, highlights and illustrates key features / bullet points clearly and appropriately	- sequences information and ideas logically - manages all aspects of cohesion well - uses paragraphing sufficiently and appropriately	- uses a wide range of vocabulary fluently and flexibly to convey precise meanings - skilfully uses uncommon lexical items but there may be occasional inaccuracies in word choice and collocation - produces rare errors in spelling and/or word formation	- uses a wide range of structures - the majority of sentences are error-free - makes only very occasional errors or inappropriacies
7	- covers the requirements of the task - (Academic) presents a clear overview of main trends, differences or stages - (General Training) presents a clear purpose, with the tone consistent and appropriate - clearly presents and highlights key features / bullet points but could be more fully extended	- logically organises information and ideas; there is clear progression throughout - uses a range of cohesive devices appropriately although there may be some under-/over-use	- uses a sufficient range of vocabulary to allow some flexibility and precision - uses less common lexical items with some awareness of style and collocation - may produce occasional errors in word choice, spelling and/or word formation	- uses a variety of complex structures - produces frequent error-free sentences - has good control of grammar and punctuation but may make a few errors
6	- addresses the requirements of the task - (Academic) presents an overview with information appropriately selected - (General Training) presents a purpose that is generally clear; there may be inconsistencies in tone - presents and adequately highlights key features / bullet points but details may be irrelevant, inappropriate or inaccurate	- arranges information and ideas coherently and there is a clear overall progression - uses cohesive devices effectively, but cohesion within and/or between sentences may be faulty or mechanical - may not always use referencing clearly or appropriately	- uses an adequate range of vocabulary for the task - attempts to use less common vocabulary but with some inaccuracy - makes some errors in spelling and/or word formation, but they do not impede communication	- uses a mix of simple and complex sentence forms - makes some errors in grammar and punctuation but they rarely reduce communication

Band	Task Achievement	Coherence and Cohesion	Lexical Resource	Grammatical Range and Accuracy
5	▪ generally addresses the task; the format may be inappropriate in places ▪ (Academic) recounts detail mechanically with no clear overview; there may be no data to support the description ▪ (General Training) may present a purpose for the letter that is unclear at times; the tone may be variable and sometimes inappropriate ▪ presents, but inadequately covers, key features / bullet points; there may be a tendency to focus on details	▪ presents information with some organisation but there may be a lack of overall progression ▪ makes inadequate, inaccurate or over-use of cohesive devices ▪ may be repetitive because of lack of referencing and substitution	▪ uses a limited range of vocabulary, but this is minimally adequate for the task ▪ may make noticeable errors in spelling and/or word formation that may cause some difficulty for the reader	▪ uses only a limited range of structures ▪ attempts complex sentences but these tend to be less accurate than simple sentences ▪ may make frequent grammatical errors and punctuation may be faulty; errors can cause some difficulty for the reader
4	▪ attempts to address the task but does not cover all key features / bullet points; the format may be inappropriate ▪ (General Training) fails to clearly explain the purpose of the letter; the tone may be inappropriate ▪ may confuse key features / bullet points with detail; parts may be unclear, irrelevant, repetitive or inaccurate	▪ presents information and ideas but these are not arranged coherently and there is no clear progression in the response ▪ uses some basic cohesive devices but these may be inaccurate or repetitive	▪ uses only basic vocabulary which may be used repetitively or which may be inappropriate for the task ▪ has limited control of word formation and/or spelling; ▪ errors may cause strain for the reader	▪ uses only a very limited range of structures with only rare use of subordinate clauses ▪ some structures are accurate but errors predominate, and punctuation is often faulty
3	▪ fails to address the task, which may have been completely misunderstood ▪ presents limited ideas which may be largely irrelevant/repetitive	▪ does not organise ideas logically ▪ may use a very limited range of cohesive devices, and those used may not indicate a logical relationship between ideas	▪ uses only a very limited range of words and expressions with very limited control of word formation and/or spelling ▪ errors may severely distort the message	▪ attempts sentence forms but errors in grammar and punctuation predominate and distort the meaning
2	▪ answer is barely related to the task	▪ has very little control of organisational features	▪ uses an extremely limited range of vocabulary; essentially no control of word formation and/or spelling	▪ cannot use sentence forms except in memorised phrases
1	▪ answer is completely unrelated to the task	▪ fails to communicate any message	▪ can only use a few isolated words	▪ cannot use sentence forms at all
0	▪ does not attend ▪ does not attempt the task in any way ▪ writes a totally memorised response			

Band	Task Response	Coherence and Cohesion	Lexical Resource	Grammatical Range and Accuracy
9	▪ fully addresses all parts of the task ▪ presents a fully developed position in answer to the question with relevant, fully extended and well supported ideas	▪ uses cohesion in such a way that it attracts no attention ▪ skilfully manages paragraphing	▪ uses a wide range of vocabulary with very natural and sophisticated control of lexical features; rare minor errors occur only as 'slips'	▪ uses a wide range of structures with full flexibility and accuracy; rare minor errors occur only as 'slips'
8	▪ sufficiently addresses all parts of the task ▪ presents a well-developed response to the question with relevant, extended and supported ideas	▪ sequences information and ideas logically ▪ manages all aspects of cohesion well ▪ uses paragraphing sufficiently and appropriately	▪ uses a wide range of vocabulary fluently and flexibly to convey precise meanings ▪ skilfully uses uncommon lexical items but there may be occasional inaccuracies in word choice and collocation ▪ produces rare errors in spelling and/or word formation	▪ uses a wide range of structures ▪ the majority of sentences are error-free ▪ makes only very occasional errors or inappropriacies
7	▪ addresses all parts of the task ▪ presents a clear position throughout the response ▪ presents, extends and supports main ideas, but there may be a tendency to over-generalise and/or supporting ideas may lack focus	▪ logically organises information and ideas; there is clear progression throughout ▪ uses a range of cohesive devices appropriately although there may be some under-/over-use ▪ presents a clear central topic within each paragraph	▪ uses a sufficient range of vocabulary to allow some flexibility and precision ▪ uses less common lexical items with some awareness of style and collocation ▪ may produce occasional errors in word choice, spelling and/or word formation	▪ uses a variety of complex structures ▪ produces frequent error-free sentences ▪ has good control of grammar and punctuation but may make a few errors
6	▪ addresses all parts of the task although some parts may be more fully covered than others ▪ presents a relevant position although the conclusions may become unclear or repetitive ▪ presents relevant main ideas but some may be inadequately developed/unclear	▪ arranges information and ideas coherently and there is a clear overall progression ▪ uses cohesive devices effectively, but cohesion within and/or between sentences may be faulty or mechanical ▪ may not always use referencing clearly or appropriately ▪ uses paragraphing, but not always logically	▪ uses an adequate range of vocabulary for the task ▪ attempts to use less common vocabulary but with some inaccuracy ▪ makes some errors in spelling and/or word formation, but they do not impede communication	▪ uses a mix of simple and complex sentence forms ▪ makes some errors in grammar and punctuation but they rarely reduce communication
5	▪ addresses the task only partially; the format may be inappropriate in places ▪ expresses a position but the development is not always clear and there may be no	▪ presents information with some organisation but there may be a lack of overall progression ▪ makes inadequate, inaccurate or over-	▪ uses a limited range of vocabulary, but this is minimally adequate for the task ▪ may make noticeable errors in	▪ uses only a limited range of structures ▪ attempts complex sentences but these tend to be less accurate than simple sentences

Band	Task Response	Coherence and Cohesion	Lexical Resource	Grammatical Range and Accuracy
(5)	• conclusions drawn • presents some main ideas but these are limited and not sufficiently developed; there may be irrelevant detail	• use of cohesive devices • may be repetitive because of lack of referencing and substitution • may not write in paragraphs, or paragraphing may be inadequate	• spelling and/or word formation that may cause some difficulty for the reader	• may make frequent grammatical errors and punctuation may be faulty; errors can cause some difficulty for the reader
4	• responds to the task only in a minimal way or the answer is tangential; the format may be inappropriate • presents a position but this is unclear • presents some main ideas but these are difficult to identify and may be repetitive, irrelevant or not well supported	• presents information and ideas but these are not arranged coherently and there is no clear progression in the response • uses some basic cohesive devices but these may be inaccurate or repetitive • may not write in paragraphs or their use may be confusing	• uses only basic vocabulary which may be used repetitively or which may be inappropriate for the task • has limited control of word formation and/or spelling; errors may cause strain for the reader	• uses only a very limited range of structures with only rare use of subordinate clauses • some structures are accurate but errors predominate, and punctuation is often faulty
3	• does not adequately address any part of the task • does not express a clear position • presents few ideas, which are largely undeveloped or irrelevant	• does not organise ideas logically • may use a very limited range of cohesive devices, and those used may not indicate a logical relationship between ideas	• uses only a very limited range of words and expressions with very limited control of word formation and/or spelling • errors may severely distort the message	• attempts sentence forms but errors in grammar and punctuation predominate and distort the meaning
2	• barely responds to the task • does not express a position • may attempt to present one or two ideas but there is no development	• has very little control of organisational features	• uses an extremely limited range of vocabulary; essentially no control of word formation and/or spelling	• cannot use sentence forms except in memorised phrases
1	• answer is completely unrelated to the task	• fails to communicate any message	• can only use a few isolated words	• cannot use sentence forms at all
0	• does not attend • does not attempt the task in any way • writes a totally memorised response			

CHAPTER 4

VOCABULARY OFTEN MISUSED
AND OVERUSED
& HOW TO DEAL WITH IT

Verba movent, exempla trahunt.
(Words move people, examples draw them.)

This Chapter is particularly significant for both your Speaking and Writing tests. I have collected a huge number of words that candidates overuse or misuse in the test. I am also providing copious substitutes to help you achieve score 7 and higher (part of the criteria is to show a broad range of vocabulary). However, make sure you use them correctly in your writing and pronounce them right during your Speaking Test. Good luck!

1. **MAYBE** /ˈmeɪbi/ adverb, noun

COMMON MISTAKE!
NOTE: Do not use 'maybe' when asked about your preferences! It ruins logic in your answer!
For example: Do you like to visit museums? Maybe. (x)

- possibly /ˈpɒsəbli/ adv.
- conceivably /kənˈsiːvəb(ə)li/ adv.
- perhaps /pə(r)ˈhæps/ adv.
- perchance /pə(r)ˈtʃɑːns/ formal, adv. (more suitable for writing)
- apparently /əˈpærəntli/ adv.
- in all likelihood /ˈlaɪklihʊd/ phr. = almost certainly
- in all probability /ˌprɒbəˈbɪləti/ phr.
- most likely /məʊst ˈlaɪkli/ phr.
- one can assume that… /əˈsjuːm/ phr.
- presumably /prɪˈzjuːməbli/ adv.
- to all appearances /əˈpɪərənsiz/ phr.
- probably /ˈprɒbəbli/ adv.
- for all I know = phr. used to emphasize that you do not know something

2. **ADVANTAGE VS. DISADVANTAGE** /ədˈvɑːntɪdʒ/ vs. /ˌdɪsədˈvɑːntɪdʒ/ noun

NOTE: advantages and disadvantages of sth
e.g. *There are multiple advantages and disadvantages of studying abroad.*
PAY ATTENTION TO PREPOSITIONS!!!

All pairs below can be used instead of advantage/disadvantage:

- reasons for sth vs. reasons against sth /ˈriːz(ə)nz/
- arguments for sth vs. arguments against sth /ˈɑː(r)gjʊmənts/
- strengths of sth/to do sth vs. weaknesses of/in sth /streŋθs/ vs. /ˈwiːknəsɪz/
- pluses of sth vs. minuses of sth /plʌsɪz/ vs. /ˈmaɪnəsɪz/
- plus factors of sth vs. minus factors of sth
  /ˈplʌs fæktə(r)z/ vs. /ˈmaɪnəs fæktə(r)z/
- pros of sth vs. cons of sth /prəʊz/ vs. /kɒnz/
- benefits of sth vs. drawbacks of sth /ˈbenɪfɪts/ vs. /ˈdrɔːˌbæks/
- good points of sth vs. bad points of sth /ˈgʊd pɔɪnts/ vs. /ˈbæd pɔɪnts/
- profits in sth/doing sth vs. hindrances to sth /ˈprɒfɪts/ vs. /ˈhɪndrənsɪz/
- assets to sth vs. impediments to sth /ˈæsets/ vs. /ɪmˈpedɪmənts/

- ✍ conveniences of sth vs. inconveniences of sth
  /kənˈviːniənsɪz/ vs. /ˌɪnkənˈviːniənsɪz/
- ✍ strong points of sth vs. weak points of sth
  /ˈstrɒŋ pɔɪnts/ vs. /ˈwiːk pɔɪnts/

Words below are to be used separately (not as a pair) and can be used both in singular and plural forms:

Advantage:

- ✍ blessing of sth /ˈblesɪŋ/
- ✍ value of sth /ˈvæljuː/
- ✍ plus point of sth /ˈplʌs pɔɪnt/
- ✍ virtue of sth/in doing sth /ˈvɜː(r)tʃuː/
- ✍ boon to/for sth /buːn/
- ✍ fruit of sth /fruːt/
- ✍ aid to sth /eɪd/
- ✍ gain to sth /ɡeɪn/
- ✍ perquisite of sth /ˈpɜː(r)kwɪzɪt/ (formal)
- ✍ perk of sth /pɜː(r)k/
- ✍ pay-off of sth /ˈpeɪɒf/ (informal)
- ✍ beauty of sth /ˈbjuːti/

Disadvantage:

- ✍ liability to sth /ˌlaɪəˈbɪləti/
- ✍ handicap to/of sth /ˈhændiˌkæp/
- ✍ limitation of sth /ˌlɪmɪˈteɪʃ(ə)n/
- ✍ disamenity /ˌdɪsəˈmiːnɪti/ (best used at the end of the phrase, e.g. *Two main sources of disamenity are tourism and weather.*)
- ✍ flaw in sth /flɔː/
- ✍ defect in sth /ˈdiːfekt/
- ✍ trouble with sth /ˈtrʌb(ə)l/
- ✍ catch in sth /kætʃ/
- ✍ disbenefit of/to sth /dɪsˈbenɪfɪt/ (formal)
- ✍ downside of sth /ˈdaʊnˌsaɪd/ (informal)
- ✍ hang-up in sth /ˈhæŋ ʌp/ (AmE, informal)
- ✍ weak link in the chain (informal)

3. **DELICIOUS** /dɪˈlɪʃəs/ adjective

> NOTE: You cannot say 'very delicious',
> e.g. ~~French food is very delicious.~~
> Instead say: French food is very tasty.

- ☞ tasty /'teɪsti/
- ☞ palatable /'pælətəb(ə)l/
- ☞ appetizing /'æpəˌtaɪzɪŋ/
- ☞ mouth-watering /'maʊθ wɔːtə(r)ɪŋ/
- ☞ juicy /'dʒuːsi/
- ☞ succulent /'sʌkjʊlənt/ = tender, juicy and tasty
- ☞ toothsome /'tuːθs(ə)m/
- ☞ savoury /'seɪvəri/
- ☞ tempting /'temptɪŋ/
- ☞ melting in the mouth
- ☞ delectable /dɪ'lektəb(ə)l/ (formal)
- ☞ nectareous /nek'tɛːrɪəs/ (formal)
- ☞ ambrosial /æm'brəʊziəl/ (formal)
- ☞ delish /dɪ'lɪʃ/ (informal)
- ☞ scrumptious /'skrʌmpʃəs/ (informal) = extremely appetizing
- ☞ yummy /'jʌmi/ (informal)
- ☞ lip-smacking /'lɪp smækɪŋ/ (informal)
- ☞ flavoursome /'fleɪvə(r)səm/
- ☞ inviting /ɪn'vaɪtɪŋ/
- ☞ very enjoyable /'ɪn'dʒɔɪəb(ə)l/
- ☞ yum-yum /jʌm 'jʌm/ (informal)
- ☞ moreish /'mɔːrɪʃ/ (BE, informal)
- ☞ sapid /'sæpɪd/ = having a strong, pleasant taste

4. **TO RELAX** /rɪ'læks/ verb

Note: This verb is intransitive, which means you cannot say:
~~Relax yourself/myself!~~ (x)
e.g. *Jogging relaxes me.*

- ☞ to rest /rest/
- ☞ to unwind /ʌn'waɪnd/
- ☞ to wind down /waɪnd 'daʊn/
- ☞ to loosen up /luːs(ə)n 'ʌp/
- ☞ to de-stress /diː'stres/
- ☞ to tranquilize /'træŋkwɪlaɪz/
- ☞ to unbend /ʌn'bend/ (informal)
- ☞ to take things easy
- ☞ to let your hair down
- ☞ to put your feet up
- ☞ to chill (out) /tʃɪl/ (informal)
- ☞ to veg out /vedʒ 'aʊt/
- ☞ to chillax /tʃɪl'æks/ (informal)
- ☞ to ease up /iːz'ʌp/
- ☞ to calm down /kɑːm 'daʊn/

- ↻ to become less tense
- ↻ to slack off /slæk'ɒf/ (informal)
- ↻ to sit back /sɪt 'bæk/
- ↻ to unbutton /ʌn'bʌt(ə)n/
- ↻ to kick back /kɪk'bæk/ (AmE, informal)

5. **SCHOOL** /skuːl/ noun

- ↻ college /'kɒlɪdʒ/ = after high school
- ↻ academy /ə'kædəmi/ = place of study in a specific field e.g. a police academy
- ↻ institute /'ɪnstɪˌtjuːt/ = an educational organization e.g. the Institute of Social Studies
- ↻ educational institution /ˌedjʊ'keɪʃ(ə)nəl ˌɪnstɪ'tjuːʃ(ə)n/
- ↻ university /ˌjuːnɪ'vɜː(r)səti/
- ↻ alma mater /ˌælmə 'mɑːtə(r)/ = a school that one once attended

6. **A SKILL** /skɪl/ noun

- ↻ ability to do sth /ə'bɪləti/
- ↻ skillfulness of sth /'skɪlf(ə)lnes/
- ↻ aptitude for sth /'æptɪˌtjuːd/
- ↻ handiness for sth /'hændines/
- ↻ adeptness at sth /ə'deptnəs/
- ↻ deftness /'deftnes/ = quick and neat skill
- ↻ adroitness /ə'drɔɪtnɪs/ = cleverness or skill
- ↻ talent for sth /'tælənt/
- ↻ knack for sth /næk/
- ↻ technique for sth /tek'niːk/
- ↻ expertise /ˌekspə(r)'tiːz/ = an expert skill in a particular field
- ↻ expertness /'ekspɜː(r)tnɪs/
- ↻ finesse /fɪ'nes/ = a skill of being able to handle delicate situations
- ↻ mastery of sth /'mɑːstəri/
- ↻ artistry /'ɑː(r)tɪstri/ = a creative skill
- ↻ competence in sth /'kɒmpɪtəns/
- ↻ dexterity in sth/with sth /dek'sterəti/ = a skill in performing tasks, especially with hands
- ↻ prowess /'praʊes/ = a great skill or ability
- ↻ capability of doing sth/to do sth /ˌkeɪpə'bɪləti/
- ↻ virtuosity /ˌvɜː(r)tʃʊ'ɒsəti/ = a great skill in music or another artistic pursuit
- ↻ strength /streŋθ/
- ↻ skill set /'skɪl set/

7. **ENVIRONEMNT** /ɪn'vaɪrənmənt/ noun

- ↻ habitat /'hæbɪtæt/ = a natural home of plants and other organisms
- ↻ territory /'terət(ə)ri/ = an area (both physical and mental)

- ↻ surroundings /sə'raʊndɪŋz/
- ↻ environs /ɪn'vaɪrənz/ = the surrounding area
- ↻ conditions /kən'dɪʃ(ə)nz/
- ↻ the natural world /ðə 'nætʃ(ə)rəl wɜ:(r)ld/
- ↻ nature /'neɪtʃə(r)/
- ↻ the Earth /ði: 'ɜ:(r)θ/
- ↻ the planet /ðə 'plænɪt/
- ↻ the ecosystem /ði: 'i:kəʊˌsɪstəm/
- ↻ the biosphere /ðə 'baɪəʊˌsfɪə(r)/
- ↻ Mother Nature /'mʌðə(r) 'neɪtʃə(r)/
- ↻ wildlife /'waɪldˌlaɪf/
- ↻ flora and fauna /'flɔ:rə ən'fɔ:nə/
- ↻ domain /dəʊ'meɪn/ = a physical area or sphere of knowledge

8. **CITY** /'sɪti/ noun

- ↻ metropolis /mə'trɒpəlɪs/ = a capital/chief city of a country or region
- ↻ town /taʊn/ = smaller than city
- ↻ conurbation /ˌkɒnɜ:(r)'beɪʃ(ə)n/ = an extended urban area
- ↻ megalopolis /ˌmegə'lɒpəlɪs/
- ↻ metropolitan area /ˌmetrə'pɒlɪt(ə)n 'eəriə/
- ↻ concrete jungle /'kɒŋkri:t 'dʒʌŋg(ə)l/ = has high density of modern buildings
- ↻ urban sprawl /'ɜ:(r)bən sprɔ:l/ = an uncontrolled expansion of urban areas
- ↻ micropolis /maɪkrəʊ'pəlɪs/ = a small city
- ↻ cosmopolis /ˌkɒzmə'pəlɪs/ = a city occupied by people from many different countries
- ↻ municipality /mju:ˌnɪsɪ'pæləti/ = a city with local government
- ↻ metroplex /'metrəʊpleks/
- ↻ the big smoke /ðə bɪg'sməʊk/ (informal)

9. **NOWADAYS** /'naʊəˌdeɪz/ adverb

- ↻ These days, … /'ði:z deɪz/
- ↻ At the present time, …
- ↻ In this day and age, …
- ↻ Currently, … /'kʌrəntli/
- ↻ Presently, …
- ↻ In modern times, …
- ↻ Contemporarily, …
- ↻ In these times, …
- ↻ In this present climate, …
- ↻ In the present circumstances, …
- ↻ Things being what they are, …

10. **LITTLE & FEW** /ˈlɪt(ə)l & ˈfjuː/ determiner

> *NOTE: Remember to use 'little' with uncountable nouns,*
> *whereas 'few' with countable ones.*

> *UN = Uncountable Noun*
> *CN = Countable Noun*

- ☞ hardly any + UN/CN /ˈhɑː(r)dli ˈeni/
- ☞ not much + UN /nɒt mʌtʃ/
- ☞ slight + CN /slaɪt/
- ☞ scant + UN/CN /skænt/
- ☞ limited + UN/CN /ˈlɪmɪtɪd/
- ☞ minimal + UN /ˈmɪnɪm(ə)l/
- ☞ negligible + UN/CN /ˈneglɪdʒəb(ə)l/
- ☞ scarcely any + UN/CN /ˈskeə(r)sli/
- ☞ a small number of + CN /ə smɔːl ˈnʌmbə(r) əv/
- ☞ one or two + CN /wʌn ɔː(r) ˈtuː/
- ☞ a handful of + CN /ə ˈhæn(d)fʊl əv/
- ☞ a couple of + CN /ə ˈkʌp(ə)l əv/
- ☞ a bit of + UN /ə ˈbɪt əv/

11. **DEVICE** /dɪˈvaɪs/ noun

- ☞ gadget /ˈgædʒɪt/ = a novel device
- ☞ implement /ˈɪmplɪmənt/ = a piece of equipment for a particular purpose
- ☞ utensil /juːˈtens(ə)l/
- ☞ tool /tuːl/
- ☞ apparatus /ˌæpəˈreɪtəs/ = technical equipment
- ☞ instrument /ˈɪnstrʊmənt/
- ☞ hardware /ˈhɑːd(r)ˌweə(r)/
- ☞ machine /məˈʃiːn/
- ☞ mechanism /ˈmekəˌnɪz(ə)m/
- ☞ equipment /ɪˈkwɪpmənt/
- ☞ paraphernalia /ˌpærəfə(r)ˈneɪliə/
- ☞ impedimenta /ɪmˌpedɪˈmentə/
- ☞ resource /rɪˈzɔː(r)s/
- ☞ contrivance /kənˈtraɪv(ə)ns/ = a skilfully created tool
- ☞ contraption /kənˈtræpʃ(ə)n/ = a complicated and strange machine

12. **VILLAGE** /ˈvɪlɪdʒ/ noun

- ☞ hamlet /ˈhæmlət/ = smaller than a village
- ☞ settlement /ˈset(ə)lmənt/
- ☞ little town /ˈlɪt(ə)l ˈtaʊn/

↻ one-horse town (informal) /wʌnˈhɔ:(r)s ˈtaʊn/

↻ dorp /dɔ:(r)p/

↻ whistle-stop /ˈwɪs(ə)l stɒp/

13. **MUCH & MANY** /mʌtʃ &ˈmeni/ determiner

NOTE: Remember to use ‘much’ with uncountable nouns, whereas ‘many’ with countable ones.
UN = Uncountable Noun
CN = Countable Noun

↻ a lot of/lots of + UN/CN /əˈlɒt əv & ˈlɒts əv/

↻ a great/large amount of + UN /əˈ greɪt/lɑ:(r)dʒ əˈmaʊnt əv/

↻ plenty of + UN/CN /ˈplenti əv /

↻ ample + UN /ˈæmp(ə)l/ = enough

↻ copious + UN/CN /ˈkəʊpiəs/

↻ plentiful + UN/CN /ˈplentɪf(ə)l/

↻ abundant in + UN/CN /əˈbʌndənt/

↻ considerable + UN/CN /kənˈsɪd(ə)rəb(ə)l/

↻ numerous + CN /ˈnju:mərəs/

↻ a great/good deal of + UN/CN /əˈgreɪt/gʊd di:l əv/

↻ countless + CN /ˈkaʊntləs/

↻ innumerable + CN /ɪˈnju:mərəb(ə)l/

↻ a multitude of + CN /ə ˈmʌltɪˌtju:d əv/

↻ multitudinous + CN /ˌmʌltɪˈtju:dɪnəs/

↻ profuse + CN /prəˈfju:s/

↻ an abundance of + CN/UN /ən əˈbʌndəns əv/

↻ several + CN /ˈsev(ə)rəl/

↻ multiple + CN /ˈmʌltɪp(ə)l/

↻ substantial + UN/CN /səbˈstænʃ(ə)l/

14. **PEOPLE/POPULATION** /ˈpi:p(ə)l/ noun

↻ individuals /ˌɪndɪˈvɪdʒuəlz/

↻ citizens /ˈsɪtɪz(ə)nz/

↻ masses /ˈmæsɪz/

↻ community /kəˈmju:nəti/

↻ natives /ˈneɪtɪvz/

↻ denizens /ˈdenɪz(ə)nz/

↻ society /səˈsaɪəti/

↻ humans /ˈhju:mənz/

↻ residents /ˈrezɪd(ə)nts/

↻ inhabitants /ɪnˈhæbɪtənts/

↻ citizenry /ˈsɪtɪz(ə)nri/ can be followed by both singular and plural verb

↻ public /ˈpʌblɪk/

- folks /fəʊks/
- humanity /hjuːˈmænəti/
- persons /ˈpɜː(r)s(ə)ns/
- the human race /ðə ˈhjuːmən reɪs/
- mortals /ˈmɔː(r)t(ə)ls/

15. **TO INCREASE** /ɪnˈkriːs/ verb
(ESPECIALLY IMPORTANT FOR WRITING TASK 1)

NOTE: You can also use this phrase: <u>on the increase</u>.
e.g. The numbers of tourists visiting England every year are on the increase.

!!! Get it right: increase (n.)

Don't use <u>increase of</u> when you want to say what is increasing.
Use <u>increase in</u>:
(x) Is death penalty connected with the increase ~~of~~ conservative judges?
(✓)Is death penalty connected with the increase in conservative judges?

Use <u>increase of</u> with a number or percentage when you want to talk about the amount by which something increases.
There has been an <u>increase of</u> nearly 20% in spending on public safety.

- to grow /grəʊ/
- to get larger /lɑː(r)dʒə/
- to rise /raɪz/
- to escalate /ˈeskəleɪt/ = to increase rapidly
- to rocket /ˈrɒkɪt/ = to increase very rapidly and suddenly
- to intensify /ɪnˈtensɪfaɪ/
- to spread /spred/ = used most often with an area
- to mount up /maʊnt ˈʌp/ = to grow more numerous or larger
- to enlarge /ɪnˈlɑː(r)dʒ/
- to expand /ɪkˈspænd/
- to climb /klaɪm/
- to soar /sɔː(r)/ = increase rapidly above the usual level
- to shoot up /ʃuːtˈʌp/ = to rise suddenly
- to extend /ɪkˈstend/
- to multiply /ˈmʌltɪplaɪ/
- to pile up /paɪlˈʌp/
- to accumulate /əˈkjuːmjʊleɪt/
- to inflate /ɪnˈfleɪt/
- to magnify /ˈmægnɪfaɪ/
- to amplify /ˈæmplɪˌfaɪ/
- to become greater /bɪˈkʌm ˈgreɪtə/
- to advance /ədˈvɑːns/

- ✍ to swell /swel/
- ✍ to proliferate /prəˈlɪfəreɪt/ = to increase rapidly in numbers
- ✍ to go through the roof (informal)
- ✍ to boost /buːst/
- ✍ to enhance /ɪnˈhɑːns/
- ✍ to widen /ˈwaɪd(ə)n/
- ✍ to hike up /haɪkˈʌp/ (informal)

16. **TO DECREASE** /diːˈkriːs/ verb
(ESPECIALLY IMPORTANT FOR WRITING TASK 1)

NOTE:
!!! Get it right: decrease (n.)

Don't use decrease of when you want to talk about what is decreasing.
Use decrease in:
(x) The programme has not led to the expected decrease of crime.
(✓) The programme has not led to the expected decrease in crime.

Use decrease of with a number or percentage, when you want to talk about the amount by which something decreases:
These graphs show a decrease of 15 per cent over the past year.

- ✍ to lessen /ˈles(ə)n/
- ✍ to reduce /rɪˈdjuːs/
- ✍ to drop /drɒp/
- ✍ to diminish /dɪˈmɪnɪʃ/
- ✍ to decline /dɪˈklaɪn/
- ✍ to dwindle /ˈdwɪnd(ə)l/ = to decrease gradually
- ✍ to abate /əˈbeɪt/ = to become smaller or less intense
- ✍ to subside /səbˈsaɪd/
- ✍ to ebb /eb/ = to lessen gradually
- ✍ to plummet /ˈplʌmɪt/ = to decrease rapidly
- ✍ to plunge /plʌndʒ/ = to fall suddenly
- ✍ to cut down /kʌt ˈdaʊn/
- ✍ to curtail /kɜː(r)ˈteɪl/ = to reduce in extent or quantity
- ✍ to deplete /dɪˈpliːt/ = to use up (resources, supply)
- ✍ to minimize /ˈmɪnɪmaɪz/
- ✍ to become less /bɪˈkʌm ˈles/
- ✍ to go down /ɡəʊ ˈdaʊn/
- ✍ to slide /slaɪd/
- ✍ to shrink /ʃrɪŋk/
- ✍ to trim /trɪm/
- ✍ to wane /weɪn/ (neg. in meaning) = to decrease in power
- ✍ to die down /daɪˈdaʊn/

⟳ to slump (informal) /slʌmp/ = to decline substantially

17. **NUTRITIOUS** /njuːˈtrɪʃəs/ adjective

⟳ full of nutrients /fʊl əv ˈnjuːtrɪənts/
⟳ nutritive /ˈnjuːtrətɪv/
⟳ healthful /ˈhelθfl/
⟳ sustaining /səˈsteɪnɪŋ/
⟳ nourishing /ˈnʌrɪʃɪŋ/
⟳ wholesome /ˈhəʊls(ə)m/
⟳ health-giving /ˈhelθ ɡɪvɪŋ/
⟳ beneficial /ˌbenɪˈfɪʃ(ə)l/
⟳ substantial /səbˈstænʃ(ə)l/
⟳ invigorating /ɪnˈvɪɡəˌreɪtɪŋ/
⟳ strengthening /ˈstreŋθ(ə)nɪŋ/

18. **LATEST** /ˈleɪtɪst/ adjective

⟳ most recent /məʊst ˈriːs(ə)nt/
⟳ newest /ˈnjuːwest/
⟳ just released /dʒʌst rɪˈliːst/
⟳ up-to-the-minute /ʌp tə ðə ˈmɪnɪt/
⟳ up-to-date /ʌp tə ˈdeɪt/
⟳ state-of-the-art /steɪt əv ðə ˈɑː(r)t/
⟳ current /ˈkʌrənt/
⟳ contemporary /kənˈtemp(ə)r(ə)ri/
⟳ fashionable /ˈfæʃ(ə)nəb(ə)l/
⟳ in fashion /ɪnˈfæʃ(ə)n/
⟳ in vogue /ɪnˈvəʊɡ/
⟳ trendy /ˈtrendi/
⟳ modern /ˈmɒdə(r)n/
⟳ space-age /ˈspeɪs eɪdʒ/ = very modern, technologically advanced
⟳ hip /hɪp/ = following the latest fashion (clothes, music)
⟳ ahead of its time /əˈhed əv ɪts ˈtaɪm/
⟳ just out /dʒʌst ˈaʊt/
⟳ hot /hɒt/

19. **PHENOMENON** /fəˈnɒmɪnən/ noun

⟳ occurrence /əˈkʌrəns/
⟳ happening /ˈhæp(ə)nɪŋ/
⟳ situation /ˌsɪtʃuˈeɪʃ(ə)n/
⟳ circumstance /ˈsɜː(r)kəmstəns/
⟳ case /keɪs/
⟳ status quo /ˌsteɪtəs ˈkwəʊ/

- ↻ event /ɪˈvent/
- ↻ incident /ˈɪnsɪd(ə)nt/
- ↻ episode /ˈepɪsəʊd/
- ↻ fact /fækt/
- ↻ occasion /əˈkeɪʒ(ə)n/
- ↻ state of affairs /steɪt əv əˈfeə(r)z/

20. **CONVENIENT** /kənˈviːniənt/ adjective

- ↻ nearby /ˌnɪə(r)ˈbaɪ/ = not far away
- ↻ suitable /ˈsuːtəb(ə)l/ = appropriate for sb or sth
- ↻ appropriate /əˈprəʊpriət/
- ↻ fitting /ˈfɪtɪŋ/ = meeting the standard required
- ↻ suited /ˈsuːtɪd/
- ↻ timely /ˈtaɪmli/ = opportune
- ↻ favourable /ˈfeɪv(ə)rəb(ə)l/
- ↻ well situated /wel ˈsɪtʃueɪtɪd/ = of a place
- ↻ handy /ˈhændi/
- ↻ practical /ˈpræktɪk(ə)l/
- ↻ easy-to-use /ˈiːzi tə ˈjuːz
- ↻ well-designed /wel ˈdɪˈzaɪnd/
- ↻ user-friendly /ˈjuːzə(r)ˈfren(d)li/
- ↻ user-oriented /ˈjuːzə(r) ˈɔːrientɪd/
- ↻ functional /ˈfʌŋkʃ(ə)nəl/
- ↻ serviceable /ˈsɜː(r)vɪsəb(ə)l/
- ↻ at hand /ət ˈhænd/
- ↻ within reach /wɪðˈɪn ˈriːtʃ/ = nearby
- ↻ accessible /əkˈsesəb(ə)l/ = able to be reached
- ↻ at your disposal /ət jə(r) dɪˈspəʊz(ə)l/
- ↻ useful /ˈjuːsf(ə)l/
- ↻ labour-saving /ˈleɪbə(r) ˈseɪvɪŋ/
- ↻ opportune /ˈɒpə(r)tjuːn/
- ↻ expedient /ɪkˈspiːdiənt/ = convenient and practical (but might be immoral)
- ↻ at you fingertips (informal)
- ↻ just round the corner (informal) = nearby

21. **GAP & DIFFERENCE** /gæp/ & /ˈdɪfrəns/ noun

- ↻ chasm between A & B /ˈkæz(ə)m/
- ↻ split between A & B/in sth /splɪt/
- ↻ contrast between A & B/to sth /ˈkɒntrɑːst/
- ↻ disparity between A & B /dɪˈspærəti/ = a great difference
- ↻ divergence of sth /daɪˈvɜː(r)dʒ(ə)ns/ = conflict in opinions, interests etc.
- ↻ imbalance of sth /ɪmˈbæləns/ = a lack of proportion
- ↻ dissimilarity between A & B /dɪˌsɪmɪˈlærəti/

↻ distinction between A & B /dɪˈstɪŋkʃ(ə)n/

↻ variation of sth /ˌveərɪˈeɪʃ(ə)n/ = a different version of sth

↻ polarity between A & B /pəʊˈlærəti/ = a contradiction

↻ contradistinction /ˌkɒntrədɪˈstɪŋkʃ(ə)n/ = A is in contradistinction to B

↻ unlikeness to/from sth /ənˈlaɪknəs/

↻ discrepancy between sth /dɪsˈkrepənsi/

↻ clash of A & B /klæʃ/

22. **DATA & INFORMATION** /ˈdeɪtə/ & /ˌɪnfə(r)ˈmeɪʃ(ə)n/ noun
(ESPECIALLY IMPORTANT FOR WRITING TASK 1)

↻ details /ˈdiːteɪlz/

↻ particulars /pə(r)ˈtɪkjʊlə(r)z/

↻ facts /fækts/

↻ figures /ˈfɪgə(r)z/

↻ statistics /stəˈtɪstɪks/

↻ specifics /spəˈsɪfɪks/

↻ material /məˈtɪəriəl/

↻ input /ˈɪnpʊt/

↻ features /ˈfiːtʃə(r)z/

23. **NUMBER** /ˈnʌmbə(r)/ noun
(ESPECIALLY IMPORTANT FOR WRITING TASK 1)

↻ numeral /ˈnjuːmərəl/

↻ figure /ˈfɪgə(r)/

↻ digit /ˈdɪdʒɪt/

↻ unit /ˈjuːnɪt/

↻ tally (a tally of = total) /ˈtæli/

↻ group /gruːp/

↻ statistics /stəˈtɪstɪks/

↻ sum /sʌm/

↻ count /kaʊnt/

24. **TO IMPROVE** /ɪmˈpruːv/ verb
(Noun 1 improves Noun 2)

↻ to make sth better

↻ to better /ˈbetə(r)/

↻ to boost /buːst/

↻ to ameliorate /əˈmiːliəreɪt/

↻ to amend /əˈmend/

↻ to refine /rɪˈfaɪn/ = to improve by making small changes

↻ to augment /ɔːgˈment/

↻ to remedy /ˈremədi/

- ☞ to enhance /ɪnˈhɑːns/
- ☞ to correct /kəˈrekt/
- ☞ to enrich /ɪnˈrɪtʃ/
- ☞ to revitalize /riːˈvaɪtəlaɪz/ = to imbue with vitality
- ☞ to redeem /rɪˈdiːm/
- ☞ to optimize /ˈɒptɪmaɪz/
- ☞ to perfect /pə(r)ˈfekt/
- ☞ to polish /ˈpɒlɪʃ/
- ☞ to touch sth up /tʌtʃ ˈʌp/
- ☞ to mend /mend/
- ☞ to revamp /ˌriːˈvæmp/ = to give sth a new form, appearance
- ☞ to advance /ədˈvɑːns/
- ☞ to make headway /meɪk ˈhedˌweɪ/ = to make progress
- ☞ to perk up (informal) /pɜː(r)k ˈʌp/
- ☞ to give a facelift to (informal)
- ☞ to do up (informal)
- ☞ to fix up (informal)

25. **THE PERIOD OF A & B** /ˈpɪəriəd/ time phrase
(ESPECIALLY IMPORTANT FOR WRITING TASK 1)

- ☞ the time of + how many years, months, days /taɪm/
- ☞ the stretch of + how many years, months, days /stretʃ/
- ☞ the duration of + how long /djʊˈreɪʃ(ə)n/
- ☞ the period from A to B /ˈpɪəriəd/
- ☞ from A to B
- ☞ decade (10 years) /ˈdekeɪd/
- ☞ the span of + how long /spæn/
- ☞ the session of + how long /ˈseʃ(ə)n/
- ☞ the cycle of + how long /ˈsaɪk(ə)l/
- ☞ over + how many + year period
- ☞ between A and B

26. **PROBLEM** /ˈprɒbləm/ noun

- ☞ difficulty /ˈdɪfɪk(ə)lti/
- ☞ trouble /ˈtrʌb(ə)l/
- ☞ complication /ˌkɒmplɪˈkeɪʃ(ə)n/
- ☞ difficult situation /ˈdɪfɪk(ə)lt ˌsɪtʃuˈeɪʃ(ə)n/
- ☞ snag (informal) /snæg/
- ☞ drawback /ˈdrɔːˌbæk/
- ☞ stumbling block /ˈstʌmb(ə)lɪŋ blɒk/
- ☞ obstacle /ˈɒbstək(ə)l/
- ☞ hurdle /ˈhɜː(r)d(ə)l/
- ☞ hiccup /ˈhɪkʌp/

- setback /ˈsetˌbæk/
- predicament /prɪˈdɪkəmənt/
- plight /plaɪt/
- mishap /ˈmɪsˌhæp/ (informal)
- dilemma /dɪˈlemə/
- quandary /ˈkwɒndəri/ = to be in a quandary
- hassle /ˈhæs(ə)l/ (informal)
- pickle /ˈpɪk(ə)l/ (informal)
- tight spot /taɪt ˈspɒt/ (informal)
- dire straits /ˈdaɪə(r) streɪts/ (informal) = to be in dire straits
- catch-22 situation (informal)
- conundrum /kəˈnʌndrəm/

27. **A KIND OF** /kaɪnd/ phrase

- a sort of /sɔː(r)t/
- a type of /taɪp/
- a variety of /vəˈraɪəti/
- a class of /klɑːs/
- a category of /ˈkætəg(ə)ri/
- of this/his etc. ilk /ɪlk/

28. **TO CAUSE** /kɔːz/ verb

- to bring about /brɪŋ əˈbaʊt/
- to give rise to /gɪv ˈraɪz tə/
- to lead to /liːd/
- to result in /rɪˈzʌltɪn/
- to create /kriˈeɪt/
- to generate /ˈdʒenəreɪt/
- to bring on /brɪŋ ˈɒn/
- to precipitate /prɪˈsɪpɪteɪt/
- to promote /prəˈməʊt/
- to foster /ˈfɒstə(r)/
- to prompt /prɒmpt/
- to provoke /prəˈvəʊk/
- to trigger /ˈtrɪgə(r)/
- to make sth happen /meɪk ˈhæpən/
- to induce /ɪnˈdjuːs/
- to form /fɔː(r)m/

29. **TREND** /trend/ noun
    (ESPECIALLY IMPORTANT FOR WRITING TASK 1)

- tendency in + place/to do sth /ˈtendənsi/

- ✍ current of sth /ˈkʌrənt/
- ✍ variability /ˌveəriəˈbɪlɪtɪ/
- ✍ direction /daɪˈrekʃ(ə)n/
- ✍ orientation /ˌɔ:riənˈteɪʃ(ə)n/
- ✍ flow /fləʊ/
- ✍ drift /drɪft/
- ✍ inclination for/to/towards sth /ˌɪŋklɪˈneɪʃ(ə)n/

30. **OPPORTUNITY** /ˌɒpə(r)ˈtjuːnəti/ noun

- ✍ chance of sth/to do sth /tʃɑːns/
- ✍ right set of circumstances /raɪt setəv ˈsɜ:(r)kəmstənsɪz/
- ✍ occasion for sth /əˈkeɪʒ(ə)n/
- ✍ opening for sth /ˈəʊp(ə)nɪŋ/
- ✍ window of opportunity /ˈwɪndəʊ əv ˌɒpə(r)ˈtjuːnəti/
- ✍ possibility of sth /ˌpɒsəˈbɪləti/
- ✍ scope for sth /skəʊp/
- ✍ break in sth /breɪk/ (informal)

31. **RULE** /ruːl/ noun

- ✍ regulation /ˌreɡjʊˈleɪʃ(ə)n/
- ✍ directive /daɪˈrektɪv/ = an official instruction
- ✍ canon /ˈkænən/ = a general law, rule
- ✍ fiat /ˈfiːæt/ = a decree
- ✍ stipulation /ˌstɪpjʊˈleɪʃ(ə)n/ = a condition needed for an agreement
- ✍ guidelines /ˈgaɪdˌlaɪnz/
- ✍ principle /ˈprɪnsəp(ə)l/
- ✍ standard /ˈstændə(r)d/
- ✍ law /lɔː/
- ✍ ordinance /ˈɔ:(r)dɪnəns/ = a decree
- ✍ commandment /kəˈmɑːn(d)mənt/ = a divine rule to be observed strictly
- ✍ restriction /rɪˈstrɪkʃ(ə)n/
- ✍ tenet /ˈtenɪt/ = in religion or philosophy
- ✍ axiom /ˈæksiəm/ = an established truth
- ✍ criterion /kraɪˈtɪəriən/

32. **CLOTHES** /kləʊðz/ noun

- ✍ clothing /ˈkləʊðɪŋ/
- ✍ apparel /əˈpærəl/ = usually unusual or formal clothes
- ✍ attire /əˈtaɪə(r)/
- ✍ dress /dres/
- ✍ garments /ˈgɑ:(r)mənts/
- ✍ outfit /ˈaʊtfɪt/ = a set of clothes worn together

- ✐ raiment /ˈreɪmənt/ (formal)
- ✐ wardrobe /ˈwɔː(r)drəʊb/ = all clothes one has
- ✐ gear /ɡɪə(r)/ (informal)

33. __WORK__ /wɜː(r)k/ noun

Meaning 'occupation, job':

- ✐ employment /ɪmˈplɔɪmənt/ = work that you are paid for regularly
- ✐ profession /prəˈfeʃ(ə)n/ = a job that you need special qualifications to do
- ✐ trade /treɪd/ = a job you are trained to do
- ✐ career /kəˈrɪə(r)/
- ✐ calling /ˈkɔːlɪŋ/ = a job that you consider important
- ✐ vocation /vəʊˈkeɪʃ(ə)n/ = a job that you do because you feel it is your purpose in life
- ✐ pursuit /pə(r)ˈsjuːt/ = an activity you enjoy
- ✐ field /fiːld/ = a type of work that you do
- ✐ line of business
- ✐ metier /ˈmetieɪ/ = a type of work that you are good at
- ✐ livelihood /ˈlaɪvlihʊd/ = sth you do that provides money
- ✐ craft /krɑːft/ = a skill you need for a particular profession
- ✐ workmanship /ˈwɜː(r)kmənʃɪp/ = the skill you use in making sth
- ✐ call /kɔːl/ = a strong feeling of wanting to do sth, esp. as a career
- ✐ gig /ɡɪɡ/ = a piece of work you do for money, esp. if you're self-employed
- ✐ post /pəʊst/ = a job, esp. with a lot of responsibility

Meaning 'task to do':

- ✐ assignment /əˈsaɪnmənt/
- ✐ undertaking /ˈʌndə(r)ˌteɪkɪŋ/ = a difficult task
- ✐ job /dʒɒb/
- ✐ chore /tʃɔː(r)/ = an ordinary job done regularly
- ✐ responsibility /rɪˌspɒnsəˈbɪləti/
- ✐ duty /ˈdjuːti/
- ✐ mission /ˈmɪʃ(ə)n/ = an important task
- ✐ service /ˈsɜː(r)vɪs/ = duties done for sb
- ✐ labour /ˈleɪbə(r)/
- ✐ effort /ˈefə(r)t/
- ✐ toil /tɔɪl/ = a very hard work, esp. physical work
- ✐ heavy lifting (informal) /ˈhevi ˈlɪftɪŋ/ = difficult work that needs a lot of effort
- ✐ challenge /ˈtʃæləndʒ/ = sth that needs a lot of skill, energy and determination to deal with

34. **TO WORK** /wɜ:(r)k/ verb

Meaning 'to be employed':

↷ to be employed
↷ to have a job
↷ to earn a living
↷ to collaborate /kəˈlæbəreɪt/ = to work with sb in order to produce sth
↷ to volunteer /ˌvɒlənˈtɪə(r)/= to do some work without getting paid
↷ to be your own boss = to work for yourself

Meaning 'to labour':

↷ to toil /tɔɪl/ = to work hard doing sth difficult, esp. physical work
↷ to labour /ˈleɪbə(r)/
↷ to exert yourself /ɪgˈzɜ:(r)t/ = to use a lot of physical or mental effort
↷ to drudge /drʌdʒ/ = to do boring work
↷ to slave /sleɪv/ = to be forced to work
↷ to slog /slɒg/ (informal) = to do difficult or boring job, for a long time
↷ to peg away /peg/ (informal) = to do something with determination
↷ to boil the ocean (informal) = to try to do sth very difficult
↷ to strive /straɪv/ = to make a lot of effort to achieve sth

35. **TO HELP** /help/ verb

(Meaning: sth helps sth else)

↷ to aid /eɪd/
↷ to support /səˈpɔ:(r)t/
↷ to assist /əˈsɪst/
↷ to be of assistance /əˈsɪst(ə)ns/
↷ to do sth for
↷ to be of use
↷ to guide /gaɪd/
↷ to cooperate /kəʊˈɒpəreɪt/ = to work with
↷ to back /bæk/
↷ to contribute to /kənˈtrɪbju:t/
↷ to promote /prəˈməʊt/ = to support sth
↷ to boost /bu:st/
↷ to give a boost to
↷ to relieve /rɪˈli:v/ = used specially for pain
↷ to alleviate /əˈli:vieɪt/ (formal)
↷ to assuage /əˈsweɪdʒ/ = to make an unpleasant feeling less severe
↷ to lessen /ˈles(ə)n/
↷ to remedy /ˈremədi/ = to solve sth

↻ to ameliorate /əˈmiːliəreɪt/ (formal) = to improve sth

↻ to mitigate /ˈmɪtɪgeɪt/ (formal) = to reduce harmful effects of sth

36.　**KNOWLEDGE** /ˈnɒlɪdʒ/ noun

↻ comprehension of sth /ˌkɒmprɪˈhenʃ(ə)n/ = the ability to understand sth

↻ grasp of sth /grɑːsp/

↻ command of sth /kəˈmɑːnd/ = often used for languages

↻ mastery of sth /ˈmɑːstəri/ = often used for languages

↻ expertise in sth /ˌekspə(r)ˈtiːz/ = special knowledge you get from experience, training or study

↻ learning sth /ˈlɜː(r)nɪŋ/ = the process of gaining knowledge

↻ erudition /ˌeruˈdɪʃ(ə)n/ (formal) = great knowledge gained through reading or studying

↻ education /ˌedjʊˈkeɪʃ(ə)n/

↻ wisdom /ˈwɪzdəm/ = knowledge gained over a long period

↻ cognition /kɒgˈnɪʃ(ə)n/ (formal) = the process of understanding things

↻ familiarity with sth /fəˌmɪliˈærəti/ = knowledge of sth because you have learnt or experienced it before

↻ schooling /ˈskuːlɪŋ/ = the education you get at school

↻ knowhow (informal) = knowledge needed to do sth, esp. practical

↻ discernment /dɪˈsɜː(r)nmənt/ = the ability to make good judgments about art, music or books

↻ proficiency in sth /prəˈfɪʃ(ə)nsi/ = a high degree of ability

↻ savoir-faire /ˌsævwɑː(r) ˈfeə(r)/ = the ability to behave correctly, esp. in a social situation

37.　**HOLIDAY** /ˈhɒlɪdeɪ/ noun

Meaning ‘vacation’ (AmE):

↻ trip /trɪp/

↻ leave (UN) /liːv/ = to be on leave

↻ leave of absence /ˈæbs(ə)ns/

↻ time off

↻ day off

↻ break from sth /breɪk/

↻ awayday

↻ rest

↻ furlough /ˈfɜː(r)ləʊ/ = when you are allowed to be away from a job or the army

↻ sickie /ˈsɪki/ (BrE) = a day when you say you are ill because you do not want to go to work

↻ respite from sth /ˈrespaɪt/ = a short period of rest from a difficult or unpleasant situation

↻ sojourn /ˈsɒdʒə(r)n/ (formal) = when you stay in a place that is not your home

↻ getaway /ˈgetəˌweɪ/ (informal) = a short holiday

↻ (take) French leave = time away from your job without asking for permission

Meaning 'a national holiday':

- festival /ˈfestɪv(ə)l/
- public holiday
- bank holiday
- legal holiday
- feast day /fiːst/
- celebration of sth /ˌseləˈbreɪʃ(ə)n/
- holy day = related to religion, e.g. Sunday

38. **CULTURE** /ˈkʌltʃə(r)/ noun

- intellectual achievement /ˌɪntəˈlektʃuəl əˈtʃiːvmənts/
- cultivation of sth /ˌkʌltɪˈveɪʃ(ə)n/
- good taste /ɡʊdˈteɪst/ = the ability to judge if sth is good or bad
- sophistication of sth /səˌfɪstɪˈkeɪʃ(ə)n/ = high quality culture
- civilization /ˌsɪvəlaɪˈzeɪʃ(ə)n/
- way of life
- customs /ˈkʌstəmz/
- traditions /trəˈdɪʃ(ə)nz/
- heritage /ˈherɪtɪdʒ/
- mores /ˈmɔːreɪz/ (formal) = traditional practices and values
- inheritance /ɪnˈherɪt(ə)ns/
- background /ˈbækˌɡraʊnd/
- ancestry /ˈænsestri/
- heredity /həˈredəti/ = the genetic process by which characteristics are passed on
- lifestyle /ˈlaɪfˌstaɪl/
- habits /ˈhæbɪts/
- the spirit of the times/age = the ideas, beliefs of a particular period of time

39. **TO PREVENT** /prɪˈvent/ verb

- to stop sth /stɒp/
- to put a stop to sth
- to avert sth /əˈvɜː(r)t/ = to prevent sth bad from happening
- to avoid sth /əˈvɔɪd/
- to keep from sth
- to halt sth /hɔːlt/
- to fend off sth /fend/ = to protect from sth negative
- to ward off sth /wɔː(r)d/
- to hinder sth /ˈhɪndə(r)/
- to hamper sth /ˈhæmpə(r)/
- to obstruct sth /əbˈstrʌkt/
- to foil sth /fɔɪl/

- ⟲ to counteract sth /ˌkaʊntərˈækt/ = to reduce the negative effect of sth by doing sth positive
- ⟲ to inhibit sth /ɪnˈhɪbɪt/
- ⟲ to preclude sth /prɪˈkluːd/ (formal)
- ⟲ to prohibit sth /prəʊˈhɪbɪt/
- ⟲ to debar sth /dɪˈbɑː(r)/ = to prevent officially
- ⟲ to stave off sth /steɪv/
- ⟲ to thwart sb /θwɔː(r)t/ = to prevent sb from doing sth they want to do
- ⟲ to restrain sth/sb from sth/sb /rɪˈstreɪn/
- ⟲ to impede sth /ɪmˈpiːd/
- ⟲ to block sth /blɒk/
- ⟲ to obviate sth /ˈɒbvieɪt/ (formal) = to get rid of sth
- ⟲ to interfere with sth /ˌɪntə(r)ˈfɪə(r)/
- ⟲ to head off sth = to prevent sth from taking place
- ⟲ to squash sth /skwɒʃ/
- ⟲ to knock sth on the head (informal)
- ⟲ to get in the way of sth (informal)

40. **TO GRADUATE** /ˈɡrædʒueɪt/ verb

- ⟲ to pass your final exams /pɑːs/
- ⟲ to qualify as + profession /ˈkwɒlɪfaɪ/
- ⟲ to complete one's studies
- ⟲ to get one's diploma /dɪˈpləʊmə/
- ⟲ to get one's degree
- ⟲ to certify /ˈsɜː(r)tɪfaɪ/

41. **THING (SOMETHING)** /θɪŋ/ noun

- ⟲ characteristic of sth /ˌkærɪktəˈrɪstɪk/
- ⟲ attribute of sth/sb /ˈætrɪˌbjuːt/
- ⟲ trait /treɪt/
- ⟲ feature /ˈfiːtʃə(r)/
- ⟲ point /pɔɪnt/
- ⟲ aspect /ˈæspekt/
- ⟲ facet of sth /ˈfæsɪt/
- ⟲ side /saɪd/
- ⟲ particular /pə(r)ˈtɪkjʊlə(r)/
- ⟲ angle /ˈæŋɡ(ə)l/
- ⟲ factor /ˈfæktə(r)/
- ⟲ notion /ˈnəʊʃ(ə)n/
- ⟲ element /ˈelɪmənt/

42. **TO CONSIST OF STH** /kənˈsɪstəv/ verb
    (ESPECIALLY IMPORTANT FOR WRITING TASK 1)

  - ♫ to be composed of /kəmˈpəʊzd/
  - ♫ to include sth /ɪnˈkluːd/
  - ♫ to contain sth /kənˈteɪn/
  - ♫ to take in sth
  - ♫ to incorporate sth /ɪnˈkɔː(r)pəreɪt/
  - ♫ to embody sth /ɪmˈbɒdi/
  - ♫ to involve sth /ɪnˈvɒlv/
  - ♫ to encompass sth /ɪnˈkʌmpəs/
  - ♫ to cover sth /ˈkʌvə(r)/
  - ♫ to embrace sth /ɪmˈbreɪs/ (formal)
  - ♫ to be made up of
  - ♫ to be formed of

43. **RICH** /rɪtʃ/ adjective

  - ♫ wealthy /ˈwelθi/
  - ♫ affluent /ˈæfluːənt/ = rich enough to buy things for pleasure
  - ♫ well-off (informal)
  - ♫ well-to-do = rich and belonging to an upper class family
  - ♫ prosperous /ˈprɒsp(ə)rəs/ = rich and successful
  - ♫ opulent /ˈɒpjʊlənt/ (formal) = used for things, e.g. opulent surroundings
  - ♫ comfortably off
  - ♫ moneyed /ˈmʌnid/
  - ♫ well-heeled /ˌwel ˈhiːld/ (informal)
  - ♫ made of money (informal)
  - ♫ rolling in it (informal)
  - ♫ loaded /ˈləʊdɪd/ (informal)
  - ♫ filthy rich /ˈfɪlθi rɪtʃ/ (informal)
  - ♫ stinking rich (informal)
  - ♫ nouveau riche /ˌnuːvəʊ ˈriːʃ/ = became rich recently

44. **POOR** /pɔː(r)/ or /pʊə(r)/ adjective

  - ♫ impoverished /ɪmˈpɒvərɪʃt/
  - ♫ poverty-stricken /ˈpɒvə(r)ti ˈstrɪkən/
  - ♫ badly off
  - ♫ in need
  - ♫ hard-up
  - ♫ bankrupt /ˈbæŋkrʌpt/
  - ♫ penniless /ˈpenɪləs/
  - ♫ as poor as a church mouse
  - ♫ without means

- destitute /ˈdestɪtjuːt/
- deprived /dɪˈpraɪvd/ = not having things essential for a comfortable life
- underprivileged /ˌʌndə(r)ˈprɪvəlɪdʒd/ = not having as many opportunities as others
- disadvantaged /ˌdɪsədˈvɑːntɪdʒd/
- lowly /ˈləʊli/ = with a low material status
- needy /ˈniːdi/
- penurious /pəˈnjʊəriəs/ (formal) = extremely poor
- impecunious /ˌɪmpɪˈkjuːniəs/ (formal)
- indigent /ˈɪndɪdʒ(ə)nt/ (formal)
- dirt-poor (informal)
- broke /brəʊk/ (informal)
- flat broke (informal)
- skint /skɪnt/ (BrE, informal)
- strapped for cash (informal)
- not having a penny to your name (informal)
- on the breadline /ˈbredˌlaɪn/ (BrE, informal)
- moneyless
- unable to make ends meet
- pauperized /ˈpɔːpəraɪzd/

45. **PART** /pɑː(r)t/ noun
(ESPECIALLY IMPORTANT FOR WRITING TASK 1)

- slice of sth /slaɪs/
- piece of sth /piːs/
- fragment of sth /ˈfrægmənt/
- portion of sth /ˈpɔː(r)ʃ(ə)n/
- fraction of sth /ˈfrækʃ(ə)n/
- proportion of sth /prəˈpɔː(r)ʃ(ə)n/
- component of sth /kəmˈpəʊnənt/
- element of sth /ˈelɪmənt/
- bit of sth /bɪt/
- constituent of sth /kənˈstɪtjʊənt/
- section of sth /ˈsekʃ(ə)n/
- division of sth /dɪˈvɪʒ(ə)n/
- module of sth /ˈmɒdjuːl/
- factor in sth /ˈfæktə(r)/
- aspect of sth /ˈæspekt/
- facet of sth /ˈfæsɪt/
- particle of sth /ˈpɑː(r)tɪk(ə)l/
- scrap of sth /skræp/ = a small part
- share in sth/of sth /ʃeə(r)/
- branch of sth /brɑːntʃ/

50

46. **TO PROTECT** /prəˈtekt/ verb

- ↻ to safeguard /ˈseɪfˌɡɑː(r)d/
- ↻ to keep sth/sb safe
- ↻ to keep sth/sb from harm
- ↻ to preserve /prɪˈzɜː(r)v/
- ↻ to shield /ʃiːld/
- ↻ to insulate /ˈɪnsjʊleɪt/
- ↻ to hedge /hedʒ/ = to protect yourself from risks involving money
- ↻ to shelter /ˈʃeltə(r)/
- ↻ to secure /sɪˈkjʊə(r)/
- ↻ to watch over
- ↻ to inoculate /ɪˈnɒkjʊleɪt/ = to protect sb against a particular disease
- ↻ to screen sth from sth /skriːn/ = to hide sth/sb by being in front of them
- ↻ to harbour /ˈhɑː(r)bə(r)/

47. **FAMOUS** /ˈfeɪməs/ adjective

- ↻ well-known
- ↻ celebrated for sth /ˈseləˌbreɪtɪd/
- ↻ renowned as/for doing sth /rɪˈnaʊnd/
- ↻ fabled /ˈfeɪb(ə)ld/ = famous because of being extremely good, beautiful or interesting
- ↻ legendary /ˈledʒ(ə)nd(ə)ri/ = famous for a long time
- ↻ notorious /nəʊˈtɔːriəs/ = famous for sth bad
- ↻ infamous /ˈɪnfəməs/ = famous for sth bad
- ↻ illustrious /ɪˈlʌstriəs/ = famous because of what they have achieved
- ↻ the one and only = used for introducing a famous person
- ↻ acclaimed /əˈkleɪmd/ = publicly written and talked about in an admiring way
- ↻ world-famous
- ↻ noted /ˈnəʊtɪd/
- ↻ distinguished /dɪˈstɪŋgwɪʃt/
- ↻ eminent /ˈemɪnənt/
- ↻ honoured /ˈɒnə(r)d/
- ↻ esteemed /ɪˈstiːmd/
- ↻ glorious /ˈglɔːriəs/
- ↻ prominent /ˈprɒmɪnənt/ = important and well-known
- ↻ venerable /ˈven(ə)rəb(ə)l/ = very old, wise and respected
- ↻ your name on everyone's lips
- ↻ having (made) a name for yourself

48. **TO SHOW** /ʃəʊ/ verb
(ESPECIALLY IMPORTANT FOR WRITING TASK 1)

- ↻ to illustrate /ˈɪləstreɪt/
- ↻ to depict /dɪˈpɪkt/

- ☞ to display /dɪˈspleɪ/
- ☞ to present /prɪˈzent/
- ☞ to exhibit /ɪgˈzɪbɪt/
- ☞ to uncover /ʌnˈkʌvə(r)/
- ☞ to demonstrate /ˈdemənˌstreɪt/
- ☞ it is visible/clear/obvious from… that /ˈvɪzəb(ə)l/klɪə(r)/ˈɒbvɪəs/
- ☞ to reveal /rɪˈviːl/
- ☞ to disclose /dɪsˈkləʊz/
- ☞ to divulge /daɪˈvʌldʒ/
- ☞ to make sth clear
- ☞ to manifest /ˈmænɪfest/ (formal)

49.   **TO STUDY** /ˈstʌdi/ verb

- ☞ to cram (for an exam) /kræm/
- ☞ to learn /lɜː(r)n/
- ☞ to be taught
- ☞ to investigate /ɪnˈvestɪgeɪt/ = to try to get detailed information
- ☞ to inquire into /ɪnˈkwaɪə(r)/
- ☞ to research /rɪˈsɜː(r)tʃ/ or /ˈriːsɜː(r)tʃ/
- ☞ to look into
- ☞ to analyse /ˈænəlaɪz/
- ☞ to examine /ɪgˈzæmɪn/
- ☞ to explore /ɪkˈsplɔː(r)/
- ☞ to review /rɪˈvjuː/
- ☞ to train /treɪn/
- ☞ to revise /rɪˈvaɪz/ = to read and learn information that you have studied in order to prepare for an exam
- ☞ to read up on/about sth = to get information on a particular subject by reading a lot about it
- ☞ to major in sth /ˈmeɪdʒə(r)/ = to study sth as your main subject at college or university
- ☞ to scrutinize /ˈskruːtɪnaɪz/ = to examine sth very carefully
- ☞ to peruse /pəˈruːz/ = to read sth
- ☞ to pore over sth /pɔːrˈəʊvə(r)/ = to examine sth very carefully and in a lot of detail
- ☞ to contemplate /ˈkɒntəmˌpleɪt/
- ☞ to ponder /ˈpɒndə(r)/
- ☞ to deliberate /dɪˈlɪbəreɪt/ = to think about or discuss sth very carefully
- ☞ to swot /swɒt/ (informal) = to study hard, esp. before an exam
- ☞ to mug up on sth (informal) = to quickly learn sth or check that you know it
- ☞ to bone up (informal) = to study hard in order to prepare for a test, meeting etc.

50.   **STUDENT** /ˈstjuːd(ə)nt/ noun

- ☞ scholar /ˈskɒlə(r)/ = sb who studies a particular subject and knows a lot about it
- ☞ undergraduate /ˌʌndə(r)ˈgrædʒuət/
- ☞ graduate /ˈgrædʒuət/ (AmE) = sb still studying after receiving a first university degree

- ✑ postgrad /ˈpəʊstˌgræd/ (BrE) = a postgraduate
- ✑ grad student
- ✑ pupil /ˈpjuːp(ə)l/
- ✑ schoolchild /ˈskuːlˌtʃaɪld/
- ✑ novice /ˈnɒvɪs/ = sb who is beginning to learn a skill or subject
- ✑ alumnus /əˈlʌmnəs/ = sb who was a student at a particular school, college or university
- ✑ fresher /ˈfreʃə(r)/ (BrE) = a student in their first year at university
- ✑ freshman /ˈfreʃmən/ (AmE) = a student in their first year at university
- ✑ sophomore /ˈsɒfəˌmɔː(r)/ (AmE) = a student in the second year of a US college or high school
- ✑ senior /ˈsiːniə(r)/ (AmE) = a student in the last year of high school or university
- ✑ schoolboy /ˈskuːlˌbɔɪ/
- ✑ schoolgirl /ˈskuːlˌgɜː(r)l/
- ✑ disciple /dɪˈsaɪp(ə)l/
- ✑ learner /ˈlɜː(r)nə(r)/
- ✑ trainee /ˌtreɪˈniː/
- ✑ apprentice /əˈprentɪs/ = sb who works for a particular person or company in order to learn

51. **DIFFERENT** /ˈdɪfrənt/ adjective

- ✑ dissimilar /dɪˈsɪmɪlə(r)/
- ✑ unlike /ʌnˈlaɪk/
- ✑ contrasting /kənˈtrɑːstɪŋ/
- ✑ contrastive /kənˈtrɑːstɪv/
- ✑ divergent /daɪˈvɜː(r)dʒ(ə)nt/
- ✑ varying /ˈveəriɪŋ/
- ✑ disparate /ˈdɪsp(ə)rət/ (formal)
- ✑ poles apart
- ✑ incompatible /ˌɪnkəmˈpætəb(ə)l/ = not able to work together
- ✑ mismatched /mɪsˈmætʃt/
- ✑ conflicting /ˌkənˈflɪktɪŋ/
- ✑ clashing /ˈklæʃɪŋ/
- ✑ alternative /ɔːlˈtɜː(r)nətɪv/
- ✑ distinct /dɪˈstɪŋkt/
- ✑ at odds
- ✑ a far cry (informal)
- ✑ worlds apart
- ✑ different as chalk and cheese

52. **FOR EXAMPLE** /fərɪgˈzɑːmp(ə)l/ phrase

- ✑ for instance, … / … for instance /fər ˈɪnstəns/
- ✑ By way of illustration, … /ˌɪləˈstreɪʃ(ə)n/
- ✑ such as …
- ✑ Like…
- ✑ …in particular /pə(r)ˈtɪkjʊlə(r)/

53

- Namely… /ˈneɪmli/
- …, to wit: … /wɪt/ (formal) = that is to say
- …, specifically… /spəˈsɪfɪkli/
- …, viz., … /vɪz/ (formal) = in other words
- …, videlicet … (My family has 4 people, viz., mother, brother, sister and I.)
- …, i.e. … (formal) = that is
- …, inasmuch as… /ˌɪnəzˈmʌtʃ æz/ (formal)
- … being … /ˈbiːɪŋ/ = to give explanation of sth
- for one thing … (for another thing)
- in other words …
- … is a case in point
- the epitome of /ɪˈpɪtəmi/ = the best possible example of sth
- e.g. /ˌiː ˈdʒiː/ (formal) = for example
- as an example/instance
- say…
- … to give as an illustration

53.   **DEVELOPMENT** /dɪˈveləpmənt/ noun

- evolution /ˌiːvəˈluːʃ(ə)n/
- growth /ɡrəʊθ/
- maturation /ˌmætʃʊˈreɪʃ(ə)n/
- expansion /ɪkˈspænʃ(ə)n/
- enlargement /ɪnˈlɑː(r)dʒmənt/
- progress /ˈprəʊɡres/
- invention /ɪnˈvenʃ(ə)n/
- advance /ədˈvɑːns/
- blossoming /ˈblɒs(ə)mɪŋ/
- elaboration /ɪˌlæbəˈreɪʃ(ə)n/
- furtherance /ˈfɜː(r)ðərəns/
- unfolding /ʌnˈfəʊldɪŋ/
- extension /ɪkˈstenʃ(ə)n/
- spread /spred/
- improvement /ɪmˈpruːvmənt/

54.   **TO DEVELOP** /dɪˈveləp/ verb

- to grow /ɡrəʊ/
- to expand /ɪkˈspænd/
- to spread /spred/
- to advance /ədˈvɑːns/
- to progress /prəʊˈɡres/
- to evolve /ɪˈvɒlv/
- to mature /məˈtʃʊə(r)/
- to thrive /θraɪv/

54

- ☞ to flourish /ˈflʌrɪʃ/
- ☞ to blossom /ˈblɒs(ə)m/
- ☞ to set in motion = to initiate
- ☞ to augment /ɔːɡˈment/
- ☞ to broaden /ˈbrɔːd(ə)n/
- ☞ to reinforce /ˌriːɪnˈfɔː(r)s/
- ☞ to refine /rɪˈfaɪn/
- ☞ to improve /ɪmˈpruːv/
- ☞ to polish /ˈpɒlɪʃ/
- ☞ to perfect /pə(r)ˈfekt/
- ☞ to foster /ˈfɒstə(r)/
- ☞ to nurture /ˈnɜː(r)tʃə(r)/
- ☞ to amplify /ˈæmplɪˌfaɪ/
- ☞ to elaborate /ɪˈlæbəreɪt/
- ☞ to unfold /ʌnˈfəʊld/

55. **TECHNOLOGY** /tekˈnɒlədʒi/ noun

- ☞ scientific knowledge
- ☞ bleeding edge /ˈbliːdɪŋedʒ/ = very new and not yet fully tested
- ☞ fifth-generation (adj.) = very advanced and includes artificial intelligence
- ☞ high tech /haɪˈtek/ (adj.) = especially electronics
- ☞ nanotechnology /ˈnænəʊtekˌnɒlədʒi/ = building very small parts, using molecules and atoms
- ☞ cutting edge /ˈkʌtɪŋˈedʒ/ (adj.)
- ☞ cleantech /ˈkliːnˌtek/ = technology which provided benefits such as clean energy, environmentally sustainable products
- ☞ cybernetics /ˌsaɪbə(r)ˈnetɪks/ = makes copies of natural things, for example artificial body parts
- ☞ intermediate technology /ˌɪntə(r)ˈmiːdiət tekˈnɒlədʒi/ = used in developing countries, based on cheap materials available there

56. **HEALTHY** /ˈhelθi/ adjective

To describe people:

- ☞ in good health
- ☞ in good trim /trɪm/
- ☞ fit /fɪt/
- ☞ in tip-tip shape
- ☞ vigorous /ˈvɪɡ(ə)rəs/
- ☞ a picture of health (informal)
- ☞ thriving /ˈθraɪvɪŋ/
- ☞ blooming /ˈbluːmɪŋ/
- ☞ well /wel/
- ☞ in condition /kənˈdɪʃ(ə)n/
- ☞ in fine fettle /ˈfet(ə)l/

- sturdy /ˈstɜː(r)di/
- robust /rəʊˈbʌst/
- strong /strɒŋ/
- hale /heɪl/
- able-bodied /ˌeɪb(ə)l ˈbɒdid/
- healthsome
- hardy /ˈhɑː(r)di/ (informal)
- fit as a fiddle /ˈfɪd(ə)l/ (informal)
- right as rain (informal)
- in the pink (informal)

To describe things:

- healthful /ˈhelθfl/
- wholesome /ˈhəʊls(ə)m/
- good for one
- beneficial /ˌbenɪˈfɪʃ(ə)l/
- salubrious /səˈluːbriəs/
- nutritious /njuːˈtrɪʃəs/
- nourishing /ˈnʌrɪʃɪŋ/
- bracing /ˈbreɪsɪŋ/
- invigorating /ɪnˈvɪɡəˌreɪtɪŋ/
- stimulating /ˈsɪmjʊleɪtɪŋ/
- therapeutic /ˌθerəˈpjuːtɪk/ = sth that makes you feel better

57. **UNHEALTHY** /ʌnˈhelθi/ adjective

To describe people:

- sickly /ˈsɪkli/ = often ill
- in poor health
- ailing /ˈeɪlɪŋ/ = ill and weak
- indisposed /ˌɪndɪˈspəʊzd/ (formal)
- frail /freɪl/
- morbid /ˈmɔː(r)bɪd/
- ill /ɪl/
- unfit /ʌnˈfɪt/
- fragile /ˈfrædʒaɪl/ = not strong or healthy
- unfit /ʌnˈfɪt/
- unwell /ʌnˈwel/
- infirm /ɪnˈfɜː(r)m/
- feeble /ˈfiːb(ə)l/
- debilitated /dɪˈbɪlɪteɪtɪd/
- diseased /dɪˈziːzd/
- pasty /ˈpeɪsti/ = looking pale and not healthy

56

To describe things:

- harmful /ˈhɑː(r)mf(ə)l/
- detrimental /ˌdetrɪˈment(ə)l/
- destructive /dɪˈstrʌktɪv/
- damaging /ˈdæmɪdʒɪŋ/
- deleterious /ˌdelɪˈtɪəriəs/
- malign /məˈlaɪn/
- insalubrious /ˌɪnsəˈluːbriəs/ (formal)
- unwholesome
- noxious /ˈnɒkʃəs/
- morbid /ˈmɔː(r)bɪd/
- insalutary /ɪnˈsæljʊt(ə)ri/ (formal)
- debilitating /dɪˈbɪlɪˌteɪtɪŋ/

58. **GOVERNMENT** /ˈgʌvə(r)nmənt/ noun

- administration /ədˌmɪnɪˈstreɪʃ(ə)n/
- authority /ɔːˈθɒrəti/
- leadership /ˈliːdə(r)ʃɪp/
- cabinet /ˈkæbɪnət/ = a group of members of a government chosen by the leader of the government to give advice to him/her
- apparatus /ˌæpəˈreɪtəs/ = people and organizations involved in some aspect of government
- bureaucracy /bjʊəˈrɒkrəsi/ = the people employed to run government organizations
- executives /ɪgˈzekjʊtɪvz/
- regime /reɪˈʒiːm/ = a government that controls the country, esp. in a strict or unfair way

59. **SHOULD** /ʃʊd/ modal verb

- you'd better + verb
- need to /niːd/
- must /mʌst/
- might /maɪt/
- could /kʊd/
- be forced to /fɔː(r)st/
- be compelled to /kəmˈpelt/
- be required to /rɪˈkwaɪə(r)d/
- be obliged to /əˈblaɪdʒd/
- can /kæn/
- may /meɪ/
- ought to /ɔːt/

60. **SOCIETY** /səˈsaɪəti/ noun

- the community /kəˈmjuːnəti/

57

↻ the general public
↻ the people
↻ mankind /mænˈkaɪnd/
↻ individuals /ˌɪndɪˈvɪdʒuəlz/
↻ the many
↻ citizenry /ˈsɪtɪz(ə)nri/
↻ population /ˌpɒpjʊˈleɪʃ(ə)n/
↻ nation /ˈneɪʃ(ə)n/
↻ public /ˈpʌblɪk/
↻ humanity /hjuːˈmænəti/
↻ elite /ɪˈliːt/ = a small group of people with a lot of advantages
↻ nobs /nɒbs/ (informal) = rich and with a high social position
↻ the grass roots = ordinary people in a society
↻ folks /fəʊks/
↻ your fellow men = other people

61.   **FOOD** /fuːd/ noun

↻ nourishment /ˈnʌrɪʃmənt/ = food necessary for life, growth and health
↻ sustenance /ˈsʌstənəns/ = food and drink
↻ daily bread /ˈdeɪli bred/
↻ edibles /ˈedɪb(ə)lz/
↻ refreshments /rɪˈfreʃmənts/ = sth to eat or drink during an event, e.g. party, meeting
↻ meals /miːlz/ = an occasion when you eat, esp. breakfast, lunch or dinner
↻ provisions /prəˈvɪʒ(ə)nz/ = food needed esp. for a journey
↻ rations /ˈræʃ(ə)nz/ = food provided for people who do not have enough and for soldiers
↻ solids /ˈsɒlɪdz/
↻ foodstuff /ˈfuːdˌstʌf/ (formal)
↻ nutrition /njuːˈtrɪʃ(ə)n/ = food as sth that keeps you healthy
↻ subsistence /səbˈsɪstəns/ = the smallest amount of food that you need to stay alive
↻ feed /fiːd/ = food given to animals
↻ fodder /ˈfɒdə(r)/ = food, esp. hay or straw, for animals
↻ diet /ˈdaɪət/ = the food that you usually eat
↻ dish /dɪʃ/
↻ delicacy /ˈdelɪkəsi/ = a rare or expensive type of food
↻ cuisine /kwɪˈziːn/ = food you can eat in a particular place (country, region)
↻ viands /ˈvaɪəndz/ (formal)
↻ eatables /ˈiːtəb(ə)lz/ (informal)
↻ nosh /nɒʃ/ (BrE, informal)
↻ groceries /ˈgrəʊsəriz/ = food you buy regularly

62.   **FASHIONABLE** /ˈfæʃ(ə)nəb(ə)l/ adjective

↻ chic /ʃiːk/
↻ smart /smɑː(r)t/

58

- elegant /ˈelɪgənt/
- stylish /ˈstaɪlɪʃ/
- designer /dɪˈzaɪnə(r)/
- modish /ˈməʊdɪʃ/
- in vogue /ɪnˈvəʊg/
- in /ɪn/
- popular /ˈpɒpjʊlə(r)/
- prevailing /prɪˈveɪlɪŋ/
- current /ˈkʌrənt/
- on-trend
- latest /ˈleɪtɪst/
- up-to-the-minute
- up-to-date
- contemporary /kənˈtemp(ə)r(ə)ri/
- modern /ˈmɒdə(r)n/
- trendy /ˈtrendi/ (informal)
- all the rage /reɪdʒ/ (informal)
- hot /hɒt/ (informal)
- natty /ˈnæti/ (informal)
- glitzy /ˈglɪtsi/ (informal) = bright, exciting and attractive but with no real value
- snazzy /ˈsnæzi/ (informal)
- funky /ˈfʌŋki/ (informal)
- hip /hɪp/ (informal)
- dressed to the nines (informal)
- dressed to kill
- fancy /ˈfænsi/
- flashy /ˈflæʃi/ = very expensive, used to impress people
- upmarket /ʌpˈmɑː(r)kɪt/ = designed for rich people
- ritzy /ˈrɪtsi/ (informal) = expensive and fashionable
- swanky /ˈswæŋki/ (informal) = expensive and fashionable

63. **TO ALLOW** /əˈlaʊ/ verb

- to permit /pə(r)ˈmɪt/
- to let /let/
- to enable /ɪnˈeɪb(ə)l/ = to give sb the ability or opportunity to do sth
- to authorize /ˈɔːθəraɪz/ = to give official permission
- to sanction /ˈsæŋkʃ(ə)n/ = to give official approval for an action
- to warrant /ˈwɒrənt/
- to approve /əˈpruːv/
- to say yes to (informal)
- to give your consent to /kənˈsent/
- to agree to /əˈgriː/
- to put up with (informal)
- to okay /ˌəʊˈkeɪ/ (informal)

- ⟳ to give the green light to (informal)
- ⟳ to mandate /mænˈdeɪt/ = to give sb the authority to do sth
- ⟳ to grant /grɑːnt/ = to allow sb to have or do what they want

64. **HOME TOWN** /ˈhəʊm taʊn/ noun

- ⟳ place of origin /ˈɒrɪdʒɪn/
- ⟳ place of birth /bɜː(r)θ/
- ⟳ native town /ˈneɪtɪv/
- ⟳ native country /ˈneɪtɪv/
- ⟳ fatherland /ˈfɑːðə(r)lænd/
- ⟳ mother country
- ⟳ home /həʊm/
- ⟳ roots /ruːts/
- ⟳ provenance /ˈprɒvənəns/
- ⟳ source /sɔː(r)s/
- ⟳ cradle /ˈkreɪd(ə)l/ = a place where sth began
- ⟳ homeland /ˈhəʊmˌlænd/ = the country you come from
- ⟳ motherland /ˈmʌðə(r)ˌlænd/
- ⟳ my native soil /sɔɪl/ = country of birth

65. **SMALL** /smɔːl/ adjective

- ⟳ tiny /ˈtaɪni/
- ⟳ bitty /ˈbɪti/ = made up of many small parts that do not fit together
- ⟳ diminutive /dɪˈmɪnjʊtɪv/ = very short or small
- ⟳ insufficient /ˌɪnsəˈfɪʃ(ə)nt/ = not enough
- ⟳ limited /ˈlɪmɪtɪd/
- ⟳ little /ˈlɪt(ə)l/
- ⟳ meagre /ˈmiːgə(r)/ = smaller or less than you want or need
- ⟳ microscopic /ˌmaɪkrəˈskɒpɪk/ = very small
- ⟳ mini /ˈmɪni/
- ⟳ minute /maɪˈnjuːt/
- ⟳ narrow /ˈnærəʊ/ = small in width
- ⟳ petite /pəˈtiːt/
- ⟳ pocket-sized /ˈpɒkɪt ˌsaɪzd/ = small enough to fit in your pocket
- ⟳ petty /ˈpeti/
- ⟳ pint-sized /ˈpaɪnt ˌsaɪzd/ (informal)
- ⟳ puny /ˈpjuːni/ = small, thin, weak (person, animal)
- ⟳ scanty /ˈskænti/ = not much, less than needed
- ⟳ slight /slaɪt/ = small in size, amount or degree
- ⟳ small-scale /smɔːl skeɪl/
- ⟳ teensy /ˈtiːnzi/ (informal)
- ⟳ teeny /ˈtiːni/ (informal)
- ⟳ trifling /ˈtraɪf(ə)lɪŋ/ = not very important

- trivial /ˈtrɪviəl/ = not important, serious or valuable
- undersized /ˌʌndə(r)ˈsaɪzd/ = smaller than normal
- wee /wiː/
- minuscule /ˈmɪnɪˌskjuːl/ = extremely small
- compact /ˈkɒmpækt/ or /kəmˈpækt/
- cramped /kræmpt/ = small and crowded
- poky /ˈpəʊki/ = small and uncomfortable
- miniature /ˈmɪnətʃə(r)/
- infinitesimal /ˌɪnfɪnɪˈtesɪm(ə)l/ = extremely small
- teeny weeny (informal)
- paltry /ˈpɔːltri/ = small in number, not important
- midget /ˈmɪdʒɪt/ = smaller than the usual size

66.   **BIG** /bɪg/ adjective

- large /lɑː(r)dʒ/
- great /ɡreɪt/
- bulky /ˈbʌlki/ = too big to be carried easily
- colossal /kəˈlɒs(ə)l/ = extremely large
- enormous /ɪˈnɔː(r)məs/
- extensive /ɪkˈstensɪv/ = very large in amount or degree
- gigantic /dʒaɪˈɡæntɪk/ = extremely large
- hefty /ˈhefti/ = large and heavy
- huge /hjuːdʒ/
- humongous /hjuːˈmʌŋɡəs/ (informal) = extremely large and impressive
- immense /ɪˈmens/ = extremely large
- massive /ˈmæsɪv/
- ponderous /ˈpɒndərəs/ = moving slowly because of being big and heavy
- roomy /ˈruːmi/ = large and providing you with a lot of space
- spacious /ˈspeɪʃəs/ = for rooms, buildings etc.
- substantial /səbˈstænʃ(ə)l/ = large in amount or degree
- tremendous /trəˈmendəs/ = to emphasize that sth such as an amount, achievement, feeling is extremely great
- vast /vɑːst/
- king-size /ˈkɪŋ ˌsaɪz/
- mondo /mˈɒndəʊ/ (informal) = very large or impressive
- sizeable /ˈsaɪzəb(ə)l/ = fairly large
- mammoth /ˈmæməθ/ = very large
- whopping /ˈwɒpɪŋ/ (informal) = extremely large
- ginormous /dʒaɪˈnɔː(r)məs/ (informal) = extremely large
- mega /ˈmeɡə/ (informal) = extremely large

67.   **OPINION** /əˈpɪnjən/ noun

- belief /bɪˈliːf/

- judgement /ˈdʒʌdʒmənt/
- view /vjuː/
- viewpoint /ˈvjuːˌpɔɪnt/
- point of view
- idea /aɪˈdɪə/
- perception /pə(r)ˈsepʃ(ə)n/
- stance /stæns/
- standpoint /ˈstæn(d)ˌpɔɪnt/
- impression /ɪmˈpreʃ(ə)n/
- sentiment /ˈsentɪmənt/
- assumption /əˈsʌmpʃ(ə)n/
- assessment /əˈsesmənt/
- conception /kənˈsepʃ(ə)n/
- notion /ˈnəʊʃ(ə)n/
- way of thinking
- thought /θɔːt/
- school of thought
- conviction /kənˈvɪkʃ(ə)n/
- persuasion /pə(r)ˈsweɪʒ(ə)n/
- attitude /ˈætɪˌtjuːd/
- estimation /ˌestɪˈmeɪʃ(ə)n/ (formal)
- stand /stænd/ = an opinion that you state publicly

68. **GOOD** /ɡʊd/ adjective

Meaning 'pleasant':

- acceptable /əkˈseptəb(ə)l/
- admirable /ˈædm(ə)rəb(ə)l/
- commendable /kəˈmendəb(ə)l/
- congenial /kənˈdʒiːniəl/
- deluxe /dəˈlʌks/
- excellent /ˈeksələnt/
- exceptional /ɪkˈsepʃ(ə)nəl/
- favourable /ˈfeɪv(ə)rəb(ə)l/
- first-class
- first-rate
- gratifying /ˈɡrætɪˌfaɪɪŋ/
- honourable /ˈɒn(ə)rəb(ə)l/
- marvellous /ˈmɑː(r)vələs/
- precious /ˈpreʃəs/
- prime /praɪm/
- reputable /ˈrepjʊtəb(ə)l/
- satisfactory /ˌsætɪsˈfækt(ə)ri/
- shipshape /ˈʃɪpˌʃeɪp/ = in good condition

- ⟳ spanking /ˈspæŋkɪŋ/
- ⟳ splendid /ˈsplendɪd/
- ⟳ sterling /ˈstɜː(r)lɪŋ/ = for work or character
- ⟳ stupendous /stjuːˈpendəs/ = very impressive
- ⟳ superb /sʊˈpɜː(r)b/
- ⟳ tip-top = extremely good

Meaning 'moral':

- ⟳ admirable /ˈædm(ə)rəb(ə)l/
- ⟳ blameless /ˈbleɪmləs/
- ⟳ charitable /ˈtʃærɪtəb(ə)l/
- ⟳ dutiful /ˈdjuːtɪf(ə)l/
- ⟳ ethical /ˈeθɪk(ə)l/
- ⟳ exemplary /ɪgˈzempləri/
- ⟳ guiltless /ˈgɪltləs/
- ⟳ honest /ˈɒnɪst/
- ⟳ honourable /ˈɒn(ə)rəb(ə)l/
- ⟳ inculpable /ɪnˈkʌlpəb(ə)l/
- ⟳ innocent /ˈɪnəs(ə)nt/
- ⟳ irreproachable /ˌɪrɪˈprəʊtʃəb(ə)l/
- ⟳ lily-white
- ⟳ praiseworthy /ˈpreɪzˌwɜː(r)ði/
- ⟳ pure /pjʊə(r)/
- ⟳ respectable /rɪˈspektəb(ə)l/
- ⟳ righteous /ˈraɪtʃəs/
- ⟳ tractable /ˈtræktəb(ə)l/
- ⟳ upright /ˈʌpraɪt/
- ⟳ virtuous /ˈvɜː(r)tʃʊəs/

Meaning 'skilled':

- ⟳ able /ˈeɪb(ə)l/
- ⟳ accomplished /əˈkʌmplɪʃt/
- ⟳ adept /əˈdept/
- ⟳ adroit /əˈdrɔɪt/
- ⟳ competent /ˈkɒmpɪtənt/
- ⟳ dexterous /ˈdekst(ə)rəs/ = able to use your hands skillfully
- ⟳ expert /ˈekspɜː(r)t/
- ⟳ proficient /prəˈfɪʃ(ə)nt/
- ⟳ proper /ˈprɒpə(r)/
- ⟳ qualified /ˈkwɒlɪfaɪd/
- ⟳ satisfactory /ˌsætɪsˈfækt(ə)ri/
- ⟳ serviceable /ˈsɜː(r)vɪsəb(ə)l/ = good enough to be used for a particular purpose but not very attractive

- ↻ skillful /ˈskɪlf(ə)l/
- ↻ suited /ˈsuːtɪd/
- ↻ talented /ˈtæləntɪd/
- ↻ thorough /ˈθʌrə/

Meaning 'useful':

- ↻ advantageous /ˌædvənˈteɪdʒəs/ = likely to make sth/sb more successful
- ↻ ample /ˈæmp(ə)l/
- ↻ appropriate /əˈprəʊpriət/
- ↻ apt /æpt/ = good at learning, suitable (name, description, comment)
- ↻ auspicious /ɔːˈspɪʃəs/ = showing signs of success
- ↻ beneficial /ˌbenɪˈfɪʃ(ə)l/
- ↻ congruous /ˈkɒŋgruəs/
- ↻ decent /ˈdiːs(ə)nt/
- ↻ desirable /dɪˈzaɪrəb(ə)l/
- ↻ favouring /ˈfeɪvə(r)ɪŋ/
- ↻ fitting /ˈfɪtɪŋ/
- ↻ opportune /ˈɒpə(r)tjuːn/
- ↻ profitable /ˈprɒfɪtəb(ə)l/
- ↻ propitious /prəˈpɪʃəs/ = with the conditions needed for a successful result
- ↻ salubrious /səˈluːbriəs/
- ↻ salutary /ˈsæljʊt(ə)ri/ = an experience that has a good effect although it is unpleasant
- ↻ seemly /ˈsiːmli/
- ↻ unobjectionable /ʌnəbˈdʒekʃ(ə)nəb(ə)l/

Meaning 'kind':

- ↻ altruistic /ˌæltruˈɪstɪk/
- ↻ approving /əˈpruːvɪŋ/ = very supportive
- ↻ beneficent /bəˈnefɪs(ə)nt/ = doing things that are intended to help people
- ↻ benevolent /bəˈnev(ə)lənt/
- ↻ charitable /ˈtʃærɪtəb(ə)l/
- ↻ considerate /kənˈsɪd(ə)rət/
- ↻ gracious /ˈgreɪʃəs/
- ↻ humane /hjuːˈmeɪn/
- ↻ humanitarian /hjuːˌmænɪˈteəriən/
- ↻ merciful /ˈmɜː(r)sɪf(ə)l/
- ↻ obliging /əˈblaɪdʒɪŋ/ = willing to help
- ↻ philanthropic /ˌfɪlənˈθrɒpɪk/
- ↻ well-disposed /ˌwel dɪˈspəʊzd/

69. **BAD** /bæd/ adjective

Meaning 'unpleasant, poor':

- ☞ abominable /əˈbɒmɪnəb(ə)l/
- ☞ amiss /əˈmɪs/
- ☞ atrocious /əˈtrəʊʃəs/
- ☞ beastly /ˈbiːstli/ (informal)
- ☞ bottom out = very low level
- ☞ bummer /ˈbʌmə(r)/ (informal)
- ☞ cheesy /ˈtʃiːzi/ = of poor quality
- ☞ crappy/ˈkræpi/ (very informal)
- ☞ crummy /ˈkrʌmi/ (informal)
- ☞ defective /dɪˈfektɪv/ = not working correctly
- ☞ diddly /ˈdɪdli/ (AmE, informal) = nothing
- ☞ downer /ˈdaʊnə(r)/ (n.) = sth that makes you sad or disappointed
- ☞ dreadful /ˈdredf(ə)l/
- ☞ erroneous /ɪˈrəʊniəs/ = not correct
- ☞ faulty /ˈfɔːlti/
- ☞ gross /grəʊs/
- ☞ grungy /ˈgrʌndʒi/ (informal) = dirty and smelling bad
- ☞ icky /ˈɪki/ (informal) = very unpleasant to touch, look at, smell or taste
- ☞ inadequate /ɪnˈædɪkwət/ = not enough
- ☞ inferior /ɪnˈfɪəriə(r)/
- ☞ junky /ˈdʒʌŋki/ (informal)
- ☞ lousy /ˈlaʊzi/ (informal)
- ☞ sleazy /ˈsliːzi/
- ☞ slipshod /ˈslɪpʃɒd/ = done in a careless way
- ☞ substandard /ˌsʌbˈstændə(r)d/
- ☞ unacceptable /ˌʌnəkˈseptəb(ə)l/

Meaning 'harmful':

- ☞ damaging /ˈdæmɪdʒɪŋ/
- ☞ deleterious /ˌdelɪˈtɪəriəs/
- ☞ detrimental /ˌdetrɪˈment(ə)l/
- ☞ hurtful /ˈhɜː(r)tf(ə)l/
- ☞ injurious /ɪnˈdʒʊəriəs/ (formal) = causing harm or damage
- ☞ ruinous /ˈruːɪnəs/

Meaning 'immoral':

- ☞ base /beɪs/
- ☞ corrupt /kəˈrʌpt/
- ☞ delinquent /dɪˈlɪŋkwənt/ = behaving in an immoral way (criminal)
- ☞ evil /ˈiːv(ə)l/
- ☞ iniquitous /ɪˈnɪkwɪtəs/
- ☞ sinful /ˈsɪnf(ə)l/
- ☞ vicious /ˈvɪʃəs/

- ↻ vile /vaɪl/
- ↻ villainous /ˈvɪlənəs/
- ↻ wicked /ˈwɪkɪd/

Meaning 'decayed':

- ↻ mouldy /ˈməʊldi/
- ↻ off /ɒf/
- ↻ putrid /ˈpjuːtrɪd/
- ↻ rancid /ˈrænsɪd/
- ↻ rotten /ˈrɒt(ə)n/
- ↻ sour /ˈsaʊə(r)/
- ↻ spoiled /spɔɪld/

Meaning 'sorry, sad':

- ↻ apologetic /əˌpɒləˈdʒetɪk/
- ↻ conscience-stricken /ˈkɒnʃ(ə)ns ˈstrɪkən/
- ↻ contrite /ˈkɒntraɪt/ or /kənˈtraɪt/
- ↻ crestfallen /ˈkrestˌfɔːlən/ = sad and disappointed, esp. when sth has not succeeded
- ↻ dejected /dɪˈdʒektɪd/ = lost all hope because they have failed at sth
- ↻ disconsolate /dɪsˈkɒnsələt/
- ↻ down /daʊn/
- ↻ downhearted /ˌdaʊnˈhɑː(r)tɪd/
- ↻ regretful /rɪˈgretf(ə)l/
- ↻ remorseful /rɪˈmɔː(r)sf(ə)l/
- ↻ woebegone /ˈwəʊbɪˌgɒn/ (formal) = looking sad

70. **SURE** /ʃɔː(r)/ or /ʃʊə(r)/ adjective

- ↻ confident /ˈkɒnfɪd(ə)nt/
- ↻ gutsy /ˈgʌtsi/ = brave and determined
- ↻ unhesitating /ʌnˈhezɪˌteɪtɪŋ/
- ↻ clear /klɪə(r)/
- ↻ convinced /kənˈvɪnst/
- ↻ doubtless /ˈdaʊtləs/
- ↻ enduring /ɪnˈdjʊərɪŋ/
- ↻ beyond doubt /bɪˈjɒnd daʊt/
- ↻ clinched /klɪntʃt/
- ↻ confirmed /kənˈfɜː(r)md/
- ↻ firm /fɜː(r)m/
- ↻ fixed /fɪkst/
- ↻ for a fact
- ↻ genuine /ˈdʒenjuɪn/
- ↻ indisputable /ˌɪndɪˈspjuːtəb(ə)l/

- guaranteed /ˌgeærənˈtiːd/
- positive /ˈpɒzətɪv/
- undeniable /ˌʌndɪˈnaɪəb(ə)l/
- unquestionable /ʌnˈkwestʃ(ə)nəb(ə)l/
- unshakable /ʌnˈʃeɪkəb(ə)l/
- sealed /siːld/
- certain /ˈsɜː(r)t(ə)n/
- definite /ˈdef(ə)nət/
- dogmatic /dɒgˈmætɪk/ = so sure that your beliefs are right that you expect others to accept them
- unmistakable /ˌʌnmɪˈsteɪkəb(ə)l/
- unfaltering /ʌnˈfɔːltərɪŋ/ (formal)
- unwavering /ʌnˈweɪv(ə)rɪŋ/
- precise /prɪˈsaɪs/
- irrevocable /ɪˈrevəkəb(ə)l/ = impossible to change
- pukka /ˈpʌkə/ (BrE, informal) = real
- as sure as eggs is eggs (informal)

71. **BEAUTIFUL** /ˈbjuːtəf(ə)l/ adjective

- alluring /əˈlʊərɪŋ/ or /əˈljʊərɪŋ/
- seductive /sɪˈdʌktɪv/
- angelic /ænˈdʒelɪk/
- appealing /əˈpiːlɪŋ/
- bewitching /bɪˈwɪtʃɪŋ/
- enchanting /ɪnˈtʃɑːntɪŋ/
- charming /ˈtʃɑː(r)mɪŋ/
- fascinating /ˈfæsɪneɪtɪŋ/
- classy /ˈklɑːsi/ (informal)
- elegant /ˈelɪgənt/
- cute /kjuːt/
- delightful /dɪˈlaɪtf(ə)l/
- highly pleasing /ˈhaɪli ˈpliːzɪŋ/
- divine /dɪˈvaɪn/
- perfect /ˈpɜː(r)fɪkt/
- dazzling /ˈdæzlɪŋ/
- adorable /əˈdɔːrəb(ə)l/
- dainty /ˈdeɪnti/ = small and attractive in a delicate way
- exquisite /ɪkˈskwɪzɪt/
- gorgeous /ˈgɔː(r)dʒəs/
- graceful /ˈgreɪsf(ə)l/
- magnificent /mægˈnɪfɪs(ə)nt/
- marvellous /ˈmɑː(r)vələs/
- ravishing /ˈrævɪʃɪŋ/
- splendid /ˈsplendɪd/
- stunning /ˈstʌnɪŋ/

- sublime /sə'blaɪm/
- glamorous /'glæmərəs/
- hunky /'hʌŋki/ (informal) = usually of a man
- magnetic /mæg'netɪk/
- mesmeric /mez'merɪk/
- tempting /'temptɪŋ/
- radiant /'reɪdiənt/
- voluptuous /və'lʌptʃʊəs/ = usually of a woman
- striking /'straɪkɪŋ/
- pulchritudinous /'pʌlkrɪtjuːdɪnəs/ (formal)
- smashing /'smæʃɪŋ/ (informal)
- out of this world (informal)
- drop-dead gorgeous (informal)

72. **NICE** /naɪs/ adjective

Meaning 'likable':

- amiable /'eɪmiəb(ə)l/
- charming /'tʃɑː(r)mɪŋ/
- commendable /kə'mendəb(ə)l/ (formal) = deserving praise
- considerate /kən'sɪd(ə)rət/ = thinking about the feelings and needs of other people
- cordial /'kɔː(r)diəl/
- courteous /'kɜː(r)tiəs/ = polite
- genial /'dʒiːniəl/
- groovy /'gruːvi/ (informal)
- ingratiating /ɪn'greɪʃiˌeɪtɪŋ/ = done in an attempt to get sb's approval (smile, nod)
- nifty /'nɪfti/ (informal) = easy to use, skilful
- unpresumptuous /ʌnprɪ'zʌmptʃuəs/ = showing a lot of respect
- well-mannered

Meaning 'precise':

- accurate /'ækjʊrət/
- befitting /bɪ'fɪtɪŋ/
- cultured /'kʌltʃə(r)d/
- dainty /'deɪnti/ = small and attractive in a delicate way
- discerning /dɪ'sɜː(r)nɪŋ/ = Showing good judgement about things, able to tell whether something is valuable or well made
- exact /ɪg'zækt/
- fastidious /fæ'stɪdiəs/ = caring about small details, keeping everything tidy
- genteel /dʒen'tiːl/ = polite well-educated person who is shocked by anything rude
- meticulous /mɪ'tɪkjʊləs/ = very thorough and caring about details
- neat /niːt/
- refined /rɪ'faɪnd/ = very polite and well-educated

68

- trim /trɪm/ = attractive person
- well-bred /ˌwel ˈbred/ = with good manners and good education

73. **INTERESTING** /ˈɪntrəstɪŋ/ adjective

- absorbing /əbˈzɔː(r)bɪŋ/ = worth all your attention
- affecting /əˈfektɪŋ/ = making you feel strong emotions
- alluring /əˈlʊərɪŋ/ or /əˈljʊərɪŋ/
- attractive /əˈtræktɪv/
- captivating /ˈkæptɪˌveɪtɪŋ/
- charismatic /ˌkærɪzˈmætɪk/ = used for people
- compelling /kəmˈpelɪŋ/
- delightful /dɪˈlaɪtf(ə)l/
- enchanting /ɪnˈtʃɑːntɪŋ/
- engaging /ɪnˈɡeɪdʒɪŋ/
- engrossing /ɪnˈɡrəʊsɪŋ/ = extremely interesting
- enthralling /ɪnˈθrɔːlɪŋ/
- entrancing /ɪnˈtrɑːnsɪŋ/
- exceptional /ɪkˈsepʃ(ə)nəl/
- gripping /ˈɡrɪpɪŋ/
- intriguing /ɪnˈtriːɡɪŋ/
- inviting /ɪnˈvaɪtɪŋ/
- magnetic /mæɡˈnetɪk/ = able to attract people strongly
- pleasurable /ˈpleʒ(ə)rəb(ə)l/ (formal)
- prepossessing /ˌpriːpəˈzesɪŋ/ (formal)
- readable /ˈriːdəb(ə)l/ = easy and pleasant to read
- riveting /ˈrɪvɪtɪŋ/ = extremely interesting
- stimulating /ˈstɪmjʊˌleɪtɪŋ/
- stirring /ˈstɜːrɪŋ/ = causing strong emotions
- striking /ˈstraɪkɪŋ/ = unusual
- thought-provoking /ˈθɔːt prəˌvəʊkɪŋ/ = makes you think of new ideas
- unputdownable /ˌʌnpʊtˈdaʊnəb(ə)l/ (informal) = of a book that is so interesting you don't want to stop reading it
- buzzworthy /ˈbʌzˌwɜː(r)ði/ = likely to create interest and attention
- nail-biting = exciting
- water cooler (n.) = esp. a TV programme that is so interesting that people talk about it at work the next day

74. **BORING** /ˈbɔːrɪŋ/ adjective

- arid /ˈærɪd/
- characterless /ˈkærɪktə(r)ləs/ = very ordinary
- cloying /ˈklɔɪɪŋ/ = too much of something hence not interesting
- colourless /ˈkʌlə(r)ləs/
- commonplace /ˈkɒmənˌpleɪs/

- dead /ded/ = of a place where not much happens
- drab /dræb/
- dull /dʌl/
- humdrum /ˈhʌmdrʌm/
- insipid /ɪnˈsɪpɪd/
- interminable /ɪnˈtɜː(r)mɪnəb(ə)l/ = continuing for a long time in a boring way
- irksome /ˈɜː(r)ks(ə)m/
- lifeless /ˈlaɪfləs/
- monotonous /məˈnɒtənəs/
- plebeian /pləˈbiːən/ = typical of sb from a low social class, an insulting word
- prosaic /prəʊˈzeɪɪk/ = lacking imagination or excitement
- repetitious /ˌrepəˈtɪʃəs/ = done many times hence boring
- spiritless /ˈspɪrɪtles/
- stale /steɪl/ = not new, original
- stodgy /ˈstɒdʒi/ = boring and difficult to read
- tame /teɪm/
- tedious /ˈtiːdiəs/ = boring and lasting too long
- tiresome /ˈtaɪə(r)s(ə)m/ = making you feel bored
- trite /traɪt/
- vapid /ˈvæpɪd/
- wearisome /ˈwɪəris(ə)m/ = making you feel tired or bored
- mundane /ˌmʌnˈdeɪn/ = ordinary
- dreary /ˈdrɪəri/ = making you feel bored or unhappy
- unimaginative /ˌʌnɪˈmædʒɪnətɪv/
- uninspiring /ˌʌnɪnˈspaɪərɪŋ/
- jejune /dʒɪˈdʒuːn/ (formal) = understanding or describing ideas in a way that is too simple
- samey /ˈseɪmi/ (BrE, informal)
- dull as ditchwater/dishwater (informal)
- mind-numbing /ˈmaɪndˈnʌmɪŋ/ = extremely boring

75. **SO-SO** /səʊˈsəʊ/ adjective, adverb

- settled /ˈset(ə)ld/ = not likely to change
- tolerable /ˈtɒl(ə)rəb(ə)l/ = satisfactory but not very good
- average /ˈæv(ə)rɪdʒ/
- enough /ɪˈnʌf/
- fair to middling /feə(r)təˈmɪd(ə)lɪŋ/ (informal)
- fairish /ˈfeə(r)ɪʃ/
- mediocre /ˌmiːdiˈəʊkə(r)/
- medium /ˈmiːdiəm/
- passable /ˈpɑːsəb(ə)l/
- run-of-the-mill (informal)
- moderate /ˈmɒd(ə)rət/
- adequate /ˈædɪkwət/
- undistinguished /ˌʌndɪˈstɪŋgwɪʃt/ = not special

- ☞ no great shakes (informal)
- ☞ suboptimal /ˌsʌbˈɒptɪm(ə)l/ (formal) = not of the highest quality
- ☞ underwhelming /ˌʌndə(r)ˈwelmɪŋ/ = not impressive

76. **IMPORTANT** /ɪmˈpɔː(r)t(ə)nt/ adjective

- ☞ eminent /ˈemɪnənt/ = for people
- ☞ influential /ˌɪnfluˈenʃ(ə)l/
- ☞ leading /ˈliːdɪŋ/
- ☞ main /meɪn/
- ☞ major league (AmE)
- ☞ meaningful /ˈmiːnɪŋf(ə)l/
- ☞ paramount /ˈpærəmaʊnt/
- ☞ prime /praɪm/
- ☞ principal /ˈprɪnsəp(ə)l/
- ☞ prominent /ˈprɒmɪnənt/ = important and well-known
- ☞ significant /sɪɡˈnɪfɪkənt/
- ☞ substantial /səbˈstænʃ(ə)l/ = important or real
- ☞ valuable /ˈvæljʊb(ə)l/
- ☞ momentous /məʊˈmentəs/ = very important because of having an effect on future events
- ☞ noteworthy /ˈnəʊtˌwɜː(r)ði/
- ☞ relevant /ˈreləv(ə)nt/
- ☞ salient /ˈseɪliənt/ (formal) = fact, issue, feature
- ☞ vital /ˈvaɪt(ə)l/ = necessary, essential
- ☞ essential /ɪˈsenʃ(ə)l/
- ☞ key /kiː/ = very important
- ☞ weighty /ˈweɪti/
- ☞ grave /ɡreɪv/ = very serious (situation)
- ☞ far-reaching /ˌfɑː(r) ˈriːtʃɪŋ/ = affecting a lot of people or things in an important way
- ☞ pivotal /ˈpɪvət(ə)l/
- ☞ epoch-making /ˈiːpɒkˌmeɪkɪŋ/ = having an important effect on the future
- ☞ world-shattering /ˈwɜː(r)ld ˈʃæt(ə)rɪŋ/
- ☞ seminal /ˈsemɪn(ə)l/ (formal) = of a piece of writing or music
- ☞ foremost /ˈfɔː(r)məʊst/
- ☞ prestigious /preˈstɪdʒəs/ = admired and respected
- ☞ notable /ˈnəʊtəb(ə)l/ = interesting enough to be mentioned
- ☞ esteemed /ɪˈstiːmd/ = for people
- ☞ crucial /ˈkruːʃ(ə)l/ = extremely important
- ☞ fundamental /ˌfʌndəˈment(ə)l/ = essential to the existence or success of sth

77. **STRANGE** /streɪndʒ/ adjective

- ☞ odd /ɒd/
- ☞ peculiar /pɪˈkjuːliə(r)/ = strange in an unpleasant way
- ☞ curious /ˈkjʊəriəs/ = unusual and interesting

- ☞ queer /kwɪə(r)/
- ☞ weird /wɪə(r)d/
- ☞ bizarre /bɪˈzɑː(r)/
- ☞ eccentric /ɪkˈsentrɪk/ = used for sb's behaviour
- ☞ offbeat /ˈɒfˌbiːt/ (informal)
- ☞ abnormal /æbˈnɔː(r)m(ə)l/ = in a way that is worrying or wrong
- ☞ uncommon /ʌnˈkɒmən/ = rare
- ☞ surreal /səˈrɪəl/ = so strange you don't believe it's real
- ☞ perplexing /pə(r)ˈpleksɪŋ/ = confusing
- ☞ inexplicable /ˌɪnɪkˈsplɪkəb(ə)l/ = impossible to explain
- ☞ uncanny /ʌnˈkæni/ = strange and mysterious
- ☞ singular /ˈsɪŋjʊlə(r)/ (formal) = strange and unusual
- ☞ freaky /ˈfriːki/ (informal) = very strange and a bit frightening
- ☞ wacky /ˈwæki/ (informal) = funny or silly
- ☞ oddball /ˈɒdˌbɔːl/ (n., informal) = sb whose behaviour is strange
- ☞ off-the-wall (informal)
- ☞ novel /ˈnɒv(ə)l/ = unusual
- ☞ exotic /ɪgˈzɒtɪk/
- ☞ idiosyncratic /ˌɪdiəʊsɪŋˈkrætɪk/ = strange and not shared by others
- ☞ outlandish /aʊtˈlændɪʃ/ = extremely strange and unusual
- ☞ edgy /ˈedʒi/ = of music, films, books etc. that are strange in a way that is interesting or exciting
- ☞ atypical /ˌeɪˈtɪpɪk(ə)l/
- ☞ anomalous /əˈnɒmələs/
- ☞ out of the ordinary
- ☞ puzzling /ˈpʌz(ə)lɪŋ/ = confusing or difficult to solve
- ☞ eerie /ˈɪəri/ = strange and mysterious, sometimes frightening
- ☞ fishy /ˈfɪʃi/ (informal) = not completely right or honest
- ☞ quirky /ˈkwɜː(r)ki/ = slightly strange

78. **FAT** /fæt/ adjective

- ☞ overweight /ˌəʊvə(r)ˈweɪt/ = heavier than you should be
- ☞ bulky /ˈbʌlki/ = big, wide and solid
- ☞ chunky /ˈtʃʌŋki/ = short and wide
- ☞ corpulent /ˈkɔː(r)pjʊlənt/
- ☞ heavy /ˈhevi/
- ☞ hefty /ˈhefti/ = large and heavy
- ☞ obese /əʊˈbiːs/ = too fat
- ☞ plump /plʌmp/ = slightly fat
- ☞ stout /staʊt/ = slightly fat
- ☞ weighty /ˈweɪti/
- ☞ chubby /ˈtʃʌbi/ (informal) = slightly fat, like a baby or a young child
- ☞ large /lɑː(r)dʒ/
- ☞ portly /ˈpɔː(r)tli/ = fairly fat
- ☞ paunchy /ˈpɔːntʃi/

- ↻ potbellied /ˈpɒtˌbelɪd/ = with a large stomach that sticks out
- ↻ beer-bellied = with a fat stomach from drinking too much beer
- ↻ meaty /ˈmiːti/ = big with a lot of fat or muscle
- ↻ of ample proportions /əvˈæmp(ə)l prəˈpɔː(r)ʃ(ə)nz/
- ↻ heavyset = big and strong
- ↻ plus-size (informal)
- ↻ big-boned (informal)
- ↻ tubby /ˈtʌbi/ (informal) = slightly fat
- ↻ roly-poly /ˌrəʊli ˈpəʊli/ (informal) = short and fat
- ↻ buxom /ˈbʌks(ə)m/ = of a woman, fat in an attractive way, with large breasts

79.   **VERY** /ˈveri/ adjective, adverb

- ↻ really /ˈrɪəli/
- ↻ enormously /ɪˈnɔː(r)məsli/ = extremely
- ↻ excessively /ɪkˈsesɪvli/
- ↻ extremely /ɪkˈstriːmli/
- ↻ greatly /ˈɡreɪtli/
- ↻ highly /ˈhaɪli/
- ↻ hugely /ˈhjuːdʒli/
- ↻ remarkably /rɪˈmɑː(r)kəbli/
- ↻ strikingly /ˈstraɪkɪŋli/
- ↻ terribly /ˈterəbli/ (informal)
- ↻ unusually /ʌnˈjuːʒʊəli/
- ↻ vastly /ˈvɑːs(t)li/
- ↻ truly /ˈtruːli/
- ↻ absolutely /ˈæbsəluːtli/
- ↻ amply /ˈæmp(ə)li/
- ↻ certainly /ˈsɜː(r)t(ə)nli/
- ↻ considerably /kənˈsɪd(ə)rəbli/
- ↻ deeply /ˈdiːpli/
- ↻ eminently /ˈemɪnəntli/
- ↻ exceedingly /ɪkˈsiːdɪŋli/
- ↻ incredibly /ɪnˈkredəbli/
- ↻ indispensably /ˌɪndɪˈspensəb(ə)li/
- ↻ largely /ˈlɑː(r)dʒli/
- ↻ notably /ˈnəʊtəbli/
- ↻ particularly /pə(r)ˈtɪkjʊlə(r)li/
- ↻ pretty /ˈprɪti/
- ↻ exceptionally /ɪkˈsepʃ(ə)nəli/
- ↻ tremendously /trəˈmendəsli/
- ↻ immensely /ɪˈmensli/
- ↻ acutely /əˈkjuːtli/
- ↻ abundantly /əˈbʌndəntli/
- ↻ decidedly /dɪˈsaɪdɪdli/

- ↻ supremely /sʊˈpriːmli/
- ↻ mightily /ˈmaɪtɪli/
- ↻ ever so (BrE, informal)
- ↻ awfully /ˈɔːf(ə)li/ (informal)
- ↻ seriously /ˈsɪəriəsli/ (informal)
- ↻ mega /ˈmegə/ (informal) = extremely
- ↻ dead /ded/ (informal)
- ↻ thoroughly /ˈθʌrəli/
- ↻ indeed /ɪnˈdiːd/ = used following 'very', e.g. The book was very good indeed.

80. **HOW ARE YOU ?** phrase

- ↻ What's up? (informal)
- ↻ How do you do? (BrE, formal)
- ↻ How is it hanging? (informal)
- ↻ How is it going?
- ↻ How are you getting on?
- ↻ How've you been?
- ↻ How's life?
- ↻ What have you been up to?
- ↻ How's everything?
- ↻ What's going on?
- ↻ How are things?
- ↻ How are you doing?
- ↻ What's happening with you?
- ↻ What's new?
- ↻ What's new with you?
- ↻ What'cha been up to lately? (AmE, informal)
- ↻ Anything new?
- ↻ What's shakin'? (AmE, informal)
- ↻ How's life been treating you?

81. **I' M FINE. THANK YOU.** phrase

- ↻ Very well, thank you. And you?
- ↻ Fine.
- ↻ Great.
- ↻ Good.
- ↻ Not bad.
- ↻ Nothing much.
- ↻ Nothing special.
- ↻ Nothing new.
- ↻ Not much.
- ↻ Very well.
- ↻ Excellent.

☞ Splendid.

82.   **CROWDED** /ˈkraʊdɪd/ adjective

☞ filled /fɪld/
☞ packed /pækt/ = extremely crowded
☞ jammed /dʒæmd/
☞ congested /kənˈdʒestɪd/= with so many vehicles or people that it's difficult to move around
☞ crammed /kræmd/
☞ cramped /kræmpt/
☞ teeming with /ˈtiːmɪŋ/
☞ swarming with /swɔː(r)mɪŋ/
☞ overflowing with /ˌəʊvə(r)ˈfləʊɪŋ/
☞ jam-packed (informal) = completely full
☞ packed like sardines /saː(r)ˈdiːnz/ (informal) = for people
☞ chock-a-block (informal) = very full
☞ thick on the ground (informal) = if things or people are thick on the ground, there are many of them
☞ nuts to butts (AmE, informal)
☞ full /fʊl/
☞ dense /dens/
☞ bulging /ˈbʌldʒɪŋ/ = completely full
☞ fill to bursting
☞ thronged /θrɒŋd/ = full of people
☞ populous /ˈpɒpjʊləs/ = (nation, city, area etc.) where many people live
☞ bursting at the seams /siːmz/
☞ wall-to-wall = filled completely
☞ standing room only = no place to sit
☞ crawling with /krɔːlɪŋ/

83.   **RURAL** /ˈrʊərəl/ adjective

☞ country /ˈkʌntri/
☞ rustic /ˈrʌstɪk/
☞ pastoral /ˈpɑːst(ə)rəl/
☞ agricultural /ˌægrɪˈkʌltʃ(ə)rəl/
☞ agrarian /əˈɡreəriən/ (formal)
☞ bucolic /bjuːˈkɒlɪk/ = pleasant
☞ sylvan /ˈsɪlv(ə)n/ (formal) = relating to a forest
☞ up-country (adv.) = of an area that is far away from towns
☞ countrified /ˈkʌntrifaɪd/ = showing disapproval

84.   **URBAN** /ˈɜː(r)bən/ adjective

☞ metropolitan /ˌmetrəˈpɒlɪt(ə)n/ = belonging to a big city

- municipal /mjuːˈnɪsɪp(ə)l/ = relating to a place with its own local government
- civic /ˈsɪvɪk/
- built-up = with lots of buildings
- megalopolitan /ˌmegəˈlɒpəlɪtən/
- overdeveloped /ˌəʊvə(r)dɪˈveləpt/ = with too many buildings
- urbanized /ˈɜː(r)bənaɪzd/ = changed into cities after being countryside
- uptown /ʌpˈtaʊn/
- inner-city
- suburban /səˈbɜː(r)bən/
- citified
- townie /ˈtaʊni/ (n.) = sb who lives in a town and doesn't know anything about the countryside

85.   **DEPEND ON/UPON** /dɪˈpend/ verb
       (A depends on B)

- rely on /rɪˈlaɪ/
- hinge on /hɪndʒ/
- be dependent on /dɪˈpendənt/
- rest on /rest/
- revolve around /rɪˈvɒlv/
- be subject to /ˈsʌbdʒɪkt/
- hang on /hæŋ/
- be decided by
- be determined by /dɪˈtɜː(r)mɪnd/
- be based on /beɪst/
- ride on /raɪd/
- be contingent on /kənˈtɪndʒ(ə)nt/ (formal)
- in accordance with /əˈkɔː(r)d(ə)ns/ (formal)
- according to /əˈkɔː(r)dɪŋ/
- be conditional on /kənˈdɪʃ(ə)nəl/
- be up to

86.   **TRADITIONAL** /trəˈdɪʃ(ə)nəl/ adjective

- conventional /kənˈvenʃ(ə)nəl/
- classic /ˈklæsɪk/
- customary /ˈkʌstəməri/
- habitual /həˈbɪtʃuəl/ = often done
- accustomed /əˈkʌstəmd/ (formal)
- conservative /kənˈsɜː(r)vətɪv/
- ceremonial /ˌserəˈməʊniəl/
- established /ɪˈstæblɪʃt/
- fixed /fɪkst/
- set /set/
- long-established

- time-honoured = done in the same way for a very long time
- age-old = very old
- historic /hɪˈstɒrɪk/
- folk /fəʊk/
- unwritten /ʌnˈrɪt(ə)n/ = known by everyone but no written down or official
- standard /ˈstændə(r)d/
- orthodox /ˈɔː(r)θədɒks/
- ritual /ˈrɪtʃuəl/
- ancestral /ænˈsestrəl/
- antediluvian /ˌæntidɪˈluːviən/ = very old, old-fashioned
- archaic /ɑː(r)ˈkeɪk/ = old and no longer used
- out-of-date
- grand old /grænd/ = old, well-known, usually popular

87. **HISTORICAL** /hɪˈstɒrɪk(ə)l/ adjective

- former /ˈfɔː(r)mə(r)/
- prior /ˈpraɪə(r)/
- ancient /ˈeɪnʃ(ə)nt/
- bygone /ˈbaɪgɒn/
- of yore /jɔː(r)/ (formal) = of a period in history a very long time ago
- chronicled /ˈkrɒnɪk(ə)ld/
- early /ˈɜː(r)li/ = used about periods of history
- retrospective /ˌretrəʊˈspektɪv/ = relating to sth that happened in the past
- documented /ˈdɒkjʊˌmentɪd/
- recorded /rɪˈkɔː(r)dɪd /
- archival /ɑː(r)ˈkaɪv(ə)l/

88. **TO AGREE WITH** /əˈgriː/ verb

- to concur with /kənˈkɜː(r)/
- to get on with
- to be of one mind with
- to be of the same opinion with
- to share the view with
- to be at one with
- to come to an agreement with
- to accord with /əˈkɔː(r)d/ (formal)
- to see eye to eye with (informal)
- to go along with (informal)
- to meet halfway (informal)
- to be in agreement with /əˈgriːmənt/
- to be of like mind
- to subscribe to sth /səbˈskraɪb/ = to agree with an idea
- to be united with /juːˈnaɪtɪd/

89. **TO DISAGREE WITH** /ˌdɪsəˈgriː/ verb

- ↻ to conflict with /kənˈflɪkt/
- ↻ to clash with /klæʃ/
- ↻ to contradict sth/sb /ˌkɒntrəˈdɪkt/
- ↻ to differ from /ˈdɪfə(r)/
- ↻ to beg to differ
- ↻ to vary /ˈveəri/
- ↻ not to see eye to eye with sb
- ↻ to be at odds with
- ↻ to be at loggerheads with /ˈlɒgə(r)ˌhedz/ = to disagree strongly
- ↻ to quarrel with /ˈkwɒrəl/
- ↻ to bicker with /ˈbɪkə(r)/ = to argue about sth that isn't important
- ↻ to wrangle with /ˈræŋg(ə)l/ = to argue for a long time
- ↻ to squabble with /ˈskwɒb(ə)l/ = to argue about sth that isn't important
- ↻ to contend with /kənˈtend/ = to have to deal with problems to achieve sth
- ↻ to dispute with /dɪˈspjuːt/
- ↻ to dissent /dɪˈsent/ (formal) = to express strong disagreement
- ↻ to fall out (informal) = to quarrel
- ↻ to oppose /əˈpəʊz/
- ↻ to argue against
- ↻ to reject sth /rɪˈdʒekt/
- ↻ to take issue with sth/sb
- ↻ to be (at) daggers drawn /ˈdægə(r)z/ /drɔːn/ = to be angry towards each other
- ↻ to contest sth /kənˈtest/ = to state formally that you disagree with sth
- ↻ to challenge sth/sb /ˈtʃæləndʒ/
- ↻ to be at variance with /ˈveəriəns/
- ↻ to debate sth/with sb /dɪˈbeɪt/
- ↻ to cross swords with /sɔː(r)dz/
- ↻ to lock horns with /hɔː(r)nz/
- ↻ to gainsay sth/sb /ˌgeɪnˈseɪ/ (formal)

90. **FAVOURITE** /ˈfeɪv(ə)rət/ adjective

- ↻ preferred /prɪˈfɜː(r)d/
- ↻ favoured /ˈfeɪvə(r)d/
- ↻ pet /pet/
- ↻ best-loved
- ↻ dearest /ˈdɪərəst/
- ↻ treasured /ˈtreʒə(r)d/
- ↻ esteemed /ɪˈstiːmd/ (formal) = admired and respected
- ↻ dear /dɪə(r)/ = liked very much
- ↻ precious /ˈpreʃəs/ = loved and valued by sb
- ↻ longed-for (formal) = wanted for a long time
- ↻ most-liked

91. **TO LIKE** /laɪk/ verb

- ⮑ to delight in sth/doing sth /dɪˈlaɪt/
- ⮑ to find pleasant /ˈplez(ə)nt/
- ⮑ to take pleasure in sth/doing sth /ˈpleʒə(r)/
- ⮑ to take to sb/sth = to begin to like sth/sb
- ⮑ to appeal to /əˈpiːl/
- ⮑ to appreciate /əˈpriːʃɪˌeɪt/
- ⮑ to be fond of /fɒnd/
- ⮑ to find attractive
- ⮑ to be keen on /kiːn/
- ⮑ to adore /əˈdɔː(r)/
- ⮑ to hold dear
- ⮑ to cherish /ˈtʃerɪʃ/
- ⮑ to relish /ˈrelɪʃ/
- ⮑ to revel in /ˈrev(ə)l/ (formal) = to enjoy doing sth
- ⮑ to have a soft spot for (informal)
- ⮑ to dig (informal)
- ⮑ can't get enough of sth
- ⮑ to be attached to
- ⮑ to have a liking for
- ⮑ to think well of
- ⮑ to admire /ədˈmaɪə(r)/
- ⮑ to fancy /ˈfænsi/
- ⮑ to be infatuated with /ɪnˈfætjueɪtɪd/
- ⮑ to carry a torch for
- ⮑ to be crazy about (informal)
- ⮑ to have a crush on (informal)
- ⮑ to have a thing for (informal)
- ⮑ to take a shine to /ʃaɪn/
- ⮑ to be partial to /ˈpɑː(r)ʃ(ə)l/
- ⮑ to have a penchant for /ˈpɒ̃ʃɑ̃n/
- ⮑ to have a passion for /ˈpæʃ(ə)n/
- ⮑ to be mad about (informal)
- ⮑ to be hooked on /hʊkt/ (informal)
- ⮑ to get a kick out of (informal)

92. **TO DISLIKE** /dɪsˈlaɪk/ verb

- ⮑ to detest /dɪˈtest/
- ⮑ to object to /əbˈdʒekt/
- ⮑ to loathe /ləʊð/
- ⮑ to abhor /əbˈhɔː(r)/ (formal)
- ⮑ to abominate /əˈbɒmɪneɪt/ (formal)
- ⮑ to regard with distaste

- ⟳ to shun /ʃʌn/ = to deliberately avoid
- ⟳ to despise /dɪˈspaɪz/
- ⟳ to scorn /skɔː(r)n/
- ⟳ to lump /lʌmp/
- ⟳ to disfavour /dɪsˈfeɪvə(r)/ (formal)
- ⟳ to disrelish (formal)
- ⟳ to hate sb's guts (informal)
- ⟳ to not stand the sight of (informal)
- ⟳ to not be sb's cup of tea (informal)
- ⟳ be sick to the back teeth of (informal)
- ⟳ be no love lost between (informal)
- ⟳ to deplore /dɪˈplɔː(r)/ (formal)
- ⟳ to find sth/sb distasteful /dɪsˈteɪstf(ə)l/
- ⟳ to be averse to /əˈvɜː(r)s/
- ⟳ to have an aversion to /əˈvɜː(r)ʃ(ə)n/
- ⟳ to shrink form /ʃrɪŋk/ = to not be willing to do sth difficult
- ⟳ to shudder at /ˈʃʌdə(r)/
- ⟳ to find sth/sb repellent /rɪˈpelənt/
- ⟳ to be unable to stomach (informal)

93. **TO BUY** /baɪ/ verb

- ⟳ to acquire /əˈkwaɪə(r)/
- ⟳ to obtain /əbˈteɪn/
- ⟳ to shop around
- ⟳ to stock up on /stɒk/
- ⟳ to invest in /ɪnˈvest/ = to buy sth you need and will use a lot
- ⟳ to merchandize /ˈmɜː(r)tʃ(ə)ndaɪz/ (formal)
- ⟳ to panic-buy /ˈpænɪk baɪ/ = when you buy a lot of sth cause you're worried there is not enough of it available
- ⟳ to purchase /ˈpɜː(r)tʃəs/ (formal)
- ⟳ to snap up /snæpˈʌp/ (informal) = to buy sth as soon as it becomes available
- ⟳ to splash out on sth /splæʃ/ (informal) = to buy sth expensive
- ⟳ to pick up /pɪkˈʌp/ (informal)
- ⟳ to procure /prəˈkjʊə(r)/ = to obtain sth with effort
- ⟳ to get hold of (informal)
- ⟳ to snatch up /snætʃˈʌp/ (informal)
- ⟳ to score /skɔː(r)/ (informal)

94. **EASY** /ˈiːzi/ adjective

- ⟳ effortless /ˈefə(r)tləs/
- ⟳ uncomplicated /ʌnˈkɒmplɪˌkeɪtɪd/
- ⟳ undemanding /ˌʌndɪˈmɑːndɪŋ/
- ⟳ straightforward /ˌstreɪtˈfɔː(r)wə(r)d/

- foolproof /ˈfuːlˌpruːf/ = of a plan, method that is so well designed that it cannot go wrong
- manageable /ˈmænɪdʒəb(ə)l/
- painless /ˈpeɪnləs/
- natural /ˈnætʃ(ə)rəl/
- a piece of cake (informal)
- cushy /ˈkʊʃi/ (informal)
- a doddle /ˈdɒd(ə)l/ (informal) = very easy to do
- a cake walk (informal)
- a walk in the park (informal)
- easy as ABC (informal)
- easy-peasy /ˌiːzi ˈpiːzi/ (BrE, informal)
- easy as pie (informal)
- child's play (informal)
- not rocket science (informal)
- elementary /ˌelɪˈment(ə)ri/
- trouble-free /ˈtrʌb(ə)l ˈfriː/
- facile /ˈfæsaɪl/ = too simple to be able to deal with a real situation
- no sweat /swet/ (informal)
- smooth sailing /ˈsmuːðˈseɪlɪŋ/ (informal) = progress of a plan without problems

95. **EXPENSIVE** /ɪkˈspensɪv/ adjective

- high-priced
- high-cost
- costly /ˈkɒs(t)li/ (formal)
- exorbitant /ɪgˈzɔː(r)bɪtənt/
- extortionate /ɪkˈstɔː(r)ʃ(ə)nət/
- overpriced /ˌəʊvə(r)ˈpraɪst/ = worth less than its price
- extravagant /ɪkˈstrævəgənt/ = costing more than reasonable
- lavish /ˈlævɪʃ/
- steep /stiːp/ (informal) = of a price, very high
- pricey /ˈpraɪsi/ (informal)
- sky-high (informal) = of a price, very high
- costing an arm and a leg (informal)
- costing the earth (informal)
- daylight robbery (informal)
- exclusive /ɪkˈskluːsɪv/ = available only to people with lots of money
- select /sɪˈlekt/ = very expensive
- luxurious /lʌgˈzjʊəriəs/
- sumptuous /ˈsʌmptʃuəs/ = impressive, expensive and of high quality
- high-class = very good quality and very expensive
- spendy (informal)
- big-ticket (informal)

96. **CHEAP** /tʃiːp/ adjective

- low-priced
- reasonable /ˈriːz(ə)nəb(ə)l/
- low-cost
- affordable /əˈfɔː(r)dəb(ə)l/
- bargain (n.) /ˈbɑː(r)gɪn/ = sth you buy that costs less than normal
- cut-price = cheaper than the normal price
- knock-down (BrE, informal) = at a reduced price
- rock-bottom = at a very low price
- budget /ˈbʌdʒɪt/
- economical /ˌiːkəˈnɒmɪk(ə)l/
- cheap-rate
- on special offer
- value-for-money
- a good buy
- bargainous (informal)
- a snip /snɪp/ (BrE, informal) = sth that costs less than you expect
- for a song (informal) = at a very cheap price
- dirt-cheap (informal)
- dog cheap (informal)
- on a shoestring /ˈʃuːˌstrɪŋ/ (informal) = using or having very little money
- cheap and cheerful = not expensive and of reasonable quality
- reasonably priced
- downmarket /ˈdaʊnˌmɑː(r)kɪt/
- cut-rate
- bargain-basement = an area in a large shop where you can buy things cheaply, often of low quality

97. **FRIENDLY** /ˈfren(d)li/ adjective

- amiable /ˈeɪmiəb(ə)l/
- affable /ˈæfəb(ə)l/
- genial /ˈdʒiːniəl/
- convivial /kənˈvɪviəl/ = friendly and making you feel welcome
- cordial /ˈkɔː(r)diəl/
- neighbourly /ˈneɪbə(r)li/
- companionable /kəmˈpænjənəb(ə)l/
- approachable /əˈprəʊtʃəb(ə)l/
- receptive /rɪˈseptɪv/ = willing to listen
- hospitable /hɒˈspɪtəb(ə)l/
- amicable /ˈæmɪkəb(ə)l/
- well-disposed /ˌwel dɪˈspəʊzd/
- good-natured /ˌgʊd ˈneɪtʃə(r)d/
- pally /ˈpæli/ (informal)

- chummy /ˈtʃʌmi/ (informal)
- folksy /ˈfəʊksi/ (AmE, informal)
- genuine /ˈdʒenjuɪn/ = sincere
- welcoming /ˈwelkəmɪŋ/
- bubbly /ˈbʌbli/ = lively, happy and friendly
- congenial /kənˈdʒiːniəl/ = enjoying the company of others
- gregarious /grɪˈgeəriəs/ = enjoys being with other people
- easy to get on with
- benign /bəˈnaɪn/ (formal)
- amenable /əˈmiːnəb(ə)l/ = willing to agree with sb
- benevolent /bəˈnev(ə)lənt/ (formal) = willing to help others
- buddy-buddy /ˈbʌdiˈbʌdi/ (informal) = very friendly, esp. in a way that seems false

98. **UNFRIENDLY** /ʌnˈfren(d)li/ adjective

- standoffish /ˌstændˈɒfɪʃ/ = behaving in a formal way that isn't friendly
- aloof /əˈluːf/
- distant /ˈdɪstənt/ = doesn't show their feelings
- unapproachable /ˌʌnəˈprəʊtʃəb(ə)l/
- inhospitable /ˌɪnhɒˈspɪtəb(ə)l/
- unneighbourly /ˌʌnˈneɪbə(r)li/
- unwelcoming /ʌnˈwelkəmɪŋ/
- chilly /ˈtʃɪli/
- frosty /ˈfrɒsti/
- wintry /ˈwɪntri/ = deliberately unfriendly
- hostile /ˈhɒstaɪl/ = behaving in a way threatening towards others
- strained /streɪnd/ = not relaxed or friendly
- antagonistic /ænˌtægəˈnɪstɪk/ = disliking sb/sth very much and showing it in their behaviour
- ill-disposed /ˌɪl dɪˈspəʊzd/
- surly /ˈsɜː(r)li/ = unfriendly and rude
- inimical /ɪˈnɪmɪk(ə)l/ (formal)
- churlish /ˈtʃɜː(r)lɪʃ/ = impolite and unfriendly
- stony /ˈstəʊni/ = not friendly and not showing any emotion
- ill-natured /ˌɪl ˈneɪtʃə(r)d/
- uncongenial /ˌʌnkənˈdʒiːniəl/
- starchy /ˈstɑː(r)tʃi/ (informal) = very formal and not showing much feeling

99. **BUSY** /ˈbɪzi/ adjective

Meaning 'at the moment':

- occupied with sth /ˈɒkjʊpaɪd/
- engaged in sth /ɪnˈgeɪdʒd/
- unavailable /ˌʌnəˈveɪləb(ə)l/

- ☞ having a previous engagement
- ☞ having a prior appointment
- ☞ tied up (informal)
- ☞ in the thick of it (informal)
- ☞ busy as a bee (informal)
- ☞ engrossed in sth /ɪnˈɡrəʊst/
- ☞ load down with sth = having a lot to deal with
- ☞ knee-deep in sth = having a lot of work or problems
- ☞ immersed in sth /ɪˈmɜː(r)st/
- ☞ rushed off your feet = very busy
- ☞ involved in sth /ɪnˈvɒlvd/
- ☞ swamped with sth /swɒmpt/
- ☞ up to one's neck
- ☞ absorbed in sth /əbˈzɔː(r)bd/

Meaning ‘busy day’:

- ☞ lively /ˈlaɪvli/
- ☞ strenuous /ˈstrenjuəs/
- ☞ tiring /ˈtaɪərɪŋ/
- ☞ swarming /swɔː(r)mɪŋ/
- ☞ vibrant /ˈvaɪbrənt/
- ☞ teeming /ˈtiːmɪŋ/
- ☞ bustling /ˈbʌs(ə)lɪŋ/
- ☞ hectic /ˈhektɪk/
- ☞ frantic /ˈfræntɪk/
- ☞ eventful /ɪˈventf(ə)l/

Meaning ‘a busy person’:

- ☞ active /ˈæktɪv/
- ☞ time-poor /ˌtaɪmˈpɔː(r)/ = with very little free time
- ☞ lively /ˈlaɪvli/
- ☞ diligent /ˈdɪlɪdʒ(ə)nt/ = works very hard
- ☞ energetic /ˌenə(r)ˈdʒetɪk/
- ☞ industrious /ɪnˈdʌstriəs/
- ☞ assiduous /əˈsɪdjuəs/ = hard-working and thorough
- ☞ restless /ˈres(t)ləs/ = not able to keep still
- ☞ sedulous /ˈsedjʊləs/ (formal) = showing continuous hard work and determination
- ☞ on the go (informal)
- ☞ having your hands full (informal)
- ☞ fully stretched (informal)
- ☞ rushed/run off your feet (informal) = very busy
- ☞ snowed under /snəʊd/ (informal) = with too much work to deal with
- ☞ on the trot (informal) = busy doing sth tiring

↻ as busy as a bee

↻ hard at it (informal) = doing sth in a fast busy way

100. **ENJOYABLE** /ɪnˈdʒɔɪəb(ə)l/ adjective

↻ pleasant /ˈplez(ə)nt/

↻ delightful /dɪˈlaɪtf(ə)l/

↻ pleasurable /ˈpleʒ(ə)rəb(ə)l/

↻ smashing /ˈsmæʃɪŋ/ (BrE, informal)

↻ ace /eɪs/ (informal) = very good

↻ brill /brɪl/ (informal)

↻ fab /fæb/ (informal)

↻ mega /ˈmegə/ (informal)

↻ epic /ˈepɪk/ = extremely enjoyable

↻ entertaining /ˌentə(r)ˈteɪnɪŋ/

↻ amusing /əˈmjuːzɪŋ/ = funny or entertaining

↻ diverting /daɪˈvɜː(r)tɪŋ/

↻ engaging /ɪnˈɡeɪdʒɪŋ/

↻ to one's liking /ˈlaɪkɪŋ/

↻ marvellous /ˈmɑː(r)vələs/

↻ magnificent /mæɡˈnɪfɪs(ə)nt/

↻ splendid /ˈsplendɪd/

↻ fabulous /ˈfæbjʊləs/

↻ terrific /təˈrɪfɪk/ (informal)

↻ magic /ˈmædʒɪk/ (informal)

↻ killer /ˈkɪlə(r)/ (informal)

NATIVE SITUATIONAL SPOKEN EXPRESSIONS

Sometimes it is difficult for students to react in social situations, e.g. when it is somebody's birthday
or when someone falls ill.
Here are a few handy solutions!

- Goodbye. See you next week!

    - Yes, cheerio, take care.

- I forgot my wife's birthday.

    - Oh dear, so you're in the doghouse again?

(to be in the doghouse = someone is angry with you because you have done something wrong

- My wife and I are celebrating our 25th wedding anniversary tonight.

  - Oh, congratulations.

- Who was that man I saw you with last night?

  - Mind your own business!

- I waited for the bus for half an hour, then three came along at once.

  - How typical!

- I've just eaten six hot dogs and now I've got a terrible stomachache.

  - That'll teach you.

- If you look at my girlfriend again, I'll kill you!

  - Oh yes, you and whose army?

- Thanks for inviting me to dinner.

  - You're welcome. Come in and make yourself at home.

- I'm brilliant! My teacher says I'm the best student in her class.

  - Stop blowing your own trumpet!

- Have a nice weekend.

  - Same to you./Likewise.

- What shall we have for dinner?

  - I could murder a curry.
    (meaning I am starving right now)

- Please don't tell anyone my secret.

  - Don't worry, my lips are sealed.

- I'm tired. I'm going to bed.

  - Night night, sweet dreams!

- I'm going to spend the weekend sitting in front of the television.

- Get a life!

- These chocolates look delicious.

  - Hands off!

- Have you had enough to eat?

  - I'm absolutely stuffed!
    (meaning: can't eat any more)

- I can't come to your party.

  - Oh, what a shame!

- I've just won $10,000.

  - No way! You are pulling my leg!

- I've got some amazing news.

  - Fire away, I'm all ears.
- By the time I'm 30, I'll be a millionaire and married to a supermodel.

  - In your dreams!

- I've heard that you're going to give me a surprise party for my birthday.

  - Oh no, who let the cat out of the bag?

- Achhhhhoooooooooo! (sneezing)

  - Bless you!

- Men are much more intelligent than women.

  - What a complete rubbish!

- Come on, let's go or we'll be late.

  - Hang on, give me a moment!

- What are you going to get me for my birthday?

  - Never you mind. Wait and see!

- I'm feeling a bit miserable at the moment!

- - Cheer up!

- Can we have your decision?

  - Let me sleep on it!

- I, er, um, well, you know, the thing is, you see, well…

  - Come on, spit it out!

- Come on darling, give me a great big kiss and then have a dance with me.

  - Go and take a running jump!
    (meaning : go away!)

- I'm taking my IELTS exam tomorrow!

  - Good luck. I'll be keeping my fingers crossed for you!

- Can I borrow your mobile to make a quick call?

  - Sure. Be my guest!

- It's my birthday today.

  - Is it? Oh, well, many happy returns!

- I promise not to be late from now on.

  - Yeah right, that'll be the day.

- My girlfriend left me last week.

  - Oh dear, so you're on the shelf again.
    (meaning: unlikely to find a partner or get married, usually because of being too old)

- Do you know Patrick James?

  - No, the name doesn't ring a bell.

- I'm sorry, but I forgot to do my homework again.

  - Again? It's time you pulled your socks up, young man.

- I failed my driving test again!

  - Oh, bad luck!

- What's the name of that restaurant we went to last week?

  - It's on the tip of my tongue. I'll remember it in a minute.

- Have you ever been to hospital?

  - No, touch wood!

- Excuse me, could you take our picture?

  - Sure. Ok, say cheese everyone!

- I'm afraid I've run out of coffee. I can only offer you tea.

  - That's all right. Any port in a storm.

CHAPTER 5

COMMON SPEAKING TOPICS & POSSIBLE QUESTIONS
VOCABULARY NEEDED FOR BAND 6 & HIGHER

Quot homines, tot sententiae
(As many men as many opinions)

PART 1 TOPICS

1. **Advertisements**
   - Do you trust advertisements? Why/why not?
   - How do you feel about advertisements? Why?
   - What kinds of adverts do you like? Why/why not?
   - What effects do ads have on people?
   - Do you think there are too many advertisements nowadays? Why/why not?
   - Have you ever bought anything tempted by an advert? Why?
   - What qualities should a good advertisement have? Why?
   - What kinds of advertisements affect people most? Why?
   - Do you think it is okay for children to advertise a product? Why/why not?
   - How do you feel about celebrities endorsing the big brands? Why?
   - Which advertisement is your favourite one? Why?
   - Is there a lot of advertising in your country? Why/why not?
   - Do you pay more attention to adverts on TV or in magazines? Why?
   - Do you watch advertisements on TV? Why/why not?
   - Do you watch advertisements on the Internet? Why/why not?
   - Would you like to watch TV without adverts? Why/why not?
   - Have you ever bought anything because of an advertisement? Why/why not?
   - Do you often see advertisements in the street, for example posters? Why/why not?

2. **Ambitions/dreams**
   - Do you consider yourself an ambitious person? Why/why not?
   - Is it always good to be ambitious?
   - What do young people in your country dream of? Why?
   - What can a person learn if they can't reach their ambition? Why?
   - What was your childhood dream? Why?
   - Have your ambitions changed over the years? Why/why not?

3. **Animals (pets, wild animals)**
   - What is your favourite animal? Why?
   - What is your favourite wild animal? Why?
   - Do you generally like animals? Why/why not?
   - Are you a pet person? Why/why not?
   - Have you ever had a pet? Why/why not?
   - Are pets popular in your country? Why/why not?
   - Which pets are most suitable for young children? Why?
   - What animals are people not allowed to keep as pets in your country? Why?
   - Are there any laws regarding pets in your country?
   - Why do people like to have pets?
   - How much money do people spend on their pets?
   - Which animals can you see around the place you live in?
   - Can you see any birds where you live? Why/why not?
   - Is it good or bad to keep animals in the zoo?

- What are some disadvantages of keeping pets?
- Do you like to see animals in zoos? Why/why not?
- Do you think pets are faithful to their owners? Why/why not?
- What are some famous animals in your country? Why?

4. **Bags**
   - Do you have many bags? Why/why not?
   - Do you have a favourite bag? Why/why not?
   - Where do you usually buy your bags? Why?
   - Who do you think cares about bags more, men or women? Why?
   - Do you always carry a bag with you? Why/why not?
   - What items are there in your bag? Why?
   - Have you ever bought a bag on the Internet? Why/why not?

5. **Beach**
   - Do you enjoy going to the beach? Why/why not?
   - Is there a beach where you live?
   - What do you usually do at the beach? Why?
   - What can people do at the beach if the weather isn't good? Why?
   - What can a person who can't swim do at the beach?
   - Are beaches in your country free of charge? Why/why not?
   - How often do you go to the beach? Why?

6. **Being busy**
   - Which day of the week is the busiest for you? Why?
   - Do you prefer to have a lot of things to do or just a few things to do? Why?
   - When was the last time you were very busy? Why?
   - Do you enjoy the times when you are busy? Why/why not?
   - Do you ever feel stressed when you're busy? Why?
   - Do you think your life might be busier in the future? Why/why not?

7. **Being on time**
   - Do you like to be on time? Why/why not?
   - How do you feel when others are late?
   - When is it important for people to be on time? Why?
   - Do you usually wear a watch? Why/why not?
   - In your culture, is it generally important to be on time? Why?
   - Why is it so hard for some people to be on time?
   - What can people do to make sure they are on time? Why?

8. **Being patient**
   - What do you usually do when you have to wait for something, for example a bus? Why?
   - Have you ever lost your patience while waiting for something? Why?
   - Do you think you are a patient person? Why/why not?
   - Do you think people in your country are generally patient? Why/why not?

- Do you think patience is a virtue? Why/why not?
- Can a person learn to be patient? Why/why not?

9. **Being polite**
- Do you think you are a polite person? Why/why not?
- How do people in your country show politeness?
- Are good manners important in your country? Why/why not?
- Who taught you how to be polite when you were a child? How?
- Have rules of politeness been changing in your country? Why/why not?
- In what situations do you think it is necessary to be polite? Why?

10. **Bicycles**
- Do you have a bicycle? Why/why not?
- How often do you ride a bicycle? Why?
- Did you learn how to ride a bicycle when you were a child? Why/why not?
- Are bicycles popular in your country? Why/why not?
- Do you think people will ride bicycles more or less in the future? Why?

11. **Birthdays**
- Are birthdays important to you? Why/why not?
- Which birthdays are the most important to people in your country? Why?
- What do people usually do on their birthdays in your country? Why?
- When was your last birthday?
- What did you do on your last birthday? Why?
- Who do you think cares about birthdays more: children or adults? Why?
- Do you think it is important to do something special on birthdays? Why/why not?
- What do you usually do on your birthday? Why?
- What did you use to do on your birthday when you were a child? Why?

12. **Boats**
- Have you ever been on a boat? Why/why not?
- Are there any boats in you city? Why/why not?
- Are boats popular where you live? Why/why not?
- How do people use boats in your country? Why?
- Are boats a safe means of transport? Why/why not?
- Would you like to buy a boat? Why/why not?

13. **Body language & Manners**
- Is body language important in your country? Why/why not?
- In what situations is body language more important than words? Why?
- Do you think you have good manners? Why/why not?
- Are table manners important in your culture? Why/why not?
- In what situations can lack of manners be a problem? Why?
- Who taught you good manners? How?
- Should parents teach their children manners? Why/why not?

14. **Books & Reading**
- Do you like reading? Why/why not?
- How often do you read? Why?
- What's your favourite book? Why?
- What kinds of books do you like to read? Why?
- Have you ever read a book in English? Why?
- When did you learn to read? Why?
- Where do you usually read books? Why?
- Is reading a good hobby? Why/why not?

15. **Buildings**
- What kind of building do you live in? Why?
- What are some typical buildings where you live? Why?
- How do you like modern buildings? Why?
- Are there a lot of historical buildings where you live? Why?
- Do you think historical buildings should be kept? Why/why not?

16. **Cars**
- Do you have a car? What make is it?
- What kind of a car would you like to have? Why?
- Do you like travelling by car? Why/why not?
- Do you think it would be good if everyone had a private car? Why/why not?
- When did you last travel by car? Why?
- Is traffic heavy where you live? Why/why not?
- Should everyone learn how to drive? Why/why not?

17. **Celebrities**
- Who's you favourite celebrity? Why?
- Do you follow celebrities? Why/why not?
- Do people in your country often follow celebrities? Why/why not?
- What kinds of people usually become famous in your country? Why?
- Do old people also admire celebrities? Why/why not?
- Have you ever met a celebrity? When?
- Would you like to meet a celebrity? Why/why not?
- Would you like to be famous? Why/why not?
- Do you know any Western celebrities?
- Are celebrities important?
- Should celebrities advertise products on TV? Why/why not?

18. **Change**
- Do you like changes? Why/why not?
- What was the biggest change in your life? Why?
- Is it easy to adapt to a change? Why/why not?
- What changes are the hardest to accept in life? Why?
- Which is better, a quick change or a gradual one? Why?

- Do older people enjoy changes? Why/why not?

19. **Children's activities**
    - What did you like doing most when you were a child? Why?
    - Did you stay more indoors or outdoors in your childhood? Why?
    - How are children's activities different now from when you were younger? Why?
    - What activities are best for children? Why?
    - What activities will children enjoy in the future? Why?

20. **Clothes & Fashion**
    - What kind of clothes do you usually like to wear? Why?
    - Do you think your preference in clothes might change in the future? Why/why not?
    - Do you prefer to buy fashionable or comfortable clothes? Why?
    - What colours do you prefer to wear? Why?
    - Do you wear the same clothes to your place of work/study and at home? Why/why not?
    - How often do you buy new clothes? Why?
    - Do you prefer to go shopping for clothes alone or with other people? Why?
    - Do you or your family make your own clothes (e.g. by sewing or knitting)? Why/why not?
    - Are there any special clothes people wear during festivals?
    - Do you think it is necessary to dress formally at work? Why/why not?
    - What do you think of school/work uniforms? Why?
    - Do you think fashion is generally important? Why/why not?
    - Who chose your clothes when you were younger? Why?
    - What are you looking for when you choose clothes? Why?
    - Have you ever helped your friends choose their clothes? Why/why not?
    - Where do you get fashion information? Why?
    - Do you like traditional clothes? Why/why not?
    - Do you change into different clothes when you get home from work/school? Why/why not?
    - In your childhood, did you ever wear any special clothes for parties? Why/why not?
    - Do you think people spend too much money on clothes? Why/why not?
    - Do you think we can judge people by what they wear? Why/why not?
    - Do you think different clothes can put people into totally different moods? Why/why not?
    - Do you have a lot of clothes in the same colour? Why/why not?
    - Do you think you will wear the same or different clothes when you are older? Why?

21. **Collecting things**
    - Do you collect anything? Why/why not?
    - Do you like collecting things? Why/why not?
    - What did you collect in your childhood? Why?
    - Why do people like to collect things?
    - What benefits do you think can people get from their collections?
    - Are many people interested in collecting things? Why/why not?
    - What do people usually collect in your country? Why?
    - How do people get items for their collections?

22. Colours

- Do you have any favourite colours? Why/why not?
- What's your favourite colour? Why?
- Are colours generally important to you? Why/why not?
- What colour is the most important in your country? Why?
- Do you care about colours of your clothes?
- Do you have any colours you really dislike? Why/why not?
- How do different colours influence the way you feel? Why?
- Did you often wear bright colours in your childhood? Why/why not?
- What colour are the walls in your room? Why?
- Do you care about the colour of your car? Why/why not?

23. Computers & the Internet & IT

- How often do you use a computer? Why?
- What are some benefits of using a computer?
- What are some drawbacks of using a computer?
- Is it easy to learn how to use a computer for older people? Why/why not?
- What do you usually do online? Why?
- Where do you usually use a computer? Why?
- Do you think the information on the Internet is always accurate? Why/why not?
- Do you like making friends online? Why/why not?
- When did you first use a computer? Why?
- Is there anything you dislike about using a computer? Why?
- Do you think computers help children's education? Why/why not?
- Do you prefer desktop computers or laptops? Why?
- What influence do you think computers have on kids?
- How long do you surf the Internet every day?

24. Concentration & Memory

- Do you think you have a good memory? Why/why not?
- Do you think it's important to have a good memory? Why/why not?
- What things do people forget easily?
- What can we do to have a better memory?
- Is technology helpful in remembering things? Why/why not?
- At what time of the day do you find it easier to concentrate on your studies? Why?
- Do you prefer to work in a silent room or in a noisy one? Why?
- What can help you concentrate when you're studying for a very long time? Why?
- Was it easier for you to concentrate on your studies when you were younger? Why?

25. Cooking

- Can you cook? Why/why not?
- Do you like to cook? Why/why not?
- How often do you cook?
- Who does most of the cooking in your family? Why?
- What kind of cooking is the easiest for you?

- Which of the cooking methods is the least/the healthiest? Why?
- What was the first thing you ever cooked? Why?
- Would you like to learn how to cook? Why/why not?
- Are TV cookery shows popular in your country? Why/why not?
- Did you ever help with cooking when you were a child? Why/why not?
- Do you think children should help with cooking? Why/why not?
- Are TV culinary shows popular in your country? Why/why not?

26. **Countryside & City**
- Do you live in the countryside or in the city? Why?
- Is it better to live in the countryside or in the city? Why?
- How is countryside better than a city to live in?
- Who do you think prefers to live in the countryside? Why?
- Would you like to have a house in the countryside in the future? Why/why not?

27. **Culture**
- Do you like your culture? Why/why not?
- What's the most significant part of your culture? Why?
- What other cultures are you interested in? Why?
- Do you think foreign people are interested in your culture? Why/why not?

28. **Daily routine & Life habits**
- Do you do the same thing(s) every day of the week?
- Do you have a daily routine? Why/why not?
- Is it important to have a daily routine? Why/why not?
- What time do you usually get up? Why?
- What time do you usually go to bed? Why?
- Are your weekday and weekend routines different? How?
- What is your favourite day of the week? Why?
- Which is the busiest day of the week for you? Why?
- If you could make one change to your daily routine, what would it be? Why?

29. **Dancing**
- Do you like to dance? Why/why not?
- How often do you dance? Why?
- What's your favourite dance? Why?
- Did you ever learn how to dance? Why/why not?
- Would you like to learn dancing in the future? Why/why not?
- When do you usually dance? Why?

30. **Decoration**
- Is house decoration important to you? Why/why not?
- How do people usually decorate their houses? Why?
- What is your favourite decoration? Why?
- Are there many pictures hanging on the walls of your house? Why/why not?

- How do you take care of your daily appearance? Why?
- Who decorated your room? Why?

31. **Dictionaries**
- Do you have a dictionary? What kind?
- How often do you use a dictionary? Why?
- Do you prefer to use an electronic or a paper dictionary? Why?
- Do you think it would be interesting to write a dictionary? Why/why not?
- Would you like to receive a dictionary as a gift? Why/why not?

32. **Diets**
- Have you ever been on a diet? Why/why not?
- Do you think diets are helpful? Why/why not?
- Are most diets healthy? Why/why not?
- Do people in your country often go on a diet? Why/why not?
- What's your favourite diet? Why?
- Do you think more people will decide to go a diet in the future? Why/why not?

33. **Drawing & Painting**
- Did you learn how to paint or draw when you were at school? Why/why not?
- Is it good for children to learn to paint and draw at school? Why/why not?
- Why do some people like to hang paintings in their homes?
- Would you like to buy a painting? Why/why not?
- Who is your favourite painter? Why?
- Would you like to learn how to paint in the future? Why/why not?

34. **Driving**
- Do you know how to drive? Why/why not?
- Do you have the driving license?
- Do you prefer to be a passenger or a driver? Why?
- Do you think everyone should learn how to drive? Why/why not?
- Is driving a car easy? Why/why not?
- At what age can people drive in your country?
- Can everyone become a good driver? Why/why not?
- What cars do people in your country usually drive? Why?

35. **Eating out**
- Do you enjoy eating out? Why/why not?
- How often do you eat out? Why?
- Do you prefer to eat out alone or with other people? Why?
- What is bad about eating out? Why?
- Do many people eat out in your country? Why/why not?
- Do you think more people will eat out in the future? Why/why not?
- Do you prefer to eat out or cook by yourself? Why?

36. Economy

- If you had enough money, would you like to make an investment? Why/why not?
- What is the best investment in your opinion? Why?
- Have you ever bought an insurance policy? Why/why not?
- Is insurance policy important? Why/why not?
- Do you have an insurance policy? Why/why not?
- Have you ever made an investment? Why/why not?
- Would you like to learn about economy in the future? Why/why not?

37. Education & Studies

- Are you a student? Why/why not?
- Where do you study? Why?
- What is your major? Why?
- Do you think your subject is interesting? Why/why not?
- Would you like to change your subject? Why/why not?
- Do you like studying? Why/why not?
- Are you a good student? Why/why not?

38. English

- How did you learn English? Why?
- Do you think English is difficult or easy to learn? Why?
- Do many people in your country speak English? Why/why not?
- What is the best way to learn English? Why?
- What's the hardest thing about learning English? Why?
- When did you start to learn English? Why?
- Do you plan to continue learning English in the future? Why/why not?

39. Exams

- Do you often take exams? Why/why not?
- What was the hardest exam you've ever taken? Why?
- Do students in your country often take exams? Why/why not?
- How do you study for an exam? Why?
- Have you ever failed an exam? Why/why not?
- Do you plan to take any exams in the future? Why/why not?

40. Family

- How many people are there in your family?
- Do you live with your family? Why/why not?
- Is your family close?
- Do you have any siblings?
- How do you contribute to your family?
- Do you often visit your family members? Why/why not?
- Do you and your family go on holiday together? Why/why not?
- How many blood relatives do you have?
- What are the advantages of living in a large family? Why?

- What are the advantages of living in a small family? Why?
- What is the best place for the elderly to live? Why?
- Who usually cooks in your family? Why?
- How important is family to you? Why?

41. Festivals & Public holidays
- What is your favourite festival? Why?
- Are there many public holidays in your country? Why/why not?
- Tell me about one traditional festival in your country.
- Do you like any Western festivals? Why/why not?
- What do you usually do during a festival? Why?
- Do you think your country needs more public holidays? Why/why not?
- Which festival do you dislike? Why?

42. Films & Movies
- What is your favourite type of films? Why?
- What's your favourite film? Why?
- How often do you watch movies? Why?
- Do you think young people enjoy the same types of films as older people? Why/why not?
- Do you like watching movies? Why/why not?
- How often do you go to the cinema? Why?
- Do you prefer to watch films at home or in the cinema? Why?
- How do you feel about documentary movies? Why?
- Do you ever watch films in English? Why/why not?
- Do you use subtitles when you watch foreign films? Why/why not?

43. Flowers, Trees & Plants
- Why do you think some people like to grow flowers?
- Do you like flowers/plants/trees? Why/why not?
- What's your favourite flower/plant/tree? Why?
- Do you like to give people flowers as gifts? Why/why not?
- Are there any flowers/plants/trees in your culture that have a special meaning?
- Do you have any potted plants in your home? Why/why not?
- Is gardening a good hobby for you?
- How can forests be protected?
- Are forests popular places to visit in your country? Why/why not?
- Did you climb trees when you were a child? Why/why not?
- Would you like to live in a place with lots of trees? Why/why not?
- Is it important to protect trees? Why/why not?
- How much do you know about plants? Why?
- Did you grow any plants in your childhood? Why/why not?
- Is a plant a good gift for you? Why/why not?
- Are there a lot of trees where you live? Why/why not?
- Do you like trees? Why/why not?
- Have you ever planted a tree? Why/why not?

- Would you like to plant a tree? Why/why not?
- Are there any special trees in your culture? Why/why not?

44. Food
- Do you cook? Why/why not?
- Can you cook?
- Do you like cooking? Why/why not?
- What's your favourite food? Why?
- Do you eat at home more or eat out more? Why?
- What are some advantages of eating at a restaurant?
- What are some disadvantages of eating at a restaurant?
- Is eating together as a family important to you? Why/why not?
- What is the staple food of your country?
- Do you and your family enjoy the same types of drinks? Why/why not?
- Do you like fruit? Why/why not?
- What is your favourite fruit? Why?
- Do you prefer home-cooked meals or restaurant food? Why?
- What was your favourite food when you were a child?
- What is your favourite taste? Why?
- Do you like vegetables? Why/why not?
- What's your favourite vegetable? Why?
- Can you cook? Why/why not?
- Did you learn to cook when you were a child? Why/why not?
- What kind of food did you like when you were a child? Why?
- How do you think the restaurants can attract more customers?

45. Free time
- What do you usually do in your free time? Why?
- Do you have a lot of free time? Why?
- Do people in your country have enough free time these days? Why/why not?
- Would you like to have more free time? Why/why not?
- Do you think you will have more or less free time in the future? Why?
- Did you have more free time in the past? Why/why not?

46. Friends
- Do you have a lot of friends? Why/why not?
- Is friendship generally important to you?
- What do you usually do with your friends? Why?
- How much time do you spend with your friends? Why?
- Do you spend more time with your friends or your family? Why?
- When you choose a friend, what qualities matter to you most? Why?
- Do you have a best friend? Why/why not?
- When did you first meet your best friend?
- Is it better to have a lot of friends or just a few close friends? Why?

47. **Furniture**
    - Do you like furniture? Why/why not?
    - Do you like your furniture? Why/why not?
    - What furniture do you usually buy? Why?
    - How much money do you think is reasonable for a piece of furniture? Why?
    - What is your favourite furniture type? Why?
    - On what factors do you base your furniture choices? Why?
    - Have you ever bought any second-hand furniture? Why/why not?
    - Where do you usually buy furniture? Why?
    - Have you ever bought any furniture online? Why/why not?

48. **Gifts & Presents**
    - When do people usually exchange gifts in your culture?
    - What gifts do people usually receive in your culture?
    - What gift would you like to receive most? Why?
    - Have you ever made a DIY gift for anyone? Why/why not?
    - Do you prefer to give or receive presents? Why?
    - Is money a common gift in your culture? Why/why not?
    - What was the last gift you got and liked? Why?
    - Have you ever received a gift you did not like? Why?
    - Do you like giving people gifts? Why/why not?
    - What types of gifts do you like to receive most? Why?
    - What types of gifts did you like when you were a child? Why?
    - Have you ever bought any presents online? Why/why not?
    - Why do you think people always give presents on some occasions?
    - Are there any special rules related to choosing gifts in your culture? What are they?
    - Are there any taboos people should avoid when choosing a gift?
    - What kinds of gifts do men and women prefer? Why?
    - What kinds of gifts do older people like to receive? Why?

49. **Going abroad**
    - Why are you planning to go abroad?
    - Do you think it is necessary for you to go abroad? Why/why not?
    - What foreign customs do you know?
    - Is there anything worrying about going abroad?
    - Besides the language, what is the most difficult thing about living abroad? Why?
    - Which foreign country would you like to go to? Why?
    - Do many people in your country want to go abroad these days? Why/why not?

50. **Handmade gifts**
    - Have you ever given someone a handmade gift? Why/why not? What was it?
    - What kinds of things do people like to make as gifts? Why?
    - Have you ever received a handmade gift? Why/why not?
    - Is it easy to make a gift? Why/why not?
    - How do you feel when someone gives you a handmade gift? Why?

- How much time does it usually take to make a handmade gift? Why?

51. **Handwriting & Writing**
    - Do you often write by hand? Why/why not?
    - Do you like writing by hand? Why/why not?
    - Is your handwriting easy or difficult for others to read? Why?
    - Do you often receive handwritten cards? Why/why not?
    - Do you enjoy receiving handwritten cards or letters? Why/why not?
    - Is it possible to learn about someone's personality from their handwriting? Why/why not?

52. **Happiness**
    - Are you a happy person? Why/why not?
    - What is happiness to you? Why?
    - What do you usually do to make yourself happy? Why?
    - How can people be happier when they work? Why?
    - When is your happiest time during a day? Why?
    - Is happiness generally important to you? Why/why not?
    - Was your childhood a happy one? Why/why not?

53. **History**
    - Are you interested in history? Why/why not?
    - Did/do you like history lessons at school? Why/why not?
    - How often do you watch historical films? Why?
    - Do you ever watch TV programmes about history? Why/why not?
    - What's the best way to learn about history? Why?
    - Is the Internet a good place to learn about history? Why/why not?
    - Is there a historical event you'd like to learn more about?
    - Is there a historical figure you'd like to learn more about?

54. **Hobbies & Interests**
    - Do you have a hobby?
    - What's your biggest hobby? Why?
    - Are your hobbies now the same or different from when you were younger? Why?
    - Are hobbies important? Why/why not?
    - Do older people have hobbies? Why?
    - Should everyone have a hobby? Why/why not?
    - Do you have enough time for your hobby? Why/why not?
    - Did you have the same hobby when you were a child? Why/why not?

55. **Holidays & Vacations**
    - What do school children usually do on their holidays? Why?
    - Where did you spend your last holidays? Why?
    - Who do you prefer spend holidays with? Why?
    - Do you prefer long holidays or short ones? Why?
    - Is there anything you don't like about holidays? Why?

- Do you think holidays are necessary? Why?
- How often do you go on holidays? Why?
- Do you think you will have more time for holidays in the future? Why/why not?

56. Hometown

- Where is your hometown?
- What is your hometown famous for?
- Which part of your country do you come from?
- Has your family always lived in your hometown? Why/why not?
- What should visitors see in your hometown? Why?
- Do you like your hometown? Why/why not?
- Do you think your hometown was a good place to grow up? Why/why not?
- Is your hometown a good place for young people? Why/why not?
- Do you know your hometown's history well? Why/why not?
- What would you like to change about your hometown? Why?
- Do you know many people in your hometown?
- Is your community good for children? Why/why not?
- Is your community good for old people? Why/why not?
- What can you tell me about the character of people in your hometown?
- What is the difference in your hometown between 10 years ago and now?
- In the future, would you prefer to live in a big city or a small town? Why?
- Are there many places of interest in your hometown?
- Was your hometown a good place to grow up? Why?
- If you could change one thing about your hometown, what would it be?

57. House & Apartment

- Do you live in a house or in a flat? Why?
- How do you like the area where you live? Why?
- What places in your city would you suggest a tourist to see? Why?
- What do you like/dislike about your home? Why?
- What would your perfect house be like?
- What is your favourite room in your house? Why?
- Have you ever moved home? Why/why not?
- Do you plan to move home in the future? Why/why not?

58. Housework & Household tasks

- Do you like doing housework? Why/why not?
- Who usually does housework in your family? Why?
- Did you help your parents with household tasks when you were a child? Why/why not?
- Are you good at cooking? Why/why not?
- How can you make housework more interesting?
- Which household tasks are the worst for you? Why?
- Do you think that robots are better than humans at doing housework?
- Do you think it would be good if robots did all the housework in the future?

59. **Humour & Telling jokes**
   - Do you think you are funny? Why/why not?
   - Can you tell jokes well? Why/why not?
   - Do you often make people laugh? Why/why not?
   - Do you like to laugh? Why/why not?
   - How often do you laugh? Why?
   - Have you ever learnt any jokes? Why/why not?
   - What's the funniest joke you have ever heard? Why?
   - Do you have a sense of humour? Why/why not?
   - Do you often make friends with funny people? Why/why not?

60. **Insects**
   - Do you like insects? Why/why not?
   - What's the biggest insect you have ever seen?
   - What is one insect you really hate? Why?
   - Are you allergic to insect bites?
   - Have you ever been bitten by an insect?
   - How do you protect yourself from insects? Why?
   - Are there any special insects in your culture? Why/why not?
   - Are there many insects where you live? Why/why not?

61. **Job & Career**
   - What job do you do?
   - Do you like your job? Why/why not?
   - Are you more productive in the morning or in the afternoon? Why?
   - What's your dream job? Why?
   - What is a good job in your opinion? Why?
   - What is more important: to succeed in one's job, teamwork or individualism? Why?
   - Is it easy to find a good job in your country now? Why/why not?
   - Do people in your country often need to work overtime? Why/why not?
   - Have you made friends with people you work with? Why/why not?
   - Are you working or studying?
   - What are the main responsibilities in your job? Why?
   - How long have you been doing this job? Why?
   - Would you like to change your job? Why/why not?
   - Do you like your job? Why/why not?
   - Have you received any training related to your work?
   - If you could choose another job, what would you choose? Why?
   - Is your job important to you? Why/why not?

62. **Keeping fit & Health**
   - Are you generally a healthy person?
   - How do you keep fit? Why?
   - Do you care about staying fit? Why/why not?
   - How do people in your country stay in shape?

- ↻ How often do you check your health? Why?
- ↻ Is it important to keep fit? Why/why not?

63. **Languages**

- ↻ What languages can you speak? Why?
- ↻ What do you think about foreigners learning your language?
- ↻ Are there any difficulties in learning a foreign language?
- ↻ Do you think learning another language is good? Why/why not?
- ↻ Besides English, what languages would you like to learn? Why?
- ↻ When did you begin to learn English? Why?
- ↻ How did you learn English? Why?
- ↻ Do you think English is easy or difficult to learn? Why?
- ↻ Do you have your own ways to learn English? What are they?
- ↻ Do you think learning English is important? Why/why not?

64. **Letters & Emails**

- ↻ Do you prefer to send emails or letters? Why?
- ↻ How often do you write emails/letters? Why?
- ↻ What is special about writing letters?
- ↻ What is the biggest disadvantage of emails? Why?
- ↻ Have you ever received a handwritten letter?
- ↻ How often do you receive emails? Why?
- ↻ Who do you usually write letters or emails to? Why?
- ↻ Do you have a blog? Why/why not?
- ↻ Do you enjoy writing emails/letters? Why/why not?
- ↻ Which do you like more, calling people or writing to them? Why?
- ↻ What kinds of letters or emails are the most difficult to write? Why?
- ↻ Who do you usually receive letters or emails from? Why?
- ↻ Do you prefer to receive a letter or an email? Why?
- ↻ Do you prefer to receive a letter or a phone call? Why?

65. **Lifestyles & Habits**

- ↻ Do you think you have a high standard of living? Why/why not?
- ↻ What are your lifestyle priorities?
- ↻ How can one's lifestyle be improved?
- ↻ What's your best habit?
- ↻ What's your worst habit?
- ↻ Do you smoke?
- ↻ Is smoking a good habit?
- ↻ Do you often stay up late? Why?
- ↻ What is bad about staying up late?
- ↻ When do you usually go to bed? Why?
- ↻ What time do you normally get up in the morning? Why?

66. **Looking for a job**
   - Have you ever looked for a job? Why/why not?
   - How do people look for a job in your country? Why?
   - Is it easy or difficult to find a new job in your country? Why?
   - Are there any websites where potential employers advertise jobs?
   - How long does it take to find a job? Why?
   - Are many people unemployed in your country? Why/why not?
   - What are the most popular jobs in your country these days? Why?

67. **Managing money**
   - Are you good at managing money? Why/why not?
   - Did you learn how to manage your money? Why/why not?
   - What's the best way to manage person's money well? Why?
   - Do you have a bank account? Why/why not?
   - Do many people in your country have multiple bank accounts? Why/why not?
   - Are you good at saving money? Why/why not?
   - Have you ever saved money for something special? Why/why not?
   - How can a person learn how to save money?
   - What do young people in your country usually save for? Why?

68. **Managing time**
   - Are you good at managing your time? Why/why not?
   - What do you do to help you organise your time? Why?
   - Did you learn how to organise your time? Why/why not?
   - What would you like to do if you had more spare time? Why?
   - Is knowing how to manage time well a useful skill? Why/why not?
   - Are people in your country generally good at managing their time? Why/why not?
   - How can a lack of time management be a problem?

69. **Maps**
   - Do you have a map of your city/country? Why/why not?
   - How often do you use a map? Why/why not?
   - Did you learn how to use a map at school? Why/why not?
   - Which do you think is better, a paper map or an electronic map? Why?
   - When you're in a new city, do you even ask people for directions? Why/why not?
   - Do you think paper maps might get out of use in the future? Why/why not?

70. **Marriage & Wedding**
   - Are there any traditions about getting married in your country?
   - What is the perfect age for a person to get married? Why?
   - What in your opinion is the most important thing in a marriage? Why?
   - Do you think people spend too much money on wedding preparations? Why/why not?
   - Do you think it is good or bad to marry late? Why?
   - How do people usually celebrate a wedding in your culture?
   - Do you think both parents should take care of the children or only the woman? Why?

71. **Mobile phones & Cell phones**
   - Do you have a mobile phone?
   - How often do you use your phone? Why?
   - When did you first use a cell phone? Why?
   - Is your mobile phone important to you? Why/why not?
   - In what situations do you switch off your mobile phone? Why?
   - How often do you change your mobile phone? Why?
   - Whom do you usually call?
   - Do you enjoy long talks over the phone? Why/why not?
   - Do you prefer to make phone calls or send messages? Why?

72. **Museums & Art galleries**
   - Do you like visiting museums or art galleries? Why/why not?
   - How often do you visit museums/art galleries? Why?
   - What can you learn from visiting museums/art galleries?
   - What kinds of museums are popular in your country? Why?
   - Do you think museums should be free of charge? Why/why not?
   - Why do you think people like to go to the museums?
   - How could museums attract more people? Why/why not?
   - What museum do you remember from your childhood? Why?
   - Do you think school children should visit museums or art galleries? Why/why not?
   - Have you been to many museums? Why/why not?
   - Is it better to visit a museum alone or with others? Why?
   - Do you think working in a museum could be interesting? Why/why not?

73. **Music & Singing**
   - Do you like listening to music? Why/why not?
   - What's your favourite kind of music? Why?
   - How often do you listen to music? Why?
   - Did you like the same type of music when you were younger? Why/why not?
   - Is there any type of music you dislike? Why?
   - Have you ever learnt to play any musical instrument? Why/why not?
   - Would you like to learn to play a musical instrument? Which one? Why/why not?
   - Did you do any singing in your primary school? Why/why not?
   - How often do you sing? Why?
   - Who is your favourite singer? Why?
   - Are the lyrics of a song important to you? Why/why not?
   - What is the difference between your country's music and Western music?
   - Is it important for children to learn how to play a musical instrument? Why/why not?
   - What are the benefits of children playing a musical instrument? Why?
   - Why is it easier for children to learn how to play a musical instrument than it is for adults?

74. **Names**
   - Does your name have any special meaning?
   - Have you ever considered changing your name? Why/why not?

- Who gave you your name? Why?
- Are some names more popular than others in your culture? Why?
- Do people in your country do anything special when a child is given a name? What?
- Do people like to change their names in your culture? Why/why not?
- In your culture, do women change their names when they get married? Why/why not?

75. Nature
- Do you like nature? Why/why not?
- Do you like spending free time in places of natural beauty? Why/why not?
- How can you learn about nature?
- What's the best way to learn about nature? Why?
- Have you ever gone camping in the mountains? Why?
- Do you think the countryside is a good living place? Why/why not?

76. Neighbours
- Do you know your neighbours? Why/why not?
- Do you get along with your neighbours? Why/why not?
- Why do you think people seem to know less about their neighbours than before?
- Why is it good to have neighbours?
- What do you usually talk about with your neighbours? Why?
- Would you prefer to have old people or young people as your neighbours? Why?
- Do your neighbours help you with anything?
- Do you help your neighbours with anything?

77. News
- Do you read the news? Why/why not?
- How often do you watch the news? Why?
- Where do you usually get the news? Why?
- What kinds of news are you interested in? Why?
- Is it important to you to keep up to date with the news? Why/why not?
- Who is more interested in the news, young people or older people? Why?
- Which news do you prefer, local, domestic or international? Why?

78. Newspapers & Magazines
- Do you enjoy reading magazines or newspapers? Why/why not?
- How often do you read them?
- What's your favourite magazine or newspaper? Why?
- What magazines or newspapers are popular in your country? Why?
- Do you think people will not read magazines or newspapers in the future? Why/why not?
- Have you ever written for a magazine or a newspaper? Why/why not?
- What do you usually do with old magazines or newspapers? Why?

79. Numbers
- Which number is your favourite? Why?
- Do any numbers have a special meaning in your country?

- Which number do you dislike? Why?
- Can you choose a plate number for a car? Why/why not?
- Are you good with numbers? Why/why not?

80. **Parks & Gardens**
- How often to go to a park? Why?
- Do you like going to a park? Why/why not?
- Are there a lot of gardens where you live?
- What do you usually do in the park/garden? Why?
- Do you prefer open-air parks or indoor ones? Why?
- What is the best season to visit a park/garden? Why?
- Would you like to have more parks/gardens where you live? Why/why not?
- What kinds of plants are most common in the parks/gardens near where you live?
- When was the last time you visited a park or a garden? Why?
- Which parks are better, the ones with open spaces or lots of leisure facilities? Why?
- How could parks in your area be improved? Why?
- What kinds of parks do you like? Why?
- What kinds of people like to go to parks? Why?

81. **Parties**
- Do you often go to parties? Why/why not?
- Did you often go to parties in your childhood? Why/why not?
- What kind of parties do you usually go to? Why?
- What do you dislike about going to parties? Why?
- Do you prefer to party with friends or family? Why?
- Who do you think likes partying more, older people or younger people? Why?
- Do you enjoy parties? Why/why not?
- How do people usually organize a party in your country? Why?
- Besides singing karaoke and eating out, what else do you do at parties? Why?
- Do you prefer formal or informal parties? Why?
- Do you prefer small or big parties? Why?
- Do you prefer to organize parties at home or somewhere else? Why?

82. **Photographs**
- Do you like to take photographs? Why/why not?
- What kinds of photos do you like to take? Why?
- Is it better to take photos with a camera or a mobile phone? Why?
- Do you often share your photos with other people? Why/why not?
- What is the most important element of a good photo? Why?
- Do you think it is necessary to learn how to use a camera? Why/why not?
- Is it good or bad to edit photos? Why?
- What do you usually do with your photos after you've taken them? Why?
- Would you like to study photography in the future? Why/why not?
- When do you like to take photos? Why?
- What kinds of photos do you keep? Why?

- Do you enjoy having your photograph taken? Why/why not?
- Do you think a professional photographer is a good career? Why/why not?
- What do you think of photos in newspapers and magazines? Why?

83. **Places to read**
- What's your favourite place to read? Why?
- What makes a place a good one to read? Why?
- Do you need to have silence around you to focus on reading? Why/why not?
- Do you prefer to read on your own or with other people? Why?
- Have you ever read in a place where it was difficult to focus? Why?

84. **Playing games**
- Do you like playing games? Why/why not?
- What was your favourite game when you were a child? Why?
- Who did you play with when you were a child? Why?
- Do you ever play video games? Why/why not?
- What are some advantages of playing games? Why?
- What are some disadvantages of playing games? Why?
- Do adults also play games in your country?
- Are online games generally good or bad? Why?
- What kinds of games do people in your country like to play? Why?
- Why do you think some people become easily addicted to games?
- Do you think children in your country have enough time to play games? Why/why not?

85. **Police**
- Is being a police officer a popular job in your country? Why/why not?
- Do you know any police officers?
- What kind of person can make a good police officer? Why?
- Do people in your country respect the police? Why/why not?
- Is being a police officer dangerous? Why/why not?
- Would you like to become a police officer in the future? Why/why not?

86. **Public transport & Transportation**
- Is there a subway system in your city?
- How often do you use public transport?
- What's your favourite means of public transport? Why?
- What do you think of the transportation system in your hometown?
- Is train travel common in your country? Why/why not?
- Have you ever met any interesting people while travelling by train?
- How do children usually travel to school? Why?
- How do you usually go travelling? Why?
- Do you think it is necessary to learn how to drive? Why?
- What is the safest transportation today? Why?
- Do you often travel by train? Why/why not?
- What in the main means of public transport in your country? Why?

- How do people go to work in your hometown? Why?
- Do you prefer taxis or private cars? Why?
- What are some advantages of riding bicycles?
- Why do people like driving in your country?
- Do you think cars will be used more in the future? Why/why not?

87. **Rain**
- Do you enjoy rainy days? Why/why not?
- During which season does it often rain in your country?
- In your country, do you have too much rain or too little rain? Why?
- How does rain make you feel? Why?
- Has the weather changed in your country over the past few years? How?
- Does it rain a lot where you live?

88. **Relaxing**
- What is your favourite way to relax? Why?
- How did you relax when you were a child?
- Why do you think some people find it difficult to relax?
- Is it easy for you to relax? Why/why not?
- Can physical activity help people relax? Why/why not?
- Are holidays the best way to relax? Why/why not?
- What are the benefits of getting relaxed? Why?
- What may happen if people don't get relaxed? Why?
- What are some common ways of relaxing in your country? Why?
- What is the difference between the way people relax now and in the past?

89. **Repairing things**
- Are you good at repairing things? Why/why not?
- Do you often repair things? Why/why not?
- Have you ever repaired anything? Why/why not?
- Do you prefer to repair things or buy new ones? Why?
- Is it easy to repair things? Why/why not?
- Do you think people will not repair things in the future? Why?

90. **School & Studying**
- Do you like your school? Why/why not?
- Why did you choose to attend that school?
- When is the best time for you to study during the day? Why?
- What are you studying?
- Have you made friends with the people you study with? Why/why not?
- Did/do you like your secondary school? Why/why not?
- What lessons did/do you dislike at school? Why?
- What is your major?
- Why did you choose this major?
- What kinds of majors are available in your country? Why?

- Do you prefer to study by yourself or in a group of people? Why?
- Do you think teachers are well-paid in your country?

91. **School subjects**
    - What is/was you favourite school subject? Why?
    - What is/was your least favourite school subject? Why?
    - Which school subject do you find most useful today? Why?
    - How did you feel on your first day at school/university?
    - What is your major?
    - Are you happy you decided to study this particular subject? Why/why not?
    - Is your major popular in your country? Why/why not?
    - Is it easy to find after graduating from your major? Why/why not?
    - Do you use computers while studying at school? Why/why not?
    - Which subject do you think is unnecessary in your school? Why?
    - What kind of school do/did you attend? Why?
    - Do/did you like your school? Why/why not?
    - Is there anything you would like to change about your school?

92. **Science**
    - Are you good at science? Why/why not?
    - Did/do you enjoy science lessons at school? Why/why not?
    - What kind of a person can be a good scientist? Why?
    - Is science easy to study? Why/why not?
    - Do students in your country like science? Why/why not?
    - Do you think more people will study science in the future? Why/why not?

93. **Seasons & Weather**
    - What's your favourite season? Why?
    - What's your favourite weather? Why?
    - What is the weather like where you live at different times of year?
    - What free time activities can you enjoy during different seasons? Why?
    - What do you usually do on sunny days? And on cold days? Why?
    - Do you like rainy days? Why/why not?
    - How does rain affect your mood?
    - How does rain influence life in your country? Why?
    - What do you do in good weather? Why?
    - What do you do in bad weather? Why?
    - What is the worst weather you have ever experienced?
    - How do different kinds of weather make you feel? Why?
    - Do you ever discuss the weather with your friends? Why/why not?
    - Have you ever visited a place with extreme type of weather? Why?
    - Would you prefer to live in a place with different seasons or in a place with the same weather all the time? Why?
    - Do you ever watch weather forecasts on TV? Why/why not?
    - Is the weather important to you when you go on holidays? Why/why not?

94. **Shoes**
- Do you have many pairs of shoes? Why/why not?
- Do you have a favourite pair of shoes? Why/why not?
- Do you prefer comfortable or fashionable shoes? Why?
- How often do you buy new shoes? Why?
- Where do you usually buy new shoes? Why?
- Do you ever buy shoes online? Why/why not?

95. **Shopping & Buying things**
- Do you enjoy shopping? Why/why not?
- Where do you usually shop? Why?
- When do you usually go shopping? Why?
- Do you have a favourite shop? Why/why not?
- What types of things do you buy most often?
- What's your favourite payment method? Why?
- Have you ever bought anything online?
- Are there any advantages to shopping online?
- Are there any disadvantages to shopping online?
- Who do you like to shop with? Why?
- Do you ever go window shopping? Why/why not?
- How often do you go shopping?
- Do you prefer to buy things in big shops or small shops? Why?
- Do you often buy famous brands? Why/why not?
- Would you like to have a job in a shop? Why/why not?
- Do you prefer shopping alone or with other people? Why?
- Have you ever tried TV direct shopping? Why/why not?
- Do you know anyone who is a shopaholic?
- Do you think shopping is a good way to relax? Why/why not?
- When was the last time you went shopping? Why?
- What's your favourite time of day for shopping? Why?
- What don't you like about shopping? Why?

96. **Sky**
- Do you often look at the sky? Why/why not?
- What do you enjoy more, the sky at night or by day? Why?
- Where can you see stars clearly? Why?
- Did you learn about stars and planets at schools? Why/why not?
- Would you like to learn more about stars and planets in the future? Why/why not?
- Why do some people find looking at the sky boring?

97. **Sleep**
- How many hours a night do you usually sleep? Why?
- How many hours of sleep do you need? Why?
- Did you get more sleep in your childhood? Why/why not?
- Is a good night's sleep generally important to you? Why/why not?

- ↻ Do you ever read in bed? Why/why not?
- ↻ Do you ever have a nap during the day? Why/why not?
- ↻ What can you do to help yourself sleep better? Why?

98. Smoking
- ↻ Do you smoke? Why/why not?
- ↻ Do you think you will start smoking in the future? Why/why not?
- ↻ Do many people in our country smoke? Why/why not?
- ↻ Who smokes more often, men or women? Why?
- ↻ Should smoking be banned in public places? Why/why not?
- ↻ How is smoking harmful?
- ↻ Have you ever tried smoking? Why/why not?
- ↻ Are cigarettes expensive in your country?

99. Socializing
- ↻ Are you a sociable person? Why/why not?
- ↻ How do people in your country usually socialize? Why?
- ↻ How does technology influence socializing these days?
- ↻ Do you think people will be more or less sociable in the future? Why?
- ↻ Where do people in your country socialize?
- ↻ Is socializing easy? Why/why not?

100. Sounds
- ↻ What is your favourite sound? Why?
- ↻ Do you have a favourite sound? What is it?
- ↻ What do you think of noise? Why?
- ↻ How do you feel in a noisy place? Why?
- ↻ Do you like music? Why/why not?
- ↻ What is your favourite musical instrument? Why?
- ↻ Do you often listen to the sounds of nature? Why/why not?
- ↻ Are nature sounds important to you? Why/why not?

101. Sports
- ↻ Do you like doing sports? Why/why not?
- ↻ How often do you do sports? Why?
- ↻ What's your favourite sport? Why?
- ↻ What sports would you like to try in the future? Why?
- ↻ What is the most popular sport in your country? Why?
- ↻ Where do you usually do sports? Why?
- ↻ When is the best time for sports? Why?
- ↻ Is swimming popular in your country? Why/why not?
- ↻ How much money would you spend on your favourite sport? Why?
- ↻ What is the best sport for the elderly? Why?
- ↻ Are there any traditional sports in your country?
- ↻ Do you like swimming? Why/why not?

- Do you often watch sports? Why/why not?
- Do you prefer to watch matches or play in a match?
- What do you think of sport facilities in your city? Why?
- Do you think it's important for children to know how to swim? Why/why not?

102. Street markets
- Do you like going to street markets? Why/why not?
- Are street markets common in your country? Why/why not?
- Do you think it would be interesting to visit a street market in a foreign country? Why/why not?
- Do you think some people prefer street markets to supermarkets? Why/why not?
- What products can people find on street markets?
- What do you usually buy at street markets? Why?

103. Sunshine
- Do you like sunshine? Why/why not?
- Do you enjoy spending time outdoors when it's sunny? Why/why not?
- How does sunshine influence your mood? Why?
- What is hard for you to do outside when it's sunny? Why?
- Would you choose a place with just a little sunshine for your holidays? Why/why not?
- How can too much sunshine be harmful?

104. Swimming
- Can you swim? Why/why not?
- Have you ever learnt how to swim? Why/why not?
- Who taught you how to swim? Why?
- Do you think everyone should know how to swim? Why/why not?
- Should children learn how to swim? Why/why not?
- Is swimming easy or difficult? Why?
- How can swimming be helpful in life? Why?
- Where do people in your country usually swim?

105. Taking a break
- How often do you take breaks when you are studying or working? Why?
- What do you usually do when you take a break? Why?
- Do you ever take a nap when taking a break? Why/why not?
- How do you feel after you've taken a break? Why?
- Are breaks necessary for you? Why/why not?
- Did you have to take breaks when you were younger? Why/why not?
- How long do your breaks last? Why?

106. Teachers
- Do/did you have a favourite teacher at school? Why/why not?
- How did teachers help you in your studies? Why?
- Do you still stay in touch with any of your teachers? Why/why not?

- Would you like to become a teacher? Why/why not?
- What qualities does a good teacher have? Why?

107. Toys
- What was your favourite childhood toy? Why?
- What kinds of toys did you play with when you were a kid? Why?
- Do you still have any of your old toys? Why/why not?
- Why do you think people like to keep their toys?
- What do you think of high-tech toys? Why?
- What do you think the toys in the future would be like? Why?
- Do you think boys and girls like different toys? Why/why not?

108. Traffic
- How is the traffic in your city? Why?
- Do you often get stuck in traffic jams? Why?
- When is traffic in your city the heaviest? Why?
- How to avoid heavy traffic?
- What can the government do to lessen traffic?
- What do you do to avoid traffic? Why?

109. Travelling
- How often to do travel? Why?
- Where do you usually travel? Why?
- Do you like travelling? Why/why not?
- Do people like to travel in your culture? Why/why not?
- Would you like to travel around the world? Why/why not?
- How can a place benefit from local tourism? Why?
- Do you prefer to travel alone or with other people? Why?
- How do you feel about backpacking? Why?
- Is travelling important to you? Why/why not?

110. Visitors
- Do visitors often come to your home? Why/why not?
- When was the last time you had visitors? Why?
- What do you need to prepare when you expect visitors?
- Are there any times of the year when you have more visitors than usual? Why/why not?
- Do you often visit other people? Why/why not?
- Do you like visiting other people? Why/why not?

111. Visiting relatives
- How often do you visit your relatives? Why?
- When was the last time you visited relatives? Why?
- When you visit relatives, what do you usually do together? Why?
- Do people often visit relatives in your culture? Why/why not?
- Do you prefer to visit relatives or friends? Why?

↻ Do young people in your country enjoy visiting relatives? Why/why not?

112. Walks

↻ How often do you go for a walk? Why?

↻ Do you like going for walk? Why/why not?

↻ Is it better to go for a walk in the city or in the countryside? Why?

↻ What are some good places to go for a walk? Why?

↻ How could cities be better places for walking? Why?

↻ Do you think you will walk more or less in the future? Why?

113. Watching TV

↻ What's your favourite TV programme? Why?

↻ What features do you think a good programme should have? Why?

↻ How many hours do you spend watching TV every day? Why?

↻ Do you think some teenagers watch too much TV these days? Why/why not?

↻ What is your favourite TV channel? Why?

↻ What kinds of TV programmes do you watch when you want to relax? Why?

↻ Do you ever watch TV programmes from foreign countries? Why/why not?

↻ Has TV ever helped you in your studies? How/why not?

↻ How much television did you watch in your childhood? Why?

↻ Do you think television has changed in your country since your childhood? How?

↻ In the future, how much television will you let your children to watch? Why?

↻ Do children in your country watch too much TV? Why/why not?

↻ What types of programme would you like to see more on television? Why?

114. Weekends

↻ What do you usually do at weekends? Why?

↻ Is the weekend your favourite part of the week? Why/why not?

↻ Do you ever have to work at the weekend? Why/why not?

↻ What did you do last weekend? Why?

↻ Do you usually plan how to spend your weekends? Why/why not?

↻ Are weekends too short for you? Why/why not?

PART 2 TOPICS

THINGS/SKILLS/SITUATIONS/OCCASIONS/ACTIVITIES/EVENTS

• **a book/(foreign) film you loved/hated/you read or watched because someone recommended it to you**

VOCAB:

1. cast /kɑːst/ (n./v.) = to choose an actor for a part
2. a blurb /blɜː(r)b/ (n.) = a short text usually printed on the back cover of a book describing what that book is about, sometimes includes quotes from critics
3. a protagonist /prəʊˈtægənɪst/ (n.) = the main character in a play, film, book or story
4. an antagonist /ænˈtægənɪst/ (n.) = the protagonist's opponent
5. to please someone's appetite /ˈæpətaɪt/ (phr.) = to satisfy the feeling that you want to do or have sth
6. lines /laɪnz/ (n.) = the words that an actor says in a performance
7. twists and turns (phr.) = intricate, convoluted circumstances (in a story)
8. a vivid portrait /ˈvɪvɪd ˈpɔː(r)trɪt/ (phr.) = a clear and detailed picture of sth
9. a blockbuster /ˈblɒkˌbʌstə(r)/ (n.) = a very successful film, show, book
10. an Oscar nominee /ˌnɒmɪˈniː/ (phr.) = (person, film) officially suggested for an Oscar
11. to have a strong aversion to sb/sth /əˈvɜː(r)ʃ(ə)n/ (phr.) = to dislike sb/sth strongly
12. to be reluctant to do sth /rɪˈlʌktənt/ (phr.) = to be unwilling to so sth
13. can't stand sb/sth (phr.) = can't bear sb/sth
14. to loathe sb/sth /ləʊð/ (v.) = to dislike sb/sth very much
15. to detest sb/sth /dɪˈtest/ (v.) = to hate sb/sth
16. an audio book /ˈɔːdiəʊ bʊk/ (n.) = a book that is read out loud, usually by an actor and recorded as an MP3 file
17. a flyleaf /ˈflaɪˌliːf/ (n.) = the first or last page of a book that is next to the cover and has nothing printed on it
18. a voracious reader /vəˈreɪʃəs ˈriːdə(r)/ (phr.) = a person very keen on reading
19. a bookworm /ˈbʊkˌwɜː(r)m/ (n.) = someone who loves reading books and spends a lot of time doing it
20. to read sth from cover to cover (phr.) = from beginning to end (of a book, magazine etc.)
21. to read sth in one sitting (phr.) = at once
22. to reread sth (v.) = to read (a text) again
23. to flick through sth /flɪk/ (v.) = to turn pages of a book, magazine etc. very quickly looking at some of the pages for a very short time
24. a dull book/film /dʌl/ (n.) = a boring book/film
25. atrocious /əˈtrəʊʃəs/ (adj.) = very bad in quality
26. sentimental /ˌsentɪˈment(ə)l/ (adj.) = making people experience feelings of sadness, sympathy, love etc., especially in a deliberate and obvious way
27. full of clichés /ˈkliːʃeɪs/ (phr.) = full of ideas that are boring because people use them a lot and they are no longer original
28. a shallow character /ˈʃæləʊ/ (phr.) = not interesting
29. feeble jokes /ˈfiːb(ə)l/ (n.) = not strong enough to make people laugh

30. a wooden dialogue /ˈwʊd(ə)n ˈdaɪəlɒg/ (phr.) = without emotions
31. a mediocre acting /ˌmiːdiˈəʊkə(r)/ (phr.) = average or below average in quality
32. sb was miscast /ˌmɪsˈkɑːst/ (phr.) = given a part without being suitable for it
33. dire /ˈdaɪə(r)/ (adj.) = terrible
34. sb was unconvincing /ˌʌnkənˈvɪnsɪŋ/ (phr.) = not capable of persuading the audience
35. utter rubbish /ˈʌtə(r) ˈrʌbɪʃ/ (phr.) = absolutely terrible
36. to be bored stiff (phr.) = to be very bored
37. to be bored out of your mind (phr.) = to be extremely bored

PART 3:
- Do many people go to the cinema in your country? Why/why not?
- Is there a rating system for cinema in your country? If so, how does it work?
- What is the general trend of your national films? Why?
- Do you think fewer people go to the cinema today, compared with the past? Why/why not?
- Is it good to watch a foreign film in its original language? Why/why not?
- How important are actors for the success of the film?
- Does casting a star guarantee the success of the film? Why/why not?
- Why do you think people like different films at different stages in their lives?
- Which do you think will be more popular in the future, going out or staying at home to watch a film? Why?
- Do you think that thanks to modern technology films produced now are better? Why/why not?
- Is children's behaviour affected by the images from films? Why/why not?
- How do films and books generally influence society? Why?
- Are historical films always truthful? Why/why not?
- Should films depicting historical events rewrite history? Why/why not?
- How do you think cinematography will develop in the future? Why?
- What kinds of books do people in your country like to read? Why?
- What sorts of books are usually bestsellers in your country? Why?
- Do people in your country often buy second hand books? Why/why not?
- Do you think books might be substituted by e-books in the future? Why/why not?
- How are e-readers harmful?
- Why do we read books generally?
- Is reading a good hobby? Why/why not?
- Why does reading as a hobby suit people of all ages?
- Can we learn anything from reading fiction? If so, what?
- How can parents encourage children to read more? Why?
- What qualities does a person need to become a good writer? Why?
- Why do some writers become successful and others don't? What does it depend on?
- Why, in your opinion, some authors can only become famous after their death?
- Can authors bring social change? How?
- Who's the most successful author in your country? Why?
- Who's the most popular foreign writer in your country? Why?
- What kinds of books do children like to read in your country? Why?
- Should parents teach their children how to read before they start school? Why/why not?
- What are main benefits of reading? Why?

- Do men and women like the same kinds of books? Why?
- Why do you think some books become popular internationally? What does it depend on?
- Which is more relaxing, reading a book or watching TV? Why?
- Is reading a book a challenging pastime? Why/why not?
- Are there any famous book adaptations in the cinema at the moment? Why/why not?
- Do you think in the future people will only grab a book for pleasure and not for knowledge? Why/why not?
- Do people in your country prefer to watch a film at home or in the cinema? Why?
- What are some common things people do today in the their spare time at home?
- Do you think it is possible for most free time activities in the future to involve computers? Why/why not?
- What types of public entertainment are there available for young people in your country?
- Are places of entertainment important? Why/why not?
- Are there any places of entertainment in the countryside in your country? Why/why not? Should there be? What kind?
- How can entertainment influence education in a good way?
- Are there any rules regulating forms of entertainment on TV today? Why/why not? Should there be?
- Do you think international films and TV shows may influence one's culture in a negative way? Why/why not?
- Do people in your country like to watch English movies? Why/why not?
- Is it easy to watch films in English in your country? Why?
- Is watching films in English a good way to improve the language? Why/why not?
- Is watching a film in English the same as reading a book in English? Why/why not?
- What other foreign films (apart from English-speaking ones) are popular in your country? Why?
- Do you think daily life depicted in foreign movies is close to reality? Why/why not?
- Can we learn anything about life in another country by watching films from foreign countries? If so, what? Why/why not?
- Do we still need to travel? Is watching a foreign film enough? Why/why not?
- Is the film industry strong in your country? Why/why not?
- Why do you think cinema has become such a popular form of art?
- What does a film need to be successful? Why?
- Do you think that money invested in film production could be used in a better way? If so, how?
- In what ways are books beneficial for children?
- Whose responsibility is it to teach children how to read? Parents or teachers? Why?
- Do you think we read more or less than our predecessors? Why?
- Do you think paper books might disappear one day? Why/why not?
- Do you think the next generation will cherish books? Why/why not?
- How many people in your society cannot read?
- What problems might illiterate people face in life?
- Do you think people should be generally encouraged to read more? Why/why not?

- **a book/film about the future/a film/book based on facts/about a real person or event**

VOCAB:

1. a touching story /ˈtʌtʃɪŋ/ (phr.) = a story that is making you feel emotional
2. a nail-biting moment (phr.) = a moment that makes you very excited
3. suspenseful /səˈspensf(ə)l/ (adj.) = (a story, film) keeps you wanting to know what will happen next
4. a sob-story (n.) = a story that evokes sympathy
5. evocative scenes /ɪˈvɒkətɪv/ (phr.) = scenes which arouse memories or images
6. the ending slays me /sleɪz/ (phr.) = impresses someone, especially by making them laugh
7. an intriguing plot /ɪnˈtriːɡɪŋ/ (phr.) = a very interesting plot, especially because of being strange or mysterious
8. a multisensory experience /mʌlti ˈsensəri/ (phr.) = relating to many senses
9. soulless /ˈsəʊlləs/ (adj.) = not at all interesting or attractive
10. memoirs /ˈmemˌwɑː(r)/ (n.) = written record of a person's own life
11. lightweight /ˈlaɪtˌweɪt/ (adj.) = not complex
12. a bedtime reading (phr.) = nice to read in bed
13. heavy going (phr.) = difficult to read or understand
14. a lugubrious setting /ləˈɡuːbriəs/ (phr.) = a rather dark and gloomy setting
15. a page-turner (n.) = a very interesting and engaging story
16. an enigmatic tale /ˌenɪɡˈmætɪk/ (phr.) = a mysterious story
17. a wry humour /raɪ/ (phr.) = a humour in the face of a bad situation
18. an idealized portrayal of /aɪˈdɪəlaɪz pɔː(r)ˈtreɪəl/ (phr) = an exaggerated description of
19. graphic /ˈɡræfɪk/ (adj.) = giving a lot of detail
20. tenable /ˈtenəb(ə)l/ (adj.) = reasonable with evidence to support it

PART 3:

- What kinds of real events or people are films/books often based on? Why?
- Can we learn anything about history from such films/books? Why/why not?
- Do you think that everything in such movies/books is always true? Why/why not?
- Is it important that facts match reality? Why/why not?
- Does a film need famous actors to be successful? Why/why not?
- What factors contribute to the success of a film/book? Why?
- Why do some actors become famous all over the world?
- Do you think it is possible that in the future computer-generated characters will replace humans? Why/why not?
- Can a film/book affect public opinion? If so, in what way?
- Should there be an age restriction for some films/books? Why/why not?
- Have you seen many movies that made you think?
- Is the main aim of a book to make the reader think? Why/why not?
- Do you think in the future most leisure activities will involve electronic products? Why/why not? Is that good or bad?
- Why are books and films about the future so popular?
- Can people learn anything from watching movies/reading books about the future? Why/why not?

- Do you think that what's depicted in such books/movies may really happen in the future? Why/why not?
- In your opinion, which modern invention has been the most helpful to us so far? Why?
- Do you think in the future we will have robots to help around the house? Why/why not?
- Would it be good to have robots to do housework? Why/why not?
- How can the latest technological inventions improve our daily life, in areas like travel or shopping? Why?
- Should world leaders be concerned with planning for the world's future? Why/why not?
- Are people generally optimistic or pessimistic about the future? Why?
- Do you believe there are other living cultures on other planets? Why/why not?

- **a childhood toy you loved/was important to you in your childhood**

VOCAB:

1. a puppet /ˈpʌpɪt/ (n.) = a small model of a person or animal that you can move by pulling wires or strings, or by putting your hand inside it
2. a loyal friend /ˈlɔɪəl/ (phr.) = a friend willing to support you even in difficult times
3. handmade (adj.) = made by a person, instead of by a machine
4. to accompany sb /əˈkʌmp(ə)ni/ (v.) = to go with someone
5. to feel on the top of the world (phr.) = to be in a very good mood because things are going well for you
6. worn out (adj.) = too old or damaged to use any longer
7. a toy car (n.) = a toy in a form of a small car
8. soft (adj.) = not harsh
9. squeaky /ˈskwiːki/ (adj.) = making a short high noise
10. to play hide-and-seek (phr.) = to play a children's game in which one player lets the other players hide, and then tries to find them
11. to chase each other /tʃeɪs/ (phr.) = to follow someone quickly in order to catch them
12. a game of… (n.)
13. a teddy bear (n.)
14. to cuddle /ˈkʌd(ə)l/ (v.) = to put your arms round sth/sb and hold them close to show that you like or love them
15. a little pet shop playset (phr.)
16. a Barbie doll /ˈbɑː(r)bi/ (n.)

PART 3:

- Do you think every child has a favourite toy in their childhood? Why/why not?
- Do boys and girls like the same types of toys? Why/why not?
- What kinds of toys do children like to play with now? Why?
- What kinds of toys did children like to play with in the past? Why?
- Why do you think some children enjoy playing with everyday household objects?
- Do you think parents buy their children too many toys? Why/why not?
- What should adults take into consideration when they are buying a toy for a child? Why?
- In your opinion, should children be allowed to choose their toys in a shop? Why/why not?

↻ Do you think some parents might buy their children too many toys in order to make up for a lack of time?

↻ Do you think the toy industry will develop in the future? Why/why not?

↻ Is there any connection between toys in shops and children's film? Why?

↻ Do you think every toy should be educational? Why/why not?

↻ Do you think toy manufacturers should be responsible for educational value in their toys? Why/why not?

↻ What do you think of advertisements targeting children? Why?

↻ Do advertisements create new consumers out of children? Is it moral? Why/why not?

↻ Is it important to teach children to share their toys? Why/why not?

↻ How can toys help children's mental development?

↻ How can toys help children's physical development?

↻ How do electronic toys affect children negatively? In what ways?

↻ Do you think that boys and girls must play with different toys? Why/why not?

↻ What can parents learn about their children by observing the way they play with their toys?

↻ How can creativity be facilitated in an early childhood?

- **a domestic product you think is good/a product made in your region**

VOCAB:

1. mass production (n.) = the process of producing large quantities of goods by using machines
2. a commodity /kəˈmɒdəti/ (n.) = something that can be bought and sold
3. merchandise /ˈmɜː(r)tʃ(ə)ndaɪz/ (n.) = goods that people buy and sell
4. service-oriented /ˈsɜː(r)vɪs ˈɔːrientɪd/ (adj.) = mainly concerned with meeting customers' needs
5. reliable /rɪˈlaɪəb(ə)l/ (adj.) = can be trusted
6. produced in + place (adj.)
7. the cost of labour /ˈleɪbə(r)/ (phr.) = the cost of the workers in a particular company
8. aspects of production (phr.) = features of production
9. to be exported /ɪkˈspɔː(r)tɪd/ (v.) = (of a product) to be sent to another country so that it can be sold there
10. to launch a product /lɔːntʃ/ (phr.) = to start selling a product to the public
11. sales figures (n.) = sales numbers
12. to do market research (phr.) = to collect information about what products people like to buy
13. stiff competition (phr.) = severe competitors
14. to drum up some business (phr.) = to try to make people buy something from you

PART 3 :

↻ Do different regions in your country produce different products? Why/why not?

↻ What are some popular food products from different parts of? Why?

↻ Is it important for a particular region to have its own products? Why/why not?

↻ Do people in your country like foreign products? If so, what kind? Why?

↻ What are some popular foreign products in your country? Why?

↻ Why do you think some brands become so successful while others don't? What does it depend on?

↻ Is it good or bad for the same product to be sold in different countries? Why?

☞ What in your opinion is the greatest invention of our times? Why?

☞ Why do you think only a few chosen inventions become internationally famous?

☞ Can inventions contribute to the world problems? How?

- **a family business/small business/successful business you know**

VOCAB :

1. a niche market /niːʃ ˈmɑː(r)kɪt/ (n.) = the part of an industry that sells a particular type of product or service to the small number of customers who want it
2. to run a business (phr.) = to have a business
3. cost-cutting (n.) = actions takes to reduce the costs of a business
4. to try the hard sell (phr.) = to attempt to sell sth by being very forceful
5. brand loyalty (n.) = confidence in the particular make and a tendency always to choose it
6. to strike while the iron is hot (phr.) = to take advantage of an opportunity before the situation changes
7. up and running (phr.) = working effectively
8. a golden opportunity (n.) = a very good chance to achieve something
9. the black market (n.) = an illegal trade
10. to stay within the budget /ˈbʌdʒɪt/ (phr.) = do not exceed money available to spend
11. to mount a challenge /maʊnt/ (phr.) = to prepare for a challenge
12. a shareholder /ˈʃeə(r)ˌhəʊldə(r)/ (n.) = sb who own shares in a company
13. a dividend /ˈdɪvɪdend/ (n.) = a share of the profits of a company, paid once or twice a year to the people who own the company's shares
14. to clinch the deal /klɪntʃ/ (phr.) = to manage to win a deal
15. mergers and acquisitions /ˈmɜː(r)dʒə(r)z ænd ˌækwɪˈzɪʃ(ə)nz/ (n.) = the department in a company that is responsible for taking over other businesses
16. to go under (v.) = to fail completely and stop operating
17. an investor /ɪnˈvestə(r)/ (n.) = a person that invests money
18. to underpin sth /ˌʌndə(r)ˈpɪn/ (v.) = to be an important basic part of something, allowing it to succeed
19. a budget /ˈbʌdʒɪt/ (n.) = the amount of money an organization has to spend on something
20. a surplus /ˈsɜː(r)pləs/ (n.) = more of something than necessary
21. an emergency fund for contingencies /kənˈtɪndʒ(ə)nsiz/ (phr.) = a certain amount of money kept for something bad that might happen in the future
22. a shortfall /ˈʃɔː(r)tˌfɔːl/ (n.) = the amount of money a business lacks
23. a deficit /ˈdefəsɪt/ (n.) = the difference between the amount of money or goods that a business has and the amount that it has spent
24. to economize /ɪˈkɒnəmaɪz/ (v.) = to save money
25. to make cutbacks (v.) = to save money
26. thriving /ˈθraɪvɪŋ/ (adj.) = very successful

PART 3 :

☞ What kind of person can make a good businessperson? Why?

☞ What are some advantages of working for a family business?

☞ What are some disadvantages of working for a family business?

☞ Do you think that when it comes to working for a family business, drawbacks outweigh benefits? Why/why not?

☞ Why do some family businesses fail?

☞ Why do people start their own businesses in the first place?

☞ Can women be as good at business as men? Why/why not?

☞ What types of businesses are there in your country?

☞ In your opinion, is it better to work for a large or small business? Why?

☞ What are some reasons for small businesses to often fail in the first year?

☞ Which businesses will be most prosperous in the future? Why?

☞ Does your country do a lot of business with other countries? Why/why not?

☞ What is good about a company exporting goods?

☞ What is bad about a company exporting products?

☞ Do you think the government should regulate how many foreign products are imported into your country? Why/why not?

☞ How do multinational companies influence local markets?

- **a (family) photograph that means a lot to you/a photograph someone took of you/you took of someone**

VOCAB :

1. to capture the moment /ˈkæptʃə(r)/ (phr.) = to record the moment
2. from the right angle (phr.) = (photo) taken well
3. a memorable moment /ˈmem(ə)rəb(ə)l/ (phr.) = a moment hard to forget
4. of great sentimental value to me /ˌsentɪˈment(ə)l/ (phr.) = (photo) precious to me
5. the camera loves (whom) (phr.) = this person always look good in photos
6. photogenic /ˌfəʊtəʊˈdʒenɪk/ (adj.) = looks good in photographs
7. a snapshot /ˈsnæpˌʃɒt/ (n.) = a photograph taken without the use of professional equipment
8. a single lens reflex camera /ˈriːfleks/ (n.) = a camera in which the lens that forms the image on the film also provide the image in the viewfinder
9. a digital camera /ˈdɪdʒɪt(ə)l/ (n.) = a camera that records and stores digital images
10. framing /ˈfreɪmɪŋ/ (n.) = the way of placing an object or a person in the photograph
11. a point-and-shoot camera (n.) = an automatic camera which, when it is pointed at a subject and the shutter release is pressed, will take a properly exposed and focused photo
12. a memento /məˈmentəʊ/ (n.) = sth that you keep to remind you of a particular person, place or experience
13. camera-shy (adj.) = sb not willing to have their photograph taken
14. a scrapbook /ˈskræpˌbʊk/ (n.) = a book in which you save pictures, articles or other material
15. to treasure sth /ˈtreʒə(r)/ (v.) = to look after sth very carefully because it is valuable to you
16. to act natural /ˈnætʃ(ə)rəl/ (phr.) = to act normal (photo – not pose)
17. to develop a photo (phr.) = to make a photograph
18. a photo shop (n.) = a place where one can develop or take photographs
19. to touch a photo up with a computer programme (phr.) = e.g. to photoshop a photo
20. to remove all reflections (phr.) = to make the photograph clearer and better
21. an online photo album (phr.) = a photo album online where one can keep and share photos with friends

128

22. to have a box of old photos lying around (phr.) = to collect old photos in a box
23. a photo blog (n.) = a blog in which the postings are mainly in the form of photographs

PART 3 :
- Why do you think people like to show their photos to friends and family?
- Do you think people who take large numbers of photos while travelling miss out on sth? Why/why not?
- Are photos better than postcards? Why/why not?
- For what occasions would people hire a professional photographer? Why?
- Are family photographs important in your culture? Why/why not?
- Are photos a good way to keep record of family life/person's life? Why/why not?
- Are photographs often used in adverts? Why/why not?
- How do photos influence the way news is reported?
- Can photographs help us remember history? Why/why not?
- Why is there always a photo of a writer on their book?
- Why is there always a photo of a singer on their CD?
- What is a good photograph? Why?
- What are some main differences between a good photo and a good painting?
- Do you think the way we take photos might change in the future? How?
- Is it better to use a professional camera or a smart phone to take photos? Why?
- Why are some photographs famous?
- What kinds of skills does a person need to become a good photographer?
- Do you think that digital cameras made photography more popular? Why?
- How can photos help children learn?
- With such advanced technology, can we still trust what we see in the photographs? Why/why not?
- Do you think learning might be more visual in the future than it is now? Why/why not?
- Does every mobile phone need a camera? Why/why not?
- Which one is better: printed photos or photos on a computer screen? Why?
- Do you think people might stop developing photos in the future and keep only their digital versions? Why/why not?
- How are photos usually used in the media? Why? Is it good or bad?
- Can anyone take a good photo? Why/why not?
- What do people pay more attention to in the magazines: articles or photographs? Why?
- Do you think it is easier or more difficult to take photos now, compared with the past? Why?
- Can photos completely replace paintings in the future? Why/why not?

- **a foreign language (not English) you would like to learn in the future**

VOCAB :
1. a window to a greater world (phr.) = something that gives one a broader perspective of the world
2. a lingua franca /ˌlɪŋgwə ˈfræŋkə/ (n.) = a language that people use to communicate when they have different first languages
3. a single international language (n.) = one language being spoken in all countries
4. to preserve the individuality of cultures (phr.) = to keep different cultures unchanged

5. bilingual /baɪˈlɪŋgwəl/ (adj.) = someone who speaks two languages extremely well
6. monolingual /ˌmɒnəʊˈlɪŋgwəl/ (adj.) = someone who uses only one language
7. to get a grasp of sth /grɑːsp/ (phr.) = to comprehend sth
8. the alphabet /ˈælfəˌbet/ (n.) = a set of letters in a particular order that are used for writing a language
9. the Cyrillic alphabet /səˈrɪlɪk/ (n.) = the alphabet used to write Russian and some Central European languages
10. a syllable /ˈsɪləb(ə)l/ (n.) = a word or apart of a word that has only one vowel sound
11. hard tones (phr.) = tones that need to follow a certain intonation pattern
12. to step inside the context of a culture (phr.) = to begin to understand a culture
13. paramount /ˈpærəmaʊnt/ (adj.) = more important than other things
14. to be competent in a language /ˈkɒmpɪtənt/ (phr.) = to be good enough in a language but not especially good
15. to bridge the gap between cultures (phr.) = to bring cultures closer together
16. to converse about sth /kənˈvɜː(r)s/ (v.) = to talk about
17. to compose a plan /kəmˈpəʊz/ (phr.) = to make a plan
18. to push yourself (phr.) = to force yourself
19. an interpreter /ɪnˈtɜː(r)prɪtə(r)/ (n.) = a spoken translator
20. a mother tongue (n.) = a native language
21. Language shapes the way we think and determines what we can think about. (phr.)
22. a pictogram /ˈpɪktəgræm/ (n.) = a character representing a picture
23. an ideogram /ˈɪdiəgræm/ (n.) = a character representing an idea

PART 3 :
- What foreign languages are common in your country among students? Why?
- Do you think everyone should learn at least one foreign language? Why/why not?
- Why are some languages more popular than others?
- Why are some people better at learning languages than others? What does it depend on?
- Are foreign language lessons fun in your country? Why/why not?
- Which language is considered an international language? Why?
- Do you think your native language can become a new international language in the future? Why/why not?
- What's good about having an international language? Why?
- What are some cons of having one main language? Why?
- How closely is language related to culture? Why?
- Has your language been influenced by other languages? Which ones? Why?
- Can a person really know a culture without knowing its language? Why?
- How important is language to cultural identity? Why?

- **a game you like to play/used to play/an indoor game you enjoyed playing in your childhood**

VOCAB :
1. time flies (phr.) = time seems to be passing very quickly

2. in retrospect,... /ˈretrəʊˌspekt/ (phr.) = considering something that happened in the past, using knowledge or information that you did not have at that time
3. with hindsight /ˈhaɪn(d)ˌsaɪt/ (phr.) = understanding of a situation or event only after it has happened
4. to bond with (v.) = to develop feelings of love, friendship towards other people
5. to activate brain cells /ˈæktɪveɪt/ (phr.) = to make the brain cells start working
6. to get addicted to /əˈdɪktɪd/ (phr.) = to enjoy a particular activity very much and spend as much time as you can doing it
7. hide-and-seek (n.) = a children's game in which one player lets the other players hide and then tries to find them
8. to count to a number (phr.) = to count from 0 to e.g. 100
9. to find someone hiding (phr.)
10. the searcher (n.) = a child in hide-and-seek game that counts and looks for others
11. to ride on my father's back (phr.) = a game where a child sits on the father's back and the father pretends to be a horse
12. making house (phr.) = a game where children pretend to have an imaginary house
13. noisy (adj.) = loud
14. an amusement park (n.) = a place where people pay money to go on rides and play games to win prizes
15. an arcade /ɑː(r)ˈkeɪd/ (n.) = a place where you can play computer games, play on slot machines etc.
16. everyone's a winner (phr.) = a concept in which nobody actually wins or loses a game
17. to blow bubbles (phr.) = to play a game where a child blows balls made of soap
18. to throw a ball around (phr.) = to play with a ball
19. sophisticated games /səˈfɪstɪˌkeɪtɪd/ (phr.) = difficult games
20. a board game (n.) = an indoor game played on a board, often with pieces that are moved around it
21. chess (n.)
22. Monopoly /məˈnɒpəli/ (n.) = a board game which uses fake money to buy properties
23. hopscotch /ˈhɒpˌskɒtʃ/ (n.) = a children's game that involves jumping on a set of squares that you draw on the ground
24. to draw grids /ɡrɪd/ (phr.) = to draw squares on the ground (for hopscotch)
25. to hop into each square (phr.) = to jump into each square
26. to hop on one foot (phr.)
27. to play marbles /ˈmɑː(r)b(ə)lz/ (phr.) = a game played by children in which they roll small coloured glass balls called marbles on the ground
28. to flick the marbles /flɪk/ (phr.) = to move the marbles suddenly and quickly
29. to scatter the marbles /ˈskætə(r)/ (phr.) = to throw the marbles
30. to play charades /ʃəˈrɑːdz/ (phr.) = a game in which players guess a word or phrase from pantomimed clues

PART 3 :
- ✎ Why do you think some people prefer indoor activities?
- ✎ What are some disadvantages of indoor activities?
- ✎ What kinds of games do children like to play today? Why?
- ✎ What kind of games did children enjoy in the past? Why?

- Is it important for children to play games outside? Why/why not?
- Do children still play games outside today? Why/why not?
- Do you think that playing games is beneficial to children's imagination? Why/why not?
- Can children learn anything through playing games? If so, what?
- Should all games children play be educational? Why/why not?
- Is it good for children to get competitive while playing games? Why/why not?
- Should everyone be competitive? Why/why not?
- Are people naturally competitive or do they become competitive? Why?
- Is it good if colleagues are competitive? Why/why not?
- What problems might occur in a workplace if workers get too competitive? Why?
- Do you think that all successful people must be competitive? Why/why not?
- Is it possible to achieve success without being competitive? Why/why not?
- Do you think young people play too many games today? Why/why not?
- What types of games can make you easily addicted? Why?

- **a good habit a friend has you'd like to develop**

VOCAB :
1. self-discipline /self ˈdɪsəplɪn/ (n.) = the ability to control your behaviour so that you do what you should do
2. as is someone's wont /wəʊnt/ (phr.) = a habit of doing a particular thing
3. be in the habit of doing sth (phr.)
4. to adopt a habit /əˈdɒpt/ (phr.) = to decide to start a habit
5. to drain sb's batteries (phr.) = to me sb very tired
6. a motivation boost /buːst/ (phr.) = an increase in motivation
7. the flow of motivation comes to a stop (phr.) = there is no more motivation to do sth
8. a sustainable habit /səˈsteɪnəb(ə)l/ (phr.) = a permanent habit
9. to form achievable goals (phr.)
10. to acquire a habit (phr.) = to start a habit
11. to be a person of habit (phr.) = have a lot of habits and stick to them
12. to break the habit (phr.) = to stop a habit (usually a bad one)

PART 3 :
- Is it easy to change a bad habit? Why/why not?
- What bad habits do people usually have?
- What are some methods to change bad habits? Why?
- What good habits should children learn? Why?
- How can parents teach their children some good habits?
- In what ways do children pick up bad habits? Why?
- Is it easier to change a bad habit when we are younger or older? Why?
- Is daily routine beneficial? How?
- How can people set their daily routine?
- How can people make sure they follow their daily routine?
- Do you think that a daily routine makes life dull? Why?
- Does a daily routine kill creativity? Why/why not?

- What are main social customs in your country? Why?
- Why do you think social customs vary from culture to culture?
- Should all countries have fixed social customs? Why/why not?
- Does a society need customs? Why/why not?
- Who sets social customs? Why?
- How does globalisation affect social customs? Why?

- **a good/bad law in your country/a rule you agreed/disagreed with**

VOCAB :

1. a regulation /ˌregjʊˈleɪʃ(ə)n/ (n.) = an official rule that controls the way that things are done
2. to prohibit /prəʊˈhɪbɪt/ (v.) = to forbid
3. red tape (n.) = documents, rules or processes that cause delays
4. to put sth into practice (phr.) = to apply sth
5. to forbid /fə(r)ˈbɪd/ (v.) = to ban
6. to do sth by the book (phr.) = to follow the rules
7. well-enforced /wel ɪnˈfɔː(r)st/ (adj.) = strongly limited
8. ignored /ɪgˈnɔː(r)d/ (adj.) = not followed (law)
9. to prevent from /prɪˈvent/ (v.) = to stop from happening
10. to cut corners (phr.) = to undertake sth in what appears to be the easiest, quickest or cheapest way, especially by omitting to do sth important
11. a catch-22 situation /ˌkætʃ twentiˈtuː ˌsɪtʃueɪʃ(ə)n/ (n.) = a set of problems that is impossible to escape from because each problem must be solved first before you can solve any of the others
12. a free-for-all (n.) = an uncontrolled situation in which people are competing with each other to gain as much as they can for themselves
13. to pass new legislation /ˌledʒɪˈsleɪʃ(ə)n/ (phr.) = to pass a new law
14. to uphold an ordered society (phr.) = to make sure the society follows rules a lives in peace and order
15. to curb lawless behaviour /kɜː(r)b/ (phr.) = to control behaviour against the law
16. to be tempted into… /temptɪd/ (phr.) = to really want to do or have sth, esp. sth that is not good for you
17. juvenile delinquency /ˈdʒuːvənaɪl dɪˈlɪŋkwənsi/ (n.) = crime among young people
18. the legal age (n.) = the age at which a person takes on the rights and responsibilities of an adult
19. a disciplinary action /ˈdɪsəˌplɪnəri/ (n.) = an action which main purpose is to enforce discipline
20. a random crime (n.) = without a conscious decision
21. to be suspicious /səˈspɪʃəs/ (adj.) = to believe that sb has probably done sth wrong
22. to deter sb from doing sth /dɪˈtɜː(r)/ (v.) = to make sb decide not to do sth
23. to aid and abet sb /eɪd ænd əˈbet/ (phr.) = to help sb to commit a crime
24. a convict /ˈkɒnvɪkt/ (n.) = sb who is in prison because they have committed a crime
25. to bring sb to justice (phr.) = to arrest sb for a crime and ensure that they are tired in court
26. a legal proceeding /ˈliːg(ə)l prəˈsiːdɪŋ/ (n.) = an activity that seeks to invoke the power of a tribunal in order to enforce a law
27. crime prevention (n.) = an attempt to reduce and deter crime and criminals
28. brutality /bruːˈtæləti/ (n.) = extreme violence
29. to fall victim to sth /ˈvɪktɪm/ (phr.) = to become a victim

30. an online fraud /frɔːd/ (n.) = a crime in which the perpetrator develops a scheme using one or more elements of the Internet to deprive a person of property or money
31. to stand trial /ˈtraɪəl/ (phr.) = to be tried in a court of law
32. a repeat offender /əˈfendə(r)/ (n.) = a person who has committed a crime many times
33. to rehabilitate /ˌriːəˈbɪlɪteɪt/ (v.) = to help a criminal to return to a healthy, independent and useful life
34. to regulate and oversee /ˈreɡjʊleɪt ænd ˌəʊvə(r)ˈsiː/ (phr.) = to control and supervise
35. to impose a ban on sth (phr.) = to forbid sth
36. to abolish sth /əˈbɒlɪʃ/ (v.) = to officially get rid of a law, system or practice
37. to implement sth /ˈɪmplɪˌment/ (v.) = to make sth start to work and be used
38. to translate sth into action (phr.) = to put sth into practice
39. to take draconian measures to do sth /drəˈkəʊniənˈmeʒə(r)z/ (phr.) = to take strict action
40. government's laxity in sth /ˈlæksəti/ (phr.) = government's neglect
41. to formulate a policy /ˈfɔː(r)mjʊleɪt/ (phr.) = to make a policy
42. law and order (n.) = safe and peaceful conditions in society that result when people obey the law
43. too harsh /hɑː(r)ʃ/ (adj.) = too severe
44. anarchy and chaos /ˈænə(r)ki ænd ˈkeɪɒs/ (phr.) = when people are behaving in a way that ignores normal rules and laws and are unable to be controlled
45. a minor offence /əˈfens/ (n.) = a crime that is not very serious
46. a downright unfair law (phr.) = an extremely unfair law
47. to get fined /faɪnd/ (v.) = to be made pay an amount of money as punishment for breaking the law
48. to be arrested (v.) = to be taken to prison
49. to be sent to gaol (Br)/jail (Am) /dʒeɪl/ (phr.)
50. a minor infringement /ɪnˈfrɪndʒment/ (phr.) = a petty crime
51. to exercise authority in unjust ways (phr.) = to have some illegal dealings

PART 3 :

☞ Is it important to have rules at school? Why/why not?
☞ Should children at different ages have the same rules? Why/why not?
☞ Do you think that students should be involved in creating rules? Is that the case in your country? Why/why not?
☞ Do students in your country usually follow rules? Why/why not?
☞ Do you have any rules in schools that you consider unnecessary?
☞ Is it important to have rules at work? Why/why not?
☞ What are the most common workplace rules in your country?
☞ Do employees usually obey those rules? Why/why not?
☞ Should there be any rules specifying the number of hours people can work? Why/why not? If so, how many hours weekly would be a good choice?
☞ Is there a dress code in most companies in your country? Is it good or bad?
☞ What disadvantages can too many rules bring? Why?
☞ What are some family rules in your country? Why?
☞ Do you think that older people and younger people can easily follow the same set of rules? Why/why not?
☞ Is it possible to avoid generation gap when it comes to obeying rules? If so, how?
☞ Should governments have a say in a way parents bring up their children? Why/why not?

- ↻ What are some common punishment systems for breaking the rules in your country?
- ↻ Who usually sets the rules in your country? Why?
- ↻ Do you think your country has too many rules? Why/why not?
- ↻ Do we need law? What for?
- ↻ Why do you think law is so powerful?
- ↻ Does your country have any laws that differ from other countries? What are they?
- ↻ What do you think should be done in your country to make people follow the law more closely?
- ↻ Do you think it is important to have international law? Why/why not?
- ↻ Which jobs in your country need to work closely with the law?
- ↻ Is being a police officer a job career in your country? Why/why not?
- ↻ What kind of person can make a good policeman or policewoman? Why?
- ↻ Is being a lawyer a good career in your country? Why/why not?
- ↻ What kind of person can make a good lawyer? Why?
- ↻ Does your society follow law? Why/why not?
- ↻ In which situation would you think breaking the law is okay? Why?
- ↻ In which situations is international law indispensable? Why?
- ↻ Who establishes international law? Why?
- ↻ What problems can occur when international law is set? Why?
- ↻ Do you think in the future local laws might give way to international law? Why/why not?

- **an environmental problem**

VOCAB :
1. to enact laws on environmental protection /ɪnˈækt/ (phr.) = to make a proposal into a law
2. to increase public awareness of (phr.) = to make people more conscious of
3. noise pollution (n.) = harmful or annoying levels of noise, as from industries, airplanes etc.
4. sewage /ˈsuːɪdʒ/ (n.) = waste substances removed from houses and other buildings by a system of large underground pipes called sewers
5. shrinking habitats (phr.) = places where animals live and breed which are decreasing in size
6. carbon dioxide emissions (phr.) = carbon dioxide gas from factories, cars, etc.
7. population growth exerts severe pressure on finite resources /ˈfaɪnaɪt/ (phr.) = resources existing only in limited amounts
8. the worst case scenario /səˈnɑːriəʊ/ (phr.) = the worst possibility for the future
9. pristine environment /ˈprɪstiːn/ (phr.) = perfectly clean, unspoilt area
10. organic /ɔː(r)ˈgænɪk/ (adj.) = without chemicals
11. herbicides /ˈhɜː(r)bɪsaɪd/ (n.) = chemicals used for killing weeds
12. global warming (n.) = the slow increase in the temperature of the Earth caused partly by the greenhouse effect increasing the amount of carbon dioxide in the atmosphere
13. a recurring problem /rɪˈkɜːrɪŋ/ (phr.) = a problem happening again and again
14. an enduring solution /ɪnˈdjʊərɪŋ/ (phr.) = a solution that can last for a long time
15. a vicious circle /ˈvɪʃəs ˈsɜː(r)k(ə)l/ (n.) = a process in which the existence of a problem causes other problems, and this makes the original problem worse
16. to dispose of sth /dɪˈspəʊz/ (v.) = to get rid of something
17. an adverse effect /ˈædvɜː(r)s ɪˈfekt/ (phr.) = a negative influence

18. a non-biodegradable material /nɒnˌbaɪəʊdɪˈɡreɪdəb(ə)l/ (phr.) = a material that cannot be separated into very small parts by bacteria so that they are not harmful to the environment
19. a reusable material (phr.) = a material that can be used again
20. to use sth wastefully (phr.) = not to care how something is used
21. the biosphere /ˈbaɪəʊˌsfɪə(r)/ (n.) = the parts of the Earth's surface and atmosphere where plant and animal life can exist
22. an endangered species /ɪnˈdeɪndʒə(r)d ˈspiːʃiːz/ (n.) = a species of animal or plant that is seriously at risk of extinction
23. a dynamic equilibrium /daɪˈnæmɪk ˌiːkwɪˈlɪbriəm/ (n.) = a state of balance between continuing processes
24. the ozone layer /ˈəʊzəʊn ˈleɪə(r)/ (n.) = a layer of ozone in the Earth's atmosphere that protects the Earth from the heat of the sun
25. the atmosphere /ˈætməsˌfɪə(r)/ (n.) = the air round the Earth or round another planet
26. to cause irreversible damage /ˌɪrɪˈvɜː(r)səb(ə)l/ (phr.) = to cause damage that cannot be brought back
27. the greenhouse effect /ˈɡriːnˌhaʊs ɪˈfekt/ (n.)
28. car emissions /ɪˈmɪʃ(ə)nz/ (n.) = a gas from cars that goes into the air
29. exhaust fumes /ɪɡˈzɔːst fjuːm/ (n.)
30. respiratory diseases /ˈresp(ə)rət(ə)ri/ (n.) = diseases relating to breathing
31. soil erosion /sɔɪl ɪˈrəʊʒ(ə)n/ (n.) = the process of soil being gradually damaged by water
32. desertification /dɪˌzɜː(r)tɪfɪˈkeɪʃ(ə)n/ (n.) = the process by which fertile land become desert
33. groundwater contamination /ˈɡraʊndˌwɔːtə(r) kənˌtæmɪnˈneɪʃ(ə)n/ (phr.) = dirty or polluted groundwater
34. sea water desalination /ˌdiːsælɪˈneɪʃ(ə)n/ (n.) = the process of removing salt from sea water so that the water can be used
35. chemical fertiliser /ˈfɜː(r)təˌlaɪzə(r)/ (n.) = a natural or chemical substance added to soil in order to help plants grow
36. acid rain /ˈæsɪd/ (n.) = rain containing a high level of acid that can damage the environment
37. to be saturated with /ˈsætʃəˌreɪtɪd/ (v.) = has much of a solid substance as possible mixed in it as part of the liquid
38. to upset the ecosystem (phr.) = to unbalance the ecosystem
39. to redress the ecological bala nce /rɪˈdres/ (phr.) = to improve the ecological balance
40. industrial waste /ɪnˈdʌstriəl weɪst/ (n.) = waste produced by industrial activity
41. at the expense of sth /ɪkˈspens/ (phr.) = if one thing exists or happens at the expense of another, the second thing suffers or is not done properly because of the first
42. a natural disaster /ˈnætʃ(ə)rəl dɪˈzɑːstə(r)/ (n.) = a natural event such as a flood, earthquake or hurricane
43. an ecological degradation /ˌiːkəˈlɒdʒɪk(ə)l ˌdeɡrəˈdeɪʃ(ə)n/ (n.) = the process of the ecosystem changing into a worse condition
44. oil shortage /ɔɪl ˈʃɔː(r)tɪdʒ/ (n.) = the lack of oil supply in the world
45. to be in short supply (phr.) = available only in small quantities, so that there is not enough
46. fossil fuel /ˈfɒsəl ˌfjuːəl/ (n.) = a fuel such as coal or oil, made from decayed material from animals or plants that lived many thousands of years ago
47. solar energy /ˈsəʊlə(r)/ (n.) = energy that uses the power of the Sun's light and heat to produce electricity

48. wind energy (n.) = electrical energy obtained from harnessing the wind with windmills or wind turbines
49. light pollution (n.) = brightening of the night sky caused by street lights and other man-made sources
50. to be a nuisance /ˈnjuːs(ə)ns/ (phr.) = to be annoying and a continuing problem
51. to be plagued with /pleɪgd/ (phr.) = to be troubled or distressed by
52. a rapid industrialization /ˈræpɪd ɪndʌstrɪəlaɪˈzeɪʃ(ə)n/ (n.) = a quick development of industries on a wide scale
53. an integrated solution (n.) = a complete solution
54. major contributors to (phr.) = main reasons for
55. to be conscious of your surroundings /ˈkɒnʃəs/ (phr.) = to be aware of your environment
56. human interference with the environment (phr.) = people's involvement in the environment
57. ozone depletion /ˈəʊzəʊn dɪˈpliːʃ(ə)n/ (n.) = the reduction of ozone layer
58. the destruction of marine life /məˈriːn/ (phr.) = the destruction of what is living in the sea

PART 3

- ☞ What problems with the environment does your country have? Why?
- ☞ What measures are being taken to solve these problems? Why?
- ☞ What can individuals do help the environment? Why?
- ☞ What can the government do to help the environment? Why?
- ☞ Is it important for children to learn about the environment? Why/why not?
- ☞ Do you study about the environment at school in your country? Why/why not?
- ☞ What's the best way to learn about the environment? Why?
- ☞ What will be the biggest environmental problem in the world in the future? Why?
- ☞ How is global warming affecting the weather? Why?
- ☞ How does the environment influence the way we feel? Why?
- ☞ Should countries cooperate on solving global environmental issues? Why/why not?
- ☞ What international campaign could help raise the awareness of the environment? Why?

- **in important invention before the age of computer**

VOCAB :
1. to come into existence /ɪgˈzɪst(ə)ns/ (v.) = to begin existing
2. epoch-making /ˈiːpɒk ˈmeɪkɪŋ/ (adj.) = having an important effect on the future
3. an indispensable part of our lives /ˌɪndɪˈspensəb(ə)l/ (phr.) = a necessary part of our lives
4. to break new ground (phr.) = to do sth innovative
5. to welcome sth with open arms (phr.) = to welcome sth warmly
6. a contraption /kənˈtræpʃ(ə)n/ (n.) = a device that appears strange or unnecessarily complicated, and often badly made or unsafe
7. a brainchild /ˈbreɪnˌtʃaɪld/ (n.) = a clever system, organization or plan that sb thinks of and develops
8. a technological breakthrough /ˌteknəˈlɒdʒɪk(ə)l ˈbreɪkθruː/ (n.) = a discovery in technology
9. to revolutionize lives /ˌrevəˈluːʃəˌnaɪz/ (phr.) = to completely change the way something is done
10. influential /ˌɪnfluˈenʃ(ə)l/ (adj.) = powerful

11. a digital native /ˈdɪdʒɪt(ə)l ˈneɪtɪv/ (n.) = a person born or brought up during the age of digital technology and therefore familiar with computers and the Internet from an early age

12. labour-saving /ˈleɪbə(r) ˈseɪvɪŋ/ (adj.) = designed to reduce the amount of work needed to complete a task

13. outdated /ˌaʊtˈdeɪtɪd/ (adj.) = old and not fashionable

14. an appliance /əˈplaɪəns/ (n.) = a machine or piece of equipment that you have in your home

PART 3 :

☞ How did people live without computers?

☞ What were some commonly used items before computers took over? Why?

☞ Can we live without computers today? Why/why not?

☞ Why is it so easy to get addicted to a computer?

☞ Can computers still be useful without the Internet access? If so, how?

☞ Can computers become obsolete in the future? Why/why not?

☞ What kind of skills does a person need to be a good inventor? Why?

☞ Should inventors be responsible for how their work is used? Why/why not?

☞ Is it easy for older people to use computers? Why/why not?

- **a great achievement of yours/a situation when you received congratulations**

VOCAB :

1. rewarding /rɪˈwɔː(r)dɪŋ/ (adj.) = giving you satisfaction, pleasure or profit

2. an aspiration /ˌæspɪˈreɪʃ(ə)n/ (n.) = an ambition

3. to pay sb a compliment /ˈkɒmplɪmənt/ (phr.) = to politely congratulate or praise sb for something

4. to give praise /preɪz/ (v.) = to express warm approval or admiration of

5. to show praise on sb (phr.) = to express warm approval or admiration of

6. to win plaudits /ˈplɔːdɪts/ (phr.) = to get positive comments

7. sth is in the bag (phr.) = (of something desirable) as good as secured

8. to be in with a chance of doing sth (phr.) = the possibility that sth will happen

9. You can't make an omelette without breaking eggs. /ˈɒmlət/ (proverb) = nothing is completely one-sided

10. an outstanding success (phr.) = a great triumph /ˈtraɪʌmf/

11. an extraordinary accomplishment (phr.) = a big success

12. a golden opportunity (n.) = a very good chance to do or achieve sth

13. to seize the opportunity /siːz/ (phr.) = to make the most of a chance you have

14. don't count your chickens before they're hatched (proverb) = don't be too confident in anticipating success or good fortune before it is certain

15. by trial and error (phr.) = by experimenting with various methods of doing sth until one finds the most successful one

16. sth worked like a dream (phr.) = sth was completely successful

17. to make full preparation (phr.) = to prepare well

18. to pass sth with flying colours (phr.) = to pass sth with distinction

PART 3 :

☞ What dreams do young people in your country have? Why?

☞ What dreams do older people have? Why?

☞ Is it easy to achieve dreams? Why/why not?

☞ Can a person learn anything from not being able to achieve their dream? Why/why not?

☞ Why do people fail at achieving their dreams?

☞ When do people usually congratulate each other? Why?

☞ How do people in your culture congratulate each other?

☞ What kinds of achievements are the biggest in your country? Why?

☞ Does everyone want to achieve something? Why/why not?

☞ Who is considered the most successful person in your country? Why?

☞ Does success always bring happiness? Why/why not?

- **a group you would like to belong to/belong to/something you did in a group**

VOCAB :

1. to join a club (phr.) = to become a member of a club
2. diverse /daɪˈvɜː(r)s/ (adj.) = including people from many different cultures or races
3. to hold parties for members (phr.) = to organize parties for club members
4. people from all walks of life (phr.) = people from different parts of society
5. a social creature /ˈsəʊʃ(ə)l ˈkriːtʃə(r)/ (n.) = a communal being
6. no man is an island /ˈaɪlənd/ (phr.) = everyone is connected to their surroundings and other people
7. gregarious /ɡrɪˈɡeəriəs/ (adj.) = sb who enjoys being with others
8. to participate fully in /pɑː(r)ˈtɪsɪpeɪt/ (phr.) = to take part in
9. to become a member of (phr.) = to join sth
10. to be affiliated with /əˈfɪlieɪtɪd/ (v.) = to be connected to
11. to be allied to /ˈælaɪd/ (v.) = to work with
12. aristocratic /ˌærɪstəˈkrætɪk/ (adj.) = belonging to the aristocracy
13. omnifarious (adj.) = relating to all sorts or varieties
14. a fan club (n.) = an organization for people who like a particular famous actor, singer, player etc. very much
15. a pantheon /ˈpænθiən/ (n.) = all the famous people connected with a particular activity, for example a sport or the film industry

PART 3 :

☞ Is it important for children to interact with others? Why/why not?

☞ What things do children like to do with adults? Why?

☞ How can children learn how to interact with other people?

☞ Do you think girls and boys should play together more often? Why/why not?

☞ How important is interaction in a workplace? Why?

☞ Do you think every group needs a leader to work well? Why/why not?

☞ For what reasons don't some groups work well together?

☞ What kind of work is better done alone? Why?

☞ What contributes to the success of teamwork?

☞ With whom do we need to interact in a society? Why?

☞ Why do you think people want to be parts of groups? What does it give them?

⟳ Can group behaviour influence the behaviour of an individual? Why/why not? If so, in what ways?

⟳ Do you think our individual choices are often in conflict with the best interest of the society? Why/why not?

- **a handmade gift you made for someone/received/a special gift you received/gave to someone/you got in your childhood/a handicraft you made**

VOCAB :

1. paper-cutting (n.) = the art of cutting paper designs
2. embroidery /ɪmˈbrɔɪdəri/ (n.) = a design of coloured stitches on cloth
3. knitting /ˈnɪtɪŋ/ (n.) = the activity of knitting things
4. root carving /ˈruːtˈkɑː(r)vɪŋ/ (n.) = a traditional Chinese art form, consisting of carving and polishing tree roots into various artistic creations
5. wood carving /ˈwʊdˈkɑː(r)vɪŋ/ (n.)
6. to develop creative thinking (phr.)
7. artistic /ɑː(r)ˈtɪstɪk/ (adj.) = relating to any form of art
8. folk /fəʊk/ (adj.) = folk art, traditions or stories were developed by people in a particular region and have become traditional there
9. calligraphy /kəˈlɪɡrəfi/ (n.) = beautiful writing done using special pens or brushes
10. decorative /ˈdek(ə)rətɪv/ (adj.) = intended to look attractive rather than be useful
11. an ornament /ˈɔː(r)nəmənt/ (n.) = a small attractive object used for decoration
12. priceless /ˈpraɪsləs/ (adj.) = very valuable
13. engraving /ɪnˈɡreɪvɪŋ/ (n.) = a picture made by cutting a design into a metal plate, putting ink on it, and pressing it onto paper
14. pottery /ˈpɒtəri/ (n.) = objects such as plates and cups that are made out of clay and baked in an oven so that they become hard
15. a potter's wheel /ˈpɒtə(r)z wiːl/ (n.) = a horizontal revolving disk on which wet clay in shaped into pots or other round ceramic objects
16. jewellery making (n.) = the process of making necklaces, bracelets, rings, pendants and other types of jewellery
17. glass painting (n.) = painting on a glass surface
18. sewing /ˈsəʊɪŋ/ (n.) = work that is being sewn
19. crochet /ˈkrəʊʃeɪ/ (n.) = a handicraft in which yarn is made up into a patterned fabric by lopping yarn with a hooked needle
20. lace-making /leɪs/ (n.) = the activity of making lace
21. weaving /wiːvɪŋ/ (n.) = forming a fabric by interlacing long threads passing in one direction with others at a right angle to them
22. the heart can't be priced (phr.) = warm thoughts behind an action are the most important
23. it is a thought that counts (phr.) = not the present, but the thought is significant
24. spontaneous /spɒnˈteɪniəs/ (adj.) = without being planned
25. keeping hold of it ever since (phr.) = not having lost something
26. tight-fisted /ˌtaɪtˈfɪstɪd/ (adj.) = not generous with money
27. to be thankful for sth /ˈθæŋkf(ə)l/ (phr.) = to be grateful for sth
28. a recipient /rɪˈsɪpiənt/ (n.) = sb who receives sth

29. hard-and-fast rules of gift giving (phr.) = fixed and not able to be changed
30. corny /ˈkɔː(r)ni/ (adj.) = used so much that seem silly

PART 3 :

- How much money should people spend on a gift? Why?
- Do people in your country often give flowers as gifts? When?
- In your culture, is it good or bad to open a gift in front of the person that gave it to you? Why?
- Do people in your country often give money? Why/why not?
- On what occasions do people exchange gifts? Why?
- What factors should people consider when choosing a gift?
- Is it better to give someone a homemade gift or one bought in a shop?
- How do people feel when they receive homemade gifts? Why?
- What homemade gifts are popular in your country? Why?
- Who do you think appreciates gifts more, children or adults? Why?
- Can people get pleasure from giving gifts? Why?
- How much do advertisements influence people's gifts choices? Why?
- Do you think that some festivals are so commercialised today because of the need for gifts? Why/why not?
- Do you think that sometimes the pressure of gifts contributes to excessive consumption? How?
- What kinds of gifts do children like to receive today? Why?
- Do boys and girls like the same or different types of gifts? Why?
- What should be taken into consideration when choosing a gift for a child? Why?
- For what occasions do children in your country receive gifts?
- Are gifts important in your culture? Why/why not?
- Do gifts in your culture always need to be expensive? Why/why not?
- What kinds of gifts do business people exchange? Why?
- Do you think people offer gifts to their family members to substitute the lack of time they spend together? Why/why not?
- Do some parents give their kids too much? Does it spoil them? Why/why not?
- How can children be encouraged to give gifts to others? Why?
- How does materialistic society affect the future of a country? Why?
- Do you think handmade gifts take too much time? Why/why not?
- Is it easy to make something valuable by hand? Why/why not?
- Do you think most people prefer to receive handmade gifts to the ones bought in a shop? Why/why not?
- Can making something help develop one's creativity? Why/why not?
- Do you think girls enjoy making things more than boys? Why/why not?
- In your opinion, is it important for schools to teach creative subjects? Why/why not?
- Can playing computer games affect one's creativity in a positive way? Why/why not?
- Can a person benefit anyhow from creating something? Why/why not?
- Do you think that some companies use the word 'handmade' only to improve their sales? Why/why not?
- How can creative people contribute to the society?

- **a happy marriage/relationship**

VOCAB :

1. a nuclear family /ˈnjuːkliə(r)/ (n.) = a couple and their dependent children, regarded as a basic social unit
2. to enjoy family harmony (phr.)
3. to fall in love at first sight (phr.) = on first seeing or meeting sb
4. a breadwinner /ˈbredˌwɪnə(r)/ (n.) = the person who earns the money to support a family
5. a homemaker /ˈhəʊmˌmeɪkə(r)/ (n.) = sb who cooks, cleans and washes clothes for their family as their main job
6. compatible /kəmˈpætəb(ə)l/ (adj.) = likely to have a good relationship because of being similar
7. to be someone's type (phr.) = to be someone with the particular qualities that you find attractive
8. to think the world of someone (phr.) = to have a very high regard for sb
9. to stick together (phr.) = to remain united
10. to drift apart (v.) = if two people drift apart, their relationship gradually ends
11. an obligation /ˌɒblɪˈgeɪʃ(ə)n/ (n.) = sth one must do for legal or moral reasons
12. a better half (n.) = a spouse
13. eternal love /ɪˈtɜː(r)n(ə)l/ (n.) = long lasting love
14. to adore sb (v.) = to worship sb
15. an undying love /ʌnˈdaɪɪŋ/ (phr.) = never ending love
16. an inseparable couple /ɪnˈsep(ə)rəb(ə)l ˈkʌp(ə)l/ (phr.) = a couple in a very close relationship spending all their time together
17. a henpecked husband /ˈhenˌpekt/ (n.) = a husband who is criticized and given orders all the time by a wife
18. a trophy wife /ˈtrəʊfi/ (n.) = a young and attractive wife regarded as a status symbol for an older man
19. ecstatic /ɪkˈstætɪk/ (adj.) = extremely happy
20. jubilant /ˈdʒuːbɪlənt/ (adj.) = extremely happy because sth good has happened
21. a bond /bɒnd/ (n.) = a relationship
22. ups and downs (n.) = a succession of both good and bad experiences
23. to appreciate sb /əˈpriːʃiˌeɪt/ (v.) = to recognize the good or special person
24. to make a sacrifice (phr.) = to give up sth important for the sake of others
25. to meet sb halfway (phr.) = to make a compromise with sb
26. to be made for each other (phr.) = to be a perfect match (as a couple)
27. to drive a wedge between people /wedʒ/ (phr.) = to cause disagreement between people
28. to clear the air (phr.) = to clarify an angry or tense situation by frank discussion
29. to store up problems (phr.) = to bottle up negative feelings
30. to go through a rough patch /ˈrʌf ˈpætʃ/ (phr.) = to go through a period of difficulties
31. to live in each other's pockets (phr.) = to be closely involved with sb

PART 3 :
- ☞ Is divorce common in your country?
- ☞ What percentage of marriages end in divorce? Why?
- ☞ At what age do people in your country get married? Why? Is it too early, too late or right about time?

- Do many couples adopt children in your country? Why/why not?
- Is polygamy a crime in your country?
- How do most people meet their marriage partners? Why?
- Are arranged marriages common in your country? Why/why not?
- How do married couples usually celebrate their wedding anniversaries? Why?
- Which wedding anniversary is the most important? Why?
- What is the main difference between a wedding in your country and a Western wedding?
- Whose responsibility is it to look after children in a marriage? Why?
- What does a typical wedding in your culture look like?
- Do you think many people spend too much money on their weddings? Why?
- What role does a wife play in your culture?
- What role does a husband play in your culture?
- Were the roles of husband and wife the same or different in the past? Why?
- Do you think both husband and wife should contribute equally to raising a child? Why/why not?
- What is a typical family unit in your country?
- Do you think the size of a typical family in your country will change in the future? Why/why not?
- Should children be involved in the process of making decisions in a family? Why/why not?
- How important is family to a stable society? Why?

- **a happy surprise**

VOCAB :
1. to be taken by surprise (phr.) = to not be prepared or expecting sth
2. out of my expectations (phr.) = better than I expected
3. to throw a party (phr.) = to organize a party
4. to shower sb with sth (phr.) = to give sb many things
5. low-key (adj.) = not showy or elaborate
6. to make a big deal out of sth (phr.) = to consider sth important
7. I couldn't believe my eyes. (phr.) = I was totally shocked.
8. amazement /əˈmeɪzmənt/ (n.) = shock
9. to bowl over /bəʊl/(v.) = to surprise sb
10. flabbergasted /ˈflæbə(r)ˌgɑːstɪd/ (adj.) = very surprised
11. to leave sb open-mouthed (phr.) = to make sb shocked
12. stupefied /ˈstjuːpɪfaɪd/ (adj.) = extremely surprisedor shocked
13. to take sb's breath away (phr.) = to amaze sb
14. to astonish sb /əˈstɒnɪʃ/ (v.) = to surprise sb
15. to astound sb /əˈstaʊnd/ (v.) = to surprise or shock sb very much
16. nonplussed /ˌnɒnˈplʌst/ (adj.) = speechless
17. to take sb aback /əˈbæk/ (v.) = to shock or surprise sb

PART 3 :
- How do people in your country show happiness? Why?
- Is it important to express happiness? Why/why not?
- Do you think money can make people happy? Why/why not?

↻ Can shopping make a person happy? Why/why not?

↻ Is there any connection between happiness and health?

↻ Do you think that a person's attitude to life can affect their happiness? Why/why not?

↻ Can people learn how to be happy? Why/why not?

↻ Can moments of unhappiness teach people anything? Why/why not?

↻ Do you think that a society gets happier when it gets richer? Why/why not?

↻ Do governments focus on citizens' happiness at all? Why/why not? Should they?

↻ Can technology make people happier? Why/why not?

↻ Will scientific advances make societies happier? Why/why not?

↻ What kinds of surprises do Chines people usually prepare for their loved ones? Why?

- **a job you'd really like to have**

VOCAB :

1. to realize your personal value (phr.) = to understand how much you are worth
2. to devote yourself to sth /dɪˈvəʊt/ (phr.) = to spend a lot of time doing sth
3. a nine-to-five job (n.) = a typical office job, very predictable
4. to break one's life routine /ruːˈtiːn/ (phr.) = to change one's regular schedule
5. a flexible schedule (phr.) = an open timetable
6. to punch the clock /pʌntʃ/ (phr.) = to punch in and out (at work)
7. job security (n.) = a feeling of being able to keep one stable job for long enough
8. to be unemployed /ˌʌnɪmˈplɔɪd/ (adj.) = to be without a job
9. job satisfaction (n.) = the feeling that you have when you enjoy your job
10. a sense of fulfilment /fʊlˈfɪlmənt/ (phr.) = a feeling of satisfaction due to one's work
11. frustration /frʌˈstreɪʃ(ə)n/ (n.) = an annoyed feeling that you get when you are prevented from doing what you want
12. an excessive workload /ɪkˈsesɪv/ (phr.) = workload heavier than reasonable
13. a cushy number /ˈkʊʃi/ (phr.) = a very easy and pleasant job not involving a lot of work
14. job prospects /ˈprɒspekts/ (n.) = chances of success at work
15. an incentive /ɪnˈsentɪv/ (n.) = sth that makes you want to do sth or to work harder
16. stable /ˈsteɪb(ə)l/ (adj.) = (of a job) not changed frequently
17. a white-collar job (n.) = a job that requires workers to work in offices rather than to do physical work
18. a foreign enterprise /ˈentə(r)ˌpraɪz/ (n.) = a large business company from abroad
19. a tempting bonus /ˈtemptɪŋ ˈbəʊnəs/ (phr.) = a significant amount of money given in addition to your normal salary
20. welfare benefits /ˈwelfeə(r)/ (n.) = care provided by a company for people
21. a long-term commitment /kəˈmɪtmənt/ (phr.) = a promise to do a particular job for a long time
22. a job hopper (n.) = sb who changes companies too often
23. to take sb on (v.) = to employ sb
24. a line of work (phr.) = an area of work
25. a vocation /vəʊˈkeɪʃ(ə)n/ (n.) = a job that you do because you feel it is your purpose in life and for which you have special skills
26. to freelance/ˈfriːlɑːns/ (v.) = to sell your work or services to many different companies

27. a chief executive (n.) = the most senior person working in a company who is responsible for running it
28. a foreman/ˈfɔː(r)mən/ (n.) = a man who is in charge of a team of workers
29. to be in charge of (v.) = to be in control of sth
30. to clock in/out (v.) = to punch in/out
31. to improve one's qualifications (phr.) = to better one's skills
32. prospects for promotion /ˈprɒspekts/ (phr.) = chances to get promoted
33. to prove one's ability (phr.) = to show what one is made of
34. to work one's way up to… (phr.) = to gradually work towards promotion
35. lucrative /ˈluːkrətɪv/ (adj.) = bringing a lot of money
36. to get your foot in the door (phr.) = to have a first introduction to a job
37. a dead-end job (phr.) = a job with no prospects

PART 3 :
- ↻ Do people in your country often change jobs? Why?
- ↻ Is it good to change jobs frequently? Why/why not?
- ↻ How do graduates make their decisions about choosing jobs?
- ↻ Do you think men and women share an equal chance for job hunting? Why/why not?
- ↻ How should a boss communicate with his/her employees? Why?
- ↻ What are the most popular jobs in your country? Why?
- ↻ How can a job be satisfying?
- ↻ Why are some jobs more satisfying than others? What does it depend on?
- ↻ What types of jobs will be most popular in the future? Why?
- ↻ What jobs were popular in the past in your country? Why?
- ↻ Do schools prepare young people well for their future jobs? Why/why not?
- ↻ Who can advise young people on their future career? Why?
- ↻ Should young people listen to others' advice when it comes to choosing a career? Why/why not?
- ↻ What's the most important factor for success in one's career?
- ↻ Can a person be successful at work without having a good education? Why/why not?
- ↻ Does a company need well-motivated workers to succeed? Why/why not?
- ↻ How can employers motivate their employees?
- ↻ Is motivation intrinsic or extrinsic? Why?

- **a lesson/training session you liked/a short course you took/a lesson you will never forget**

VOCAB :
1. rote learning /rəʊt/ (n.) = learning by mechanical or habitual repetition of sth
2. to rack my brains /ræk/ (phr.) = to make a great effort to think or to remember sth
3. continual assessment /kənˈtɪnjʊəl əˈsesmənt/ (n.) = the educational policy in which students are examined continuously over most of the duration of their education
4. collaborative learning /kəˈlæb(ə)rətɪv/ (phr.) = learning in groups
5. tertiary education /ˈtɜː(r)ʃəri/ (n.) = college and universities education
6. to burn the midnight oil (phr.) = to read, study or work late into the night
7. a stairway to the society and individual success (phr.)
8. to concentrate on sth /ˈkɒns(ə)nˌtreɪt/ (v.) = to give all your attention to the thing you are doing

9. to form the basis of sth /ˈbeɪsɪs/ (phr.) = to make a good foundation for sth
10. a comprehensive coverage of sth /ˈkʌv(ə)rɪdʒ/ (phr.) = a complete presentation of sth
11. distance learning (n.) = a system in which students work at home with the help of TV and the Internet and send work to their teachers by post or email
12. to lag behind the class /læg/ (phr.) = to not be able to keep pace with other students
13. a teacher's pet (n.) = a student that everyone thinks the teacher likes best
14. to swot /swɒt/ (v.) = to study very hard, especially for an examination
15. a mediocre student (phr.) = not too good and not too bad
16. to come on in leaps and bounds (phr.) = with rapid progress

PART 3 :

- What qualifications do young people seek after today? Why?
- Is teacher-student relationship in your country good? Why/why not?
- How would you change the education system in your country? Why?
- How important is a good education system for a country's economy? Why?
- What types of education does your country offer to adults? Why?
- Why would adults still want to study?
- Should courses for adults be free? Why/why not?
- Do many adults take evening classes in your country? Why/why not?
- What are the most popular short courses in your country? Why?
- Are teachers generally respected in your country? Why/why not?
- Is being a teacher a popular job in your country? Why/why not?
- What are some disadvantages of being a teacher?
- When looking for a job, which one do you think is more helpful: high qualifications or rich experience? Why?
- What main problems do graduates face today when it comes to employment? Why?
- Is it good for a society to have highly educated citizens? Why/why not?
- Why do people take extra courses?
- What are some benefits of short courses?
- Why do you think retired people like to take courses?
- Besides providing new skills and knowledge, what other benefits do short courses have?
- Are evening classes popular in your country? Why/why not?
- Do you believe children's classes should always be fun? Why/why not?
- What kind of a person can become a good teacher of children? Why?
- Do schools in your country focus on developing children's social skills? Why/why not? Should they?
- Is it true that we are never too old to start learning something new?
- Do you think adult education should be free of charge? Why/why not?
- What kinds of classes for adults are popular in your country? Why?
- Does a person always need to further their skills and qualifications in order to get promoted or find a better job? Why?
- How is technology used in education today?
- Do you think that online classes may replace real classroom experience one day? Why/why not?
- Do you think a teacher will always be important in one's learning process? Why/why not?

- **a magazine/newspaper you often read**

VOCAB :

1. published worldwide (adj.) = published in many countries
2. sections (n.) = parts of a magazine or newspaper
3. in-depth feature stories /ˈfiːtʃə(r)/ (phr.) = detailed articles that concentrate on a particular subject
4. to model myself on sb /ˈmɒd(ə)l/ (v.) = to copy the way that someone behaves because you admire them
5. current affairs /ˈkʌrənt əˈfeə(r)z/ (n.) = political, social and economic events that are happening now and are discussed in newspapers and news
6. a tabloid /ˈtæblɔɪd/ (n.) = a newspaper with fairly small pages mostly containing storied about famous people and not much serious news
7. a broadsheet /ˈbrɔːdˌʃiːt/ (n.) = a newspaper printed on large sheets of paper containing serious news
8. a want ad (n.) = a short advertisement that put in a newspaper, for example so that you can sell sth
9. to subscribe to sth /səbˈskraɪb/ (v.) = to pay money so that you will regularly receive copies of a newspaper or magazine
10. to skim /skɪm/ (v.) = to read sth quickly and not very carefully
11. to leaf through sth /liːf/ (v.) = to turn the pages quickly and without looking at them carefully
12. an allegation /ˌæləˈɡeɪʃ(ə)n/ (n.) = a statement that someone has done sth wrong or illegal even though this has not been proved
13. a cover-up (n.) = an attempt to stop people from discovering the truth about sth, especially a crime or a serious mistake
14. scathing /ˈskeɪðɪŋ/ (adj.) = criticizing sb or sth in a very strong way
15. to leak sth to sb /liːk/ (v.) = to tell private or secret information to journalists
16. to quote sb /kwəʊt/ (v.) = to say or write words that sb else has said or written
17. mushy stuff /ˈmʌʃi/ (phr.) = silly and not sincere
18. to flip through the pages (phr.) = to read sth quickly without paying too much attention to it
19. an all-round magazine (phr.) = a comprehensive magazine
20. classy and stylish /ˈklɑːsi//ˈstaɪlɪʃ/ (adj.) = of excellent quality and showing good judgement about how to look attractive and fashionable
21. a fashion inspiration /ˌɪnspəˈreɪʃ(ə)n/ (n.) = sth that gives your new fashion ideas and the enthusiasm to create sth with them
22. to serve as a watchdog that keeps people informed (phr.) = to function as a news service provider
23. the populace can stay informed /ˈpɒpjʊləs/ (phr.) = the public can know about the latest news
24. to scan the headlines /ˈhedˌlaɪnz/ (phr.) = to look quickly through the headlines without reading the article
25. the accountability to the truth /əˌkaʊntəˈbɪləti/ (phr.) = the responsibility to report truthfully
26. to censor sth /ˈsensə(r)/ (v.) = to remove parts of an article for moral, religious or political reasons
27. a daily update /ˈʌpdeɪt/ (n.) = a report containing all the latest news and information brought up to date every day
28. creditable news /ˈkredɪtəb(ə)l/ (phr.) = news good enough to deserve some praise or admiration
29. an unbiased journalist /ʌnˈbaɪəst/ (phr.) = a journalist who reports in a fair way

PART 3 :

- What kinds of things do people in your country like to read? Why?
- Is there any difference between reading a book and reading a newspaper? Why/why not?
- Do older people read the same things as younger people? Why/why not?
- Who reads more: younger people or older people? Why?
- Is reading generally a good habit? Why/why not?
- Do you think people read less today than in the past? Why/why not?
- Why do you think some people dislike reading?
- Do you think people will read more or less in the future? Why?
- Is reading generally important? Why/why not?
- Do people in your country read enough today? Why/why not?
- How are good reading skills valuable at different stages of education? Why?
- Can reading help person's mental development? How?
- Can TV be beneficial to people's mental development? Why/why not?
- Can we learn anything from reading a magazine? What? Why/why not?
- Why do people read magazines and newspapers today?
- Is being a journalist a good career? Why/why not?
- Do you think it is exciting to write articles? Why/why not?
- What skills does a person need to be a good journalist? Why?
- Do you think that all journalists always write according to the reality? Why/why not?
- Do people in your country generally keep up with the news? Why/why not?
- Is it important to keep up with the news? Why/why not?
- Which news is more important, local or international? Why?
- Do you think in the future technology might replace newspapers and magazines? Why/why not?
- What role do social media play in spreading news?
- What are the most popular magazines or newspaper in your hometown?

- **a part of foreign culture that interests you/a place where you learnt something about foreign culture**

VOCAB :

1. to have an (positive/negative) influence on /ˈɪnfluəns/ (phr.) = to have an effect on
2. to have a great impact on /ˈɪmpækt/ (phr.) = to have a huge effect on
3. ignorance /ˈɪgnərəns/ (n.) = a lack of knowledge or facts about sth
4. when in Rome do as the Romans do (phr.)
5. a cultural exchange /ˈkʌltʃ(ə)rəl ɪksˈtʃeɪndʒ/ (n.) = a situation in which people give each other information about their own cultures
6. a religious festival /rəˈlɪdʒəs/ (phr.) = a celebration of a day important in a specific religion
7. to make sb more tolerant and open-minded /ˈtɒlərənt/ (phr.) = to open sb's mind
8. to be an eye-opener (phr.) = to show sth surprising that you did not know before
9. to eliminate preconceptions /ɪˈlɪmɪneɪt ˌpriːkənˈsepʃ(ə)nz/ (phr.) = to get rid of unproven opinions
10. to confirm one's prejudices /ˈpredʒʊdɪsɪz/ (phr.) = to strengthen one's unreasonable opinions or feelings
11. offensive /əˈfensɪv/ (adj.) = insulting

148

12. mainstream /ˈmeɪnˌstriːm/ (adj.) = considered ordinary or normal and accepted or used by most people
13. to be customary /ˈkʌstəməri/ (adj.) = usual in a particular society
14. to be unorthodox /ʌnˈɔː(r)θədɒks/ (adj.) = not following the usual rules or beliefs of your religion, society etc.
15. to be in the minority /maɪˈnɒrəti/ (phr.) = to be in a small part of a population that is different in race, religion or culture from most of the population
16. social mores /ˈmɔːreɪz/ (n.) = the traditional practices and moral values of a particular society
17. to stem from /stem/ (v.) = to be caused by
18. to assimilate into a new culture /əˈsɪmɪleɪt/ (phr.) = to begin to consider yourself part of a community or culture rather than being foreign
19. a language barrier /ˈbæriə(r)/ (n.) = the difficulties faced when people who have no language in common attempt to communicate with each other
20. primitive /ˈprɪmətɪv/ (adj.) = at a very simple stage of development
21. etiquette /ˈetɪket/ (n.) = a set of rules for behaving correctly in social situations
22. manners /ˈmænə(r)z/ (n.) = traditionally accepted ways of behaving that show a polite respect for other people
23. to frown upon sb/sth /fraʊn/ (v.) = to not approve of sth
24. respectful /rɪˈspektf(ə)l/ (adj.) = showing respect
25. an ethnic minority /ˈeθnɪk maɪˈnɒrəti/ (n.) = a group that has different national or cultural traditions from the main population
26. animosity towards sb /ˌænɪˈmɒsəti/ (n.) = a strong feeling of disliking sb/sth
27. a stereotype /ˈsteriəˌtaɪp/ (n.) = a very firm and simple idea about what a particular type of person or thing is like
28. nostalgia /nɒˈstældʒə/ (n.) = thoughts about happy time in your past
29. a dynamic culture /daɪˈnæmɪk/ (phr.) = a culture continuously changing, growing or developing
30. a huge melting pot /ˈmeltɪŋ/ (phr.) = a place where different peoples, styles, theories etc. are mixed together
31. an international community (phr.) = a community with a lot of foreigners living there
32. an illustrious culture /ɪˈlʌstriəs/ (phr.) = famous and respected

PART 3 :
- Many people like to celebrate Western festivals today, what do you think of that?
- Are people in your country curious about other cultures? Why/why not?
- How can people learn about other cultures? Why?
- What's the best way to learn about foreign cultures? Why?
- How did people learn about foreign cultures in the past? Why?
- Is it necessary to live in a foreign country to understand its culture? Why/why not?
- How does globalisation influence your culture? Why?
- Do you think international sport events could bring countries closer together? Why/why not?
- Are people in your country interested in international news? Why/why not?
- How do international news affect people's view on their own countries? Why?
- Do you think that in the future borders might disappear and all countries will be one? Why/why not?
- What's the best way to preserve cultural differences? Why?

🖒 Which cultural differences are most important to keep? Why?

🖒 Should minority languages survive? Why/why not?

🖒 Do you think that excessive travel nowadays might eliminate cultural differences in the future? Why/why not?

- **a piece of clothing you like a lot/a traditional garment from your country/something you wore for a special occasion**

VOCAB :

1. a garment /ˈgɑː(r)mənt/ (n.) = a piece of clothing
2. individuality /ˌɪndɪˌvɪdʒuˈæləti/ (n.) = the things that make sb or sth different from all others
3. creativity /ˌkriːeɪˈtɪvəti/ (n.) = the ability to create new ideas or things using your imagination
4. minimalism /ˈmɪnɪm(ə)lˌɪz(ə)m/ (n.) = using a small number of colours and very few accessories when dressing
5. to keep pace with the times (phr.) = to stay fashionable
6. to be in season (phr.) = popular during particular time of year
7. to be dressed in the height of fashion (phr.) = to be dressed in an extremely fashionable way
8. a power outfit (phr.) = formal clothes to make you seem powerful
9. to be out of season (phr.) = not fashionable anymore
10. to be hip to the current happenings (phr.) = following latest fashion
11. chic /ʃiːk/ (adj.) = fashionable and attractive in style
12. to be slaves to fashion (phr.) = people extremely dependent on fashion trends
13. to dictate the trends /dɪkˈteɪt/ (phr.) = to set trends
14. haute couture /ˌəʊt kuːˈtjʊə(r)/ (n.) = expensive and fashionable clothes
15. to lead the fads /fæds/ (phr.) = to lead sth that is popular or fashionable for only a short time
16. tailor-made /ˈteɪlə(r) meɪd/ (adj.) = designed for a particular person
17. mundane /ˌmʌnˈdeɪn/ (adj.) = ordinary and not exciting
18. drab /dræb/ (adj.) = not colourful or interesting
19. sophisticated /səˈfɪstɪˌkeɪtɪd/ (adj.) = complicated and advanced in design
20. a fashion statement (phr.) = expressions of oneself through clothes they wear
21. consumerism /kənˈsjuːməˌrɪz(ə)m/ (n.) = the belief that it is good for a country if people buy and use a lot of goods and services
22. fabric /ˈfæbrɪk/ (n.) = cloth, used for making clothes
23. a baggy garment (phr.) = a loose piece of clothing
24. to fit loosely (phr.) = a bit saggy
25. body-hugging (n.) = a skin-tight garment
26. to accentuate the figure /ækˈsentʃueɪt ðə ˈfɪgə(r)/ (phr.) = to make one's figure more noticeable
27. lace /leɪs/ (n.) = light delicate cloth with patterns of small holes in it
28. a fusion of A and B /ˈfjuːʒ(ə)n/ (phr.) = a combination of A and B
29. needlework /ˈniːd(ə)lˌwɜː(r)k/ (n.) = sewing or another activity in which you create sth using a needle, for example embroidery or crochet
30. hand-me-downs (n.) = clothes that have been passed on from another person
31. tattered /ˈtætə(r)d/ (adj.) = looks like it's in very bad condition because parts of it have been torn
32. to dress for comfort (phr.) = to wear clothes that are comfortable more than fashionable
33. to have an impeccable taste in clothing /ɪmˈpekəb(ə)l/ (phr.) = to have a perfect fashion style

34. tacky /ˈtæki/ (adj.) = looking cheap and of poor quality
35. Clothes make the man. (phr.) = the way one looks creates others view of them
36. fashion-conscious (adj.) = very interested in fashion and wanting to wear fashionable clothes, spend time in fashionable places etc.
37. breathable/ˈbriːðəb(ə)l/ (adj.) = comfortable because made of cloth that has a lot of very small holes that allow air in
38. to make a comeback (phr.) = to return to fashion again
39. gaudy /ˈɡɔːdi/ (adj.) = brightly coloured and ugly, of bad quality
40. ragged /ˈræɡɪd/ (adj.) = torn and dirty
41. to shrink /ʃrɪŋk/ (v.) = to become smaller in size
42. to blend with sth /blend/ (v.) = to mix with
43. to grow out of sth (v.) = if children grow out of clothes, they grow bigger and the clothes become too small for them
44. the key to sth /kiː/ (phr.) = the most important element
45. to conceal sth /kənˈsiːl/ (v.) = to cover sth
46. to create an illusion /ɪˈluːʒ(ə)n/ (phr.) = to make an effect different from the way things are
47. flattering /ˈflæt(ə)rɪŋ/ (adj.) = making you look more attractive

PART 3 :
- ☞ Is there any traditional costume that women/men in your country wear? Why/why not?
- ☞ Who wears traditional clothing more often? Men or women? Why?
- ☞ Do people in different parts of your country wear different types of clothes? If so, why?
- ☞ In what ways are your clothes different from the clothes your parents or grandparents wear? Why?
- ☞ Do you think fashion is generally important? Why/why not?
- ☞ How to be fashionable?
- ☞ Why has fashion been changing so quickly?
- ☞ What in your opinion is real fashion? Why?
- ☞ Do you think that everyone likes shopping? Why/why not?
- ☞ Why do some people prefer to shop with friends while others do it alone?
- ☞ Is the Internet a good place to buy clothes? Why/why not?
- ☞ Do people in your country often buy second-hand clothes? Why/why not?
- ☞ What types of clothes do people in your country wear on formal occasions? Why?
- ☞ What are the main differences between men's and women's clothes in your country? Why?
- ☞ Are people in your culture often judged by the clothes they wear? Why/why not?
- ☞ Is the fashion industry a promising field? Why/why not?
- ☞ Do you think in the future designers might use recycled materials to make their collections? Why/why not?
- ☞ How does globalisation influence the fashion industry?
- ☞ What kinds of clothes are considered formal in your culture? Why?
- ☞ Did people wear formal clothes as much in the past? Why/why not?
- ☞ Is there any connection between out lifestyles and our clothes?
- ☞ Do many companies require employees to wear uniforms in your country? Why/why not?
- ☞ Is it good to be asked to wear a uniform to work? Why/why not?
- ☞ What are the most common jobs where employees wear uniforms? Why?

- Do you think people behave differently when in uniforms? How?
- Do you think workers should be able to choose what they wear for work? Why/why not?
- How does globalization affect the clothing industry? Why?
- Do you think one day all people will wear the same style of clothes? Will national clothes disappear? Why/why not?

- **a piece of furniture you have in your home**

VOCAB :
1. to cultivate the home-like feeling (phr.) = to make sure a house feels homey
2. old-school (adj.) = traditional
3. a print of age (phr.) = visible mark of the passing time
4. clunky /ˈklʌŋki/ (adj.) = large, solid and heavy in a way that is not attractive
5. to be on the scrapheap /ˈskræpˌhiːp/ (phr.) = no longer wanted or needed, although still capable of being useful
6. as good as new (phr.) = in a very good condition
7. wear and tear /ˌweər ən ˈteə(r)/ (n.) = the changes or damage that normally happen to sth that has been used, causing it to be less useful or less valuable
8. furnishings /ˈfɜː(r)nɪʃɪŋz/ (n.) = such things as furniture, carpets and curtains
9. movables /ˈmuːvəb(ə)lz/ (n.) = a piece of furniture that can be moved from one place to another
10. sculpted /ˈskʌlptɪd/ (adj.) = very firm or straight in an attractive way
11. luxurious /lʌɡˈzjʊəriəs/ (adj.) = very expensive and comfortable
12. timeless /ˈtaɪmləs/ (adj.) = not affected by time or by changes in fashion
13. functional /ˈfʌŋkʃ(ə)nəl/ (adj.) = practical and simple
14. handwoven (adj.) = woven by hand
15. colourfast /ˈkʌlə(r)ˌfɑːst/ (adj.) = does not lose its colour when you wash it
16. versatile /ˈvɜː(r)sətaɪl/ (adj.) = able to be used in many different ways
17. classic /ˈklæsɪk/ (adj.) = beautiful in a very simple way and always fashionable
18. ephemeral /ɪˈfemərəl/ (adj.) = lasting for only a short time
19. solid /ˈsɒlɪd/ (adj.) = strong
20. coarse /kɔː(r)s/ (adj.) = rough and hard
21. elongated /ˈiːlɒŋˌɡeɪtɪd/ (adj.) = longer and narrower than is normal or natural

PART 3 :
- Do many people in your country buy second-hand furniture? Why/why not?
- What changes have there been in furniture over the past decade?
- What is the difference between furniture in your country and Western furniture?
- How do people dispose of the old furniture? Why?
- What is typical style furniture in your country?
- Do many people in your country like traditional furniture? Why/why not?
- How do people in your country furnish their homes? By themselves or with the help of decoration companies? Why?
- Is furniture in your country expensive? Why/why not?
- Do many people like antiques? Why/why not?
- Do you think people will need less furniture in the future? Why/why not?

⟳ What do you think the furniture of the future will look like? Why?

⟳ Would it be better to buy a house already fully furnished? Why/why not?

- **a piece of jewellery that is special to you**

VOCAB :

1. to be in style (phr.) = in an impressive, luxurious way
2. vintage /ˈvɪntɪdʒ/ (adj.) = old but kept in good condition because it is interesting or attractive
3. shipshape /ˈʃɪpˌʃeɪp/ (adj.) = tidy and in good condition
4. a jade pendant on a red string /dʒeɪd ˈpendənt/ (phr.) = a piece of jewellery that hangs from a chain around your neck made of a hard green substance
5. a brooch /brəʊtʃ/ (n.) = a piece of jewellery with a pin on the back that you fasten to your clothes
6. a precious stone /ˈpreʃəs/ (phr.) = a stone worth a lot of money
7. a fake stone /feɪk/ (phr.) = a stone made to look like a real one in order to trick people
8. an imitation /ˌɪmɪˈteɪʃ(ə)n/ (n.) = a copy of sth
9. costume jewellery /ˈkɒstjuːm ˈdʒuːəlri/ (n.) = jewellery made with inexpensive materials, not valuable but looks expensive
10. to go with sth (phr.) = to match sth
11. matching /ˈmætʃɪŋ/ (adj.) = with the same colour, pattern or design
12. showy /ˈʃəʊi/ (adj.) = big and expensive in a way that seems ugly
13. tacky /ˈtæki/ (adj.) = looks cheap and of poor quality or sth that shows bad taste
14. shapely /ˈʃeɪpli/ (adj.) = attractive in shape
15. an heirloom /ˈeə(r)ˌluːm/ (n.) = a valuable or special possession that has belonged to a family for many years
16. lustrous /ˈlʌstrəs/ (adj.) = bright and shiny
17. tantalizing /ˈtæntəˌlaɪzɪŋ/ (adj.) = making you feel excited or hopeful about having sth that you want
18. queenly /ˈkwiːnli/ (adj.) = looking like a queen
19. divine /dɪˈvaɪn/ (adj.) = like a god
20. magnetic /mæɡˈnetɪk/ (adj.) = able to attract and interest people very strongly
21. unblemished pearls /ʌnˈblemɪʃt pɜː(r)lz/ (phr.) = a small round jewel that is white and shiny and that grows inside the shell of an oyster, without faults
22. a handsome glossy stone (phr.) = a gorgeous shiny jewel
23. an intriguing matrix /ɪnˈtriːɡɪŋ ˈmeɪtrɪks/ (phr.) = a captivating pattern

PART 3 :

⟳ Do you have a favourite piece of jewellery? What it is?

⟳ How do people get jewellery in your country?

⟳ Do many people keep jewellery from previous generations? Why/why not?

⟳ Is jewellery in your country expensive? Why/why not?

⟳ Who makes jewellery in your country? Why?

⟳ Is it better to buy jewellery or make it by hand? Why?

⟳ Do you think men or women care about jewellery more? Why?

⟳ Why are some pieces of jewellery so expensive?

⟳ Do people spend too much money on jewellery today?

⟳ Do you think in the future people will use jewellery more or less? Why?

⟳ Does our taste in jewellery change when we grow up? Why?

⟳ Why are some pieces of jewellery more special to people than others?

- **the biggest failure you have had in your life**

<u>VOCAB :</u>

1. to add fuel to the fire (phr.) = to cause a situation or conflict to become more intense, especially by provocative comments
2. back to square one (phr.) = back to where one started, with no progress having been made
3. a lost cause (n.) = a person or thing that can no longer hope to succeed or be changed for the better
4. to beat a dead horse (phr.) = to waste energy on a lost cause
5. to fall by the wayside (phr.) = to fail to persist in an endeavour
6. the weak link (in the chain) (phr.) = the least dependable element
7. a recipe for disaster /ˈresəpi/ (phr.) = sth that is likely to lead to a particular outcome
8. infallible /ɪnˈfæləb(ə)l/ (adj.) = not capable of making mistakes
9. to go pear-shaped (phr.) = to become unsuccessful
10. to come unstuck /ʌnˈstʌk/ (phr.) = to fail completely
11. to be out of one's depth /depθ/ (phr.) = beyond one's ability to cope
12. a tricky situation /ˈtrɪki/ (phr.) = a sensitive situation
13. to be really up against it (phr.) = to face some serious but unspecified difficulties
14. to go downhill /ˌdaʊnˈhɪl/phr.) = to become worse
15. an unmitigated disaster /ʌnˈmɪtɪˌɡeɪtɪd dɪˈzɑːstə(r)/ (phr.) = an absolute tragedy
16. to miss the boat (phr.) = to be too slow to take advantage of an opportunity

<u>PART 3 :</u>

⟳ How do people usually fail in life?

⟳ Can failure teach us anything? If so, what?

⟳ How does failure make people feel? Why?

⟳ Why would some people call others a failure?

⟳ In your country, do people fail a lot? Why/why not?

⟳ Does public failure hurt more than a private one? Why/why not?

⟳ Which failures hurt the most? Why?

⟳ What could children learn from failing at something? Why?

⟳ Do you think the image of success will change in the future? Why/why not?

⟳ Is it worth trying again after a failure at something? Why/why not?

- **a piece of news you have heard lately**

<u>VOCAB :</u>

1. to make the world integrated /ˈɪntɪˌɡreɪtɪd/ (phr.) = to make the world more balanced
2. to kill time (phr.) = to make time seem to pass more quickly by doing sth instead of just waiting
3. to spread like wildfire /ˈwaɪldˌfaɪə(r)/ (phr.) = to spread with great speed

4. a hot potato (n.) = a difficult issue that people try to avoid dealing with or discussing
5. to exaggerate the facts /ɪgˈzædʒəreɪt/ (phr.) = to describe the facts in a way that makes it seem larger or more important than they really are
6. to give birth to humongous misunderstanding /hjuːˈmʌŋgəs/ (phr.) = to create a huge wrong idea
7. to cause public panic /ˈpænɪk/ (phr.) = to cause anxiety among the public
8. to be well-informed (adj.) = to know a lot about a subject or a situation
9. to distort the truth /dɪˈstɔː(r)t/ (phr.) = to change the truth
10. to be unbiased /ʌnˈbaɪəst/ (adj.) = to be fair
11. censorship /ˈsensə(r)ʃɪp/ (n.) = the process of removing parts of news that are considered unsuitable for moral, religious or political reasons
12. to blow sth out of proportion (phr.) = to present sth as more than it really is
13. to misrepresent sth /ˌmɪsreprɪˈzent/ (v.) = to give false or incorrect description of the news
14. to sweep sth under the carpet /swiːp/ (phr.) = to ignore a problem in the hope that it will be forgotten
15. There's no smoke without fire. (phr.) = there's always some reason for a rumour

PART 3 :
⟳ Do people in your country often read newspapers? Why/why not?
⟳ Where do people normally get the news? Why?
⟳ What do you think of news distortion? Why?
⟳ Why do you think more people like to read entertainment news more than political news?
⟳ Do you think people should be allowed to express their opinion about certain news online? Why/why not?
⟳ What types of news are people in your country interested in? Why?
⟳ Which age group is most interested in the news in your country? Why?
⟳ Do you think everyone should care about the news? Why/why not?
⟳ Do people always need to have immediate access to the latest news? Why/why not?
⟳ What are some disadvantages of following the news?
⟳ How do you think people will get the news in the future? Why?
⟳ Do you think people have access to too much information these days? Why/why not?
⟳ Is a news reporter a good job? Why/why not?
⟳ How are stories reported today?
⟳ How were stories reported in the past? Why?
⟳ In what ways does technology affect news reports?
⟳ Do you think we will still need news reporters in the future or will technology take care of that? Why?

• **a plant/flower/tree that is important in your country**

VOCAB :
1. a symbol of /ˈsɪmb(ə)l/ (n.) = sth that represents a particular idea
2. scented /ˈsentɪd/ (adj.) = having a pleasant smell
3. an inspiration source for artists (phr.) = sth artists get their stimuli from
4. exquisite /ɪkˈskwɪzɪt/ (adj.) = extremely beautiful and delicate
5. to express affection (phr.) = to express feelings

6. a petal /ˈpet(ə)l/ (n.) = one of the coloured parts around the centre of a flower
7. a thorn /θɔː(r)n/ (n.) = a sharp point that sticks out from the stem of a plant
8. a stem /stem/ (n.) = the long thin central part of a plant from which the leaves and flowers grow
9. a branch /brɑːntʃ/ (n.) = a part of a tree that grows out of its trunk with leaves, flowers or fruit growing on it
10. a twig /twɪg/ (n.) = a very small think branch from a tree or bush
11. a trunk /trʌŋk/ (n.) = the main part of a tree that the branches grow out of
12. fauna /ˈfɔːnə/ (n.) = all the animals that live in a particular area
13. horticulture /ˈhɔː(r)tɪ͵kʌltʃə(r)/ (n.) = the activity of growing and studying garden plants
14. a peony /ˈpiːəni/ (n.) = a plant with large pink, red, or white flowers or one of the flowers
15. a carnation /kɑː(r)ˈneɪʃ(ə)n/ (n.) = a flower with a sweet smell, often worn as a decoration on formal occasions such as weddings
16. a tulip /ˈtjuːlɪp/ (n.) = a colourful flower shaped like a cup that grows on a long stem in spring
17. a daisy /ˈdeɪzi/ (n.) = a type of small white flower with a yellow centre
18. a chrysanthemum /krɪˈsænθɪməm/ (n.) = a plant with large round brightly coloured flowers
19. a lavender /ˈlævəndə(r)/ (n.) = a plant with small purple flowers that smell nice
20. a lotus flower /ˈləʊtəs/ (n.) = an Asian water plant with large white or pink flowers
21. to fertilize /ˈfɜː(r)təlaɪz/ (v.) = to add a natural or chemical substance to soil in order to help plants grow
22. intoxicating /ɪnˈtɒksɪ͵keɪtɪŋ/ (adj.) = giving you a lot of happiness and excitement
23. a delicate fragrance /ˈdelɪkət ˈfreɪgrəns/ (phr.) = a soft pleasant smell
24. a faint smell of /feɪnt/ (phr.) = a smell of sth that is not strong
25. a pungent smell /ˈpʌndʒənt/ (phr.) = a very strong smell
26. a musty odour /ˈmʌsti ˈəʊdə(r)/ (phr.) = an unpleasant niff
27. to add compost to enrich the soil /ˈkɒmpɒst/ (phr.) = to fertilize the soil
28. to prune bushes /pruːn ˈbʊʃɪz/ (phr.) = to remove parts of bushes to make them grow better
29. to dig the ground /dɪg/ (phr.) = to make a hole in earth or sand using your hands or tools
30. to plant bulbs for the following spring /bʌlbz/ (phr.) = the parts of plants that are shaped like an onion from which a flower grows

PART 3 :

- ☞ Do many people in your country grow flowers? Why/why not?
- ☞ What are the most popular flowers to grow in your country? Why?
- ☞ Do any flowers have a special meaning in your culture? If so, which ones? What is it?
- ☞ When do people use flowers?
- ☞ Who is better at growing flowers, men or women? Why?
- ☞ Do children in your country grow trees? Why/why not?
- ☞ Should individuals grow more trees? Why/why not?
- ☞ How are trees helpful to the environment? Why?
- ☞ What are the best plants to keep in one's garden? Why?
- ☞ Do people in your culture grow their own vegetables? Why/why not?
- ☞ How can trees be used?

- **a prize you would like to win**

VOCAB :
1. a booby prize /'buːbi/ (n.) = a prize given as a joke to the last-lace finisher in a race or competition
2. a trophy /'trəʊfi/ (n.) = a large silver cur or similar object given as a prize to the winner of a competition
3. an accolade /'ækəleɪd/ (n.) = an honour given to sb for their work
4. laurel /'lɒrəl/ (n.) = a small tree with shiny dark green leaves that do not fall off in winter, often given to winners
5. a prize winner (n.) = a winner of a prize
6. a champ /tʃæmp/ (n.) = a champion
7. enticing /ɪnˈtaɪsɪŋ/ (adj.) = so good and attractive that you want to have it or do it very much
8. a seductive award /sɪˈdʌktɪv əˈwɔː(r)d/ (phr.) = a very attractive award
9. an irresistible opportunity /ˌɪrɪˈzɪstəb(ə)l/ (phr.) = an opportunity impossible to refuse

PART 3 :
- How are students rewarded in your country?
- What can students be rewarded for? Why?
- How are students punished in your country?
- What can students be punished for? Why?
- What types of prizes do students get in your country? Why?
- Should children be rewarded for their success at school? Why/why not? If so, what's the best reward?
- Do you think some parents push their children too much to win? Why/why not?
- What is a common reward system for employees in your country?
- Is rewarding best workers beneficial to the company? Why/why not? If so, how?
- Would you say the best reward is always satisfaction of doing the job well? Why/why not?
- What's the best way to reward achievements in sport? Why?
- Do you think professional sportspeople approach winning the same way amateurs do? Why/why not?
- What can happen if a sportsperson is too focused on succeeding in sports?
- Are international sporting competitions important to the world? Why/why not?

- **a show/performance you really enjoyed**

VOCAB :
1. spine-tingling /'spaɪn ˌtɪŋɡ(ə)lɪŋ/ (adj.) = very exciting
2. to be on the edge of your seat (phr.) = to be very excited and give full attention to sth
3. settings (n.) = time and place in a story
4. sound effects (n.) = the recorded sounds
5. to be scared out of your wits /wɪts/ (phr.) = to be extremely frightened
6. nail-biting /neɪl ˈbaɪtɪŋ/ (adj.) = making you feel very excited or worried
7. an adaptation /ˌædæpˈteɪʃ(ə)n/ (n.) = a show that has been made from a book or play

8. a twist /twɪst/ (n.) = a sudden situation change in a show
9. cast /kɑːst/ (n.) = all actors in a film or play
10. sensational /senˈseɪʃ(ə)nəl/ (adj.) = very exciting and surprising
11. applause /əˈplɔːz/ (n.) = the sound made by people clapping at a show
12. phenomenal /fəˈnɒmɪn(ə)l/ (adj.) = extremely impressive or surprising
13. unanimously acclaimed /juːˈnænɪməsli əˈkleɪmd/ (phr.) = publically written and talked about in an admiring way by all
14. gripping /ˈɡrɪpɪŋ/ (adj.) = very exciting and interesting
15. an audience /ˈɔːdiəns/ (n.) = a group of people who have come to a place to see or hear a film, performance etc.
16. to put on a play (phr.) = to produce a play
17. a largish theatre /ˈlɑː(r)dʒɪʃ/ (phr.) = a fairly big theatre
18. to be blown away by sth (phr.) = to be extremely impressed by sth
19. to capture the character perfectly /ˈkæptʃə(r)/ (phr.) = to express the character very well
20. facial expressions /ˈfeɪʃ(ə)l/ (n.) = motions of the muscles beneath the skin of one's face
21. acrobatics /ˌækrəˈbætɪks/ (n.) = gymnastic feats
22. a rehearsal /rɪˈhɜː(r)s(ə)l/ (n.) = an occasion when you practise for the performance of a play, concert etc.
23. an opening night (n.) = the first night that a play or other entertainment is performed
24. 'break a leg' (phr.) = used for wishing sb good luck
25. a die-hard fan (phr.) = a fan who continues supporting sth/sb in spite of opposition
26. electric atmosphere /ɪˈlektrɪk ˈætməsˌfɪə(r)/ (phr.) = extremely exciting atmosphere
27. cheers and applause /ˈtʃɪə(r)z ænd əˈplɔːz/ (phr.) = good wishes and praise expressed by clapping
28. a fuddy-duddy /ˈfʌdiˌdʌdi/ (n.) = sb who has old-fashioned attitudes and is rather boring
29. to prance about on stage /prɑːns/ (phr.) = to move in a lively confident way on stage
30. slow-paced /sləʊˈpeɪst/ (adj.) = not too fast
31. a duller /dʌlə/ (n.) = a show that is extremely boring
32. an art venue /ˈvenjuː/ (n.) = a place suitable for art shows and exhibitions
33. namby-pamby /ˌnæmbi ˈpæmbi/ (adj.) = behaving in a way that seems weak or extremely sensitive
34. to rocket the place /ˈrɒkɪt/ (phr.) = to become very successful
35. to hype the crowd /haɪp/ (phr.) = to use a lot of advertisements and other publicity to influence or interest people
36. bravo /ˌbrɑːˈvəʊ/ (interjection) = used for showing that you admire what sb has done or that you enjoyed their performance

PART 3 :
↪ What kinds of shows are most common in your country? Why?
↪ Do many people like to go to shows or performances in your country? Why/why not?
↪ What is the average cost of a show or a performance?
↪ Are shows in your country always worth watching? Why/why not?
↪ What's the difference between watching a show and watching a film? Why?
↪ Who is the most famous performer in your country today? Why?
↪ Do you have a lot of traditional shows in your culture? Why/why not?
↪ Who enjoys going to shows more, young people or older people? Why?

⮎ Do you think more or fewer people will go to performances in the future? Why?

⮎ How does technology affect the way performances are given?

⮎ Can everyone be a good a performer? Why/why not?

- **a skill you'd like to learn/something you can't do now but would like to learn/something useful someone taught you/you learnt from a member of your family**

VOCAB :
1. an exercise in frustration /frʌˈstreɪʃ(ə)n/ (phr.) = trying to stay patient while learning sth new
2. nitty-gritty /ˌnɪti ˈgrɪti/ (n.) = the most basic aspects of a situation or an activity that must be dealt with, even if they are unpleasant
3. a trick up your sleeve (phr.) = sth kept secret and in reserve for use when needed
4. to take sth in (v.) = to undertake work at home
5. to know sth like the back of your hand (phr.) = to know sth inside-out
6. to be out of practice (phr.) = not currently proficient in a particular activity or skill due to not having exercised or performed it for some time
7. an arduous process /ˈɑː(r)djuəs/ (phr.) = an extremely difficult process
8. to acquire a skill/əˈkwaɪə(r)/ (phr.) = to obtain a skill
9. an innate talent /ˌɪˈneɪt/ (phr.) = a talent you have always had
10. to consult an expert /kənˈsʌlt/ (phr.) = to turn to an expert
11. a problem-solving ability (phr.) = an ability to find solutions to difficult or complex issues
12. to have the knack of doing sth /næk/ (phr.) = to have a skill or ability to do sth
13. mediocre /ˌmiːdiˈəʊkə(r)/ (adj.) = average
14. to know sth inside out (phr.) = to know sth very well
15. to get the hang of sth /hæŋ/ (phr.) = to learn a skill or activity
16. to be rusty /ˈrʌsti/ (adj.) = a skill that is rusty has not been used recently
17. to hone a skill /həʊn/ (phr.) = to improve a skill
18. to be adept at sth /əˈdept/ (adj.) = to be skilful at doing sth
19. to be proficient in sth /prəˈfɪʃ(ə)nt/ (adj.) = to be very skilful at sth that you have learnt
20. to be out of your depth /depθ/ (phr.) = in a situation that you cannot deal with because it is too difficult or dangerous

PART 3 :
⮎ What skills can children learn at home? How?

⮎ What skills can children only learn at school? Why?

⮎ Should children learn from their parents or only their teachers? Why?

⮎ Do you think parents today have enough time to teach their children life skills? Why/why not?

⮎ Should everyone know how to use a computer? Why/why not?

⮎ What's the best way to learn how to use a computer? Why?

⮎ Why do you think it is easier for young people to learn how to use a computer?

⮎ Do older people need to know how to use a computer? Why/why not?

⮎ Do you think that learning how to use a computer is a one time deal or is it a continuous process? Why?

⮎ How does technology affect education?

⮎ What are the main advantages of using the Internet as source of information?

- What are the main disadvantages of getting information from the Internet? Why?
- Do you think computers have changed the way people think? Why/why not? If so, in what ways?
- Do you think teachers and classroom-based learning will be disposable in the future? Why/why not?
- What skills can children learn at home?
- Should children learn how to read before they reach school age? Why/why not?
- What do we learn from our mothers?
- What do we learn from our fathers?
- What skills should parents always teach children at home? Why?
- What can children learn from playing games with their parents?
- Is it better to have strict parents or more lenient parents? Why?
- What problems may parents have when teaching their children something new?
- What things should children learn at school?
- Are young children learning the same way as teenagers? What different methods should be used to teach these two groups? Why?
- Is everything we learn at school useful in our adult life? Why/why not?
- What's the most useless school subject in your opinion? Why?
- How can school knowledge be more practical?
- Who learns more easily: younger people or older people? Why?
- What kind of person can be a good children teacher? Why?
- What kind of person can be a good adults teacher? Why?
- Do we need teachers to learn? Why/why not?
- What can we learn without a teacher? Why?
- Which things require a teacher to help us learn? Why?
- In what ways can families help children do well at school?
- Are friends or family more important in youngsters' developmental process? Why?
- Does school influence one's development? In what ways?
- What can children learn from older people in their families?
- How can older people contribute to society?
- Do you think older people understand modern world? Why/why not?

- **a song that means a lot to you/from your childhood**

VOCAB :

1. a piece of music (phr.) = a song
2. a bedtime melody /ˈbedˌtaɪm ˈmelədi/ (phr.) = a song sung or played before putting a baby to sleep, very calm
3. lyrics /ˈlɪrɪks/ (n.) = the words of a song
4. comforting /ˈkʌmfə(r)tɪŋ/ (adj.) = making you feel less sad, worried or disappointed
5. gives me inner peace (phr.) = puts me at peace
6. fast rhythm /ˈrɪðəm/ (phr.) = fast tempo
7. soothing and mellow voice /ˈsuːðɪŋ ənd ˈmeləʊ/ (phr.) = a voice that has a gently calming effect
8. an inspiration /ˌɪnspəˈreɪʃ(ə)n/ (n.) = sth/sb that gives you new ideas and the enthusiasm to create sth with them
9. a lullaby /ˈlʌləbaɪ/ (n.) = a relaxing song that helps a young child go to sleep

160

10. to strengthen your willpower (phr.) = to make your drive stronger
11. a version /ˈvɜː(r)ʃ(ə)n/ (n.) = a form of a song that is different from other forms or from the original
12. a theme song of /θiːm/ (n.) = a song written specifically for a radio/TV programme, movie or a video game, etc.
13. a unique tune /juːˈniːk/ (phr.) = a very special, unusual tune
14. a lot of airplay /ˈeə(r)ˌpleɪ/ (phr.) = the big number of times a piece of music is played on the radio
15. nostalgic /nɒˈstældʒɪk/ (adj.) = making sb remember happy times in the past

PART 3 :

- ↻ What kinds of music are currently popular in your country? Why?
- ↻ Do young people enjoy the same types of music as the elderly? Why/why not?
- ↻ Is music we listen to today different from music in the past? If so, in what ways?
- ↻ Is the most popular music today enjoyed by people of all ages? Why/why not?
- ↻ Do students learn about music in your country? Should they? Why/why not?
- ↻ Should everyone learn how to play a musical instrument? Why/why not?
- ↻ Is it important for schools to teach musical ability to students? Why? How is it helpful?
- ↻ Why do people listen to music?
- ↻ Is music a part of culture? Why/why not?
- ↻ Does music always influence people in a positive way? Why/why not?
- ↻ Should government use public finances to support music (e.g. opera, theatre)? Why/why not?
- ↻ What kinds of music do children like to listen to? Why?
- ↻ What kinds of music do teenagers enjoy? Why?
- ↻ What kinds of music do older people appreciate most? Why?
- ↻ Do you think our taste in music changes as we grow older? Why/why not?
- ↻ Should children learn about music? Why/why not?
- ↻ Where is music most present in contemporary society?
- ↻ Why do you think there is always background music in shops?
- ↻ Do you think that music in public places is a form of noise pollution? Why/why not?
- ↻ Why do people create music?
- ↻ Can music help a person express who they are? Why/why not?
- ↻ Is music important to groups? Does it show who the group members are? Why/why not?
- ↻ Why is pop music so widespread around the world?
- ↻ How does pop music influence other genres? Why?
- ↻ How can music help in defining a culture? Why?

- **a souvenir you brought home from holidays/gave someone**

VOCAB :
1. charm /tʃɑː(r)m/ (n.) = sth that people believe brings them luck
2. a memento /məˈmentəʊ/ (n.) = sth that you keep to remind you of a particular person, place or experience
3. a keepsake /ˈkiːpˌseɪk/ (n.) = a small object that you keep in order to remind you of someone or something

4. a token /ˈtəʊkən/ (n.) = sth you give sb as a way of showing your feelings towards them
5. sth makes me think of (phr.) = sth reminds me of sth else
6. sth causes me to remember (phr.) = sth helps me remember
7. sth puts me in mind of (phr.) = sth reminds me of
8. to evoke /ɪˈvəʊk/ (v.) = to bring a particular emotion, idea or memory into your mind
9. a souvenir stand /ˌsuːvəˈnɪə(r)/ (n.) = a place to buy souvenirs, usually by the side of the road
10. sb swarms me when I get home (phr.) = sb surrounds me when I get home
11. to be overcharged /ˌəʊvə(r)ˈtʃɑː(r)dʒd/ (adj.) = to be asked to pay more money than is reasonable, or more money than the real price
12. to get treats from travels (phr.) = to get some little gifts or souvenirs from travels

PART 3 :
- What kinds of souvenirs do Chines people buy? Why?
- Why do people like to buy souvenirs?
- Do you think it would be a good idea for a local person to open a souvenir shop? Why/why not?
- Do many people take photos during their travel? Why/why not?
- Do people in your country usually use a camera or a phone to photograph places they visit? Why?
- Why do you think so many people like to share their photos with others on social media?
- Do people in your country write travel blogs? Why/why not?
- Do you think writing a travel blog is a good idea? Why/why not?
- What makes us remember certain events from the past and forget the others? Why?
- How can technology help us remember the past? Why?
- Do you think technology might substitute human memory in the future? Why/why not?
- Which memories do people usually want to hold on to in their older age? Why?

- **a special meal you had/would like to have/you invited friends or family to**

VOCAB :
1. staple food /ˈsteɪp(ə)l/ (n.) = food that people eat or use regularly
2. gastronomically redundant /ˌgæstrəˈnɒmɪkli rɪˈdʌndənt/ (phr.) = not needed for cooking or eating anymore
3. frozen food /ˈfrəʊz(ə)n/ (n.) = food preserved by being made extremely cold and stored at a very low temperature
4. canned food /kænd/ (n.) = food that has been preserved in a metal container without air
5. a TV dinner (n.) = a prepared prepackaged meal that only requires heating before it is ready to eat
6. to have a sweet tooth (phr.) = to like to eat sweet food
7. a candlelight dinner /ˈkænd(ə)l ˌlaɪt/ (phr.) = dinner with burning candles adding to the atmosphere
8. to take pot luck (phr.) = to choose sth when you do not know what you will get and can only hope that it will be good
9. seconds /ˈsekəndz/ (n.) = a second helping of a dish
10. nibbles /ˈnɪb(ə)lz/ (n.) = things like nuts, crisps, etc., before a meal
11. to enjoy a sumptuous meal in opulent surroundings /ˈsʌmptʃuəs/ /ˈɒpjʊlənt/ (phr.) = a rich meal in special surroundings

PART 3 :

- ⟳ Is having a meal together important in your culture? Why?
- ⟳ Why do some people choose to eat out on special occasions?
- ⟳ Do you think people will eat more at home in the future?
- ⟳ If both parents are working who can prepare meals for children in their families? Why?
- ⟳ Is food that people in your country eat every day the same or different from food eaten on special occasions? How?
- ⟳ Is there more variety of food in shops now than in the past? If so, is it good or bad for consumers? Why?
- ⟳ Do you have a lot of imported products in your country? Why/why not?
- ⟳ What are the biggest disadvantages of transporting food long distance?
- ⟳ Do people prefer to buy local products or imported ones? Why?
- ⟳ Do you think people's diet is generally healthy today? Why/why not?
- ⟳ What are some common health issues people have related to their diet nowadays?
- ⟳ How can governments encourage their citizens to be on a healthy diet?
- ⟳ How can healthy diet of public contribute to a stronger economy of the country? Why?
- ⟳ What is the most popular food people in your country often eat?
- ⟳ Do children like the same food as adults? Why/why not?
- ⟳ Do people eat healthily today? Why/why not?
- ⟳ Is the quality of food in your country good?
- ⟳ Does the food cooked at home have better quality than restaurant meals? Why?
- ⟳ What is more important when buying food? Quality or price?
- ⟳ Is your government controlling the quality of food? How?
- ⟳ Do you think there is too much food available nowadays?
- ⟳ Is there imported food available in shops in your country?
- ⟳ Why do people like to buy imported food?
- ⟳ Do you think there will still be small farms in the future?
- ⟳ How often do people in your country eat out? Why?
- ⟳ What are some cons of eating in restaurants? Why?
- ⟳ Do you think it is possible that in the future no one will cook at home? Why/why not?
- ⟳ Is the food people eat on special occasions the same or different from everyday food?
- ⟳ Is food generally important in your country during celebrations? Why/why not?
- ⟳ Do you think some people waste money on too much food for special occasions? Why/why not?
- ⟳ What's the main difference between the way food is produced now and was produced in the past?
- ⟳ Is there any connection between climate change and food production? If so, what?
- ⟳ How will science and technology change the way food is produced in the future?

- **a story from your childhood you remember well**

VOCAB :

1. a fairy tale (n.) = a traditional children's story in which magic things happen
2. moving /ˈmuːvɪŋ/ (adj.) = making you feel emotional
3. a fantasy story /ˈfæntəsi/ (n.) = a story that shows a lot of imagination and is very different from real life

4. knights and dragons /naɪts/ /ˈdrægənz/ (phr.) = a soldier who wore a suit of armour and rode a horse, and large imaginary creatures in old stories that had wings and a long pointed tail and breathed out fire

5. aliens and robots /ˈeɪliənz/ /ˈrəʊbɒts/ (phr.) = creatures from a planet other than Earth and machines that can do work by themselves, often work that humans do

6. a far-fetched scenario /ˌfɑː(r) ˈfetʃt səˈnɑːriəʊ/ (phr.) = a situation difficult to believe because it is very unlikely

7. a poignant chronicle of /ˈpɔɪnjənt ˈkrɒnɪk(ə)l/ (phr.) = a moving and sad description of a sequence of events

8. a compelling tale /kəmˈpelɪŋ ˈteɪl/ (phr.) = a powerful story that keeps you interested

9. to twiddle your thumbs /ˈtwɪd(ə)l/ (phr.) = to feel bored, with nothing to do

10. to cut a long story short (phr.) = to tell sth briefly

11. everything turned out all right in the end (phr.) = everything finished well

12. I lived to tell the well (phr.) = I survived the events

PART 3 :
☞ What kinds of stories do children like? Why?
☞ What can children learn from stories? Why?
☞ Do all children's stories need a happy ending? Why/why not?
☞ Do all children's stories need to be educational? Why/why not?
☞ Why are there always good characters and bad characters in stories?
☞ Does a story need to be true to be good? Why/why not?
☞ How real should characters in novels be?
☞ Do young people and older people like the same type of characters? Why/why not?
☞ Why do we always remember some stories from our childhood?
☞ How are stories passed on today compared with the past? Why?
☞ Why isn't traditional storytelling popular today?
☞ Are stories an important part of culture? Why/why not?
☞ How will stories be told in the future? Why?

- **a talk/speech you heard/you gave**

VOCAB :
1. to cut the mustard /ˈmʌstə(r)d/ (phr.) = to reach the expected or necessary standard
2. a famous quote /kwəʊt/ (phr.) = famous words that sb else has said or written
3. short and sweet (phr.) = not too long or complicated
4. passionate /ˈpæʃ(ə)nət/ (adj.) = enthusiastic, showing strong beliefs
5. a conference /ˈkɒnf(ə)rəns/ (n.) = a large meeting
6. to come away with a wealth of ideas (phr.) = to express a lot of ideas suddenly, in a way that shock people
7. a speaker (n.) = a person giving a speech/talk
8. a delegate /ˈdeləgət/ (n.) = sb who is chosen to represent a group of other people at a meeting
9. an audience /ˈɔːdiəns/ (n.) = a group of people who have come to a place to hear a speck/talk
10. to answer questions off the cuff (phr.) = to answer questions without planning or thinking about it first

11. to cater for all sorts of participants (phr.) = to provide everyone with everything they want or need
12. to bounce ideas off one another (phr.) = to discuss with one another
13. sb knows his/her stuff (phr.) = sb is very knowledgeable about their topic
14. to wing it (phr.) = to so sth without preparation or plans
15. to sit through sth (phr.) = to stay until the end of sth, especially if you are not enjoying it
16. to nod off (v.) = to go to sleep, especially when you do not intend to
17. to play it by ear (phr.) = to decide what to do as a situation develops rather than planning what you will do before you start
18. to ramble on for ages /ˈræmb(ə)l/ (phr.) = to talk about sth for a long time in a way that is boring, annoying or confusing

PART 3 :

- What kinds of speeches are there common in your country? Why?
- Who can be a good speaker? What skills do they need? Why?
- How to overcome stage fright?
- What is the ideal duration of a talk/speech? Why?
- What can help make a speech more interesting? Why?
- Whom would you consider the most gifted public speaker?
- Do you study public speaking when you are at school in your country? Why/why not?
- Is it easy to make a speech? Why/why not?
- How does technology affect the way we give speeches today?
- Do you think there will be no need for public speaking in the future? Why/why not?
- Where would people give speeches most often in the past in your country? Why?

- **a time when you were very busy**

VOCAB :
1. to run errands /ˈerəndz/ (phr.) = to do small jobs that involve going to collect or deliver sth
2. to be pressed for time (phr.) = to be in a hurry
3. to live and breathe sth (phr.) = to be very enthusiastic about a particular activity and spend all the time you can doing it or talking about it
4. to throw yourself into sth (phr.) = to give all your energy or attention to doing sth
5. there's no stopping sb (phr.) = it is impossible to prevent sb from doing sth
6. to get carried away (phr.) = to become so excited or involved in sth that you lose control of your feelings or behaviour
7. life's too short (phr.) = you should not waste time doing things that are not important
8. to be up to your eyes in sth (phr.) = to have a very large amount of sth to do or deal with
9. to be on the go (phr.) = very busy and active
10. a frantic schedule /ˈfræntɪk ˈʃedjuːl/ (phr.) = an urgent plan of activities or events

PART 3 :
- What things do people generally need to do every day? Why?
- Is it good to have a daily routine? Why/why not?
- What are some disadvantages of having a daily routine?

↻ Why do you think some people dislike making any changes in their daily routine?

↻ How do people usually relax?

↻ Is it important to have some quiet time from time to time? Why/why not?

↻ Can physical activity be a good way to relax? Why/why not?

↻ Has the time for leisure activity been recently reduced? Why/why not?

↻ Are people in your country usually good at managing their time? Why/why not?

↻ How can people manage their time better? In what ways?

↻ Why are some people better at managing their time than others? What does it depend on?

↻ How has technology influenced the way people manage time? Why?

↻ Are students in your country taught some ways to manage their studying time better? Why/why not?

↻ Do you think time management classes would be useful to students? Why/why not?

- **a traditional festival/event in your country**

VOCAB :

1. auspicious /ɔːˈspɪʃəs/ (adj.) = showing signs that suggest that sth is likely to be successful
2. a celebration /ˌseləˈbreɪʃ(ə)n/ (n.) = a party or special event at which you celebrate sth
3. to rejoice at /rɪˈdʒɔɪs/ (v.) = to fell very happy about sth, to celebrate sth in a happy way
4. to parade about the streets /pəˈreɪd/ (phr.) = to walk as part of an organized group in order to celebrate sth
5. a time of renewal /rɪˈnjuːəl/ (phr.) = a time of a new beginning
6. a colourful spectacle /ˈspektək(ə)l/ (phr.) = an unusual and exciting event
7. flamboyant /flæmˈbɔɪənt/ (adj.) = extremely colourful and exaggerated
8. raucous /ˈrɔːkəs/ (adj.) = very noisy
9. to commemorate /kəˈmeməreɪt/ (v.) = to respect and remember officially
10. to set off fireworks (phr.)
11. a fireworks display /dɪˈspleɪ/ (phr.) = a fireworks show
12. a public event (n.) = an event available for people in general
13. to ring in the New Year (phr.) = to ring bells to celebrate the beginning of a new year
14. a New Year's resolution /ˌrezəˈluːʃ(ə)n/ (n.) = a decision that you make on the first day of the year about the things that you intend to do or stop doing during that year
15. to go overboard (phr.) = to do more than is necessary
16. to have a blast /blɑːst/ (phr.) = to have an enjoyable experience
17. to enjoy oneself immensely /ɪˈmensli/ (phr.) = to enjoy oneself a lot

PART 3 :

↻ How are most festivals in your country different from Western ones?

↻ Why do you think so many people celebrate Western festivals these days?

↻ Does your country have any traditional food?

↻ Does your country have any traditional dresses?

↻ Do you think young people are still interested in traditional things? Why/why not?

↻ Are traditions important in a culture? Why/why not?

↻ What traditions have already disappeared from your culture? Why?

↻ What could be done to preserve traditions?

☞ Do you think that the fact that people travel more these days contributes to fewer traditions? Why/why not?

☞ Can one culture share traditions with another one? Why/why not?

☞ Should all traditions change over time? Why/why not?

☞ Do you see any activities present in your culture now that might become new traditions in the future?

- **a TV/radio programme you watch/listen to regularly/that made you laugh/you find interesting/something interesting you learnt from TV/internet**

VOCAB :

1. educational /ˌedjʊˈkeɪʃ(ə)nəl/ (adj.) = giving people useful knowledge
2. entertaining /ˌentə(r)ˈteɪnɪŋ/ (adj.) = enjoyable and fun
3. broadcast by /ˈbrɔːdˌkɑːst/ (which channel) (v.) = to be sent out by TV or radio for the public to watch/listen to
4. a sitcom /ˈsɪtkɒm/ (n.) = a TV or radio series about a particular group of characters who deal with situations in a humorous way
5. to aim at /eɪm/ (v.) = to want people to listen to it or watch it
6. hilarious /hɪˈleəriəs/ (adj.) = extremely funny
7. inspirational /ˌɪnspəˈreɪʃ(ə)n(ə)l/ (adj.) = giving you the enthusiasm to do or create sth
8. off the air (phr.) = no longer broadcasting on radio or TV
9. peak time (n.) = the prime time TV viewing hours
10. ratings /ˈreɪtɪŋz/ (n.) = the number of people who watch or listen to a particular TV or radio programme
11. to be glued to (v.) = to be looking at sth and not paying attention to anything else
12. a reality show (n.) = a show that does not use professional actors but shows real events and situations involving ordinary people
13. a quiz show (n.) = a show which is a competition for people to answer questions
14. to tune in to a radio station (phr.) = to listen to a particular radio station
15. an announcer /əˈnaʊnsə(r)/ (n.) = sb whose job is to give information about television or radio programmes in between other programmes
16. to host a show /həʊst/ (phr.) = to introduce and talk to the people taking part in a television or radio programme
17. to phone-in (v.) = to telephone a radio or television programme with a question or comment
18. at your fingertips (phr.) = if you have a subject at your fingertips, you have a thorough knowledge of it and can give useful information to others whenever they ask for it
19. a reliable source (phr.) = a true material
20. to decipher between a fact and an opinion /dɪˈsaɪfə(r)/ (phr.) = to understand the difference between a fact and an opinion
21. a hacker /ˈhækə(r)/ (n.) = sb who uses a computer to connect to other people's computers secretly and often illegally, so that they can find or change information
22. sth caught my eye (phr.) = sth got my attention
23. a groundbreaking TV /ˈɡraʊn(d)ˌbreɪkɪŋ/ (phr.) = TV that uses new methods
24. an episode /ˈepɪsəʊd/ (n.) = a part of a television or radio story that is broadcast separately and forms one of a series

167

25. cable TV /ˈkeɪb(ə)l/ (n.) = a system for broadcasting television programmes in which signals are sent through underground wires
26. constant adverts (phr.) = advertisements that always appear
27. the sole purpose is to /səʊl/ (phr.) = the only purpose it to
28. a jokester (n.) = a person fond of making or telling jokes
29. to burble away in the background /ˈbɜː(r)b(ə)l/ (phr.) = to talk fast about sth for a long time, especially in a way that annoys people because they cannot understand what you are saying
30. sth has evolved down the ages /ɪˈvɒlvd/ (phr.) = sth has changed over the years
31. a source of entertainment (phr.) = providing entertainment to people
32. to be aired on TV /eə(r)d/ (phr.) = to be broadcast
33. a couch potato /kaʊtʃ/ (n.) = sb who spends a lot of time sitting at home watching TV
34. it gets you hooked /hʊkt/ (phr.) = it attracts you
35. even if you miss an episode it's easy to catch up (phr.)

PART 3 :

- What kinds of things make children laugh? Why?
- Is it easier for children to laugh than it is for adults? Why?
- Is humour during lessons important? Why/why not?
- Is there any connection between laughter and health?
- Why do you think some people can tell great jokes while others cannot? What does it depend on?
- Is sense of humour important in a relationship? Why/why not?
- How can people from different countries understand each others' sense of humour?
- Can foreign comedy be understood and appreciated in your country?
- Can humour be helpful in politics? How?
- Should world leaders study jokes and humour from other countries? Why/why not?
- Does your country have 'black humour'? If so, what are its main themes?
- Is radio still popular in your country? Why/why not?
- What types of programmes are more suitable for the radio? Why?
- What kind of a person could make a good radio presenter? Why?
- Do you have a national radio station in your country? What is it?
- Who do you think listens to the radio more, young people or older people? Why?
- How can a local radio station serve its community?
- Are there a lot of advertisements on the radio today? Why/why not?
- Are radio advertisements effective? Why/why not?
- How did the invention of radio change people's lives?
- Do you think that listeners should pay to be able to listen to the radio? Why/why not?
- Do you think in the future the radio might be replaced by other technological forms? Why/why not?
- What kinds of TV programmes are most popular in your country? Why?
- Do people prefer to watch films at home or go to the cinema? Why?
- What are some advantages of watching a film in the cinema?
- What advantages can watching TV bring to people who live alone? Why?
- Does TV always waste time? Why/why not?
- Is the youngsters' behaviour often influenced by TV? If so, in a positive or negative way? Why?
- Is it good or bad to have such a broad variety of channels? Why?

- Are most TV channels financed by the government or through advertising? Which way do you think is better? Why?
- Do you think TV might be replaced by the newest media in the future? Why/why not?
- What kinds of TV programmes do people like to watch? Why?
- Do you think that people of different ages enjoy the same or different types of programmes? Why?
- Are there any educational programmes available on TV?
- Should all TV programmes be educational? Why/why not?
- What types of entertainment are popular in your country? Why?
- Is there a lot of advertising on TV in your country? Why/why not?
- Do most people like to see advertisements on TV? Why/why not?
- Are there any regulations on TV adverts in your country? Why/why not?
- Do you have access to international channels in your country?
- Why do you think there are so many new TV channels in the world? Do we need them all?
- What's the purpose of 24-hour news channels?
- Can international programmes contribute to global peace? How?
- Which is better, watching TV or listening to the radio? Why?
- Are there any regulations in your country on what can be shown on TV? Why/why not? Should there be?
- Can radio and TV help us learn anything? If so, what? If not, why not?
- What are the main cons of using TV and radio for educational reasons?
- Do you think other media might replace TV and radio in the future? Why/why not?
- What are some latest developments in broadcasting in your country?
- How are programmes generally founded?
- What makes a TV or radio programme high-quality?
- How much time do people in your country spend watching television? Why?
- What are the most popular TV programmes today? Why?
- Has television in your country changed recently? If so, how?
- What is the general quality of TV programmes in your country?
- Do many people prefer to watch foreign TV? Why?
- Can television be educational? How?
- What are some disadvantages of using TV to educate children?
- Is there anything adults can learn from different TV programmes? If so, what?
- What kind of impact does television have on society? Why?
- Is satellite TV going to replace local TV? Why/why not?
- Does TV determine how we understand the world today? Why/why not?
- How can the Internet be used by students in their learning process?
- Why do you think so many students prefer to use the Internet to books?
- Do you think there is a chance that the Internet might replace libraries in the future? Why/why not?
- Is social networking on the Internet common in your country? Why/why not?
- Which online social networking sites are popular in your country? Why?
- How does widespread online social networking affect friendship? Why?
- Do you think people socialize online because they like it or because they must keep up with technological advances? Why?

↻ Do you think that business people might use the Internet for their dealings more in the future? Why/why not?

↻ Has the Internet improved people's quality of life? Why/why not? If so, how?

↻ Do you think society can benefit from all the citizens using the Internet? Why/why not? How?

↻ Are we becoming too dependent on the Internet? Why/why not?

- **a useful app**

VOCAB :
1. to popularise sth /ˈpɒpjʊləraɪz/ (v.) = to make sth popular with many people
2. a dependency on sth /dɪˈpendənsi/ (n.) = addiction to sth
3. social networking /ˌsəʊʃəl ˈnetwɜː(r)kɪŋ/ (n.) = the creation and sharing of information and ideas in online communities accessed via mobile and web-based technologies
4. to interact with /ˌɪntərˈækt/ (v.) = to communicate with
5. to have a resurgence in popularity /rɪˈsɜː(r)dʒ(ə)ns/ (phr.) = to have an increase in popularity
6. instant messaging (n.) = a kind of e-mail where both people are online at the same time
7. a chat room (n.) = an online conversation between a group of people on topics chosen by them
8. an ability to send files as attachments /əˈtætʃmənts/ (phr.) = files you send at the same time as e-mail messages
9. downloading and uploading times (phr.) = the amount of time it takes to download and upload a file
10. to screen out /skriːn/ (v.) = to prevent from reaching you

PART 3 :
↻ What technological devices do people in your country use on a daily basis? Why?

↻ Do you think technology has made our lives easier? Why/why not?

↻ Does technology always save time? Why/why not?

↻ What are the biggest disadvantages of technology?

↻ Do people depend too much on technology? Why/why not?

↻ For whom is it easier to keep up with the technological changes, young people or older people? Why?

↻ Why do you think some people always need to have the latest technological gadgets?

↻ Do we need so many technological advances?

↻ Is it possible to always keep up with changes in technology? Why/why not?

↻ How does technology influence people's relationships? Why?

↻ Can we believe everything we see on the Internet? Why/why not?

↻ How can people filter the information from the Internet?

↻ What are some negative influences technology has on cultures?

- **a vehicle you would like to own**

VOCAB :
1. a hybrid car /ˈhaɪbrɪd/ (n.) = a car that uses two or more kinds of power, for example a car that can run using either petrol or electricity

2. fuel consumption /ˈfjuːəl kənˈsʌmpʃ(ə)n/ (n.) = the amount of fuel a vehicle uses
3. a gas guzzler /ˈgæs ˌgʌzlə(r)/ (n.) = a car that is expensive to drive because it uses a lot of petrol
4. a manual /automatic gearbox /ˈgɪə(r)ˌbɒks/ (n.)
5. to rev the engine /rev/ (phr.) = to press the accelerator with your foot when the vehicle is not moving in order to make the engine operate faster
6. a fender-bender (n.) = a minor accident in which vehicles are slightly damaged
7. to get a ticket (phr.) = to be fined
8. a speed trap (n.) = a place on a road where the police secretly measure how fast people are driving

PART 3 :

↷ Do many people in your country buy second-hand cars? Why/why not?

↷ How are cars usually advertised?

↷ Why do you think so many people want to have their own car?

↷ Is a car a symbol of status?

↷ What advantages does using public transport have?

↷ What disadvantages does using public transport have?

↷ Should governments promote public transport system? Why/why not?

↷ How can governments improve public transport system?

↷ Do you think big cities should have more highways? Why/why not?

↷ Should motorways have tollgates? Why/why not?

↷ How do you see your road system in the future? Why?

↷ What kinds of vehicles are common where you live? Why?

↷ How is today's transport of passengers different from the one in the past? Why?

↷ Do you think passenger transport might change in the future? How?

↷ Is there a lot of traffic in your country? Why/why not?

↷ What causes heavy traffic?

↷ How can heavy traffic be reduced?

↷ Do you think car owners should contribute to the cost of building new roads? Why/why not?

↷ What's more important to the benefit of the society, more roads or railroads? Why?

↷ Are there any regulations banning roads from being built in scenic areas? Why/why not? Should there be?

- **a website you often visit**

VOCAB :

1. to check someone' profile /ˈprəʊfaɪl/ (phr.) = to look at someone's personal details that they post on a social media website or app
2. to maintain my social network /meɪnˈteɪn/ (phr.) = to keep connections with people via social media
3. Internet is a goldmine /ˈgəʊldˌmaɪn/ (phr.) = Internet is a source of valuable information and resources
4. the age of information explosion /ɪkˈspləʊʒ(ə)n/ (phr.) = times when access to information is easy
5. provides a range of news from global updates to entertainment and sport news (phr.)
6. content is updated (phr.)

7. fact-based (adj.) = reliable as based on facts
8. the comment column /ˈkɒment ˈkɒləm/ (n.) = a part of a website where users can leave comments and opinions
9. identity theft /aɪˈdentɪti θeft/ (n.) = stealing information about someone that makes it possible to use their bank account or credit card
10. virtual reality /ˈvɜː(r)tʃʊəl riˈæləti/ (n.) = images and sounds that are produced by a computer and connected equipment to make the user feel as if they are in real three-dimensional space
11. information overload (n.)/ infobesity (n.) = a situation in which you get more information than you can deal with at one time and become tired and confused
12. a phenomenally successful website /fəˈnɒmɪn(ə)li/ (phr.) = an extremely successful website
13. a web browser /ˈbraʊzə(r)/ (n.) = a software programme that is used for finding and looking at pages on the Internet
14. a registered user /ˈredʒɪstə(r)d ˈjuːzə(r)/ (n.) = a user that has created an account to access a particular website
15. to rate sth /reɪt/ (v.) = to consider that sth has a particular quality
16. to express yourself openly (phr.) = to not be afraid to express one's opinions
17. to upload pictures /ˈʌpˌləʊd/ (phr.) = to send pictures from your computer to a larger system using the Internet
18. a bulletin board /ˈbʊlətɪn bɔː(r)d/ (n.) = a place on a computer system or on the Internet where you can leave messages and read messages from other people
19. a 24-hour Internet café (n.) = a place where you can use the Internet for a fee all day long
20. a wireless Internet set up (n.) = an Internet connection that does not need a cable
21. a huge fad /fæd/ (phr.) = sth that is very popular or fashionable for only a short time
22. to boost communication /buːst/ (phr.) = to improve communication
23. limitless entertainment on the web (phr.) = entertainment accessible without limits online
24. a search engine (n.) = a computer program used for searching for information on the Internet
25. to be logged on (v.) = to be using a computer system

PART 3 :

- What are some popular websites in your country? Why?
- Is the information you find online always reliable? Why?
- Do many people in your country play computer games online? Why/why not?
- Can we learn anything from playing online games? If so, what?
- What are main drawbacks of playing online computer games?
- Is online shopping popular in your country? Why/why not?
- Is online shopping safe? Why/why not?
- What are some pros of shopping online?
- Can the Internet help people with their studies? Why/why not? How?
- Does the Internet make people lazier in terms of learning things nowadays? Why/why not?
- Do we still need printed newspapers today?
- Do you think libraries might disappear soon? Why/why not?
- Do you think the Internet can be seen as the most significant invention of the last fifty years? Why/why not?
- In what ways does the Internet influence society?
- Can the Internet contribute to greater co-operation between countries? Why/why not? How?

⌁ How has human communication been changed by the Internet? Why?

- **an advertisement that made you buy something/you remember well**

VOCAB :

1. a time filler (n.) = sth that fills free time well
2. manipulated /məˈnɪpjʊleɪtɪd/ (adj.) = influenced by sth/sb
3. persuasive /pə(r)ˈsweɪsɪv/ (adj.) = convincing
4. a flyer /ˈflaɪə(r)/ (n.) = a sheet of printed information advertising sth
5. a trailer /ˈtreɪlə(r)/ (n.) = a brief excerpt from a film, TV or radio programme which is used to advertise sth
6. a sky-writing (n.) = words written in the sky using smoke from a plane
7. a sandwich board (n.) = an advertising poster hung at the back and front of a person who then walks around a busy area
8. to plug sth (v.) = to advertise sth
9. misleading /mɪsˈliːdɪŋ/ (adj.) = intended to make sb believe sth that is incorrect or not true
10. blatant brainwashing /ˈbleɪt(ə)nt ˈbreɪnˌwɒʃɪŋ/ (phr.) = shamelessly making sb adopt radically different beliefs by using systematic and often forcible pressure
11. tantalizingly appealing /ˈtæntəˌlaɪzɪŋli əˈpiːlɪŋ/ (phr.) = temptingly attractive
12. to bombard sb with sth /bɒmˈbɑː(r)d/ (v.) = to give sb so much information that it is difficult for them to deal with it all
13. charity ads /ˈtʃærəti ˈædz/ (n.) = advertisements encouraging people to donate money to those in need
14. flawless /ˈflɔːləs/ (adj.) = without any mistakes
15. an icon effect /ˈaɪkɒn ɪˈfekt/ (n.) = the influence famous people have on the public
16. pop-up advertising windows (phr.) = windows advertising variety of products, appearing suddenly on a computer screen when you are looking at the Internet
17. the advertising slot /slɒt/ (n.) = a time during programmes when it is arranged that an adverts will appear
18. be intensively advertised /ɪnˈtensɪvli/ (phr.) = be advertised very often and in many places
19. an advertising campaign /kæmˈpeɪn/ (n.) = a series of things such as television advertisements or posters that try to persuade people to buy a product
20. prime time (n.) = the most popular time for watching television, which is in the middle of the evening
21. hackneyed subjects /ˈhæknid/ (phr.) = subjects which have been used so often that they no longer seem interesting or original
22. media hype /ˈmiːdiə haɪp/ (n.) = the use of a lot of adverts and other publicity to influence or interest people
23. sponsorship /ˈspɒnsə(r)ʃɪp/ (n.) = money given to an organization to help to pay for sth
24. a commercial /kəˈmɜː(r)ʃ(ə)l/ (n.) = an advertisement on television or radio
25. a billboard /ˈbɪlˌbɔː(r)d/ (n.) = a large board for advertisements in an outside public place
26. a jingle /ˈdʒɪŋg(ə)l/ (n.) = a short phrase, usually with music, that is easy to remember, used for advertising sth on the radio or TV
27. ubiquitous /juːˈbɪkwɪtəs/ (adj.) = present everywhere
28. unavoidable /ˌʌnəˈvɔɪdəb(ə)l/ (adj.) = impossible to stop from happening

29. sth has far-reaching effects (phr.) = sth is affecting a lot of people
30. a ripple effect /ˈrɪp(ə)l/ (n.) = a situation in which one thing causes a series of other things to happen

PART 3 :
⟳ What are the most popular types of advertising in your country? Why?
⟳ Is music an important part of an advert? Why/why not?
⟳ Why do you think some people get annoyed with adverts?
⟳ What do you think is the general purpose of advertising?
⟳ Are people's buying behaviours affected by advertising in any way?
⟳ What features should a good advert have? Why?
⟳ How have advertisements changed in the past ten years?
⟳ Do you think that advertisements should not be directed at children? Why/why not?
⟳ Can advertising be used to convey a public health message? If so, how?
⟳ Do you enjoy living in consumer society? Why/why not?
⟳ Has the life of an individual been improved due to consumerism? Why/why not?
⟳ How does consumerism affect country's economy (both positively and negatively)?
⟳ How does consumerism affect global economy?

- **an ambition you have but not achieved yet**

VOCAB :
1. a bucket list /ˈbʌkɪt ˌlɪst/ (n.) = a lift of things you want to do before you reach a certain age, or before you die
2. persistence /pə(r)ˈsɪstəns/ (n.) = the attitude or behaviour of sb who continues to do sth in a determined way
3. to fulfil one's potential (phr.) = to reach someone's abilities
4. to have a yearning for sth /ˈjɜː(r)nɪŋ/ (phr.) = to want sth very much
5. to have a craving for sth /ˈkreɪvɪŋ/ (phr.) = to have a very strong feeling of wanting sth
6. aspiration /ˌæspɪˈreɪʃ(ə)n/ (n.) = sth that you want to achieve
7. an intent /ɪnˈtent/ (n.) = the intention to do sth
8. to pull sth off (v.) = to succeed in doing sth that is difficult
9. to score /skɔː(r)/ (v.) = to succeed in doing sth
10. to accomplish /əˈkʌmplɪʃ/ (v.) = to succeed in doing sth
11. to dream up (v.) = to think of a new idea or plan, especially one that is silly or unusual
12. My plan is to + do sth (phr.) = I intend to do
13. power-hungry (adj.) = having a strong desire for power
14. a go-getter /ˌɡəʊ ˈɡetə(r)/ (n.) = sb who is determined to succeed and who works hard to achieve this
15. zealous /ˈzeləs/ (adj.) = full of great energy, effort and enthusiasm
16. motivated /ˈməʊtɪˌveɪtɪd/ (adj.) = enthusiastic and determined to achieve success
17. slothful /ˈsləʊθf(ə)l/ (adj.) = lazy
18. lax /læks/ (adj.) = not paying enough attention to rules, or not caring enough about quality or safety

PART 3 :

↻ What are some common ambitions children have? Why?

↻ How do our ambitions change when we grow up? Why?

↻ Is it important for children to have ambitions? Why/why not?

↻ Why are some people too ambitious?

↻ Is it good for children to be too ambitious? Why/why not?

↻ Is ambition useful at work? Why/why not?

↻ Why are some people more ambitious at work than others?

↻ What qualities, apart from ambition, do people need to become successful at work? Why?

↻ What kinds of problems may people face when they are too ambitious at work?

↻ What is your definition of ambition? Why?

↻ What can people gain from having high aspirations? Why?

↻ Is everyone born ambitious? Why/why not?

↻ Do you think being ambitious is an admirable quality? Why/why not?

↻ How does society reward ambitious people? Why?

↻ How do people with aspirations contribute to the world?

- **an important letter/email/message you received/sent**

VOCAB :

1. un-environmentally friendly (adj.) = designed to harm the natural environment
2. what's written can't be undone (phr.) = written word stands as proof forever
3. ink traces /ɪŋk ˈtreɪsɪz/ (n.) = signs of ink
4. to sense sth through the lines (phr.) = to get the feeling of sth from someone's written words
5. junk mail /dʒʌŋk/ (n.) = advertising and other information sent to you by post, email, or fax, although you did not ask for it and do not want it
6. to read between the lines (phr.) = to guess sth that is not expressed directly
7. at the push of a button (phr.) = easily accessible
8. e-mail fraud /frɔːd/ (n.) = the crime of obtaining money from sb by tricking them via emails
9. e-mail spamming /ˈspæmɪŋ/ (n.) = the practice of sending emails to large numbers of people on the Internet, especially when these are not wanted
10. messy handwriting (phr.) = handwriting difficult to read
11. to avoid typos /ˈtaɪpəʊz/ (phr.) = to avoid small mistakes in a printed document
12. to be inundated with sth /ˈɪnʌndeɪtɪd/ (adj.) = to be sent much more of sth than someone can easily deal with
13. never-ending stream of emails (phr.) = continuous emails
14. to respond to sth promptly /ˈprɒmptli/ (phr.) = to respond to sth immediately
15. a jotter /ˈdʒɒtə(r)/ (n.) = a small book in which you write notes
16. to write with a stylus /ˈstaɪləs/ (phr.) = to write using an instrument used for marking a computer screen
17. a cyber jotter /saɪbə(r)/ (n.) = a small online notebook in which you write notes
18. old school (adj.) = traditional or typical of the early style of sth
19. to become a thing of the past (phr.) = to become old-fashioned
20. legible /ˈledʒəb(ə)l/ (adj.) = able to be read
21. illegible /ɪˈledʒəb(ə)l/ (adj.) = difficult or impossible to read

175

22. my hand cramps easily /kræmps/ (phr.) = I have pain in my hand caused by writing for a long time

PART 3 :

- ↻ How do people in your country usually communicate? Why?
- ↻ Can you think of any problems that short forms of communication (e.g. sms, emails) might cause?
- ↻ Do young people communicate in the same way as older people? Why/why not?
- ↻ Is information from the Internet always accurate?
- ↻ Can the information from the Internet replace teachers in the future? Why/why not?
- ↻ How did people communicate in the past?
- ↻ When is it important to speak or write formally? Why?
- ↻ How is formal communication different from the informal one?
- ↻ In what situations in life are good communication skills extremely important? Why?
- ↻ Which jobs require effective communication skills?
- ↻ Are good communication skills a talent we are born with or can we learn how to communicate better? Why?
- ↻ Could you think of any situations where communication skills would be more important than what's being said?
- ↻ Do people still write letters today? Why/why not?
- ↻ What types of letters do we receive in this day and age?
- ↻ What things are better to be written about? Why?
- ↻ What things are better to be said over the phone? Why?
- ↻ Do you think that the art of writing letters might completely disappear in the future? Why?
- ↻ How to make communication powerful? Why?
- ↻ What makes a good communicator? Why?
- ↻ What is good about communicating face to face? Why?
- ↻ What is more powerful, spoken or written word? Why?
- ↻ What's the most popular way of communicating today? Why?
- ↻ Can pictures help communication? If so, how?
- ↻ Will technology influence the way people communicate in the future? If so, how? Why/why not?
- ↻ Do you think it is possible for the world to use the same language in the future? Why/why not?
- ↻ How does it feel to receive a handwritten letter?
- ↻ Are letters still important in business world today?
- ↻ What are letter-writing disadvantages?
- ↻ What kinds of skills could be useful in writing business correspondence?
- ↻ Are letters good historical records?
- ↻ What historical information can letters provide?
- ↻ How can historians use written correspondence?
- ↻ Can current written correspondence be helpful in the future? How?

- **an interesting article you read**

VOCAB :
1. critical thinking (n.) = the objective analysis and evaluation of an issue in order to form a judgement
2. to read extensively /ɪkˈstensɪvli/ (phr.) = to read a lot
3. to arouse someone's desire to /əˈraʊz/ (phr.) = to cause sb's enthusiasm
4. well-worn themes /θiːmz/ (phr.) = topics used many times
5. a write-up (n.) = an article in a newspaper or magazine that gives the writer's opinion about sth such as a new book, play or film
6. a feature /ˈfiːtʃə(r)/ (n.) = a newspaper or magazine article that concentrates on a particular subject
7. a piece /piːs/ (n.) = an article
8. absorbing /əbˈzɔː(r)bɪŋ/ (adj.) = so entertaining that you give it all your attention
9. stimulating /ˈstɪmjʊˌleɪtɪŋ/ (adj.) = making you feel interested
10. unputdownable (adj.) = so interesting or exciting that you do not want to stop reading it

PART 3 :
- Are there a lot of libraries in your country? Why/why not?
- What types of libraries are there in your country?
- Do people in your country generally like to visit libraries? Why/why not?
- What do people usually do in libraries? Why?
- What is a good library? Why?
- Are libraries in your country free? Why/why not?
- Do many people like to read in your country? Why/why not?
- How is reading taught in schools in your country? Why?
- Do people need reading skills today? Why/why not?
- How do literate people influence societies?
- What's the most powerful printed media you've seen?
- Do you think electronic communication today is too fast? Why/why not?
- What are some disadvantages of fast communication?
- In the future, which fields of communication do you see develop even more? Why?

- **an object you like a lot/an old object your family has kept for many years/something you borrowed/lent/something you can't live without (not a phone or a computer)**

VOCAB :
1. brand new (adj.) = extremely new
2. cutting-edge (adj.) = extremely modern and advanced
3. bits and pieces (phr.) = small individual things
4. odds and ends (phr.) = small things that are all different and not valuable or important
5. innovative /ˈɪnəveɪtɪv/ (adj.) = new, original and advanced
6. a device /dɪˈvaɪs/ (n.) = a machine or piece of equipment that does a particular thing
7. up-to-date (adj.) = modern

177

8. second-hand (adj.) = owned or used by someone else before you
9. as good as new (phr.) = in almost the same good condition as before being damaged or injured
10. a genuine antique /ˈdʒenjuɪn ænˈtiːk/ (phr.) = an old object such as a piece of furniture or jewellery that is valuable because it is rare, beautiful and real
11. fully reconditioned /ˌriːkənˈdɪʃ(ə)nd/ (adj.) = completely repaired
12. packaging /ˈpækɪdʒɪŋ/ (n.) = the boxes, bottles, plastic etc used for wrapping products so that they can be sold

PART 3 :

- Why do you think some people like to keep old things?
- Should historical buildings be kept or taken down? Why?
- Do you think that objects made in the past had better quality than today? Why/why not?
- Do people in your country enjoy visiting museums? Why/why not?
- What types of museums are there in your country?
- Is a visit to a museum the best way to learn about history? Why/why not?
- What should museums do to attract more people? Why?
- Should everyone know their country's history? Why/why not?
- What are the benefits of knowing one's history?
- Are archaeological discoveries important today? Why/why not?
- What will future generations remember about our era? Why?
- What do people in your country usually borrow from their neighbours?
- What things do people prefer to borrow than buy? Why?
- Is it a good idea to borrow money? Why/why not?
- What problems might occur when we borrow things to people?
- What can we do when something we borrowed has not been returned on time? Why?
- How do people ask to have their things returned?
- Why is it difficult to ask for something to be given back?
- Do people in your country often share the ownership of something? If so, what?
- Do many people use public bikes in your country? Why/why not?
- Why are some people not willing to share the ownership or their cars or houses with others, even family members?
- Do you think in the future there might be more need for shared ownership? Why/why not?
- What are the most common things people can't live without? Why?
- Why do you think children often get attached to one particular toy?
- Who is more into recent technology, youngsters or elders? Why?
- Why do you think some people always want to buy latest technological gizmos?
- Is it easy to throw away old things? Why/why not?
- Why do you think some people find it hard to get rid of old things?
- Is your society obsessed with buying new things? Why?
- Do you think media affect our shopping decisions? Why/why not?
- Is there enough choice of products?
- Is a wide choice of products necessary? Why/why not?
- Why do people often buy things they do not really need?
- Are the same things important to contemporary people as were to our predecessors? Why/why not?

- How important is family in your culture?
- Has family been more or less important lately?
- Do you think that at different stages in life we see different things as most important? Why/why not?
- Is society too materialistic these days? Why/why not?
- What types of groups can young people belong to in your country?
- Why do you think people enjoy belonging to groups?
- Do men and women prefer the same types of groups? Why/why not?
- Do many people in your country socialize online? Why/why not?
- Is it important to socialize online in modern society? Why/why not?
- Has technology helped us be a part of a social group? Why/why not? If so, how?
- Do you think that people contact each other face to face much less these days due to technology? Why/why not?
- What makes teamwork successful? Why?
- What kind of a person can be a good team player?
- Do you think that in order to become successful one needs to be able to work in a team well? Why/why not?
- What kind of a team in better, a diverse one or the one where members bring different views in? Why?
- What kind of qualities does a good team leader need? Why?

- **something electronic you often use/you bought for your home/a time when you had a problem with a piece of equipment/a piece of equipment which you find useful**

VOCAB :

1. to cross that bridge when one comes to it (phr.) = to deal with a problem when and if it arises
2. a high-tech gizmo /ˈgɪzməʊ/ (phr.) = a small piece of equipment, especially one whose name you do not know
3. a brand /brænd/ (n.) = a product that has its own name and is made by one particular company
4. handy /ˈhændi/ (adj.) = useful
5. a feature /ˈfiːtʃə(r)/ (n.) = an important aspect of sth
6. on its last legs (phr.) = old, in bad condition and not likely to continue working
7. supersonic /ˌsuːpə(r)ˈsɒnɪk/ (adj.) = faster than the speed of sound
8. to be mechanised /ˈmekənaɪzd/ (adj.) = using machines
9. high-definition (adj.) = providing images that show a lot of detail very clearly
10. to realise the untapped potential of sth /ʌnˈtæpt/ (phr.) = to understand the unused possibilities of sth
11. essential (adj.) = completely necessary
12. a predicament /prɪˈdɪkəmənt/ (n.) = a difficult situation that is not easy to get out of
13. to smash sth up (v.) = to destroy sth completely by violently breaking it into many pieces
14. to tear sth to bits /teə(r)/ (phr.) = to damage sth completely
15. to fall to bits (phr.) = to be in a very bad condition because of being old or badly made
16. a technophile (n.) = an enthusiast of technology
17. a portable device /ˈpɔː(r)təb(ə)l/ (phr.) = a device easy to carry
18. in mint condition (phr.) = in new or perfect condition

179

19. to be subjected to wear and tear (phr.) = to undergo changes and damage that normally happen when sth is being used
20. to lag behind /læg/ (v.) = to not be as successful or advanced as sth else
21. technical jargon /ˈteknɪk(ə)l ˈdʒɑː(r)gən/ (phr.) = special words and phrases that are only understood by people who work in technology
22. to think sth through (v.) = to consider the facts about sth in an organized and thorough way
23. a storm in a teacup (phr.) = a lot of trouble about sth that is not important
24. to take the bull by the horns (phr.) = to deal with a problem in a very direct and confident way
25. to sort out the problem (phr.) = to deal with the problem successfully

PART 3 :

- What do you think are the main differences between mobile phones today and the first mobile phone?
- What kinds of technological products are popular in your country? Why?
- What main disadvantages do you see in the technological products today? Why?
- Why do you think some people always need to buy latest technological products?
- Who likes technology more, men or women? Why?
- What kind of technological devices will we use in our homes in the future?
- How does technology help in the workplace? Why?
- What do people use mobile phones for?
- Are some people too dependent on their phones today?
- What are some downsides of using a mobile phone?
- What do you think could be done to stop school children from using mobile phones during class?
- Do you think people rely on technology too much these days? Why/why not?
- Will new technological products shorten working hours? Why/why not? How?
- What types of equipment do we use on a daily basis?
- Do we really need so much equipment in our homes? Why/why not?
- Is housework load lighter today than it was in the past? Why/why not?
- Do people rely on equipment too much?
- What are some disadvantages on depending on equipment at home?
- What kinds of people can be good at designing machinery and equipment? What skills do they need? Why?
- Do schools in your country cultivate students design skills? Why/why not?
- What's the latest innovation popular in your culture?
- Do you agree that the best inventions are always very simple? Why/why not?
- How are new inventions tested before production?
- Does your government support innovation? If so, in what way?
- Should inventions be shared with other countries? Why/why not?
- How can the world benefit from the latest inventions? Why?
- Does buying a new piece of equipment make people feel better? Why/why not?
- Do we become lazier because of so much equipment around us? Why/why not?
- Do people still get their things repaired today? Why/why not?
- Why do things break?
- Is it better to fix things or just throw them away? Why?
- Should people learn how to fix certain things in life? If so, which ones? Why/why not?

↻ Should children be taught how to fix basic things at school? Why/why not?

↻ What kind of a person could be a great inventor? Why?

↻ Do you think people were more inventive in the past? Why/why not?

↻ Can anyone invent something?

↻ Is being inventive something we are born with or something we can learn?

↻ Are inventors important to a country? Why?

↻ Can inventors contribute to country's economy in any way? If so, how?

- **something expensive you would like to buy/you bought/a time when you saved money for something special/something special you would like to buy in the future/something you bought but haven't used much**

VOCAB :

1. a genius of bargaining /ˈdʒiːniəs/ (phr.) = someone who is excellent at bargaining for a lower price

2. daylight robbery (n.) = sth much too expensive

3. a rip-off (n.) = sth that is more expensive than it should be

4. a white elephant (n.) = sth that is useless and may have cost a lot of money

5. to cost an arm and a leg (phr.) = very expensive

6. bells and whistles (phr.) = the additional features that make sth attractive to use or look at

7. to have deep pockets (phr.) = to have abundant financial resources

8. is a luxury /ˈlʌkʃəri/ (phr.) = with the best and most expensive things around you

9. sth is an absolute necessity /ˈæbsəluːt nəˈsesəti/ (phr.) = sth is extremely needed

10. a spending pattern /ˈpætə(r)n/ (phr.) = the way one spends their money

11. conspicuous consumption /kənˈspɪkjʊəs kənˈsʌmpʃ(ə)n/ (phr.) = a great amount of things people buy or use

12. to be economical /ˌiːkəˈnɒmɪk(ə)l/ (adj.) = not costing or spending much money

13. to be penny-wise and pound-foolish (phr.) = not willing to spend small amounts of money, but likely to spend large amounts in a stupid way

14. a source of income (phr.) = where your money comes from

15. to scrimp and save to do sth /skrɪmp/ (phr.) = to spend money only on what is necessary and to save as much as you can

16. make ends meet (phr.) = to have just enough money to buy the things that you need

17. to be broke/skint /brəʊk/skɪnt/ (adj.) = to have no money

18. abject poverty /ˈæbdʒekt/ (n.) = complete poverty

19. to cost sb a fortune /ˈfɔː(r)tʃən/ (phr.) = to cost a lot of money

20. the bill for sth is exorbitant /ɪgˈzɔː(r)bɪtənt/ (phr.) = the bill for sth is much more than reasonable

21. a status symbol /ˈsteɪtəs/ (n.) = a possession that someone is proud of and considers to be a symbol of their money or power

22. to be acquisitive /əˈkwɪzətɪv/ (adj.) = trying to get things, especially because you want them, rather than because you need them

23. vanity /ˈvænəti/ (n.) = complete lack of importance or value

24. to tighten one's belt /ˈtaɪt(ə)n/ (phr.) = to spend less money

25. to do sth on a shoestring /ˈʃuːˌstrɪŋ/ (phr.) = on a small budget

26. to be beyond someone's means (phr.) = to cost more money than your earn

27. to be dirt-cheap (adj.) = very cheap
28. a bargain /ˈbɑː(r)gɪn/ (n.) = a lower than usual price
29. to go on a shopping spree /spriː/ (phr.) = to spend a short period shopping only
30. to keep up with the Joneses /ˈdʒəʊnzɪz/ (phr.) = to try to be as rich, successful etc as your neighbours
31. sth is selling like hot cakes (phr.) = is being sold very quickly in large quantities
32. a futuristic look /ˌfjuːtʃəˈrɪstɪk/ (phr.) = looking so modern that it seems to belong to the future
33. home delivery (n.) = have products you bought brought to your home directly
34. to fork sth out (v.) = to spend money on sth, especially when you do not want to
35. to get thrown into trash (phr.) = to be thrown away
36. personal consumption (n.) = the amount of things one eats, buys, uses
37. disposable income /dɪˈspəʊzəb(ə)l/ (n.) = income remaining after deduction of taxes and other mandatory charges, available to be spent or saved as one wishes
38. an end-of-season sale (n.) = a sale event in shops happening at the end of each season

PART 3 :
- Which is more important to most people, the quality of the product or its price?
- Is there any way a consumer can check the quality of a product before purchasing it?
- What kinds of things would most people like to buy if they had enough money? Why?
- Do you think some people overpay for products that could be bought cheaper? Why?
- Can having lots of money make a person unhappy? Why/why not?
- How do people usually become rich in your culture?
- Which is more important to become rich, luck or hard work? Why?
- Do you think everybody wants to become rich one day? Why/why not?
- What other things do you see as important in life, except for money? Why?
- Which country is the wealthiest at the moment in your opinion?
- What benefits can people enjoy living in a rich country?
- Do rich countries have any responsibility to help the poorer ones? Why/why not?
- Should one country give money to another? If so, in what situation? Should the giving country control how the money is spent? Why/why not?
- What do people in your country usually save money for? Why?
- Is it easy to save money? Why/why not?
- Who is better at saving money, men or women? Why?
- Do you think some people spend more money then they make? Why/why not?
- Is marketing making people spend more? Why?
- Do many people in your country have credit cards? Why/why not?
- Do credit cards make people spend more? Why/why not?
- Can spending money make a person happy? Why/why not?
- Are people in your country generally good at managing money? Why/why not?
- How do families decide what to spend their money on? Why?
- Do you think it is common for governments to waste public money? Why/why not?
- Do you think people spend too much time on shopping these days? Why/why not?
- What are some recent changes in shopping habits?
- How can people use the time spent on shopping more productively?
- How does advertising affect how much and what we buy?

- Does advertising have any positive effects on consumerism? Why/why not?
- Do you think all businesses need to advertise their products? Why/why not?
- Is consumerism a good contribution to the society and economy? Why/why not?
- How does consumerism influence the environment? Why?
- Do you think growth in consumerism can be sustained? Why/why not? If so, how?
- Do people in your country like shopping? Why/why not?
- Can shopping be a hobby? Why/why not?
- What are some advantages of shopping in a huge mall?
- What are some disadvantages of shopping in a huge mall?
- Which is more important, quality or price? Why?
- Do people in your country recycle? Why/why not?
- What products do people recycle most often? Why?
- What materials are easy to recycle? Why?
- Is it important to recycle? Why/why not?
- Do you think that people recycle more often now than they did in the past? Why/why not?
- Will more people recycle in the future? Why/why not?
- Is there a lot of advertising in your country? Why/why not?
- Do people believe advertisements? Why/why not?
- Is advertising in your country powerful? Why/why not?
- Do people often buy advertised products? Why/why not?
- Do advertisements make people buy unnecessary things? Why/why not?
- Does the government control advertisements in your country? Why/why not?
- What are some benefits of governmental regulations on adverts?
- What are some drawbacks of governmental regulations on adverts?

- **something you have shared with others**

VOCAB :
1. to split sth /splɪt/ (v.) = to share sth by diving it into separate parts
2. to have a hand in sth (phr.) = to help to make sth happen
3. to apportion sth /əˈpɔː(r)ʃ(ə)n/ (v.) = to divide sh between two or more people
4. to divvy up /ˈdɪvi/ (v.) = to divide or share sth
5. to share responsibilities (v.)
6. reluctant /rɪˈlʌktənt/ (adj.) = not willing to do sth
7. reticent /ˈretɪs(ə)nt/ (adj.) = not willing to provide information about sth
8. to share your experience (phr.)
9. readily given /ˈredɪli/ (adj.) = easily given
10. ungrudging /ʌnˈgrʌdʒɪŋ/ (adj.) = done willingly
11. the lion's share (phr.) = the largest part of sth
12. share and share alike (phr.) = used for saying that is is best to share things equally and fairly
13. a trouble shared is a trouble halved (proverb) = talking to someone else about one's problems helps to alleviate them
14. to share sb's sorrow/ˈsɒrəʊ/ (phr.) = to share sb's great sadness

PART 3 :

- What are the benefits of sharing?
- Do people in your country often share food during celebrations? Why/why not?
- How do you think children could be taught to share?
- Why do you think some people don't like sharing?
- Is it important to share with others? Why/why not?
- What things do children dislike sharing with others and why?
- Why is it important for children to learn how to share things at young age?
- Do people often need to share space in your country? Why/why not?
- What does sharing accommodation look like in your country? Why?
- Do people in your country often share transportation? Why/why not? On what occasions?
- Do you think that when people share something there should be some clearly established rules? Why/why not?
- How do people normally share information? Why?
- Do you think the Internet makes people share too much personal information? Why/why not?
- Should researchers share their findings with others freely? Why/why not?
- Do you think that it is necessary for countries to share information if they want to cooperate better? Why/why not?

- **useful advice you received/gave**

VOCAB :

1. to go against the grain (phr.) = to be completely different from what you feel is right for you
2. to oppose a tendency /ˈtendənsi/ (phr.) = to disagree with a habit
3. to convince sb to do sth /kənˈvɪns/ (v.) = to persuade sb to do sth
4. sb has no say in sth (phr.) = sb has no power of decision
5. to go in one ear and out the other (phr.) = used for saying that sb does not remember what you say or pay attention to it
6. to miss out on vital information /ˈvaɪt(ə)l/ (phr.) = to lose an opportunity to get important information
7. it makes sense to do sth (phr.) = it is practical and sensible to do sth
8. to take note of sth (phr.) = to try to remember sth because you think it is important
9. sth is of the essence /ˈes(ə)ns/ (phr.) = sth is very important
10. if all else fails (phr.) = used for saying that, if other methods do not succeed, there is one last thing that you can try to do
11. for what it's worth (phr.) = used when you are telling someone sth and you are not sure how useful it is
12. sth is your best bet (phr.) = the thing or action that gives the best chance of a successful result
13. to turn sb down (v.) = to not accept an offer/advice
14. If I were you, I'd… (phr.) = used for giving advice
15. If I were in your shoes, I'd… (phr.) = used for giving advice
16. to take sth into account (v.) = to consider sth when you are trying to make a decision
17. You'd better…(phr.) = used to give advice
18. Try to… (phr.) = used to give advice
19. I hadn't thought about that. (phr.) = I have no idea about it

184

20. Yes, you'll right. I'll do that. (phr.) = used when one accepts advice
21. Of course! I should have thought about that! (phr.) = used when one agrees with the advice received
22. You may be right, but here's the thing...(phr.) = used when one isn't convinced whether the advice received would work

PART 3 :
- Who usually gives personal advice in your country? Why?
- Is it better to be advised by family or friends? Why?
- Do teachers in your country often advise students on personal issues? Why/why not?
- What kind of a person can be a good advisor? Why?
- Who's the best person to give career advice in our life? Why?
- Who usually advises young people on which job to choose in your country? Why?
- Do young people follow career advice given? Why/why not?
- Is it better to listen to others' advice or make decisions alone? Why?
- What does a person need to know to be able to advice someone on their career? Why?
- Which advice on consumer goods is the most reliable one? Why?
- Where can we find reliable information about products we buy?
- Do you think that some harmful products need to be banned? Why/why not?
- Who is responsible for people's health, government, manufacturers or individuals? Why?
- What advice do young people usually need? Why?
- What's the best way to give advice to a young person? Why?
- In local communities in your country, are there any advisors one can turn to? Why/why not?
- Who could be a good community advisor? Why?
- Do you think that only old people can give good advice? Why/why not?
- Does a person need some special training to advise others? Why/why not? If so, what kind?
- What can happen if people follow advice blindly? Why?
- Do you think it is often true that what people do and advise others aren't the same things? Why/why not?
- Which is more useful, receiving a piece of advice or learning from our own mistakes? Why?

- **your favourite meal/a dish you know how to make/foreign food you have tried**

VOCAB :
1. vitamins /ˈvɪtəmɪnz/ (n.) = natural substances found in food that are necessary to keep your body healthy
2. fibre/ˈfaɪbə(r)/ (n.) = the parts of fruit, vegetables and grains that your body cannot digest
3. to be nutritious /njuːˈtrɪʃəs/ (adj.) = providing the substances that people need in order to be healthy
4. fattening /ˈfæt(ə)nɪŋ/ (adj.) = making you fat
5. savoury /ˈseɪvəri/ (adj.) = tasting of salt or spices and not sweet
6. to be a far cry from (phr.) = to be very different from sth
7. to be entirely different from /ɪnˈtaɪə(r)li/ (phr.) = to be completely different from sth
8. herbs /hɜː(r)bz/ (n.) = plants used for adding flavour to food or as a medicine

185

9. condiments /ˈkɒndɪmənts/ (n.) = things like salt, pepper or a sauce that you put on food or the table to make it taste better

10. fragrant /ˈfreɪgrənt/ (adj.) = with a pleasant smell

11. a barbecue /ˈbɑː(r)bɪˌkjuː/ (n.) = a meal at which mean and other food is cooked and eaten outside, often a meal that you invite friends to

12. to pressure cook /ˈpreʃə(r)/ (v.) = to cook with a tight lid that allows pressure of steam to cook food quickly

13. to garnish /ˈgɑː(r)nɪʃ/ (v.) = to add sth to a dish of food to make it look more attractive

14. to preserve /prɪˈzɜː(r)v/ (v.) = to prevent food from decaying by adding a chemical substance to it

15. to precook /ˌpriːˈkʊk/ (v.) = to cook sth partly so that it can be heated and eaten at a later time

16. a secret recipe /ˈsiːkrət ˈresəpi/ (phr.) = a set of instructions for cooking or preparing a particular food that only a few people know about

17. sth can touch my taste buds (phr.) = sth very tasty for sb

18. metabolism /məˈtæbəˌlɪz(ə)m/ (n.) = all the chemical processes by which cells produce the energy and substances necessary for life

19. to be a gourmet /ˈgʊə(r)meɪ/ (n.) = sb who knows a lot about good food and wine

20. to be mouth-watering (adj.) = food that smells and looks very good

21. to be disgusting /dɪsˈgʌstɪŋ/ (adj.) = extremely unpleasant

22. a pickled cabbage /ˈpɪk(ə)ld/ (n.) = a cabbage preserved in vinegar or salt water

23. to pan-fry (v.) = to fry in a pan in a small amount of fat

24. a dip /dɪp/ (n.) = a thick cold sauce for dipping pieces of food into before eating them

25. to stir-fry (v.) = to cook food quickly by moving it around in hot oil

26. a steamer /ˈstiːmə(r)/ (n.) = a container used for cooking food with steam

27. to steam /stiːm/ (v.) = to cook food with steam

28. deep-fried (adj.) = cooked in a lot of hot oil

PART 3 :

☞ Are there any rules of how to behave during meals in your country?

☞ Is it important to have meals together in your country? Why/why not?

☞ Is watching TV and eating at the same time a good habit? Why/why not?

☞ What's a typical diet in your country?

☞ Has diet in your country changed recently? Why/why not?

☞ Does advertising influence people's diet? How?

☞ Is food in school canteens usually healthy? Why/why not?

☞ How can schools encourage healthy diet?

☞ Is being a farmer a good job in your country?

☞ Is agriculture an important part of your country's culture? Why/why not?

☞ How have ways of producing food changed over the years?

☞ Can technology be helpful in food production?

☞ Do you think in the future scientific and technological developments might affect the way food is made? To what extent? How?

- **your favourite means of transport/a trip you took by public transport**

VOCAB :

1. a rickshaw /ˈrɪkˌʃɔː/ (n.) = a small vehicle with two wheels used for carrying passengers and pulled by sb riding a bicycle or walking
2. a tuk-tuk (n.) = a three-wheeled motorized vehicle used as a taxi (usually in Thailand)
3. a double-decker bus /ˌdʌb(ə)l ˈdekə(r)/ (n.) = a bus that has both an upper and a lower level where people can sit
4. to move freely (phr.) = to move without restrains
5. to do harm to (phr.) = to be harmful to
6. a transport infrastructure /ˈɪnfrəˌstrʌktʃə(r)/ (n.) = the set of transport systems that affect how well it operates
7. a road network (n.) = a system of streets and roads in a place
8. rails /reɪlz/ (n.) = metal bars that a train travels on
9. a carriage /ˈkærɪdʒ/ (n.) = one of the vehicles that are joined together to make a train
10. a compartment /kəmˈpɑː(r)tmənt/ (n.) = one of the separate spaces into which a railway carriage is divided
11. a window seat (n.) = a seat that is next to a window on a plane, trains or bus
12. an aisle seat /aɪl/ (n.) = a seat in a train, plane etc next to an aisle
13. a flight crew /kruː/ (n.) = the people involved with flying a plane including the plots, the flight engineer and the navigator
14. to be airsick /ˈeə(r)ˌsɪk/ (adj.) = to feel ill as a result of the movement of a plane
15. a passenger ship (n.) = a ship carrying people
16. to embark /ɪmˈbɑː(r)k/ (v.) = to get on a ship in order to begin a journey
17. a pier /pɪə(r)/ (n.) = a structure built out from the land over water and used for getting on and off boats
18. to be seasick /ˈsiːˌsɪk/ (adj.) = to fell ill from the movement of the boat
19. to be carsick /ˈkɑː(r)ˌsɪk/ (adj.) = to feel ill from travelling in a car
20. a convertible /kənˈvɜː(r)təb(ə)l/ (n.) = a car with a roof that can be folded back or removed completely
21. a dirigible /ˈdɪrɪdʒəb(ə)l/ (n.) = an aircraft like a large balloon with an engine
22. a four-by-four (n.) = a vehicle that has four-wheel drive
23. a vespa (n.) = an Italian brand of a scooter
24. a limousine /ˌlɪməˈziːn/ (n.) = a large expensive comfortable car in which a screen separates the driver from the passengers

PART 3 :

- What can be done to solve traffic congestion?
- What in your opinion is the biggest reason of the increasing car accidents?
- What types of public transports are there in your country?
- What is the most popular means of public transport? Why?
- What are some advantages of public transportation?
- What are some disadvantages of public transportation?
- How can more people be encouraged to use public transport instead of their private cars?
- Why do people like to use their private cars so often? Even for a short trip?

- What is the percentage of families owing a car in your country?
- Why do you think some families have more than one private car?
- Is there any way the government can limit private car ownership? If so, how?
- Do you think people will use their private cars more in the future? Why/why not?
- How can public transport be more environmentally friendly?
- What new innovative means of transport will we have in the future?

- **your favourite weather/season**

VOCAB :

1. drizzle /ˈdrɪz(ə)l/ (n/v) = very light rain
2. to hit a park/garden (phr.) = to go to a park/garden
3. to turn on my hibernation mode /ˌhaɪbə(r)ˈneɪʃ(ə)n/ (phr.) = to sleep a lot
4. torrential rain /təˈrenʃ(ə)l/ (n.) = rain that falls fast in large amounts
5. the pollution is a real killer (phr.) = the pollution is terrible
6. a catastrophe /kəˈtæstrəfi/ (n.) = an event that causes a lot of damage or makes a lot of people suffer
7. a cold snap/spell (n.) = a period of cold weather
8. a meteorological satellite /ˌmiːtiərəˈlɒdʒɪk(ə)l ˈsætəlaɪt/ (n.) = a satellite measuring weather conditions
9. humid /ˈhjuːmɪd/ (adj.) = hot and wet in a way that makes you feel uncomfortable
10. scorching /ˈskɔː(r)tʃɪŋ/ (adj.) = extremely hot
11. freezing /ˈfriːzɪŋ/ (adj.) = very cold
12. continental /ˌkɒntɪˈnent(ə)l/ (adj.) = characteristic of mainland Europe
13. monsoonal /mɒnˈsuːnəl/ (adj.) = rainy, accompanying the wet monsoon
14. tropical /ˈtrɒpɪk(ə)l/ (adj.) = from the hottest parts of the world
15. subtropical /ˌsʌbˈtrɒpɪk(ə)l/ (adj.) = from or relating to the warm parts of the world just north and south of the tropics
16. a sandstorm /ˈsæn(d)ˌstɔː(r)m/ (n.) = a strong wind in the desert that blows clouds of sand in the air
17. in the shade /ʃeɪd/ (phr.) = where sun does not go
18. cloudless sky /ˈklaʊdləs/ (phr.) = sky without any clouds
19. sweltering hot /ˈswelt(ə)rɪŋ/ (adj.) = extremely hot in an uncomfortable way
20. a heavy downpour /ˈdaʊnˌpɔː(r)/ (n.) = a large amount of rain that falls quickly
21. it's bucketing down (phr.) = to rain very hard
22. to get drenched through /drentʃt/ (phr.) = to get thoroughly wet
23. a rainbow /ˈreɪnˌbəʊ/ (n.) = a curved line of colours that appears in the sky when the sun shines while it is raining
24. to tremble with cold /ˈtremb(ə)l/ (phr.) = to shake with cold
25. sleet /sliːt/ (n.) = a mixture of snow and rain
26. to be snowed in (phr.) = to be unable to leave a place because a lot of snow has fallen there
27. to be cut off (phr.) = to not be able to leave a place due to snow

PART 3 :

- What are the main changes in weather in your country in recent years?

- Why is the weather getting worse in your opinion?
- What do people generally think about pollution?
- What pollution is the most serious one in your country?
- What can be done about pollution?
- What do you know about global warming?
- What kinds of clothes do people in your country wear at different times of year? Why?
- Do most people in your country watch the weather forecast? Why/why not?
- Can any daily activities by affected by weather? If so, how?
- How many seasons does your country have?
- How do different seasons vary in your country?
- Do you celebrate any festivals related to seasons? Why/why not?
- How do different seasons affect the country's economy?
- Has your country experienced a climate change in recent years?
- What problems might global warming bring in the future?
- Who should be responsible for controlling global warming? Why?
- How does the weather change in your country at different times of the year?
- Do you think more people like cold or warm weather? Why?
- What are some good sides of living in a cold country?
- What jobs have close connection with weather conditions?
- How can working in extremely hot or cold conditions be difficult?
- What jobs are limited to particular seasons? (farming, tourism)
- How does seasonal work affect communities?
- What are some recent climate changes in the world? Why?
- Are people generally concerned with climate change? Why/why not?
- What measures have been taken so far to tackle the climate change problem?

- **your first mobile phone**

VOCAB :
1. to speed up the pace of sth (phr.) = to make sth work faster
2. to bring liberation from sth /ˌlɪbəˈreɪʃ(ə)n/ (phr.) = to give freedom from sth
3. mute mode /mjuːt/ (n.) = a setting on your phone that allows you to keep it on but with silent option
4. to upgrade sth /ʌpˈɡreɪd/ (v.) = to make a device more powerful or effective
5. no frills (phr.) = used for referring to sth that is good enough but has no unnecessary extra features
6. the battery has run down (phr.) = the battery has stopped working
7. on the blink (phr.) = if a piece of electrical equipment is on the blink, it is not working very well
8. a manufacturer /ˌmænjʊˈfæktʃərə(r)/ (n.) = a company that makes a product
9. cumbersome /ˈkʌmbə(r)s(ə)m/ (adj.) = not simple, fast or effective enough and difficult or annoying to use
10. handy /ˈhændi/ (adj.) = useful
11. to make improvements /ɪmˈpruːvmənts/ (phr.) = to make changes for the better
12. sth has improved beyond all recognition /ˌrekəɡˈnɪʃ(ə)n/ (phr.) = sth has improved in a way that makes it impossible to recognize what it is

13. to be an instrument of social change /ˈɪnstrʊmənt/ (phr.) = to help social change
14. a SIM card /ˈsɪm ˌkɑː(r)d/ (n.) = subscriber identity module card: a small piece of plastic that is inside a mobile phone and contains information about the person who uses the phone
15. reception /rɪˈsepʃ(ə)n/ (n.) = signal strength
16. a flip phone (n.) = a small mobile phone that closes by folding in the middle to make it easier to carry
17. to be cutting out (phr.) = for a phone: to stop working
18. feature /ˈfiːtʃə(r)/ (n.) = an important part or aspect of sth
19. mobile phone culture is out of control (phr.) = everyone is crazy about mobile phones
20. to switch it off in public places (phr.) = to not use your phone in public places
21. compact /ˈkɒmpækt/ (adj.) = smaller than most things of the same kind
22. a smartphone /ˈsmɑː(r)t ˌfəʊn/ (n.) = a mobile phone that also works as a small computer, allowing you to store information and write letters and reports
23. mobile entertainment /ˌentə(r)ˈteɪnmənt/ (n.) = entertainment one can enjoy on their phone
24. useful functions /ˈfʌŋkʃ(ə)ns/ (phr.) = a handy purpose of a phone

PART 3 :
- ☞ Are phones popular in your country? Why/why not?
- ☞ When do children in your country start using mobile phones? Why?
- ☞ Is it easy for everybody to learn how to use a mobile phone? Why/why not?
- ☞ What are some drawbacks of mobile phones?
- ☞ Do people prefer to have a smart phone today? Why/why not?
- ☞ In what ways do people use mobile phones in your country? Why?
- ☞ Is texting popular in your country? Why/why not?
- ☞ Do many people use apps? Why/why not?
- ☞ What apps are the most popular in your country? Why?
- ☞ Do you think mobile phones need to have the Internet connection? Why/why not?
- ☞ Does modern technology always help people? Why/why not?
- ☞ Do you think business people might travel less due to advanced technology soon? Why/why not?
- ☞ Do you think that translation on the Internet will decrease a number of people learning foreign languages? Why/why not?
- ☞ Can modern technology help to learn a foreign language? How?
- ☞ How does technology influence communication between people?

- **something you did that was relaxing**

VOCAB:
1. bliss /blɪs/ (n.) = complete happiness
2. idle away /ˈaɪd(ə)l/ (v.) = to spend time relaxing and doing nothing
3. a dabbler /ˈdæb(ə)lə/ (n.) = a person who never keeps doing one activity for long
4. a shot in the arm (phr.) = something that quickly makes a bad situation much better
5. to ease tension /iːz ˈtenʃ(ə)n/ (phr.) = to release pressure
6. to let your hair down (phr.) = to relax and enjoy yourself because you are in a comfortable environment
7. to practise yoga /ˈjəʊgə/ (phr.) = to do yoga

8. an early night (phr.) = an occasion when you go to bed earlier than usual
9. a night out (phr.) = an evening when you go out to a cinema, theatre, party etc.
10. to unwind /ʌnˈwaɪnd/ (v.) = to begin to relax after you have been working hard or feeling nervous
11. to take your mind off sth (phr.) = to make you stop thinking or worrying about sth
12. to laze about /leɪz/ (v.) = to relax and enjoy yourself, doing no work
13. to loosen up /ˈluːs(ə)n/ (v.) = to relax or to become less serious
14. to have a kip /kɪp/ (phr.) = to have a short sleep
15. to sit in silence (phr.) = to sit without taking or any other distractions
16. to get on the dance floor (phr.) = to relax by dancing

PART 3 :
⮧ What do young people in your country like to do in their spare time?
⮧ What free time activities do the elderly enjoy?
⮧ Do you think people have enough leisure time today? Why/why not? What would they need to change to have more free time?
⮧ Are leisure activities today the same with the ones in the past? Why/why not?
⮧ Can doing nothing be relaxing? Why/why not?
⮧ In today's world, is it easy to relax? Why/why not?
⮧ Why do some people have so many troubles relaxing?
⮧ Is it important to take time off work/study regularly? Why/why not?
⮧ Do you think people will have more time for relaxation in the future? Why/why not?
⮧ Do you think people in different countries relax in the same or different way? Why?
⮧ Is the leisure industry a big one in your country?
⮧ How can the leisure industry grow even stronger in the future?

• **something you would really like to do in the future/a plan you have for your future/something you would like to do in your future (not related to work or studies)**

VOCAB :
1. to balance work and family /ˈbæləns/ (phr.) = to create a healthy level of time spent with family and spent working
2. an incentive /ɪnˈsentɪv/ (n.) = sth that makes you want to do sth or to work harder, because you know that you will benefit by doing this
3. a goal /ɡəʊl/ (n.) = sth that you hope to achieve
4. to pursue career goals /pə(r)ˈsjuː/ (phr.) = to follow your carer plans
5. to have one's heart set on sth (phr.) = to aim at sth
6. to make up one's mind (phr.) = to make a decision
7. the only fly in the ointment is /ˈɔɪntmənt/ (phr.) = the only problem that spoils sth is
8. a stepping stone in the pursuit of my dreams (phr.) = a step in a process of reaching you dreams that helps you to move forward
9. foreseeable future /fɔː(r)ˈsiːəb(ə)l/ (phr.) = future that easily be imagined before it happens
10. to go ahead with sth (v.) = to start or continue to do sth, especially after waiting for permission
11. to bring sth forward (v.) = to change the date or time of an event so that it happens earlier
12. to look ahead to sth (v.) = to think about what is likely to happen, or to plan what you are going to do in the future

13. to go according to plan /əˈkɔː(r)dɪŋ ˌtuː/ (phr.) = to go as planned

PART 3 :
- Do people in your country usually plan for the future? Why/why not?
- What kinds of plans do youngsters make in your country?
- What kinds of plans do elderly make in your country?
- Why do you think some people do not make plans?
- Is it easy to plan?
- What are some good ways to plan things?
- Should people plan? Why/why not?
- Is it true that people get better at planning things once they grow older? Why/why not?
- Can people learn anything from plans that didn't work out? If so, what?
- Is it important to plan one's retirement? Why/why not?
- How can people make sure their retirement is well-planned?
- Who usually takes care of the older family members in your country?
- Is it easy to take care of an older family member? Why/why not?
- How should the government deal with a large ageing population? Why?

- **something difficult which you did well**

VOCAB :
1. Achilles' heel /əˌkɪliːz ˈhiːl/ (n.) = a weak feature that sb or sth has that could cause failure or could be attacked
2. an arduous process /ˈɑː(r)djuəs/ (phr.) = an extremely difficult process
3. to be very rewarding /rɪˈwɔː(r)dɪŋ/ (adj.) = giving you satisfaction, pleasure or profit
4. to use lateral thinking /ˈlæt(ə)rəl/ (phr.) = to solve problems in a way where you use your imagination to try to think about it in a different or unusual way
5. willpower /ˈwɪlˌpaʊə(r)/ (n.) = the ability to control your thoughts and behaviour in order to achieve sth
6. to overcome a dilemma /dɪˈlemə/ (phr.) = to succeed in a situation in which you have to make a difficult decision
7. trial and error (phr.) = a way of finding a good method that involves trying several possibilities and learning from your mistakes
8. feeble attempts /ˈfiːb(ə)l/ (phr.) = not good enough to achieve the intended result
9. a major hurdle /ˈhɜː(r)d(ə)l/ (phr.) = a big problem
10. minor difficulties (phr.) = small problems
11. to pay off (v.) = if sth that you do pays off, it brings you some benefit
12. to bear fruit /beə(r)/ (phr.) = to have a successful result
13. You reap what you sow. (phr) = used for saying that sth happens to sb because of what they have done in the past
14. to exert yourself /ɪɡˈzɜː(r)t/ (phr.) = to use a lot of physical or mental effort
15. to come to fruition /fruːˈɪʃ(ə)n/ (phr.) = to get the result that you wanted to achieve from a plan or idea
16. gruelling /ˈɡruːəlɪŋ/ (adj.) = very difficult and involving a lot of continuous effort
17. a perennial problem /pəˈreniəl/ (phr.) = a problem that never seems to go away

18. to get to grips with sth (phr.) = to start to deal with a problem, situation or job that you have to do
19. to exacerbate sth /ɪɡˈzæsə(r)beɪt/ (v.) = to make a problem become worse
20. it's more trouble than it's worth (phr.) = used to say sth is not worth making too much effort to succeed at it
21. easier said than done (phr.) = used for telling sb that what they are advising you to do is not easy to achieve
22. to roll your sleeves up (phr.) = to prepare to work
23. sth takes some doing (phr.) = sth takes a lot of effort

PART 3 :
↪ Do most people like challenges? Why/why not?
↪ What challenges do young people need to face when they are starting their adult life? Why?
↪ Do you think that people in the past had to deal with the same kinds of problems? Why/why not?
↪ Can a little bit of difficulty help a person in any way? How?
↪ Are young people in your country generally ambitious? Why/why not?
↪ What is the biggest ambition of young people in your country today? Why?
↪ Is it generally important for young people to have ambitions? Why/why not?
↪ What can happen if someone is too ambitious?
↪ What types of jobs involve an element of risk? Why?
↪ Why do some people choose to do dangerous jobs?
↪ Who is responsible for a disaster in dangerous jobs?
↪ Should people doing risky jobs be paid more? Why/why not?

- **something you did that helped you learn another language**

VOCAB :
1. a language organization habit (phr.) = the way you organize your language studies
2. slang /slæŋ/ (n.) = words or expressions that are very informal and are not considered suitable for more formal situations
3. native pronunciation /ˈneɪtɪv prəˌnʌnsiˈeɪʃ(ə)n/ (phr.) = authentic articulation
4. drilling /drɪlɪŋ/ (n.) = learning through repetition
5. a loanword /ˈləʊnˌwɜː(r)d/ (n.) = a word from one language that is used in another language without being changed
6. lexicon /ˈleksɪkən/ (n.) = all the words and phrases in a language
7. to brush up on sth (v.) = to practise and improve your skills or knowledge of sth
8. to divert sb's attention from sth /daɪˈvɜː(r)t/ (phr.) = to distract sb from sth
9. an example sentence (phr.) = a sentence one uses with a new word to know its usage
10. context /ˈkɒntekst/ (n.) = the words surrounding a particular word that help to give it its meaning
11. ambiguous /æmˈbɪɡjuəs/ (adj.) = not clear
12. to interpret sth /ɪnˈtɜː(r)prɪt/ (v.) = to translate what sb is saying in one language into another language
13. transparent /trænsˈpærənt/ (adj.) = simple, clear and easy to understand
14. self-explanatory (adj.) = easy to understand without explanations
15. precise (adj.) = exact and accurate

16. figurative /ˈfɪɡərətɪv/ (adj.) = if you use words in a figurative way, you use them not in their normal literal meaning but in a way that makes a description more interesting or impressive
17. to sink in (v.) = to become completely understood
18. durable materials /ˈdjʊərəb(ə)l/ (phr.) = materials that are able to stay in good condition for a long time and after being used a lot
19. out of necessity /nəˈsesəti/ (phr.) = sth must be done
20. linguistically-diverse /lɪŋˈgwɪstɪkli daɪˈvɜ:(r)s/ (adj.) = including elements from many different languages
21. to enjoy learning for learning's sake /seɪk/ (phr.) = to like learning just for the benefit of learning
22. to relish the intellectual challenge /ˈrelɪʃ/ (phr.) = to get great satisfaction from the intellectual challenge
23. to open up a world of possibilities (phr.) = to broaden sb's horizons
24. to constantly be exposed to (phr.) = to be in contact with
25. to become proficient /prəˈfɪʃ(ə)nt/ (phr.) = to become very skilful at sth that you have learnt
26. immersion /ɪˈmɜ:(r)ʃ(ə)n/ (n.) = a method of teaching a foreign language in which teachers and students use only the foreign language during classes
27. a visual learner /ˈvɪʒʊəl/ (n.) = a person who learns best by seeing
28. a target language /ˈtɑ:(r)gɪt/ (n.) = the language into which a text, document or speech is translated
29. to brainstorm /ˈbreɪnˌstɔ:(r)m/ (v.) = to discuss ideas in a brainstorming discussion

PART 3 :
- ↻ What foreign languages are common in your country? Why?
- ↻ What in your opinion is the most difficult about learning a foreign language? Why?
- ↻ Who learns a foreign language faster: younger people or older people? Why?
- ↻ What's the best method to learn a foreign language?
- ↻ Is it important to know a foreign language? Why/why not?
- ↻ How does learning a foreign language benefit us?
- ↻ Are foreign languages more important in a contemporary world than they were in the past? Why/why not?
- ↻ If the whole society learns a foreign language, wouldn't that affect their culture negatively? Why?
- ↻ What are dominant languages in the world today? Why these ones?
- ↻ Do you think your native language might become dominant in the future? Why/why not?
- ↻ Is it good or bad to have one international language? Why?
- ↻ Do you think that if a country accepts one global language it also needs to accept one global culture? Why/why not?

- **a competition you would like to join/you took part in**

VOCAB :
1. to compete on a level playing field (phr.) = to compete in a situation that is fair for all the people involved
2. fair and square (phr.) = in a way that is clear and fair, so that no one can complain or disagree
3. evenly-matched /ˈi:v(ə)nli/ (adj.) = matched equally

4. to dominate /ˈdɒmɪneɪt/ (v.) = to control sth or sb
5. a cliffhanger (n.) = a situation in which it is not clear what will happen next
6. to be predictable /prɪˈdɪktəb(ə)l/ (adj.) = to happen in a way that you would expect
7. team spirit (n.) = an enthusiastic attitude towards working or playing together with other people as a team
8. good sportsmanship /ˈspɔː(r)tsmənʃɪp/ (phr.) = fair and honest behaviour in sport
9. to hammer sb /ˈhæmə(r)/ (v.) = to defeat sb
10. to set the pace /peɪs/ (phr.) = to set the speed of sth
11. to forge ahead /fɔː(r)dʒ/ (v.) = to move forwards in a strong steady way
12. to take some beating /ˈbiːtɪŋ/ (phr.) = to be damaged because of performing badly or being criticized
13. to hot up (v.) = to become very lively or exciting
14. to come out on top (phr.) = to be the best or the winner
15. a dark horse (n.) = sb who wins a race, competition, election etc that no one expected them to win
16. neck and neck (phr.) = involved in a close race, competition etc.
17. to give it your all (phr.) = to do your best
18. to give sth your best shot (phr.) = to do your best
19. to play it safe (phr.) = to avoid taking any risks
20. a close shave (phr.) = a situation in which you only just avoid sth dangerous or unpleasant

PART 3 :
- What are some common competitions people in your country can join? Why?
- Why do some people enjoy taking part in competitions more than others?
- Are competitions good or bad for children? Why?
- Can people learn anything from participating in competitions? Why/why not?
- Is motivation something we naturally have or do we need to develop it? Why?
- How should a good boss motivate his or her workers? Why?
- What is a better motivation, money or a sense of achievement? Why?
- Can children do better at school if they are brought up in a strict family? Why/why not?
- Is public recognition generally important to people in your country? Why/why not?
- What personal achievements should be recognized publicly? Why?
- Why is it important to be publically praised to some people?
- Do you think that today's pop culture sees different things as praiseworthy? Why/why not?

- **a concert you went to/a live event you have been to/would like to go to/a public/art/cultural event you attended/a place you know where people go to listen to music**

VOCAB :
1. a newsworthy event /ˈnjuːzˌwɜː(r)ði/ (phr.) = an interesting event
2. sensational /senˈseɪʃ(ə)nəl/ (adj.) = very excitingand surprising
3. a drink on the house (phr.) = a free drink
4. an open-air concert (phr.) = a concert conducted out in the open space
5. a symphony orchestra /ˈsɪmfəni ˈɔː(r)kɪstrə/ (n.) = a large orchestra that plays classical music
6. blaring music /bleə(r)ɪŋ/ (phr.) = very loud music
7. to be suffused with /səˈfjuːzd/ (v.) = to be surrounded by

8. to be steeped in /stiːpt/ (v.) = to have a lot of particular quality or thing
9. acoustic music /əˈkuːstɪk/ (n.) = without using electronic equipment
10. a composer /kəmˈpəʊzə(r)/ (n.) = sb who writes music, especially classical music
11. sonata /səˈnɑːtə/ (n.) = a piece of classical music for one instrument, usually the piano or for one instrument and a piano
12. a tune /tjuːn/ (n.) = a song or piece of music
13. to give a concert (phr.) = to perform at a concert
14. a podium /ˈpəʊdiəm/ (n.) = a small raised area where sb stands to conduct an orchestra
15. a soloist /ˈsəʊləʊɪst/ (n.) = sb who performs a musical solo
16. an accompanist /əˈkʌmpənɪst/ (n.) = sb who plays the supporting music while sb else sings or plays the main tune
17. the new and the old intermingle /ˌɪntə(r)ˈmɪŋg(ə)l/ (phr.) = the old and new mix
18. a live band (n.) = a musical group performing live
19. jam-packed with people (phr.) = full of people
20. highly spirited /ˈspɪrɪtɪd/ (adj.) = expressing opinions in a determined way
21. an expressive art form /ɪkˈspresɪv/ (phr.) = an art form that clearly shows the thoughts or feelings of the artist
22. a bit over the top (phr.) = more than what is considered normal or suitable
23. a choir /kwaɪə(r)/ (n.) = a group of singers who perform together
24. to pay through the nose for sth (phr.) = to pay much too much for sth
25. a genre /ˈʒɒnrə/ (n.) = a particular style
26. booze, merch and dope /buːz/ /mɜː(r)tʃ/ /dəʊp/ (phr.) = alcohol, good that are sold related to the band and drugs
27. a jazz trio /ˈtriːəʊ/ (n.) = a group of three musicians who play jazz music together
28. good acoustics /əˈkuːstɪks/ (phr.) = the way that sound is heard in a room, as a result of the room's shape and size
29. to bounce off the piano lid /baʊns/ (phr.) = to move energetically from the top of the piano, usually for dramatic effect during performance

PART 3:
↻ Where can children hear music?
↻ Is listening to music beneficial to children? Why/why not?
↻ Should every child learn how to play a musical instrument? Why/why not?
↻ How has popular music in your country changed over the years?
↻ Should music be available on the Internet for free? Why/why not?
↻ How has technology influenced the way music is being made today?
↻ How will music be different in the future?
↻ Is technology going to replace traditional music?
↻ How can music be helpful with memories?
↻ Why do we remember certain songs but forget others?
↻ Which way is better to express feelings, music or words? Why?
↻ Can music help cultural understanding? How?
↻ Can we live without music?
↻ Do many people in your country go to concerts today? Why/why not?
↻ What's the best place to listen to music? Why?

- Why do people enjoy live concerts?
- Is the experience one gets at a live concert different from listening to music at home? How?
- Who is the best live performer in your country? Why?
- Are concerts popular in your country?
- Are concert tickets pricey? Why/why not?
- Do you think artists will perform live more in the future? Why/why not?
- How does technology affect the way concerts are organised?

- **a family event/gathering you were a part of/from your childhood**

VOCAB :
1. a good laugh /lɑːf/ (phr.) = a fun time
2. a bit of a drag /dræg/ (phr.) = boring
3. a convivial atmosphere /kənˈvɪviəl/ (phr.) = a friendly and making you feel welcome atmosphere
4. a large feast /fiːst/ (n.) = a large meal for a lot of people in order to celebrate sth
5. to go through the hassle of cooking /ˈhæs(ə)l/ (phr.) = to trouble yourself with cooking
6. a festive season /ˈfestɪv/ (phr.) = bright and colourful in a way that makes you think of a celebration
7. to sit around the dinner table (phr.) = to sit at the table and enjoy the meal and time together
8. to catch up on our news (phr.) = to exchange the latest changes in everyone's lives
9. the whole clan /klæn/ (phr.) = a large group of families that are related to each other
10. an extended family /ɪkˈstendɪd/ (n.) = a family group that included grandparents, cousins, aunts etc.
11. to tell sidesplitting jokes /ˈsaɪdˌsplɪtɪŋ/ (phr.) = to tell extremely humorous jokes
12. a get-together (n.) = an informal social occasion
13. to stay up all night (phr.) = to not go to sleep and talk all night
14. to bring us closer together (phr.) = to strengthen the bond between us
15. You can choose your friends, but you can't choose your family. (phr.) = you should accept your family as they are because you did not choose them
16. the atmosphere turned sour /ˈsaʊə(r)/ (phr.) = the atmosphere was unpleasant, unfriendly
17. the be-all and end-all of our lives (phr.) = the main aim in our lives
18. a safety net (n.) = a plan or system that is designed to protect people or prevent serious problems
19. material and emotional needs (phr.) = the needs related to our lives and out feelings
20. strong traditions based around families (phr.)
21. to have sb's best interest at heart (phr.) = to care for someone's well-being a lot

PART 3 :
- What does a typical family in your country look like? Why?
- What are some main roles in a typical family? Why?
- Have the family roles always been this way in your country? Why/why not?
- Do you think parents treat boys and girls in the same or different way? Why?
- How can parents prepare their children well for adult life? Why?
- At what age do children become adults in your country? Do you think it's the right age? Too early? Too late?
- What skills do children need to acquire to become successful adults in the future? Why?

- Do you think children grow up too fast today? Why/why not?
- Is being an adult only about age?
- Do young people in your country experience a lot of pressure today? Why/why not? If so, from where?
- How do young people usually deal with pressure?
- How can youngsters be helped to achieve their dreams?
- Do you think that young people these days are too materialistic? Why/why not?
- What are the values of young people in your society?

- **a friend's success that made you proud**

VOCAB :

1. to be down-to-earth (adj.) = practical and sensible
2. to set priorities /praɪˈɒrətiz/ (phr.) = to pay attention to the most important things
3. motivated /ˈməʊtɪˌveɪtɪd/ (adj.) = enthusiastic and determined
4. enthusiastic /ɪnˌθjuːziˈæstɪk/ (adj.) = very interested in sth or excited by it
5. to express your admiration /ˌædməˈreɪʃ(ə)n/ (phr.) = to express your respect
6. to be supportive of sb /səˈpɔː(r)tɪv/ (adj.) = helpful and sympathetic
7. to be superior to sth/sb /sʊˈpɪəriə(r)/ (adj. = to be better than sth/sb else
8. to make a meal of sth (phr.) = to take more time or care than is necessary when you are doing sth
9. a resounding success /rɪˈzaʊndɪŋ/ (phr.) = a complete success
10. to turn out well/badly (phr.) = to have a good/bad result
11. the secret of sb's success (phr.) = a particular way of achieving success
12. a stroke of luck (phr.) = sth that happens by chance and that helps you to achieve sth
13. to realize your potential (phr.) = to understand your capabilities
14. to not put a foot wrong (phr.) = to do nothing wrong and not make any mistakes
15. to overcome obstacles /ˈɒbstək(ə)lz/ (phr.) = to succeed at solving problems
16. to go from strength to strength (phr.) = to develop or process with increasing success
17. to prop sth up /prɒp/ (v.) = to support
18. a roaring success /ˈrɔːrɪŋ/ (phr.) = a huge success

PART 3 :

- How can a student become successful at school?
- How are good students usually rewarded in schools in your country?
- Is being good at artistic subjects as important as excelling in academic subjects? Why/why not?
- In your culture, is it important to parents to have successful children? Why/why not?
- In what ways can a person become successful at work?
- How can a boss motivate his or her workers?
- Is success at work important to people in your culture? Why/why not?
- What does a person need to do to become successful?
- What problems do people need to overcome to become successful? Why?
- Is successful life really important in your culture? Why/why not?
- Does success equal happiness? Why/why not?
- What is more important for success, opportunity or ability? Why?
- Can people feel successful if they are not publically recognized? Why/why not?

- **something you are good at/bad at**

VOCAB :
1. sth is a subject very close to my heart (phr.) = sth deeply interests me
2. to be passionate about sth /ˈpæʃ(ə)nət/ (adj.) = to have very strong feelings, interest or enthusiasm about sth
3. avid /ˈævɪd/ (adj.) = very enthusiastic about sth you do regularly
4. bokeh photography (n.) = the visual quality of the out-of-focus areas of a photographic image
5. to make beaded jewellery /ˈbiːdɪd/ (phr.) = to make jewellery decorated with beads
6. compelling /kəmˈpelɪŋ/ (adj.) = interesting or exciting enough to keep your attention completely
7. time-consuming (adj.) = takes a long time to do
8. ravishing /ˈrævɪʃɪŋ/ (adj.) = very beautiful
9. a buff /bʌf/ (n.) = sb who is very interested in and knows a lot about a particular subject
10. to be a freak of sth /friːk/ (phr.) = sb who is extremely interested in a particular subject or activity
11. to be a do-gooder /ˌduː ˈɡʊdə(r)/ (n.) = sb who always tries to help people, especially people who are poor or in trouble
12. a social butterfly (phr.) = sb who is socially dynamic, networking, charismatic and gregarious
13. flower arranging (n.) = the skill of arranging flowers in an attractive way to use for decoration
14. gifted /ˈɡɪftɪd/ (adj.) = with an impressive natural ability
15. competent /ˈkɒmpɪtənt/ (adj.) = capable of doing sth in a satisfactory or effective way
16. a pastime /ˈpɑːsˌtaɪm/ (n.) = sth thay you do regularly for fun in your free time
17. a leisure pursuit /ˈleʒə(r) pə(r)ˈsjuːt/ (phr.) = a free time activity
18. a side interest (phr.) = an additional hobby
19. avocation (n.) = a hobby
20. recreational /ˌrekriˈeɪʃ(ə)n(ə)l/ (adj.) = done or used for enjoyment

PART 3 :
- What are young people in your country usually good at? Why?
- What are the elderly good at? Why?
- How can a person become good at something?
- Why are we bad at some things?
- Can we learn any skill? Why/why not?
- What does it take to become a master of something?
- Do you think people are too lazy to become good at something?
- How does technology affect the way we learn things?
- What are the most needed experts in your country? In what fields?
- What is the most difficult thing to learn? Why?
- Do you think people will become more dependent on machines in the future? Why/why not?

- **a long journey you took/a memorable trip you took/a trip you are planning to take soon/a school trip you remember well**

VOCAB :
1. to widen your view /ˈwaɪd(ə)n/ (phr.) = to increase your knowledge

2. to get a better insight into sth /ˈɪnsaɪt/ (phr.) = to get a better understanding of sth
3. to hit the road (phr.) = to start a journey
4. to stick around (v.) = to remain in a place for longer than you originally intended, especially in order to wait for sth to happen
5. to venture off the beaten path /ˈventʃə(r)/ (phr.) = to go far away from the places that people usually visit
6. to be in the middle of nowhere (phr.) = a long way from any town or city
7. an itinerary /aɪˈtɪnərəri/ (n.) = a plan of a journey that you are going to make, including information about when and where you will travel
8. luggage /ˈlʌɡɪdʒ/ (n.) = bags and suitcases that you take on a journey
9. to travel light (phr.) = travel with minimum luggage
10. to go back and forth (phr.) = to move first in one direction and then in the opposite direction many times
11. to embark on a long trip /ɪmˈbɑː(r)k/ (phr.) = to depart
12. landscapes flashing by (phr.) = landscapes passing quickly
13. a home base (n.) = a place where you start from and often finish
14. to be thrown into a totally new situation (phr.) = to experience sth completely new
15. to explore a place /ɪkˈsplɔː(r)/ (phr.) = to travel to a place in order to learn about it
16. wanderlust /ˈwɒndə(r)ˌlʌst/ (n.) = a strong wish to travel
17. to fulfil my need for adventure (phr.) = to satisfy my desire to travel
18. Have your wits about you wherever you go. (phr.) = think quickly and make sensible decisions
19. comfy /ˈkʌmfi/ (adj.) = comfortable
20. earplugs /ˈɪə(r)ˌplʌɡz/ (n.) = small pieces of plastic or rubber that you put in your ears to keep noise or water out
21. a blindfold /ˈblaɪn(d)ˌfəʊld/ (n.) = sth that is tied over sb's eyes so that they cannot see (used for sleeping while travelling)
22. to move around the cabin /ˈkæbɪn/ (phr.) = to stretch your legs on a plane
23. to stretch /stretʃ/ (v.) = to make your body as straight as possible so that your muscles become long and tight
24. to feel dehydrated /ˌdiːhaɪˈdreɪtɪd/ (adj.) = to feel weak or ill because you have lost a lot of water from your body by not drinking enough or through sweating, vomiting or having diarrhoea
25. to kill time on your trip (phr.) = to make time seem to pass more quickly by doing sth instead of just waiting
26. to recline your seat back /rɪˈklaɪn/ (phr.) = to make the back of your seat lean backwards to be more comfortable
27. to organize a trip (phr.) = to plan a trip
28. to coordinate a trip (phr.) = to be in charge of a trip
29. a permission form /pə(r)ˈmɪʃ(ə)n/ (n.) = a slip on which parents usually allow their children to attend an event or a trip
30. up-front payment (phr.) = payment made in advance
31. a chaperone /ˈʃæpərəʊn/ (n.) = a parent or teacher who goes to a school on a school trip to help to look after the children
32. a meticulously built programme /mɪˈtɪkjʊləsli/ (phr.) = a carefully prepared trip

PART 3 :

- ↪ Do you think it's better to travel alone or with other people? Why?
- ↪ Is it dangerous to travel alone? Why?
- ↪ What are the most popular travel destinations among people in your country?
- ↪ What's the best time of the year in your country to travel?
- ↪ Do you think in the future people will travel more or less?
- ↪ How has the way people travel changed over the years?
- ↪ Is backpacking a popular way of travelling in your country? Why/why not?
- ↪ Why more and more students want to have further education abroad?
- ↪ How do people usually travel? Why?
- ↪ What's the most economical means of transport? Why?
- ↪ How will people travel in the future? Why?
- ↪ Why does travel industry grow in one country but does not in another? What does it depend on?
- ↪ How do international airports influence local people?
- ↪ In the future, do you think people will travel internationally less or more? Why?
- ↪ What kinds of problems do people making a long journey need to face?
- ↪ How can one make a long journey more comfortable? Why?
- ↪ Is it better to depart on a long journey alone or with companions? Why?
- ↪ Why do so many people want to travel to foreign countries today?
- ↪ What are some necessary preparations people need to make before going abroad?
- ↪ Which foreign countries are the most popular destinations today? Why?
- ↪ How do people decide which country to visit?
- ↪ Do you think people travel overseas more now than in the past? Why/why not?
- ↪ Do you think people will travel abroad more in the future? Why/why not?
- ↪ Can travel be educational? Why/why not? If so, how?
- ↪ What can travellers learn about a country they travel to?
- ↪ Can people learn anything about themselves while travelling abroad? If so, what?
- ↪ Is travelling the best way to expand intercultural understanding? Why/why not?

- **a party you attended/held**

VOCAB :

1. a guest /gest/ (n.) = a person invited to a party
2. a housewarming party /ˈhaʊsˌwɔː(r)mɪŋ/ (n.) = a party to celebrate moving to a new house or flat
3. a fancy dress party (n.) = a party where everyone dresses up in costume as other people
4. to order sth /ˈɔː(r)də(r)/ (v.) = to ask for food or drink in a restaurant or hotel
5. a bash /bæʃ/ (n.) = a party or celebration
6. a booze-up /buːz/ (n.) = a party or social event where people drink a lot of alcohol
7. a party pooper /ˈpɑː(r)ti ˌpuːpə(r)/ (n.) = sb who is not willing to take part in an activity or who spoils other people's enjoyment of it
8. to go clubbing /ˈklʌbɪŋ/ (v.) = to go out in the evening to dance and drink in clubs
9. to light the candles /laɪt/ (phr.) = to make the candles start burning
10. the party is in full swing (phr.) = at the highest level
11. to come to an end (phr.) = to finish
12. to run the risk of waking up the neighbours (phr.) = be so loud as to wake up the neighbours

13. to put up with noise (phr.) = to tolerate the noise
14. to create a warm atmosphere (phr.) = to make people feel welcome
15. to make a cake (phr.) = to bake a cake
16. life and soul of the party (phr.) = sb who is very lively at social events
17. a bouncy castle /ˈbaʊnsi/ (n.) = a large plastic structure filled with air, and often in the shape of a castle for children to play in
18. refreshments /rɪˈfreʃmənts/ (n.) = sth to eat or drink during a party
19. a host/hostess /həʊst/ˈhəʊstɪs/ (n.) = a person who invites sb to a party
20. to lay on food and drink /leɪ/ (phr.) = to provide food and drink
21. to make a contribution to sth /ˌkɒntrɪˈbjuːʃ(ə)n/ (phr.) = sth that you do or bring to help make a party successful
22. a lot of clearing up (phr.) = a lot of things to clean after a party
23. disposable plates and cutlery /dɪˈspəʊzəb(ə)l/ (phr.) = plates and cutlery that will be thrown away after they are used
24. a gatecrasher /ˈɡeɪtˌkræʃə/ (n.) = a person that goes to a party without having been invited
25. deafening music (phr.) = very loud music
26. to drown out the conversation /draʊn/ (phr.) = to prevent a conversation from being heard by making a louder noise
27. to liven things out /ˈlaɪv(ə)n/ (phr.) = to make things more interesting or exciting
28. to get carried away (phr.) = to become so excited or involved in sth that you lose control of your feelings or behaviour
29. to socialize /ˈsəʊʃəlaɪz/ (v.) = to spend time with other people socially
30. the more the merrier (phr.) = used for saying that you will be happy if more people come or take party in what you are doing
31. a party animal (n.) = sb who enjoys going to lots of parties
32. to hang out (v.) = to spend time in a particular place or with particular people

PART 3 :

↻ How often do people throw family parties in your country? Why?
↻ What special occasions do people in your country celebrate as a family? Why?
↻ Are parties generally important to families? Why? In what way?
↻ Do people in your culture celebrate now in the same way they used to? If not, what changed?
↻ Where would most people typically throw a party? Why?
↻ Is there any traditional festival that only cities or villages would celebrate? What is it?
↻ What do people usually do at local celebrations? Why?
↻ Are young people still interested in local celebrations? Why/why not?
↻ Do old people enjoy taking part in local celebrations? Why/why not?
↻ Where do most national celebrations in your country come from? What's their origin?
↻ Why do you think there are so many global festivals, e.g. International Women's Day or New Year? Is it good for the local culture? Why/why not?
↻ What new celebrations can we expect in the future? Why?
↻ Do you think future generations will still hold on to traditional celebrations? Why/why not?
↻ Is tradition still important? Why/why not?

- **a perfect day off**

VOCAB :
1. to soothe your nerves /suːð/ (phr.) = to make you more calm and relaxed
2. to get refreshed from hard work /rɪˈfreʃt/ (phr.) = to feel more lively and comfortable after a long time of work
3. the tension melts away /ˈtenʃ(ə)n/ (phr.) = the feeling of being nervous or worried that you cannot relax goes away
4. ideal (adj.) = as good as you can imagine
5. utopian /juːˈtəʊpiən/ (adj.) = based on the idea that life can be perfect
6. too good to be true (phr.) = so good that you cannot believe that such a situation is possible or can continue
7. to unbutton /ʌnˈbʌt(ə)n/ (v.) = to relax
8. to take a load off someone's mind (phr.) = to bring someone relief from anxiety
9. in the back of beyond (phr.) = a remote or inaccessible place
10. in the sticks (phr.) = rural areas
11. in the middle of nowhere (phr.) = a place that is remote and isolated
12. impulsive /ɪmˈpʌlsɪv/ (adj.) = done suddenly, without thinking what the result will be
13. spur-of-the-moment (adj.) = sudden and not planned or thought about carefully

PART 3 :
- How much free time do people in your country have?
- What do people in your country usually do in their spare time? Why?
- How many days off do people get? Is it enough?
- Do people plan their days off? Why/why not?
- What day of the week is the best for a day off? Why?
- How have leisure activities changed over the years? Why?
- Do you think people will have more free time in the future? Why/why not?
- How does the lack of spare time affect people's well-being?
- How do people apply for a day off in your country?
- What are some common reasons people give for a personal day off?

- **a picnic you went on/meal outdoors you enjoyed**

VOCAB :
1. a picnicker /ˈpɪknɪkə/ (n.) = a person having a picnic
2. an outdoor meal /ˌaʊtˈdɔː(r)/ (phr.) = a meal outdoors
3. an alfresco meal /ælˈfreskəʊ/ (phr.) = eaten outside, in the open air
4. a cookout /ˈkʊkˌaʊt/ (n.) = an informal meal eaten outside with food usually cooked over a fire or on a barbecue
5. a barbecue /ˈbɑː(r)bɪˌkjuː/ (n.) = a meal at which meat and other food is cooked and eaten outside
6. paper plates and cutlery /ˈkʌtləri/ (phr.) = plates made of paper and the knives, forks and spoons that you use for eating food
7. a picnic basket /ˈbɑːskɪt/ (n.) = a container for carrying things needed for a picnic

8. a blanket /ˈblæŋkɪt/ (n.) = a thick cover made of wool or another material that you use to sit on while having a picnic
9. a thermos flask /ˈθɜː(r)məs flɑːsk/ (n.) = a container that keeps liquids hot or cold
10. snacks (n.) = a small amount of food that you eat between meals
11. finger food (n.) = food served in such a form and style that it can conveniently be eaten with the fingers
12. a cooler /ˈkuːlə(r)/ (n.) = a machine uses for keeping liquids cold
13. an esky /ˈeski/ (n.) = a container for keeping food and drinks cold that you can carry around with you
14. refreshments /rɪˈfreʃmənts/ (n.) = sth to eat or drink during an event such as a meeting or party
15. Frisbee /ˈfrɪzbi/ (n.) = a round piece of plastic that you throw to another person in a game played outside
16. a picnic hamper /ˈhæmpə(r)/ (n.) = a picnic basket
17. a rug /rʌg/ (n.) = a small carpet that covers part of a floor

PART 3 :
↪ When do people eat outdoors in your culture? Why?
↪ Are picnics common in your country? Where? Why/why not?
↪ Who enjoys picnics more, young people or older people? Why?
↪ What are some advantages of eating outdoors?
↪ What are some disadvantages of having a meal outdoors?
↪ Do people prefer to eat at home or in a restaurant? Why?
↪ Can you provide some advantages of eating at home?
↪ What are some disadvantages of eating in a restaurant?
↪ Was people's diet healthier in the past? Why/why not?
↪ How does unhealthy diet influence society?
↪ What can a government do to rise public's awareness of healthy food?
↪ Can most people in your country cook? Why/why not?
↪ Should young people study traditional recipes from their countries? Why/why not?
↪ How can a country promote its cuisine globally?
↪ Is it good to promote a country's cuisine in the world? Why/why not?
↪ Is there a lot of foreign food in your country? Why/why not?
↪ Do you think individual national cuisines will survive in the future?
↪ Is there any type of food that people all around the world enjoy eating?

- **a school subject you liked/disliked/people ask you for information about/interests you now**

VOCAB :
1. promising /ˈprɒmɪsɪŋ/ (adj.) = likely to be successful or very good
2. an elective class /ɪˈlektɪv/ (n.) = a class that you choose to do, rather than one that you must do
3. a curriculum /kəˈrɪkjʊləm/ (n.) = the subjects that students study at a particular school
4. theoretical knowledge /ˌθɪəˈretɪk(ə)l/ (phr.) = knowledge based on theories or ideas instead of on practical experience
5. to be curious about /ˈkjʊəriəs/ (adj.) = eager to know
6. do not rely on linear thinking /ˈlɪniə(r)/ (phr.) = do not rely on thinking in one dimension only

7. academic performance /ˌækəˈdemɪk/ (n.) = results of studying at school
8. a standardised test /ˈstændə(r)daɪz/ (n.) = a test that is administered and scored in a consistent, standard manner
9. to be ingrained in you /ɪnˈɡreɪnd/ (adj.) = has been in your for a long time and cannot easily be changed
10. to soak sth in (v.) = to spend time experiencing and enjoying sth
11. to wade through sth (v.) = to read or deal with a lot of boring information
12. to crack the books /kræk/ (phr.) = to study
13. to not have the foggiest idea (phr.) = to know nothing about sth
14. a mature student /məˈtʃʊə(r)/ (phr.) = a sensible student
15. to play truant /ˈtruːənt/ (phr.) = to skip classes without permission
16. coursework /ˈkɔː(r)sˌwɜː(r)k/ (n.) = school work that a student must do as part of a course of study

PART 3 :

☞ Do primary school children study the same subjects when they are in secondary school? Why?
☞ How many years do students stay at school in your country?
☞ Is school generally important to us? Why/why not?
☞ Besides knowledge, what else do we get from going to school?
☞ Are there any activities held by schools in your country? What kind?
☞ Do you think it is good to have an equal number of boys and girls at school? Why/why not?
☞ Is general knowledge important? Why/why not?
☞ Can television contribute to increasing people's general knowledge? Why/why not?
☞ How can we use general knowledge in everyday life?
☞ Are TV quizzes and shows popular in your country? Why/why not?
☞ What's the best source of knowledge, in your opinion? Why?
☞ Do teachers in your country encourage students to ask questions during classes? Why/why not?
☞ Should teachers encourage students to ask questions in class? Why/why not?
☞ Is finding information quickly more important than finding the correct information? Why/why not?
☞ What are some disadvantages of the Internet as a source of information?
☞ What kind of person is suitable for conducting academic research? Why/why not?
☞ Should scientific discoveries be widely shared? Why/why not?
☞ Which areas of research are the most promising ones in your country at the moment? Why?
☞ Which areas of research will excel in the future? Why do you think so?
☞ What are the most popular subjects among high school students in your country? Why?
☞ What makes a subject interesting?
☞ How can a teacher make his or her subject more appealing to students?
☞ In your opinion, which subjects shouldn't be taught at schools in the future?
☞ What new subjects should be taught at schools in the future? Why?
☞ How can teachers help struggling students?
☞ Is a lot of homework really necessary to comprehend a subject better? Why/why not?
☞ Do schools in your country teach practical subjects? (driving, cooking, doing housework) Should they?
☞ In your country, can you choose the subjects you'd like to study in high school? Why/why not?

- What is the age when students are allowed to leave school and finish their education in your country?
- Is it better to study in a single-sex school or in a co-educational school? Why?
- Is it important for children to enjoy what they study? Why/why not?
- Which classes are usually fun in your country? Why?
- Should children study many different subjects or just a few subjects? Why?
- Can television be a reliable source of knowledge?
- What's the best source of knowledge? Why?
- Can older people be a good source of knowledge? Why/why not?
- What kind of a person can be good at researching things?
- In which academic fields is research extremely crucial? Why?
- Who should fund academic projects? Why?
- Do you think that too much time and money is being spent on research these days? Why/why not?

- **a situation when you encountered a wild animal/an interesting animal/an animal you'd like to have**

VOCAB :

1. to be fascinated by /ˈfæsɪneɪtɪd/ (adj.) = to be very interested or attracted by
2. to live a carefree life /ˈkeə(r)ˌfriː/ (phr.) = to live happily without any worries, problems or responsibilities
3. to behave aggressively /əˈgresɪvli/ (phr.) = to behave in an angry that shows you want to fight or attack sb
4. a divine animal /dɪˈvaɪn/ (phr.) = an animal treated like a god
5. to be on the verge of extinction /ɪkˈstɪŋkʃ(ə)n/ (phr.) = close to stop existing
6. cruel /ˈkruːəl/ (adj.) = sb who is cruel enjoys causing pain to other people or animals
7. outrageous /aʊtˈreɪdʒəs/ (adj.) = very shocking or unreasonable
8. a demise of /dɪˈmaɪz/ (n.) = the time when sth stops existing
9. affection /əˈfekʃ(ə)n/ (n.) = a feeling of liking and caring about sb/sth
10. faithfulness /ˈfeɪθf(ə)lnes/ (n.) = used about a dog who behaves like a friend
11. loyal /ˈlɔɪəl/ (adj.) = willing to support or to be a friend
12. a companion /kəmˈpænjən/ (n.) = sb who is with you
13. a cage /keɪdʒ/ (n.) = a container made of wire or metal bars and used for keeping birds or animals in
14. inhumane /ˌɪnhjuːˈmeɪn/ (adj.) = treating people or animals in a very cruel way
15. to be held in captivity /kæpˈtɪvəti/ (phr.) = when animals are kept in a place such as a park or zoo instead of living in their natural environment
16. a sanctuary /ˈsæŋktʃuəri/ (n.) = a special area where animals live in a natural environment protected from people
17. a safari park (n.) = a large area of land where wild animals are kept so that people can drive through and watch them
18. biodiversity /ˌbaɪəʊdaɪˈvɜː(r)səti/ (n.) = the variety of different types of plant and animal life in a particular region
19. to maltreat /mælˈtriːt/ (v.) = to be violent or cruel to an animal

20. an aquarium /əˈkweəriəm/ (n.) = a glass or plastic container that fish and other water animals are kept in
21. animal rights (n.) = a belief that animals should be treated well by people and not killed or used for scientific experiments
22. animal exploitation /ˌeksplɔɪˈteɪʃ(ə)n/ (phr.) = unfair treatment of animals
23. a food chain (n.) = the natural process in which one living thing is eaten by another
24. a bird of prey /preɪ/ (n.) = a bird that hunts and eats other animals
25. animal testing (n.) = tests done on animals
26. a habitat /ˈhæbɪtæt/ (n.) = the type of place that a particular animal usually lives in
27. wildlife /ˈwaɪldˌlaɪf/ (n.) = animals, birds and plants that live in natural conditions
28. flora /ˈflɔːrə/ (n.) = all the plants that grow in a particular region
29. fauna /ˈfɔːnə/ (n.) = all the animals that live in a particular area
30. to make good companions (phr.) = to be good friends
31. to crave companionship /kreɪv/ (phr.) = to want company desperately
32. stray animals /streɪ/ (phr.) = animals lost or without a home

PART 3 :
↻ Are zoos popular in your country? Why/why not?
↻ Can zoos educate children? How?
↻ Who likes to visit zoos more, younger people or older people? Why?
↻ Is it right to keep animals in cages? Why/why not?
↻ What wild animals are common in your country?
↻ Why do some people like to keep pets?
↻ How do people use animals for their own benefit? (e.g. furs, cooking)
↻ Do you think animals need to be killed?
↻ Do you think science can provide alternative products so that animals could be saved? How?
↻ How are endangered species protected in your country?
↻ How does an increase in population influence the wildlife? Why?
↻ Are safari parks good for animals? Or only for people? Why?
↻ Do you think countries should work together to save endangered species these days? If so, how?
↻ What's the best way to learn about animals? Why?
↻ Do you have biology classes in schools? Why/why not?
↻ Are TV programmes about wildlife a good way to learn about animals? Why/why not?
↻ Is it beneficial for children to have pets? Why/why not?
↻ Can a child learn anything from having a pet? If so, what? Why/why not?
↻ How can rare animals be saved?
↻ Do you think keeping rare animals in zoos is the best way to keep them safe? Why/why not?
↻ Is it possible for governments to protect rare animals in the wild? Why/why not?
↻ What can you and me do to help save rare animals? Why?
↻ How would you describe a relationship between humans and animals?
↻ Is it morally right to use animals for scientific research? Why/why not?
↻ Should people generally care about animal extinction? Why/why not?
↻ How do you see the relationship between humans and animals in the future? Why?

- **a situation when you had to be polite/friendly with someone you didn't like**

VOCAB :

1. impeccable manners /ɪmˈpekəb(ə)l/ (phr.) = perfect ways of behaving that show a polite respect for others
2. exemplary behaviour /ɪgˈzempləri/ (phr.) = excellent so that others should try to copy it
3. cheeky /ˈtʃiːki/ (adj.) = behaving in a way that does not show respect
4. insolent /ˈɪnsələnt/ (adj.) = rude, especially when you should be showing respect
5. downright rude /ˈdaʊnˌraɪt/ (phr.) = extremely rude
6. disgraceful /dɪsˈgreɪsf(ə)l/ (adj.) = extremely bad or shocking
7. to return the favour /ˈfeɪvə(r)/ (phr.) = sth that you do for someone because they have helped you in some way
8. to be politically correct (phr.) = not offensive
9. conventions /kənˈvenʃ(ə)nz/ (n.) = ways of behaving that are generally accepted as being normal and right
10. conduct /ˈkɒndʌkt/ (n.) = the way sb behaves
11. etiquette /ˈetɪket/ (n.) = a set of rules for behaving correctly in social situations
12. social graces /ˈgreɪsɪz/ (phr.) = social behaviour
13. propriety /prəˈpraɪəti/ (n.) = behaviour that follows accepted social or moral standards

PART 3 :

- How do people show politeness in your culture?
- In what situations is being polite extremely important? Why?
- Should a person be as polite to a stranger as they are to a family member? Why/why not?
- Is there any difference between being polite and being friendly?
- Do people always express what they feel or think? Why/why not?
- How can children learn not to say what they think in certain situations?
- Are there any situations when you think it is better not to say what you think or feel? If so, what are they?
- Is it possible to always be honest? Why/why not?
- Why are foreigners sometimes seen as impolite when visiting your country?
- Should visitors adapt to the place they are in? Why/why not?
- Is politeness generally important in your culture? Why/why not?
- Do you think some cultures see politeness as more important than others? What does it depend on?
- In what situations do people need to be friendly to someone they dislike?
- Do you think that sometimes people only seem friendly but aren't? Why?
- What is the point of pretending to be friendly with someone?
- What are some main ways in which people can manipulate others into giving them what they don't want to give?
- Do you think it is better to be direct about things we want? Why/why not?
- Can impatient people ever get what they want? Why/why not?
- Can a person come across as too nice? When? Is it good?
- How important is non-verbal communication in your country?
- What universal body language do people in your country use? Why?

↷ Is it possible to judge whether someone is lying by looking into the person's eyes? Why/why not?

↷ How can people who do not speak a common language communicate effectively? Why?

- **a time when you received good service from a company/shop/restaurant**

VOCAB :

1. impeccable /ɪmˈpekəb(ə)l/ (adj.) = perfect
2. sluggish /ˈslʌgɪʃ/ (adj.) = rather slow
3. courteous /ˈkɜː(r)tiəs/ (adj.) = polite
4. overbearing /ˌəʊvə(r)ˈbeərɪŋ/ (adj.) = too confident
5. sullen /ˈsʌlən/ (adj.) = unwilling to smile
6. brusque /bruːsk/ (adj.) = quick and rude
7. off-putting /ˌɒfˈpʊtɪŋ/ (adj.) = makes you feel you do not want to go there again
8. to go out of their way (phr.) = do everything possible
9. a prompt reply to any query /ˈkwɪəri/ (phr.) = a quick reply to a question or enquiry
10. to be responsive to complaints (phr.) = to listen, take sth seriously and then act
11. accommodating /əˈkɒməˌdeɪtɪŋ/ (adj.) = willing to understand and help
12. obliging /əˈblaɪdʒɪŋ/ (adj.) = willing and happy to do things for you
13. incompetent /ɪnˈkɒmpɪt(ə)nt/ (adj.) = failing through insufficient skill, knowledge or training
14. shoddy /ˈʃɒdi/ (adj.) = poor quality
15. substandard /ˌsʌbˈstændə(r)d/ (adj.) = below the standard expected
16. uncooperative /ˌʌnkəʊˈɒp(ə)rətɪv/ (adj.) = not supportive
17. a huge backlog of orders (phr.) /ˈbækˌlɒg/ = number of orders which are waiting to be dealt with
18. a sense of urgency /ˈɜː(r)dʒ(ə)nsi/ (phr.) = a feeling that your request is important or urgent
19. a helpline (n.) = a telephone number where you can get help if you have problems
20. to put sb on hold (phr.) = to make sb wait
21. under guarantee/warranty /ˌgærənˈtiː/ˈwɒrənti/ (phr.) = having a written promise by a company to repair or replace a faulty product

PART 3 :

↷ What kinds of jobs need to deal with the public on a daily basis in your country? Why?

↷ What kind of a person can be good at a service job? Why?

↷ Do most companies offer training to their staff? Why/why not?

↷ Do you think people working at service jobs should be trained on a regular basis? Why/why not?

↷ How do companies in your country deal with problems?

↷ From your experience, do most companies respond quickly to a problem brought by a customer? Why?

↷ What should a company do if the product they sold is faulty?

↷ What are the best ways to avoid complaints and problems with their products?

↷ What factors contribute to the success of a company? Why?

↷ What are the biggest challenges most international companies face when doing business abroad? Why?

↷ Do you think happy staff is important to most companies in your country? Why/why not? Should they be?

↻ Would you say a successful company needs to be innovative? Why/why not?

• **a situation when you helped someone/when someone helped you**

<u>VOCAB :</u>
1. One good turn deserves another. (phr.) = used for saying that you should be kind to sb who has been kind to you
2. to lend a helping hand (phr.) = to help sb
3. to be of service to sb /ˈsɜ:(r)vɪs/ (phr.) = to help or be useful to someone
4. to do sb a favour (phr.) = used to ask for help
5. to give sb a leg-up (phr.) = to help sb to make progress, especially in their career
6. to get sb out of a tight spot (phr.) = to help sb out of a difficult situation
7. to save sb's bacon (phr.) = to help sb to avoid a difficult or unpleasant situation
8. boosterish /ˈbu:stə(r)ɪʃ/ (adj.) = supporting sth enthusiastically and often uncritically
9. eager to please (phr.) = willing to do anything that other people want
10. appreciative /əˈpri:ʃətɪv/ (adj.) = showing that you are grateful
11. indebted to /ɪnˈdetɪd/ (adj.) = grateful to sb for their help
12. to be in sb's debt /det/ (phr.) = to owe gratitude to someone for a service or favour
13. beholden /bɪˈhəʊld(ə)n/ (adj.) = feeling an obligation to do sth for someone who has helped you in the past

<u>PART 3 :</u>
↻ What are main benefits of helping others?
↻ How do people in one community usually help each other? In what way?
↻ Do you think now people help others as much as in the past? Why?
↻ How can adults teach children that it's good to help others?
↻ Can children be helpful to the elderly? How?
↻ What can boys and girls be helpful with? Why?
↻ Do many people in your country do some volunteering? Why/why not?
↻ What's the most common way of volunteering in your country? Why?
↻ Can volunteers also benefit from helping others? How?
↻ Why do some people like to do unpaid jobs?
↻ What kinds of problems might they meet when they do unpaid work?
↻ What international aid organisations do you know of?
  Do they work in your country? Why/why not?
↻ Are charity organizations always trustworthy? Why/why not?
↻ Are large charities always more efficient than local charities? Why/why not?
↻ Can international aid projects add to stable international relations between countries? How?
↻ Do you think colleagues should help each other at work? Why/why not?
↻ What are some main responsibilities that employers have towards their employees? Why?
↻ Is it important for a company to provide leisure facilities for its workers? Why/why not?
↻ Should one country send help to another in times of a natural disaster? Why/why not?
↻ Do countries need to share their innovations in science and medicine with others? Why/why not?
↻ Do you think different countries will cooperate more in the next couple of years? Why/why not?
↻ In what types of jobs do people always need to help others?

- What kind of a person would choose a job that requires helping others?
- Do you think people whose jobs require helping others should be paid more? Why/why not?
- How can an individual help in the community? In what ways?
- Do you think everyone should do some volunteering? Why/why not?
- Who usually makes decisions regarding communities in your country? Why?
- What can we do create a global community? Why?
- What makes people feel a part of a global community?
- Do you think we might have one language used everywhere in the world in the future? Why/why not?
- Do you think if everyone spoke the same language the world would be a better place? Why/why not?
- What would have to be changed to create an ideal world? Why?

- **a sport event you watched/attended/your favourite sport/an exciting sport**

VOCAB :

1. to make you vigorous /ˈvɪg(ə)rəs/ (phr.) = to make you full of energy, enthusiasm or determination
2. to train people to have a quick response (phr.) = to train people to have a quick reaction
3. to cultivate team spirit /ˈkʌltɪveɪt/ (phr.) = to develop the ability to work in a team
4. to mould sb's temperament /məʊld/ (phr.) = to shape sb's character
5. to burn the fat (phr.) = to lose calories and get slimmer
6. blood pumping through my veins (phr.) = to make sb feel more energetic
7. adrenalin rush /əˈdrenəlɪn/ (phr.) = a surge of a hormone increasing rates of blood circulation
8. a gym membership /ˈmembə(r)ʃɪp/ (n.) = a member card to a gym
9. mental profits (phr.) = psychological benefits
10. a strenuous sport /ˈstrenjuəs/ (phr.) = a demanding sport
11. exhaustion /ɪgˈzɔːstʃ(ə)n/ (n.) = a feeling of being extremely tired and without energy
12. to build up stamina /ˈstæmɪnə/ (phr.) = to develop the ability to work hard over a long period of time without getting tired
13. an outlet for one's energy /ˈaʊtˌlet/ (phr.) = a way of expressing one's energy
14. to let off steam (phr.) = to express your feelings of anger or excitement without harming anyone
15. to qualify for /ˈkwɒlɪfaɪ/ (v.) = to reach a particular stage of a competition by competing successfully in an earlier stage
16. a knockout stage of the competition /ˈnɒkaʊt/ (phr.) = a competition in which the player or team that loses a game does not take part in later games
17. a runner-up (n.) = a person or team that does not win a competition or race but is second or close to winning
18. victory /ˈvɪkt(ə)ri/ (n.) = winning a competition, game, race etc.
19. to be in poor form (phr.) = to be out of shape
20. a good run (phr.) = a running time that energizes one
21. unbeaten /ʌnˈbiːt(ə)n/ (adj.) = if a team, player is unbeaten, they have never been defeated in a competition
22. to go to pieces (phr.) = to be so nervous or worried that you cannot behave in a sensible way

23. to dominate the game /ˈdɒmɪneɪt/ (phr.) = to play much better than your opponents in a game or sport
24. a means of therapy /ˈθerəpi/ (phr.) = a form of treatment for an illness or medical condition
25. a gymnasium /dʒɪmˈneɪziəm/ (n.) = a large hall or room with special equipment for doing physical exercises
26. to stimulate brain chemicals (phr.) = to make one think better
27. to deliver oxygen and nutrients to your tissues (phr.)
28. sth helps your entire cardiovascular system /ˌkɑː(r)diəʊˈvæskjʊlə(r)/ (phr.) = sth helps your heart and blood vessels
29. upset sleep pattern (phr.) = abnormal sleep
30. to endorse fitness /ɪnˈdɔː(r)s/ (phr.) = to express support for being fit

PART 3 :

↻ Do you think non-competitive sports are real sports? Why/why not?
↻ Why do you think some people do sports while others don't? What does it depend on?
↻ What are some favourite leisure activities of your generation? And of your parents' generation? Why?
↻ What is your country's national sport? Why?
↻ Does your country do well at the Olympics in any particular sport?
↻ Why are some sports popular in some countries but not in others?
↻ Do men do sports more than women? Why/why not?
↻ What physical exercise do primary school/secondary school children do?
↻ What are the benefits of children playing sports at school?
↻ Does playing sports at school have any negative sides?
↻ Is it better to watch sports live or on TV? Why?
↻ What changes have there been in your country over the past 20 years in children's games and activities?
↻ In your country, do you think people are becoming less active these days? Why?
↻ If people are good at a particular sport, should they join the competition? Why/why not?
↻ What are the most popular sports to watch on TV in your country? Why?
↻ Are sports TV programmes a good chance for families to spend time together? Why/why not?
↻ Do you think we will see more sport on TV in the future? Why/why not?
↻ Who is the most admired sportsperson in your country? Why?
↻ What qualities does a person need to become a successful sportsperson? Why?
↻ Do you think some sport stars make too much money? Why/why not?
↻ Would it be good for a country to be a host of international sport event? Why/why not?
↻ Should commercial sponsors be allowed to finance international sport events? Why/why not?
↻ How can international sport events influence international relations between countries?
↻ Which sports are popular in your country? Why?
↻ Do you think as many people do sports today as in the past? Why/why not?
↻ Are PE classes important in your country? Why/why not?
↻ What sports do children practise in schools in your country?
↻ Is competition always healthy? Why/why not?
↻ Do children always need to be rewarded for schoolwork? Why/why not?
↻ How else can teachers encourage students to work hard if not through rewards?

- ⟳ Is there a lot of competition in a contemporary society? What kind?
- ⟳ Which jobs would benefit from competitive spirits? Why?
- ⟳ How important is cooperation in society? Why?
- ⟳ How can different countries cooperate?
- ⟳ Should countries cooperate? Why/why not?
- ⟳ Why do you think some people enjoy doing dangerous sports?
- ⟳ What character traits does a person need to be good at dangerous sports?
- ⟳ Do you think governments should impose laws controlling dangerous sports? Why/why not?
- ⟳ Is there a lot of sport on TV in your country?
- ⟳ Which sports do people like to watch most? Why?
- ⟳ Do you think that sport television programmes can encourage people to take up sports? Why/why not?
- ⟳ Is doing sport as a hobby comparable with doing it as a career? Why/why not?
- ⟳ What is more important to be successful at sports, training or natural ability? Why?
- ⟳ Why do you think some sportspeople are able to affect societies?

- **a team project that you participated in/a project you did as a part of your studies**

VOCAB :

1. to compromise /ˈkɒmprəmaɪz/ (v.) = to come to an understanding
2. a happy medium (n.) = a way of doing sth that is between extreme positions or is satisfactory to everyone
3. well-organized /ˈɔː(r)gənaɪzd/ (adj.) = well planned and executed
4. a social creature /ˈkriːtʃə(r)/ (phr.) = a social being
5. a common goal (n.) = a group goal
6. to boost morale /məˈrɑːl/ (phr.) = to increase the amount of enthusiasm that a group of people feel about their situation
7. to foster team spirit (phr.) = to promote team spirit
8. collaboration /kəˌlæbəˈreɪʃ(ə)n/ (n.) = working together
9. a mutual feedback /ˈmjuːtʃuəl/ (phr.) = a feedback given to each other
10. to pool diverse skills /puːl/ (phr.) = to share different skills in order to work more effectively together
11. to fit in (v.) = to belong to a group
12. to undermine the work of the team /ˌʌndə(r)ˈmaɪn/ (phr.) = to make the work of the team become gradually less effective or successful
13. to stifle individual enterprise and initiative /ˈstaɪf(ə)l/ (phr.) = to stop one's project from developing normally
14. two heads are better than one (phr.) = it's helpful to have the advice or opinion of a second person
15. to stimulate discussion /ˈstɪmjʊleɪt/ (phr.) = to encourage discussion
16. to use a clipboard /ˈklɪpˌbɔː(r)d/ (phr.) = to use a small board that you can attach papers to
17. a gigantic workload /dʒaɪˈgæntɪk/ (phr.) = a very heavy workload

PART 3 :
- ⟳ What kinds of activities should be done in a team rather than individually? Why?

- ↻ Can we learn anything from being a part of a team? If so, what?
- ↻ Are many tasks in your country done in a team? Why/why not?
- ↻ How can being a part of a team benefit children? Why?
- ↻ Does every team need a leader? Why/why not?
- ↻ What personality traits does a person need to have to be a good team member?
- ↻ What are some factors, apart from people, which make a team successful?
- ↻ What problems can team members meet? Why?
- ↻ Should creative people be a part of a team? Why/why not?
- ↻ Should creative people work alone to do their best work? Why/why not?
- ↻ What are some disadvantages of belonging to clubs?
- ↻ Do you think recent technology might reduce the need for group work in the future? Why/why not?
- ↻ How does belonging to a group benefit older people?
- ↻ Do you think people's behaviour changes when they are in a group? Why?
- ↻ Why do teenagers have the need to belong to a group?
- ↻ Why some people prefer not to be a part of group?
- ↻ Should countries join others in trade? Why/why not?
- ↻ Do you think the biggest global problems can only be tackled by international organizations? Why/why not?
- ↻ Do you think it is possible to have just one universal government? Would that be good? Why?
- ↻ Do you think children in your country have too much homework? Why/why not?
- ↻ Can doing homework help students? Why/why not? If so, in what ways?
- ↻ Should very young children be given homework as well? Why/why not
- ↻ What things can students learn outside the classroom?
- ↻ Do we still need teachers?
- ↻ Why do you think some parents decide to home school their children?
- ↻ Can a subject be learnt well without classes?
- ↻ Do all university students in your country have a computer? Why/why not?
- ↻ How can studying be troublesome for a student who does not have a computer? Why?
- ↻ Do university students use the Internet too much? Why/why not?
- ↻ Can the Internet be a reliable source of information for university students? Why/why not?
- ↻ Is it possible for computer-based learning to replace class-based teaching in the future? Why/why not?

- **a time when you lost something**

VOCAB :
1. to go down the drain (phr.) = completely lost or wasted
2. to be in vain (phr.) = without success
3. to be looking for a needle in a haystack (phr.) = to be looking for sth that is almost impossible to find
4. to misplace sth /ˌmɪsˈpleɪs/ (v.) = to put sth in the wrong place and lose it
5. to lose track of sth (phr.) = to no longer know where sth is
6. lackadaisical /ˌlækəˈdeɪzɪk(ə)l/ (adj.) = doing sth in a lazy or careless way that shows you are not really interested in it

7. slap-happy (adj.) = silly and not thinking about what you are doing
8. shambolic /ʃæmˈbɒlɪk/ (adj.) = very badly organized
9. disorganized /dɪsˈɔ:(r)ɡənaɪzd/ (adj.) = sb who is disorganized does not deal with things in a clear or sensible way
10. to have a memory like a sieve (phr.) = an extremely bad memory
11. scatterbrained /ˈskætə(r)ˌbreɪnd/ (adj.) = not thinking in an organized way and often forgetting or losing things
12. tense /tens/ (adj.) = nervous and not relaxed
13. to mislay sth /mɪsˈleɪ/ (v.) = to lose sth for a time, especially because you cannot remember where you put it
14. to be in the hot seat (phr.) = to be in a difficult position

PART 3 :
- What things do people lose most often? Why?
- What things are easy to get lost? Why?
- How can one find what they lost?
- Is police helpful in looking for lost things? Why/why not?
- Should people offer a reward to a person who finds what they've lost? Why/why not?
- In what situation is it easy to lose focus? Why?
- How can people pay better attention to what they are doing?
- Why do you think some people always lose things? What does it depend on?
- Can technology be helpful in remembering things?
- How can we make sure we won't lose something? Why?
- How does losing something make us feel? Why?
- Do you think people are too attached to their things these days? Why/why not?

- **a time when you forgot to do something**

VOCAB :
1. to fail to remember (phr.) = to forget
2. to disremember (v.) = to forget
3. to neglect sth (v.) = to fail to do sth you should do
4. to overlook sth /ˌəʊvə(r)ˈlʊk/ (v.) = to fail to notice or remember sth
5. absent-minded (adj.) = likely to forget things
6. amnesiac (n.) = sb who has amnesia
7. sth slipped my mind (phr.) = I completely forgot about sth
8. to blank out (v.) = to try not to think about sth or try to forget it
9. to pay no heed to sth /hiːd/ (phr.) = to not consider sth at all
10. oblivion /əˈblɪviən/ (n.) = a situation in which sth has been completely forgotten

PART 3 :
- What things are usually hard to remember? Why?
- How can people remember things better? Why?
- What jobs require a great memory? Why?
- Is a good memory something we are born with or a skill we learn as we grow? Why?

- ☺ Can anyone practise their memory? How?
- ☺ Why do some people remember things better than others?
- ☺ Do you think that technology makes people lazy so that they don't have to remember so many things? Why/why not?
- ☺ Why is it important to remember certain moments or things in life?
- ☺ Do our memories change over time or stay the same? Why?
- ☺ What do you think two people present at the same event might remember it completely differently? What does it depend on?
- ☺ Is our personal sense of identity connected with our memories? Why/why not?

- **a time when you met a friend you haven't seen for a long time/a school friend you remember well**

VOCAB :
1. come hell or high water (phr.) = even though there may be problems or difficulties
2. to lead a busy life (phr.) = to never have free time
3. for old times' sake (phr.) = so that you can remember a happy time in the past
4. to be tied up at work (phr.) = to be very busy at work
5. Absence makes the heart grow fonder. (phr.) = you feel more attention for those you love when parted from them
6. to bump into sb /bʌmp/ (v.) = to meet sb unexpectedly
7. to get in touch with sb (phr.) = to speak or write to sb, especially after you have not spoken to them for a long time
8. to catch up with sb (v.) = to talk to sb whom you have not seen for some time in order to find out what he or she has been doing in the interim
9. sb looks a million dollars (phr.) = sb looks extremely good
10. to get hold of sb (phr.) = to manage to talk to sb, on the phone or directly
11. to hear from sb (v.) = if you hear from sb, they write to you, phone you, email you etc.
12. to drop sb a line (phr.) = to write a short letter to someone

PART 3 :
- ☺ How can we find our old friends?
- ☺ Is it easier to locate our old friends today than it was in the past? Why/why not?
- ☺ What are main advantages of finding old friends?
- ☺ What are main disadvantages of finding old friends?
- ☺ Are friends generally important? Why?
- ☺ Why do you think some friendships last while others break?
- ☺ What kind of friendship is able to survive for many years?
- ☺ Should people make friends with people who are similar to them or different? Why?
- ☺ Should people make friends with people of different ages? Why/why not?
- ☺ Is friendship between a man and a woman possible? Why/why not?
- ☺ How do social websites affect friendships today?
- ☺ Are friendships made online as strong as the ones made face to face? Why/why not?
- ☺ Do you think technology has brought people together or took them further apart? Why?
- ☺ What is the best way to maintain friendships? Why?

- Do you go to class reunions? Why/why not?
- Are class reunions common in your country? If so, how often do they happen?
- Why do you think some people choose not to join their class reunion?
- Is seeing your classmates again the same with staying in touch online? Why/why not?
- Can people from different countries become friends? How?
- What kinds of problems might occur between friends from different cultures?
- Should international leaders be friends? Why/why not?
- Do you think childhood friendships are the strongest? Why/why not?
- Is it better to have a just a few close friends or a lot of friends? Why?
- What's the best way to meet new people in your country? Why?
- Is it easy to make friends today? Why/why not?
- Was it easier to make friends in the past? Why/why not?
- Do many people in your country make friends via the Internet? Why/why not?
- Is making friends online safe? Why/why not?
- How do friends influence us? Why?
- Should parents choose friends for their children? Why/why not?
- In what situations may friends become more important than person's family? Why?
- What's the most important factor in friendship? Why?
- Should friends be always honest with each other? Why/why not?

- **a time when you moved to a new house/school**

VOCAB :
1. a standard of upright conduct /ˈʌpraɪt/ (phr.) = rules of appropriate behaviour
2. self-paced learning (phr.) = learning process in which you decide how fast to study
3. a penthouse /ˈpentˌhaʊs/ (n.) = a luxury flat at the top of the building
4. high-rise flat (n.) = a flat in a tall, modern building with a lot of floors
5. core curriculum (phr.) = the most important and basic subjects that all school students must study
6. extracurricular activities /ˌekstrəkəˈrɪkjʊlə(r)/ (phr.) = things that you do at school that aren't part of your course
7. coeducation /ˌkəʊedjʊˈkeɪʃ(ə)n/ (n.) = the system of educating students of both sexes in the same class or college
8. a single sex school (n.) = a type of school where only one sex studies
9. a mixed-ability class (n.) = a class designed for students with different levels of educational ability
10. to feel out of one's element /ˈelɪmənt/ (phr.) = to feel unhappy and uncomfortable in a situation
11. to be attuned to /əˈtjuːnd/ (adj.) = to be familiar with sth and able to deal with it in a sensitive way
12. to blend in with (v.) = to be similar to others
13. to fit in with (v.) = to belong
14. to stand out from (v.) = to be easy to notice because of being different
15. peer pressure (n.) = the influence that other people of your own age or social class have on the way you behave or dress
16. to feel out of place (phr.) = to feel uncomfortable in a particular situation or place
17. to find a niche for oneself /niːʃ/ (phr.) = to find sth that is suitable for you

PART 3 :

- ☞ Do people in your culture often move homes? Why/why not?
- ☞ What are some reasons for which people would move to a new home?
- ☞ Do people in your country often change jobs? Why/why not?
- ☞ What are main reasons for changing schools in your country?
- ☞ What problems do people face when they move homes?
- ☞ What are the biggest pros of living in the same place for many years? Why?
- ☞ Is it easy to accept change? Why/why not? What does it depend on?
- ☞ Do children handle changes better than adults? Why/why not?
- ☞ Can work changes influence one's family life? Why/why not? If so, how?
- ☞ Which is better, a sudden change or a gradual one? Why?
- ☞ Should every society be mobile? Why/why not?
- ☞ How important is good education when it comes to social mobility? Why?
- ☞ What do you think people's economic situation usually depend on?
- ☞ Has globalisation made it easier or harder for people to improve their lives? Why?

- **a time when you were asked to give your opinion in a questionnaire/survey**

VOCAB :

1. to carry out a survey /ˈsɜː(r)veɪ/ (phr.) = to conduct a survey
2. to submit my opinion /səbˈmɪt/ (phr.) = to give your opinion
3. I suggested that… (phr.)
4. scrutiny /ˈskruːtɪni/ (n.) = careful examination of sb/sth
5. a poll /pəʊl/ (n.) = an occasion when a lot of people are asked what they feel about sth
6. to riposte /rɪˈpɒst/ (v.) = to reply in a quick and clever way
7. to put forward (v.) = to offer an opinion
8. to hint /hɪnt/ (v.) = to say what you are thinking or feeling in an indirect way
9. to imply /ɪmˈplaɪ/ (v.) = to suggest that you think sth without saying it directly
10. a query /ˈkwɪəri/ (n.) = a question that you ask because you want information
11. a viewpoint /ˈvjuːˌpɔɪnt/ (n.) = an opinion
12. a stance /stæns/ (n.) = an attitude or view about sth
13. to be of the opinion (phr.) = to think that

PART 3 :

- ☞ Where are people usually asked to fill a questionnaire in your country? Why?
- ☞ Do people like to answer survey questions? Why/why not?
- ☞ What are some common topics of surveys?
- ☞ Are TV surveys popular in your country? Why/why not?
- ☞ Can the results of public surveys be trusted? Why/why not?
- ☞ Do you think people always answer truthfully to the survey? Why/why not?
- ☞ Are most questionnaires anonymous? Why/why not?
- ☞ Do you think companies take survey results into account when launching a new product? Why/why not?
- ☞ Do you think in the future people will only fill online questionnaires? Why/why not?

- **a time when you were late for something**

VOCAB :
1. punctuality is not my middle name /ˌpʌŋktʃuˈæləti/ (phr.) = being on time is not my strongest quality
2. on the dot (phr.) = at exactly the time you mention
3. an urgent matter /ˈɜː(r)dʒ(ə)nt/ (phr.) = sth that needs to be dealt with immediately
4. to schedule things accordingly /ˈʃedjuːl/ (phr.) = to plan things well
5. an oppressive deadline /əˈpresɪv/ (phr.) = a deadline that worries you
6. to prioritize sth ruthlessly /praɪˈɒrɪtaɪz ˈruːθləsli/ (phr.) = to decide in what order you should do things without compassion for others
7. to stick to your priorities (phr.) = to follow your plans according to their importance
8. to keep sb waiting (phr.) = to make sb stay in one pace or do nothing until you are ready to see or talk to them
9. right at the last minute (phr.) = when it is almost too late
10. to anticipate /ænˈtɪsɪpeɪt/ (v.) = to think that sth will probably happen
11. a rigorous time limit /ˈrɪgərəs/ (phr.) = a strict deadline
12. to procrastinate /prəʊˈkræstɪneɪt/ (v.) = to delay doing sth until later, usually sth that you do not want to do
13. better late than never (phr.) = used for telling sb you are happy that they did something, but wish they had done it earlier

PART 3 :
- Why are people usually late?
- Is being late in your country considered rude? Why/why not?
- What kinds of excuses do people usually give when they are late?
- How late is too late, according to your culture?
- Are students often late to class in your country? Why/why not?
- How do teachers usually punish late students in your country?
- Are workers often late to work in your country? Why/why not?
- What are some common punishments companies have for being late?
- Do you think punctuality is important? Why/why not?
- Can everyone learn punctuality? Why/why not?
- What can people do to help them remember to be on time?

- **a traffic jam you experienced**

VOCAB :
1. poisonous fumes /ˈpɔɪz(ə)nəs fjuːmz/ (phr.) = harmful gases
2. to swallow the traffic jam /ˈswɒləʊ/ (phr.) = to put up with the traffic jam
3. to suffocate passengers /ˈsʌfəkeɪt ˈpæsɪndʒə(r)/ (phr.) = to not provide enough fresh air to breath for passengers (on a bus)
4. a traffic flow /fləʊ/ (phr.) = a traffic movement

5. a rush hour (n.) = the time of day when there are a lot of cars on the road because most people are travelling to or from work
6. a traffic bottleneck /ˈbɒt(ə)l‿nek/ (phr.) = a place where a road is blocked by heavy traffic
7. to inch along /ɪntʃ/ (v.) = to move very slowly
8. bumper-to-bumper (adj.) = in a long line of vehicles that are close together and moving very slowly
9. the volume of traffic /ˈvɒljuːm/ (phr.) = the number of vehicles on the road
10. traffic density /ˈdensəti/ (phr.) = the degree to which traffic is heavy
11. to be jam-packed (adj.) = completely full
12. a commuter /kəˈmjuːtə(r)/ (n.) = sb who travels regularly to and from work
13. at the intersection /ˈɪntə(r)‿sekʃ(ə)n/ (phr.) = at the place where roads cross each other
14. to jam on the brakes /dʒæm/ (phr.) = to brake with force (of a driver)
15. a chronic problem /ˈkrɒnɪk/ (phr.) = a problem that is always happening or returning and is very difficult to solve
16. a traffic warden (n.) = sb whose job is to check that vehicles are legally parked
17. to jump the lights (phr.) = to ignore a red traffic light and keep driving
18. a long tailback /ˈteɪl‿bæk/ (n.) = a line of slow or stopped traffic
19. road rage /reɪdʒ/ (n.) = anger or violence between drivers because of difficult driving conditions
20. a head-on collision /kəˈlɪʒ(ə)n/ (phr.) = two vehicles hitting each other directly in the front

PART 3 :
- Is traffic heavy in cities in your country? Why?
- What percentage of families own a car in your country?
- What percentage of families own more than one car?
- Do people in your country use skateboards, rollerblades or electric scooters to commute?
- How much has traffic increased since your grandparents' time? Why?
- When is the traffic in your city the heaviest? Why?
- What can people do when they get stuck in a traffic jam? Why?
- Do you think traffic in big cities in your country might get heavier in the future? Why/why not?
- What are some ways traffic is managed in your country?
- What can the government do to improve traffic congestion problem? Why?
- Can building more motorways help improve traffic? Why/why not?
- In what ways is public transport useful to the improvement of traffic? Why?
- How does heavy traffic influence the environment? Why?
- Do you think governments should impose taxes on lorries? Why/why not?
- Is a decrease in travel a good solution to the problem of global warming? Why/why not?

- **an occasion when visitors came to your home/when you visited someone's home/someone who visited your home/an interesting person you met**

VOCAB :
1. offbeat /ˈɒf‿biːt/ (adj.) = unusual, often in an interesting way
2. eccentric /ɪkˈsentrɪk/ (adj.) = often behaving in slightly strange or unusual ways
3. mannered /ˈmænə(r)d/ (adj.) = behaving in a way that is extremely formal and not natural

4. rounded /ˈraʊndɪd/ (adj.) = combining different aspects to produce a result that is complete or well developed
5. first impressions are more lasting (phr.) = the first feeling stays for long
6. an unexpected visit /ˌʌnɪkˈspektɪd/ (phr.) = a surprising visit, because you did not expect it at all
7. to drop in on sb (v.) = to make a short visit somewhere
8. to come over (v.) = to visit sb
9. We're expecting company this evening. (phr.) = We have invited guests for this evening.
10. Make yourself comfortable. (phr.) = used to make guests relaxed and feeling welcome
11. to return a visit (phr.) = to visit sb because they visited you in the past
12. vivacious /vɪˈveɪʃəs/ (adj.) = lively and attractive
13. enigmatic /ˌenɪɡˈmætɪk/ (adj.) = mysterious and difficult to understand
14. on the surface /ˈsɜː(r)fɪs/ (phr.) = on the outside
15. don't judge a book by its cover (phr.) = used for saying that you should not form an opinion about sb/sth only from their appearance
16. misleading /mɪsˈliːdɪŋ/ (adj.) = intended or likely to make someone believe sth that is incorrect or not true
17. a virtue /ˈvɜː(r)tʃuː/ (n.) = a good quality or habit that a person has
18. cunning /ˈkʌnɪŋ/ (adj.) = sb who uses their intelligence to get what they want, especially be tricking or cheating people
19. to pop over (v.) = to pay someone a short visit
20. to get a warm welcome (phr.) = to be welcomed by hosts
21. a friend of a friend (phr.) = an acquaintance
22. a cliché conversation /ˈkliːʃeɪ/ (phr.) = a conversation that is boring because it's not longer original
23. to joke around (v.) = to have fun
24. to show up empty-handed /ˌempti ˈhændɪd/ (phr.) = to visit sb without a gift

PART 3 :
- ☞ Do people often visit each other's homes in your culture? Why/why not?
- ☞ When people in your country have visitors, how do they usually prepare for the visit?
- ☞ Is it polite to bring a gift if visiting sb's home for the first time? If so, what kind of a gift would be appropriate?
- ☞ In the past, when people visited others in your culture, how was it different from now?
- ☞ Is it important to invite people to one's home in your culture? Why/why not?
- ☞ Do you think people in your country are hospitable? Why/why not?
- ☞ When people in your country travel, would they prefer to stay at a hotel or at friends'? Why?
- ☞ What are some advantages of staying at your friends' place when travelling?
- ☞ What kinds of services are people in your country looking for in a hotel? Why?
- ☞ Do you think hotel staff should be trained? Why/why not?
- ☞ What's the worst hotel service you have ever heard of?
- ☞ How can foreign countries make visitors feel welcome? What can they do? Why?
- ☞ Do you think it's important that foreigners adapt to your country's local customs? Why/why not?
- ☞ How does tourism influence international relations between countries? Why?
- ☞ What in your opinion is the best way to get to know a person? Why?
- ☞ How do people in your country usually make friends? Why?

↻ Is it possible to really know someone when you first meet them? Why/why not?

↻ What qualities do you look for in a friend? Why?

↻ What kind of person could never be your friend? Why?

↻ How important is person's family in developing one's personality? Why?

↻ Are friends also important to help us form our character? How? Why/why not?

↻ When do you think is a child's personality formed? At what age?

↻ Can a person change their personality? How?

↻ What personality traits are valued today? Was it the same in the past? Why/why not?

↻ When looking for a job, do you think one's personality can make a difference? Or only their abilities matter? Why?

↻ Is it possible that most people will become more introverted in the future due to technological advancement? Why/why not?

- **a walk you took**

VOCAB :

1. a relaxing stroll /strəʊl/ (phr.) = a walk that is not hurried, often just for pleasure
2. to keep up with sb (v.) = to go at the same speed with sb
3. to get out of breath (phr.) = to breathe fast and with difficulty, for example because you have been walking too fast
4. to take sb along (phr.) = to bring sb somewhere
5. to slow sb down (phr.) = to walk too slow for sb's else
6. to set off (v.) = to begin a journey
7. to fall behind (v.) = to move more slowly than others so that you are behind them
8. Get a move on! (phr.) = used for telling someone to hurry
9. a military march /mɑː(r)tʃ/ (phr.) = a walk by a group of soldiers in which each person matches the speed and movements of the others
10. to saunter /ˈsɔːntə(r)/ (v.) = to walk in a slow and relaxed way
11. a promenade /ˌprɒməˈnɑːd/ (n.) = a place to walk, usually next to a beach
12. a ramble /ˈræmb(ə)l/ (n.) = a long walk in the countryside for enjoyment

PART 3 :

↻ Do people in your country enjoy taking walks? Why/why not?

↻ How often do people usually take a walk? Why?

↻ What are the most common places for people to take a walk? Why?

↻ Is it necessary to have good weather during a walk? Why/why not?

↻ How does the environment influence the number of people taking walks these days?

↻ Why do people like to have a walk?

↻ Why don't some people ever take walks?

↻ What else do people in your country like to do to stay fit? Why?

↻ Who enjoys walking more, young people or older people? Why?

↻ Do you think people will walk more in the future? Why/why not?

- **a wedding you attended/heard about**

VOCAB :
1. a wedding gown /gaʊn/ (n.) = a wedding dress
2. a tuxedo /tʌkˈsiːdəʊ/ (n.) = a man's black or white jacket worn on formal occasions
3. to cry in delight /dɪˈlaɪt/ (phr.) = to cry out of happiness
4. to witness a joyful moment /ˈwɪtnəs/ (phr.) = to see something happy happen
5. a banquet /ˈbæŋkwɪt/ (n.) = a formal meal prepared for a large number of people on an important occasion
6. a ceremony /ˈserəməni/ (n.) = a formal public event with special traditions
7. to pronounce man and wife /prəˈnaʊns/ (phr.) = to formally state that a couple are now married to each other
8. newlyweds /ˈnjuːliˌwedz/ (n.) = a man and a woman who have not been married to each other for very long
9. a limo /ˈlɪməʊ/ (n.) = a large expensive comfortable car
10. to take a vow /vaʊ/ (phr.) = to commit to a marriage
11. a sedan chair /sɪˈdæn/ (n.) = a covered seat on two long poles that was used in the past for carrying an important person around
12. a red veil /veɪl/ (phr.) = a thin red piece of cloth worn over a woman's head and often partly over her face
13. a priest /priːst/ (n.) = a man who performs religious duties in Christianity, such as a wedding
14. a pastor /ˈpɑːstə(r)/ (n.) = a priest or minister in some Christian churches
15. to exchange wedding rings (phr.)
16. to be showered with a handful of rose petals (phr.) = when guests throw petals of roses at the newlyweds in front of a church after the ceremony
17. to throw the bouquet (phr.) = when a bride throws her flowers behind her and one of her unmarried female guests catch them, which means she will get married soon too
18. to propose a toast (phr.) = to raise a glass and wish all the best to the newlyweds
19. cake-cutting (n.) = the moment when newlyweds officially cut their wedding cake together
20. a hen party (n.) = a celebration for a woman who is about to get married, in which only her women friend take part
21. a stag night (n.) = an occasion when a group of men celebrate together because one of them is soon to be married
22. to go on honeymoon /ˈhʌniˌmuːn/ (phr.) = to go on a holiday that two people take after they get married
23. a dowry /ˈdaʊri/ (n.) = money and property that, in some cultures, a woman's family gives to her husband when they get married
24. to tap one' glass /tæp/ (phr.) = to pour liquid into a glass
25. to pop the question (phr.) = to ask someone to marry you

PART 3 :
- At what age do people in your country get married? Why?
- How is traditional wedding in your culture celebrated? Why?
- Does everyone enjoy going to weddings? Why/why not?
- How has the way weddings are conducted changed over the years? Why?

- How do you think people will celebrate weddings in the future? Why?
- Who usually pays for a wedding?
- Are weddings expensive in your country? Why/why not?
- What special activities do people like to have during their weddings? Why?
- Are there a lot of couples in your country who decide not to get married?
- Why do people get married in your culture?
- Why some people don't want to get married?
- What are some common wedding gifts in your country?

- **an event that changed your life in a good way/influenced you a lot**

VOCAB :

1. to amend sth /əˈmend/ (v.) = to make changes to improve sth
2. to get a new lease of life (phr.) = to become more energetic and active than before
3. to assimilate sth /əˈsɪmɪleɪt/ (v.) = to help sb feel that they are part of a community rather than feeling foreign
4. to resist change /rɪˈzɪst/ (phr.) = to oppose or fight change
5. to enforce change /ɪnˈfɔː(r)s/ (phr.) = to make sure that change is made
6. a sweeping change /ˈswiːpɪŋ/ (phr.) = a change that is wide in range or effect
7. a subtle change /ˈsʌt(ə)l/ (phr.) = a delicate and not obvious change
8. to facilitate change /fəˈsɪləteɪt/ (phr.) = to make change possible
9. an ongoing consultation process /ˌkɒns(ə)lˈteɪʃ(ə)n/ (phr.) = a continuous discussion between people before they make a decision
10. to implement sth /ˈɪmplɪˌment/ (v.) = to make sth work and be used
11. to be at the crossroads /ˈkrɒsˌrəʊdz/ (phr.) = to be at the point when you have to make an important decision about what to do next

PART 3 :

- Who do you think can adapt more easily to change, children or adults? Why?
- What are some benefits of change in people's lives?
- Do you think it's a good idea to change jobs often? Why/why not?
- What are some benefits of staying in one job for a long time?
- Do people in your country generally like changes? Why/why not?
- How often do people change jobs in your country? Why?
- What benefits does keeping the same job for many years have?
- Why do some people decide to change jobs more often than others?
- Why do you think more and more people decide to live and work abroad?
- What kinds of problems may a person face when living in a new country? Why?
- Is it easier for young people or older people to adapt to changes? Why?
- Do people need to make more changes now than in the past? Why/why not?
- How can society benefit from having adaptable citizens?
- What kind of threat does too quick of a change pose to society?
- What are some common celebrations in your culture?
- How do people in your culture usually celebrate? Why?
- Does everyone like to join family celebrations in your country? Why/why not?

224

- Do young people enjoy family celebrations today? Why/why not?
- What national celebrations do you have in your country?
- Do people in your country prefer national or family celebrations? Why?
- What does a traditional wedding look like in your culture?
- Are weddings important in your culture? Why/why not?
- Who is responsible for organising a wedding in your culture? Why?
- Who pays for a wedding in your culture? Why?
- Do you think people spend too much money on their weddings today? Why?
- Do many people in your country follow Western wedding trends? Why/why not?
- At what age do people in your country usually get married? Why?
- Why do you think some people decide to get married at a later age?
- What's the most important factor in choosing a marriage partner? Why?
- Is it important to marry someone with the same education level? Why/why not?
- What are male roles in a typical marriage in your country?
- What are female roles in a typical marriage in your country?
- Do you think that spousal roles will change in the future? Why/why not?

- **an experience that made you laugh/cry**

VOCAB :
1. to shed crocodile tears /ˈkrɒkədaɪl ˌtɪə(r)z/ (phr.) = to cry out of sadness that is not sincere
2. to be in stitches (phr.) = to be laughing a lot
3. to burst into tears (phr.) = to suddenly start crying
4. to pull sb's leg (phr.) = to tell someone sth that is not true, as a joke
5. a practical joke (n.) = a trick that is intended to surprise sb or make them look silly
6. to laugh your head off (phr.) = to laugh heavily
7. to have a good laugh about sth (phr.) = to have fun
8. the joke fell flat (phr.) = the joke did not make anyone laugh
9. no laughing matter (phr.) = sth that should be treated seriously
10. to keep a straight face (phr.) = to look serious even though you are in a funny situation

PART 3 :
- What kinds of things make people laugh? Why?
- What kinds of things make people cry? Why?
- Are comedy programmes popular on TV in your country? Why/why not?
- Is there any difference between comedy on TV and comedy in books (e.g. comic books)? Why/why not?
- Is comedy often used in advertising? Why/why not?
- Why do people like to laugh?
- Why are some things funny to some people but not to others?
- Do you think men and women find the same things funny? Why/why not?
- Can laughter be beneficial to our health? If so, how?
- Is it important to laugh together in a relationship? Why/why not?
- Can humour be useful when learning a foreign language? How?
- Do you think jokes can be adequately translated from one language to another? Why/why not?

225

↻ Is it important to understand the humour of the country when learning a foreign language? Why/why not?

↻ Can humour be helpful in international relations? How?

- **an important/difficult decision you made**

VOCAB :

1. to be between a rock and a hard place (phr.) = to be in a position in which you have to choose between two things that are not good
2. soul-searching (n.) = careful thought about your beliefs, attitudes, or actions because you think it is important to behave in an honest and moral way
3. in advance /əd'vɑːns/ (phr.) = in preparation for a particular time or event in the future
4. beforehand /bɪ'fɔ:(r)hænd/ (adv.) = before a particular event: used especially for talking about sth done in preparation for the event
5. to draw up a plan (phr.) = to make a plan
6. to intend to do sth /ɪn'tend/ (v.) = to have a plan in your mind to do sth
7. to have mixed feelings about sth (phr.) = to not be certain how you feel about sb/sth
8. to be up in the air (phr.) = not yet decided
9. to be still wavering between A and B /'weɪvə(r)ɪŋ/ (phr.) = to not be certain about what to say or do
10. a train of thought (phr.) = a series of thoughts
11. to weigh sth up /weɪ/ (v.) = to consider the good and bad aspects of sth in order to reach a decision about it
12. to follow the gut feeling (phr.) = to follow the feeling that you are certain is right
13. to rush into a decision (phr.) = to make a decision without first thinking carefully about it
14. to go with the majority view (phr.) = to follow what most people think
15. to have a mind of your own (phr.) = to think for yourself
16. to lack the courage of your convictions (phr.) = to not be certain what one believes in
17. I always go for… (phr.) = I always choose
18. to be a toss-up (n.) = the act of throwing a coin into the air and making a decision based on which side the coin falls on
19. the lesser of two evils (phr.) = the less unpleasant or harmful of two possible choices
20. to be in two minds about sth (phr.) = to not be certain about sth or to have difficulty in making a decision

PART 3 :

↻ Do young people in your country usually make their own decisions or do they tend to listen to other's advice? Whose? Why?

↻ What kind of a person can be a good advisor? Why?

↻ How do young people in your country get advice about what career to choose?

↻ What is the most important piece of advice you would give to today's youth? Why?

↻ What kind of things should friends advise on? Why?

↻ What kind of things should family advise on? Why?

↻ Do schools in your country teach students problem solving skills?

↻ Should schools teach how to make decisions? Why/why not?

- What are the most important decisions in person's life? Why?
- Do you think that contemporary decisions are more complex than those in the past? Why/why not?
- How do media influence our decisions?
- Should feelings be taken into consideration when making a decision? Why/why not?
- How do societies choose decision makers? Why?
- Can individuals affect decisions made by large companies? How?
- Should different countries cooperate when it comes to making decisions? Why/why not?
- What are some crucial decisions the world is waiting for today?

• **an interesting event in history you would like to know more about**

VOCAB :
1. to be famous for (adj.) = to be known for
2. to be well-known for (adj.)
3. Gone are the days when…(phr.) = the past is over
4. remote ancestors /rɪˈməʊt ˈænsestə(r)z/ (phr.) = relatives from distant past
5. to vanish /ˈvænɪʃ/ (v.) = to disappear
6. to succeed sb to the throne /səkˈsiːd/ (phr.) = to replace sb in the line to the throne
7. to accede sb to the throne /əkˈsiːd/ (phr.) = to formally become a king, queen
8. to seize power /siːz/ (phr.) = to gain control
9. to usurp power /juːˈzɜː(r)p/ (phr.) = to take over sth without having rights to do so
10. to abuse power /əˈbjuːz/ (phr.) = to use power in a bad, dishonest way
11. a feudal period /ˈfjuːd(ə)l/ (phr.) = a time when ordinary people do not have many rights
12. a medieval period /ˌmediˈiːv(ə)l/ (phr.) = a time relating to the period of European history between about the year 1000 ad and the year 1500
13. the Renaissance /rɪˈneɪs(ə)ns/ (n.) = the period in Europe between the 14th and 16th centuries
14. a chariot /ˈtʃæriət/ (n.) = a vehicle with two wheels and no roof that was pulled by horses in races and battles in ancient times
15. a cart /kɑː(r)t/ (n.) = a vehicle with four wheels and no roof that is pulled by a horse and is used for carrying things
16. a stagecoach /ˈsteɪdʒˌkəʊtʃ/ (n.) = a vehicle pulled by horses, used in the past for carrying people, letters and goods
17. a historian /hɪˈstɔːriən/ (n.) = sb who studies or writes about events in history
18. a historical figure /hɪˈstɒrɪk(ə)l ˈfɪɡə(r)/ (n.) = an important person from the past

PART 3 :
- Do most people like to visit historical places? Why/why not?
- What historical sites are the most popular ones among tourists in your country? Why?
- Do people still like to go to museums? What for?
- Are museums useful when learning about history? How?
- Are historical buildings kept only for tourists? Why/why not?
- Should entrance be free to historical sites in your country? Why/why not?
- Do you study History in schools? Is it interesting? Why/why not?
- What topics do History lessons usually cover?

- Are most students interested in history or do they find it boring? Why?
- How can teachers kindle students' interest in history? In what ways? Why?
- What can we learn from our history?
- How can our past benefit our present?
- Is it possible to understand the past? How?
- What do you think will our century be remembered for? Is it worth studying in the future? Why/why not?
- How can we learn about important historical figures?
- Why are some historical figures remembered by generations while others seem to be quickly forgotten?
- Could any important figures from the past serve as role models for today's youth? Why/why not?
- Do you think people learn more from their successes in the past or their failures? Why?
- What lessons will future generations learn from our times?

- **an interesting/boring/important (phone) conversation you had with someone you didn't know**

VOCAB :
1. ad nauseam / ˌæd ˈnɔːziæm/ (adv.) = if you do or say sth ad nauseam, you repeat it so many times that it annoys other people
2. to get sth off one's chest (phr.) = to talk to sb about sth that has been worrying you, so that you feel better about it
3. to pick the receiver (phr.) = to pick up a part of a phone you need to hear and speak, especially on an old-fashioned phone
4. chit-chat (n.) = a friendly conversation about things that are not very important
5. a tete-a-tete / ˌtet ə ˈtet/ (n.) = a private conversation between two people
6. to hang up on sb (v.) = to stop using a telephone at the end of a conversation
7. to get through to sb (v.) = to make sb understand what you are
8. to mishear /mɪsˈhɪə(r)/ (v.) = to not hear sth correctly
9. a crank call /kræŋk/ (n.) = a telephone call made to disturb, annoy or trick sb, often anonymously
10. to slam down the phone /slæm/ (phr.) = to hit sth against or onto a surface with great force
11. out of the blue (phr.) = happening in a way that is sudden and unexpected

PART 3 :
- What kind of a person can be a good communicator?
- In which jobs are good communication skills essential? Why?
- Are people born with good spoken communication skills or can they learn them? Why?
- Can anyone be trained to communicate well? Why/why not?
- How do children learn to speak?
- Do you think adults talk to children the same way they talk to other adults? Why/why not?
- Who can learn a foreign language more easily: a child or an adult? Why?
- Can humans communicate with animals? If so, in what ways?
- Do you think in the future there will be robots able to speak like a human being? Why/why not?
- Why do we need to be able to speak?
- What problems would a person who can't speak meet in her or his life?
- What kinds of people enjoy chatting with others? Why?

↻ What makes a person unwilling to chat? Why?

↻ Do you think women are generally more talkative than men? Why/why not?

↻ In what ways is talking face-to-face better than over the phone?

↻ Is it easy to discuss personal problems with others? Why/why not?

↻ Why is it sometimes easier to discuss a problem with a stranger rather than a family member?

↻ Do you think that talking about a problem can be helpful? How?

↻ Why do you think so many people are willing to go on national TV and discuss their personal problems?

↻ Is social networking important in your country? Why/why not?

↻ Are social networking websites popular? Why/why not?

↻ Who likes to be involved in social networking more: younger people or older people?

↻ Why are some older people not willing to join social networking circles?

↻ How does social networking influence human relations?

↻ Has the concept of friendship changed due to a widespread social networking? Why/why not?

↻ Do men and women talk about the same or different things? Why?

↻ Is a phone conversation the same as a face-to-face contact? Why/why not?

↻ In your culture, is it polite to argue or disagree with people? Why/why not? If so, in what situations?

↻ Do people often give presentations in your culture? Why/why not?

↻ When do people in your country need to give a presentation?

↻ Do people often give presentations in English? Why/why not?

↻ Are visual aids helpful to the presenter? How?

↻ What's the hardest part of giving a presentation? Why?

↻ Should presenters tell jokes? Why/why not?

↻ Are you taught how to speak in public when you go to school? Why/why not?

↻ Do you think public speaking is a skill useful to everyone? Why/why not?

↻ When in life can public speaking come in handy?

↻ What qualities does an effective public speaker have?

↻ How do media affect public speaking?

• **an occasion that made you angry/embarrassed/disappointed**

VOCAB :

1. a bitter pill to swallow (phr.) = an unpleasant fact or situation that is difficult to accept
2. to keep calm (phr.) = to not get anxious or nervous
3. to be indifferent to sth /ɪnˈdɪfrənt/ (adj.) = lacking interest in sth
4. awkward /ˈɔːkwə(r)d/ (adj.) = difficult to deal with and embarrassing
5. to be ill at ease (phr.) = to not be confident or relaxed
6. to be annoyed at/with sb for sth /əˈnɔɪd/ (adj.) = to feel slightly angry or impatient
7. to be irritated about/at/with/by sb/sth /ˈɪrɪˌteɪtɪd/ (adj.) = to be annoyed or impatient about sth
8. to be furious at/about sth /ˈfjʊəriəs/ (adj.) = extremely angry
9. to be enraged at/by sb/sth /ɪnˈreɪdʒd/ (adj.) = extremely angry
10. to lose one's temper (phr.) = to suddenly become angry
11. to hit the roof (phr.) = to become very angry

12. to go berserk /bə(r)'zɜ:(r)k/ (adj.) = to become violent and uncontrolled because you are very angry

13. to get on sb's nerves (phr.) = to make sb feel annoyed or nervous

14. to infuriate sb /ɪn'fjʊərieɪt/ (v.) = to make sb extremely angry

15. to be in tears (phr.) = to cry a lot

16. devastated (adj.) = feeling very shocked and upset

17. to be gutted /'gʌtɪd/ (adj.) = to be extremely disappointed

18. hysterical /hɪ'sterɪk(ə)l/ (adj.) = behaving in an uncontrolled way because you are extremely excited, afraid or upset

19. appalled /ə'pɔ:ld/ (adj.) = offended or shocked very much by sth, because it is extremely unpleasant or bad

20. stunned /stʌnd/ (adj.) = very shocked or upset

21. no such luck (phr.) = used for saying that sth good that might have happened did not happen

22. to be sick and tired of sth (phr.) = to be very unhappy about sth

23. to be at the end of your tether /'teðə(r)/ (phr.) = to feel very upset because you are no longer able to deal with a difficult situation

24. to go off the deep end (phr.) = to unexpectedly become very angry, especially without a good reason

25. to scream your head off (phr.) = to laugh, shout etc. very loudly

26. to have egg on your face (phr.) = to be embarrassed or appear stupid because sth that you tried to do has gone wrong

27. all hell broke loose (phr.) = used for saying that sth happened that made people angry or upset and they started fighting or arguing

PART 3 :
↻ What makes people angry? Why?
↻ In what situations do people often feel embarrassed? Why?
↻ When do people feel most disappointed? Why?
↻ What can a person do to change negative feelings into positive ones? Why?
↻ Who gets angry more easily: young people or older people? Why?
↻ In your culture, how do people feel when they do something wrong? Why?
↻ What is the best way to deal with anger? Why?
↻ Do people in your culture show emotions? Why/why not?
↻ When is it not appropriate to show emotions in your culture? Why?
↻ Did people react emotionally to certain situations in the past? Why/why not?
↻ How can strong emotions affect one's health?
↻ Where can a person emotionally unstable look for help in your country?

• **an occasion/something/an event from your childhood that made you happy**

VOCAB :
1. a philosophical question /ˌfɪlə'sɒfɪk(ə)l/ (phr.) = a question related to philosophy
2. a meaningful life purpose /'mi:nɪŋf(ə)l/ (phr.) = an important goal in life
3. a new day is always a gift (phr.) = used to explain that every day should be cherished

4. happiness is contagious /kənˈteɪdʒəs/ (phr.) = happiness spreads quickly from one person to another

5. 'Life is lie a box of chocolates '(Forest Gump) (quote) = life is full of surprises, you never know what will happen next

6. count your blessings (phr.) = to realize that there are good things about your situation, as well as bad ones; used to tell sb they should not complain

7. in retrospect /ˈretrəʊˌspekt/ (phr.) = considering sth that happened in the past, using knowledge or information that you did not have at the time

8. a sleepover /ˈsliːpˌəʊvə(r)/ (n.) = a children's party at which all the guests stay the night at one person's house

9. When I look back, I appreciate… (phr.) = used to talk about the past

10. babyhood (n.) = the time of yourlife when you were a baby

11. springtime of life /ˈsprɪŋˌtaɪm/ (phr.) = first stage of life

12. salad days (n.) = the period when one is young and inexperienced

13. juvenescence /ˌdʒuːvəˈnes(ə)ns/ (n.) = the state of being young

14. nonage /ˈnəʊnɪdʒ/ (n.) = the period of immaturity or youth

15. an incident /ˈɪnsɪd(ə)nt/ (n.) = an event or occurrence

16. a bash /bæʃ/ (n.) = a party or celebration

17. to recall /rɪˈkɔːl/ (v.) = to remember sth

18. to look back on (v.) = to think about a time or event in the past

PART 3 :

↪ How do people in your culture usually express their feelings?

↪ Do you think most people are happy? Why/why not?

↪ What is happiness?

↪ How can a person become happier?

↪ Between what people think you are and what you really are, which one is more important to you? Why?

↪ Can money make us happy? Why/why not?

↪ What usually makes us happy? Why?

↪ Can too much money make a person unhappy? Why/why not?

↪ Can work make people happy? Why/why not?

↪ Do you think people work better if they are happy? Why/why not?

↪ Is it common for people to rely on their work when it comes to their happiness?

↪ How can a person change their life if they feel unhappy?

↪ Is happiness understood today as the same concept as it was in the past? Why/why not?

↪ Do you think that people today focus too much on their own happiness neglecting everyone around them? Why/why not?

↪ Are individuals responsible for the happiness of others? Why/why not?

↪ Are we born happy or do we become happy as we grow?

↪ Is happiness a feeling or a state of mind?

↪ What kinds of things do people like to keep from their childhood? Why?

↪ Why are photographs from early years so important to some people?

↪ Can a song remind a person about something happy from their childhood?

↪ What makes a childhood a happy one? Why?

- Do you think that childhood that children experience today is the same or different from their parents' childhood? Why?
- Is childhood an important stage in life? Why/why not?
- What contributes to children's quick development? Why?
- Do you think that children grow up faster today? Why/why not?
- Who can deal with the modern world better, children or their parents? Why?

- **an occasion when somebody lied to you/you lied to somebody**

VOCAB :

1. honesty is the best policy (phr.) = it's always good to be honest
2. to be economical with the truth /ˌiːkəˈnɒmɪk(ə)l/ (phr.) = to say things that are not true or to not tell everything that you know
3. to talk sth up (v.) = to discuss sth in a way that makes them seem more interesting or attractive
4. fair and square (phr.) = in a way that is clear and fair, so that no one can complain or disagree
5. to embellish sth /ɪmˈbelɪʃ/ (v.) = to make a story more interesting by adding details, especially ones that are not completely true
6. to gloss over sth (v.) = to ignore or avoid unpleasant facts
7. unpalatable truth /ʌnˈpælətəb(ə)l/ (phr.) = truth that is unpleasant to accept or think about
8. to detect sth /dɪˈtekt/ (v.) = to prove sth
9. an awful interrogation /ɪnˌterəˈgeɪʃ(ə)n/ (phr.) = a terrible process of asking sb a lot of questions in an angry or threatening way
10. to catch sb out (v.) = to show that sb is not telling the truth
11. to feel utterly humiliated /ˈʌtə(r)li hjuːˈmɪlieɪt/ (phr.) = to feel completely ashamed
12. to distort sth /dɪˈstɔː(r)t/ (v.) = to change sth such as information as that it is no longer true or accurate
13. phoney /ˈfəʊni/ (adj.) = sb who is phoney pretends to be friendly, clever, kind etc.
14. to deceive sb /dɪˈsiːv/ (v.) = to trick sb by giving a false idea about sth
15. a white lie (n.) = a lie told to avoid making sb upset, not for your own advantage or in order to harm sb else
16. falsehood /ˈfɔːlshʊd/ (n.) = a statement that is not true
17. a half-truth (n.) = a statement that is only partly true or gives only some of the facts
18. a fib /fɪb/ (n.) = a lie about sth that is not important
19. to keep the truth from sb to spare their feelings (phr.) = to lie in order not to upset sb
20. to lose face (phr.) = to no longer impress people or be respected by them, especially by showing that you are not in control of a situation
21. to face up to the truth (phr.) = to accept the truth
22. to cover sth up /ˈkʌvə(r)/ (v.) = to hide sth
23. to prevent the facts from coming to light (phr.) = to keep the truth to yourself
24. to have sth on your conscience /ˈkɒnʃ(ə)ns/ (phr.) = used when sth is causing you to feel guilty
25. to pull the wool over sb's eyes (phr.) = to try to trick or cheat sb by giving them wrong information
26. I wasn't born yesterday. (phr.) = used to remind sb that one isn't naïve

PART 3 :

- What do people usually lie about in your culture? Why?
- Is there any situation when a lie is told for good reasons? Why/why not?
- Do you think everyone lies sometimes? Why/why not?
- How can white lies escalate into bigger problems?
- How can one tell if someone's not telling the truth?
- Do you think all lies eventually come out? Why/why not?
- How can technology help find out the truth about crimes?
- Why do you think witnesses do not always agree on what they saw?
- Do you think advanced methods of investigation might discourage people from committing crimes? Why/why not?
- What is the value of honesty?
- Is honesty generally important in your culture? Why/why not?
- Should parents teach their children to always be honest? Why/why not?
- Do you think that people generally expect public figures to be honest?
- Can a person expect honesty when they aren't always honest? Why/why not?
- What other qualities are important in people? Why?

- **an occasion when you got lost somewhere**

VOCAB :

1. all's well that ends well (phr.) = used for saying that a situation that did not start in a good way has ended in a way that is satisfactory or pleasing
2. to lose your way (phr.) = to not know where you are or how to get to where you want to go
3. a landmark /ˈlæn(d)ˌmɑː(r)k/ (n.) = a famous building or object that you can see and recognize easily
4. a reference point (n.) = a fixed place that you use to help you to find your way or to see where other things are
5. to navigate /ˈnævɪɡeɪt/ (v.) = to find and follow a path through a difficult place
6. to orientate /ˈɔːriənteɪt/ (v.) = to orient
7. an atlas /ˈætləs/ (n.) = a book of maps
8. a GPS /ˌdʒiː piː ˈes/ (n.) = global positioning system: a system for finding exactly where you are anywhere in the world using satellites
9. I'm not good at topography. /təˈpɒɡrəfi/ (phr.) = I don't know much about maps and features of land.
10. to have a terrible sense of direction (phr.) = to have a bad ability to know without guidance the direction in which you are moving

PART 3 :

- What's the best way to find our way? Why?
- Do you learn how to read a map at school? Why/why not?
- Do you think everyone should know how to read a map? Why/why not?
- Is being able to read a map a useful skill today? Why/why not?
- Why do you think some people are better at directions than others?

↻ Do you think people today rely too much on their phones to help them find the way? Why/why not?

↻ Why do people like to travel to new places?

↻ Is it important to learn about the place before going there? Why/why not?

↻ What preparations should people make before going to a new place? Why?

↻ What problems may people face when going to a new place? Why?

↻ Is everyone born with a need of exploration? Why/why not?

↻ How did people explore places in the past?

↻ What are the biggest challenges with exploring places today?

↻ Should certain places be explored internationally? Why/why not?

↻ Who should fund scientific explorations? Why?

- **an outdoor activity you would like to try for the first time/you often do**

VOCAB :

1. to get in shape by (doing sth) (phr.) = to get in a good physical condition by doing sth
2. in the open air (phr.) = outside
3. outdoor clothing (n.) = clothes sutaible to wear outdoors
4. a windproof jacket /ˈwɪn(d)pruːf/ (n.) = a jacket that gives protection from the wind
5. a rainproof jacket /ˈreɪnpruːf/ (n.) = a jacket that gives protection from rain
6. a campsite /ˈkæmpˌsaɪt/ (n.) = a place where people on holiday can stay in tents or other temporary shelters, usually with toilets and a supply of water
7. a canyon /ˈkænjən/ (n.) = a long deep valley with very steep sides made of rock
8. a cliff /klɪf/ (n.) = the steep side of an area of high land
9. a desert /ˈdezə(r)t/ (n.) = a large area of land with few plants and little water and where the weather is always dry
10. a gorge /ɡɔː(r)dʒ/ (n.) = a deep valley with high straight sides where a river has cut through rock
11. a stream /striːm/ (n.) = a small narrow river
12. a trail /treɪl/ (n.) = a path in the countryside
13. to build a fire (phr.) = to make a bonfire
14. to leave no trace (phr.) = to leave no sign that sb was present somewhere
15. to abseil /ˈæbseɪl/ (v.) = to climb down the front of a large rock or a tall building while holding onto a rope
16. to traverse /trəˈvɜː(r)s/ (v.) = to move over or across an area
17. a bug spray (n.) = a chemical used to keep insects away from you
18. a cooking stove /stəʊv/ (n.) = a machine that provides heat for cooking
19. a first aid kit (n.) = a small box or bag with the things that you would need to treat sb if they were injured or suddenly became ill
20. a torch /tɔː(r)tʃ/ (n.) = a small electric light operated by batteries that you hold in your hand
21. a flashlight /ˈflæʃˌlaɪt/ (n.) = an American word for a torch
22. hiking shoes (n.) = shoes made specifically for hiking hills and mountains
23. matches /ˈmætʃɪz/ (n.) = small sticks that produce a flame when rubbed against a rough surface
24. a tent (n.) = a shelter made of cloth and supported with poles and ropes
25. a sleeping bag (n.) = a warm bag that you sleep in, especially when camping

PART 3 :

- What are some benefits of outdoor activities?
- Do you think shopping is an outdoor activity? Why/why not?
- How can children benefit from outdoor activities?
- Do you think people have enough physical activity these days? Why/why not?
- What outdoor activities are popular among people of different ages in your country? Why?
- How can people find more chances to do some physical activity in their busy schedules?
- Are there any physical activities that you'd consider harmful?
- What can team sports teach people?
- Should children often take part in team competitions?
- What disadvantages do competitions have?
- Why do you think so many people like to watch team sports?
- Do most people like to do any extreme sports?
- Why do you think extreme sports' popularity has risen lately?
- What risk factors do extreme sports have?
- Why would people do extreme sports despite their dangers?
- Does everyone like physical risk? Why/why not?
- Should everyone try a risky sport at least once? Why/why not?

- **recent changes in your hometown**

VOCAB :

1. suitable for /ˈsuːtəb(ə)l/ (adj.) = right for a particular purpose, person or situation
2. scenery /ˈsiːnəri/ (n.) = natural things such as trees, hills and lakes that you can see in a particular place
3. to be born and bred (phr.) = used for saying where sb was born and grew up
4. sth takes your breath away (phr.) = sth is very amazing, beautiful or inspiring
5. it is getting better/worse (phr.) = things are becoming better/worse
6. no longer a place like home (phr.) = used when a place does not remind you of home, usually due to negative changes
7. sth sprouted like mushrooms /spraʊtɪd/ (phr.) = sth appeared suddenly in big numbers
8. relentless urbanization /rɪˈlentləs ˌɜː(r)bənaɪˈzeɪʃ(ə)n/ (phr.) = a continual process by which cities grow bigger
9. the influx of /ˈɪnflʌks/ (n.) = a large number of people or things coming to a particular place
10. a car-free zone (n.) = space in the city where cars are not allowed
11. central business district (CBD) /ˌsiː biː ˈdiː/ = the area of a city where the most important businesses and shops are located
12. noisy and smoggy /smɒgi/ (phr.) = loud and polluted
13. to be rendered obsolete by sb /ˈrendə(r) ˌɒbsəˈliːt/ (phr.) = to be announced as no longer used and replaced by sth newer
14. to be displaced by sth /dɪsˈpleɪst/ (phr.) = to be taken place by sth else
15. population ageing /ˈeɪdʒɪŋ/ (phr.) = the population is becoming old
16. a birth rate (n.) = the officially recorded number of births in a particular year or place
17. population density /ˈdensəti/ (phr.) = the number of people in a place
18. overcrowded /ˌəʊvə(r)ˈkraʊdɪd/ (adj.) = containing too many people

19. old-fashioned /ˌəʊld ˈfæʃ(ə)nd/ (adj.) = no longer modern or fashionable
20. avant-garde /ˌævɒŋˈgɑː(r)d/ (adj.) = very modern and may shock people because it is so different from what has gone before
21. a critical juncture /ˈdʒʌŋktʃə(r)/ (phr.) = a very important stage in a process
22. A has fundamentally changed B /ˌfʌndəˈment(ə)li/ (phr.) = A has changed B in a very important or basic way
23. to be a milestone /ˈmaɪlˌstəʊn/ (n.) = an event or achievement that marks an important stage in a process
24. sth is no longer a necessity (phr.) = sth isn't needed anymore
25. thriving economy /ˈθraɪvɪŋ/ (phr.) = very successful economy
26. sluggish economy /ˈslʌgɪʃ/ (phr.) = not improving as quickly as necessary
27. to transform sth /trænsˈfɔː(r)m/ (v.) = to make sth completely different
28. to evolve /ɪˈvɒlv/ (v.) = to gradually change and develop over a period of time

PART 3 :
- Why do cities change?
- What affects changes in places?
- How have cities in your country changed over the years?
- How do you see the future change in cities?
- Does the countryside also evolve? How?
- Is it easy to keep up with the changes around us? Why/why not?
- Who adjusts more easily to a change, young people or older people? Why?
- How do technological advances influence places?
- Is the government controlling the extent of changes in your country? Why/why not?
- Can a change be bad? How?
- Do you think we will not be able to catch up with the changes around us in the future?
- How does a change make one feel? Why?

- **something you did last weekend/last summer or winter holidays/perfect holidays away from home/a time when you stayed away form home**

VOCAB :
1. booked solid /ˈsɒlɪd/ (phr.) = completely booked (of a hotel)
2. to escape reality (phr.) = to avoid everyday life
3. a holidaymaker /ˈhɒlɪdeɪˌmeɪkə(r)/ (n.) = a person who is visiting a place for their holiday
4. to have the time of your life (phr.) = to have a wonderful time
5. to book a flight (phr.) = to reserve a flight
6. to flock to /flɒk/ (v.) = to gather together in a large group because there is sth interesting
7. a backpacker /ˈbækˌpækə(r)/ (n.) = sb who travels around an area on foot or public transport, often carrying a backpack
8. a souvenir /ˌsuːvəˈnɪə(r)/ (n.) = sth that you buy during a holiday or at a special event to remind you later of being there
9. a travel agency (n.) = a business that helps people plan holidays and make travel arrangements
10. to book a package tour (phr.) = to reserve a holiday arranged by a travel company for a fixed price that included the cost of your hotel and transport

11. peak season /piːk/ (phr.) = a time in the year when most tourists visit a place
12. slack season /slæk/ (phr.) = not busy season
13. jet lag (n.) = the feeling of being very tired and sometimes confused because you have travelled quickly on a plane across parts of the world where the time is different
14. commercialized /kəˈmɜː(r)ʃəlaɪzd/ (adj.) = changed from sth enjoyable or important into sth that exists to make a profit
15. a holiday resort /rɪˈzɔː(r)t/ (n.) = a place where a lot of people go on holiday, usually one with a lot of hotels, bars etc.
16. to go on your own (phr.) = to go alone
17. holiday snaps /snæps/ (phr.) = a photo taken without the use of professional equipment on holidays
18. vibrant /ˈvaɪbrənt/ (adj.) = lively and exciting
19. to laze around /leɪz/ (v.) = to relax and enjoy yourself, doing no work
20. off the beaten track (phr.) = far away from the places that people usually visit
21. a trek /trek/ (n.) = a walk that seems long and difficult
22. to get away from it all (phr.) = to talk about sth different from what you should be talking about
23. remote /rɪˈməʊt/ (adj.) = far away from other cities or people
24. unspoiled /ʌnˈspɔɪld/ (adj.) = a place that has not been changed in ways that make it less beautiful or enjoyable
25. to recharge your batteries (phr.) = to regain energy

PART 3 :
- What are the most popular holiday destinations in your country? Why?
- Which are the main holiday times for people in your country?
- What sorts of holidays are popular among people in your country?
- Are holidays longer now than in the past? Why/why not?
- Do you think some professionals (e.g. doctors, teachers) should have longer holidays than others? Why/why not?
- What benefits can going away on holidays bring? Why?
- How is staying at home during holidays good? Why?
- What factors should people take into consideration when choosing their holiday destination? Why?
- What preparations need to be made before going on holidays? Why?
- Should people learn something about the culture of the place they want to visit? Why/why not?
- How can time-off be beneficial to workers? Why?
- What advantages do companies offering good holiday packages have? Why?
- Why do you think some people never go on holidays?
- Why is it so difficult for some people to go on holidays?
- Why do people like to travel away from home?
- How do people prefer to travel long-distance today? Why?
- How did people travel long-distance in the past? Why?
- Why do you think some people have the money, have the time but never travel anywhere?
- What can one learn from travelling? Why?
- Do young people experience travels the same way as older people? Why/why not?
- Isn't it just enough to watch remote places on TV? Why do people need to go there in person?

↪ What's the best way to remember person's travel? Why?

↪ How does globalisation affect people's travel? Why?

↪ Does the fact that more and more people travel make the world more similar? Why/why not?

↪ How does excessive travel influence the environment? Why?

↪ Should the number of world travellers be decreased? If so, how? Who should be responsible for that?

↪ When people travel, do they prefer to stay at hotels or with friends and relatives? Why?

↪ Do you think we should help around the house when we are guests? Why/who not?

↪ Do you think that staying at friend's place can feel the same as being at home? Why/why not?

↪ What factors do people in your country take into consideration when choosing a hotel? Why?

↪ How important is it for service to be friendly towards hotel customers? Why?

↪ Are luxurious facilities really needed? Why?

↪ Is the hospitality industry well developed in your country? Why/why not?

↪ Do many people seek jobs in the hospitality industry? Why/why not?

↪ Are there any rules set for the restaurants and hotels in your country? If so, who sets them? Why?

↪ Do you think the hospitality industry is important to your country? Why/why not? If so, in what way?

- **your favourite way of communicating with others**

VOCAB :

1. preferable /ˈpref(ə)rəb(ə)l/ (adj.) = more suitable or useful than sth else
2. sth caters to the demand and economic situation /ˈkeɪtə(r)z/ (phr.) = sth provides what is necessary
3. economical /ˌiːkəˈnɒmɪk(ə)l/ (adj.) = not costing or spending much money
4. time-saving (adj.) = designed to help you to do sth more quickly
5. information highway /ˈhaɪˌweɪ/ (phr.) = the fastest way to provide information
6. to stay in touch (phr.) = to stay in communication
7. across the miles (phr.) = between long distances
8. to go door to door (phr.) = to take sb directly from one place to the place they need to go to
9. to put pen to paper (phr.) = to start writing sth
10. freedom of expression (phr.) = the right to say and do whatever you want
11. to protect whistleblowers (phr.) = to protect sb who reports dishonest or illegal activities within an organization to sb in authority
12. to break down barriers /ˈbæriə(r)z/ (phr.) = to remove problems
13. to get your wires crossed (phr.) = if two people get their wires crossed, they become confused because they each think that the other one is talking about sth else
14. government snooping (phr.) = to secretely try to get private information
15. to be hooked on social networking (phr.) = to be very attracted by social networking
16. to be glued to a screen (phr.) = to be looking at the screen and not paying attention to anything else
17. automation /ˌɔːtəˈmeɪʃ(ə)n/ (n.) = a system that uses machines to do work instead of people

PART 3 :

↪ What is the most common way to communicate with others in your culture? Why?

⊙ What kinds of problems do people need to face when using phones?

⊙ Is talking to a person face to face just like talking to someone on the phone? Why/why not?

⊙ Do people in your culture still write letters? If so, when?

⊙ Some people prefer to write a letter than an email. Why do you think that is?

⊙ What are some disadvantages of letters?

⊙ What are some disadvantages of emails?

⊙ Were letters important to people in the past? Why/why not?

⊙ Do you think in the future people will only write emails and traditional letters will disappear? Why/why not?

⊙ How do modern means of communication affect people's work?

⊙ Is it good to be able to be contacted 27/4? Why/why not?

⊙ How does modern technology influence the quality of relationships between people?

- **how you learnt about science when you were at school**

VOCAB :

1. to analyse /ˈænəlaɪz/ (v.) = to study or examine sth in detail
2. a genius /ˈdʒiːniəs/ (n.) = sb who is much more intelligent or skilful than other people
3. to learn sth by heart (phr.) = to memorize sth
4. students' autonomy /ɔːˈtɒnəmi/ (phr.) = the power to make their own decisions by students in their learning process
5. a scientific breakthrough /ˌsaɪənˈtɪfɪkˈbreɪkθruː/ (phr.) = a discovery in science
6. the advent of sth /ˈædvent/ (n.) = the introduction of a new idea etc.
7. to supersede sth/supplant sth /ˌsuːpə(r)ˈsiːd/səˈplɑːnt/ (v.) = to replace sth because it's more useful or more modern
8. genetic engineering (n.) = the practice or science of adding genes to a living thing
9. to experiment with sth /ɪkˈsperɪˌment/ (v.) = to try ne ideas, methods or activities in order to find out what results they will have
10. to satisfy human curiosity /ˈsætɪsfaɪ/ (phr.) = to give one's curiosity what it needs
11. a hard-won discovery (phr.) = a discovery achieved only after a lot of effort
12. artificial intelligence (n.) = the use of computer technology to make computers and other machines think and do things in the way that people can
13. to propose a hypothesis /haɪˈpɒθəsɪs/ (phr.) = to suggest an idea that attempts to explain sth but has not yet been tested or proved
14. a phenomenon /fəˈnɒmɪnən/ (n.) = an event or situation that can be seen to happen or exist
15. empirical evidence /ɪmˈpɪrɪk(ə)l/ (phr.) = evidence based on real experience or scientific experiments rather than on theory
16. repeatable procedures /prəˈsiːdʒə(r)z/ (phr.) = a way of doing sth that is often repeated
17. a facet of sth /ˈfæsɪt/ (n.) = an aspect of sth
18. a biased interpretation of the results /ˈbaɪəst/ (phr.) = an unfair interpretation of the results
19. to come under close scrutiny /ˈskruːtɪni/ (phr.) = to be carefully examined
20. to verify the results /ˈverɪfaɪ/ (phr.) = to check the results
21. to replicate sth /ˈreplɪkeɪt/ (v.) = to make sth again in the same way as before

PART 3 :

- ↻ When do students in your country start learning science? Is it too early? Why/why not?
- ↻ Do you think young children should learn science? Why/why not?
- ↻ Who is usually more into science, boys or girls? Why?
- ↻ How can children learn about science outside school?
- ↻ Can learning science influence children's development process? In what way?
- ↻ What are some of the most important areas of science today?
- ↻ Who should fund scientific research? Why?
- ↻ Should scientists from different countries share their discoveries with others? Why/why not?
- ↻ Do you think a scientist should be responsible for how their discovery is used? Why/why not?
- ↻ What's the main purpose of science?
- ↻ Can scientists be trusted? Do they always work bearing in mind the well-being of the ordinary people? Why/why not?
- ↻ Should there be rules controlling scientific research? Why/why not? If so, who should set them? Why?

- **the process of getting a driving license in your country**

VOCAB :

1. reckless driving /ˈrekləs/ (n.) = driving without thinking about the possible bad effects of your actions
2. drink-driving (n.) = driving after you have drunk too much alcohol
3. to impair a person's driving ability /ɪmˈpeə(r)/ (phr.) = to make a person's ability to drive less effective
4. to get somewhere safe and sound (phr.) = to get somewhere without problems
5. to go over the speed limit (phr.) = to drive faster than the law allows
6. to block sb/sth in (v.) = to stop sb from moving their car out of a place
7. to flag sb down (v.) = to wave at the driver of a car so that they stop
8. to pull over (v.) = to stop by the side of the road
9. at a snail's pace (phr.) = very slowly
10. to fill up the car (phr.) = to deliver petrol to the car
11. a driving school (n.) = a school where you can study how to drive a car
12. a theoretical test /ˌθɪəˈretɪk(ə)l/ (phr.) = a test asking questions about driving rules one needs to take to be able to get a driver's licence
13. a road test (phr.) = a practical test where one needs to show they can drive a car
14. a penalty point (n.) = an official note made on your driving licence because you have done sth wrong while driving

PART 3 :

- ↻ At what age do people in your country start driving? Why?
- ↻ Do you think people in your country are good drivers? Why/why not?
- ↻ Who makes a better driver, a man or a woman? Why?
- ↻ Is it easy to pass a driving test in your country? Why/why not?
- ↻ Are cars expensive in your country?
- ↻ What makes of cars are the most popular in your country? Why?

- What is the system of penalties for bad driving?
- Do road accidents happen often in your country? Why/why not?
- What are some common reasons for road accidents?
- Do you think we will drive different types of vehicles in the future? If so, what kind?
- How does a large number of cars affect environment? Why?

- **something you do to stay healthy**

VOCAB :

1. a wholesome diet /ˈhəʊls(ə)m/ (phr.) = a diet consisting of food that is good for you
2. an unhealthy diet (phr.) = a diet consisting of food that is bad for you
3. greasy /ˈgriːsi/ (adj.) = prepared with a lot of oil or fat
4. beauty sleep (n.) = sleep considered to be sufficient to keep one looking young and beautiful
5. to cut down on sth (v.) = to reduce the amount of sth
6. an intake of /ˈɪnteɪk/ (n.) = the amount of sth that you eat or drink
7. a fast food junkie (phr.) = a person who is addicted to eating fast food
8. a carbonated drink /ˈkɑː(r)bəˌneɪtɪd/ (phr.) = with small bubbles of air in it
9. dietary habits /ˈdaɪət(ə)ri/ (phr.) = habits related to the foods that sb eats
10. protein-rich food /ˈprəʊtiːn/ (phr.) = food such as meat, eggs, milk that people need in order to grow and be healthy
11. genetically-modified food /dʒəˌnetɪkli ˈmɒdɪfaɪd/ (phr.) = food that has its genetic structure changed in order to make it look or taste better
12. to minimise the risk of sth /ˈmɪnɪmaɪz/ (phr.) = to reduce the risk of sth
13. to keep one's figure (phr.) = to stay in shape
14. to be health-conscious (adj.) = concerned about how healthy one's diet and lifestyle are
15. an exercise regimen /ˈredʒɪmən/ (phr.) = a programme of exercise for improving your health
16. self-discipline (n.) = the ability to control your behaviour so that you do what you should do
17. an immune system (n.) = the system in your body that protects you against diseases
18. sth has taken its toll on one's health (phr.) = sth has harmed or damaged one's health
19. a chronic disease /ˈkrɒnɪk/ (n.) = a serious disease which lasts for a long time
20. to contract a disease /kənˈtrækt/ (phr.) = to become infected with a disease
21. to feel under the weather (phr.) = to not feel too well
22. high cholesterol /kəˈlestərɒl/ (phr.) = too much of a substance found in the blood and the cells of the body
23. high blood pressure (phr.) = a medical condition when blood flows from your heart around your body in an abnormal way
24. a workout /ˈwɜː(r)kaʊt/ (n.) = an occasion when you do physical exercise
25. agile /ˈædʒaɪl/ (adj.) = able to move quickly and easily
26. stiff /stɪf/ (adj.) = with pain in muscles and unable to move easily
27. sluggish /ˈslʌgɪʃ/ (adj.) = not moving as quickly as usual
28. a splitting headache /ˈsplɪtɪŋ/ (phr.) = a very bad pain in your head
29. to put sb at their ease (phr.) = to make sb relaxed
30. an ounce of prevention is worth a pound of cure (phr.) = it is easier to stop sth from happening in the first place than to repair the damage after it has happened

31. your body heals and repairs itself (phr.) = used to tell someone that their ailing can be healed on its own

32. vitamin supplementation /ˈvɪtəmɪntˌsʌplɪmenˈteɪʃ(ə)n/ (phr.) = the process of adding all necessary vitamins to food in order to keep your body healthy

33. to cut down on sugar and caffeine /ˈkæfiːn/ (phr.) = to reduce sugar and a substance in coffee and tea that makes you feel awake

34. a breakfast skipper (phr.) = a person who never eats breakfast

35. a toxin /ˈtɒksɪn/ (n.) = a poisonous substance that causes disease

36. isometric exercises /ˌaɪsəʊˈmetrɪk/ (phr.) = exercises involving isometrics

37. to make a conscious effort to eat healthily (phr.) = to decide to eat healthily

38. quantifiable health benefits /ˈkwɒntɪˌfaɪəb(ə)l/ (phr.) = benefits to health that can be measured or seen

PART 3 :

↪ What are the most common ways for people in your country to stay fit?

↪ Do people of all ages care about their health in your country? How?

↪ Do men and women do the same things to stay fit? Why/why not?

↪ Do you think doing sports or exercises is the best way to stay fit? Why/why not? What is?

↪ Why do you think some people don't do anything to help them stay healthy today?

↪ Do you have Physical Education at school in your country? Do students like it? Why/why not?

↪ What can schools do to inspire students to stay fit?

↪ What's the best way to reduce stress, either from work or school? Why?

↪ Do you think that old people care more about their health than young people? Why?

↪ Whose responsibility is it to keep people healthy? Why?

↪ Are there any government campaigns to raise public health awareness? Why/why not? Do you think there should be?

↪ What could governments do to protect citizens' health?

↪ Do you think it is easy to relax for most people? Why/why not?

↪ What lifestyle changes could people make to improve their health?

↪ Do schools in your country teach children about the importance of health? Why/why not? Should they?

↪ How can media affect people's understanding of health?

↪ Do you think doctors should explain the importance of health to people or only treat their health problems? Why?

↪ How do employers in your country look after their workers' health? Why?

↪ Are there any governmental laws protecting employees' health in your country? Why/why not?

↪ How important is the general health of the society?

PLACES

• **a beautiful house/apartment/you visited (and liked)/you room/your favourite room in your home/an ideal home you would like to have in the future**

VOCAB :

1. decent decoration /ˈdiːs(ə)nt/ (phr.) = good decoration

2. fancy furniture /ˈfænsi/ (phr.) = expensive and fashionable furniture
3. Feng Shui /ˌfʌŋ ˈʃweɪ/ (n.) = a Chinese philosophy which states that the position of buildings and the arrangement of objects in the home affects the health and well-being of people living there
4. minimalism /ˈmɪnɪm(ə)lˌɪz(ə)m/ (n.) = using the smallest possible range of materials, colours, decorations etc.
5. cramped /kræmpt/ (adj.) = small and crowded
6. to raise the social status (phr.) = to increase your position in society
7. newly bought (adj.) = just bought
8. south-facing (adj.) = a place facing the south
9. spacious /ˈspeɪʃəs/ (adj.) = having a lot of space inside
10. a bungalow /ˈbʌŋgəˌləʊ/ (n.) = a house that is all on one level
11. a villa /ˈvɪlə/ (n.) = a large house with a big garden in a warm country or region
12. cosy /ˈkəʊzi/ (adj.) = warm and comfortable
13. wide window-sill with lilies in full bloom (phr.)
14. an apartment complex (phr.) = a block of flats
15. a landlord/landlady /ˈlæn(d)ˌlɔː(r)d/ˈlæn(d)ˌleɪdi/ (n.) = a man/woman who owns a house, flat or room that people can rent
16. a tenant /ˈtenənt/ (n.) = sb who rents a flat from a person who owns it
17. a lease /liːs/ (n.) = a legal contract in which you agree to pay to use sb else's building for a specific period of time
18. a mortgage /ˈmɔː(r)gɪdʒ/ (n.) = a legal agreement in which you borrow money from a bank in order to buy a house
19. to flip a house (phr.) = the act of purchasing a home with the intention of selling it in the near future for a profit
20. a wooded lot (phr.) = a lot with many trees
21. a floor plan (phr.) = how the inside of the house is set up
22. a ritzy area /ˈrɪtsi/ (phr.) = neighbourhood where homes are expensive and fancy
23. student digs /dɪgz/ (phr.) = a room or flat that you rent to live in as a student
24. with all the mod cons /ˌmɒd ˈkɒnz/ (phr.) = with all the equipment in your house that make life easy and comfortable

PART 3 :
- What type of housing is most common in your country? Why?
- Are houses in urban areas the same or different from houses in the countryside? Why?
- Do people in your country usually own their houses or rent them? Why?
- Do people of different ages prefer to live in different types of houses? Why?
- What materials are often used in modern housing? Why?
- What materials were used in traditional housing in your country? Why?
- Do cities in your country have many homeless people? Does anyone help them? If so, how?
- What are most common housing problems in your country?
- Do more people prefer small or large rooms? Why?
- Do you think everyone likes to have at least one room to themselves? Why/why not?
- How can a person make their room more pleasant?

- Do you think that the looks of a given business site's reception area contribute to the success of that business? Why/why not? How?
- Can a workplace's layout influence the way workers do their jobs? Why/why not?
- Should workers be allowed to personalize their desks? Why/why not?
- Are buildings in different countries designed in the same or different way? Why?
- How are modern buildings different from buildings in the past?
- Should environment be taken into consideration when planning buildings in the future? Why/why not?
- Do most people prefer to live in the countryside or city? Why?
- Do you think most youngsters prefer to live in a house? Why/why not?
- Where do older people like to live? Why?
- Do many people design their own homes? Why/why not?
- Are traditional types of houses still important to build? Why/why not?
- Can global warming influence the style of houses we will have in the future? Why/why not?
- Should modern houses only be built in the city? Why/why not?
- Who controls building construction in your country?
- Is it government's responsibility to provide housing for its citizens? Why/why not?
- What are the biggest drawbacks of living in a high-rise building?
- What are the main advantages of living in the countryside?
- What factors should be taken into account when designing a house? Why?
- Is it important for urban buildings to look beautiful? Why/why not?
- Are there any regulations regarding urban housing? If so, who sets them?
- Should historic buildings be kept?
- Do historic buildings waste public's money? Why/why not?
- Are outdoor spaces needed in towns? Why/why not?
- Do you think town centres should be mainly commercial areas or residential ones? Why?
- What are the most common types of homes in your country?
- What were some common types of homes in the past?
- What is the best type of home for a family? Why?
- What are some advantages of living in an old house?
- What are some disadvantages of living in an old house?
- How do people in your country choose a place to live in?
- Is it important to live close to family members? Why/why not?
- How can small homes be better than big homes?
- What makes an area a popular one for living in your country?
- What makes a house a home?
- Why would people choose to live in the countryside?
- How can governments encourage more people to live in rural areas?
- Can people in your country build a house wherever they want in the countryside? Why/why not?
- Do you think that life in the countryside is peaceful and harmonious? Why/why not?
- How can people living in the countryside benefit from the harmony in rural areas?

- **a café/a restaurant you love going to**

VOCAB :

1. grotesque /ɡrəʊˈtesk/ (adj.)
2. to be a regular at (place) (phr.) = to go to a place often to eat
3. to dine /daɪn/ (v.) = to eat dinner
4. to specialize in (what kind of food) /ˈspeʃəlaɪz/ (phr.) = to be an expert in a particular part of a subject or profession
5. a chef /ʃef/ (n.) = sb who cooks food in a restaurant as their job
6. a fussy eater /ˈfʌsi/ (phr.) = a person who has very particular demands when eating
7. dietary requirements /ˈdaɪət(ə)ri/ (phr.) = special things sb can't eat
8. teetotal /tiːˈtəʊt(ə)l/ (adj.) = sb who never drinks alcohol
9. to be wined and dined (phr.) = to be invited out to restaurants
10. attentive service (phr.) = kind service
11. takes my mind off work (phr.) = allows me not to think about work
12. to hang around (v.) = to spend time in a place waiting or doing nothing
13. food hygiene /ˈhaɪdʒiːn/ (phr.) = food cleanliness
14. food supplies (phr.) = the amount of food available to eat
15. it's down a small street (phr.) = it's not on the main road
16. a real best kept secret (phr.) = a treasure
17. on the outskirts /ˈaʊtˌskɜː(r)ts/ (phr.) = not downtown
18. to dip sth in vinegar /dɪp/ (phr.) = to put a piece of food into vinegar for better flavour before eating it
19. picturesque /ˌpɪktʃəˈresk/ (adj.) = attractive
20. to enjoy your meal without feeling rushed (phr.) = to eat slowly for pleasure
21. to make a mess on my clothes (phr.) = to spill some food or drinks over your clothes
22. alcoholic beverages /ˌælkəˈhɒlɪk/ (phr.) = drinks containing alcohol
23. filling /ˈfɪlɪŋ/ (adj.) = makes you feel full quickly
24. good/bad digestion /daɪˈdʒestʃ(ə)n/ (phr.) = good/bad ability to digest food
25. café latte /ˈkæfeɪ ˈlɑːteɪ/ (n.) = a drink made by mixing espresso (strong coffee) with ot milk with lots of bubbles of air in it
26. jasmine tea /ˈdʒæzmɪn/ (n.) = tea made of a climbing plant with white, yello or pink flowers that have a strong smell
27. a bite to eat /baɪt/ (n.) = a small piece of food
28. leftovers /ˈleftˌəʊvə(r)z/ (n.) = the food that remains at the end of a meal after you have finished eating
29. a doggy bag (n.) = a bag or box that you take home from a restaurant, containing the food that you did not finish eating

PART 3 :

- ↪ Why do you think people go to a restaurant when they want to celebrate?
- ↪ Do people in your country often eat in restaurants? Why/why not?
- ↪ Why would people in your country choose to dine in a restaurant?
- ↪ What are main disadvantages of eating in restaurants in your country?
- ↪ Are fast food restaurants popular in your country? Why/why not?

☞ What place would you call a good restaurant? Why?

☞ Which one is better, a small local restaurant or a large international chain? Why?

☞ Apart from food, what else can make a restaurant successful? Why?

☞ Are the most expensive restaurants always the best ones? Why/why not?

☞ Do people look at diets differently now than in the past? Why/why not?

☞ Should governments provide advice on healthy food to the public? Why/why not?

☞ How will food production change in the future? Will science change what we eat? Why/why not?

- **a colourful place you have been to/an unforgettable place/an unusual place you have been to/you visited for a short time but would like to go back to**

VOCAB :

1. visual tiredness /ˈvɪʒʊəl/ (phr.) = tired of the things you see
2. eye-catching (adj.) = attractive or unusual and therefore noticed
3. a theme park /θiːm/ (n.) = a large park where people pay to play games and have fun and where all the entertainment is designed according to one theme
4. to gaze at sth /geɪz/ (v.) = to look at sb or sth for a long time
5. breathtaking /ˈbreθˌteɪkɪŋ/ (adj.) = extremely impressive or beautiful
6. out of the ordinary (phr.) = unusual or different
7. pastel colours /ˈpæst(ə)l/ (phr.) = pale soft colours
8. a tinge of green /tɪndʒ/ (phr.) = a bit of green
9. scintillating /ˈsɪntɪˌleɪtɪŋ/ (adj.) = very impressive, interesting or clever
10. jazzy /ˈdʒæzi/ (adj.) = bright, colourful and attractive
11. buzzworthy /ˈbʌzˌwɜː(r)ði/ (adj.) = likely to create interest and attention

PART 3 :

☞ What are the most common types of landscapes in your country? Why?

☞ Why do you think people enjoy looking at natural landscapes?

☞ How can large numbers of tourists damage natural areas?

☞ What kinds of people enjoy exploring new areas?

☞ Why do people have the need to explore remote parts of the world?

☞ What kind of a person could be a good explorer? Why?

☞ How can explorers finance their journeys?

☞ Do you think our way of life is affected by our area of living?

☞ Is it important for cultures to vary? Why/why not?

☞ Would it be good to have just one universal culture across the world? Why/why not?

☞ Why are some phenomena so widespread in the world?

☞ What colours do people in your country choose when it comes to decorating their homes? Why?

☞ Do you think men and women would choose the same colours to paint their walls in? Why/why not?

☞ How can colours of our surroundings affect the way we feel?

☞ Is colour usually important in things you buy? Why/why not?

☞ Can certain colours make people buy more? Why/why not?

☞ Why do you think business people always wear dark colours?

☞ What role does colour play in advertising? Why?

- ☞ Are colours and pictures important for a course book? Why/why not?
- ☞ How can pictures help students study?
- ☞ Do think bright adverts add to the cityscape? Why/why not?
- ☞ Would you say people pay too much attention to appearance nowadays?
- ☞ What places are suitable for a short visit in your country? Why?
- ☞ Do you think one can really know a place after a short stay? Why/why not?
- ☞ What are the biggest advantages of a short trip over a long journey?
- ☞ Why do you think some people like to go back to the place they visited before?
- ☞ Do you think a second visit to the same place feels the same as the first one? Why/why not?
- ☞ Do many people in your country choose to go to the same holiday spot every year? Why/why not?
- ☞ Is tourism developing in your country?
- ☞ Do you think people should first get to know their own country before they travel abroad? Why/why not?
- ☞ Is it important for tourists to be aware of cultural differences when they travel? Why/why not?
- ☞ Do you think tourism industry might change in the future? Why/why not? If so, how?

- **a country you would like to visit/you visited and would like to visit again/you think is interesting**

VOCAB :

1. to adapt to /əˈdæpt/ (v.) = to change your ideas or behaviour so that you can deal with a new situation
2. to deal with the sense of loss (phr.) = to handle the loss of sth well
3. to get used to patterns of learning (phr.) = to become familiar with ways of learning
4. to go abroad /əˈbrɔːd/ (phr.) = to go to a foreign country
5. to go overseas /ˈəʊvə(r)siːz/ (phr.) = to go to a country across the sea from your country
6. affordable accommodation /əˈfɔː(r)dəb(ə)l/ (phr.) = cheap enough for ordinary people to afford
7. allure /əˈlʊə(r)/ (n.) = a special, exciting and attractive quality that sb or sth has
8. a national anthem /ˈænθəm/ (n.) = the official song of a particular country that people sing on special occasions
9. currency /ˈkʌrənsi/ (n.) = money that is used in a particular country
10. a native language /ˈneɪtɪv/ (n.) = the first language that we learn in the country where we were born
11. a flag /flæg/ (n.) = a piece of cloth decorated with the pattern and colours that represent a country
12. a landmark /ˈlæn(d)ˌmɑː(r)k/ (n.) = a famous building or object that you can see and recognize easily
13. a culture shock (n.) = the nervous and confused feeling that people sometimes get when they arrive in a place that has a very different culture from their own
14. a cross-cultural experience (phr.) = an experience involving different cultures
15. heritage /ˈherɪtɪdʒ/ (n.) = the art, buildings, traditions and beliefs that a society considers important to its history and culture
16. bizarre gestures /bɪˈzɑː(r) ˈdʒestʃə(r)/ (phr.) = strange movements that communicate feelings
17. to make a false assumption /əˈsʌmpʃ(ə)n/ (phr.) = to have the wrong idea about sth

PART 3 :

- What are the benefits of foreign travel? Why?
- Has foreign tourism in your country changed in the past few years? How?
- Besides tourism, what other reasons do people have to go overseas?
- Is it important to respect local cultures when travelling abroad? Why/why not?
- Why do people like to travel abroad?
- Are tourists generally good or bad for a country? In what ways?
- How can too many tourists be a downside?
- Why do you think some people want to study abroad?
- Why do you think some people choose to work abroad for a few years?
- Do you think that living abroad feels the same as just visiting a particular country as a tourist? Why/why not?
- What kinds of problems do people face when they live abroad?
- How can living abroad benefit children?
- Should a country have a good relationship with its neighbours? Why/why not?
- How can a country maintain a good relationship with its neighbours?
- In what ways can different countries cooperate with each other?
- Which is more crucial, international cooperation or national interest? Why?
- What are the most popular countries your countrymates like to travel to? Why these ones?
- Why do people decide to travel abroad?
- How is travelling abroad different from travelling domestically?
- Is tourism good or bad for a country? Why?
- What advantages can tourism bring to your country? Why?
- What disadvantages can tourism bring to your country? Why?
- Do you think that tourism might need to change because of environmental issues? Why/why not?
- Can living in a foreign country ever feel like being home? Why/why not?
- Do you think we perceive a foreign country in the same way when we live there and travel there? Why/why not?
- Should people adapt to the culture of the country they decide to live in? Why/why not?
- Is speaking the local language really necessary? Why/why not?
- How does globalisation influence differences between cultures?

- **a historical place you visited**

VOCAB :

1. to be located /ləʊˈkeɪtɪd/ (adj.) = to exist in a particular place
2. reputation /ˌrepjʊˈteɪʃ(ə)n/ (n.) = the opinion that people have about how good or bad sb or sth is
3. an attractive spot (phr.) = an appealing place to visit
4. a fabulous panoramic view of /ˌpænəˈræmɪk/ (phr.) = a great view of a large area of land or sea around you
5. an original style (phr.) = a special style
6. world-renowned /rɪˈnaʊnd/ (adj.) = famous
7. to date back to (v.) = to be made or begun at a particular time in the past
8. the annals of sth /ˈæn(ə)lz/ (n.) = the official records of sth, arranged according to its date

9. ancient /ˈeɪnʃ(ə)nt/ (adj.) = relating to people who lived thousands of years ago and to their way of life
10. bustling /ˈbʌs(ə)lɪŋ/ (adj.) = full of noise and activity, usually pleasant and interesting
11. a contemporary feel (phr.) = a modern quality
12. a fairly compact city /ˈkɒmpækt/ (phr.) = a small city but arrange in a way that uses space very effectively
13. touristy /ˈtʊərɪsti/ (adj.) = designed for tourists or full of tourists
14. momentous /məʊˈmentəs/ (adj.) = very important because of having an effect on future events
15. a sight /saɪt/ (n.) = a place to visit
16. a memorial /məˈmɔːriəl/ (n.) = a structure built to remind people of a famous person or event

PART 3 :
↝ Do people in your country enjoy visiting historical places? Why/why not?
↝ What historical places are the most popular today? Why?
↝ Were people more into visiting historical places in the past? Why/why not?
↝ Are visits to historical sites in your country free? Why/why not?
↝ What's the best way to learn about history? Why?
↝ How can history help us at present?
↝ In what ways can people learn about history? Why?
↝ Can watching historical movies be helpful in learning about the past? Why/why not?
↝ Do you think historical films should always depict history accurately? Why/why not?
↝ Is it important for an individual to know his or her country's history?
↝ Why do you think there are so many different versions of history? What does it depend on?
↝ How do you think future generations will remember our century? Why?

• **a leisure centre/sports centre you often go to**

VOCAB :
1. endurance /ɪnˈdjʊərəns/ (n.) = the ability to continue doing sth physically difficult
2. flexibility /ˌfleksəˈbɪləti/ (n.) = the ability to bend or move easily
3. a physical capacity /kəˈpæsəti/ (phr.) = energy
4. to be on a crash diet (phr.) = to attempt to lose weight in a very short time
5. an open-style lobby /ˈlɒbi/ (phr.) = the area inside the sports centre
6. aerobics /eəˈrəʊbɪks/ (n.) = very active physical exercises done while listening to music, often in a class
7. to burn calories /ˈkæləriz/ (phr.) = to lose some units of energy from food through physical exercise
8. a sedentary job /ˈsed(ə)nt(ə)ri/ (phr.) = a job involving a lot of sitting and not much exercise
9. blood circulation /ˌsɜː(r)kjʊˈleɪʃ(ə)n/ (phr.) = the continues movement of blood around your body
10. muscle strength /ˈmʌs(ə)l/ (phr.) = the power your muscles have
11. to feel refreshed /rɪˈfreʃt/ (phr.) = to feel more lively and comfortable after you have rested, washed, eaten etc.
12. to feel invigorated /ɪnˈvɪɡəreɪtɪd/ (phr.) = to feel full of energy
13. state-of-the-art facilities (phr.) = very modern facilities
14. a gym /dʒɪm/ (n.) = a large hall or room with special equipment for doing physical exercises

15. a treadmill /ˈtredˌmɪl/ (n.) = a piece of exercise equipment with a flat moving surface that you walk or run on while staying in the same place
16. a stationary bike /ˈsteɪʃ(ə)n(ə)ri/ (n.) = an exercise bike
17. a cross-trainer (n.) = a piece of exercise equipment with parts that you stand on and parts that you hold, allowing you to move your legs and arms backwards and forwards
18. a personal trainer (n.) = someone whose job is to make you fit by showing you how to exercise effectively
19. a sauna /ˈsɔːnə/ (n.) = a small hot wooden room that people sit in in order to sweat
20. weight training (n.) = exercise that involves lifting weights, especially using equipment in a gym
21. Pilates /pɪˈlɑːteɪz/ (n.) = a form of exercise in which you develop the muscles in your abdomen in order to control your body movement and protect your back
22. Zumba /ˈzʊmbə/ (n.) = an exercise programme based mainly on Latin American dancing and music
23. water aerobics (n.) = aerobics exercise in fairly shallow water such as in a swimming pool
24. jazz dancing /dʒæz/ (n.) = dancing including a broad range of dance styles

PART 3 :

- ↻ Do people in your country often go to leisure centres? Why/why not?
- ↻ What can people do in sport centres?
- ↻ Who enjoys going to a leisure centre more, young people or older people? Why?
- ↻ Were sport centres popular in your country in the past? Why/why not?
- ↻ Do you think more of fewer people will visit leisure centres in the future? Why?
- ↻ Are leisure centres free of charge in your country?
- ↻ Do you think the government should sponsor sport centres? Why/why not?
- ↻ Why do you think some people can't keep up the habit of exercising regularly?
- ↻ Why don't some people exercise at all?
- ↻ How can leisure centres contribute to local communities? Why?
- ↻ What's the best location for a sport centre? Why?

- **a library you often use**

VOCAB :

1. shabby /ˈʃæbi/ (adj.) = old and in bad condition
2. well-equipped /ɪˈkwɪpt/ (adj.) = with a lot of useful items
3. a librarian /laɪˈbreəriən/ (n.) = someone who works in a library or who is in charge of a library
4. to turn a deaf ear to the students' inquiry (phr.) = to ignore students' problem entirely
5. to be absorbed in study /əbˈzɔː(r)bd/ (phr.) = to be so interested or involved in study that you do not notice anything else
6. reference materials /ˈref(ə)rəns/ (phr.) = books with information
7. a bookworm /ˈbʊkˌwɜː(r)m/ (n.) = sb who enjoys reading books and spends a lot of time doing it
8. bibliography /ˌbɪbliˈɒɡrəfi/ (n.) = a list of books, articles etc that sb has used for finding information for a piece of work they have written
9. inter-library loan (phr.) = system where libraries exchange books with one another
10. to cram for an exam (phr.) = to study intensively for a short time
11. airy /ˈeəri/ (adj.) = with a lot of fresh air and space

12. an almanac /ˈɔːlməˌnæk/ (n.) = a publication, usually issued annually, containing facts and statistics
13. an anthology /ænˈθɒlədʒi/ (n.) = a compilation of writings or poems from one or more authors focusing on a particular subject
14. a catalogue /ˈkætəlɒg/ (n.) = a list of records that represent the holdings of a library
15. a database /ˈdeɪtəˌbeɪs/ (n.) = an organized collection of information
16. stacks /stæks/ (n.) = shelves where the books and other library materials are located

PART 3 :
- Do you think government should input more money in libraries or should citizens pay to use them? Why?
- Do many people go to libraries in your country? Why/why not?
- Did people go to libraries more often in the past? Why/why not?
- Do you think people will stop using libraries one day? Why/why not?
- Who enjoys libraries more, young people or older people? Why?
- Apart from reading, what can one do in a library? Why?
- Are resources available in libraries still useful? Why/why not?
- Do you think all libraries should be computerized? Why/why not?

- **a park/garden you visited/a place in the open air you have been to**

VOCAB :
1. to be bathed in sunshine /bɑːθt/ (phr.) = to be covered by sunshine
2. brushy trees /ˈbrʌʃi/ (phr.) = trees covered in brushwood
3. a botanic garden /bəˌtænɪk ˈgɑː(r)d(ə)n/ (n.) = an establishment where plants are grown for display to the public and often for scientific study
4. unique natural scenery (phr.) = a special place with nature
5. to be encircled by /ɪnˈsɜː(r)k(ə)ld/ (adj.) = to be completely surrounded by
6. a pine tree /paɪn/ (n.) = a tall tree with thin sharp leaves called needles that do not fall off in winter, and hard brown fruits called cones
7. a fir /fɜː(r)/ (n.) = a tall tree with thin sharp leaves that do not fall off in winter, it produces large hard brown fruits called cones
8. a maple tree /ˈmeɪp(ə)l/ (n.) = a tree that grows mainly in northern countries and has wide
9. multicoloured flowers /ˌmʌltiˈkʌlə(r)d/ (phr.) = flowers of many different colours
10. spectacular /spekˈtækjʊlə(r)/ (adj.) = extremely impressive
11. charming /ˈtʃɑː(r)mɪŋ/ (adj.) = very attractive and pleasant
12. sth makes your eyes dazzled to death /ˈdæz(ə)ld/ (phr.) = sth impresses you a lot, with its beauty
13. smashing /ˈsmæʃɪŋ/ (adj.) = very good or impressive
14. the cute dews dancing on the petals of flowers /djuːz/ (phr.) = small drops of water that form on the ground during the night and look like they are dancing
15. like a fairyland /ˈfeərɪlænd/ (phr.) = like an imaginary place where fairies live
16. evergreen trees /ˈevə(r)ˌgriːn/ (phr.) = trees covered in green leaves all year long, not only in summer
17. a flowerbed /ˈflaʊə(r)ˌbed/ (n.) = an area in a garden or park where flowers are grown
18. autumn foliage /ˈfəʊliɪdʒ/ (phr.) = the leaves of plants and tress in autumn

19. a bush /bʊʃ/ (n.) = a plant that is smaller than a tree and has a lot of thin branches growing close together
20. a campground /ˈkæmpˌɡraʊnd/ (n.) = an American word for a campsite (Br.)
21. to come into bloom/blossom /bluːm ˈblɒs(ə)m/ (phr.) = (of a tree or plant) to be covered with flowers
22. to bear fruit (phr.) = to produce fruit
23. to imitate the best of nature /ˈɪmɪteɪt/ (phr.) = to copy the beauty of nature
24. a site /saɪt/ (n.) = a place where you can stay in a tent or caravan
25. a gentle slope going down to a pond (phr.) = a gentle slide of a hill or a mountain ending in a pond
26. a shed /ʃed/ (n.) = a small building, usually made of wood, in which you store things
27. a butterfly /ˈbʌtə(r)ˌflaɪ/ (n.) = a flying insect with large colourful wings
28. to scatter seeds /ˈskætə(r) siːdz/ (phr.) = to throw seeds in order to plant sth
29. a meadow /ˈmedəʊ/ (n.) = a field where grass and wild flowers grow

PART 3 :
- Who do you think should be responsible for the public parks or gardens in your city? Why?
- How important is it for a country to have a national park? Why?
- Why do people generally enjoy visiting parks and gardens?
- Should the entrance to parks and gardens be free? Why?
- How do people in your country use gardens around their homes?
- Is it important for children to have a garden to play in? Why/why not?
- What do people in your country usually grow in their private gardens? Why?
- Is it a good idea to grow your own food in the garden? Why?
- Are there a lot of public gardens where you live?
- What do people like to do in public gardens? Why?
- Do people in your country often visit public gardens? Why/why not?
- Who like going to gardens more, young people or older people? Why?
- How could your government develop more green areas where you live?
- Do you study about food at schools in your country?
- Are people in your country generally aware of where food comes from? Why/why not?
- Are you encouraged in your country to grow your own food? Why/why not?
- Do you think if people knew how to grow their own food, the environment would be cleaner? Why/why not?
- How can children benefit from growing things? Why?
- When do people usually use flowers? What for?
- Why do you think some people enjoy having their own garden?
- What are main benefits of growing your own food? Why?
- Why do you think city dwellers complain about the lack of green spaces?
- Should we pay to visit city parks? Why/why not?
- Can city parks be taken over by modern houses in the future? Why/why not?
- Does your country have a national park?
- How does your country protect wildlife and natural landscapes? Why?
- Should the public be allowed to visit protected areas? Why/why not?
- How do you see the future of national parks or protected areas? Why?

252

- **a place near water/lake/river/sea you really liked/a seaside place you would like to visit/leisure activity near the sea**

  ## VOCAB :
  1. to overlook the ocean /ˌəʊvə(r)ˈlʊk/ (phr.) = to have a view at the ocean from above
  2. to enjoy the unbroken coastline (phr.) = to appreciate the coastline that is not damaged
  3. transparent water /trænsˈpærənt/ (phr.) = water clear enough to see through it
  4. a cool breeze /briːz/ (phr.) = a refreshing light wind
  5. to witness happiness and sorrows /ˈwɪtnəs/ (phr.) = to see happiness and unhappiness
  6. flow /fləʊ/ (n.) = the movement of the sea in towards the land
  7. a reservoir /ˈrezə(r)ˌvwɑː(r)/ (n.) = a lake where water is stored so that is can be supplied to the houses in an area
  8. a stream /striːm/ (n.) = a small narrow river
  9. a canal /kəˈnæl/ (n.) = an artificial river
  10. tide /taɪd/ (n.) = the way that the level of the sea regularly rises and falls during the day
  11. tropical scenes /ˈtrɒpɪk(ə)l/ (phr.) = scenes in the hottest parts of the world
  12. attractive nature (phr.) = impressive nature
  13. a deluxe sea-view room /dəˈlʌks/ (phr.) = a room which has a sea view and is more expensive than others because of its better quality
  14. a luxury suite /ˈlʌkʃəri swiːt/ (phr.) = an expensive set of rooms
  15. crystal clear water (phr.) = very clear water
  16. reflecting the blue sky (phr.) = showing the image of the blue sky
  17. swimming in it is just like a fantasy (phr.) = swimming somewhere feels amazing
  18. radiant sunshine /ˈreɪdiənt/ (phr.) = very bright sunshine
  19. intoxicating flowers /ɪnˈtɒksɪˌkeɪtɪŋ/ (phr.) = flowers giving you a lot of happiness or excitement
  20. mouth-watering seafood (phr.) = very tasty seafood
  21. to soak up the sunshine (phr.) = to spend time experiencing the sunshine
  22. murky /ˈmɜː(r)ki/ (adj.) = dark and difficult to see through usually because of dirt in the water
  23. a deckchair /ˈdekˌtʃeə(r)/ (n.) = a light chair made of canvas (strong cloth) on a wooden frame that you can fold up, used for sitting on outside in warm water, especially at the beach
  24. a beach umbrella (n.) = a huge umbrella designed to protect you from the sun on the beach
  25. to sunbathe /ˈsʌnˌbeɪð/ (v.) = to sit or lie in the sun so that your skin becomes darker
  26. sunburn /ˈsʌnˌbɜː(r)n/ (n.) = the condition of having red sore skin that is caused by staying in the sun for too long
  27. to get tanned /tænd/ (phr.) = to get darker skin than before because of spending time in the sun
  28. a suntan lotion (n.) = a lotion that you rub onto your skin to stop it from being burned by the sun
  29. sunstroke /ˈsʌnˌstrəʊk/ (n.) = a dangerous physical condition that results when your body temperature gets too hot
  30. to dive /daɪv/ (v.) = to jump into water
  31. to splash about /splæʃ/ (v.) = to move around noisily in water
  32. wetlands /ˈwetlændz/ (n.) = low land that is often covered with water from the lake, river, or sea next to it
  33. to be inland /ˈɪnlənd/ (phr.) = not near a coast
  34. water-skiing (n.) = a sport in which you stand on skis and ride on the surface of water while being pulled behind a boat

35. jet skiing (n.) = driving a Jet Ski
36. water polo (n.) = a game played in water by two teams of seven players who get points by throwing a ball into the opponent's goal
37. to wiggle your toes in the sand /ˈwɪɡ(ə)l/ (phr.) = to make short quick movements from side to side in the sand
38. to splash in the waves /splæʃ/ (phr.) = to hit the surface of the water nosily for fun
39. to build sand castles (phr.) = to make castles out of sand on the beach
40. a beach-goer (n.) = a person who goes to the beach regularly
41. to snorkel /ˈsnɔː(r)k(ə)l/ (v.) = to swim under water using a snorkel
42. powdery sand /ˈpaʊd(ə)ri/ (phr.) = sand like powder
43. a gondola /ˈɡɒndələ/ (n.) = a long narrow boat with curved ends that you move using a long pole

PART 3 :
- What's the most popular seaside place for people in your country to visit? Why?
- Why do you think so many people like to go to the seaside for their holidays?
- Who enjoys holidays by the sea, children or adults? Why?
- What activities can a person do on the beach?
- Do you think in the future more or fewer people will be going to the seaside? Why?
- What can you do at the seaside when the weather isn't too good? Why?
- Do many people choose to travel by sea today? Why/why not?
- What are some advantages of travelling by sea?
- Can a person learn anything during travelling by sea? What?
- Did people travel by sea more in the past? Why/why not?
- What goods are usually transported by sea? Is it safe? Why/why not?
- Do you think there should be some international regulation concerning fishing? Why/why not?
- Some people claim it's better to dispose rubbish into the sea than dump it on land. What do you think? Why?
- What main problems do seas have? How can they be solved? Why?
- Are there any health benefits of spending time by the sea? If so, what are they?
- What kinds of jobs need the sea?
- What are some advantages of travelling by the sea?
- What are some disadvantages of travelling by the sea?
- Are goods still transported by the sea today? Why/why not?
- Do you think goods will be still transported by the sea in the future? Why/why not?
- What marine resources do we lack?
- How is global warming affecting the marine organisms?
- How can fish be protected?
- Do you think scientists will continue exploring the undersea?
- Is exploration or the underworld beneficial or harmful to the environment? Why?
- What water sports do people in your country usually do? Why?
- Why do people generally enjoy doing water sports?
- Is there any historical value to water where you live?
- Is oil as important as water? Why/why not?
- Is technology going to be helpful with solving the problem of water shortage in the world? Why/why not?

- ↻ What leisure activities do people in your country do with water?
- ↻ In your opinion, should everyone learn to swim? Why/why not?
- ↻ How can spending time by the lake affect people's well-being?
- ↻ Is there enough water in the world?
- ↻ Which world regions suffer from water shortage? Why?
- ↻ How is water important to us?
- ↻ What needs to be done to make people realize how important a resource water is?
- ↻ How can people save water on a daily basis?
- ↻ How can governments encourage masses to save water?
- ↻ How is the sea important to a country?
- ↻ Is the sea still used for trade? Why/why not?
- ↻ Why do scientists explore the bottom of the sea?
- ↻ Is the exploration of the outer space necessary? Why/why not?
- ↻ How do you see the future of the sea?
- ↻ Is marine life going to survive in the future? Why/why not?
- ↻ Do you think parents should teach their children how to swim? Why/why not?
- ↻ Is water freely available to everyone in your country? Why/why not?
- ↻ How does water consumption vary in the rural areas and in the urban areas?
- ↻ Do you think the world might experience water shortage in the future? Why/why not? If so, what could be done to prevent it?

- **a place of natural beauty you found truly beautiful/you would like to visit**

VOCAB :
1. everything exists together in a delicate balance /ˈdelɪkət/ (phr.) = there is a pleasant balance between all
2. an picturesque landscape /ˌpɪktʃəˈresk/ (phr.) = and attractive area of land
3. open spaces (phr.) = areas of protected or conserved land on which development is indefinitely set aside
4. remote /rɪˈməʊt/ (adj.) = far away from other cities, towns or people
5. tranquil /ˈtræŋkwɪl/ (adj.) = calm, still and quiet
6. serene /səˈriːn/ (adj.) = calm and peaceful
7. far away from the hustle and bustle of city life (phr.) = away from liveliness of the city
8. to relieve stress /rɪˈliːv/ (phr.) = to make stress less unpleasant
9. to be dotted with /ˈdɒtɪd/ (adj.) = to be present in many parts of the place
10. snow-capped mountains /ˈsnəʊ kæpt/ (phr.) = mountains that have snow on the top
11. winding paths /ˈwaɪndɪŋ pɑːθs/ (phr.) = paths with a lot of bends
12. gentle rolling hills /ˈrəʊlɪŋ/ (phr.) = hills that continue for a long distance
13. undulating hills /ˈʌndjʊleɪtɪŋ/ (phr.) = hills that move gently up and down in the shape of waves on the sea
14. iridescent trees /ˌɪrɪˈdes(ə)nt/ (phr.) = trees changing colours in different types of light
15. a shimmering reflection in the lake /ˈʃɪmə(r)ɪŋ/ (phr.) = a gentle and slightly shaking reflection in the lake
16. awe-inspiring (adj.) = making you feel great respect and admiration, sometimes fear
17. exhilarating /ɪgˈzɪləˌreɪtɪŋ/ (adj.) = making you feel extremely happy, excited, and full of energy

18. deciduous trees /dɪˈsɪdjuəs/ (phr.) = trees that lose all their leaves each autumn
19. vegetation /ˌvedʒəˈteɪʃ(ə)n/ (n.) = plants and trees
20. to save natural resources (phr.) = to use valuable substances such as wood and oil in a smart way

PART 3 :
↪ What are some popular places of natural beauty in your country?
↪ Do people in your country often go to places of natural beauty? Why/why not?
↪ What benefits can a visit to a place of natural beauty bring?
↪ Which do you find more interesting to visit, a place of natural beauty or a city? Why?
↪ Are places of natural beauty protected in your country? If so, in what ways?
↪ Do you think tourism has a negative effect on places of natural beauty? Why/why not?
↪ What can be done to protect places of natural beauty?
↪ Whose responsibility is it to protect places of natural beauty? Why?
↪ Do industries exploit places of natural beauty in your country? If so, in what ways?
↪ Can a city be beautiful? Why/why not?
↪ How can we have more greenery in cities?
↪ Do people need nature to be happy? Why/why not?
↪ Is it better to describe the beauty of nature in words or pictures? Why?
↪ Why has nature been an inspiration to so many artists?

* **a school you attended in your childhood**

VOCAB :
1. a boarding school (n.) = a school in which most or all of the students live during the part of the year that they go to lessons
2. a campus /ˈkæmpəs/ (n.) = an area of land containing all the main buildings of a university
3. a dormitory /ˈdɔː(r)mɪtri/ (n.) = a large room where a lot of people sleep, for example in a school or army camp
4. school premises /ˈpremɪsɪz/ (phr.) = the buildings and land that a school uses
5. tons of homework /tʌnz/ (phr.) = a lot of homework
6. high pressure of exams (phr.) = stress related to exams
7. to have butterflies in your stomach (phr.) = to feel very nervous about sth, for example exams
8. an auditorium /ˌɔːdɪˈtɔːriəm/ (n.) = a large room or building used for meetings, lectures, or public performances
9. a computer laboratory /ləˈbɒrət(ə)ri/ (n.) = a building or large room where students study Computer Science
10. a science lab (n.) = a place where students study science, equipped with all necessary things
11. brightly coloured (adj.) = with strong colours
12. concrete /ˈkɒŋkriːt/ (adj.) = made of concrete
13. elegant /ˈelɪɡənt/ (adj.) = beautiful in a simple way
14. pebbledashed /ˈpeb(ə)lˌdæʃt/ (adj.) = made of cement mixed with a lot of small pebbles and spread over the outside walls of a house
15. single-storey (adj.) = (of a building) with just one level
16. hideous /ˈhɪdiəs/ (adj.) = very ugly

17. timbered /ˈtɪmbə(r)d/ (adj.) = a timbered building has outside walls made completely or partly of wood

PART 3 :

- ↻ What are the main differences between schools in urban areas and schools in the suburbs?
- ↻ Is it important to have options of extra-curriculum activities at school? Why/why not? What kinds of activities?
- ↻ Should school facilities by available to society?
- ↻ Which is more important: good teachers or good amenities? Why?
- ↻ What kind of a person can be a good children teacher? Why?
- ↻ What qualities does a good teacher need? Why?
- ↻ Do you think teachers give children too much homework today? Why/why not?
- ↻ Is it better to attend a big school or a small one? Why?
- ↻ Do children learn better in big or small classes? Why?
- ↻ Is it easy to make friends in large schools? Why/why not?
- ↻ Is competition fiercer in big schools? Why/why not?
- ↻ Do you think students who go to a large school are at an educational advantage? If so, how? Why/why not?
- ↻ Do you study any social subjects in schools in your country? Why/why not?
- ↻ Do schools have any other functions apart from the educational one?
- ↻ How can schools teach students social skills? Why?
- ↻ Whose input is more important when it comes to teaching social behaviours: school's or parents'? Why?
- ↻ Do you think schools in your country prepare their students well for the future social life? Why/why not?

- **a shop/shopping mall/street you often go to/that you like**

VOCAB :

1. a wide selection of goods (phr.) = a variety of items to choose from
2. décor /ˈdekɔː(r)/ (n.) = the style of decoration and furniture in a building
3. a customer /ˈkʌstəmə(r)/ (n.) = a person or company that buys goods or services
4. a commodity /kəˈmɒdəti/ (n.) = something that can be bought and sold, especially a basic food product or fuel
5. modest in price /ˈmɒdɪst/ (phr.) = not too expensive
6. high in quality (phr.) = of very good quality
7. the highlight is /ˈhaɪˌlaɪt/ (phr.) = the most exciting, impressive or interesting part of sth
8. neons /ˈniːɒnz/ (n.) = fluorescent lighting or signs using neon or another gas, used for advertising
9. to go window shopping (phr.) = to look at things in shop windows but not buying anything
10. to become widely available (phr.) = to be easily accessible to all
11. final clearance /ˈklɪərəns/ (phr.) = the time when shops are selling out most of their goods at a lower price
12. a boutique /buːˈtiːk/ (n.) = a small fashionable shop, especially one that sells clothes
13. retail therapy (phr.) = the activity of shopping in order to make yourself feel happier
14. a chain store (n.) = one of a group of shops that all belong to the same person or company

15. to sell the atmosphere (phr.) = to attract more customers due to good atmosphere in a shop
16. intimate /ˈɪntɪmət/ (adj.) = private and friendly and makes you feel relaxed and comfortable
17. a fancy wallpaper /ˈwɔːlˌpeɪpə(r)/ (phr.) = a very nice thick paper on walls inside a house decorating them
18. stuffed sofas /stʌft/ (phr.) = sofas filled with a soft material
19. an alley /ˈæli/ (n.) = a narrow street or passage between or behind buildings
20. a cobbled street /ˈkɒb(ə)ld/ (phr.) = a street covered with round cobblestones
21. street musicians (phr.) = musicians performing on the street for money
22. an impulse shopper /ˈɪmpʌls/ (phr.) = a person who does shopping based on strong feelings they have to buy things
23. to go somewhere in search of sth (phr.) = to go somewhere hoping to find sth
24. a price tag (n.) = a label on a product that says how much it costs
25. to shop till you drop (phr.) = to shop for a very long time until one is extremely tired
26. to browse /braʊz/ (v.) = to look at things in a shop without being sure whether you want to buy anything
27. to be after a particular thing (phr.) = to be looking for a specific thing in a shop
28. to have an eye for a bargain (phr.) = to be very good finding good deals
29. to shop around (v.) = to go to several shops before you decide what particular thing to buy
30. to be distracted by cheap offers (phr.) = to buy sth just because it's cheap and not for its excellent quality
31. spending spree /spriː/ (phr.) = a short period of time you spend shopping
32. bargain hunting /ˈhʌntɪŋ/ (phr.) = looking for bargains
33. to indulge in /ɪnˈdʌldʒ/ (v.) = to allow yourself to have or do sth that you enjoy
34. crippling financial debts /ˈkrɪplɪŋ/ (phr.) = financial problems causing damage or more problems
35. a regular customer (phr.) = a person who always shops in the same place
36. to stand in line (phr.) = to queue for sth
37. stalls (n.) = large tables or small buildings that are open at the front, used for selling things or for giving people information
38. a vendor /ˈvendə(r)/ (n.) = sb who sells sth, but not in a shop
39. a knick-knack (n.) = a small cheap object used as a decoration
40. to stroll along /strəʊl/ (v.) = to walk without hurrying, often for pleasure

PART 3 :
↻ Which is better, shopping in a large shopping mall or a small local shop? Why?
↻ What are the usual working hours of shops in your country?
↻ Do you think certain shops should be open 24/7? Why? Which ones?
↻ Why do so many people like to spend time in shopping malls?
↻ How are shopping malls bad for the environment?
↻ Is Internet shopping popular in your country? Why/why not?
↻ Is Internet shopping safe? Why/why not?
↻ Why has the popularity of Internet shopping grown in recent years?
↻ What are main advantages of Internet shopping?
↻ What are main disadvantages of shopping online?
↻ How does Internet shopping influence local shops?
↻ Do you think people generally spend too much these days? Why/why not?

- What are some reasons for increase in consumerism?
- Can consumerism be a good thing for a country? In what way?
- How does consumerism influence society negatively?
- Are credit cards encouraging consumerism? Why/why not?
- Does everyone have the responsibility to get involved in local community's activities? Why/why not?
- How does technology influence local communities?

- **a tourist attraction in your country worth visiting**

VOCAB :

1. a tourist attraction (n.) = a place to visit that is very popular with tourists
2. to generate tax revenue /ˈdʒenəreɪt/ (phr.) = to produce the income that is gained by governments through taxation
3. a cultural mosaic /məʊˈzeɪɪk/ (phr.) = sth that consists of a combination of different cultures
4. to show sb the sights (phr.) = to take sb to see the most famous places
5. a sightseeing tour /ˈsaɪtˌsiːɪŋ/ (n.) = a tour that focuses on travelling around a place to see the interesting things in it
6. a date of foundation (phr.) = a time in the past when sth was started
7. to date back to (v.) = to be made or begun at a particular time in the past
8. ancient /ˈeɪnʃ(ə)nt/ (adj.) = very old
9. medieval /ˌmediˈiːv(ə)l/ (adj.) = relating to the period of European history between about the year 1000 ad and the year 1500
10. a fine example of (Gothic, Baroque, Renaissance) architecture (phr.) = a great representation of architecture
11. to be preserved /prɪˈzɜː(r)vd/ (adj.) = to be taken care of (a place or building) in order to prevent it from being destroyed
12. remains /rɪˈmeɪnz/ (n.) = the part of something that is left after the rest has been finished, used, or destroyed
13. to restore /rɪˈstɔː(r)/ (v.) = to clean and repair sth old and dirty so that it looks the same as it did originally
14. a monument /ˈmɒnjʊmənt/ (n.) = a place of historical importance, for example an old building
15. to escape the crowd (phr.) = to go where there are not many people
16. hordes of people /hɔː(r)dz/ (phr.) = (neg.) crowds
17. fortification /ˌfɔː(r)tɪfɪˈkeɪʃ(ə)n/ (n.) = the process of making buildings, walls etc stronger in order to defend a place
18. awe-inspiring (adj.) = it fills you with a sense of the power and beauty of what you are looking at
19. to be worth seeing (phr.) = to be worth a visit
20. little known (adj.) = not so popular
21. a notable feature /ˈnəʊtəb(ə)l ˈfiːtʃə(r)/ (phr.) = an interesting part
22. the charm of the place /tʃɑː(r)m/ (phr.) = a pleasant quality that attracts people
23. to wander around /ˈwɒndə(r)/ (v.) = to travel from place to place, especially on foot, without a particular direction or purpose
24. an imperial palace /ɪmˈpɪəriəl ˈpæləs/ (n.) = a very large building used as the official home of a royal family, president, emperor

25. ceremonial /ˌserəˈməʊniəl/ (adj.) = a ceremonial event follows a formal or traditional pattern
26. to exemplify/ɪgˈzemplɪfaɪ/ (v.) = to be a typical example of something
27. a sightseeing fanatic /fəˈnætɪk/ (phr.) = sb who loves sightseeing very much
28. in the heart of (phr.) = in the central part of sth
29. trashed with litter (phr.) = full of rubbish
30. a signature landmark (phr.) = a special spot
31. off the tourist trail (phr.) = not on the main tourist path
32. an unexplored ancient village (phr.) = a very old village that not many people have visited yet

PART 3 :
↻ What types of tourist attractions can visitors enjoy in your country?
↻ What are the most popular tourist sites in your country?
↻ Have most people visited famous places in their country? Why/why not?
↻ Is it important for citizens to know and see tourist attractions? Why/why not?
↻ Are tourist attractions free in your country? Why/why not?
↻ What's the best way to visit tourist attractions? Why?
↻ Do you think people of different ages enjoy different attractions? Why/why not?
↻ What can children learn from visiting famous spots?
↻ Do schoolchildren often go on trips to famous places? Why/why not?
↻ Is it better to go on a guided tour or individually when visiting famous attractions? Why?
↻ How does tourism affect country's economy?
↻ How do international tourists influence local cultures? Why?
↻ How do huge numbers of visitors affect natural places?
↻ Should the number of visitors to places of natural beauty be controlled? If so, how?
↻ Do you think that if people want to contribute to environmental protection they shouldn't visit places of natural beauty? Why/why not?

• **a town/city you visited as a tourist**

VOCAB :
1. a flourishing place /ˈflʌrɪʃɪŋ/ (phr.) = a successful place
2. brain drain (n.) = a situation in which a country's most intelligent people, especially scientists, go to another country in order to make more money or to improve their living or working conditions
3. my kind of place (phr.) = a place that suits my taste
4. cosmopolitan /ˌkɒzməˈpɒlɪt(ə)n/ (adj.) = showing the influence of many different countries and cultures
5. a metropolis /məˈtrɒpəlɪs/ (n.) = a big city
6. a city-dweller /ˈdwelə(r)/ (n.) = a person who lives in a city
7. anonymity /ˌænəˈnɪməti/ (n.) = a situation in which something has no interesting or unusual features
8. to be amazed by its magnificence (phr.) = to be shocked by its perfection
9. to get a better insight into the history of /ˈɪnsaɪt/ (phr.) = to understand the history of a place better
10. rapid development /ˈræpɪd/ (phr.) = quick improvement
11. renovated /ˈrenəveɪtɪd/ (adj.) = made old look new again by repairing and improving it

260

12. to be marked by /mɑː(r)kt/ (adj.) = to be noticeable because of sth
13. a perfect layout /ˈleɪaʊt/ (phr.) = a really good way in which the different parts of sth are arranged
14. a sleepless city /ˈsliːpləs/ (phr.) = a city that is always vibrant, even at night
15. an industrial city /ɪnˈdʌstriəl/ (phr.) = a city with many industries
16. a historical city (phr.) = a city where an important event in history happened
17. a wide choice of entertainment (phr.) = a variety of places where one can go to have fun
18. bustling /ˈbʌs(ə)lɪŋ/ (adj.) = full of noise and activity and usually pleasant and interesting
19. urban sprawl /ˈɜː(r)bən sprɔːl/ (n.) = a very large area of buildings, industries etc that has spread from a city into the countryside surrounding it, especially in a way that is not attractive
20. lively bars and restaurants (phr.) = bars and restaurants with many customers
21. an inner city (n.) = an area near the centre of a large city where a lot of poverty and other social problems exist
22. shops are boarded up (phr.) = shops are closed as their windows and doors are covered with wooden boards
23. upmarket shops /ʌpˈmɑː(r)kɪt/ (phr.) = shops for people who have a lot of money
24. a pavement café (n.) = a restaurant with tables and chairs outside on the pavement or on a street where vehicles do not normally go
25. an office block (n.) = a large building that contains many offices
26. a retail park (n.) = an area where there are several large shops together in one place, especially furniture shops and electrical shops

PART 3 :
- What amenities do modern cities have?
- Do you think cities will grow bigger and bigger in the future? Why?
- What kinds of attractions do tourists like to see? Why?
- In what way can tourism boost local economy?
- What are some disadvantages of having too many tourists in the city?
- Why do some people prefer to live in the countryside?
- What are the biggest drawbacks of living in a big city?
- What problems do people always face in a city?
- What problems do people always face in the countryside?
- Have there been any changes in styles of buildings where you live in the past 20 years?
- Should historical buildings be preserved or should they make room for apartments? Why?
- Does the government control urban development in your country?
- Do you think modern architecture should match the traditional style of buildings in your country? Why/why not?
- What kind of a person enjoys living in a city? Why?
- What advantages can a city offer to families with children? Why?
- Why do you think so many people migrate to cities today?
- What are the biggest problems cities experience today?
- How do city problems affect people's lives?
- Do you think that people living in the countryside have no problems or different problems? Why?
- Who is in charge of city planning in your country? Why?
- What causes small cities to develop into large ones? Why?
- Is planning necessary for a city to grow? Why/why not?

↻ Do you think that future cities will be entirely different from present ones? Why/why not?

- **a working place you saw/your working place/the best working place you've ever had**

VOCAB :

1. an employee-friendly environment (phr.) = a place where all employees feel welcome
2. to work long hours for low pay (phr.) = to work too much for not enough money
3. a demanding job /dɪˈmɑːndɪŋ/ (phr.) = a job that needs a lot of time, ability and energy
4. a contract /ˈkɒntrækt/ (n.) = a written legal agreement between two people or businesses that says what each must do for the other or give to the other
5. routine work /ˌruːˈtiːn/ (phr.) = ordinary work and not interesting or special
6. to be well-staffed /stɑːft/ (adj.) = to have enough people to work
7. to be short-staffed (adj.) = to not have enough people to work
8. stress-induced diseases /ɪnˈdjuːst/ (phr.) = diseases cause by stress
9. the pace of work /peɪs/ (phr.) = the speed at which sb works
10. occupational hazard /ˌɒkjʊˈpeɪʃ(ə)nəl ˈhæzə(r)d/ (phr.) = sth that could be dangerous or could cause damage related to your job
11. a backbreaking task /ˈbækˌbreɪkɪŋ/ (phr.) = a task that is physically very hard and tiring
12. to work around the clock (phr.) = to work all day and all night
13. telecommuting /ˈtelikəˌmjuːtɪŋ/ (n.) = working from home on a computer and sending work to the office over telephone lines, by modem or fax
14. a teleconference /ˈteliˌkɒnf(ə)rəns/ (n.) = a meeting held among people in different places using an electronic communications system
15. on-the-job training (phr.) = training received while already working
16. a relocation allowance /ˌriːləʊˈkeɪʃ(ə)n əˈlaʊəns/ (n.) = an amount of money sb gets because they need to move to another city for their job
17. a subsidized canteen /ˈsʌbsɪdaɪzd kænˈtiːn/ (phr.) = a place where meals are served at work at low price
18. a performance-related bonus scheme /skiːm/ (phr.) = a system where employees receive bonus depending on their performance at work
19. a benefits package (n.) = a list of extra money or other advantages that you get in addition to your salary from you employer
20. to intervene to resolve the problem /ˌɪntə(r)ˈviːn/ (phr.) = to become involved in the problem in order to solve it
21. proactive /prəʊˈæktɪv/ (adj.) = taking action and making changes before they need to be made, rather than waiting until problems develop
22. to blow sth up out of proportion (phr.) = to make a situation seem much worse than it really is
23. to pass the buck (phr.) = to make sb else deal with sth that you should take responsibility for

PART 3 :
↻ What facilities are necessary for a good working/studying place? Why?
↻ Is it important for a workplace to make you feel happy? Why/why not?
↻ Do you think that some people work too much? Spend too much time in their workplace? Why/why not?
↻ Is studying place really the best place to get knowledge? Why/why not?

262

- What kinds of jobs can people do from home? Why?
- Is it common in your country for people to work from home?
- What kind of unpaid work can be done from home?
- Is volunteering an important job, too? Why/why not?
- Do you think in the future more people might like to work from home? Why? Who would that be?
- What is the connection between modern workplaces and environment?
- What businesses can easily be 'environmentally friendly'? Why?
- Are most businesses in your country 'environmentally friendly'? Why/why not?
- Do you think that large institutions should share the responsibility of environment protection with the government? If so, to what extent? In what way? Why?
- Should students have a say in the way their study place looks like? Why/why not?
- Should school campuses take natural environment into consideration? Why/why not?

- **an exhibition you really enjoyed/a work of art (a statue, painting etc.) you have seen and liked**

VOCAB :
1. to pay a visit to (phr.) = to go somewhere
2. huge number of visitors (phr.) = many people visiting a place
3. a pavilion /pəˈvɪliən/ (n.) = a building or tent at an exhibition or show
4. philistinism /ˈfɪlɪstɪˌnɪz(ə)m/ (n.) = inability to appreciate art or culture
5. a detractor /dɪˈtræktə(r)/ (n.) = a critic
6. the public wised up /waɪzd/ (phr.) = became more sophisticated
7. the art was dumbed down /dʌmd/ (phr.) = became less intellectual
8. to vote with your feet (phr.) = to stop coming
9. sth is deemed mad /diːmd/ (phr.) = sth is considered mad
10. visually literate /ˈvɪʒʊəli ˈlɪt(ə)rət/ (phr.) = educated with regard to art
11. to be inured to criticism /ɪˈnjʊə(r)d/ (phr.) = to not be affected by criticism
12. highbrow /ˈhaɪˌbraʊ/ (adj.) = intended for educated people
13. dazzling /ˈdæzlɪŋ/ (adj.) = inspiring great admiration because it is brilliant in some way
14. evocative /ɪˈvɒkətɪv/ (adj.) = calling up images and memories
15. exquisite /ɪkˈskwɪzɪt/ (adj.) = having rare beauty
16. peerless /ˈpɪə(r)ləs/ (adj.) = better than any other
17. to illustrate the motifs /ˈɪləstreɪt/ (phr.) = to show the ideas
18. to illuminate sth /ɪˈluːmɪneɪt/ (v.) = to make sth clear and easier to understand
19. a long queue /kjuː/ (phr.) = a long line of people waiting for sth
20. to tour around /tʊə(r)/ (v.) = to be performed or shown in several different places
21. stunning /ˈstʌnɪŋ/ (adj.) = very impressive or beautiful
22. to suit all tastes (phr.) = to be liked by everyone
23. a masterpiece /ˈmɑːstə(r)ˌpiːs/ (n.) = an excellent painting, book, piece of music etc, or the best work of art that a particular artist, writer, musician etc has ever produced
24. iconic /aɪˈkɒnɪk/ (adj.) = very famous and well known, and believed to represent a particular idea
25. modern art (n.) = art related to the present time
26. ancient art (n.) = art related to thousand of years ago
27. performance art (n.) = the art form that combines visual art with dramatic performance

263

28. cultural art (n.) = art related to the culture of a particular group, county or society
29. a delicacy /ˈdelɪkəsi/ (n.) = the quality of being delicate in appearance, colour, taste or smell
30. a form of human expression (phr.) = a way of showing one's emotions
31. graffiti /grəˈfiːti/ (n.) = words or pictures drawn on walls in public places
32. massive /ˈmæsɪv/ (adj.) = very large in amount or degree
33. to present its subject matter vividly (phr.) = to express the main idea very clearly
34. to provoke emotional response /prəˈvəʊk/ (phr.) = to cause a reaction based on feelings
35. multifarious /ˌmʌltɪˈfeərɪəs/ (adj.) = consisting of many different types
36. love and art can be linked (phr.) = there's a connection between love and art
37. art is everlasting /ˌevə(r)ˈlɑːstɪŋ/ (phr.) = art exists forever
38. to fill the void /vɔɪd/ (phr.) = to bring back sth that is needed but not present at the moment
39. a manifestation of /ˌmænɪfeˈsteɪʃ(ə)n/ (n.) = evidence that sth exists

PART 3 :

- ☞ What kinds of cultural events do people like to go to in your country? Why?
- ☞ Is it expensive to go to such events?
- ☞ What type of art is popular in your country? Why?
- ☞ Do you think older and younger people enjoy the same or different types of art? Why?
- ☞ Why do you think some people enjoy going to art galleries?
- ☞ Why do you think some people dislike going to art exhibitions?
- ☞ What is the value of art?
- ☞ Why do we need art?
- ☞ Do you think artists are paid enough?
- ☞ Is it reasonable for governments to purchase works of art to be displayed in public places? Why/why not?
- ☞ Why are some pieces of art more valuable than others?
- ☞ What is art?
- ☞ Whose job is it to critique works of art? Why?
- ☞ What's the main difference between a well-made object and a work of art?
- ☞ Do you think an advertisement can be a form of art? Why/why not?
- ☞ Can everyone become a good artist? Why/why not?
- ☞ What skills does a person need to create a work of art? Why?
- ☞ Do you think children should learn art? Why/why not?

- **an old building/a modern/an unusual/an important building you visited/in your city/museum you visited**

VOCAB :

1. sth is conveniently located in (phr.) = it is very easy to get there
2. sophisticated /səˈfɪstɪˌkeɪtɪd/ (adj.) = knowing and understanding a lot about a complicated subject
3. shabby /ˈʃæbi/ (adj.) = old and in bad condition
4. run-down (adj.) = in bad condition because no one has spent money on repairs
5. a modern skyscraper /ˈskaɪˌskreɪpə(r)/ (phr.) = a very tall building

6. a circular driveway /'sɜː(r)kjʊlə(r) 'draɪv weɪ/ (phr.) = a space in front of a building to drive in or park a car in a shape of a circle

7. a large fountain /'faʊntɪn/ (phr.) = a huge structure through which a stream of water is pumped into the air and falls down again

8. a lobby /'lɒbi/ (n.) = the area just inside the entrance to a hotel, theatre, or other large building

9. flooded with natural light /'flʌdɪd/ (phr.) = covered in natural light

10. a chandelier /ˌʃændə'lɪə(r)/ (n.) = a large light that hangs from a ceiling and has branches for holding electric lights or candles

11. scrolls and calligraphy on the walls /skrəʊlz//kə'lɪɡrəfi/ (phr.) = long rolls of paper with ancient writing on and beautiful writing done using special pens or brushes

12. lanterns hanging from the ceiling /'læntə(r)ns/ (phr.) = lights inside a transparent container with a handle for carrying it

13. stunning /'stʌnɪŋ/ (adj.) = very impressive or beautiful

14. an escalator /'eskə leɪtə(r)/ (n.) = a set of moving stairs that take people from one level to another in a large building

15. to remain intact /ɪn'tækt/ (phr.) = not harmed or damaged

16. under construction /kən'strʌkʃ(ə)n/ (phr.) = being built

17. dilapidated /dɪ'læpɪ deɪtɪd/ (adj.) = old and in bad condition

18. elegant /'elɪɡənt/ (adj.) = attractive because they are beautiful in a simple way

19. to be a showcase for /'ʃəʊ keɪs/ (phr.) = an event that emphasizes the good qualities of sth

20. to represent sth /ˌreprɪ'zent/ (v.) = to be a sign or symbol of sth

21. well-ventilated /'ventɪleɪtɪd/ (adj.) = with fresh air

22. spacious /'speɪʃəs/ (adj.) = with a lot of space inside

23. to be an eyesore /'aɪ sɔː(r)/ (n.) = sth that is ugly or unpleasant to look at, especially a building

24. to be a blot on the landscape /blɒt/ (phr.) = sth that makes a place look less attractive, for example an ugly building

25. a commercial building /kə'mɜː(r)ʃ(ə)l/ (phr.) = a building full of offices related to business

26. a residential building /ˌrezɪ'denʃ(ə)l/ (phr.) = a building where all flats are for living

27. to convert sth into /kən'vɜː(r)t/ (v.) = to change from on to another

28. formerly owned by (phr.) = previously belonged to

29. to fall into decay /dɪ'keɪ/ (phr.) = to be gradually destroyed

30. ultra-modern (adj.) = incorporating ideas, styles or techniques only recently developed or available

31. ruins /'ruːɪnz/ (n.) = the parts of a building that remain after it has been severely damaged

32. an artefact /'ɑː(r)tɪ fækt/ (n.) = an object that was made a long time ago and is historically important, for example a tool or weapon

PART 3 :
- ☞ Do most people in your country think it is worth keeping historical buildings? Why/why not?
- ☞ Does you country have many historical buildings? Why/why not?
- ☞ Can we learn anything from visiting a historical building? If so, what?
- ☞ Whose responsibility is it to look after historical buildings? Why?
- ☞ What is the traditional style of housing in your country?
- ☞ Has the style of houses in your country changed in the past few years? Why/why not? How?

- Do you think that we need the same or different types of houses at different stages of our lives? Why?
- What kinds of houses will we have in the future? Why?
- Are buildings in your country usually well-designed? Why/why not?
- Can climate of a place influence the way buildings are constructed? In what way?
- Is it important for buildings to match the landscape surrounding them? Why/why not?
- Who is usually responsible for town planning in your country? Why?
- Do you think most cities in your country are well-planned? Why/why not?
- Should all buildings in a city look similar? Why/why not?
- What can governments do with old, abandoned buildings?
- How do high-rise buildings affect people's lifestyle?
- How could homes be more environmentally friendly?
- Do you think we might have homes built underground or underwater in the future? Why?

- **a zoo or a wildlife park that you have visited**

VOCAB :

1. survival of the fittest (phr.) = the continued existence of organisms that are best adapted to their environment, with the extinction of others, as a concept in the Darwinian theory of evolution
2. a cage /keɪdʒ/ (n.) = a container made of wire or metal bars and used for keeping birds or animals in
3. a menagerie /məˈnædʒəri/ (n.) = a large collection of wild animals kept in cages etc
4. a safari park (n.) = a large area of land where wild animals are kept so that people can drive through and watch them
5. a zoological garden /ˌzuːəlɒdʒɪk(ə)l ˈgɑː(r)d(ə)n/ (n.) = a large place where many types of wild animals are kept, usually in cages, so that people can see them
6. wildlife conservation /ˌkɒnsə(r)ˈveɪʃ(ə)n/ (phr.) = the protection of wildlife
7. to study animal behaviour (phr.) = to investigate how animals behave
8. artificial environment /ˌɑː(r)tɪˈfɪʃ(ə)l/ (phr.) = environment made by people instead of being natural
9. natural habitat /ˈnætʃ(ə)rəl ˈhæbɪtæt/ (n.) = the type of place that a particular animal usually lives in or a particular plant usually grows in, for example a desert, forest, or lake
10. unethical /ʌnˈeθɪk(ə)l/ (adj.) = morally wrong, or against accepted standards of behaviour, especially in a particular profession
11. to stroke an animal /strəʊk/ (phr.) = to gently move your hand over skin, hair, or fur of an animal
12. to hear a loud roar of a lion /rɔː(r)/ (phr.) = to hear a loud deep sound that a lion makes
13. the tiger was in a fit of anger (phr.) = the tiger has a sudden uncontrollable outbreak of anger
14. an animal sanctuary /ˈsæŋktʃuəri/ (phr.) = a special area where animals live in a natural environment protected from people
15. wilderness /ˈwɪldə(r)nəs/ (n.) = an area of land where people do not live or grow crops and where there are no buildings
16. a tasteless exhibition /ˈteɪs(t)ləs/ (phr.) = an exhibition that is ugly or unpleasant
17. brutal /ˈbruːt(ə)l/ (adj.) = extremely violent
18. ill-treated (adj.) = treated in a cruel or unkind way
19. well looked after (adj.) = treated well

20. saved from extinction (phr.) = saved from dying

PART 3 :
- ⟳ Are there many zoos in your country?
- ⟳ Who enjoys going to the zoo?
- ⟳ Are animals kept in zoos treated well? Why/why not?
- ⟳ Are there any wildlife parks in your country?
- ⟳ Where should wildlife parks be located?
- ⟳ Should entrance to zoos and wildlife parks be free of charge? Why/why not?
- ⟳ Is the best way to protect animals keeping them in captivity? Why/why not?
- ⟳ Should children visit zoos? Why/why not?
- ⟳ What can the government do to protect animals?
- ⟳ Do you think more species will become endangered in the future? Why/why not?

PEOPLE

- **a character from a traditional story/a film character/a book character**

VOCAB :
1. sensational /sen'seɪʃ(ə)nəl/ (adj.) = very exciting and surprising
2. a big fan of /fæn/ (phr.) = sb who likes watching or listening to sth such as a sport, films or music very much or who admires a famous or important person very much
3. thought-provoking /'θɔːt prə‚vəʊkɪŋ/ (adj.) = interesting in a way that makes you think of new ideas or that changes your attitude to something
4. to be in tears (phr.) = to be crying
5. tearjerker /'tɪə(r)‚dʒɜː(r)kə(r)/ (n.) = a sad film or story that makes you cry
6. a leading actor /'liːdɪŋ/ (n.) = the main actor
7. a supporting role /sə'pɔː(r)tɪŋ/ (n.) = an important role but not the main part
8. a hero /'hɪərəʊ/ (n.) = the main male character of a book, film, or play, who usually has good qualities
9. a heroine /'herəʊɪn/ (n.) = the main female character of a book, film, or play, who usually has good qualities
10. courage /'kʌrɪdʒ/ (n.) = the ability to do something that you know is right or good, even though it is dangerous, frightening, or very difficult
11. dignity /'dɪgnəti/ (n.) = the impressive behaviour of someone who controls their emotions in a difficult situation
12. humility /hjuː'mɪləti/ (n.) = a way of behaving that shows that you do not think that you are better or more important than other people
13. to inspire sb /ɪn'spaɪə(r)/ (v.) = to give someone the enthusiasm to do or create something
14. an idealist /aɪ'dɪəlɪst/ (n.) = sb who is idealistic
15. a hypocrite /'hɪpəkrɪt/ (n.) = a person who claims to have certain moral principles or beliefs but behaves in a way that shows they are not sincere
16. a snob /snɒb/ (n.) = someone who thinks they are better than other people, usually because of their social class

17. to look down on sb (v.) = to think that you are better or more important than someone else, or to think that something is not good enough for you
18. malicious /məˈlɪʃəs/ (adj.) = unkind and showing a strong feeling of wanting to hurt someone

PART 3 :
- What characters do children like? Why?
- What characters do older people prefer? Why?
- Do you think every story needs a bad character? Why/why not?
- How can the writer make his or her characters more believable? Why?
- What makes a character a great one?
- Do you think authors often base their characters on real people? Why/why not?
- Why do we remember certain characters and forget others straight away?
- What kinds of characters will become famous in the future? Why?
- Were characters in the past created differently than the current ones?
- How does technology affect the way characters are portrayed? Why?
- What characters are the most famous in your culture? Why?
- Does your culture have any superheroes? Why/why not?
- Does every culture need a superhero? Why/why not?
- How can characters influence children in a negative way?

- **a family member you like to spend time with/you'd like to work in the future with**

VOCAB :
1. to be the apple of someone's eye (phr.) = the person that someone loves most of all and is very proud of
2. like chalk and cheese (phr.) = used for saying that two people or things are completely different from each other
3. sb is always there for you (phr.) = you can always rely on this person
4. spontaneous /spɒnˈteɪniəs/ (adj.) = happening in a natural way without being planned or thought about
5. down-to-earth (adj.) = practical and sensible
6. passionate /ˈpæʃ(ə)nət/ (adj.) = showing or expressing strong beliefs, interest, or enthusiasm
7. with integrity /ɪnˈtegrəti/ (phr.) = the quality of always behaving according to the moral principles that you believe in, so that people respect and trust you
8. blood is thicker than water (phr.) = used for saying that family relationships are usually stronger than other types of relationships
9. your own flesh and blood (phr.) = someone's relative
10. to fight like cat and dog (phr.) = to fight or argue often or with a lot of anger
11. there's little love lost between them (phr.) = there's some kind of misunderstanding between them
12. to take sb for granted (phr.) = to expect someone to always be there and do things for you even when you do not show that you are grateful
13. to have a lot in common with sb (phr.) = to have the same features as something else
14. to enjoy each other's company (phr.) = to like spending time together
15. to fall out with sb (v.) = to have an argument with sb

268

16. to get on like a house on fire (phr.) = to become good friends very quickly and have a lot to talk to each other about
17. to have our ups and downs (phr.) = to be sometimes happy and sometimes not

PART 3 :
- Is family in your culture generally important? Why?
- Do young people like to spend time with old people? Why/why not?
- How can people maintain a good family relationship after they have moved overseas?
- Do many families have only one child in your country? Why/why not?
- Who usually takes care of the house in a typical family in your culture?
- Is it generally important to spend time with the family in your country? Why/why not?
- How can time spent with older people benefit the young?
- With whom do young people spend most time in your country? Why?
- How would you describe a typical family relationship in your country? Why?
- Do you think that family relationships become more important as people grow older? Why/why not?
- Why are some families stronger than others?
- What do you think a family unit will look like in the future? Why?
- Do many people establish relationships online today? Why/why not?
- Are social media popular in your country? Why/why not? Which ones?
- What are the main advantages of having friends on social media? Why?
- What are the main disadvantages of having friends on social media? Why?
- How does increased use of social media influence relationships between people? Why?
- Do people often work for family businesses in your culture? Why/why not?
- Is it a good idea to work for a family business? Why/why not?
- What kinds of family businesses are common in your country? Why?
- What are some cons of working for a family business? Why?
- Why do you think some people, despite having the opportunity, don't want to work for a family business?
- Is it better to work for a large or a small company? Why?
- Do people in your country stay with one company for many years or change jobs often? Which is better and why?
- Would you say working in a large corporation is too impersonal? Why?
- How does globalisation affect the ways people do business today? Why?
- How does the Internet influence the ways people do business today? Why?
- Do you think small businesses have a future on the market? Why/why not?
- What potential changes do you see in the way people will work in the future? Why?

- **a famous person/celebrity/sportsperson (domestic/international)/a famous foreigner in your country/you would like to meet**

VOCAB :
1. moral values (phr.) = the recognition between what is right and wrong
2. an upright citizen /ˈʌpraɪt/ (phr.) = an honourable and honest citizen
3. to praise sb /preɪz/ (v.) = to express strong approval or admiration for sb/sth, especially in public

4. a constant centre of attention (phr.) = always in the middle of things
5. to play a major role in sb's life (phr.) = to be important in sb's life
6. a trademark /'treɪdˌmɑː(r)k/ (n.) = a name or design belonging to a particular company, used on its products
7. happy-go-lucky (adj.) = a happy-go-lucky person tends not to worry about the future
8. a chatterbox /'tʃætə(r)ˌbɒks/ (n.) = sb who talks a lot
9. to give sb the red-carpet treatment (phr.) = to treat sb better, as privileged or a distinguished visitor
10. to worship sb /'wɜː(r)ʃɪp/ (v.) = to feel or show respect and love for a god
11. to make a scene /siːn/ (phr.) = to act irrationally and aggressively in public
12. a lame duck (n.) = sb who is not successful and needs a lot of help and support
13. libel /'laɪb(ə)l/ (n.) = the illegal act of writing things about someone that are not true
14. defamation /ˌdefə'meɪʃ(ə)n/ (n.) = the offence of writing or saying something bad about someone that is not true and makes people have a bad opinion of them
15. to hobnob /'hɒbˌnɒb/ (v.) = (neg.) to be friendly with sb who is famous
16. fifteen mins of fame (phr.) = a brief period of fame that a person enjoys before fading back into obscurity
17. to preserve one's integrity /prɪ'zɜː(r)v/ (phr.) = to keep one's character and moral values from changing
18. to meet sb in person (phr.) = to meet with the actual person face to face
19. sth is part and parcel of being famous (phr.) = sth is an aspect of being famous that has to be accepted
20. paparazzi /ˌpæpə'rætsi/ (n.) = photographers who follow famous people in order to take photographs of them that newspapers and magazines will buy
21. extravagant lifestyles /ɪk'strævəgənt/ (phr.) = lifestyles costing a lot of money
22. to dominate the headlines /'dɒmɪneɪt/ (phr.) = to be the most important issue on the headlines
23. a public figure /'fɪgə(r)/ (n.) = a well-known person
24. to court media publicity /kɔː(r)t/ (phr.) = to try to impress the media in order to get more attention from them
25. scandal /'skænd(ə)l/ (n.) = talk or reports in the newspapers or on television about shocking events involving important people
26. in the public eye (phr.) = the state of being known or of interest to people in general, especially through the media
27. in the headlines /'hedˌlaɪnz/ (phr.) = a part of the most important stories in the news
28. an athletic talent /æθ'letɪk/ (phr.) = a person very talented at sports
29. record-breaking /'rekɔː(r)dˌbreɪkɪŋ/ (adj.) = faster, longer, larger etc than anything that has been done before
30. a tabloid /'tæblɔɪd/ (n.) = a newspaper with fairly small pages mostly containing stories about famous people and not much serious news
31. to suffer from press intrusion /ɪn'truːʒ(ə)n/ (phr.) = to be a victim of media interrupting your peaceful and private life
32. to pry into sb's life /praɪ/ (phr.) = to be interested in someone's personal life in a way that is annoying or offensive
33. rehab /'riːˌhæb/ (n.) = the process of helping someone to give up drugs or alcohol
34. to rock sb/sth (v.) = to shock, surprise or frighten sb

35. rumour /ˈruːmə(r)/ (n.) = unofficial information that may or may not be true
36. to be under the microscope /ˈmaɪkrəˌskəʊp/ (phr.) = to be under critical examination
37. to make a name for yourself (phr.) = to become well-known
38. fame comes at a price (phr.) = being famous has its own disadvantages
39. fame can go to someone's head (phr.) = fame can make someone conceited
40. an instant star /ˈɪnstənt/ (phr.) = sb who became famous very quickly
41. to fall by the wayside (phr.) = to not be successful or effective any longer
42. to cast a shadow over sth (phr.) = to make a situation seem less hopeful and more likely to end badly

PART 3 :

- Why do you think some people who died long time ago are still famous today?
- What are some advantages of being famous?
- What kinds of people are famous in your country? Why?
- Many teenagers worship stars today. Do you think it is right or wrong? Why?
- Is 'celebrity effect' a positive or a negative phenomenon in your opinion?
- How can famous people handle gossip?
- How can celebrities contribute to the society?
- Some famous people earn a lot of money without doing much work. What's your opinion on that?
- What kinds of people usually become celebrities in your country? Why?
- What kinds of people could become celebrities in the past? Why?
- Do you think media focus too much on famous people? Why/why not?
- Why are so many people interested in celebrities' private lives?
- Is bad publicity also beneficial to celebrities? In what way?
- Why do you think some people really want to become famous?
- We live in the celebrity culture today. Do you think some people simply become celebrities overnight because the society needs them?
- How does celebrity worship influence societies?
- How does being famous affect a person's family?
- Do you think everyone would like to be famous? Why/why not?
- Can a person become famous without having any special talents? Why/why not?
- Are celebrities important to a society? Why/why not?
- Why do young people often copy famous people?
- How are celebrities responsible for their societies?
- How can celebrities be involved in raising a country's profile?
- Which sports are popular in your country? Why?
- Which sports do people like to watch in your country? Why?
- Do you think most people enjoy being a part of sports competitions? Why/why not?
- Should children do sports? Why/why not?
- Who is the most successful sportsperson in your country? Why?
- What qualities do people need to become champions?
- How is technology becoming more crucial to sports?
- Do you think sportspeople are generally paid too much? Why/why not?
- Why do you think some sports are more internationally recognized than others?

↻ How should big sports events be funded? Why?

↻ How can fame influence a celebrity's child?

↻ How do you think people feel when their fame ends?

↻ Does every society need celebrities? Why?

↻ What are some reasons for which foreigners come to your country?

↻ Can a person become famous without having any special talents?

↻ Why do you think some people stay famous for many years while others are forgotten after a short while?

↻ What are the main advantages of being famous?

↻ What are the main disadvantages of being famous?

↻ Does being famous mean being powerful? Why/why not?

↻ Do you think that young people copy famous people? Why/why not? Is it good or bad?

↻ How can celebrities use their fame to help other people?

↻ Should celebrities be involved in solving world problems? Why/why not?

↻ How can a country benefit from having international stars?

↻ Do you think celebrities should endorse products? Why/why not?

↻ Do you think that star's nationality matters? Why/why not?

↻ Do you think that people will become more famous internationally in the future? Why/why not?

• **a good neighbour/something a stranger did sth to help you/something you did to help your neighbour/your neighbourhood**

VOCAB :

1. a sense of belonging (phr.) = a feeling that one is a part of a certain place
2. harmonious /hɑː(r)ˈməʊniəs/ (adj.) = friendly and peaceful
3. a busybody /ˈbɪziˌbɒdi/ (n.) = someone who is very interested in other people's private lives and activities and tries to get involved in them in a way that is annoying
4. a close-knit community /ˌkləʊs ˈnɪt/ (phr.) = consisting of people who do a lot of activities together and look after one another
5. a sense of alienation /ˌeɪliəˈneɪʃ(ə)n/ (phr.) = the feeling that you do not belong in a particular society, place, or group
6. an occupant /ˈɒkjʊpənt/ (n.) = someone who uses a room, building, area of land, seat, bed, or other place during a period of time
7. to live next door to sb (phr.) = to live in the building, room next to yours or next to another
8. to move in (v.) = to start living in a different house or flat
9. to break the ice (phr.) = to do or say sth that makes people feel less shy or nervous in a social situation
10. to get along (v.) = to like each other and to be friendly to each other
11. to have sth in common with sb (phr.) = to have the same features as sb else
12. to help sb out (v.) = to help sb in a difficult situation
13. to lock sb out (v.) = to prevent someone from coming into a room or building by locking the door
14. to keep sb company (phr.) = to spend time with sb so that they will not feel lonely
15. to lend sb a hand (phr.) = to help sb
16. disruptive /dɪsˈrʌptɪv/ (adj.) = causing difficulties
17. vicinity /vəˈsɪnəti/ (n.) = the area near a particular place

18. purlieus /ˈpɜː(r)ljuːz/ (n.) = the outer areas of a place
19. a quiet nabe /ˈneɪb/ (phr.) = a quiet neighbourhood
20. the hood /hʊd/ (n.) = the neighbourhood where you live in a city or town
21. loud music blasting out (phr.) = continuous noise made by loud music
22. to do sth at an unearthly hour /ʌnˈɜː(r)θli/ (phr.) = to do sth at a time of day, especially very early, that is not a reasonable time to speak to or to see sb

PART 3 :
- Do you think people know their neighbours like they used to? Why?
- What qualities make a person a good neighbour? Why?
- What neighbourhood, in your opinion, is the best one for a child to grow up in? Why?
- Are neighbourhoods depicted on TV real?
- What facilities are necessary for a good neighbourhood? Why?
- How can neighbours build stronger relationships? Why?
- Why do you think people feel attached to the area where they grew up?
- Is it easy or difficult to establish a sense of identity with a new place? Why?
- Do you have many minorities in your country?
- Do you think differences in clothes and customs should be preserved? Why/why not?
- What kinds of problems might occur where people come from different ethnic groups?
- Do people prefer to listen to/read local news or national news? Why?
- Which aspects of life should be governed nationally and which locally? Why?
- How can people help their neighbours? Why?
- Is it important for people to help their neighbours? Why/why not?
- What are some advantages of neighbours helping each other?
- Why do you think some people, despite having a chance, don't want to help their neighbours?
- How are modern neighbourhoods in the city different from the past?
- Do people living in cities know their neighbours? Why/why not?
- Can a large city feel lonely? Why/why not?
- How can modern people get more involved into their community lives?
- Do many people in your country volunteer? Why/why not?
- What are some ways of volunteering in your country? Why?
- How do people volunteer abroad?
- Should the government support volunteer organisations? Why/why not?
- How can the government support volunteer organisations? Why?
- Can a volunteer benefit in any way from helping others? How?
- What are some common ways neighbours help each other?
- Do younger people willingly help older people in their neighbourhood today?
- What kinds of problems can occur among neighbours? How can they be solved?
- Do people contribute to their local communities in your culture?
- How can individuals improve their local communities?
- How can one volunteer in a local community?
- Why do some people decide to volunteer to help others and others do not?
- Do you think that everyone should experience some volunteer work before his or her actual employment? Why/why not?
- Do people in your country generally respect others? Why/why not?

273

⟳ Is modern society less concerned with the needs of other people? Why/why not?

⟳ Do you think tourists are always respectful towards locals? Why/why not?

⟳ How can international organizations promote cooperation between countries? In what ways?

- **a good parent**

VOCAB :

1. to go above and beyond (phr.) = to do more than necessary for sb
2. a carrot and stick method (phr.) = a mixture of promises and threats to persuade sb to do sth
3. to take after sb (v.) = to look or behave like an older relative
4. sth runs in the family (phr.) = if a skill or talent runs in the family, it means all family member have it
5. to follow in sb's footsteps (phr.) = to do the same work or achieve the same success as someone else before you
6. to turn a blind eye to sth (phr.) = to pretend you do not notice something, because you should do something about it but you do not want to
7. to be a chip off the old block (phr.) = to look or behave like one of your parents
8. under the same roof (phr.) = in the same home
9. to put sb in a straitjacket /ˈstreɪtˌdʒækɪt/ (phr.) = to restrict sb's freedom
10. the responsibility for sth falls on sb (phr.) = sb is accountable for sth
11. to shirk one's responsibilities for sth /ʃɜː(r)k/ (phr.) = to avoid accepting responsibility for sth
12. to fulfil one's responsibilities /fʊlˈfɪl/ (phr.) = to do what you must do
13. to deny sb the freedom to do sth (phr.) = to not allow sb to do sth
14. there is no substitute for sth/sb /ˈsʌbstɪˌtjuːt/ (phr.) = used for saying that nothing else is good or useful enough to replace something
15. to cause friction between… and… /ˈfrɪkʃ(ə)n/ (phr.) = to cause disagreement
16. conflicts arise /əˈraɪz/ (phr.) = conflicts begin
17. core values (phr.) = the most important beliefs of a person or group
18. unspoken rules (phr.) = rules not expressed in words, usually because other people already understand
19. to be hereditary /həˈredət(ə)ri/ (adj.) = passed from a parent to a child
20. to be estranged from sb /ɪˈstreɪndʒd/ (adj.) = not seeing sb very often, especially because of having fought with them
21. an empty nester /ˌempti ˈnestə(r)/ (n.) = a parent whose children are adults and have left their parents' home
22. a family bond (phr.) = a relationship one has with family members
23. the sense of obligation /ˌɒblɪˈgeɪʃ(ə)n/ (phr.) = the feeling of duty
24. to take sth for granted (phr.) = to expect something always to happen or exist in a particular way, and to not think about any possible problems or difficulties
25. to be grateful to sb /ˈgreɪtf(ə)l/ (adj.) = feeling that you want to thank someone because they have given you something or have done something for you
26. charity begins at home (phr.) = used for saying that you should look after yourself, your own family, friends, or country before you start helping other people
27. to feel homesick /ˈhəʊmˌsɪk/ (phr.) = feeling sad and alone because you are far from home
28. to have fond recollections of sth /fɒndˌrekəˈlekʃ(ə)nz/ (phr.) = to have warm memories of sth

274

29. love and devotion /dɪˈvəʊʃ(ə)n/ (phr.) = love and admiration or loyalty
30. to love, honour and cherish sb /ˈɒnə(r)/ (phr.) = to love, respect and appreciate sb
31. child-rearing /rɪərɪŋ/ (n.) = the process of bringing up a child or children
32. maternal instinct /məˈtɜː(r)n(ə)l ˈɪnstɪŋkt/ (phr.) = the bond between a mother and her child
33. nurturing instinct /ˈnɜː(r)tʃərɪŋ/ (phr.) = an ability to care for a young child
34. the generation gap (n.) = the difference in opinions or behaviour between older and younger people which often causes problems between them
35. a breadwinner /ˈbredˌwɪnə(r)/ (n.) = the person who earns the money to support a family
36. a homemaker /ˈhəʊmˌmeɪkə(r)/ (n.) = someone who cooks, cleans, and washes clothes for their family as their main job
37. like chalk and cheese (phr.) = very different from each other
38. to reprimand sb in private /ˈreprɪˌmɑːnd/ (phr.) = to tell sb in a serious way but in private that sth they have done is wrong
39. a creature of habit (phr.) = someone who likes to do the same thing at the same time every day
40. to go to great length to hold the family together (phr.) = to try in a very determined way to keep the family relationship strong
41. a shoulder to cry on (phr.) = someone who listens to you with sympathy when you talk about your problems
42. to give sb a helping hand (phr.) = to help sb

PART 3 :
↷ Are children close with their parents in your culture? Why/why not?
↷ Do you think it's good for children to be close with their parents? Why/why not?
↷ What do children usually do with their dads?
↷ What do children usually do with their mums? Why?
↷ Can everyone be a good parent? Why/why not?
↷ Can a person learn how to be parent? Why/why not?
↷ How do parents influence their children?
↷ How does a loss of a parent affect a child's development? Why?
↷ At what age do people in your country usually decide to have a baby? Why?
↷ Are parents respected in your culture?
↷ What conflicts often occur between parents and their children? Why?
↷ Do you think parents will stop being their children's role models in the future? Why/why not?

* **a good student you know**

VOCAB :
1. to be good with figures /ˈfɪgə(r)z/ (phr.) = to be good at counting and calculating, usually good at Maths
2. to have an eye for detail (phr.) = to be able to spot little things easily
3. to induce cramming /ɪnˈdjuːs/ (phr.) = to cause sb study hard in order to learn a lot in a short time
4. well-rounded (adj.) = including a good balance of various subjects
5. to slack off (v.) = to take things easy
6. conscientious /ˌkɒnʃiˈenʃəs/ (adj.) = working hard and careful to do things well
7. sedulous /ˈsedjʊləs/ (adj.) = showing continued hard work, effort and determination

8. meticulous /mɪˈtɪkjʊləs/ (adj.) = very thorough and with careful attention to detail
9. studious /ˈstjuːdɪəs/ (adj.) = tending to study and read a lot
10. diligent /ˈdɪlɪdʒ(ə)nt/ (adj.) = working very hard and very carefully
11. unflagging /ʌnˈflægɪŋ/ (adj.) = not changing or becoming weaker
12. with your nose to the grindstone /ˈɡraɪndˌstəʊn/ (phr.) = working very hard
13. punctual /ˈpʌŋktʃuəl/ (adj.) = arriving at the time agreed on
14. sb always meets deadlines /ˈdedˌlaɪnz/ (phr.) = sb always finishes a task by the date it was agreed on

PART 3 :

- What kind of a student is considered a good one in your culture? Why?
- Can a student be good at all subjects?
- What does it take to be a good student, hard work or talent? Why?
- Is the idea of a good student always related to good grades? Why/why not?
- Is it important to study well in your country? Why/why not?
- How can good studies help students in their adult life? Why?
- Are bad students treated worse in your country? Why/why not?
- How important is education in your country? Why?
- Do you think more people care about education today than in the past? Why/why not?
- Does success in education guarantee success in life? Why/why not?

- **a historical figure**

VOCAB :

1. a bygone era /ˈbaɪɡɒn ˈɪərə/ (phr.) = a period of time in the past
2. to break the traditional view (phr.) = to change the stereotype
3. to pursue individuality /pə(r)ˈsjuː/ (phr.) = to seek strong personality
4. legendary /ˈledʒ(ə)nd(ə)ri/ (adj.) = very famous or well known for a long time
5. a hero /ˈhɪərəʊ/ (n.) = someone who has done something brave, for example saving a person's life or risking their own life
6. an anti-hero (n.) = a main character in a story who does not have the qualities that a hero usually has, such as being morally good
7. infamous /ˈɪnfəməs/ (adj.) = well known for something bad
8. a brave man/woman /breɪv/ (phr.) = a heroic man/woman
9. a man/woman of courage /ˈkʌrɪdʒ/ (phr.) = a man/woman with the ability to do something that you know is right or good, even though it is dangerous, frightening, or very difficult
10. lion-hearted /ˌlaɪən ˈhɑː(r)tɪd/ (adj.) = brave and determined
11. a conqueror /ˈkɒŋkərə(r)/ (n.) = someone who has taken control of land or people by force
12. a liberator /ˈlɪbəreɪtə/ (n.) = a person who frees people from sth/sb controlling them
13. to emancipate /ɪˈmænsɪpeɪt/ (v.) = to give freedom and rights to someone
14. a Good Samaritan /səˈmærɪt(ə)n/ (n.) = a person who helps someone they do not know who is in trouble
15. to engage in a fight for freedom (phr.) = to get involved in activities that lead to freedom

16. to crusade /kruːˈseɪd/ (v.) = to work hard for a long time to achieve something that you strongly believe is morally right

PART 3 :
- What historical figures are popular in your country? Why?
- Are historical figures always a good example to follow? Why/why not?
- What Western historical figures do people in your country know about?
- How did people become famous in the past? Why?
- What current celebrities do you think next generations will remember? Why?
- Why does history remember some people and forget the others?
- Can we learn anything from history? What?
- How do stories about historical figures survive till now?
- Are young people in your country generally interested in history? Why/why not?

- **a popular actor (domestic/international)/a comic actor popular in your country/an artist/an entertainer you admire**

VOCAB :
1. an outstanding performance /aʊtˈstændɪŋ/ (phr.) = an extremely impressive performance
2. to be on the edge of your seat (phr.) = to be very excited and interested in sth because you want to know what happens next
3. an overnight success (phr.) = sth has become famous very quickly but usually fame doesn't last too long
4. a consummate actor/actress /kənˈsʌmət/(phr.) = an actor/actress showing great skill at acting
5. cinematography /ˌsɪnəməˈtɒɡrəfi/ (n.) = the job or skill of making films
6. overrated /ˌəʊvəˈreɪtɪd/ (adj.) = not as good as people say
7. far-fetched /ˌfɑː(r) ˈfetʃt/ (adj.) = impossible to believe
8. risqué /ˈrɪskeɪ/ (adj.) = slightly immoral and likely to shock some people
9. moving /ˈmuːvɪŋ/ (adj.) = making you feel strong emotion, esp. pity or sadness
10. memorable /ˈmem(ə)rəb(ə)l/ (adj.) = you remember it long after
11. to be panned /pænd/ (adj.) = to be very negatively criticized
12. to be universally lauded /lɔːdɪd/ (phr.) = to be highly praised
13. up-and-coming (adj.) = likely to become very famous or successful
14. to be miscast /ˌmɪsˈkɑːst/ (phr.) = wrong person for the role
15. an encore /ˈɒŋkɔː(r)/ (n.) = call from the audience to repeat the performance
16. a standing ovation /əʊˈveɪʃ(ə)n/ (phr.) = the audience stood up and applauded

PART 3 :
- Why are some actors more popular than others in your country?
- Do you think many youngsters try to copy the behaviour of famous actors? Is that good or bad? Why?
- Do you think actors are paid too much for their work? Why/why not?
- What is the most popular kind of entertainment for children in your country? Why?
- Do all children like to visit a circus? Why/why not?
- Is circus popular in your country? Why/why not?

☝ Do you think that children's entertainment must always be educational? Why/why not?

☝ Do men and women like the same type of entertainment? Why/why not?

☝ Are computer games popular in your country?

☝ Which age group likes to play computer games most? Why?

☝ Do you think all entertainment in the future will be related to technology? Why/why not?

• **a singer/band you like listening to/popular in your country**

VOCAB :

1. to keep a low profile /ˈprəʊfaɪl/ (phr.) = to try to stop people from noticing you
2. glamorous /ˈɡlæmərəs/ (adj.) = attractive, rich and famous
3. a debut album /ˈdeɪbjuː ˈælbəm/ (n.) = a first collection of several songs recorded on a CD or as an MP3 file etc.
4. to top the chart (phr.) = to go to the top of a hit list
5. to be musically-inclined /ɪnˈklaɪnd/ (adj.) = extremely interested in music
6. sb can't carry a tune (phr.) = sb can't sing musical notes correctly
7. to be tone deaf (adj.) = to be unable to sing a tune correctly because you cannot hear the difference between musical notes
8. a pop chart (n.) = a record chart that is ranking recorded music according to popularity
9. to be just another flash in the pan (phr.) = to be popular just for a very short time
10. a smash hit /smæʃ/ (n.) = a song that is extremely successful
11. to have what it takes (phr.) = to have the necessary qualities for success
12. to love the sound of someone's voice (phr.) = to adore sb's voice
13. a songster/songstress (n.) = male/female: a person who sings and/or writes songs skilfully
14. a diva /ˈdiːvə/ (n.) = a famous female singer of popular music
15. a songbird /ˈsɒŋˌbɜː(r)d/ (n.) = a bird that makes a beautiful sound or a female singer
16. heartwarming /ˈhɑː(r)tˌwɔː(r)mɪŋ/ (adj.) = making you feel happy, usually because other people are being kind
17. emotive /ɪˈməʊtɪv/ (adj.) = causing strong feelings

PART 3 :

☝ Where do people in your country go to listen to music? Why?

☝ Are concerts popular in your country? Why/why not?

☝ What are some advantages of listening to live music?

☝ What are some disadvantages of listening to live music?

☝ Has technology influenced the way people listen to music? If so, how?

☝ Do you learn about music when you go to school in your country? Why/why not?

☝ Why do some people decide to learn how to play a musical instrument?

☝ Should everyone play a musical instrument? Why/why not?

☝ What is the best age to start learning how to play a musical instrument? Why?

☝ Can everyone become good at playing a musical instrument? What does it depend on?

☝ Is music an important part of your culture? Why/why not?

☝ Why do think people often feel patriotic when listening to their national anthem?

☝ Does your culture have a lot of traditional music?

☝ Do you think traditional music might be replaced by modern music in the future? Why/why not?

278

- ☞ What types of singers are popular in your country today? Why?
- ☞ Do you think everyone can learn how to sing well? Why/why not?
- ☞ How can a good singing voice be helpful in life?
- ☞ Why do some songs become successful while others don't?
- ☞ What qualities does a song need to become a hit?
- ☞ Do you think today's music industry is more into making money than making good music? Why/why not?
- ☞ How do you think will music change in the future?
- ☞ How does technology affect the way music is made?
- ☞ Why do we need music?
- ☞ Does the society need music? Why/why not?
- ☞ Is it important to teach children about a country's traditional music? Why/why not?
- ☞ Should everyone appreciate music? Why/why not?
- ☞ Do you think governments should fund music teaching? Why/why not?
- ☞ Should the government fund the development of music? Why/why not?

- **a successful person you know/your boss/(someone you know who is) a good leader**

VOCAB :

1. enormous persuasive skills /pə(r)'sweɪsɪv/ (phr.) = skills that help one make people agree to do or believe what they want them to
2. to work well under pressure (phr.) = to handle work pressure well
3. a good communicator /kə'mjuːnɪˌkeɪtə(r)/ (phr.) = a person who is understood well
4. to climb the career ladder /kə'rɪə(r) c'lædə(r)/ (phr.) = to get promoted
5. to be ahead of your time (phr.) = to be innovative and radical by the standards of the time
6. to be labour-intensive (adj.) = a labour-intensive industry or process needs a lot of people to do the work
7. to be self-reliant /rɪ'laɪənt/ (adj.) = able to do things for yourself and not depend on other people
8. to be self-sufficient /sə'fɪʃ(ə)nt/ (adj.) = able to provide everything that you need by yourself, without help from other people
9. to be a self-made man/woman (phr.) = a person who was born poor or otherwise disadvantaged, but who achieved great economic or moral success thanks to their own hard work and ingenuity
10. to show initiative /ɪ'nɪʃətɪv/ (phr.) = to show that you are able to decide in an independent way what to do and when to do it
11. to do sth of one's own accord /ə'kɔː(r)d/ (phr.) = to do something without being asked, forced, or helped by someone else
12. to be tenacious /tə'neɪʃəs/ (adj.) = a tenacious person is very determined and is not willing to stop when they are trying to achieve something
13. perseverance /ˌpɜː(r)sɪ'vɪərəns/ (n.) = a determined attitude that makes you continue trying to achieve something difficult
14. a go-getter /ˌgəʊ 'getə(r)/ (n.) = someone who is determined to succeed and who works hard to achieve this
15. to go from rags to riches (phr.) = used for describing a situation in which someone who has been very poor becomes very rich
16. to be under someone's thumb (phr.) = to be completely controlled by someone else

279

17. to have a finger in every pie (phr.) = to be involved in a lot of different things
18. to throw your weight around (phr.) = to use your authority to tell other people what to do in a rude and unpleasant way

PART 3 :
- What kind of a person can make a good boss? Why?
- Who makes better bosses, men or women? Why?
- What problems do bosses face every day? Why?
- What is success?
- In which areas of life can people become successful? Why?
- How can a person achieve success? Why?
- Is being successful important in your culture? Why/why not?
- How does success change people?
- Can successful people have real friends? Why/why not?
- Do you think the concept of success will change in the future? Why/why not?
- Does everyone yearn success? Why/why not?
- What are the main advantages of being someone's boss? Why?
- In a typical family, who is usually the leader? Why?
- Do you think the head of the family might be woman in the future? Why/why not?
- Do you think it is easy to make decisions for the whole family? Why/why not?
- What kind of decisions do family leaders need to make?
- Who is generally better at making decisions, men or women? Why?
- What kind of a person can make a good manager? Why?
- Do you think managers should make their decisions by themselves or should they involve their employees? Why?
- Who is more important for a company's success, good managers or good workers? Why?
- Do you think it is fair for managers to make a lot more money than workers? Why/why not?
- What makes a good leader? Why?
- Why do you think some people want to be leaders in the first place?
- Do you think everyone wants to be a leader? Why/why not?
- Can a person learn how to be a good leader? Why/why not? If so, how?

- **a teenager you know/a child you know**

VOCAB :
1. to act out (v.) = to express your thoughts or feelings through your words or behaviour
2. antisocial behaviour /ˌænti'səʊʃ(ə)l/ (phr.) = used when sb is not interested in meeting other people or not enjoying friendly relationships with them
3. to be well-behaved /ˌwel bɪ'heɪvd/ (adj.) = a well-behaved child or animal behaves in a way that is polite or gentle and does not upset people
4. adolescence /ˌædə'les(ə)ns/ (n.) = the period of your life when you change from being a child to being a young adult
5. a healthy outlook on life (phr.) = a good attitude towards life
6. a well-adjusted adult /ˌwel ə'dʒʌstɪd/ (phr.) = an adult that is mentally strong and able to deal with problems without becoming very upset

280

7. to drop out of school (phr.) = to leave school before you have finished what you intended to do
8. to skip school /skɪp/ (phr.) = to avoid going to school
9. to come of age (phr.) = to reach the age when you are legally an adult
10. to feel inhibited /ɪnˈhɪbɪtɪd/ (phr.) = to feel too embarrassed or not confident enough to do sth
11. to be the black sheep of the family (phr.) = to not be approved of by the other members of the family
12. obedient /əˈbiːdiənt/ (adj.) = doing what a person, law, or rule says that you must do
13. disobedient /ˌdɪsəˈbiːdiənt/ (adj.) = deliberately doing the opposite of what someone in authority has told you to do, or deliberately not obeying rules
14. unruly /ʌnˈruːli/ (adj.) = very difficult to control
15. to be cheeky to sb /ˈtʃiːki/ (adj.) = behaving in a way that does not show respect, especially towards someone who is older or more important
16. a childish prank /ˈtʃaɪldɪʃ præŋk/ (phr.) = a silly trick that you play on sb to surprise them
17. to nurture /ˈnɜː(r)tʃə(r)/ (v.) = to provide the care and attention necessary for a young child to grow and develop
18. to have an impact on sth /ˈɪmpækt/ (phr.) = to have an influence on sth
19. peer pressure (n.) = the influence that other people of your own age or social class have on the way you behave or dress
20. a broken home (phr.) = a family where the parents are divorced or do not live together, and the children suffer as a result
21. permissive /pə(r)ˈmɪsɪv/ (adj.) = allowing someone a large amount of freedom to behave as they choose
22. rebellious /rɪˈbeljəs/ (adj.) = opposing authority or accepted ways of doing things
23. to run wild (phr.) = to grow without discipline
24. authoritarian /ɔːˌθɒrɪˈteəriən/ (adj.) = controlling everything and forcing people to obey strict rules and laws
25. a detrimental effect on sth/sb /ˌdetrɪˈment(ə)l/ (phr.) = a harmful or damaging influence on sth/sb
26. to pull your weight (phr.) = to do your fair share of work
27. messy /ˈmesi/ (adj.) = very untidy or dirty
28. to nag /næg/ (v.) = to frequently ask someone to do something that they do not want to do
29. fuss /fʌs/ (n.) = a lot of unnecessary worry or excitement about something
30. to lay down rules (phr.) = to state the rules clearly
31. to dent sb's trust /dent/ (phr.) = to diminish sb's trust
32. trivial worries /ˈtrɪviəl/ (phr.) = worries that are not very important or serious
33. to keep things in perspective /pə(r)ˈspektɪv/ (phr.) = to judge things in a sensible way
34. to articulate how you feel /ɑː(r)ˈtɪkjʊleɪt/ (phr.) = to express feelings clearly and effectively
35. as good as gold (phr.) = extremely well behaved
36. a middle-child syndrome /ˈsɪnˌdrəʊm/ (phr.) = a set of feelings related to being a middle-child
37. to put sb on a pedestal /ˈpedɪst(ə)l/ (phr.) = to admire or love someone so much that you believe they have no faults
38. to lavish sth on sb /ˈlævɪʃ/ (v.) = to give sb a lot of sth

PART 3 :
↪ Did you enjoy your teenage years in your country? Why/why not?
↪ When do teenagers become adults in your country? Why?

281

↺ Do teenagers behave the same way as children? Why/why not?

↺ Do teenagers in your country respect older people? Why/why not?

↺ Do you think young people today have a more enjoyable life than in the past? Why/why not?

↺ Do schools in your country prepare young people well for their future responsibilities as adults? Why/why not?

↺ Should young people be given more responsibilities at a younger age? Why/why not?

↺ What are some main problems teenagers have? Why?

↺ What problems can teenagers with too much money and freedom cause?

↺ Who influences society more: older people or younger people? Why?

↺ Do you think that influence of younger and older people might change in the future? If so, how?

- **a travel companion you enjoyed your journey with/an adventurous person you know**

VOCAB :

1. a party animal (n.) = sb who enjoys going to lots of parties
2. to be good company (phr.) = sb who people enjoy spending time with
3. to stick together (v.) = to remain close together and support one another
4. there's safety in numbers (proverb) = being in a group of people makes you feel more confident or secure about taking action
5. to offer moral support (phr.) = to offer support or help, the effect of which is psychological rather than physical
6. a great way to bond (phr.) = a great way to strengthen a relationship with sb
7. to come closer together (phr.) = to make a relationship stronger
8. to share hairy moments /ˈheəri/ (phr.) = to share moments that are difficult or dangerous
9. a live wire /ˌlaɪv ˈwaɪə(r)/ (n.) = a person who has a lot of energy and is interesting to be with
10. a bright spark (phr.) = someone who is clever or who has a clever idea
11. full of beans (phr.) = very lively and full of energy
12. to stick your neck out (phr.) = to take a risk by saying or doing sth that could be wrong or could make other people react angrily
13. to play it safe (phr.) = to avoid taking any risks
14. it is down to the psychological make-up of a person (phr.) = sth depends on a person's character
15. a sensation seeker se (phr.) = sb who always looks for excitement
16. to be at risk from sth (phr.) = to be in a situation in which sth unpleasant or dangerous could happen to you
17. to take a chance on a long shot (phr.) = to do sth even though it involves risk and even if it is not likely to be successful

PART 3 :

↺ Is it better to travel alone or with other people? Why?

↺ What kind of a person can make a good travel companion? Why?

↺ Do people in your country travel a lot? Why/why not?

↺ Do you think people will travel more in the future? Why/why not?

↺ Who is more adventurous: young people or older people? Why?

↺ What qualities does a person need to have to be adventurous?

↺ Why are some people not scared of anything?

- Do adventurous people travel more? Why/why not?
- What are some examples of adventures people can take on in your country?
- Are adventurous TV programmes popular in your country? Why/why not?
- Are travel programmes popular in your country? Why/why not?

- **an intelligent person**

VOCAB :

1. multilingual /ˌmʌltiˈlɪŋgwəl/ (adj.) = able to speak several different languages well
2. college-educated (adj.) = sb who went and graduated from college
3. to be gifted/talented /ˈgɪftɪd/ˈtæləntɪd/ (adj.) = to have an impressive natural ability
4. to be bilingual /baɪˈlɪŋgwəl/ (adj.) = sb who is able to speak two languages extremely well
5. a smart alec (n.) = sb who behaves in an annoying way by trying to show how clever they are
6. to be monolingual /ˌmɒnəʊˈlɪŋgwəl/ (adj.) = speaking, writing or using only one language
7. a Renaissance man/woman /rɪˈneɪs(ə)ns/ (phr.) = a man/woman who knows a lot about many different subjects and has many practical skills and abilities
8. to be versatile /ˈvɜː(r)sətaɪl/ (adj.) = having a wide range of different skills and abilities
9. a prodigy /ˈprɒdədʒi/ (n.) = a young person who has a natural ability to do sth extremely well
10. to know sth backwards/inside out (phr.) = to be very familiar with sth
11. a self-taught person (phr.) = sb who learnt a skill by themselves
12. as bright as a button (phr.) = very clever
13. quick-witted /ˌkwɪk ˈwɪtɪd/ (adj.) = able to think of good ideas or good answers quickly
14. a genius /ˈdʒiːniəs/ (n.) = sb who is much more intelligent or skilful than other people
15. a mastermind /ˈmɑːstə(r)ˌmaɪnd/ (n.) = someone who plans a difficult or complicated operation
16. a great intellect /ˈɪntəlekt/ (phr.) = sb who is extremely intelligent
17. a brainiac /ˈbreɪniak/ (n.) = sb who is exceptionally clever
18. an egghead /ˈegˌhed/ (n.) = someone who has a lot of knowledge and intelligence and is only interested in academic subjects

PART 3 :

- Do you often meet intelligent people?
- In what ways can a teacher sparkle students' interest in learning?
- What qualities does a teacher need to be considered a good teacher?
- Who should be more involved in developing children's intelligence: their parents or teachers? Why?
- Have you ever met a genius?
- Do you think that being highly intelligent makes a person lonely and unhappy? Why/why not?
- Are geniuses selfish? Why/why not?
- Who decides whether a person can be called a genius or not?
- Do you think that modern society focuses too much on intelligence? Why/why not?
- Can technology increase someone's intelligence? Why/why not?
- Do you think human intelligence has limits? Why/why not?

- **an old person you admire/respect/have met/you like spending time with/something you like doing with the elderly**

VOCAB :

1. conventional /kənˈvenʃ(ə)nəl/ (adj.) = sb who follows the usual and accepted opinions and ways of behaving, especially without questioning them
2. vigorous /ˈvɪg(ə)rəs/ (adj.) = full of energy, enthusiasm, or determination
3. a granny flat /ˈgræni ˌflæt/ (n.) = a set of rooms for an elderly person, connected to a relative's house
4. to be out of touch with sth (phr.) = to no longer have recent knowledge or information about sth
5. to be fond of /fɒnd/ (v.) = to like sb/sth a lot
6. hale and hearty /heɪl ænd ˈhɑː(r)ti/ (phr.) = strong and healthy
7. as fit as a fiddle /ˈfɪd(ə)l/ (phr.) = very fit
8. a bonding mechanism /ˈmekə ˌnɪz(ə)m/ (phr.) = a way to bond with sb
9. to keep sb company (phr.) = to spend time with sb
10. to wear your heart on your sleeve (phr.) = to make your feelings obvious to other people
11. to be getting on (a bit) (phr.) = fairly old
12. hard of hearing /ˈhɪərɪŋ/ (adj.) = unable to hear well
13. sb lives life to the fullest (phr.) = sb lives and enjoys life as much as possible
14. inner strength (phr.) = the strength sb has inside of themselves
15. to radiate cheerfulness /ˈreɪdieɪt ˈtʃɪə(r)f(ə)lnəs/ (phr.) = to show happiness in your expression or behaviour
16. a deep-rooted sense of respect (phr.) = a strong (because you felt it for a long time) feeling of admiration
17. to be held in high regard (phr.) = to be admired or respected very much
18. tai chi /ˌtaɪ ˈtʃiː/ (n.) = a Chinese activity that involves doing very slow physical exercises to make your mind relax and improve your body's balance
19. as a form of (phr.) = as a way of
20. to remain active /rɪˈmeɪn/ (phr.) = to stay active even at the old age
21. considerate /kənˈsɪd(ə)rət/ (adj.) = thinking about the feelings and needs of other people
22. early in her/his life (phr.) = in sb's young age
23. to teach sb an invaluable lesson /ɪnˈvæljuəb(ə)l/ (phr.) = to teach sb something extremely useful
24. a senior /ˈsiːniə(r)/ (n.) = older
25. to have the final say (phr.) = to have the responsibility for making a decision, although others can give their opinions first
26. you can't teach an old dog new tricks (phr.) = used for saying that it is very difficult to make someone do something in a new way when they have been doing it their own way for a long time

PART 3 :

↻ Are older people generally respected in your country? Why/why not?
↻ How can old people be useful to their families?
↻ What can young people learn from the elderly?
↻ Is it good for grandparents to raise their grandchildren? Why/why not?
↻ Can older people learn anything from the youngsters? If so, what?
↻ Do you think young people today pay enough attention to the elderly people? Why/why not?

- With whom do older people usually live in your country?
- What kind of a person can be a good caretaker of an old person? Why?
- Should older people always live with their families? Why/why not?
- Who should pay for elderly care? Why?
- How can older people be helpful to society by still working?
- Is it good or bad for a country to have a set retirement age? Why?
- At what age do people in your country retire?
- What is the condition of society where the majority are the elderly?
- Does your country have a pension system for the elderly? If so, is it enough for them to live on their own? Why/why not?
- What are the advantages of being old?
- What are the main disadvantages of being old?
- Do old people have better lives now than in the past? Why/why not?
- Do you think that the lives of the older people might improve in the future? Why/why not?
- When is a person considered old in your culture?
- Why do you think there is often a generation gap between the old and the young?
- What is the retirement age in your country?
- Why do you think some employers do not want to hire older people?
- How can older people contribute to the country's politics?
- What do people like to do together as a family in your country? Why?
- Should families spend time together outdoors? Why/why not?
- What are some of the advantages children can enjoy when both parents work outside the house?
- Do people get their moral values only from their family members? Why/why not?
- With whom do we spend most time in our lives? Why?
- Should a person spend time with different people or similar ones? Why?
- Is time spent alone needed? What for?
- How should workers behave towards their employers? Why?
- How should managers treat their employees? Why?
- Do you think our behaviour adapts to the people we are with? Why/why not?
- Do you think people's behaviour changes if they meet someone rich or famous? Why/why not? If so, how?
- What relationships are the most important in our lives? Why?
- Which relationships shape our personality? Why?
- Why do you think some people are loners while others are very sociable?
- Do you think that a relationship can only be successful if two people's characters are similar? Why/why not?
- What personality traits are generally difficult to deal with? Why?
- How can technology benefit older people?
- What benefits can a company gain through employing older people? Why?
- What aspects of contemporary life are difficult for the elderly to accept? Why?

- **someone who you think is handsome/beautiful**

VOCAB:
1. to be very arty /'ɑː(r)ti/ (adj.) = showing a great interest in art, but in a way that may not be sincere
2. stunning /'stʌnɪŋ/ (adj.) = very impressive or beautiful
3. shoulder-length hair (phr.) = hair that end by one's shoulders
4. chubby cheeks /'tʃʌbi/ (phr.) = cheeks that are slightly fat but in a cute way
5. ginger hair /'dʒɪndʒə(r)/ (phr.) = orange-brown hair
6. freckles /'frek(ə)lz/ (n.) = small brown spots on sb's skin
7. beauty is only skin-deep (proverb) = a pleasing appearance is not a guide to character
8. alluring /ə'lʊərɪŋ/ (adj.) = attractive in an exciting way
9. glamorous /'glæmərəs/ (adj.) = attractive and interesting in an exciting and unusual way
10. bewitching /bɪ'wɪtʃɪŋ/ (adj.) = very attractive
11. exquisite /ɪk'skwɪzɪt/ (adj.) = extremely beautiful and delicate
12. magnificent /mæg'nɪfɪs(ə)nt/ (adj.) = very impressive and beautiful, good or skilful
13. drop-dead gorgeous /'gɔː(r)dʒəs/ (adj.) = extremely attractive
14. hunky /'hʌŋki/ (adj.) = physically strong and sexually attractive

PART 3:
- Are the clothes people wear important in your culture? Why/why not?
- Can the clothes make somebody more beautiful or handsome? Why? How?
- Do companies need to use beautiful models to sell clothes? Why/why not?
- How can being beautiful be helpful in life?
- Is being beautiful always a good thing? When would it not be so good? Why?
- Why do you think people appreciate beauty in nature so much?
- Which landscapes do people consider beautiful? Why?
- Can a city be beautiful? If so, how?
- What can describe natural beauty better, words or pictures? Why?
- Do you think society is generally too obsessed with physical beauty today?
- Have the perceptions of beauty been the same over the years? Why/why not?
- Which is more important, physical or inner beauty? Why?
- Should people conform to the mass vision of beauty? Why/why not?
- What do some contemporary people do to become more beautiful? Why?

- **someone you know who has an interesting job/an unusual job you would like to do/a job that is important in your country**

VOCAB:
1. a team player (n.) = sb who works well with other people as part of a group
2. to work non-stop (phr.) = to work all the time
3. a glass ceiling /'siːlɪŋ/ (n.) = an unfair system that prevents some people, especially women, from reaching the most senior positions in a company or organization

4. to discriminate against sb /dɪˈskrɪmɪneɪt/ (v.) = to treat sb unfairly because of their religion, race or other personal features

5. a pecking order /ˈpekɪŋ ˌɔː(r)də(r)/ (n.) = a system where some people have the right to get promotions before others

6. atypical /ˌeɪˈtɪpɪk(ə)l/ (adj.) = not usual or typical

7. unorthodox /ʌnˈɔː(r)θədɒks/ (adj.) = not following the usual rules or beliefs of your religion, society etc.

8. peculiar /pɪˈkjuːliə(r)/ (adj.) = strange, often in an unpleasant way

9. a workaholic /ˌwɜː(r)kəˈhɒlɪk/ (n.) = someone who spends most of their time working and has little interest in other things

10. a devout employee /dɪˈvaʊtˌemplɔɪˈiː/ (phr.) = a very enthusiastic worker

PART 3 :

- ↻ What types of jobs do young people in your country like to choose? Why?
- ↻ How do people in your country choose their jobs?
- ↻ In what ways are large companies different from small companies?
- ↻ Why do some people prefer to work in small companies?
- ↻ Do men and women in your country enjoy the same types of jobs? Why/why not?
- ↻ What makes people decide to do a certain job? What factors?
- ↻ Can young people in your country get any advice about their future jobs? If so, where from?
- ↻ Do many students in your country have part-time jobs? If so, what kind?
- ↻ Is it good for a student to have a part-time job? Why/why not?
- ↻ Do students have any practical subjects at universities in your country?
- ↻ What is the unemployment rate in your country?
- ↻ Does your government support the unemployed?
- ↻ Should the government support the unemployed? Why/why not?
- ↻ What is the retirement age in your country? Is it the same for men and women?
- ↻ Do pensioners have enough financial support to lead a decent life? Why/why not?
- ↻ Are working conditions in your country generally good?
- ↻ Does the government control working conditions in your country? If so, how?
- ↻ What factors do people base their decision of a particular job on?
- ↻ Which one do you think is more useful today, experience or formal study? Why?
- ↻ Do people often change jobs in your country? Why/why not?
- ↻ Do people in your country care if they like the job they have? Why/why not?
- ↻ Is job satisfaction necessary? Why/why not?
- ↻ Why do some people need to have a balance between work, family and their social life?
- ↻ How does globalisation affect job market in your country?
- ↻ What are some disadvantages of working in a foreign country?
- ↻ What kinds of jobs do you think might disappear in the future? Why?
- ↻ Is it easy or difficult to choose one's career? Why?
- ↻ How important are qualifications to land a good job today? Why?
- ↻ Do any companies pay their workers to get further qualified? Why/why not?
- ↻ Would many people in your country be willing to relocate to another country for work? Why/why not?
- ↻ How does the fact that some people relocate for work influence their family life?

- ↻ Do you think people will change careers more often in the future? Why/why not?
- ↻ At what age can people legally start a full-time job in your country? Is it too early, too late or right about time? Why?
- ↻ Is it easy to find a good job in your country? Why?
- ↻ Do you think that working conditions have improved over the years? Why/why not?
- ↻ Do you think schools prepare students well for their future working life? Why/why not?
- ↻ What skills do current employers look for in their workers? Why?
- ↻ Do you think everyone should graduate from a university? Why/why not?
- ↻ How can a large number of university-educated people contribute to the society?
- ↻ Why do you think people are after some jobs but not so interested in others?
- ↻ What are some downsides of putting work before family? Why?
- ↻ How will migration affect work in your country in the future? Why?
- ↻ What social changes are significant to the job market? Why?

- **someone you know who is good at cooking**

VOCAB :
1. to be all fingers and thumbs (phr.) = to be unable to do a small difficult job because you cannot control your fingers well enough
2. cooking utensils /juːˈtens(ə)lz/ (phr.) = sth that you use for cooking
3. to have cookouts /ˈkʊkˌaʊts/ (phr.) = to have an informal meal eaten outside with food usually cooked over a fire or on a barbecue
4. to burn sth to a crisp /krɪsp/ (phr.) = to burn sth completely
5. the best thing since sliced bread (phr.) = a person or thing that someone thinks is excellent or likes very much
6. to chop sth up /tʃɒp/ (v.) = to cut food into pieces
7. cuisine /kwɪˈziːn/ (n.) = a particular style of cooking food, especially the style of a particular country or region
8. a cordon bleu cook /ˌkɔː(r)dɒ̃ ˈblɜː/ (phr.) = a cook that shows the highest standard of quality in his/her cooking
9. to fix some food (phr.) = to cook sth
10. to rustle up /ˈrʌs(ə)l/ (v.) = to quickly produce something such as a meal using whatever is available
11. a palatable dish /ˈpælətəb(ə)l/ (phr.) = a dish that tastes good
12. finger-licking (adj.) = delicious
13. sth melts in your mouth (phr.) = sth tastes very good

PART 3 :
- ↻ Do people in your country cook at home a lot? Why/why not?
- ↻ Did people cook more in the past? Why/why not?
- ↻ Is it important for families to have meals together? Why/why not?
- ↻ Do you think people might cook less in the future? Why/why not?
- ↻ Is the food in school canteens in your country tasty? Why/why not?
- ↻ Do you think boys also need to learn how to cook? Why/why not?
- ↻ Do you think everyone should learn how to cook? Why/why not?

- Should children learn how food is produced? Why/why not?
- Do schools in your country pay attention to providing enough nutrition to students? Why/why not?
- Do people discuss healthy food? Why/why not?
- Should an individual be concerned about how healthy today's food is? Why/why not?
- What kinds of information should the food industry provide to consumers about the food they buy? Why?
- Are there any rules or regulations regarding food safety in your country? Why/why not? Should there be? What kind?

- **your best friend**

VOCAB :
1. to carry sb's burden (phr.) = to share something difficult that happened to sb else
2. common values (phr.) = similar principles
3. a heart-to-heart talk (phr.) = a very private conversation between two people, usually concerning their personal feelings
4. a web pal (n.) = a friend you only know online
5. soulmates /ˈsəʊlˌmeɪts/ (n.) = people who feel close to each other in spirit and understand each other deeply
6. a lifelong companion (phr.) = friend who was with you all your life
7. inseparable /ɪnˈsep(ə)rəb(ə)l/ (adj.) = very close
8. a bosom pal /ˈbʊz(ə)m/ (phr.) = a very close friend
9. sb is after your own heart (phr.) = someone who has the same opinions as you on a particular subject
10. a kindred spirit /ˈkɪndrəd/ (phr.) = someone who likes or cares about the same things as you do
11. to bury the hatchet /ˈhætʃɪt/ (phr.) = to become friendly with someone again after a disagreement
12. to keep one's word (phr.) = to do what one has promised
13. mutual trust /ˈmjuːtʃuəl/ (phr.) = trust which is felt both ways
14. to socialize with sb /ˈsəʊʃəlaɪz/ (v.) = to spend time with other people socially, for example at a party
15. to get along with (v.) = to like each other and be friendly to each other
16. A is the complete opposite of B (phr.) = A is entirely different from B
17. to be on the same wavelength /ˈweɪvˌleŋθ/ (phr.) = to understand the way that another person thinks because you often have the same ideas and opinions as they do
18. to not see eye to eye with sb (phr.) = to not agree with sb or to not have the same opinion as them
19. a fair-weather friend (phr.) = someone who only wants to be your friend when things are going well for you
20. to stab sb in the back (phr.) = to do something bad that is not loyal to someone who trusts you
21. to console sb at times of sorrow /kənˈsəʊl/ (phr.) = to try to make sb feel better when they are unhappy
22. joys and sorrows (phr.) = happy and unhappy times
23. to confide in sb /kənˈfaɪd/ (v.) = to tell sb a secret or discuss your private feelings with them
24. innermost thoughts /ˈɪnə(r)ˌməʊst/ (phr.) = most personal and private thoughts
25. to suppress your feelings /səˈpres/ (phr.) = to stop yourself from feeling emotions

26. vulnerable /ˈvʌln(ə)rəb(ə)l/ (adj.) = someone who is vulnerable is weak or easy to hurt physically or mentally

27. pent up emotions /ˌpent ˈʌp/ (phr.) = pent up emotions are strong feelings, for example anger, that you do not express so that they gradually become more difficult to control

28. to stick up for sb (v.) = to speak in support of a person or an idea, belief, or plan, especially when no one else will

29. through thick and thin (phr.) = under all circumstances, no matter how difficult

30. birds of a feather flock together (phr.) = used for saying that people of a similar type tend to support and agree with each other

PART 3 :
↻ Why do we need friends?
↻ How do people make friends in your country?
↻ Do you think that parents should be concerned about the friends their children have? Why/why not?
↻ Is it easy to make friends in your country? Why/why not?
↻ What is the best way to make friends?
↻ Which do you think is better: a friend you have had from childhood or a friend from your adulthood? Why?
↻ Why do you think so many people make friends online today?
↻ Is it safe to establish friendships online? Why/why not?
↻ Is it wise to tell all our secrets to friends? Why/why not?
↻ What is the best way to communicate with friends?
↻ Why do you think some friends drift apart?

• **your colleague/classmate/a polite person**

VOCAB :
1. average Joe (phr.) = for males: a very average person
2. plain Jane (phr.) = for females: a very average person
3. sb is my opposite number (phr.) = has the same job as me
4. a good rapport /ræˈpɔː(r)/ (phr.) = a good relationship/communication
5. to be someone's peer /pɪə(r)/ (n.) = to be of the same age as another person
6. to talk shop (phr.) = to talk about work
7. sb has an attitude problem (phr.) = sb's behaviour is strange and causing disagreements with others
8. to be an eager beaver /ˈiːɡə(r) ˈbiːvə(r)/ (n.) = sb who is extremely enthusiastic and enjoys working extremely hard
9. to be an indicator of ability /ˈɪndɪˌkeɪtə(r)/ (phr.) = to show ability
10. interpersonal skills /ˌɪntə(r)ˈpɜː(r)s(ə)nəl/ (phr.) = skills involving relationships between people
11. to be forward-looking /ˈfɔː(r)wə(r)d ˌlʊkɪŋ/ (adj.) = looking at the future in a positive way and happy to try new ideas and methods
12. a wet blanket (n.) = someone who spoils other people's fun by being negative and complaining
13. quick-witted /ˌkwɪk ˈwɪtɪd/ (adj.) = able to think of good ideas or good answers quickly
14. shrewd /ʃruːd/ (adj.) = able to judge people and situations very well and to make good decisions

15. ruthless /ˈruːθləs/ (adj.) = willing to make other people suffer so that you can achieve your aims
16. to come across as (phr.) = if someone or something comes across in a particular way, you have a particular opinion of them when you meet them or see them
17. pushy /ˈpʊʃi/ (adj.) = extremely determined to get what you want, even if it annoys other people
18. to strike sb as sth (phr.) = to make someone have a particular opinion or feeling
19. conscientious /ˌkɒnʃiˈenʃəs/ (adj.) = working hard and careful to do things well
20. charisma /kəˈrɪzmə/ (n.) = a strong personal quality that makes other people like you and be attracted to you
21. assertive /əˈsɜː(r)tɪv/ (adj.) = behaving in a confident way in which you are quick to express your opinions and feelings
22. to get up your nose (phr.) = to annoy you a lot

PART 3 :
☞ Do you make friends with your classmates in your country? Why/why not?
☞ Do people usually stay in touch after they've graduated from school? Why/why not?
☞ Is it important to make friends with classmates? Why/why not?
☞ What kind of people are more likeable? Why?
☞ Do people cooperate with their colleagues? Why/why not?
☞ Is it important to get along with our colleagues? Why/why not?
☞ Are people in your country generally polite? Why/why not?
☞ Is it easier to make friends with polite people? Why/why not?
☞ Should we make friends with people similar to us or different from us?
☞ What can disagreements with others teach us?

- **your favourite teacher/a good teacher that influenced you/someone who taught you a useful skill**

VOCAB :
1. to promote equality /prəˈməʊt ɪˈkwɒləti/ (phr.) = to support the state of being equal, especially in having the same rights, status and opportunities
2. a disruptive student /dɪsˈrʌptɪv/ (phr.) = a student causing interruptions in class
3. to put theory into practice (phr.) = to use what you've learnt in reality
4. first-hand experience /ˌfɜː(r)stˈhænd/ (phr.) = experience obtained directly from sb who is involved in sth
5. to kindle someone's interest in sth /ˈkɪnd(ə)l/ (phr.) = to start a strong interest in sth
6. to inspire sb /ɪnˈspaɪə(r)/ (v.) = to give sb the enthusiasm to do or create sth
7. to build a close rapport between /ræˈpɔː(r)/ (phr.) = to build a strong relationship between
8. 'a mediocre teacher tells, a good teacher explains and a great teacher inspires'/ˌmiːdiˈəʊkə(r)/ (quotation)
9. strict /strɪkt/ (adj.) = someone who is strict has definite rules that they expect people to obey completely
10. lenient /ˈliːniənt/ (adj.) = if a person or system is lenient, they punish someone less severely than they could
11. to have a lasting impact on sb (phr.) = to have a long-term influence on sb

12. to be grateful to sb /ˈɡreɪtf(ə)l/ (adj.) = feeling that you want to thank someone because they have given you something or have done something for you
13. to sparkle a passion for sth /ˈspɑː(r)k(ə)l/ (phr.) = to light a love for sth
14. to credit sb for /ˈkredɪt/ (v.) = to admit sb's contribution to sth
15. the best teacher of the year (phr.) = a title given to one teacher at a school every year, chosen via students votes usually

PART 3 :
- Why do some people like to be teachers?
- What qualities a good teacher should have? Why?
- What difficulties do teachers need to confront today?
- Should children be punished at school? If so, how?
- Do you think one day teachers can be replaced by computers? Why/why not?
- Are there any problems with education in your country? What are they?
- How can education in your country be improved? Why?
- Do you think single-sex school are a good idea? Why/why not?
- Are there many private schools in your country?
- What's the main difference between a public and a private school in your country?
- When should children go to school? Why?
- Do you think it is good to assign a lot of homework to children? Why/why not?

- **your role model/a person you wanted to be similar to when you were growing up**

VOCAB :
1. at someone's beck and call (phr.) = available to do things for another person whenever they want
2. to set a good example (phr.) = to make a good model to follow
3. to meet someone's expectations /ˌekspekˈteɪʃ(ə)nz/ (phr.) = to rise up to sb's belief in you
4. to fall short of someone's expectation (phr.) = to not to rise up to sb's belief in you
5. to be someone's mentor /ˈmentɔː(r)/ (phr.) = to be an experienced person who helps sb who has less experience, especially in their job
6. to take sb under your wing (phr.) = to look after sb, especially if you are older or more experienced
7. to set the benchmark for sth /ˈbentʃˌmɑː(r)k/ (phr.) = to set a standard for sth
8. to be sb's source of inspiration (phr.) = to be very inspirational to sb
9. approachable nature /əˈprəʊtʃəb(ə)l/ (phr.) = with friendly personality and easy to talk to
10. to be the backbone and guiding light of sb /ˈbækˌbəʊn/ (phr.) = to make sb strong and show them a right way to do things
11. characteristics of a hero (phr.) = features of a hero
12. selfless /ˈselfləs/ (adj.) = caring about other people's needs and problems more than your own
13. philanthropy /fɪˈlænθrəpi/ (n.) = the belief that you should help people, especially by giving money to those who need it
14. for the common good (phr.) = for the benefit of everyone
15. humble /ˈhʌmb(ə)l/ (adj.) = not proud and not thinking that you are better than other people

PART 3 :

- How do famous people influence children? Why?
- What kinds of famous people do children like in your country? Why?
- Do you think famous people should always set a good example for children? Why/why not?
- Is it ethically acceptable for companies to use celebrities to advertise children's products? Why/why not?
- Is growing up in your country a nice experience? Why/why not?
- How is growing up today different from growing up twenty years ago? Why?
- Do you think most children in your country are independent from their parents? Why/why not?
- How independent should children be from their parents? Why?
- How can parents teach their children to become more independent? Why?
- At what age do children in your country become adults? Why?
- What are the most important needs of children? Why?
- Do you think child welfare in your country is good? Why/why not?
- Is it easy to be a parent? Why/why not?
- In your opinion, should parents be trained how to bring up their children? Why/why not?
- How could the government promote the importance of child welfare?

- **your favourite writer/a famous writer**

VOCAB :

1. sb's legacy lives on /ˈlegəsi/ (phr.) = sth that sb has achieved continues even after their death
2. sb has a large following (phr.) = to have a large group of people who support or admire the work or ideas of a particular person or organization
3. an autobiography /ˌɔːtəubaɪˈɒgrəfi/ (n.) = a book about your life that you write yourself
4. a biography /baɪˈɒgrəfi/ (n.) = a book that someone writes about someone else's life
5. posthumously acclaimed /ˈpɒstjuməsli əˈkleɪmd/ (adj.) = publicly written and talked about in an admiring way after one's death
6. an author /ˈɔːθə(r)/ (n.) = someone who writes books, articles etc, especially as their job
7. a wordsmith /ˈwɜːdsmɪθ/ (n.) = a skilled used of words
8. a scribbler /ˈskrɪblə(r)/ (n.) = a writer, especially one who is considered not to be very good
9. prominent /ˈprɒmɪnənt/ (adj.) = important and well known
10. to have one's name in lights (phr.) = to be vey famous
11. enthralling /ɪnˈθrɔːlɪŋ/ (adj.) = so exciting that you give it all your attention
12. creativity /ˌkriːeɪˈtɪvəti/ (n.) = the ability to create new ideas or things using your imagination
13. visionary /ˈvɪʒən(ə)ri/ (adj.) = original and showing a lot of imagination
14. innovative /ˈɪnəveɪtɪv/ (adj.) = new, original and advanced

PART 3 :

- What kind of people can be good writers? Why?
- What skills does a person need to write interestingly? Why?
- Who is the most famous writer in your country?
- What foreign writers are famous in your country? Why?
- Is it easy to write a book? Why/why not?
- Why do people read books?

- Are writers paid enough for their work? Why/why not?
- Can a person learn how to write well?
- How long does it take to write a good book? Why?
- Do publishers get too much money from book sales? Why/why not?
- Do you think people will write and publish more books in the future? Why/why not?

CHAPTER 6

WRITING TYPES
TASK 1 & TASK 2
HOW TO WRITE WELL

Lapsus calami
(Error of the pen)

TASK 1

- you will have about 20 minutes for this task
- do not underestimate it, focus on it as much as you will on your essay
- it is worth 40% of your final writing score
- do not write fewer than 150 words, as you will be penalized for it
- do not write more than 150 words, as you will surely make more mistakes and you are more likely to lose logic (+10% is acceptable)
- do not describe all the data
- spot the significant information: the highest point, the lowest point, etc.
- classify the most important details that need to be included
- decide on the tense you will use throughout your writing
- group the information
- contrast and compare data
- do not write a conclusion
- use formal style, do not use colloquial English
- do not present personal opinions
- avoid using personal pronouns
- paraphrase as much as you can as to avoid repetitive vocabulary
- do not forget to write an overview (one or two sentences summarising the general trends or information given in the graph, chart or diagram), it can come at the beginning, in the middle or at the end of your summary

TYPES OF QUESTIONS:

- **a table**

What are the main features?
- high numbers
- low numbers
- the biggest contrasts
- the closest similarities

Necessary words
- a row
- a column
- a box
- a trend

The proportion of income adults and children spent on 4 common items in the UK in 1998

	food	electronic equipment	music	videos
adults	25%	5%	5%	1%
men	14%	10%	5%	2%
women	39%	1%	5%	0.5%
children	10%	23%	39%	12%
boys	9%	18%	38%	18%
girls	11%	5%	40%	17%

EXEMPLAR REPORTS:
(All reports provided here would achieve Band 8 &9)

1. *The tables show the results of a survey of students who defer their degrees. The first table shows reasons why some students prefer to stay at home in their own country. The second table shows why others choose to travel overseas.*
    Summarise the information by selecting and reporting the main features, and make comparisons where relevant.

Reasons for staying at home	%
Easier to find paid work	26
Already speak the language	25
Cheaper to stay with family	18
Dangers of travel	12
Lack of money	12
Other reasons	7

Reasons for travelling overseas	%
Learning about a new culture	25
Adventure and excitement	24
Help people in poorer countries	15
Get away from parents	14
Make new friends	12
Other reasons	10

Many students choose to defer the start of their degree courses and take a gap year. Some prefer to stay in their home countries. Conversely, some like to travel to other countries. The tables compare the reasons why they choose either to travel abroad or stay at home.

26% of the students who stay in their own countries want to find paid work, and find this easier at home. In the same way, 25% prefer to stay in a country where they can already speak the language. In contrast to this, 25% want to travel to learn about a different culture, nearly the same as the 24% who are looking for adventure and excitement overseas.

The third most popular reason for staying at home is to save money. 18% stated that they did so because it was cheaper to stay with their families. On the other hand, 14% of those who travel do it because they want to get away from their parents. A similar percentage, 15%, would like to help people in poorer countries, compared with 12% who are looking for new friends. The same percentage of deferring students stay at home because they do not have enough money to go overseas. 10% of the travellers and 7% of the other group stated other reasons for their choices.

In general, it would appear that the main reasons for staying at home are related to finance. By contrast, those who travel are more concerned with having fun and gaining experience before starting university.

2. *The table shows the average band scores for students from different language groups taking the IELTS Academic Paper in 2003.*
Summarise the information by selecting and reporting the main features, and make comparisons where relevant.

	Listening	Reading	Writing	Speaking	Overall
Hindi	6.78	6.38	6.62	6.86	6.73
Malayalam	6.31	6.13	6.49	6.52	6.43
Russian	6.35	6.13	6.11	6.69	6.38
Spanish	6.27	6.42	6.08	6.64	6.41

The table illustrates the breakdown of scores for the IELTS Academic Paper in 2003. IT shows separate scores for all four sections (Listening, Reading, Writing and Speaking), together with the overall score for students from four different language groups around the world.

From an overall perspective, Hindi speakers achieved the highest grades with an average score of 6.73 across all four sections. Moreover, they scored the highest of all four language groups in three of the four sections, namely Listening, Writing and Speaking.

Malayalam speakers scored the second highest scores overall, closely followed by Spanish and Russian speakers. Although Malayalam speakers did not do so well in the Reading, Speaking and Listening sections compered to Russian and Spanish speakers, there was a significant difference in their grades for the Writing section. These grades were high relative to Russian and Spanish candidates. Surprisingly, Spanish speakers, who achieved the second lowest results overall, achieved the highest results of all four language groups for the Reading section.

As a final point, it is interesting to note that the scores for each section show that all students on average scored the highest marks for the Speaking section and the lowest marks for the Reading section.

3. *The tables below provide information on rental charges and salaries in three areas of London. Write a report for a university lecturer describing the information shown below.*

	Weekly rents per property (£/w)				Salaries needed (£/year)		
Area	**1 bed**	**2 bed**	**3 bed**		**1 bed**	**2 bed**	**3 bed**
Notting Hill	375	485	738		98,500	127,500	194,000
Regent's Park	325	450	650		85,500	118,000	170,500
Fulham	215	390	600		56,500	102,500	157,500

The tables show two sets of related information: the relative cost, in pounds, of renting a property with one, two or three bedrooms in three different suburbs of London and an indication of the kind of annual salary you would need to be earning to rent in these areas.

Of the three areas mentioned, Notting Hill is the most expensive with weekly rents starting at £375 (salary of approximately £100,000) and rising to £738 per week for a 3-bedroom property. To afford this, one would require a salary in the region of £200,000 per annum. Alternatively, Fulham is the cheapest area shown with rents ranging from £215 per week for a one-bedroom property to £600 per week for a 3-bedroom one. To rent in this area, salaries need to fall between £85,000 and £170,000, depending on the number of bedrooms required. For those able to pay in the middle price range for accommodation, Regent's Park might be a more suitable district.

- **a graph/a line graph**

Necessary words :
- data points
- straight line segments
- an x-axis (horizontal)
- a y-axis (vertical)
- peaks (ups)
- troughs (downs)

300

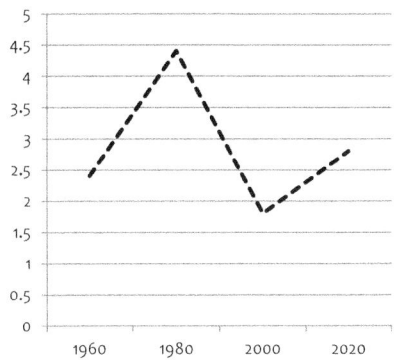

1. Single-variable line graph

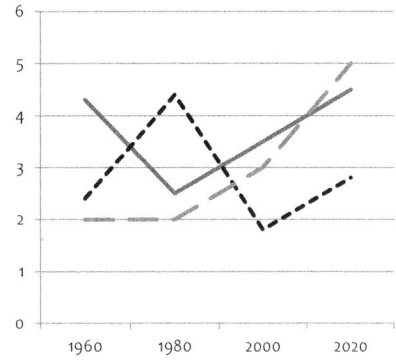

2. Multiple-variable line graph

EXEMPLAR REPORTS:
(All reports provided here would achieve Band 8 & 9)

1. *The graph below gives information about Dubai gold sales in 2002.*
Summarise the information by selecting and reporting the main features, and making comparisons where relevant.

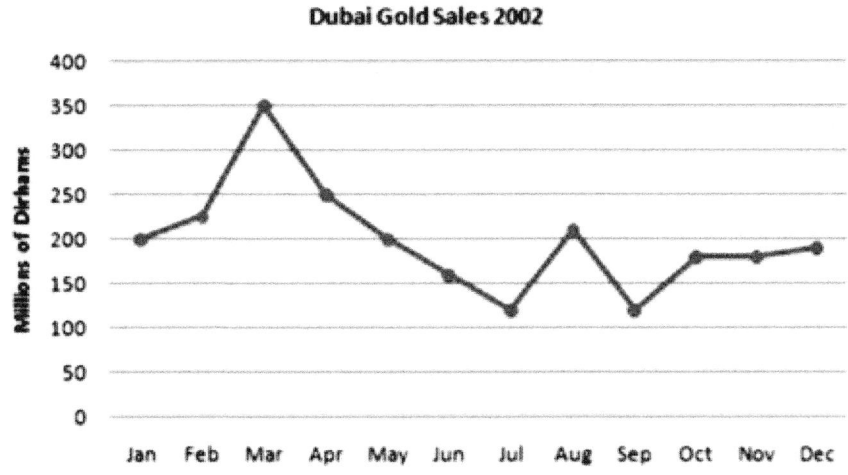

The diagram given illustrates how gold sales in Dubai fluctuated over a period of 12 months. Overall, gold sales in Dubai remained relatively unchanged in 2002, at their highest in March while weakest in July and September.

301

It is observed that in the first month of 2002, gold sales stood at 200 million dirhams and rose slightly to reach about 225 million in February. This was followed by another increase, although much steeper, in March when sales were almost 125 million dirhams higher than February. However, this upward trend was suddenly broken and sales plummeted dramatically over the next 4 months to reach a little over 100 million dirhams in July. August sales showed a significant rise back to January levels as figures nearly doubled, but this was not to last as they dropped again in September to the same level as they were in July. October came with a small increase of about 100 million dirhams in sales, after which sales figures levelled off and remained static over the last two months of 2002.

2. *The charts show the number of international students in the USA by subject and country. Summarise the information by selecting and reporting the main features, and make comparisons where relevant.*

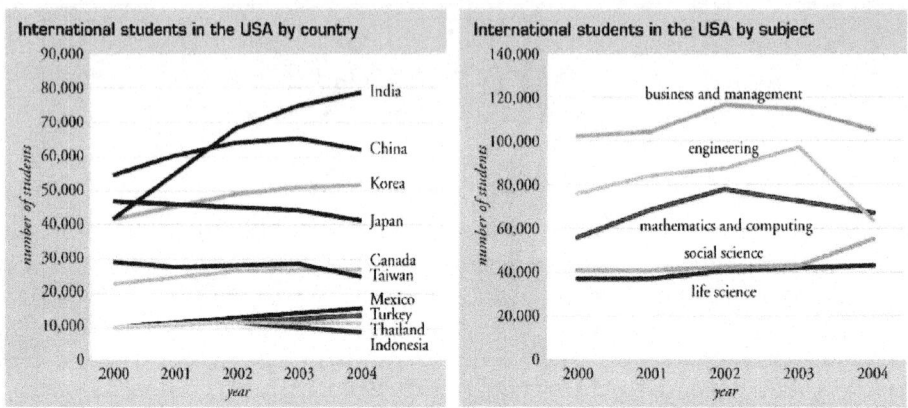

The charts show changes in numbers of overseas students studying in the USA between the years 2000 and 2004.

The first chart shows that numbers of students from India doubled over a four-year period, shooting up from 40,000 to 80,000 by 2004. The second largest group were the Chinese, although during 2003 there was a noticeable downward trend. Overall, numbers remained relatively stable at between 50,000 and 60,000. Numbers of Korean students meanwhile rose steadily to around 50,000, while numbers of students from Japan declined gradually to 40,000 by 2004. Numbers of Taiwanese students also fell from 30,000 by about 5,000, to be overtaken by the Canadians at the end of 2003. Student figures from Mexico, Turkey, Thailand and Indonesia showed little change, remaining at approximately 10,000.

The second chart reveals that the most popular subject for international students was business and management. Numbers rose significantly in 2001, but then gradually declined to around 100,000 by 2004. Crowd studying engineering plummeted in 2003 from 90,000 to 60,000, slightly less than mathematics and computing by the end of the year. Student statistics in social and life sciences were both stable at around 40,000 until 2003, when digits studying social science showed a significant increase of over 50,000 students.

3. *The graphs below show average monthly temperature and rainfall in two places in South Africa. Summarise the information by selecting and reporting the main features, and make comparisons where relevant.*

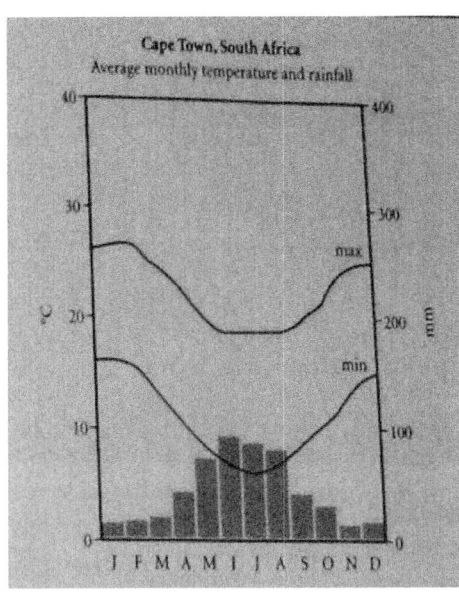

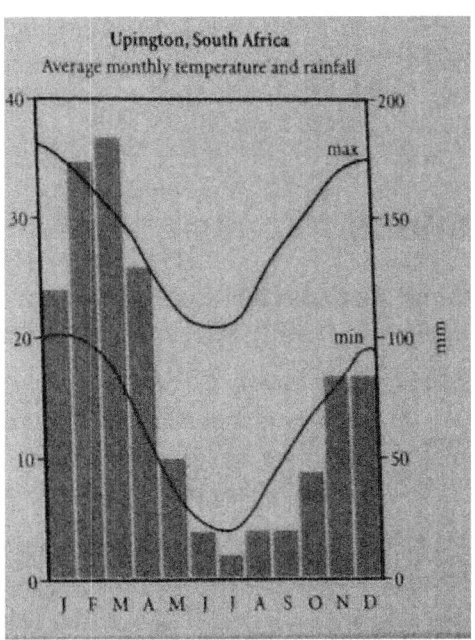

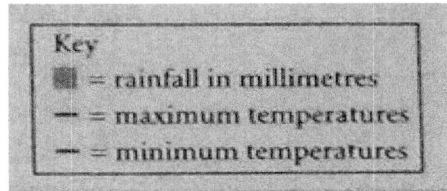

The graphs provide climatic information for Cape Town and Upington in South Africa. The red and blue lines plot average maximum and minimum monthly temperatures, while the orange bars show average rainfall.

From the line graphs it can be seen that there is less fluctuation in temperature in Cape Town than in Upington, where maximum temperatures reach over 35 degrees C in January (the highest temperatures in Cape Town are well below 30 degrees C). Both places are at their coolest in June and July. In Upington, temperatures rise steeply again through August and September, whereas in Cape Town, the increase is more gradual.

Also, Upington is much wetter than Cape Town outside the months of June to September. March is the wettest month in Upington, with an average rainfall of around 180 millimetres. In contrast, Cape Town has hardly any rain in the period November to March. Its peak rainfall is in June, when it receives approximately 100 millimetres.

- **a bar chart**

Necessary words::
- ✎ rectangular bars
- ✎ values
- ✎ plotted vertically/horizontally
- ✎ axes

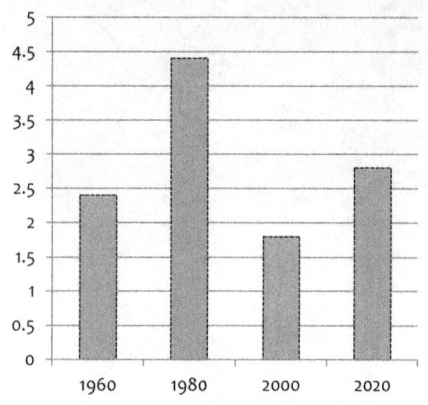

1. Single-variable bar chart

2. Multiple-variable bar chart

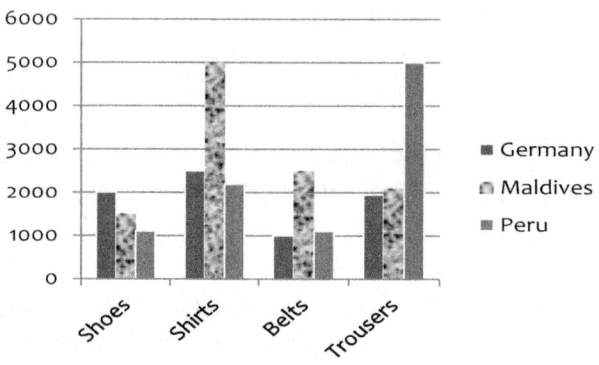

3. Comparison bar chart

1. The bar chart below shows a survey of a group of young professionals aged 20-30 years old who were asked to state which factors motivated them to succeed.
Write a report for a university lecturer describing the information shown below.

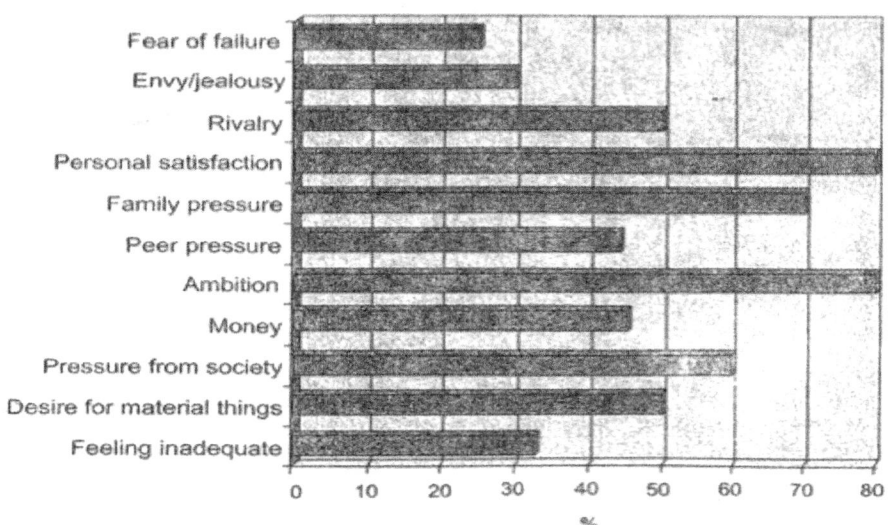

Factors motivating people to succeed

The bar chart depicts the results of a survey of young professionals (between 20 and 30 years old), who were asked to state which points they thought gave them an incentive to achieve success. It is clear that success among the survey takers depends mainly on self-motivating factors.

The aspects are divided into three main groups, namely personal (both positive and negative) and external ones, with the former being the larger of the two. In the first group, 'Personal satisfaction' and 'Ambition' are mentioned by 80% of respondents with 'Desire for material things' and 'Money' being given by 50% and 45%, respectively. Of the more negative personal factors, 'Rivalry' is cited by 50% of surveyees as being a factor motivating them to succeed. Other factors that make up this latter sub-group are 'Feeling inadequate', 'Envy/Jealousy' and 'Fear of failure' at 34%, 30% and 25% respectively.

Among the external factors, the highest rating goes to 'Family pressure', which is quoted by 70% of the poll sample, followed by 'Pressure from society' at 60% and 'Peer pressure' at 45%.

2. The graph below shows the value in thousands of dollars of three companies selling farming equipment every five years from 1960 and their projected value from 2007 to 2012. Farm Implements Ltd did not start trading until 1980.
Write a report for a university lecturer describing the information shown below.

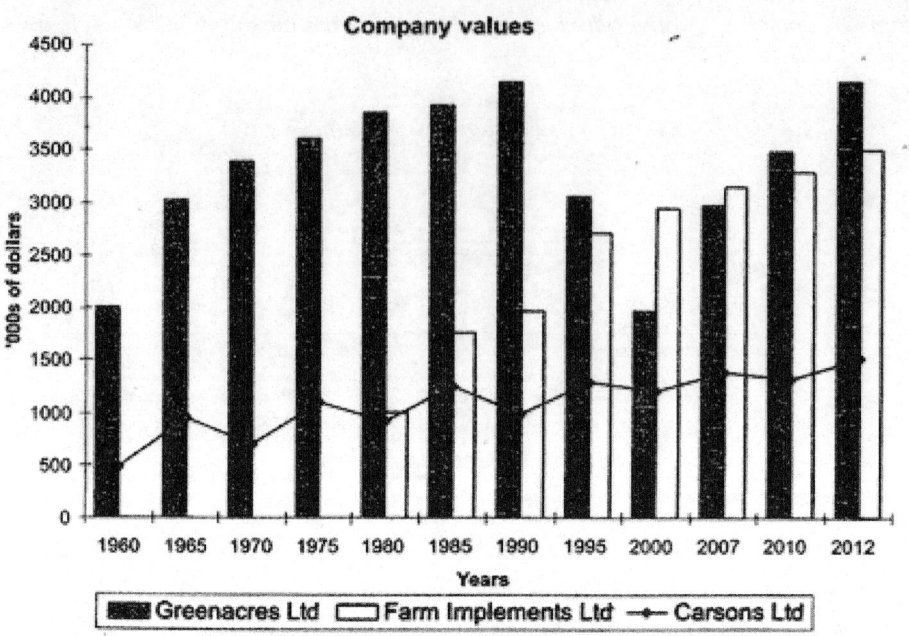

The chart shows the value in dollars of three companies selling farming equipment every five years from 1960 until 2000 and their estimated values up to 2012.

Whilst Greenacres Ltd more than doubled in value between 1960 and the year 1990, rising from 2 million dollars to just over 4 million, the value dropped by approximately 25% by 1995 and then by another third by the year 2000, when it was valued at 2 million dollars. In contrast, the trend for Carsons Limited was steadily upwards with some fluctuations and a doubling in value from 500,000 dollars to one million by the year 2000. The third company, Farm Implements Ltd, was not set up until 1980. However, by the year 2000, its value stood at approximately 2 million dollars, doubling from its 1980 value of 1 million. Farm Implements Ltd, is expected to increase in value gradually until 2012.

Until 2012, Greenacres Ltd and Carsons Ltd are both expected to increase in value with the former recovering to match the peak of just above 4 million dollars last seen in 1990. Similarly, Carsons Ltd is set to continue its steady increase reaching a value of 1.5 million dollars by 2012.

3. The chart shows components of GDP in the UK from 1992 to 2000.
Summarise the information by selecting and reporting the main features and make comparisons where relevant.

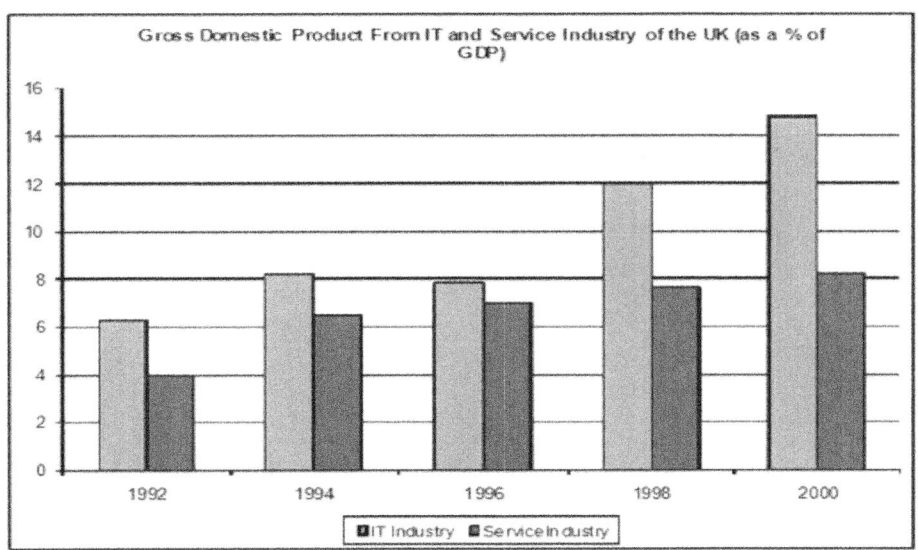

The bar chart depicts the gross domestic product generated from the IT and Service Industry in the UK from 1992 to 2000. It is measured in percentages. Overall, it can be seen that both increased as a percentage of GDP, but IT remained at a higher rate throughout this entire time.

At the beginning of the period, in 1992, the Service Industry accounted for 4 per cent of GDP, whereas IT exceeded this, at just over 6 per cent. Over the next four years, the levels became more similar, with both components standing between 6 and just over 8 per cent. IT was still higher overall, though it dropped slightly from 1994 to 1996.

However, over the following four years, the patterns of the two components were noticeable different. The percentage of GDP from IT increased quite sharply to 12 in 1998 and then nearly 15 in 2000, while the Service Industry stayed nearly the same, increasing to only 8 per cent. At the end of the period, the percentage of GDP from IT was almost twice that of the Service Industry.

- **a pie chart**

Necessary words:
- a sector
- a piece
- a proportion
- a percentage

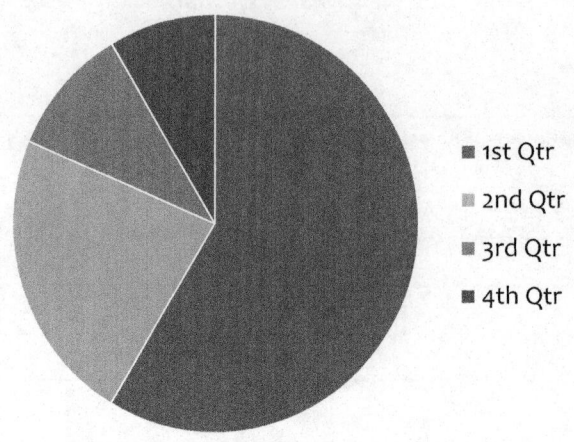

1.   The charts below give information about world spending and population.
Summarise the information by selecting and reporting the main features, and make comparisons
where relevant.

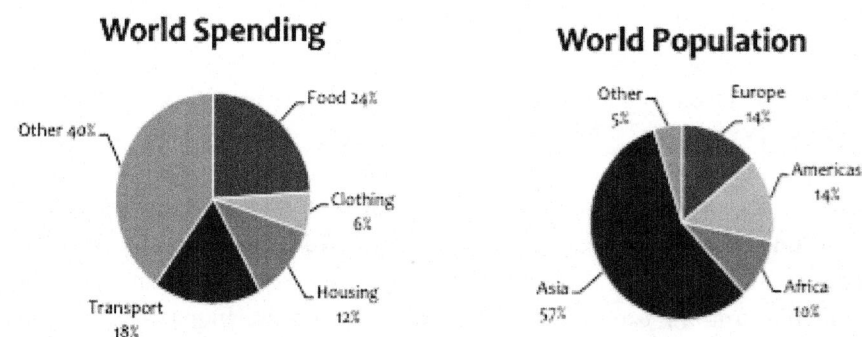

The first pie chart compares the shares of four major items in global expenditure. It is observed that the most significant amounts are paid for food (almost a quarter of global expenditure) and transport (almost 20%), while housing also accounts for a considerable proportion. The least among the four is spent on clothing (merely 6 per cent) and the remaining 40% is spent on a variety of other items.

The second diagram illustrates how global population is distributed. According to this chart, there is a significant difference between the population of Asia and that of other continents since 3 out of every 5 human beings live in Asia. Europe and the Americas share similar proportions and together are host to roughly one-third of the world's population, while the inhabitants of Africa form a mere one-tenth.

Obviously, four items are responsible for three-fifths of the overall spending around the world, the most prominent share being that of food. Moreover, the largest group of humans populates Asia, where the population outnumbers that of the rest of the world by 3 to 2.

2. *Write a report for a university lecturer describing the information below.*

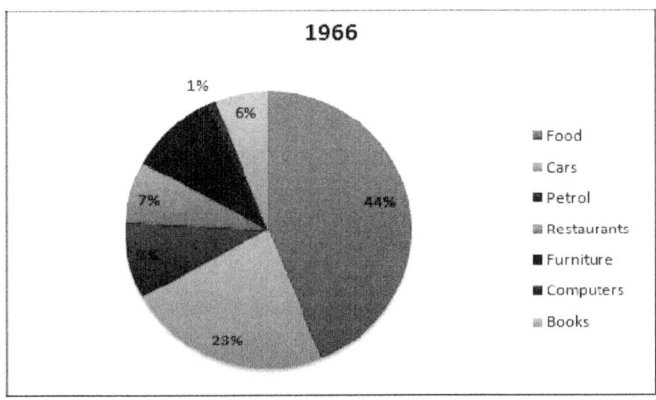

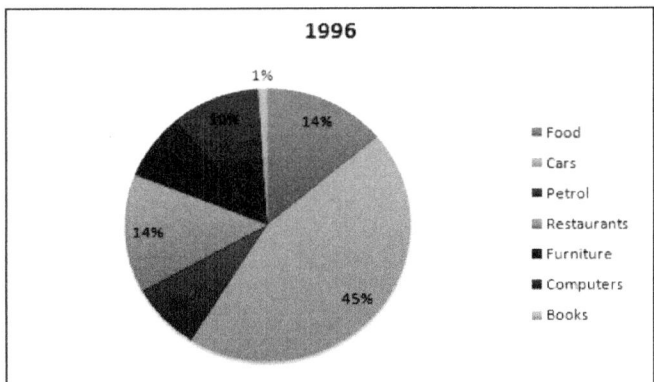

The pie charts show changes in American spending patterns between 1966 and 1996. It is visible that increased amounts spent on cars, computers, and eating out were made up for by drops in expenditure on food and books.

Food and cars made up the two biggest items of expenditure in both years. Together they comprised over half of household spending. Food accounted for 44% of spending in 1966, but this dropped by two thirds to 14% in 1996. However, the outlay on cars doubled, rising from 23% in 1966 to 45% in 1996.

Other areas changed significantly. Spending on eating out doubled, climbing from 7% to 14%. The proportion of salary spent on computers increased dramatically, up from 1% in 1996 to 10% in 1996. Yet, as computer expenditure rose, the percentage of outlay on books plunged from 6% to 1%.

3.   *Write a report for a university lecturer describing the information in the two graphs below.*

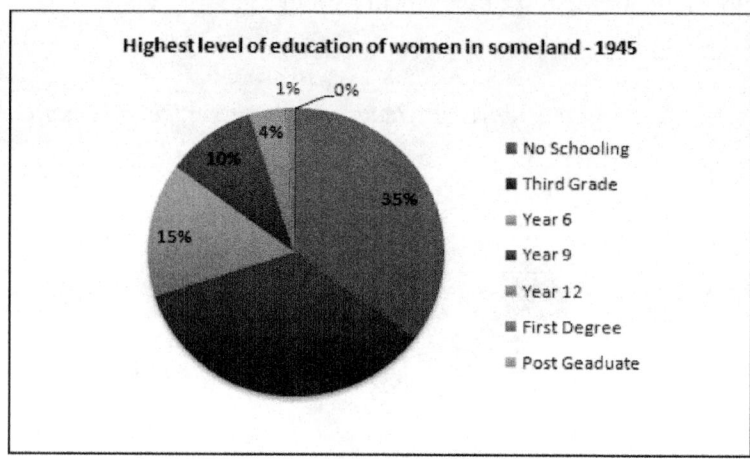

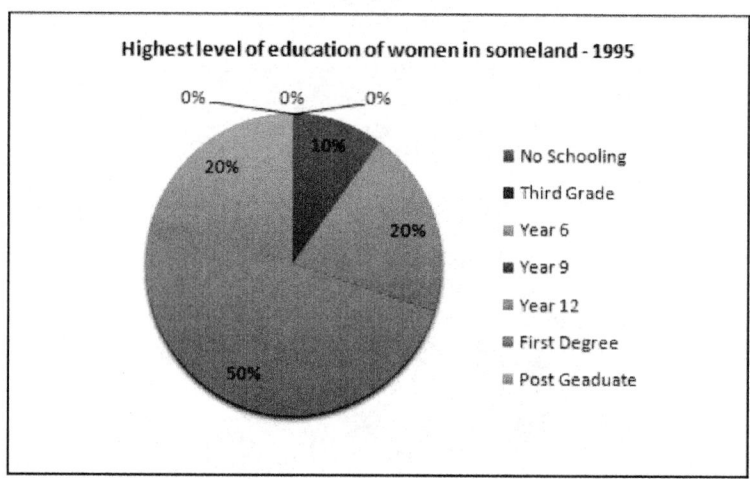

The pie charts compare the highest level of education achieved by women in Someland across two years, 1945 and 1995. It can be clearly seen that women received a much higher level of education in Someland in 1995 than they did in 1945.

In 1945 only 30% of women completed their secondary education and 1% went on to a first degree. No women had completed post-graduate studies. This situation had changed radically by 1995. In that year, 90% of women in Someland had completed secondary education and of those, half had graduated from an initial degree and 20% had gone on to postgraduate studies. From the other end of the scale it is visible that by 1995 all girls were completing lower secondary, although 10% ended their schooling at this point. This is in stark contrast with 1945 when only 30% of girls completed primary school, 35% had no schooling at all and 35% only completed the third grade.

310

- **a process diagram/a flow chart/a cycle diagram**

TIPS :

- ↻ try to answer these questions to yourself first:
  - What happens?
  - How does it happen?
  - What is the purpose of this diagram?
  - What principles are involved?
  - How does it work?
  - Why does it work that way?
- ↻ make sure you understand what the important stages of the flow chart or diagram are
- ↻ make sure to check the order in which stages come in
- ↻ do not include minor details
- ↻ maintain logical order of your writing
- ↻ use adequate linking expressions
- ↻ write the whole passage with unity and coherence

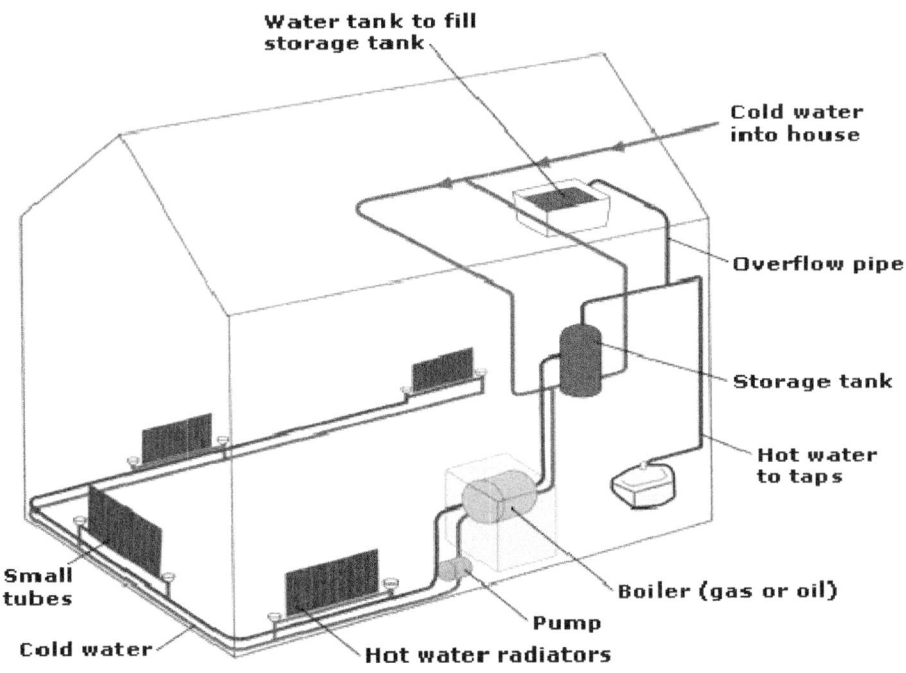

Grammar :

- use Present Simple to report actions which happen regularly in a process
- for natural events (rain, clouds formation, erosion etc.) use the active forms of verbs
- for artificial events use the passive forms of verbs as the human subjects are usually ignored in order to focus on what is being done
- use 'by' when you need to report that a tool is used to perform a stage of a process
  for tools = It is done using/through the use of a...
  for methods = It is done through/via...

EXEMPLAR REPORTS:
(All reports provided here would achieve Band 8&9)

1. The diagram below shows the process of using water to produce electricity. Summarise the information by selecting and reporting the main features, and make comparisons where relevant.

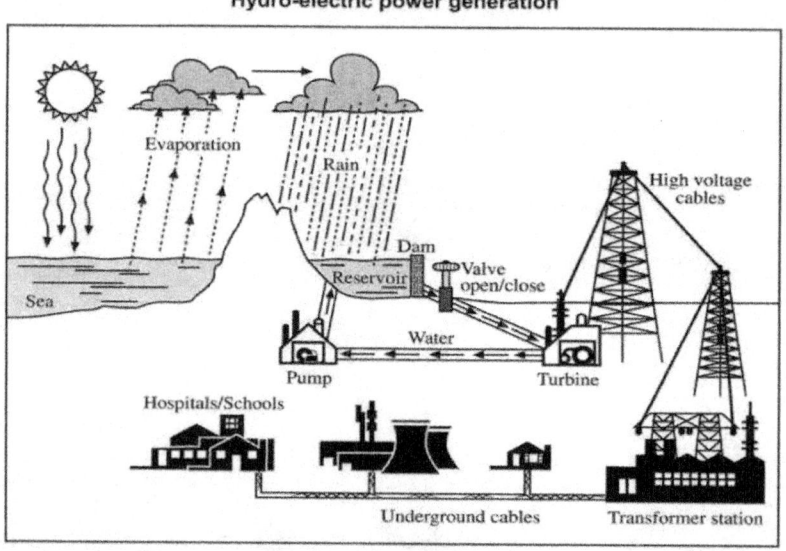

Hydro-electric power generation

The picture explains the process through which water is used to produce electrical power. All in all, it comprises over ten stages. It is clear that hydroelectric power is generated using water from the sea through a relatively sophisticated procedure.

The process begins when seawater is heated by the sun and evaporates to form small clouds in the sky. Next, they merge into a storm cloud, which then rains over the mountain. This rainwater is gathered in the reservoir behind a dam. The following steps involve a pipe which connects the reservoir to a turbine as well as a pump, and is controlled using a valve. Once this valve is opened, water flows into the turbine and rotates it to produce electrical current, following which it is pumped back into the reservoir. After this, the electricity produced by the turbine is transferred to the transformer station through high voltage cables. The last stage happens when the electrical power is being delivered to domestic and industrial consumers as well as educational and medical facilities.

2. The diagram shows how an Internet search engine works.
Summarise the information by selecting and reporting the main features, and make comparisons
where relevant.

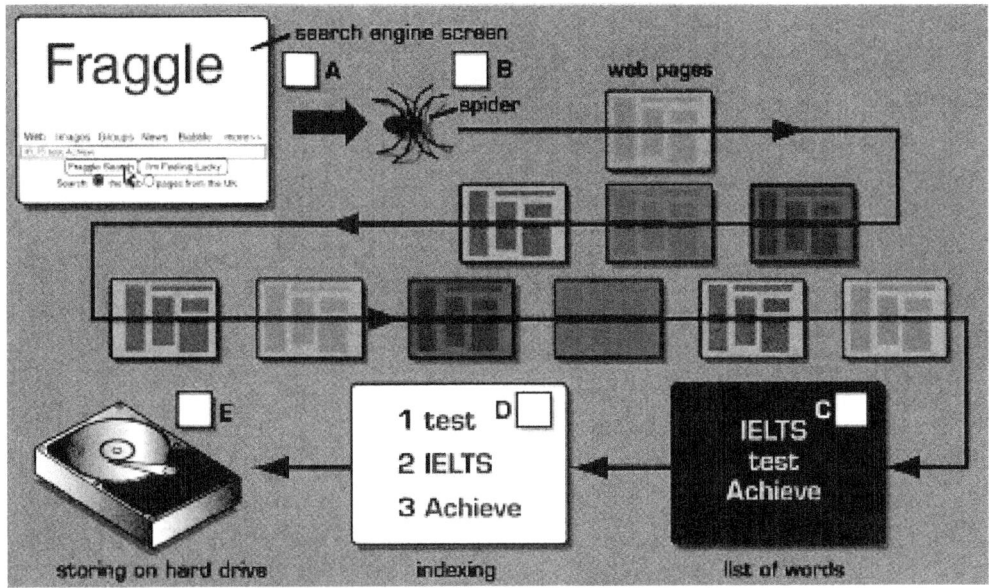

To do an Internet search, a web browser or a search engine are used. They are programmes that help people find information from hundreds of thousands of webpages. According to the picture, there are five stages in the process of finding information on the Internet.

The first step of the procedure is that the user tells the search engine what to look for. This is done by typing in the key words of the topic: the more words are typed, the narrower the search will be. Subsequently, a programme called a spider starts to search for the information on the most popular websites and most heavily used servers. At the same time, the information on these sites is recorded and then the links to the other sites should be followed so that the search spreads over the most popular parts of the web.

In the next stage, the search engine builds a list of words, and notes where these words are found. After that, it orders and presents the information in a way one can use, giving links to the pages according to how often the word appears on a webpage. The final part of the procedure is that the search engine saves the data to be accessed later, meaning that the website that was looked at previously can be easily found.

3.   *The diagram shows how an ATM transactions work worldwide.*
Summarise the information by selecting and reporting the main features, and make comparisons where relevant.

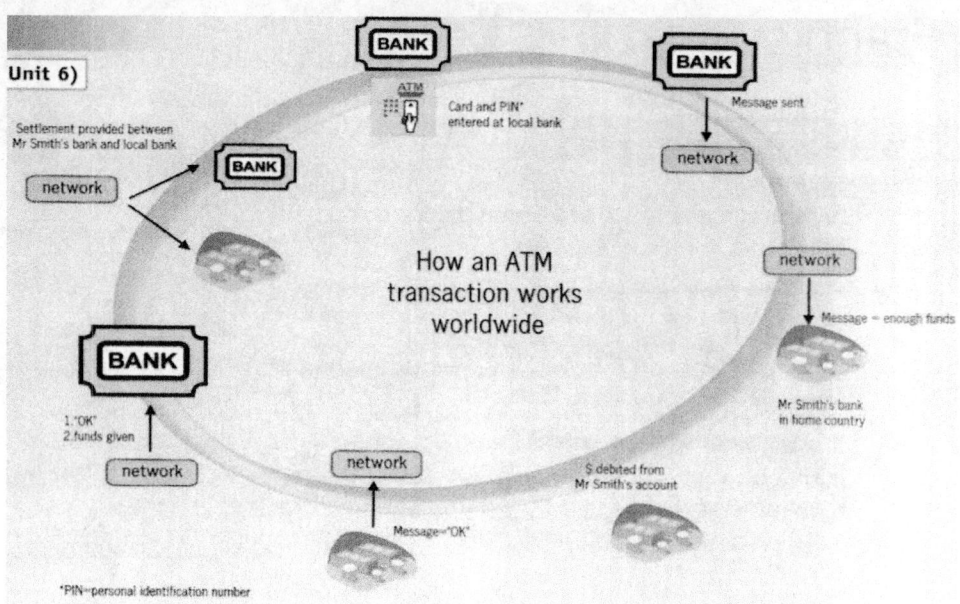

The diagram shows how a transaction works at au automated teller machine in five steps, allowing us to withdraw money from any participating bank in the world.

First of all, Mr Smith inserts his card and PIN into the ATM at a local bank abroad. An electronic message is sent to the central network which is passed on to Mr Smith's own bank in his home country. The local bank will not dispense the cash until it knows the funds are available in Mr Smith's own account.

As soon as the home country bank receives the request and checks the balance, the money is debited from the account. The bank then replies to the message via the network, stating that the local bank can provide Mr Smith with the amount requested. Mr Smith retrieves the money and his card and goes on his way. Later that day a settlement occurs between the two banks facilitated by the central network.

- **a map**

TIPS :
- look at the map and make sure you understand what it shows
- use lots of location words
- describe objects, including their shape, size, colour, location, condition, texture, purpose etc.
- check if all the essential information from the picture is in your description
- focus on the key information as there will be too much information for you to describe in great detail
- try to paraphrase words written on the map

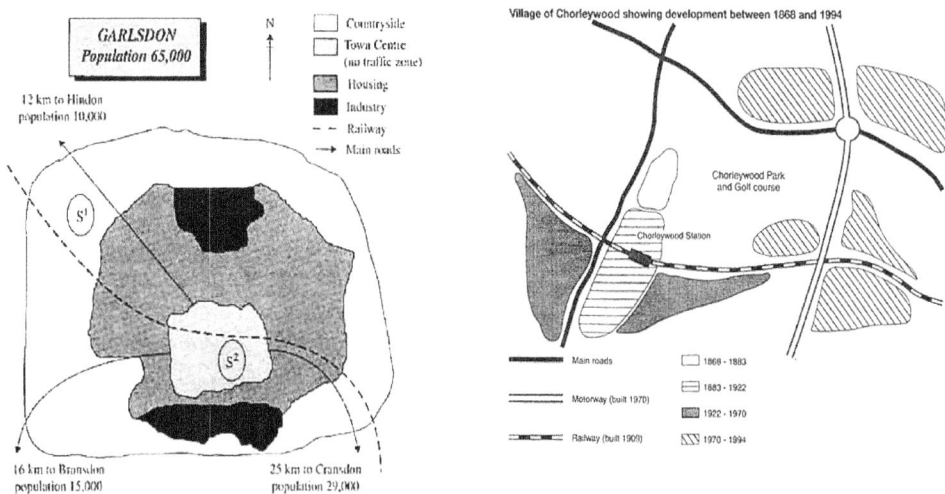

1. Comparison map   2. Development map

Useful vocabulary for describing positions on maps:

- at the top/bottom
- on the right/left side
- in the right/left side
- in the middle
- along
- across from
- opposite to
- close to
- adjacent to
- next to
- beside
- 10 miles from
- 10 miles to the right of
- 10 miles north of

Useful vocabulary for maps:

- residential area: an area that has lots of houses and some schools
- industrial area: an area that has lots of factories
- commercial area: an area that has lots of stores
- warehouse: a building where things are kept until they are sold
- parking lot: an area where people can park cars
- woodland: an area with lots of trees
- intersection: the pint where several streets meet
- to replace sth: to take the place of sth
- to expand: to become larger
- to construct: to build
- to develop: to make
- to remove: to get rid off
- to modify: to change
- to demolish: to destroy a building or other structure completely
- proximity: closeness

EXEMPLAR REPORTS:
(All reports provided here would achieve Band 8&9)

1. *The map below is of the town of Garlsdon and shows two possible sites for a new supermarket. Summarise the information by selecting and reporting the main features, and make comparisons where relevant.*

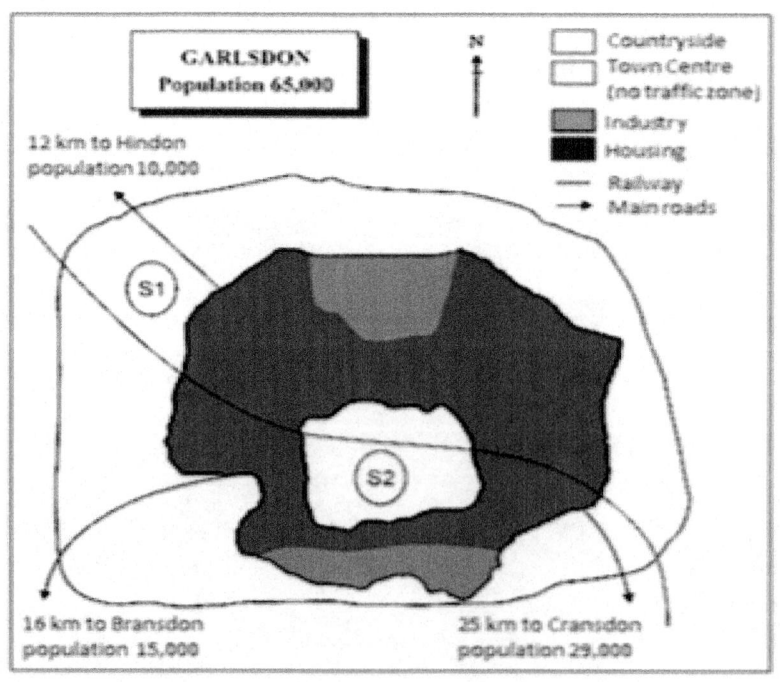

The first potential location (S1) is outside the town itself, and is sited just off the main road to the town of Hindon, lying 12 kilometres to the north-west. This site is in the countryside and so would be able to accommodate a lot of car parking. This would make it accessible to shoppers from both Hindon and Garlsdon who could travel by car. Since it is also close to the railway line linking the two towns to Cransdon (25 km to the south-east), a potentially large number of shoppers would also be able to travel by train.

In contrast, the suggested location, S2, is right in the town centre, which would be good for local residents. Theoretically the store could be accessed by road or rail from the surrounding towns, including Bransdon, but as the central area is a no-traffic zone, cars would be unable to park and access would be difficult.

Overall, neither site is appropriate for all the towns, but for customers in Cransdon, Hindon and Garlsdon, the out-of-town site (S1) would probably offer more advantages.

2. *The map below shows changes in a village named Chorleywood (1868-1994).*
Summarise the information by selecting and reporting the main features, and make comparisons where relevant.

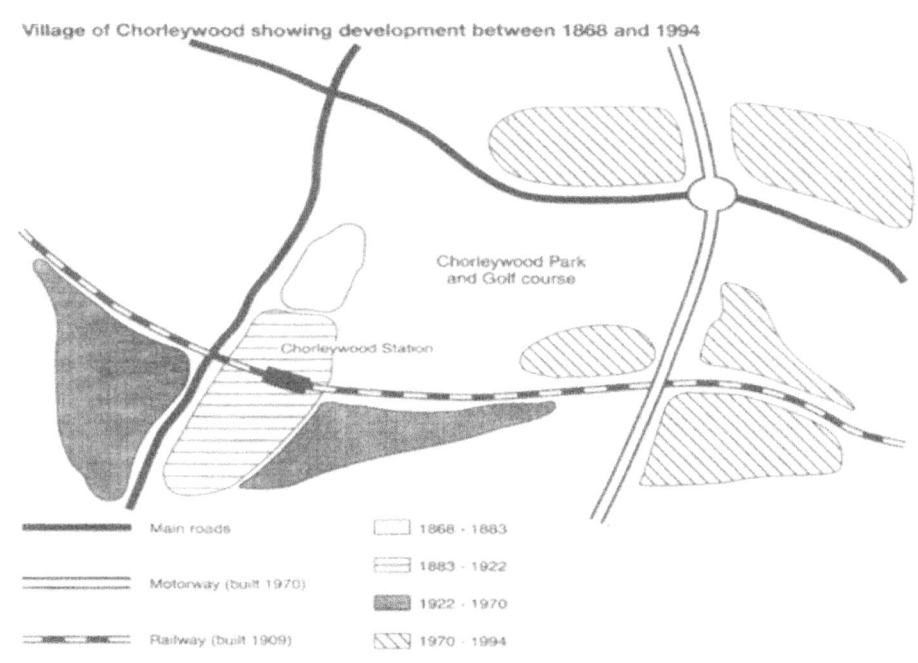

The map depicts the growth of a village called Chorleywood between 1868 and 1994. It is clear that the village grew as the transport infrastructure was improved. Four periods of development are shown on the map, and each of the populated areas is near to the main roads, the railway of the motorway.

From 1868 to 1883, Chorleywood covered a small area next to one of the main roads. Chorleywood Park and Golf Course is now located next to this original village area. The village grew along the main road to the south between 1883 and 1922, and in 1909 a railway line was built crossing this area from west to east. Chorleywood station is in this part of the village.

The expansion of Chorleywood continued to the east and west alongside the railway line until 1970. At that time, a motorway was built to the east of the village, and from 1970 to 1994, further development of the village took place around motorway intersections with the railway and one of the main roads.

3. *Below is a map of the city of Brandfield. City planners have decided to build a new shopping mall for the area, and two sites, S1 and S2 have been proposed. Summarise the information by selecting and reporting the main features and make comparisons where relevant.*

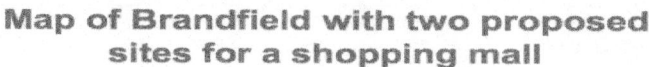

Map of Brandfield with two proposed sites for a shopping mall

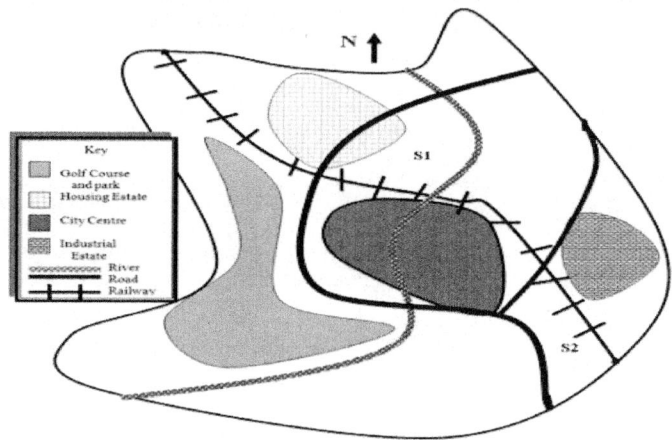

The map illustrates plans for two possible sites for a shopping mall in the city of Bradfield. It can be seen that the two sites under consideration are in the north and the south east of the town.

The first possible site for the shopping mall, S1, is just north of the city centre, above the railway line, which runs from the south east of the city to the north west. If it is built here, it will be next to a large housing estate, thus providing easy access for those living on the estate and in the city centre. It will also be next to the river, which runs through the town.

The site in the south east, S2, is again just by the railway line and fairly close to the city centre, but it is near to an industrial estate rather than housing.

There is a main road that runs through the city and is close to both sites, thus providing good road access to either location. A large golf course and park in the west of the town prevents this area from being available as a site.

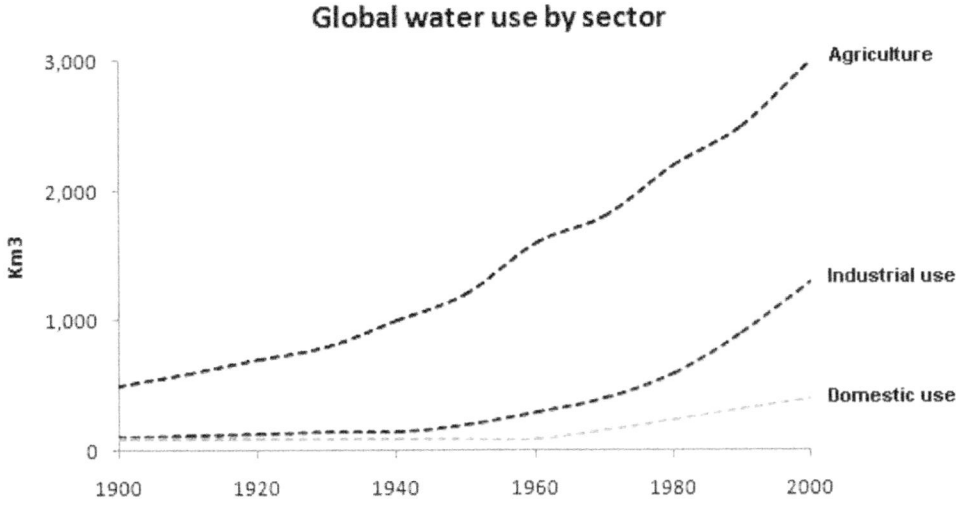

Global water use by sector

Country	Population	Irrigated land	Water consumption per person
Brazil	176 million	26,500 km²	359 m³
Democratic Republic of Congo	5.2 million	100 km²	8 m³

Vocabulary for comparing & contrasting:

- use a good number of comparative adjectives (e.g. more productive, higher, hotter, etc.)
- use structures to compare and contrast like: more… than…, far less… than…, as… as…, twice as much… as…, three times more… than…, slightly more … than…, the same… as…
- a considerable/significant/notable/slight/marginal difference between… and…
- strikingly/broadly/fairly similar to…
- A similar trend can be observed in…
- The results for…, however, reveal a markedly different trend.
- to compare: both, same, also, like, analogous to, similar, similarly, alike, whereas, each, likewise, just as, in the same way, akin to, as well as, on a similar note
- comparative phrases:
  - …and…both have…
  - Both…and…are…
  - …and…are the same because…
  - …also has…
  - …is like… because…
  - Similarly, …is…

319

- …is similar to… in many ways because…and…
- Whereas…is…, …is…and…
- …and…are alike because…
- …is just as difficult as…because…

- to contrast: different, but, although, different from, however, one difference, on the other hand, in comparison, by contrast, by comparison, instead of, in contrast to, conversely, even though, unlike, on the contrary, yet, despite, differ, variation, otherwise
- contrasting phrases :
    - …is…different than…because…
    - …is…, but…is…
    - Although…has…, …has…
    - …is… However, …is…
    - …is… On the other hand, …is…
    - Even though…has…, …has…
    - …and…differ because…
    - …is unlike…because…
    - …has…, yet…has…
    - …is… On the contrary, …is…
    - Despite having…, …is different because…
    - One variation between…and… is that …has…

___EXEMPLAR REPORTS:___
___(All reports provided here would achieve Band 8&9)___

1. *The charts below give information about travel to and from the UK, and about the most popular countries for UK residents to visit.*
Summarise the information by selecting and reporting the main features, and make comparisons where relevant.

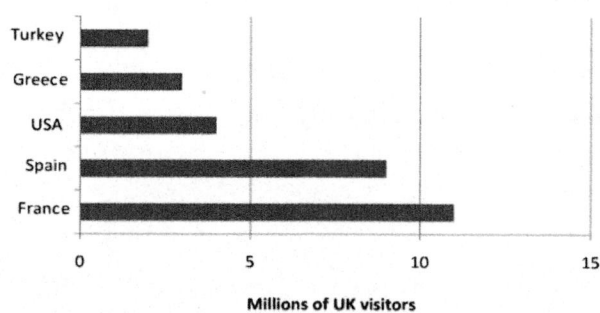

Most popular countries visited by UK residents 1999

Turkey, Greece, USA, Spain, France

Millions of UK visitors

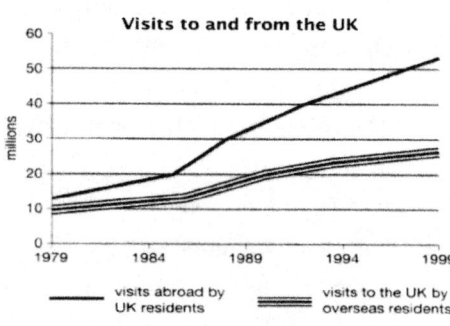

Visits to and from the UK

millions

1979 1984 1989 1994 1999

visits abroad by UK residents
visits to the UK by overseas residents

The first diagram compares changes in the number of British tourists who travelled abroad with that of foreign visitors to the United Kingdom over the last 20 years of the previous century. According to the graph, the former initially stood at more than 12 million and grew six-fold at the end of the survey. In comparison, the latter number was slightly less than that of the British tourists at the beginning of this period and experienced similar yet less intensive trends, reaching approximately half as high by the end of the century.

The bar chart reveals the top 5 countries visited by the British in the last year of the above survey. It can be observed that while France and Spain absorbed the largest numbers of British tourists with about 11 and 9 million visits respectively, Turkey was the least popular among the five, visited by only about 30% as many British travellers as France.

Overall, tourism from and to the United Kingdom boomed in the 1980s and 90s. Moreover, most of the trips made by the British abroad were to 5 countries only.

2. *The charts show the percentage of the food budget the average family spent on restaurant meals in different years. The graph shows the number of meals eaten in fast food restaurants and sit-down restaurants.*
Give reasons for your answer and include any relevant examples from your own knowledge or experience.

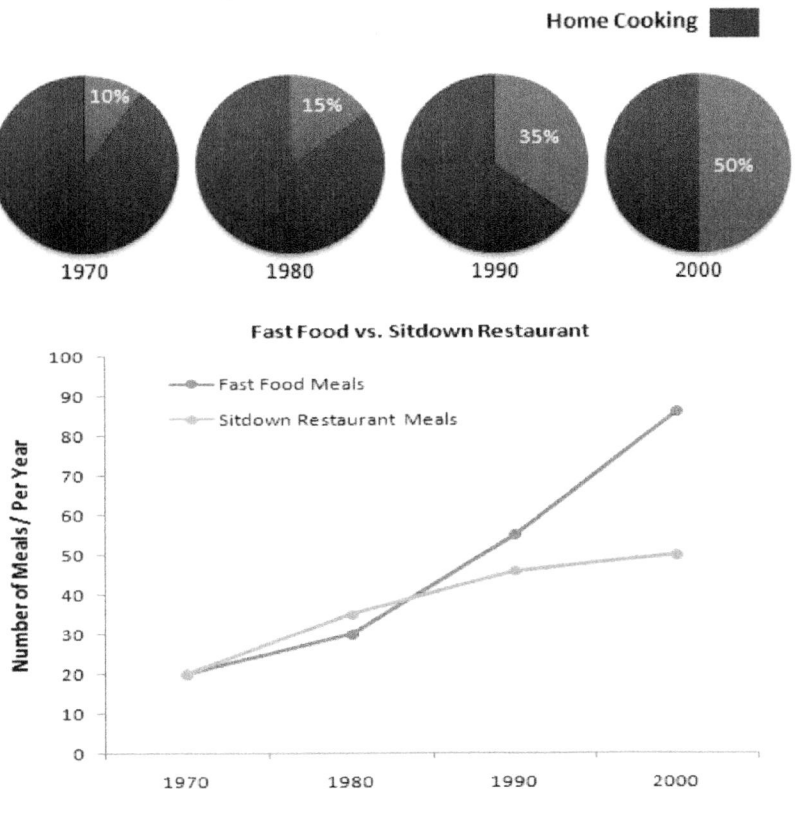

Over the past 30 years, the average family has dramatically increased the number of meals that they eat at restaurants. The percentage of the family's food budget spent on restaurant meals steadily climbed. Just 10 per cent of the food budget was spent on restaurant meals in 1970, and 15 per cent in 1980. That percentage more than doubled in 1990, to 35 %, and rose again in 2000 to 50%.

Where families eat their restaurant meals also changed during that 30-year period. In 1970, families ate the same number of meals at fast food and sit-down restaurants. In 1980, families ate slightly more frequently at sit-down restaurants. However, since 1990, fast food restaurants serve more meals to the families than the sit-down restaurants do. Most of the restaurant meals from 2000 were eaten at fast food restaurants. If this pattern continues, eventually the number of meals that families eat at fast food restaurants could double the number of meals they eat at sit-down restaurants.

3.   *The table below shows CO2 emissions for different forms of transport in the European Union. The pie chart shows the percentage of European Union funds being spent on different forms of transport.*
Give reasons for your answer and include any relevant examples from your own knowledge or experience.

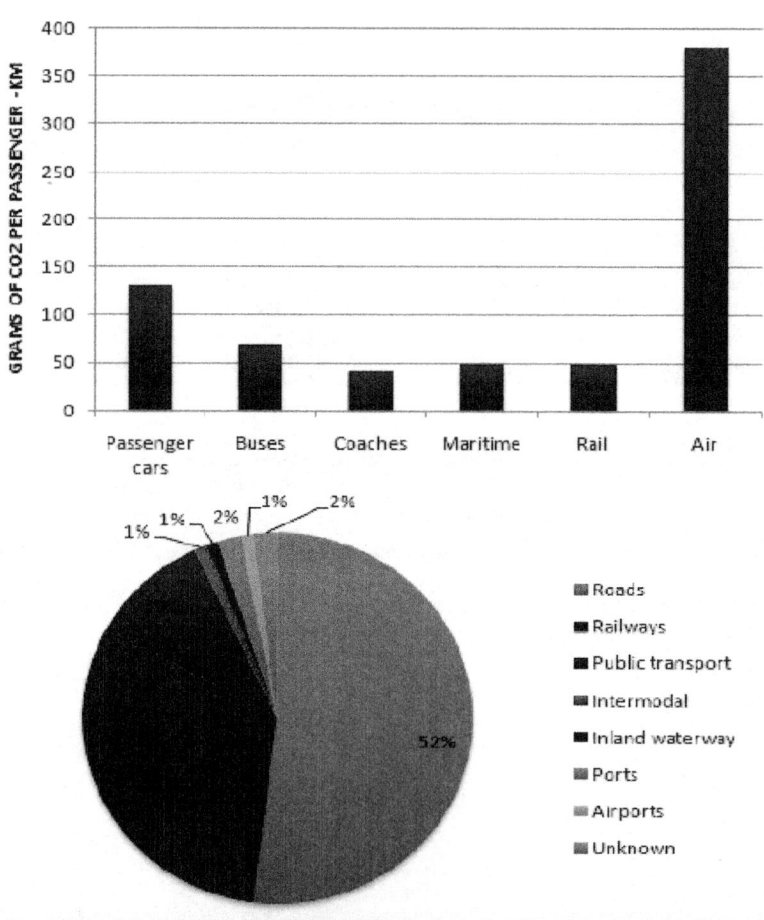

The chart shows CO2 emissions per passenger kilometre for various methods of transport in the European Union while the pie chart shows European Union spending on transport. Flying by air produces by far the greatest CO2 emissions, approximately three times as much as passenger cars which are the next largest producers. Very little is spent by the EU on air travel while roads make up more than half of the EU transport budget.

Trains produce about three times less CO2 emissions per passenger kilometre than passenger cars and eight times less than air travel. Nearly a third of EU transport funds are spent on railways.

Ships are a clean form of transport and produce about the same amount of CO2 per passenger kilometre as trains do. However, only 2 per cent of EU funds are spent on ports. A further one per cent is spent on inland waterways.

Coaches are the cleanest form of transport. Emissions of CO2 per passenger kilometre from coaches are half those of buses. Buses emit less than half as much CO2 per passenger kilometre as cars. The European Union spends 10 per cent of its transport budget on public transport, such as buses and coaches.

HOW SHOULD YOU BUILD YOUR REPORT?

For single graphs/charts:
1. Introduction: 1 paragraph (1-2 sentences), introduce the topic, paraphrase the prompt (do not copy it), give a brief overview and present a trend
2. Two main body paragraphs: organize and group the information, summarize it and analyse it by contrasting and comparing where necessary (depending on the prompt), select what is important, do not present all the information given

For double graphs/charts:
1. Introduction: Write two sentences: introduce each chart separately (in one sentence) and present a trend.
2. Two main body paragraphs: 1. show main points for each chart, compare the charts
                                            2. compare the information from both charts
   NOTE: Do not write a conclusion. This task does not require you to present any personal opinions or write anything beyond the information provided.

How to write a good INTRODUCTION?

Always paraphrase the prompt by:
- using derivatives of a word
   e.g. contribute (v.) – contribution (n.)
- converting active sentences into passive once and vice versa
   e.g.   ~~Children used the books more eagerly when they were illustrated.~~

The books were used more eagerly when they were illustrated.

- using synonyms and antonyms

  e.g.   ~~The graph provides information on the number of cars bought…~~

  The chart shows data on the figure of cars purchased…

- making changes, e.g.:
  - graph = line/bar graph
  - chart = line/bar chart
  - diagram = figure
  - shows = illustrates etc.
  - proportion = percentage
  - information = data (requires a plural verb)
  - the number of = the figure of
  - people in the USA = Americans
  - from 1999 to 2009 = between 1999 and 2009
  - from 1999 to 2009 = over a period of 10 years
  - how to produce = the process of producing
  - in three countries = in the UK, France and Spain (i.e. name the countries)

PREPARE FOR THIS TASK (about 2-3 minutes)

- Study the question carefully. Make sure you understand instructions correctly.
- Think about the outline. Make note of some pertinent points.
- Note the times given for correct use of tenses.
- Make sure your ideas are arranged logically with appropriate connectors.
- Do not neglect to proofread your report. It will help you identify grammatical errors and correct them before the examiner reads it.

USEFUL VOCABULARY FOR TASK 1

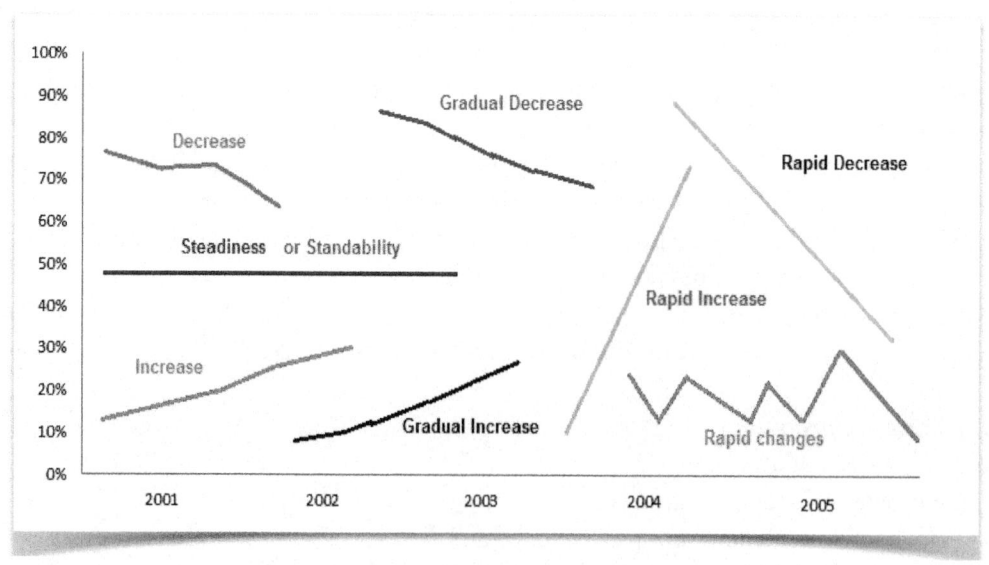

✓ **For general statements/introduction:**
- According to the…,
- As shown in the…,
- As can be seen from the…,
- We can see from the…,
- It is manifested from the…,
- It is visible from the…,
- It can be learnt from…,
- It is clear/apparent from…,
- The …shows/indicates/illustrates/reveals/represents/depicts…
- As the … shows,
- As is illustrated by the…

✓ **For time frames:**
- from… to…
- between… and…
- for (one month etc.)
- for a period of (how many years)
- over the (next month etc.)
- over the (25-year period etc.)
- during the (10-year period etc.)
- throughout the period
- in (1999 etc.)
- in (the next two decades etc.)
- before/after
- around/about
- (in) the period from… to…
- from that time on
- after that
- then
- in the 1980s
- in years to come
- in the winter months
- in the first quarter of the year (3 months)
- in the second half of the year

✓ **For quantity:**
- the amount of (with uncountable nouns)
- figure (n.)
- the total quantity = the total amount
- the whole of the (with uncountable nouns)
- the majority (with singular or plural verbs)
- the maximum = the largest
- quantity (with countable nouns)

- the number of (with plural nouns)
- the total
- the total number
- all of the
- the whole amount
- the full amount
- the greatest amount
- the greatest number
- the minimum
- percent (used with a number)
- percentage (not used with a number but with adjectives)
- the proportion of (with plural nouns)

✓ **For age groups :**
- age group/profile/bracket/range/cohort
- People aged…
- …-… year-olds

✓ **Verbs related to measurement:**
- be
- constitute
- equal
- include
- stand at
- make up
- comprise
- account for
- record
- become
- consist of
- amount to
- represent
- reach

✓ **Useful mathematical expressions:**
- half (n.)
- halve (v.) (divided by two)
- double (n./v.) (times two)
- triple (n.)
- treble (v.) (times three)
- quadruple (v.) (times four)
- threefold (adj.) (three times as much)
- quarter (n./v.) (times four)
- multiply (v.)

- divide (v.)
- average (adj./v./n.)
- total (adj./v.)
- partial (adj.) (not complete)
- equal (adj./n)
- fraction (n.)
- one-third
- one-fifth
- two-thirds
- two-fifths

TREND (a general direction in which something is developing or changing)

- tendency
- current
- variability
- direction
- orientation

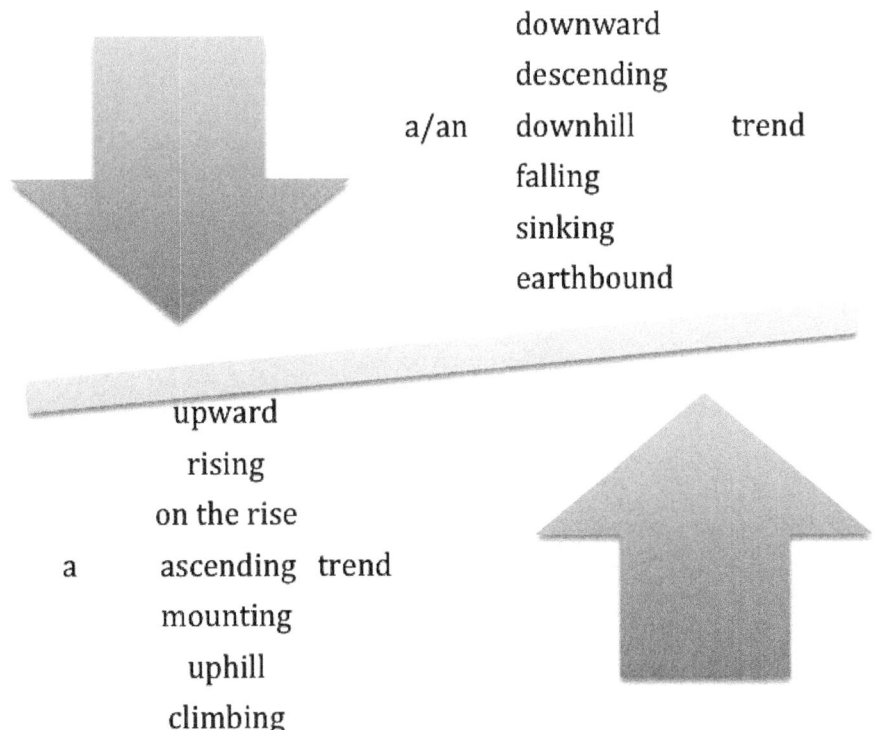

Grammar for describing trends
(for tense reference see Appendices in this book)

- Use Simple Past if the data represents actions from the past
- Use Simple Present (for graphs, charts and tables) if the task represents changes or actions which happen regularly
- Use Passive Voice for processes and cycles
- Use Present Perfect for the trend that begins in the past and continues till now
- Use Future Simple to report the value a trend will reach in the future years

Phrases for future predictions:

Predictions		
Expectations		
Anticipations	reveal	
Forecasts	show	(that) sth will drop dramatically.
Estimates	indicate	
Evaluations		
Calculations		

Or use passive structures:

	predicted
	expected
	anticipated
It is	forecast that sth will drop dramatically.
	estimated
	evaluated
	calculated

POSITION (a place where something is located)

Nouns = a levelling off at
a plateau at

Verbs = stand at
level off at
plateau at
level out at
stabilize at
reach a high peak/low at
reach + number

HOW THINGS CHANGE (v. + adv.)

Big/fast change:
- dramatically
- sharply (fast)
- significantly
- highly
- severely
- considerably
- extremely
- excessively
- widely
- drastically
- substantially
- hugely
- enormously
- tremendously
- remarkably
- rapidly (fast)
- quickly (fast)
- swiftly (fast)
- steeply (fast)
- crucially
- strikingly
- notably
- briskly (fast)
- exponentially (a high degree of change)

Medium change:
- carefully
- noticeably
- markedly
- moderately
- to a certain extent
- vaguely

Small/slow change:
- slightly
- minimally
- gradually (slow)
- slowly (slow)

- at a slow pace
- steadily
- bit by bit
- little by little
- slowly but surely
- marginally

Unexpected change:
- suddenly
- unexpectedly
- abruptly

NO CHANGE or SMALL CHANGE

NO CHANGE (v.):
- To remain at + number
- To remain constant/steady/static/stable
- To stay flat
- To stay/remain unchanged at + number
- To become flat
- To flatten out
- To plateau
- To bottom out
- To be stable
- To keep at
- To shift

A CHANGE (n.)
- a minor/slight change
- a modification
- an alteration
- an adjustment

TO COMPARE (two tables/graphs/bar charts/pie charts/maps/diagrams):

- There is a

considerable	difference	between A and B.
constant	discrepancy	
sudden	dissimilarity	
noticeable	contrast	
great	distinction	
	differentiation	
	divergence	

330

disparity
polarity
deviation
gap
contradistinction

- The greatest difference occurred + when/where?
- In contrast to B, A is (larger/smaller etc.)   by + number.
- In comparison with B, A is….
- A is just/approximately under/over + how many times larger/smaller than B.
- A is under/over twice/three times as large/great/high as B.
- A is considerably higher/greater than B.
- A is almost/roughly as large/high as B.

TO FLUCTUATE (v.)

- To fluctuate around + number/time
- To remain between A and B
- To vary
- To be unstable
- To alter
- To swing
- To oscillate
- To rise and fall
- To undulate

A FLUCTUATION (n.)

- a minor/slight fluctuation
- a variation
- a shift
- an alternation
- a swing
- an oscillation
- an unsteadiness
- a rise and fall
- an undulation

TO INCREASE (VERB) :

- to rise by/to
- to go up by/to
- to build up
- to expand
- to climb by/to

- to rocket to/by (big)
- to take off (big)
- to reach a new high at
- to reach a peak at
- to escalate
- to grow to/by
- to soar (big)
- to shoot up (big)
- to boom
- to double
- to triple
- to surge
- to intensify
- to mount up
- to multiply
- to inflate
- to magnify
- to amplify
- to elevate
- to skyrocket (big)

AN INCREASE (NOUN):
- a tightening up of
- a rise of
- a growth of
- a progress in
- a climb
- an expansion of
- a doubling in + N. (two)
- a trebling in + N. (three)
- a boom
- a surge
- an escalation
- a multiplication
- an inflation
- a magnification
- an amplification
- an extension
- an elevation
- an increment
- an upsurge

TO DECREASE (VERB):

- to decline to/by
- to diminish to/by
- to fall to/by
- to dip to/by
- to drop to/by
- to dive to/by (big change)
- to plummet to/by (big)
- to crash to/by (big)
- to reach a new low of
- to reach a trough at
- to plunge to/by (big)
- to slump to/by
- to deteriorate
- to go down to/by
- to lessen
- to reduce
- to dwindle
- to abate
- to subside
- to ebb
- to curtail
- to deplete
- to minimize

A DECREASE (NOUN):

- a decline of
- a drop of
- a slump of
- a reduction in
- a plunge
- a deterioration in
- a plummet
- a weakening of
- a fall of
- a relaxation of
- a change of
- a crash
- a downturn
- a diminution
- a wane

- an ebb

TASK 2

- you will have about 40 minutes for this task
- plan, plan, plan! it only takes a minute (it can be in a form of a diagram, rough notes or pictures etc.) but adds to your logic significantly
- it is worth 60% of your final writing score
- do not write fewer than 250 words, as you will be penalized for it
- do not write more than 250 words, as you will surely make more mistakes and you are more likely to lose logic (+10% is acceptable)
- use Academic English (that means no slang, colloquial language, contractions etc.)
- you will be asked to discuss a subject of general interest (see a comprehensive list of topics in this chapter)
- you will need to present your opinion and justify it, offer solutions to a problem or speculate about future trends
- use a variety of structures for a higher score
- think in English when writing, do not translate word for word from your language!
- decide which points will be written as topic sentences and think about how they will be developed into paragraphs
- use topic sentences to clearly identify the main theme in each paragraph
- try to develop each paragraph in a convincing way (this may be done through the use of examples, explanations, details, logical inferences, causes and effects, or comparisons and contrasts)
- ensure that your paragraphs are arranged in logical order (each should contain an appropriate connective word to ensure a smooth transition between paragraphs)
- if the topic requires your opinion, make sure you state it clearly in your introduction, support it throughout your answer and re-state it (in a different way) in the conclusion
- include both simple and complex sentences (with more than one clause) in your essay
- proofread your essay and check for grammar and punctuation mistakes

TYPES OF ESSAYS ON IELTS

1. Opinion or agree/disagree essays

They present the writer's personal opinion concerning the topic, clearly stated and supported by reasons and/or examples.

The opposing viewpoint and reason should be included in a separate paragraph before the closing one, together with an argument that shows it is an unconvincing viewpoint.

The writer's opinion should be included in the introduction, and summarised/restated in the conclusion.

If you see the following key words in the prompt:

- ☞ To what extent/How far do you agree/think…?
- ☞ …agree or disagree?
- ☞ … Discuss.
- ☞ Give your opinion.

HOW TO PLAN AND ORGANIZE *OPINION* ESSAY?

Below is the plan. Follow it in order to write coherently.

Introduction
Paragraph 1
State the topic and your opinion clearly
Main Body
Paragraph 2 & 3 & 4 or 2 & 3
(depending on the number of ideas you have)
Viewpoints & reasons, examples
Paragraph 5 or 4
Opposing viewpoint & reasons, examples
Conclusion
Final Paragraph
Summarise & restate your opinion

EXEMPLAR ESSAYS:
(All essays presented below would obtain Band 8&9)

1. *These days many people discuss genetic engineering. What is your stand on this issue?*

By and large, genetic modification of the living organisms is essentially based on changing information in their genes. This process is known as recombinant DNA technology. The genes carry pivotal details about each particular cell, which are passed on through generations.

Firstly, genetic engineering is the subject of controversy. The proponents claim it can bring more benefits than risks. For instance, I consider genetic modification the best solution to famine due to the fact that we can already buy 'improved' food in shops. Secondly, gene therapy has been recently stated as the way to fight cancer and haemophilia. To my mind, such genetically modified organisms have the potential to help prevent many terminal diseases. Thirdly, those organisms are likely to speed up the production of vaccines or hormones. For this reason, I think GMOs will considerably matter in the development of DNA researches as well as clinical trials. For example, the defective gene will be replaced by the proper one. Owing to the factors mentioned above, I strongly advocate the phenomenon of GMOs as an extremely advantageous one.

On the contrary, the opponents of this issue perceive it as an attempt to interfere with nature. I totally agree with them. Creating new forms of life using such methods as gene modification is immoral. People should not take over God's power. I believe there are some mysteries in the Universe which should not be controlled by human beings, cloning in particular. This genetic modification entails many drawbacks. If we manage to clone a human embryo, we will immediately long for cloning entire nations. Such possibility could bring despair if we created another Adolf Hitler. I personally believe that our human tendency to gain immortality is highly inappropriate. We are not responsible enough to wield all the world's power because, as history shows, we often take advantage of it.

All things considered, I can definitely place myself among adversaries of the genetic modification. Even though it has amazing potential to improve our lives, still the question of the user's intention remains. I am not deeply convinced that humans are able to keep within bounds when it comes to such a crucial matter.

2. *"Although the position of women in society today has improved, there is still a great deal of sexual discrimination." Do you agree?*

Throughout this century, the role of women within society has changed, and the majority of people feel that this change is for the better. More women work than ever before, and it is accepted in Western culture that many women now have careers. Nonetheless, in my opinion there is still a great deal of sexual discrimination against women within society, and the belief that sexual equality has been achieved is not altogether accurate.

To begin with, many women find it very difficult to return to work after having children. The main reason for this is that there are rarely any provisions made for childcare in the workplace and, in these cases, women are forced to find someone to look after the children while they are at work. Obviously, this can prove to be a time-consuming and expensive process, yet it must be done if mothers are to be able to resume their careers.

Secondly, the traditional views of the position of women within society are so deeply ingrained that they have not really changed. For instance, not only is the view that women should stay at home and look after their family still widely held, but it is reinforced through images seen on television programmes and advertisements. An example of this is that few men are ever seen doing housework on television, since this is traditionally thought of as "a woman's job".

Thirdly, since families often need two incomes in order to enjoy a good standard of living, a woman finds herself doing two jobs: one at home and one at the office. So, it could be said that a woman's position has, in fact, deteriorated rather than improved, with the result that women carry the burdens of equality but get none of the benefits.

In contrast, there are some people who claim that the problem of sexual discrimination no longer exists. They point out that women do, after all, have legal rights intended to protect them from discrimination. In addition, a few women are now beginning to reach top positions as judges, business leaders and politicians, while a number of other previously all-male professions are operating their ranks to women. Nonetheless, these examples are not the norm and discrimination is still very much with us.

Taking these points into consideration, I would say that the position of women has improved only slightly. While rules and laws have changed, it is the deep-rooted opinions of people within society which are taking a longer time to evolve. Needless to say, until these attitudes have changed, sexual discrimination will remain a problem which we all need to face and fight against.

3. *It is inevitable that as technology develops so traditional cultures must be lost. Technology and tradition are incompatible – you cannot have both together. To what extent do you agree or disagree?*

Undeniably, technological advancement has rapidly eroded traditional culture we inherited from our ancestors. Traditional games, musical instruments, performances and celebrations are given less and less attention in this era of globalization.

To illustrate, traditional games such as kites and spinning tops have given way to the new, modern and sophisticated video games. Children nowadays are more interested in playing video games rather than traditional games which they deem old-fashioned. Apart from this, traditional instruments such as banjos are being replaced by new innovations such as pianos and electric guitars.

In addition, the number of traditional performances organized such as the Chinese Opera have also been decimated over the past few decades. This is mainly due to creation of idiot boxes which broadcast a variety of TV shows, making traditional performances pale in comparison with all the comedies and soap operas broadcasted.

Indeed, traditional culture is slowly being wiped out by the strong current of technology. However, they are not mutually incompatible. In other words, both of them can exist together. Concrete steps can be taken in order to bring these forgotten traditional cultures back into our society. One way of doing this is to educate our younger generation on our traditional cultures. Traditional games can be introduced as a kind of a sport in schools. Parents also play a major role in educating their children to appreciate traditions which have been passed down from generation to generation. Traditional performances and the use of traditional musical instruments can be revived through the promotion by the media.

In conclusion, the strong current of technological advancement has indeed washed out some of our traditions; nevertheless, those two issues are not mutually incompatible. We can preserve our treasured traditions which reflect our origins and roots but at the same time manage to develop our country with full utilization of technology.

2. <u>For and against essays (also called: pros and cons essays)</u>

They present both sides of an issue, discussing points in favour of a particular topic as well as those against, or the advantages and disadvantages of a particular question.

Each point should be supported by justifications, examples, and/or reasons.

The writer's own opinion should be presented only in the final paragraph.

If you see the following key words in the prompt:

- advantages
- merits
- benefits
- upsides
- positive effects
- disadvantages
- demerits
- drawbacks
- downsides
- negative effects etc.
- Some people…
- Others…
- Discuss the arguments on both sides…
- How..?

HOW TO PLAN AND ORGANIZE *FOR AND AGAINST* ESSAY?

Below, I present two alternative plans. Both are equally good.

Introduction	Introduction
Paragraph 1	***Paragraph 1***
State topic (without stating your opinion)	State topic (summary of topic without stating your opinion)
Main Body	**Main Body**
Paragraphs 2 or 2&3	***Paragraph 2***
(depending on the number of ideas you have)	First argument for & against
Arguments for & justifications, examples or reasons	***Paragraph 3***
Paragraphs 3 or 4&5	Second argument for & against
Arguments against & justification, examples or reasons	
Conclusion	**Conclusion**
Final Paragraph	***Final Paragraph***
Balanced consideration or direct/indirect opinion	Balanced consideration or direct/indirect opinion

A *for and against essay* can end in <u>a balanced consideration</u> in which you restate that there are points for and against the topics, or it can end by expressing <u>an opinion</u> in which case you state directly that you are either in favour or against the topic.

Conclusion expressing balanced considerations/opinion indirectly:

In conclusion,	it can/must be said/claimed that…
On balance,	it seems/appears that…
All things considered,	it would seem that…
Taking everything into account/consideration,	it is clear/obvious that…
To conclude,	there is no/little doubt that…
To sum up,	it is true to say that…
All in all,	although it must be said that…
Finally/Lastly,	it is likely/unlikely/possible/ foreseeable that…
	it may be concluded/said that…
	the best course of action would be to…
	achieving a balance between… would be…

All things considered, the obvious conclusion to be drawn is that…

There is no absolute answer to the question of…

In the light of this evidence, it is clear/obvious/etc. that…

In conclusion,		clear/apparent		evidence
All in all,	it is	plain/obvious	from	the above points
To sum up,		evident /foregoing		arguments

Conclusion expressing opinion directly:

In conclusion,	it is my belief/opinion that…
On balance,	I (firmly) believe/think that…
All things considered,	I am inclined to believe that…
Taking everything into account/consideration,	I am convinced that…
To conclude,	I (do not) agree that/with…
To sum up,	
All in all,	

Taking everything into account, I therefore conclude/feel/believe (that)…

For the above-mentioned reasons, therefore, I (firmly) believe that…

EXEMPLAR ESSAYS:
(All essays presented below would obtain Band 8&9)

1. More and more people decide to undergo plastic surgeries these days. Discuss both pros and cons of this issue.

There has been a vast increase in the interest in the plastic surgery in the last decade. Not only do people undergo a surgery to get rid of scars, crooked noses and such but they also want to improve their appearance. Breast enlargement, hair implants, rhinoplasty, facelift or a tummy tuck are broadly common. This issue has both advantages and disadvantages.

To start with, there are cases when plastic surgery seems to be a need. Nasty scars or serious complexion illnesses are to be removed immediately. Sometimes even protruding ears can pose an obstacle to happiness. The eventual patient is likely to feel miserable or depressed because of such flaws. The greatest advantage of plastic surgery is the improvement of one's self-esteem. For instance, such surgical interventions as breast augmentation or hair implants have a great ability to make people more pleased with their image. Besides this, being subjected to operations frequently means significant amelioration of health. Just as liposuction for obese people, which sometimes is the only solution to prevent them from having a heart attack or diabetes. Likewise varicose vein removal helps people move properly and kills their pain. There are surely more positive sides of plastic surgery that would convince its opponents to its usefulness.

On the other hand, plastic surgery is bound up with dreadful pain as well as a huge danger. Recovery takes months while patient is bedridden not able to function normally without doctors' assistance. This case can turn out to be vastly exhausting both physically and mentally. In addition, financial aspect is often off-putting. It is available only for people who are wallowing in money, namely celebrities and businessmen. They want to change their looks out of boredom or on a whim. Nonetheless, this reason is not strong enough to discourage many of them from undergoing risky procedures. And, deciding on such an extreme change of a body construction, one should definitely find a skilled doctor, who would explain all the benefits and risks related to plastic surgery. In short, downsides to body reconstruction are certainly worth a thought.

To recapitulate, plastic surgery undoubtedly has its pros and cons. Although it is surely true that in many cases it is inevitable, there are still instances when it is just one's dreams fulfillment. Therefore, the person thinking it over should take into consideration arguments for and against.

2. "Greater freedom does not necessarily lead to greater happiness". Discuss.

Over the years, mankind has recognised the need for personal and social freedom, and this is perhaps one of the most important social advancements ever made. However, whether it has led to increased personal happiness is highly debatable; many people would argue that greater freedom has led to increased social disorder and personal dissatisfaction.

Firstly, it is true that people are now more at liberty to choose how to live their lives. For example, in the Western world at least, the choice of where to live, what career to pursue and which religion to follow has never been greater. In addition to this, people have more leisure time in which to enjoy a wider range of recreational activities. On the other hand, it can be argued that this increased freedom can lead people to take things for granted and expect too much from life. As an example of this, the greater choice of material goods available has resulted in people quickly growing bored with their possessions. Consequently, no sooner have they acquired something new than they tire of it. They find short-term happiness in material goods and entertainment, but boredom and frustration soon send them looking for fresh distractions.

Secondly, social and moral attitudes have become less rigid. This has allowed for a greater variety of lifestyles and more freedom in human relations. This is illustrated by the fact that pupils and teachers now treat each other as equals, and parent-child relationships are now much more relaxed. Nevertheless, some people believe that this increase in freedom has resulted in the escalation of social problems. They argue that the current lack of discipline has given rise to a breakdown in the traditional family and the decay in educational standards as well as the rise in juvenile delinquency.Thus, it may be said that society is becoming more and more dangerous because of the very fact that people are more open-minded than they were in the past.

To conclude, there is evidence both to support and refute the view that greater freedom does not necessarily lead to greater happiness. On the one hand, people have more opportunities to raise their standard of living. On the other hand, the many examples of protest, strikes and criminal activities which are a feature of modern society are a sign that although people may be free, they are not necessarily happier.

3. *It is sometimes argued that too many students go to university, while others claim that a university education should be a universal right. Discuss both sides of the argument and give your own opinion.*

In some advanced countries, it is not unusual for more than 50% of young adults to attend college or university. Critics, however, claim that many university courses are worthless and young people would be better off gaining skills in the workplace. In this essay, I will examine both sides of this argument and try to reach a conclusion.

There are several reasons why university has become a popular choice for young people. First, growing prosperity in many parts of the world has increased the number of families with money to invest in their children's future. At the same time, falling birth rates mean that one- or two-child families have become common, increasing the level of investment in each child. It is hardly surprising, therefore, that young people are willing to let their families support them until the age of 21 or 22. Furthermore, millions of new jobs have been created in knowledge industries, and these jobs are typically open only to university graduates.

However, it often appears that graduates end up in occupations unrelated to their university studies. It is not uncommon for an English literature major to end up working in sales, or an engineering graduate to retrain as a teacher, for example. Some critics have suggested that young people are just delaying their entry into the workplace, rather than developing professional skills. A more serious problem is that the high cost of a university education will mean that many families are reluctant to have more than one child, exacerbating the falling birth rates in certain countries.

In conclusion, while it can be argued that too much emphasis is placed on university education, my own opinion is that the university years are a crucial time for personal development. If people enter the workplace aged 18, their future options may be severely restricted. Attending university allows them time to learn more about themselves and make a more appropriate choice of their career.

3. Problem-solution essays

They suggest solutions to problems and analyse the problems and their possible solutions. Also, expected results or consequences are presented.

The writer's opinion may be mentioned, directly or indirectly, in the introduction and/or conclusion.

If you see the following key words in the prompt:

- ☞ problems
- ☞ reasons
- ☞ solutions
- ☞ advice
- ☞ steps
- ☞ recommendations

HOW TO PLAN AND ORGANIZE *PROBLEM-SOLUTION* ESSAY?

Below is the plan. Follow it in order to write coherently.

Introduction
Paragraph 1
State the problem and its cause(s)/consequence(s)
Main Body
Paragraphs 2&3 or 2&3&4 or 2&3&4&5 (depending on the number of the ideas you have)
Suggestions & results
Conclusion
Final Paragraph
Summarise your opinion

USEFUL EXPRESSIONS: PROBLEMS & SOLUTIONS

Steps	should		so as to	solve/overcome…
Measures	must	be taken	in order to	combat/deal with…
	could			eradicate…

Serious attempts to halt/prevent/solve… must be made.

One (possible)			solve/overcome			
Another		way to	combat/deal with	this problem		would be…
An alternative			eradicate	the problem (of)…		is…

People	should focus	their/		to solve/overcome the problem of…	
Governments		our attention		to improve the situation of…	
We		on ways		to reduce the impact of…	on society…

If steps/measures were taken to…   the effect/result/
If… happened/were to happen,   consequence
If attempts were made to address the problem   would be…
By (+ing)…, we/governments /etc., can ensure that/prevent…
The… situation could be improved if…
It would be a good idea if…

The	effect/consequence	of (+noun/-ing)	would	be…
	outcome/result		might	

EXEMPLAR ESSAYS:
(All essays presented below would obtain Band 8&9)

1.   What could be done to improve the lives of the elderly?

For many elderly people the latter part of their life is not a time to relax and enjoy retirement, but rather a difficult and unhappy period, owing to financial worries, falling health and loneliness. As life expectancy increases, the average person lives well beyond the age of retirement. As a result, the elderly make up an ever-increasing percentage of society, which makes it more important than ever for a real effort to be made in improving the lives of senior citizens.

One way to deal with the situation would be to ensure that the elderly have enough money on which to live. Obviously, when a person stops working, they still require a source of income to cover their basic needs such as food, accommodation and heating. A clear solution to the problem is for the government to make sure that the state pension is adequate for these needs. Furthermore, free financial advice should be made available to retired people so that the stress of worrying about money could be reduced as far as possible.

Steps should also be taken to overcome problems the elderly face as a result of deteriorating health due to old age, and inadequate health-care provisions. Again, the responsibility should fall to the government to provide access to the best health care available, which may necessitate paying for residential homes where the elderly can have round-the-clock nursing, or, at the very least, providing medication free of charge to all people over a certain age. As a result, old people would enjoy not only better health, but also peace of mind from the knowledge that they need not fear falling ill and being unable to pay for treatment.

The lives of old people could also be improved if attempts were made to address the problem of social isolation, which so many of them face. If we organised trips for the elderly to community centres, visits from social workers or free bus passes to allow pensioners greater mobility, the effect would be to alleviate the problem of loneliness which marks the lives of so many old people living alone and far from their families.

One final suggestion, which would help enormously, is to change the attitude of the community towards its older members, who are all too often seen as a burden on society and dismissed as having little to do with modern life. We need to be taught from an early age to respect the views of old people, and appreciate their broader experience of life. This would help society as a whole, and encourage the appreciation of the role that old people can still play today.

To sum up, there are several measures which could be taken to improve the lives of old people. If the government and individuals alike were to help, it would make retirement and old age a time to look forward to, rather than dread.

2. *Crime in developed countries is one of the biggest problems in society. It is often said that crime is one of the main things that makes their quality of life poorer. What are the causes of the problem and what measures can be taken to reduce it?*

In this essay, I will outline the mains reasons why crime is still a problem even in developed countries, and suggest some measures which might be taken to control it.

In my opinion, most people commit crimes because they want something they cannot have. If everyone in society had an equal amount of money, there would be no need for people with lower incomes to be envious of those who drive fast cars and live in big houses. Advertising intensifies the desire for luxury goods and celebrity lifestyles, and although it is necessary to promote sales and improve the economy, it can encourage feelings of greed and jealousy. In addition to this, young people are particularly vulnerable to peer pressure. They may be influenced by their friends to start taking drugs or stealing cars for fun. Nevertheless, some rebellious behaviour in young people is normal and perhaps even healthy. It needs to be channelled into other types of activities.

I feel that there are three ways in which crime can be reduced. Firstly, most developed countries have a large and well-paid police force. However, that force spend most of their time in cars. They need to be more visible on the street. Secondly, young people need to be educated about how they can contribute to society. Finally, parents should be more responsible. They have children, yet they do not control their behaviour. Consequently, children grow up without learning the rules of society.

On the whole, I do not believe that we can ever rid our society of all crime, but if the measures I have suggested here were taken, I am convinced that we would see an improvement. What is more, none of these suggestions would be expensive to apply.

3. *Giving aid to poorer countries does not work. The richer nations have given billions of dollars to poorer nations, but while some nations have benefited, many more are still poor. What are the causes of the problem and what measures can be taken to reduce it?*

It is true that money given to developing nations rarely seems to have any effect in the long term. In this essay, I will give some reasons why this happens, and suggest ways the situation can be improved.

As I see it, the main reason aid money is ineffective is corruption. In developing countries, civil servants, teachers and policemen are paid so little that they are unable to live on their salaries. For this reason, they are forced to take money for favours, and as a result, those who cannot afford to pay bribes will not receive fair treatment, justice or a good education. Because of this corrupt administration system, money goes missing before it can reach the people it is intended for. Consequently, the gap between the rich and the poor become wider, and so we see tyrants and dictators living in palaces while their people starve.

It seems to me that poorer nations would benefit more from education and training than financial aid. Professionals from all fields can donate some of their time to teaching local people new skills, and as a consequence, they will be able to teach others in turn. As poverty is caused by ignorance, so education is the key to prosperity. When financial donations are made, foreign governments need the money does not disappear. Thus, it is more likely to be used for the development of the country's infrastructure, and for helping the poor and needy.

All in all, the problem of world poverty cannot be solved by money alone. Nations need to work together on long-term projects, sharing their knowledge and skills so that each person has something valuable to offer to their community.

HOW TO QUICKLY MAKE A PLAN OF YOUR ESSAY?

EXAMPLES:

1. Write about the following topic:
   Some people believe that professional sportsmen and women are paid too much money nowadays in relation to their usefulness to society.
   Do you agree or disagree?

Here is one possible way of designing as essay plan. It only takes up to two minutes but helps with logic and cohesion a lot.

Paragraph plan:

PARA 1	Introduction
	- outline topic
	- give my basic opinion (agree/disagree)
PARA 2	Salaries/prospects of top sports players
	- include examples: David Beckham?
PARA 3	Salaries of other 'useful' jobs
	- doctors
	- teachers
	- firefighters
PARA 4	Role of sport in society
PARA 5	Conclusion
	- restate my opinion
	- finish with a strong sentence

2. Write about the following topic:

The amount of sport shown on television every week has increased significantly and this is having an impact on live sports events.
Do you think the benefits of having more televised sport are greater than the disadvantages?

Here is another possible way of designing as essay plan.

Mind map:

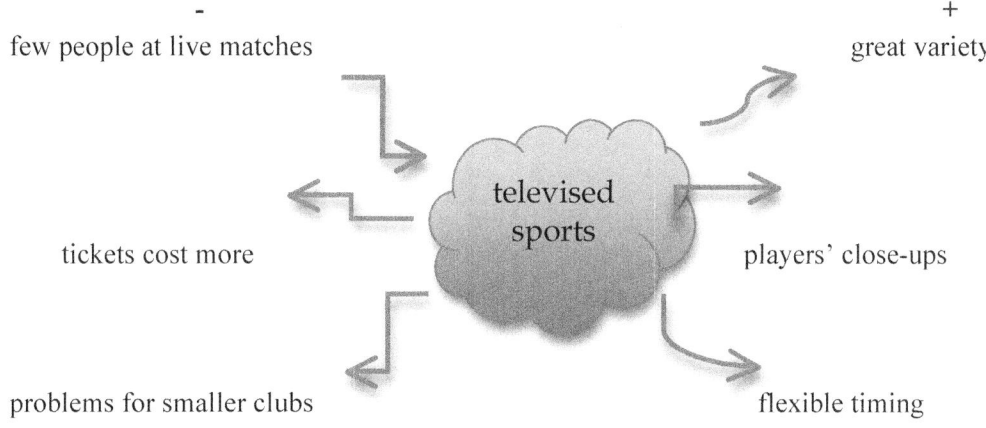

THE DISCUSSION CLOCK

When planning your essay you may refer to the discussion clock ideas. It is a useful "brainstorming" technique, as it helps examine a topic from various viewpoints and decide on points to include in your essay.

347

Keep in mind that a topic may not relate to all the aspects presented in the discussion clock.
Remember that for each viewpoint you have thought of, there is usually an opposing argument. Think of the opposing arguments as well when planning your essay.

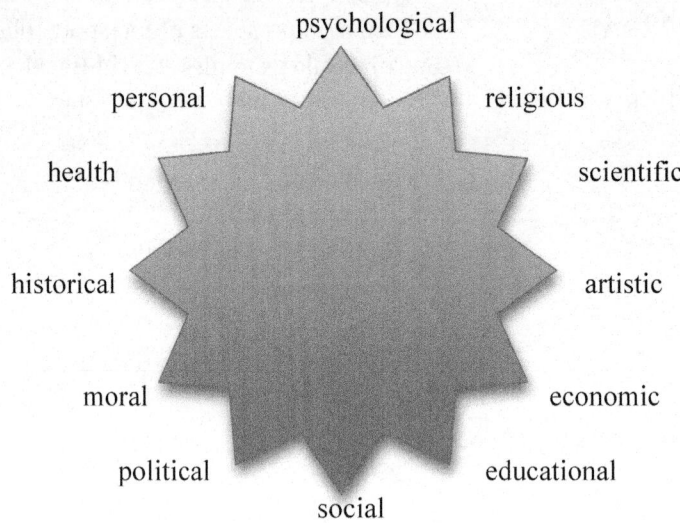

USEFUL STATEMENTS for writing paragraphs

INTRODUCTION to the paragraph

- ✓ It is generally/widely believed/accepted that…
- ✓ It is quite clear/apparent that…
- ✓ It is common nowadays for… to…
- ✓ There is a public debate that…
- ✓ It goes without saying that…
- ✓ There is an ever-increasing/ever-growing number of…
- ✓ Recently the phenomenon has aroused much concern…
- ✓ Recently the issue has been brought into focus…
- ✓ Many nations have been faced with the problem…
- ✓ One of the controversial questions is…
- ✓ One of the heated issues is…
- ✓ Nowadays there is a growing tendency…
- ✓ Nowhere in history has the issue been more visible than…
- ✓ There is a growing awareness…
- ✓ It is worthwhile to investigate this issue from different aspects.
- ✓ This essay would like to look into some of the causes and give possible solutions.
- ✓ This issue has aroused a heated debate recently.
- ✓ There has been no shortage of heated discussion on the issue.

1st SUPPORTING SENTENCE in a paragraph

- ✓ It is well known that…
- ✓ Everybody knows that…
- ✓ It is often the case that…
- ✓ No one can deny the fact that…
- ✓ There is no denying that…
- ✓ There is no doubt that…
- ✓ It is crucial to mention the indisputable fact that…
- ✓ One thing that is of great significance is that…
- ✓ It can be expressed as follows…
- ✓ The chief reason why… is that…
- ✓ We have every reason to believe that…
- ✓ It should be borne in mind that…

2nd SUPPORTING SENTENCE in a paragraph

- ✓ However, …
- ✓ On the other hand, …
- ✓ It can also be argued that…
- ✓ It is also well known that…
- ✓ Another special consideration in this case is that…
- ✓ … should not be neglected.
- ✓ There is some truth in this, but there is much to be said for…
- ✓ Despite…,
- ✓ In spite of…,
- ✓ But the reverse is also the case.
- ✓ One thing which is equally important is that…
- ✓ But that is only part of the explanation. Perhaps the most remarkable about… is…
- ✓ Another equally essential consideration is…
- ✓ … may be further supported by…
- ✓ Apart from this, another aspect is…

CONCLUSION in a paragraph

- ✓ In conclusion, therefore, although…, …
- ✓ From what has been discussed above, a conclusion may be drawn that…
- ✓ In summary, it is important…
- ✓ Obviously, if no reaction is taken, it is likely that…
- ✓ A second look needs to be taken to…, otherwise…
- ✓ It might be time to take… into account.
- ✓ It is urgent that effective measures should be taken to…
- ✓ Apparently,…

HOW TO USE PUNCTUATION CORRECTLY?

Many of my own students do not know how to use punctuation in English correctly. Here are some tips for improvement.

Comma (,)

- ➪ to set off something that existed before and which is clearly defined

  e.g. It has been years since I read 'Hamlet', which is not my favourite book.

- ➪ to set off the adverbial clause when it comes before the main clause

  e.g. In case of an emergency, the teacher should call for an ambulance immediately.

- ➪ to set apart appositives (normally noun phrases that are placed side by side, with one element serving to identify the other in a different way)

  e.g. Barrack Obama, the current president of the United States, will visit China next year.

- ➪ to set apart the participial phrase from the rest of the sentence

  e.g. The speaker, sipping water, began to make a presentation.

- ➪ to separate successive nouns, verbs or adjectives in a sentence

  e.g. I like to chat, sing, dance, and eat at the party. (Note: A comma is used before the final *and* in a list of three or more items.)

- ➪ to set off a transition word or phrase when a pause is needed for clarity or emphasis

  e.g. We could, however, talk about it later.

- ➪ to separate an adverbial phrase from the rest of the sentence

  e.g. They tried, in spite of my protests, to swim during storm.

Colon (:)

- ➪ to come before an extended explanation

  e.g. I have done shopping today: three kilograms of potatoes and a carton of milk.

- ➪ to introduce a list, often follows *namely, such as, as follows*

  e.g. Please provide the following documents in order to apply for a visa, namely: passport, visa application, and a fee receipt.

Semicolon (;)

- ➪ to separate two independent thoughts in a sentence that otherwise would have been separated by using a conjunction such as *and* or *but*

  e.g. The speech was too boring; it went on for hours.

Question mark (?)

- ➪ to indicate a direct question being asked (avoid in academic writing!)

  e.g. Does anyone have any questions regarding the topic?

Exclamation mark (!)

- ➪ to indicate a strong and emotional response

  e.g. I wish you were here!

Hyphen (-)

- ➪ in compound nouns

e.g. Everyone wishes their children had more self-discipline.
- ✎ in a compound adjective that precedes a noun
  e.g. a second-hand car

Parentheses ( )
- ✎ to enclose words and phrases independent of the sentence, such as explanatory notes, omissions, and comments that are not written by the author
  e.g. William Shakespeare (1564-1616) was an English poet, playwright, and actor.
- ✎ to enclose words not directly relevant to the main topic of the sentence but too important to omit
  e.g. Optimistic people (like myself) always seem to look at the bright side of things.
- ✎ to add examples
  e.g. The new camera has many features (including fish lens and bokeh) that will be very beneficial to my future work.

Inverted commas (single ' ' or double " ")
- ✎ for book titles use double inverted commas
  e.g. My favourite book is "Hamlet".

HOW TO USE THE CORRECT STYLE AND AVOID COMMON ERRORS?

Do not:
- use abbreviations: here's, it's, don't, shouldn't etc.
  Instead write: here is, it is, do not, should not
- use a lot of
  Instead write: many (countable nouns), a great deal of (uncountable nouns)
- place *And, But* or *So* at the beginning of your sentences
- write sentences that are incomplete
  Instead: make sure all of your sentences have a main clause (with a verb)
- use *big*
  Instead write: large
- use redundant words or phrases (ones that provide information that is so obvious it is not worth stating)
- use colloquial expressions, phrasal verbs, idioms
  e.g. put up with, be over the moon about sth
- use simplistic vocabulary
  e.g. Experts *say* they *think* this is *bad*, …
- write a series of short sentences
  e.g. many people think so. They are wrong.
- use simple linking words except for variety
  e.g. and, but, so, etc.
- use very emotional language
  e.g. *I absolutely detest* people who…
- express personal opinions too strongly, instead use milder expressions

e.g. ~~I know...~~ It seems to me that...

- use over-generalisation
  e.g. *All* politicians are corrupted.
- refer blindly to statistics without accurate reference to their source
  e.g. *A recent study* showed... - which study?
- use clichés
  e.g. Rome was not built in a day.
- use personal examples
  e.g. In my school...

Do:

- use Present Participle clauses for compact style
  e.g. ~~Between 1860 and 1900 the temperature remained steady. During that time the temperature rose and fell by no more that 0.1 Centigrade.~~
  Instead write: Between 1860 and 1900 the temperature remained steady, *rising* and *falling* by no more than 0.1 Centigrade.
- use prepositions *at* and *with*
  e.g.   Australia came next, *with* a total of 42,215 students.
  By far the greatest proportion of electricity was generated by oil, *at* 59%.
- use parentheses ( )
  e.g. Europe, with the greatest consumption per head of cigarettes (over 200) was...
- make sure you followed the 'agreement' rule
  - subject + verb (check both are singular/plural)
  - pronoun + noun (check both are singular/plural)
  - number + noun (a plural is needed with anything above 'one')
  - after phrases such as *kind of* (+ singular), *one of* (+ plural noun + singular verb), *a number of* (+ plural noun + singular verb) etc.
  - after *many* (+ plural)
  - after *every/each* (+ singular)
- use passive voice, impersonal constructions
  e.g. It is argued that...
- use a range of advanced vocabulary (verbs, adjectives, abstract nouns, etc.)
  e.g. heated debate concerning the controversial issue...
- use formal linking words/phrases (for a full list of those check Chapter 7)
  e.g. furthermore, however, nonetheless, etc.
- use complex sentences with a variety of links, depended clauses, etc.
  e.g. Although it is widely accepted that compulsory military service, which provides an army with abundant manpower, is beneficial to a country's ability to defend itself, closer analysis of military efficiency suggests that it is advanced weaponry which plays a crucial role in...
- use inversion, especially in conditionals
  e.g. Never has this been more obvious...
- use generalisations
  e.g. In *most developed countries*, education...
- use sequencing

e.g. Firstly, Secondly , etc.
- make references to other sources
  e.g. Experts have proved that…
- use quotations, either word-for-word or in paraphrase, being careful to identify the source
  e.g. As Winston Churchill said, "…

INCLUDING QUOTATIONS IN YOUR ESSAY

It is always great to be able to quote academics but if you do so, make sure you do it in a correct way. You will find a comprehensive list of quotations in this book's Appendices.

Are there any expected standards for using quotations in an essay? Yes, there are. The most important one is that you should not give the impression of being the author of the quotation. That would amount to plagiarism. Here are a set of rules to clearly distinguish your writing from the quotation:

- ✓ Sometimes, you describe the quotation in your own words before using it. In this case, you should use a colon (:) to indicate the beginning of the quotation. Then begin the quotation with a quotation mark ("). After you have completed the quotation, close it with a quotation mark ("). Here is an example:

Sir Winston Churchill made a witty remark on the attitude of a pessimist: "A pessimist sees the difficulty in every opportunity; an optimist sees the opportunity in every difficulty."

- ✓ Sometimes the sentence in which the quotation is embedded does not describe the quotation, but merely introduces it. In this case, do away with the colon. Simply use the quotation marks. Here is an example:

Sir Winston Churchill once said "A pessimist sees the difficulty in every opportunity; an optimist sees the opportunity in every difficulty." "

- ✓ As far as possible, you should mention the author and the source of the quotation. For instance:

In Shakespeare's play As You Like It, Touchstone says to Audrey in the Forest of Arden "The fool doth think he is wise, but the wise man knows himself to be a fool." (Act V, Scene I).

- ✓ Ensure that the source of your quotation is authentic. Also, verify the author of your quotation.

WRITING TOPICS & KEY IDEAS FOR ESSAYS

My students often complain that they can't come up with any ideas for the topic of their essays, so here I am providing ideas! No more complaining guys ☺
Feel free to use these ideas in you Speaking Test as well!
For your convenience, topics are presented in an alphabetical order.

1. ## ACCIDENTS
   CAUSES: bad driving habits, drunk driving, over-confidence of the drivers, violation of essential rules (e.g. speeding and driving recklessly), distraction, carelessness, tiredness, navigational errors, poor road conditions, defective equipment, deficiencies in the vehicle, poor visibility, poor weather conditions, relaxation of driving and safety law, lack of law enforcement and inadequate public education on this issue
   SOLUTIONS: promote public education (e.g. workshops and free booklets), redesign and reshape poor roads, equip roads and streets with necessary facilities (e.g. put up more road signs, install speed control devices, provide more speed bumps and humps), reduce car insurance, toughen driving laws, treat law-breakers more harshly (e.g. revoke the delinquents' driving license)

2. ## ACID RAIN
   EFFECTS: causes extensive damage to vegetation, water resources, natural ecosystem and living organisms (e.g. aquatic ecosystems are seriously threatened by acidic water); causes many health problems (e.g. skin disorders); endangers the wildlife (e.g. extinct species); damages agricultural products and often makes heavy losses; is highly corrosive, so it can damage the stonework of buildings and statues
   HOW TO PREVENT IT: use environmentally-friendly and renewable sources of energy (since sulphur dioxide, a major contributor to acid rain, is released to the atmosphere by burning fossil fuels and wood); impose vehicle emission standards to control pollutants; introduce more efficient laws to deal with the environmental issue; encourage industries to move to suburbs by providing enough incentives and other financial assistance

3. ## ADDICTION
   CAUSES & CONTRIBUTING FACTORS: weak willpower, personality deficiencies, family breakdown, poor family environment, regular use of tobacco products, recreational drug use, peer pressure, joblessness, relaxation of laws
   HOW TO HELP THE ADDICTS: through addiction rehabilitation programmes: occupational therapy, vocational training, job placement, life skills training, community education, family support, behavioural therapy, medical treatment, counselling sessions to build up the addict's character, preventative programmes; provide ongoing training for educators and treatment providers (Prevention is better than cure!)
   MEASURES TO ADDRESS DRUG ADDICTION: promote public education, take action against drug trafficking, limit the availability of addictive drugs by tightening up the laws on drug possession

EFFECTS: psychological problems (e.g. anxiety, loneliness, self-pity, self-blame, hopelessness, concentration disorders and learning disabilities); physiological and physical problems (e.g. lung cancer, respiratory diseases); destroys human spirit and mental capabilities; destroys family relationships, major cause of family breakdown; is the root of many crimes

4. **ADOPTION**
ROLE: to promote the welfare of disadvantaged children; gives adoptive parents the ability to fulfill their dreams of having a child; provides adoptive children with a two-parent home and sometimes siblings; provides permanent, secure and nurturing environment for the child; promotes the well-being of children, birth-parents and adoptive families

5. **ADVERTISING**
PROS: helps heighten competition, lower prices, introduce new products and services; helps people find their latent needs; raises people's awareness; provides people with a lot of useful information; enables consumers to make intelligent choices
CONS: uses tricky and catchy slogans to persuade people to buy things they don't need; creates unreal needs; most products are flashy and poor in quality but heavily hyped; tempting and misleading; works through suggestion, gives people unrealistic expectations; affects people's shopping habits; focuses on sales promotion only; often misinforms; uses unethical and unacceptable methods (e.g. gimmicks to target people to buy new products)
ROLE OF CONSUMERS' ASSOCIATION: to protect consumers from unsafe products, to help consumers file formal complaints and deal with profiteering and overcharging

6. **AGING & THE ELDERLY CARE**
CAUSES OF EARLY AGING: genetic and environmental factors; poor lifestyles, inferior nutrition, low activity levels, excessive weight gain, harmful environmental elements (e.g. excessive UV light exposure, air pollution)
SUGGESTIONS TO DELAY AGING: having a healthy lifestyle; a balanced diet and healthy eating habits; sensible weight control; regular physical exercises; proper exercise and relaxation; plenty of rest; adequate sleep; proper medical care (e.g. regular check-ups and screening); regular use of quality supplements; having a skin care programme and protection from ultraviolet light; adequate attention to spiritual needs

7. **AGRICULTURE**
ROLE: contributes to the GDP and GNP of countries, forms the backbone of the rural economy, reduces rural poverty, provides food security, provides a variety of job opportunities, contributes to natural beauty and scenic landscapes
SUGGESTIONS TO DEVELOP AGRICULTURE: stabilising markets, guaranteeing a minimum price for agricultural products, supporting farmers with educational and technical assistance, reducing production costs and increasing productivity by offering equipment leasing services, constructing efficient irrigation networks, setting fair standards of living for the farmers population, offering financial support and loans in order to promote agricultural activities

8. **AIDS**
   CAUSES: transmitted through using contaminated and shared blood products, sexual contact with an infected partner
   SUGGESTIONS TO PREVENT AIDS: educate people on how the disease is spread, promote moral values, make testing services and anti-HIV drugs available, set up HIV prevention workshops and counselling sessions designed to increase people's awareness

9. **AIR POLLUTION**
   CAUSES: burning fossil fuels, emission of hazardous pollutants from factories and vehicles (e.g. carbon dioxide, carbon monoxide)
   EFFECTS: health problems (e.g. respiratory diseases, eye irritation, premature newborn babies), destruction of the ozone layer, global warming, damage to natural resources, ecosystem degradation, poor air quality
   HOW TO MINIMISE AIR POLLUTION: implement energy efficiency programmes, introduce vehicle emission standards, expand car replacement programmes (new cars with old cars), extend environmentally-friendly means of transport, expand public transport facilities (e.g. park-and-ride terminals, carpool facilities, obligatory regular check-ups for cars), use of more efficient engines and modern exhaust-filtering devices, use cleaner fuels (e.g. unleaded petrol), develop tree-planting programmes

10. **ANIMAL TESTING**
    FOR: many medical treatments and procedures have been developed from experiments on animals, a ban on the use of animals will prevent the possible production of certain vaccines, provides scientists with important data to treat human diseases; legislation in most countries set standards for animal testing and laboratories have guidelines to prevent cruelty
    AGAINST: animals have the right to live their own lives peacefully and we are not to meddle just because we can; many experiments cause discomfort, suffering, harm, pain and death; there are other alternatives available (e.g. computer simulation); results are not applicable to humans; it is cruel, inhumane and unethical

11. **ART**
    EFFECTS: to express feelings, convey opinions, transmit values, connect people with a common vision, enhance the sensitivity of humans, encourage self-expression, creativity and innovation, sharpen and enlighten the mind, encourage analytical thinking, stimulate imagination, enhance critical thinking by presenting new ideas, raise questions, promote dialogue, bridge the gap among cultures, bring joy through harmony, colour and form; a way of self-fulfillment, a universal language that can be enjoyed by different people; is inspiring; life without art would be dull and incomplete

12. **ASTROLOGY**
    FOR: can be used for describing the character of individuals and increasing self-awareness; helps us gain new perspectives about ourselves, understand our strengths and weaknesses; is a tool of empowerment; promotes self-understanding and self-discovery; helps us predict impending events and other issues; is harmless and amusing

AGAINST: promotes fatalism, superstition and illusion; is irrational and unscientific; promotes the worst thing in the world, i.e. uncritical thinking; has no acceptable mechanism; its principles are invalid; it has failed hundreds of tests

13. **AUTOMATION**

PROS: higher product quality, greater production capacity and higher output, efficient use of materials, reduced factory lead times and fewer worker health problems; has helped to reduce the workload and operational costs; robots are used to perform a wide range of tasks that require speed, flexibility and high level of precision that result in greater control and consistency of product quality; labour saving machines can be programmed to perform the same tasks over and over (most production lines are repeatable and self-checking); robots aren't impressed by human behaviour; gives humans an opportunity to relieve from repetitive, hazardous and unpleasant tasks

CONS: unemployment, redundancies and layoffs, high capital expenditure and ongoing maintenance costs are required to invest in automated machines; purchased equipment become outdated and are not usually compatible with new devices

14. **BRAIN DRAIN**

CAUSES & CONTRIBUTING FACTORS: 'Push' factors include economic instability, shortage of educational and research facilities, desire for higher qualifications, poor working conditions, limited career prospects, low salaries, unemployment, desire for a better urban life, political unrest and conflicts; 'Pull' factors include better economic prospects, modern educational systems, better research facilities, better opportunities for higher qualifications, prestige of foreign training, higher salaries and incomes, better employment opportunities, higher standards of living, attraction of overseas life

EFFECTS: hinders sustainable development and economic growth; is a burden to the economy; the national budget spent on the education of students who ultimately contribute to economies of other countries

SUGGESTIONS TO ADDRESS BRAIN DRAIN: ensure economic stability, provide adequate educational facilities, support think tanks and researchers financially, provide elites with necessary facilities

15. **BRIBERY**

CAUSES & CONTRIBUTING FACTORS: inefficient administrative systems, mismanagement, a lack of well-defined or rigid laws, incomplete regulations and laxity of administrative laws, poor law enforcement, financial problems, low salaries

EFFECTS: against organisational code of ethics, abuse of power and authority, hinders sustainable development and economic growth, causes a growing gap between the rich and the poor

SUGGESTIONS TO PREVENT BRIBERY: promote moral values, define efficient administrative systems, introduce stricter laws, impose heavy penalties on bribery

16. **CHARITY**

MISSIONS OF CHARITIES: to relieve human suffering, improve living conditions of the needy, help disadvantaged people who live in poverty, provide necessary facilities for depressed areas, provide accommodation assistance, provide medical care for low-income families and individuals, improve educational standards, raise donation for victims of natural disasters, promote public awareness about different social issues, support and strengthen families, provide low-interests loans for low-income earners, provide employment opportunities, support people who suffer from physical and mental diseases, assist the disabled by providing free training courses, adoption services, aid to immigrants, public education, supply of expensive medical equipment and services

17. CHILDCARE

ROLE OF CHILDCARE: promote the physical, mental, emotional, intellectual and social development of children, provide a variety of health-promoting and disease-preventing services (e.g. providing a warm, safe, homelike and nurturing environment for children)

TYPES OF CHILDCARE: family daycare, childcare providers, nursery schools, caregivers, trained teachers, pre-school centres, after-school care programmes, in-home care programmes

18. CHILD LABOUR

CAUSES: inefficient labour laws, a lack of law enforcement, decline in education opportunities, socio-economic problems (e.g. family poverty, family breakdown, child abuse)

EFFECTS: affects the intellectual development of the child, endangers the child's learning ability, prevents many children from attending school, causes heath issues, damages children's mental health and causes irreversible physical harm, contributes to adult unemployment (as children are hired at lower wages), is exploitative, against moral principles

19. CHILDHOOD

It is a time filled with happy memories of carefree play and excitement.

Plays an important role in building character, developing personality, and enhancing intellectual abilities. It is the best time to promote social and emotional development, modify or correct unfavourable traits, teach or learn good habits, such as proper exercise and good eating habits.

It is the best time to learn lifelong skills.

20. CHILDREN'S EDUCATION

ROLE: provide a safe learning atmosphere, teach basic knowledge of reading, writing and arithmetic, develop physical and intellectual growth of children, teach social skills, interpersonal interaction and how to be a part of a peer group

21. CITY LIFE

PROS: gives us an opportunity to become familiar with different cultures, customs, traditions; has recreational facilities, cultural places, shopping opportunities; urban areas have higher standard of living (e.g. better health care systems, better sanitation services, more educational facilities, more job opportunities); life's more attractive and vibrant

CONS: air pollution, overcrowding, increased traffic jams, higher rate of crime, depression, tension and mental disorders, life is fast-paced, hectic, stressful and mechanical, not much of a community spirit

22. CLIMATE

EFFECTS: affects people's daily routines, work patterns, leisure activities, sleeping habits, lifestyles, life expectancy, health conditions, the type of agricultural products, eating and drinking habits, our character types and moods, the natural environment, vegetation types, soil formation, animal life, livestock, natural resources, migration patterns, building styles and materials due to the specific needs of people, the economic development of an area; there is a link between climate and population distribution

23. COMPUTER GAMES

PROS: have many educational benefits such as they help children develop problem-solving and analytical skills (e.g. drawing conclusions, seeking alternatives, making predictions), increase cognitive skills and encourage practical experience, encourage creativity, initiatives and mental power; teach and reinforce academic subjects (e.g. some computer games enhance mathematical skills); are entertaining; teach children how to be a team player (as they offer a multiplayer function)

CONS: encourage violent tendencies (e.g. aggression, antisocial behaviour, recklessness), show graphic fight scenes, language tends to be violent, decrease interaction and social skills, can cause psychological and mental problems (tension), take up much of children's leisure time

24. COMPUTERISATION

PROS: speed, accuracy, adaptability, compatibility, high memory capabilities, ability to perform complex tasks (e.g. performing mathematical, logical and statistical operations), important for storing, presenting and processing data, designing and modelling simulated operations and controlling machinery; contribute to higher output, offer many features (e.g. the Internet, e-mail)

CONS: we are becoming increasingly dependent on computers; downsizing of industries (which leads to dismissal of workers, higher unemployment rates), damage of office community, jobs become more mechanical and soulless, diminished rapport with people, the privacy of humans can be invaded, made life more complicated and stressful

25. COUNTRYSIDE

PROS: gives us an opportunity to enjoy views of areas, get peace and quiet far from urban stress, get away from the hustle and bustle of city life; many cultural areas; the greenness of nature is spectacular; provides many outdoor activities (e.g. swimming, fishing, hiking); low cost of living; people are friendlier than city dwellers; a strong sense of unity; crime rate is low

CONS: isolation, shortage or lack of educational facilities (e.g. fewer universities), shortage or lack of medical facilities (e.g. fewer hospitals), shortage or lack of recreational and cultural facilities; not much privacy (as everyone knows one another); low level of income, low-paced and uneventful life

26. CRIME

CAUSES: personality disorders and deficiencies, poor parenting, family breakdowns, lack of a proper family life, lack of decent housing, poor education, educational problems, drug and alcohol abuse, prolonged unemployment, financial problems, social injustice and inequality, relaxation of criminal laws, lack of law enforcement

SOLUTIONS: cultural measures, e.g. programmes intended to strengthen family values and re-educate offenders; economic measures, e.g. providing job opportunities, raising public welfare, increasing income levels; crime deterrent measures, e.g. adopting stricter laws and punishment-oriented approaches (prison should serve four functions: isolation, punishment, rehabilitation and deterrence); social factors, e.g. eliminate any kind of discrimination, provide equal opportunities for all people (which requires a long-term plan and social participation)

27. **CULTURAL HERITAGE**

   ROLE: contributes to greater cultural cohesion of communities, plays a major role in providing a legacy for future generations, promotes a sense of national and regional identity, plays a key role in shaping our environment, contributes to the attractiveness of our environment, contributes to the transmission of culture, reflects the history, customs and social values of our past generations, has a key role in attracting tourists

28. **CULTURE**

   COMPONENTS: thoughts, feelings, attitudes, unwritten rules, history, folklore, literature, art, music, learned beliefs, customs, shared values, traditions and norms of people who are unified by race, language, nationality, religion and common beliefs

   ROLE OF CULTURE: to enrich national identity, promote national integration, strengthen understanding among ethnic groups, ensure social stability, transmit accepted values

29. **CULTURE SHOCK**

   SYMPTOMS: feelings of uncertainty, homesickness, extreme sadness, acute nostalgia, loneliness, depression, withdrawal, a sense of disorientation, moodiness, frustration, emotional and physical discomfort

   SOLUTIONS: learn as much as you can about your host country before you arrive, learn the rules of social conduct, history and the language of the host country, immerse yourself in the new culture, get accustomed with your immediate surroundings, establish a routine as soon as possible, include physical activity into your routine, stay busy and get involved in activities that you enjoy, develop a hobby, join a club, meet people who share similar interests, find a friend to be a 'cultural informant' in order to gain a proper perspective on people's culture

30. **DIET**

   EFFECTS: helps you enhance your overall health, increase your energy level, improve your immune system, reduce the risk of health problems (e.g. high blood pressure and diabetes)

   SUGGESTIONS TO ACHIEVE A HEALTHY DIET: eat the right kinds of food (wholesome meals), avoid overeating, eat the right amount of food at each meal, eat several meals to prevent hunger, cut down on salt and sugar, choose healthier cooking methods (e.g. steaming, poaching, baking, stir-frying), measure what you eat and then analyse your food records (this helps maintain normal body weight), make sure you provide enough calories and all the necessary daily nutrients

   FOOD PYRAMID: is a basic guide which gives information about food and nutrition, helps us follow a healthy balanced diet; each group is equally important and plays a unique role in health (if any piece is removed, the pyramid will be incomplete)

31. **DISABILITY**

   HOW TO HELP PEOPLE WITH DISABILITIES:

   Civic and community access facilities: to support the disabled through greater access to public places, e.g. wide exit doors, reserved car parks and telephone ramps

   Medical services: purchasing medical equipment, nursing and day care, health seminars and counselling

Employment opportunities: to empower the disabled to gain access to appropriate work opportunities by providing vocational programmes and supporting them to enter and maintain in the labour market

Educational assistance: to empower the disabled to acquire knowledge and build capabilities that enable them to choose a quality life that they desire by providing educational opportunities

Supportive services: accommodation support, retirement pension, and disability insurance benefits, financial incentives, such as tax rebates could be offered to smaller companies who hire disabled workers

32. DISTANCE LEARNING

PROS: learning can be personalised and customised to meet the learner's needs; a great way to study at a personal speed and intensity without waiting for the slower pace of the average classroom (you don't need to keep up with he pace of the group); educational materials can be easily downloaded; more flexible deadlines; flexibility to study in any locations; no time spent commuting to classes; flexibility for those with irregular work schedules; you set your own time; accessibility for those with restricted mobility (e.g. the disabled and the elderly); flexibility for those with family responsibilities (e.g. parents with young children at home); lower tuition fees

CONS: lower quality of education compared with 'on-campus education'; not many aspects of a true campus or traditional classrooms (e.g. no research or lab facilities); time involved to learn how to use the system or software; lag time between students' input and teachers' feedback, occasional technology problems, lack of socialisation; lack of teamwork and contact between peers; academic honesty of online students; assessment difficulties

33. DIVORCE

CAUSES: lack of understanding and tolerance, personality differences, selfishness, weak commitment to lifelong marriage, inter parental conflicts, interference of parents, financial reasons, prolonged marital conflicts, lack of communication, grown-up problems, failed expectations, unmet needs, inadequate preparation for marriage, drug addiction

EFFECTS: psychological traumas (e.g. anxiety, tension, depression and feelings of guilt for both parties involved); destroys family unit; weakens society; causes financial difficulties; children face emotional problems and are more likely to have marital problems and choose unstable partners; causes psychological difficulties and damages the emotional development of children

SUGGESTIONS TO REDUCE DIVORCE: premarital counselling, marriage education, stronger divorce laws to preserve the integrity of marriage and safeguard family relationship

34. DOPING

EFFECTS: against the athletic spirit, ethical principles, sport values and fair play; gives an unfair advantage over the rivals; is hazardous to the physical and mental health of athletes; hurts the public faith; destroys the spirit of a healthy competition (sportsmanship); damages the credibility and reputation of sporting achievements; tarnishes reputation of athletes

SOLUTIONS: to promote cultural measures; more educational programmes to enlighten the athletes about the consequences associated with consuming doping; doping test should be carried out at all official competitions; heavier penalties and long-term suspensions; stricter laws

35. EDUCATION

ROLE: to provide people with sufficient knowledge of skills in reading, writing and arithmetic; prepare us for life by providing relevant knowledge, skills, attitudes and ideas for more fulfilling, productive and satisfying lives; direct children's growth emotionally; nurture children to become good citizens; develop personalities and intellectual skills; enhance interpersonal relationships; expand knowledge; develop critical thinking skills; sharpen, broaden and deepen the mind; provide us with real-life experiences; familiarize individuals with the norms and values of society; increase social mobility

CURRICULUM: school curricula should be more concerned with the needs of the society; should enhance employment prospects by proving life skills; should offer essential knowledge that makes connections to real life; more practical courses should be included; lessons should be learner-friendly; should balance the theoretical and practical aspects of the course; content should be designed to help students achieve their future goals

FEATURES OF A GOOD UNIVERSITY: being recognised by professional bodies, providing students with high quality education, having qualified teaching staff, creating a supportive and stimulating atmosphere, offering modern and accessible facilities and services (e.g. athletic facilities, career counselling services)

36. ENERGY

ENERGY EFFICIENCY: energy saving programmes contribute to the economic growth, sustainable development, higher productivity, revenue creation, expense reduction, the improvement of the environment

37. ENVIRONMENT

ALARMING FACTS: air pollution, water pollution from industrial emissions, illegal dumping, waste disposal, overfishing, radioactive contamination, noise pollution, deforestation

EFFECTS: health problems, food crisis, poor water quality, loss of biological diversity, endangered marine life, erosion and soil degradation, desertification, depletion of the ozone layer

HOW TO PROTECT THE ENVIRONMENT: impose stricter environmental standards; enforce related laws; establish protective zones of natural scenery; phase out indiscriminate logging (forests are valuable sources); increase public awareness; apply renewable materials and energy; use environmentally-friendly alternatives to control fossil emissions and other sources of greenhouse gases; apply efficient waste disposal systems that include waste treatment, recycling, disposal facilities, waste collection and designing sanitary landfills

38. FAME

PROS: allows your opinions to be heard; you can be the role model or even the superhero of many people; having admirers, supporters and fans can be enticing and satisfying; can bring you respect, status and popularity; you would have power, influence and probably wealth

CONS: brings nothing but misery; can ruin your personal life and privacy; famous people are bothered by photographers and the press (which causes insecurity); causes confusion of identity and disorientation; causes relationship problems; can ruin real friendships; doesn't necessarily bring popularity

39. FAMILY

THE ROLE OF FAMILY: it is the most basic unit of any society; it is the source of identity, inspiration, love, affection, strength, comfort, security, support and encouragement; provides guidance and protection for its members; plays a key role in the emotional and behavioural development of children; plays a significant role in the development of adult achievements; its role is to nurture relationships, transfer the values and initiate the young into culture

40. FAMILY TIES

ROLE: family gatherings play an important role in nurturing family relationships; family togetherness helps family members solve their problems more easily; family ties build common interests and strengthen family relationships; develop interpersonal skills

SUGGESTIONS FOR FAMILY TIES: eating meals together whenever possible; helping family members with housework; attending their sports events or activities and giving positive feedback; watching a TV programme the whole family likes; having a family night out; exercising together; doing chores together; driving them whenever possible; sharing a hobby together; going on family holidays

41. FAMINE

CAUSES: droughts, earthquakes, poor weather and lack of rainfall; civil war, overpopulation, unfair distribution of resources, inadequate food production, low agricultural productivity, failure of harvest due to climatic conditions; lack of water resources leads to deforestation and ultimately results in famine

EFFECTS: poverty, starvation, malnutrition, mass death, extinction of animals, starvation of livestock, outbreaks of diseases (e.g. pestilence), mass migration (e.g. illegal immigration), economic failure and increase in requests for overseas food

HOW TO PREVENT IT: allocate financial assistance intended to support farmers (e.g. subsidies, grants, loans), develop agriculture-related technologies (e.g. mechanization of agriculture and irrigation systems), population control

42. FASHION & CLOTHING

PROS: better appearance, industrial benefits (clothing, textile, cosmetics), mass production makes prices lower; provides employment; adds colours and beauty to life; provides us with more choices; shows us the lifestyle features of communities; is a means of self-expression

CONS: can be against the values and norms of a community; most fashionable clothes are just eye-catching, flashy and poor in quality; purchased clothes often get discarded; not focused on warmth, comfort or durability; only intends to make profits (fashion slaves are exploited); new fashions impose unwanted costs (a burden to a family budget); a lot of time needs to be spent to keep up with fashion; influences people in a bad way when it comes to purchasing decisions or shopping habits (to persuade people to spend money on things they don't need)

43. FEAR

CAUSES: ignorance, misinformation, uncertainty of the future, a series of events in childhood, unsolved issues from the past, having a traumatic experience, lack of confidence, illusion, psychological disorders, an unknown situation

EFFECTS: keeps you from making positive changes in your life; persuades you to set easier goals and do less than you are capable of; keeps you from asserting yourself; affects creativity and productivity; negatively impacts abilities and success; keeps you from taking risks; causes a number of behavioural problems (e.g. indecisiveness, hesitation, confusion); affects physical conditions (e.g. increased heart rate, high blood pressure); affects daily life, relationships and personal growth

HOW TO OVERCOME FEAR: become aware of it, identify the ways you express fear, recognise the situations which trigger fear, use behavioural techniques to reduce fear and stress, analyse your fear and see how irrational they are, try not to obsess with fearful thoughts

44. FESTIVALS

ROLE: instill a sense of patriotism; promote a sense of national and cultural identity; encourage a feeling of community pride and unity; bring diverse groups of people together; preserve history, traditions, shared values and morals of a country; commemorate past events; revive local traditions; contribute to community participation; entertain and educate

45. FIELD TRIPS & EXTRACURRICULAR ACTIVITIES

ROLE: provide students with numerous opportunities to interact with peers; complement the curriculum; provide outdoor learning opportunities; encourage teamwork, creativity, responsibility, life skills, interpersonal skills, self-improvement; educate and entertain; strengthen the interest areas of students; help working parents

46. FILM

FEATURES OF A GOOD FILM: a good scenario and plot, action, sequences, special effects, graphics, sound effects, professional crew (e.g. directors, producers, light and sound technicians, actors etc.); well-defined characters and clever dialogues; well-written; well-directed; enlightening, illuminating, educational, constructive, entertaining, interesting, visually stunning; keeps viewers eager to see what happens next; provokes discussion; makes audiences inspired by its message; involves the viewer in the story (with both empathy and sympathy); can change viewer's mood

47. FRIENDSHIP

QUALITIES OF A GOOD FRIEND(SHIP): honest, trustworthy, loyal, reliable, dependable, kind, affectionate, sympathetic, devoted, considerate, helpful, supportive, caring, selfless, consistent, encouraging, inspiring, tolerant, confidant, positive, open-minded, forward-looking, thoughtful, level-headed, well-humoured; respects your privacy; provides companionship and emotional support; stands by you when you are in trouble; is always open to new ideas; respects your opinion; never breaks confidence; accepts you totally with all your limitations and weaknesses

48. GENERATION GAP

CAUSES: difference in age, cultural norms, experiences, opinions, values and attitudes; new electronic technologies

EFFECTS: mistrust, communication breakdown and family problems

SUGGESTIONS TO BRIDGE GENERATION GAP: public education, strengthen common points (e.g. counselling sessions); revive shared values

49. GLOBAL WARMING

CAUSES: increase of gases which trap the heat of the sun (e.g. CO2); natural changes in climatic patterns; excessive use of fossil fuels; emission of industrial pollutants and deforestation

EFFECTS: natural disasters (e.g. floods, droughts, blizzards, heat waves, wild fires, hurricanes, earthquakes); rising sea levels; reshaping shorelines; melting ice in the poles; retreating glaciers; increasing the spread of diseases

SOLUTIONS: impose and enforce tougher laws to reduce air pollution; develop energy efficiency programmes to limit carbon emission; develop environmentally-friendly alternatives (e.g. solar-powered cars); encourage green space development programmes (e.g. tree-planting programmes); promote initiatives intended to heighten people's awareness about this issue

50. GLOBALISATION

FOR: speed of transport for goods and people; increased liquidity of capital allows investors in developed countries to invest in developing countries; promotes economic growth; increased flow of communications allows information to be shared between individuals and corporations around the world; makes the nations more homogenous; promotes equality of opportunity; ties the world together; brings welfare and peace; promotes cultural cohesion

AGAINST: destroys local economies and small businesses; spreads a materialistic attitude (consumption as a path to prosperity); the greater risk of diseases transferred unintentionally between nations

51. GM (GENETICALLY MODIFIED) FOOD

FOR: better texture; increased nutritional value; better flavour and colour; more efficient use of land; longer shelf life; greater yield; reduced weeds; elimination of allergy-causing properties; easier shipment; greater resistance to environmental changes

AGAINST: we don't know of the steps involved before GM food are made available for sale; haven't been tested adequately for their safety; we don't know enough about this science; altering genes could lead to unforeseen problems; potentially dangerous (may cause diseases); pests can be developed (DNA changes); 'tampering with nature' by mixing genes among species isn't right; regulation and control standards vary from country to country (no international regulatory system)

52. HAPPINESS

DEFINITIONS: subjective, depending on the person's mentality; ability to keep positive perspectives; ability to have a clear sense of purpose; satisfaction; being in good health; loving relationships; peaceful environments; philosophical view of life; world view; type of personality; success; delight; safety; to lead a happy life: 'Do what you like and like what you do'

53. HIGH-RISE BUILDINGS

PROS: occupy only a small area of land; provide lots of floor space; contribute to the area's vibrancy; withstand powerful earthquakes (designed and tested by computer simulations); higher standard of accommodation and convenience; contribute to the image of an area; national or regional symbol of the city; reflect the culture of society

CONS: all look the same; ruin the distinguished features of cities; have no real character; ruin the view of natural features; cause a negative impact on the rural landscapes; spoil the overall appearance of skylines; make cities and lifestyles more heterogeneous; intensify social problems (e.g. noticeable class distinction); endanger the lives of people (safety standards may be sacrificed to profits)

54. HISTORY

ROLE: enriches our understanding of ourselves; helps us learn about our origins, backgrounds, ideas, traditions and institutions that have shaped the development of our country; gives us a sense of connection with the past; brings people together and reminds us of the memories that we share; enables us to avoid repeating the mistakes of the past; is illuminating; allows us to understand and conclude how past human actions impact the present and the future; teaches us many lessons of life; helps us to think more logically and make informed judgements about current and future events; enlightens future generations

55. HOBBIES

BENEFITS OF HOBBIES: provide relief from stress; provide entertainment and relaxation; contribute to productive leisure time; provide educational opportunities to enhance life experience; increase problem-solving capabilities; build character; encourage social interaction; teach self-expression; boost creativity, confidence, accomplishment and discipline

56. HOLIDAY

OUTDOOR RECREATION: CAMPING, CLIMBING, HIKING, PICNICKING: a way to renew and strengthen our relationships; encourage family bonding; build lifelong friendships; get close to nature; get away from the hustle and bustle of everyday life; provide a chance to get peace and quiet; contribute to people's overall well-being by providing opportunities for physical fitness and stress reduction activities; give us a great chance to relax and have fun (enthusiasm for work is renewed after a break); can be educational ('learn by doing' approach); teach us how to adjust to new environments and various social situations; help us increase self-reliance, maturity, independence, leadership skills; help us develop team work skills; teach us how to take responsibility for others; encourage social connectedness; help us widen our horizons

TRAVELLING & SIGHTSEEING: show the importance of non-school education (as simple procedures like buying a train ticket or changing currency are mastered); help us familiarise ourselves with the highlights of different cities; give us opportunities to get familiar with places of interest, tourist attractions, landmarks, lifestyles and traditions of other cities; allow us to explore the diversity of different cultures

ADVENTURE: excitement, danger, novelty, exploring, being exposed to an unknown outcome, thrills (that we cannot get in ordinary life), character and confidence building

EDUCATIONAL TOURS & EXCURSIONS: broaden the mind; promote the cross-cultural understanding among nations; learn about other people, history, lifestyles, cultures, customs and languages

57. HOME SCHOOLING

PROS: promotes family involvement and parental contribution; encourages transmission of parental values to children; allows parents to tailor the curriculum to their personal talents of their children (lessons can be efficiently customised to each child's needs); allows a flexible schedule; allows to speed up or slow down the material in order to match their child's developmental readiness in various subjects; children can spend more time in areas which interest them; students are more self-directed and have a greater depth of knowledge

CONS: prevents peer interaction; hinders social development of children; students are more likely to become unsociable; prevents children from being exposed to the ideas and beliefs of others

58. HOMELESSNESS

CAUSES: personal irresponsibility, family conflicts, family breakdown, health problems, psychological and mental diseases, drug abuse, poverty, lack of adequate job skills, substandard wages, joblessness, lack of affordable housing, forced evictions, natural disasters

EFFECTS: social exclusion, deprivation of basic human needs, social isolation, health problems, psychological disorders, poor mental health, loss of confidence, unemployment

SOLUTIONS: supportive services, e.g. empowering the homeless to be financially independent by providing decent jobs and emergency assistance (housing subsidy policies, emergency shelters)

59. HOUSING

CAUSES OF HOUSING SHORTAGE: overpopulation, internal and external migration, lack of balance between supply and demand in housing market, shortage of existing houses

SUGGESTIONS TO PROTECT LOW-INCOME FAMILIES: affordable rental houses and home ownership initiatives; schemes designed to provide grants and subsidised loans to assist people in meeting their housing needs; 'mass construction programmes' (to provide low-income families with affordable housing)

EFFECTS OF POOR HOUSING: long-term health problems (e.g. respiratory problems, rheumatic diseases); social isolation; poor performance (at school and work)

60. ILLITERACY

CAUSES: family poverty, overpopulation, inadequate educational facilities, low parental education, social exclusion

EFFECTS: low self-esteem, restricted social participation opportunities, irrational fear of new technologies, poor employment opportunities, high unemployment, increase in poverty

SOLUTIONS: eliminate poverty, provide free education for vulnerable and disadvantaged people, devise programmes in order to fight illiteracy (e.g. compulsory primary education)

61. INDUSTRIAL RELATIONS/CONFLICTS

CAUSES: collision of interests between workers and employers; poor pay and wage disputes; heavy physical work; lack of mutual respect; poor working conditions; long irregular working hours; inflexible hours; forced overtime; lack of insurance coverage; lack of job security; limited career promotion; discrimination and inequalities; unfair dismissals and layoffs; redundancy payment problems; retirement issues; hazardous duties; lack of labour productivity; poor performance of workers; irresponsibility of workers who don't follow the regulations; disruptive strikes;

miscommunication; lack of holiday entitlements; lack of well-defined job descriptions; unclear roles; unreasonable expectations

SOLUTIONS: encourage any creativity and self-development (e.g. providing reasonable financial assistance as a motivator); provide and facilitate a situation in which employees can upgrade their professional skills; provide a friendly work atmosphere with team-focused activities; consider workers' welfare; respect workers' rights; ensure the safety of workers; provide opportunities for growth; ensure greater protection against unfair dismissals

62. THE INTERNET

PROS: facilitates the flow and dissemination of information; has changed the quality and quantity of information; helps people gain access to all sort of information quickly; allows for interaction around the world at a relatively low cost; enables people to form communities in new and unique relationships (e.g. discussion forums, where people can easily communicate and share their ideas); provides many learning opportunities and research activities; the most important features of the Internet include e-mail, online conversation, information retrieval, e-commerce, online shopping, online learning and browsing the Internet for downloading different material

CONS: unsupervised children of the Internet (children are being inundated with dangerous information); lots of websites which promote immorality in society; 'copy and paste academic assignments'; loss of privacy; the Internet addiction causes irregular sleeping patterns; can cause isolation; hacking, spam, viruses, cookies and credit card fraud

63. JOB

FEATURES OF A GOOD JOB: financially-rewarding (high-paid/high-earned); a reasonable level of salary is ensured; provides a sense of accomplishment; is emotionally fulfilling (job satisfaction); provides meaningful and challenging learning experiences to improve job skills; prospects for promotion; job security

QUALITIES OF A GOOD EMPLOYEE: creative, well-educated, well-trained, well-informed, well-adjusted, energetic, self-directed, highly responsible, efficient, well-organised, business like, personable, punctual, dependable, a self-starter, a good goal setter, flexible enough to carry out tasks outside of job description, respects the chain of commands, has a sense of loyalty, motivated

QUALITIES OF A GOOD EMPLOYER: understanding, reliable, open-minded, tolerant, responsive, approachable, considerate, positive, encouraging, supportive, treats all subordinates fairly, has high regards for his or her employees; always tries to promote good morale among the employees; always considers employees' welfare and rights (e.g. providing decent benefits package and insurance coverage); protects the health and safety of his or her employees; tries to provide a friendly working atmosphere

QUALITIES OF A GOOD COLLEAGUE: helpful, supportive, understanding, co-operative, has a pleasant personality, easy to get along with, covers for you willingly when you can't come or fall behind in your work

PROMOTION CRITERIA: education, competency, productivity, technical skills, innovation, analytical ability, seniority, experience, enthusiasm, energy level, flexibility, loyalty, integrity, expertise, creativity, initiative, determination, decisiveness, willpower, perseverance, diligence, leadership skills, interpersonal abilities, communication skills

64. JUVENILE DELIQUENCY

CAUSES:

Psychological problems: inferiority complexes, suppressed desires, personality disorders

Family-related factors: family dominance, inadequate family care, parental permissiveness, family neglect, lack of parental control, lack of a proper upbringing, family poverty

Educational factors: educational failure, truancy, school dropouts

Peer-related factors: peer pressure, poor relationships with peers

SOLUTIONS:

Supportive programmes: youth employment opportunities, after-school programmes, public recreation programmes, family support services, parent education, initiatives introduced to provide the youth with social skills, family involvement as a key component of school improvement

Deterrent and prevention efforts: compulsory primary education, prevention of child abuse (e.g. child labour), prevention measures, enacting legislation to deter young people from committing crime

65. INTERNATIONAL LANGUAGE

FOR: For example: Esperanto is a very logical language, it has been designed to be easy; most roots are internationally understood; it has a productive system of word formation, the grammar is very regular. One international language: prevents language discrimination, no languages are advantaged ('equality for everyone'); helps nations be closer; contributes to removing conflicts and wars; helps with tourism, business and science

AGAINST: For example: Esperanto is not of much use, the number of speakers is very limited; without history, culture, roots; can't translate great literature into Esperanto; doesn't evolve; lacks the technical vocabulary to make a suitable and modern language; isn't easy to learn; artificial, unattractive and soulless

66. LAW

ROLE: provides correction; promotes equality, justice and fairness; ensures privacy, tranquillity, well-being and happiness; protects people from discrimination; ensures orderly public life; protects individuals' rights; ensures the stability of society; maintains peace and discipline in the country; protects the safety and welfare of people; preserves community standards and morality; deters, prevents, punishes and encourages; settles private arguments and disputes among individuals and businesses; protects the rights of the citizens in various walks of life; protects citizens; punishes those who violate the laws; provides punishment for those who do not follow the established rules of conduct; safeguards the public from crimes and criminals; makes the society a safer place to live in

67. LIFE EXPECTANCY

CONTRIBUTING FACTORS: genetic characteristics, personality type, regular exercise, sufficient physical activities, weight control, food quality, healthy diet, medical care, good use of nutritional supplements, adequate sleep, climatic conditions, family support, income levels, avoiding tobacco use

68. MARRIAGE

ROLE: provides a solid foundation for society; enriches family values; is the safest relationship for both men and women; prevents many social problems (e.g. sexual immorality); brings health benefits (e.g. fewer symptoms of depression, better physical and emotional health); has a positive effect on physiological functions of adults; allows for higher saving rates and greater life satisfaction; protects against the feeling of loneliness; allows us to grow in character

CRITERIA: should be based on mutual understanding, sympathy, affection, love, warmth, mutual tolerance, sacrifice and commitment; an ideal partner is honest, open-minded, outgoing, fun-loving, helpful, supportive, goal-oriented, assertive, reliable, dedicated, devoted, encouraging, understanding, patient, dignified, thoughtful and sympathetic

69. MASS MEDIA

ROLE: to educate, inform and entertain people; to portray social problems; to communicate and share information; to serve to build a healthy and progressive society; to help create community; to shape people's opinions; to bring about a greater awareness; to form and reflect public opinions; to instill social values

70. MEMORY

CAUSES OF FORGETFULNESS: tiredness, concentration problems, stress and general anxiety, emotional problems, alcohol abuse; aging; Alzheimer's disease; certain brain conditions (e.g. stroke)

MEMORY IMPROVEMENT TECHNIQUES: convince yourself that you have a good memory; avoid being negative; relax and don't tire or put yourself under pressure to recall the information you want (a relaxed mind is able to recall the information in a better way); exercise daily (regular exercise improves circulation and efficiency throughout the body and makes you more alert and relaxed); try meditation ('mindfulness' meditation allows for a better focus and better memory); sleep well (regular sleep patterns serve to give brain rest); keep your brain active by developing new mental skills (e.g. learning a new language, challenging your brain with puzzles and games); reduce stress; try to improve your observational skills; have vivid and memorable images (you remember things more easily if you visualise); repeat things you need to remember (the more time you hear, see or think about something, the more certainly you'll remember it); group things to make it easier to remember; try categorising the individual things; organise your life (e.g. keep item that you frequently need in the same place every time)

71. MIGRATION

CAUSES: 'push factors': natural disasters (e.g. earthquakes), periodic or chronic food crisis, high population density, poverty, political unrest; 'pull factors': higher living standards in other countries, better labour market conditions, better income opportunities

PROS: makes the culture of the host country richer; creates a greater social diversity that can bring about increased understanding between people of different countries

CONS: is associated with many problems including cultural disputes, economic problems, income inequality, overcrowding, spread of diseases, unplanned city development, housing shortage; causes a huge burden on the social welfare of the host country; can damage the job market; threatens local culture and community cohesion

72. **MODERN LIFE**

PROS: has made our lives easier and more comfortable; new time-saving machines are being made to meet the specific needs of people; has brought about convenience; has reduced household chores; allows people to enjoy a higher standard of living

CONS: has made people of all ages less active which can lead to many health problems; is associated with psychological problems (e.g. depression, stress, anxiety, tension, psychological pressure and mental disorders); too fast-paced, mechanical and stressful; brings materialistic outlook; results in environmental problems (e.g. air pollution); too competitive (people are constantly trying to have more and more)

73. **MUSIC**

PROS: to increase cognitive abilities and activate your brain; to clear your mind; to release physical tension; to fill you with positive energy; to give a sense of peace; to alter your mood; to give you a positive outlook on life; can be used as treatment to cure various diseases (music therapy); can increase productivity; can be relaxing, calming, restful, inspiring

CONS: certain types of music can stimulate negative emotions (e.g. violence, aggression, rebellion, criminal behaviour, suicidal tendencies); some music can attract isolated and depressed youth and feed their feelings with despair and hostility; certain types of music can damage the hearing mechanism and nervous system

74. **NATURAL DISASTERS**

EXAMPLES: drought, earthquake, flood, forest fire, tidal wave, hurricane, cyclone, severe storm, landslide, volcanic eruption, overflowing of rivers and lakes

HOW TO DEAL WITH THEM: deliver relief supplies and vital first aid to victims (e.g. medical care, mass shelters, presence of trained emergency services and international rescue crews); enhance safety standards; increase anti-earthquake construction standards; ensure high standards of buildings (should be solidly built, well-structured, resistant); building materials should be based on quality and durability; public awareness-raising programmes (e.g. educate people how to face natural disasters); precautionary measures to enhance safety standards (prepare people for disasters); advance warning to predict natural disasters

75. **NOISE POLLUTION**

CAUSES: industrial operations, urban development activities (e.g. construction activities), transportation systems (e.g. air, road, rail traffic, car horns), car alarms, air conditioners

LONG-TERM EFFECTS: psychological and psychological health problems (e.g. hearing loss, sleeplessness, mental disorders, emotional disturbances, long-term stress, aggression, distraction, tension, lost productivity, reduced efficiency)

SOLUTIONS: apply technical measures (e.g. plant trees along main roads, technical adjustments); changes in operation methods; reduce the noise at source to prevent its transmission; raise public awareness through various programmes (e.g. seminars intended to inform people about the effects of noise pollution); impose stricter laws

76. **OBESITY**

CAUSES: overeating, poor diet, bad eating habits (e.g. regular consumption of high-calorie foods and compulsive eating disorders), unhealthy lifestyles (e.g. excessive sleep, lack of exercise, inadequate physical activity, regular use of medications); genetics factors; hormonal, metabolic and physiological factors

EFFECTS: shorter life span; posture problems; sleep disorders; breathing problems; increased risk of diabetes; high blood pressure; high cholesterol; increased risk of heart attacks and heart failure; limited choice of clothing; feeling of embarrassment; negative impacts on social contacts; lower self-esteem; discrimination in job market

HOW TO PREVENT OBESITY: follow a balanced diet; choose healthier cooking methods (e.g. steaming, boiling); count the number of calories needed for a healthy diet; cut down on carbohydrates and sugar (e.g. limit sugary drinks); limit fat intake by avoiding deep fried foods; eat wholesome meals; increase physical activities; have a regular fitness programme; use medical weight loss therapies; prescribed medications

77. OVERPOPULATION

CAUSES: high birth rate, high immigration rate, decreased rate of mortality, availability of health services

EFFECTS: decline in life quality, unhygienic living conditions, housing shortage, higher land prices, higher rents, increased illiteracy, decline in education quality, lower quality of public services, decline in public health, higher rate of unemployment, lower wages, depletion of natural resources, deforestation, growth of urban sprawl, increased level of pollution, food and water shortage

HOW TO CONTROL POPULATION GROWTH: increase people's awareness, apply family planning and counselling programmes; making contraception available to the public; start initiatives to control birth rate (e.g. give special tax deduction for the couples who have only one or two children)

78. PARENTING

PARENTAL RESPONSIBILITIES: to provide a supportive environment for raising children; to take care of the physical and emotional needs of children; to provide children with love, guidance, inspiration and direction; to give children adequate freedom to build their own character; to help children learn social skills; to nurture their talents; to be consistent and not to discriminate against children

FAMILY UPBRINGING: contributes to the personality development and success of children; instills the necessary values to make the lives of children more sustainable; makes children well-adjusted, self-directed and self-made

79. PERSONALITY

COMPONENTS: genetic factors like inheritance, physical qualities, psychological features, appearance, natural features of temperament, natural talents, cognitive potentials, intellectual abilities; personal interests and preferences; life goals, values, personal beliefs, expectations, desires, tendencies, general attitudes; self-perception, life experiences, family size, family living conditions, education, social environment, social skills

HOW TO IMPROVE PERSONALITY: be interested in people; assume that people like you; admit your weaknesses; attend social gatherings; learn new things; associate with people who are successful and happy

80. **PETS**

PROS: act as companions for people who live alone; provide a link between humans and nature (e.g. dogs are useful for protection and serve as guides for the disabled, they can also help their owners exercise); keeping pets promotes a sense of caring and responsibility in children; help children develop responsible attitudes; give amusement to their owners

CONS: transmit contagious diseases and cause many health problems (e.g. allergies, asthma, skin irritations); they are expensive to keep (food, medical treatment); communities carry costs of animals that have been abandoned by irresponsible owners; can cause serious distress to neighbours and residents (barking, attacking, biting, straying, etc.)

81. **POVERTY**

CAUSES: personal laziness, death in family, joblessness, lack of work effort, lack of work skills, low income, death of wage-earner, slow income growth, illiteracy, inadequate education, poor health, high cost of housing, divorce, natural disasters, lack of equal opportunities in society, unfair distribution of wealth, overpopulation, ineffective economic systems, limited employment opportunities

EFFECTS: poor health, early death even from preventable and treatable diseases, dangerous living conditions, hunger, poor nutrition, illiteracy, family separation, family conflicts, high rate of crime, mental and psychological problems, long-term stress, hopelessness, despair, diminished intellectual capabilities, school dropouts, child abuse

SOLUTIONS: establish employment opportunities for low-income and disadvantages families; develop entrepreneurship schemes; increase assistance programmes for the needy and poverty-stricken families (e.g. welfare schemes and income support); ensure minimum level of health care services; support food distribution programmes to assist depressed areas; eradicate inequalities; improve economic growth by providing suitable opportunities for economic activities; population control (long-term solution)

82. **PUBLIC TRANSPORT**

ROLE: benefits: reduced pollution, personal safety, fewer number of accidents, less traffic congestion, environmentally-friendly, run with alternative forms of energy, cost-efficient (compared with private cars), makes communities more equal by providing different forms of transportation for the needy, creates a sense of community, brings commuters closer

HOW TO DEVELOP AND IMPROVE PUBLIC TRANSPORT: make it faster, more comfortable and more convenient (e.g. provide more bus lanes); devise programmes intended to encourage people to use public transport (e.g. free rides, discounts on passes); develop public transportation services and infrastructures in urban and rural areas by allocating enough budgets to modernise the transport systems

83. **RECYCLING**

BENEFITS: more efficient use of natural resources (inorganic waste is separated from organic household refuse and used for future recycling); conservation of energy; reduced demand of new materials; prevention of pollution; safe disposal of hazardous materials; prevention of illegal dumping; less amount of garbage; reduced overhead and waste disposal costs; saving landfill space

84. SATELLITE

ROLE: earth observation purposes (mapping the topography and shape of the ocean's surface); space exploration purposes (information obtained about other planets); traffic controlling, navigation, vehicle tracking and positioning; military purposes (e.g. military surveillance and detection); long distance communications and remote imaging (e.g. internet communications); distance and online learning (virtual universities); data relay (radio and television broadcasts); environmental applications (e.g. weather forecasts, meteorological observation, climate monitoring, volcanic eruption predictions, earthquake predictions, ocean temperatures, studying the ozone layer and the atmosphere, space explorations); telemedicine (delivery of health services via remote telecommunications)

85. SCHOOL & PARENTAL DISCIPLINE

GOALS OF SCHOOL DISCIPLINE: to teach students to behave in a way that is acceptable and contributes to academic achievement and educational success; to create a safe environment to learn in; to maintain effective learning conditions; to reinforce appropriate school behaviour; to instill self-discipline; to help students develop self-control; to strengthen children's ability to cooperate with peers; to promote positive behaviour of self-respect, mutual respect, care and consideration

EFFECTS OF PHYSICAL PUNISHMENT: antisocial behaviour (e.g. lying, stealing, cheating, bulling); aggression; feeling of hurt; resentment; violence; hate; humiliation; lower self-esteem; failure; frustration

86. SMOKING

CAUSES: personal tendencies; character flaw; peer pressure; poor family environment; family pressure; stress; lack of confidence; poor education; tobacco advertising increases the number of smokers

EFFECTS: bad breath; stained teeth; premature skin aging; respiratory problems (e.g. coughing, wheezing, shortness of breath, asthma); health problems (e.g. higher risk of lung cancer, heart attack); expensive habit; leads to addiction; passive smoking is also harmful (why non-smokers should be bothered by the unhealthy lifestyle choices of smokers)

HOW TO QUIT SMOKING: nicotine replacement therapy (e.g. nicotine gum, patches, inhalers, regular exercise); behaviour change therapies (e.g. replacing one habit with another, counselling sessions)

87. SPACE EXPLORATION

FOR: more efficient worldwide communications; the only help for overpopulation in the future; the only justifiable alternative with depleting natural resources; provides knowledge about the origin of the solar system; allows us to discover whether life exists anywhere else; serves the essential interests of most nations

AGAINST: imposes huge amount of cost; burdens tax payers; the allocated budget could be better spent on basic needs; there are more important social issues which need urgent attention like poverty, youth unemployment, pollution etc.; puts human life in danger

88. SPORT

PHYSICAL EFFECTS OF DOING SPORTS: healthy life, promotion of physical fitness; staying fit and in shape; to restore energy and vitality; to strengthen bones and muscles; to boost blood circulation; to develop a greater awareness of body; to improve body posture and flexibility; to improve immune system; to reduce the risk of heart attacks; to prevent diseases (e.g. obesity, high blood pressure)

MENTAL EFFECTS OF DOING SPORTS: to improve mental health; to build self-confidence; to enhance mental and emotional well-being; to lift your spirit; to clear your mind and keep your mind focused; to think more positively; to give you a sense of accomplishment; to relieve stress; to control anxiety; to overcome long-term strains; to sharpen your memory; to increase concentration and mental power

EFFECTS OF MENTAL SPORTS (e.g. CHESS): memory development; logical thinking abilities; intellectual skills; creativity skills; analytical thinking skills; cognitive skills; problem solving skills; critical thinking abilities

EFFECTS OF INDIVIDUAL SPORTS: promote self-discipline and a sense of personal responsibility; allow lots of personal expression both physically and mentally

EFFECTS OF TEAM SPORTS: promote teamwork, interpersonal skills, coordination skills, social interaction skills, leadership abilities, communication skills, loyalty, interdependence, group unity, a sense of duty; develop friendship and social skills while enhancing self-esteem and health; promote self-control and self-discipline by abiding the rules of the game; teach us how to achieve a common goal and accept responsibility; teach us about dealing with success and failure

89. SPORTING EVENTS

ROLE: promote tourism (which in the long run can be streamlined into socio-economic development efforts of countries); provide fair and equal opportunities for all participants to compete; encourage interaction among cultures (international sporting events); deepen understanding and friendship among nations through competitions; promote a sense of cohesion and national identity; bring people of diverse cultures together; promote international cooperation; release people's patriotic emotions in a safe way; provide many job opportunities; serve the interests of a large number of people; promote national pride in countries

90. SPORTSMANSHIP

ROLE: good sportsmanship is playing fair, following the rules of the game, respecting the judgement of referees and officials, treating opponents with respect, congratulating winners promptly and willingly, accepting the game's outcome without complaints and excuses, talking courteously to everyone before, during and after games and events (including teammates, opponents, coaches, officials and spectators), accepting the result of one's actions gracefully; avoid blaming teammates for mistakes or poor team performance; avoid all acts of poor sportsmanship (e.g. trash talking, showboating, humiliating, taunting opponents); it promotes worldwide culture of peace and encourages teamwork, cooperation, tolerance, self-esteem and character development of participants

91. STRESS

CAUSES: acute stress: disorganization, hormonal imbalance, lack of confidence, physical surroundings, crammed schedule, poor time management, heavy workload, lack of understanding, unfamiliar situations (e.g. new technologies); chronic stress: work pressure, unsolved problems, powerlessness, dysfunctional family relationships, long-term relationship problems, long-term unemployment, poverty, financial problems

EFFECTS: mental symptoms: memory problems, difficulty in making decisions, inability to concentrate, poor judgements, confusion, repetitive thoughts, apathy, mental irritation, weaker performance; emotional symptoms: restlessness, depression, anxiety, tension, anger, resentment; physical symptoms: sleep disturbances, fatigue, rapid heartbeat, high blood pressure, weight gain or loss, eating disorders, isolation from others, nervous habits (e.g. nail biting)

HOW TO RELIEVE OR COPE WITH STRESS: meet our spiritual needs: apply relaxation techniques (e.g. meditation); use medication; remove the stressor; give up unrealistic expectations; take a quick mental break; have proper nutrition; exercise regularly; rest sufficiently

92. SUCCESS

CONTRIBUTING FACTORS: positive thinking, motivation, willpower, determination, stamina, self-improvement, interpersonal skills, social skills, confidence level, self-esteem, self-trust, diligence, seriousness, self-discipline, patience, experience, creativity, intelligence, calculated risks, careful planning, perseverance (it's important to keep trying)

DEFINITIONS: setting and achieving one's personal goals; true peace of mind; having a good family life; a certain level of career advancement; academic achievement; having financial ability to afford whatever needed; lack of confidence is a psychological barrier to success

93. TOURISM

PROS: promotes international understanding and cooperation among nations; is a significant source of revenue; provides job opportunities; encourages regional development; increases foreign exchange earnings; enhances higher standard of living for local communities

CONS: can cause environmental destruction, damage to ecosystem and serious forms of pollution; can cause cultural degradation (debase the host culture, displace locals); uses up natural resources; deprives the local population from their natural rights to use these resources

94. TRAFFIC

CAUSES: bad weather, poor signal timing, car accidents, inadequate roadway capacity, insufficient number of roads, substandard road conditions, increased number of cars (roads and transport services suffer when they are overused); urban sprawl and unplanned urban growth in large cities

HOW TO REDUCE TRAFFIC: apply automated traffic management systems; improve public transport systems; encourage people to use more public transport; provide carpooling facilities; establish car sharing schemes; ease traffic jams through radio reports; impose vehicle emission laws; introduce a regulatory system planned to limit the number of cars on the roads (e.g. odd-even number plates policy); ban private cars from entering certain areas of the city; increase the number of roads; provide a safe network of walking and cycling routes

95. TV

PROS: a powerful tool to educate viewers around the world; provides people with inspiration, ideas and knowledge; holds families together; serves the particular interests of individuals and groups; a fast way to find out about the latest news from all over the world; the main source of information for most people; a convenient source of entertainment; affordable (compared with other means of entertainment); an important forum for discussing and putting forward various issues

CONS: can stop family members from communicating with each other; children spend too many hours passively watching TV; TV addiction can lead to poor academic performance and result in physical complications (e.g. obesity); makes children lose important social skills; passive TV watching damages sleep patterns; misinforms people (propaganda tool by some governments); shows lots of violence (which contributes to aggressive behaviour of the youth and consequently leads to social disorder)

96. UNEMPLOYMENT

CAUSES: high expectations of job seekers; low level of education; lack of job experience; personal laziness; unavailability of suitable jobs; inadequate vocational training; excessive unemployment benefits; overpopulation; lack of planned balance between the educational output and economic expansion; depressed and unstable economy can lead to high unemployment rate

EFFECTS: Individual effects: lower self-esteem, substantial loss of life satisfaction, financial problems, divorce and ruined families, increased participation in illegal activities, psychological disorders (e.g. hopelessness, apathy and depression); Social effects: poverty, higher crime rates, internal and external migration of labour; Economic effects: slowdown in economic growth, recession

SOLUTIONS: increase economic growth, improve job skills through education (e.g. offering training programmes for unskilled and low skilled workers); open the market to national and private investments; increase labour market flexibility; encourage entrepreneurship programmes for increasing employment opportunities

97. URBAN SPRAWL

CAUSES: unplanned city development, unlicensed construction, the growth of urban infrastructure, inefficient land use patterns, fragmented municipal governments, increased rural migrations, population growth

EFFECTS: Environmental impact: loss of agricultural lands which leads to lower food production; degradation of water resources; inadequate sewage disposal systems; loss of natural vegetation; poor air quality; ugly suburban landscapes; destruction of wildlife habitats; Social impact: loss of community identity; loss of community spirit and values; marked disparities in wealth between cities and suburbs; traffic congestion; longer community times; Economic impact: increased public costs; higher tax burdens; increased energy consumption; increased unemployment rate; urban infrastructure decline

98. VIOLENCE

CAUSES: social inequalities; lack of a proper upbringing; poor home life; psychological problems; behavioural problems; personal frustration; superiority and inferiority complexes; financial pressure; relaxation of criminal laws; lack of law enforcement; learned patterns of behaviour; teen parties and gangs; certain types of films can provoke violence

SOLUTIONS: ensure equal opportunities in different aspects of social life; take preventive measures (e.g. impose certain laws to prevent violence); promote public education (e.g. educate people how to overcome their angry feelings)

99. **WATER POLLUTION**

CAUSES: domestic waste, polluted agricultural runoff, industrial emission, washout of poisonous chemicals from dumps, leakage from disposal sites, inadequate sewage treatment, sewage discharge, soil erosion, excessive use of synthetic and inorganic substances in industries

EFFECTS: endangers human life and natural ecosystems; destroys water quality; causes great loss in agriculture; is a threat to the underwater life; causes many life-threatening health problems (e.g. cholera, typhoid)

SOLUTIONS: Preventive programmes: enact tougher laws; Supervisory role of authorities: sea dumping should be strictly prohibited; Technical measures: design efficient waste disposal systems to prevent water pollution (e.g. provide recycling and disposal facilities); Educational programmes: increase public awareness; offer programmes intended to encourage public participation

100. **ZOO**

FOR: built to conserve and protect animals that are threatened in their natural environment; provide quality care for animals; place a higher priority on animal welfare (e.g. veterinary and medical care ensure good physical conditions for animals); have careful breeding programmes; are educational; create basic research opportunities; provide communities with an opportunity to observe rare and endangered species of animals in their natural behaviour; provide public entertainment; allow interaction between humans and animals; provide significant biological resources; create income (obtained money can be spent on environmental issues)

AGAINST: are cruel and inhumane; humans have no right to interfere with the natural environment of animals; keeping animals captive causes suffering; lots of risks (e.g. animal diseases can be transferred, in case of an incident animals cannot escape); cause environmental problems

CHAPTER 7

DISCOURSE MARKERS FOR BOTH SPEAKING AND WRITING (E.G. LINKING WORDS FOR COHESION)

Est modus in rebus.
(There is a middle course in all things.)

Conversational fillers (used in speaking only):

- mm
- uh
- um
- er
- erm
- yeah
- ok
- oh
- well
- you know
- ok then
- right
- I mean
- I guess
- I would have to say
- actually
- really
- in fact
- as a matter of fact
- sort of
- kind of
- you can imagine
- like
- as you know

When you can't remember a given word, you can replace it with a vague word (speaking only):

- for objects: thingy, thingummy, thingumajig, thingumabob, whatsit, whatchamacallit, whatnot
- for people: whatshisname (for a man), whatshername (for a woman), whosit

To express your personal opinion:

- In my opinion/point of view,
- As far as I know/see/understand,
- I (really) think/believe/am convinced that
- Frankly/honestly speaking, (for speaking only)
- To be frank/honest, (for speaking only)
- I would like to say/appeal/express (for speaking only)
- I feel that (for speaking only)
- I suppose that
- I assume that
- I doubt that
- I guess that

- In my impression, (for speaking only)
- In my eyes, (for speaking only)
- To my mind,
- To my way of thinking,
- I am convinced that
- It strikes me that
- It is my (firm) belief/opinion/view/conviction (that)
- I am inclined to believe that
- It seems/appears to me that
- As far as I am concerned
- My opinion is that
- I (definitely) feel/think that
- Personally,
- In my experience, (for speaking only)
- Speaking for myself, (for speaking only)
- If you ask me, (for speaking only)
- From my point of view,
- As I see it, (for speaking only)
- In my estimation,
- In my book, (for speaking only)
- For my money, (for speaking only)
- To the best of my knowledge,

To express a memory (for speaking only):

- In my memory,
- As far as I can remember,
- If I remember correctly, it should be
- I still remember that
- In retrospect,
- As far as I recall,
- As I look back on
- When I think back on/to

To emphasize a point:

- I have to admit that (for speaking only)
- It is (definitely) true that
- There is no doubt that
- I have noticed that (for speaking only)
- Indeed,
- Naturally,
- Clearly,
- Obviously,
- Of course,

382

- Needless to say,
- It is obvious that
- In point of fact
- As a matter of fact,
- In truth,
- If truth be told, (for speaking only)
- Admittedly,

To add more points:

- Equally,
- Also,
- Again,
- Indeed,
- Additionally,
- as well as
- What is more,
- Furthermore,
- Apart from this/that,
- In addition (to this),
- Moreover,
- Besides (this),
- …not to mention the fact that…
- Not only…, but also…
- There is another side to the issue/argument/question of…

To compare or contrast:
(remember to use comparatives)

- There are many differences
- The main difference is
- whereas/while (X is… whereas/while Y is…)
- Comparatively speaking,
- They are similar in some ways such as
- but
- in contrast to
- however,
- by contrast
- nevertheless,
- nonetheless,
- although
- instead of
- yet,
- even though
- apart from

- as opposed to
- except for
- unlike
- even so
- still
- regardless of (the fact that)
- In spite of (the fact that)
- Despite (the fact that)
- likewise
- Opponents of… argue that
- The fact that… contradicts the belief/idea that
- While it is true to say that…, in fact
- On the other hand,
- On the contrary,
- While/although…, it cannot be denied that
- Conversely,
- It may be the case that…, but
- granted that
- Alternatively,
- compared with
- in comparison with/to
- in the same way/manner
- similarly, again
- also
- as…as.
- more…than
- twice as…as
- less…than
- in like manner

To talk about the past:
(remember to use past tenses)

- In the past…
- At one time…
- Back then…
- X years ago…
- When I was young…
- Last (week, year, etc.)…
- If my memory serves me (well/right/correctly)

To talk about the present:
(remember to use present tenses)

- Nowadays,

384

- These days,
- Currently,
- Presently,
- At the moment,
- These days,
- Today,
- At the present time,
- In these times,
- In this day and age,
- Now,
- At this moment in time,
- In the present climate,

To speculate (extremely useful for problem-solution essay): (try to use First Conditional)

- I think, in the future…
- will (definitely)/won't
- will (probably)/won't
- I doubt that … will…
- might/might not/could
- I think we'll probably see a lot of changes…
- It's unlikely that we'll have…
- I bet (that)…
- I imagine (that)…
- The chances are that…
- In all probability,
- My guess is that…
- There's just a chance that…
- I wouldn't be surprised if…
- it can/could/may/might…
- it is possible/probably/(un)likely/foreseeable/certain that…
- … is (un)likely to/bound to/certain to/possible/probable…
- The likelihood/possibility/probability of (-ing/noun) is…

To explain reasons:

- The main reason/cause/ground/motive/aim for this is…
- I think it's because…
- I think there are several reasons for this…
- Owing to (the fact that)…
- Due to (the fact that)…
- …because of
- …because/as/since…
- The reason why… is that…

- It explains why…
- For this reason…
- Therefore,
- If…then…
- on the grounds that…
- since
- as
- In view of…,
- on account of
- given that
- Seeing that…
- …now that…

To agree (for speaking):

- That's true.
- I completely/entirely agree.
- I agree to a certain extent/point.
- Absolutely.
- I couldn't agree more.
- On the whole, I think these arguments are fair.
- I quite agree.
- I thin you're absolutely right.
- That's a very good point.
- You've got a very good point there.
- I fully support what you say.
- Exactly!

To disagree (for speaking):

- I'm not sure I entirely agree.
- I disagree.
- I don't' agree (at all).
- But don't you think that…?
- I see what you mean, but…
- But isn't it really a question of…?
- But what about…?
- But surely…?
- I take your point, but…
- Yes, but on the other hand…
- But all the evidence suggests that…
- I'm afraid I can't agree with you on this matter.
- I wouldn't say that.
- I can't accept that.

To ask for clarification (for speaking only):

- Could you repeat that, please?
- I'm sorry, I didn't catch what you said about…, please?
- I'm not sure what you mean.
- Sorry, but I'm not quite clear on…
- I beg your pardon.
- I'm sorry, could you repeat what you said about…, please?
- Pardon?
- Would you please rephrase it? (applies only to Part 3)
- So what you're saying is that…
- Am I correct in assuming that…?
- Let me just make sure – your point/question is (that)…
- If I have understood you correctly, your point is that…

To list points/enumerate:

- First of all,
- First(ly),
- In the (first, second, etc.) place,
- To begin with,
- The first (reason) is
- Second(ly),
- Third(ly),
- Finally,
- To start with,
- Last(ly),
- Next,
- On top of (that)…,
- Then,
- After this/that,
- Afterwards,
- Last but not least,
- For one thing,
- For another thing,
- The (first, second, next, last) point I'd like to make is…

To express similarity:

- in the same way
- likewise
- similarly
- accordingly
- equally (important)
- not only…but (also)

- the same
- in a similar way
- in a similar fashion
- both … and …
- as well as
- also
- too
- like x, y…
- as…as…
- just as x, y…
- just as x, so y…

To quote:

- As X sais/says, "…"
- As X wrote/writes, "…"
- As X commented/comments, "…"
- As X observed/observes, "…"
- As X pointed/points out, "…"
- To quote from X, "…"
- It was X who said that, "…"
- This example is given by X: "…"
- According to X, "…"
- X claims that, "…"
- X found that, "…"
- The opinion of X is that, "…"
- As X stated/states, "…"

To summarize/conclude:

- In conclusion,
- In summary,
- In short,
- Lastly,
- To conclude,
- To sum up,
- Finally,
- All in all,
- Taking everything into account/consideration,
- On the whole,
- All things considered,
- On balance,
- For the above mentioned reasons,
- Therefore I feel that,
- Briefly,
- To put it briefly,

388

- In all,
- In brief,
- To summarise,
- In a nutshell,
- Basically,
- Unquestionably,
- Undoubtedly,
- Summarizing,
- To recapitulate,
- To recap,
- So,
- As a final point,
- Eventually,
- Altogether,
- Hence,
- Overall,
- Thus,
- Last but not least,

To give examples:

- for example
- for instance
- in particular
- particularly
- such as
- that is to say
- namely
- a (good) case in point is…
- to illustrate
- in the following manner
- take… as an example/instance
- as an illustration
- A better example of this can be best provided by…
- The most familiar example of this is…
- … is generally cited as an example of…
- All available evidence points to the fact that…
- Nothing could be more apparent than the evidence that…
- like…
- especially
- The fact that shows/illustrates that…
- as (evidence of)…
- thus
- to illustrate
- to show what (I mean)

- specifically
- let us (take the case of)
- in support of this
- to demonstrate .
- e.g.,
- As proof of that,
- including
- by way of illustration
- case in point
- viz.,
- to wit.

To express effect/show results/consequences:

- as a result
- consequently
- hence
- so
- therefore
- thereby
- thus
- for this reason
- as a consequence (of)
- on this/that account
- it follows that
- if…were to happen, the effect/result would be
- this results in
- this leads to…
- …is due to…
- …is brought about/by/because…
- then
- in which case
- since
- …,if so,…
- …,if not,…
- …otherwise,…
- …caused…
- …contributes to…

To infer/clarify:

- in other words
- in that case
- then
- (or) else

- otherwise
- The chances are that…
- Probably, there is some truth in the idea that…
- It makes no difference whether…
- That is (to say)…
- To put it another way,
- which means that…
- put simply,
- to clarify
- to explain
- to rephrase it
- to put it more (simply),
- basically
- i.e., (that is)

To give alternatives:

- alternatively,
- on the other hand,
- then again
- either…or…
- (better) still
- the alternative is

To refer to other sources (for reference):

- With reference to…
- According to…
- regarding…
- concerning…
- with respect to
- with regard to
- in regard to
- in reference to
- to turn to
- as for…
- incidentally
- The work of X indicates/reveals/shows that…
- Turning to X, one finds that…
- In a study of Y, X found that…
- As X has indicated…

To express purpose/intention:

- so that

- so as to
- in order to
- in case
- with the purpose/intention of
- to
- for

To make general statements:

- As a (general) rule,
- By and large,
- Generally,
- In general,
- On the whole,
- In most cases,
- All things considered,
- All in all,
- For the most part,
- In the main,
- As a rule,
- Overall,
- On average,

To make partially correct statements:

- In some cases,
- Up to a point,
- To a certain extent/degree,
- To some extent/degree,
- In a sense,
- In a way,
- To a limited extent,
- This is partly true (but)
- There is some truth in (this)

To state other people's opinion:

- It is popularly believed that…
- People often claim that…
- It is often alleged that…
- Some people argue that…
- Many argue that…
- Most people feel that…
- Some people point out that…
- Contrary to popular belief,

To express condition:

- on the condition that
- provided (that)
- providing (that)
- only if
- as long as
- in the event of
- in the event that
- if
- in case
- whether (or not)
- otherwise
- or (else)
- presuming (that)
- assuming (that)
- on the assumption that
- given (that)
- with the provision that
- with/on the understanding that
- contingent to

To express time:

- when
- whenever
- before (that time)
- till
- after (a while)
- since (then)
- as
- while
- now that
- afterwards
- at first/last/the same time
- thereafter
- in the end
- meanwhile
- concurrently
- soon
- as soon as
- finally
- next
- immediately
- in the future

- subsequently
- at that time
- so far
- somewhat
- earlier
- shortly
- over the next (2 days, month, etc.)
- as long as

Miscellaneous
(adverbs and phrases may be used at the beginning of sentences to show how the sentence which follows relates to the rest of the text):

- Admittedly, (used to introduce a concession or recognition that sth is true or is the case)
- All things considered,
- As a general rule,
- Astonishingly, (= surprisingly)
- Broadly, (= in general)
- By and large, (= on the whole)
- Characteristically, (= typically)
- Clearly, (= without doubt)
- Coincidentally, (= happening by chance)
- Conveniently,
- Curiously, (= strangely)
- Disappointingly,
- Equally, (= to the same extent or degree)
- Essentially, (= basically)
- Explicitly, (= in a clear and detailed way)
- Even so, (= in spite of that)
- Eventually, (= in the end)
- Fortunately,
- Fundamentally, (= essentially)
- Generally speaking,
- Interestingly,
- Ironically,
- In essence, (= fundamentally)
- In general,
- In particular,
- In practice,
- In reality,
- In retrospect, (= when looking back)
- In hindsight (= when looking back)
- In theory,
- In view of this,
- More interestingly,

- More seriously,
- More specifically,
- Naturally,
- On balance,
- Obviously,
- On reflection,
- Overall,
- Paradoxically, (= self-contradictory)
- Potentially, (= possibly)
- Predictably,
- Presumably,
- Primarily, (= firstly)
- Probably,
- Remarkably,
- Seemingly, (= apparently)
- Significantly,
- Surprisingly,
- Theoretically,
- To all intents and purposes, (= essentially)
- Typically,
- Ultimately, (= in the end)
- Understandably,
- Undoubtedly,
- Unfortunately,
- With hindsight,

APPENDICES

FAMOUS QUOTATIONS

"After all is said and done, more is said than done."	Aesop
"When I was born, I was so surprised I didn't talk for a year and a half.	Gracie Allen
"I'm not afraid to die. I just don't want to be there when it happens."	Woody Allen
"The secret of life is not to do what you like, but to like what you do."	Anonymous
"Love is not about who you live with. It's about who you can't live without."	Anonymous
"A real friend is someone who walks in when the rest of the world walks out."	Anonymous
"Opportunity may knock only once, but temptation leans on the doorbell."	Anonymous
"Good supervision is the art of getting average people to do superior work."	Anonymous
"Wit is educated insolence."	Aristotle
"Education is the best provision for the journey to old age."	Aristotle
"One swallow does not make the spring."	Aristotle
"Pleasure in the job puts perfection in the work."	Aristotle
"We are what we repeatedly do."	Aristotle
"Wishing to be friends is quick work, but friendship is a slow ripening fruit."	Aristotle
"There is safety in numbers."	Anonymous
"The worst solitude is to be destitute of sincere friendship."	Sir Francis Bacon
"Knowledge is power."	Sir Francis Bacon
"Behind every great fortune there is a crime."	Honore de Balzac
"An error doesn't become a mistake until you refuse to correct it. "	Orlando A. Battista
"When one door closes, another opens; but we often look so long and so regretfully upon the closed door that we do not see the one which has opened for us.	Alexander Graham Bell
"Happiness lies in good health and a bad memory."	Ingrid Bergman
"Only a fool learns from his own mistakes. The wise man learns from the mistakes of others."	Otto von Bismarck
"Ability is nothing without opportunity."	Napoleon Bonaparte
"Glory is fleeting, but obscurity is forever."	Napoleon Bonaparte
"Never interrupt your enemy when he is making a mistake."	Napoleon Bonaparte
"The heart has reasons that reason does not understand."	Jacques Bossuet
"Never stand begging for that which you have the power to earn."	Miguel de Cervantes
"There are people who have money and people who are rich."	Coco Chanel
"Don't ever take a fence down until you know the reason it was put up."	G. K. Chesterton
"A woman uses her intelligence to find reasons to support her intuition."	G. K. Chesterton
"The price of greatness is responsibility."	Winston Churchill

"We make a living by what we get. We make a life by what we give."	Winston Churchill
"A pessimist sees the difficulty in every opportunity; an optimist sees the opportunity in every difficulty."	Winston Churchill
"Success is the ability to go from one failure to another with no loss of enthusiasm."	Winston Churchill
"If you are going through hell, keep going."	Winston Churchill
"A lie gets halfway around the world before the truth has a chance to get its pants on."	Winston Churchill
"History will be kind to me for I intend to write it."	Winston Churchill
"Gratitude is not only the greatest of virtues, but the parent of all others.	Cicero
"Progress is the injustice each generation commits with regard to its predecessors."	E.M. Cioran
"I believe in luck; how else can you explain the success of those you dislike?"	Jean Cocteau
"Our greatest glory is not in never falling, but in rising every time we fall."	Conficius
"Respect yourself and others will respect you."	Conficius
"Nothing in life is to be feared; it is only to be understood."	Marie Curie
"The only difference between me and a madman is that I'm not mad."	Salvador Dali
"Have no fear of perfection; you'll never reach it."	Salvador Dali
"It is not the strongest of the species that survives, nor the most intelligent, but the one most responsive to change."	Charles Darwin
"It's the friends you can call up at 4 a.m. that matter."	Marlene Dietrich
"Talk to a man about himself and he will listen for hours."	Benjamin Disraeli
"The greatest good you can do for another is not just share your riches, but reveal to him his own."	Benjamin Disraeli
"Little things affect little minds."	Benjamin Disraeli
"The secret of success is constancy of purpose."	Benjamin Disraeli
"Pure love and suspicion cannot dwell together: at the door where the latter enters, the former makes its exit.	Alexandre Dumas
"All for one and one for all."	Alexandre Dumas
"Genius is one percent inspiration and ninety-nine percent perspiration."	Thomas Edison
"Only two things are infinite - the universe and human stupidity, and I'm not sure about the former."	Albert Einstein
"When you are courting a nice girl, an hour seems like a second. When you sit on a red-hot cinder, a second seems like an hour. That's relativity."	Albert Einstein
"Not everything that can be counted counts, and not everything that	Albert Einstein

counts can be counted."	
"The difference between genius and stupidity is that genius has its limits."	Albert Einstein
"It's not that I'm so smart, it's just that I stay with problems longer."	Albert Einstein
"Anyone who has never made a mistake has never tried anything new."	Albert Einstein
"Before God we are all equally wise - and equally foolish."	Albert Einstein
"Great spirits have always encountered violent opposition from mediocre minds."	Albert Einstein
"Gravitation cannot be held responsible for people falling in love."	Albert Einstein
"I never think of the future. It comes soon enough."	Albert Einstein
"In case of dissension, never dare to judge till you've heard the other side."	Euripides
"Man's best possession is a sympathetic wife."	Euripides
"A writer is congenitally unable to tell the truth, and that is why we call what he writes fiction."	William Faulkner
"Obstacles are those frightful things you see when you take your eyes off your goal."	Henry Ford
"You can't build a reputation on what you are going to do."	Henry Ford
"The biggest mistake people make in life is not trying to make a living at doing what they most enjoy."	Malcolm Forbes
"To accomplish great things, we must not only act, but also dream; not only plan but also believe."	Anatole France
"Most fools think they are only ignorant."	Benjamin Franklin
"Blessed is he who expects nothing, for he shall never be disappointed."	Benjamin Franklin
"Creative minds have always been known to survive any kind of bad training."	Anna Freud
"Men are more moral than they think, and far more immoral than they can imagine."	Sigmund Freud
"We cannot teach people anything; we can only help them discover it within themselves."	Galileo Galilei
"I believe in equality for everyone, except reporters and photographers."	Mahatma Gandhi
"You must be the change you wish to see in the world."	Mahatma Gandhi
"Live as if you were to die tomorrow; learn as if you were to live forever.	Mahatma Gandhi
"Nothing strengthens authority as much as silence"	Charles de Gaulle
"Graveyards are full of indispensable men."	Charles de Gaulle
"Formula for success : rise early, work hard, strike oil."	J. Paul Getty
"Money isn't everything but it sure keeps you in touch with your children."	J. Paul Getty
"If you can actually count your money, then you're not a rich man."	J. Paul Getty
"All the world over I will back the masses against the classes."	William Gladstone

"Enjoy when you can and endure when you must."	Johann Wolfgang van Goethe
"Whatever you can do or dream, begin it."	Johann Wolfgang van Goethe
" A man can stand anything except a succession of ordinary days."	Johann Wolfgang van Goethe
"Talent develops in tranquillity, character in the full current of human life."	Johann Wolfgang van Goethe
"Never confuse movement with action."	Ernest Hemmingway
"Drama is life with the dull bits cut out."	Alfred Hitchcock
"Forty is the old age of youth; fifty is the youth of old age."	Victor Hugo
"Life is the flower for which love is the honey."	Victor Hugo
"Intelligence is the wife, imagination is the mistress, memory is the servant."	Victor Hugo
"Maybe this world is another planet's hell."	Aldous Huxley
In matters of style, swim with the current; in matters of principle, stand like a rock."	Thomas Jefferson
"Our brightest blazes are commonly kindled by unexpected sparks."	Samuel Johnson
"When making your choices in life, do not forget to live."	Samuel Johnson
"Love is the wisdom of the fool and the folly of the wise."	Samuel Johnson
"Science is organized knowledge. Wisdom is organized life."	Immanuel Kant
"Forgive your enemies, but never forget their names."	John F. Kennedy
"When written in Chinese, the word crisis is composed of two characters. One represents danger, the other represents opportunity."	John F. Kennedy
"Man is still the most extraordinary computer of all."	John F. Kennedy
"Liberty without learning is always in peril; learning without liberty is always in vain.	John F. Kennedy
"Education: the inculcation of the incomprehensible into the indifferent by the incompetent."	John Maynard Keynes
"In the end we will remember not the words of our enemies but the silence of our friends."	Martin Luther King
"Take everything you like seriously, except yourselves."	Rudyard Kipling
"Gardens are not made by sitting in the shade."	Rudyard Kipling
"The absence of alternatives clears the mind marvellously."	Henry Kissinger
"The nice thing about being a celebrity is that if you bore people they think it's their fault."	Henry Kissinger
"We can live without religion and meditation, but we cannot survive without human affection."	Dalai Lama
"Life is what happens to you when you are busy making other plans."	John Lennon
"In the end it's not the years in your life that count; it's the life in your years."	Abraham Lincoln

"Nearly all men can stand adversity, but if you want to test a man's character, give him power."	Abraham Lincoln
"You cannot escape the responsibility of tomorrow by evading it today."	Abraham Lincoln
"You can fool all of the people some of the time, some of the people all of the time, but you can't fool all of the people all of the time."	Abraham Lincoln
"No enterprise is more likely to succeed than one concealed from the enemy until it is ripe for execution."	Niccolo Machiavelli
"People ask for criticism, but they only want praise."	W. Somerset Maugham
"It is cruel to discover one's mediocrity only when it is too late."	W. Somerset Maugham
"To the soul, there is hardly anything more healing than friendship."	Thomas Moore
"Tact is the knack of making a point without making an enemy."	Isaac Newton
"The advantage of a bad memory is that one enjoys several times the same good things for the first time."	Friedrich Nietzsche
"What doesn't kill you will make you stronger."	Friedrich Nietzche
"When one has much to put into them, a day has a hundred pockets."	Friedrich Nietzsche
"We don't see things as they are; we see things as we are."	Anais Nin
"Life shrinks or expands in proportion to one's courage."	Anais Nin
"Burdens become light when cheerfully borne."	Ovid
"In the field of observation, chance favours only the prepared mind."	Louis Pasteur
"The chief enemy of creativity is good taste."	Pablo Picasso
"The mind is not a vessel to be filled, but a fire to be kindled."	Plutarch
"Fools rush in where angels fear to tread."	Alexander Pope
"You don't stop laughing because you grow old; you grow old because you stop laughing."	Michael Pritchard
"The voyage to discovery is not in seeking new landscapes but in having new eyes."	Marcel Proust
"If you wish to avoid seeing a fool, you must break your mirror."	Francois Rabelais
"A statesman is a successful politician who is dead."	Thomas Brackett Reed
"Instruction ends in the schoolroom, but education ends only with life."	F.W. Robertson
"Many people despise wealth but few know how to give it away."	F. de la Rochefoucauld
"Men give away nothing so liberally as their advice."	F. de la Rochefoucauld
"The only thing we have to fear is fear itself."	Franklin D. Roosevelt
"The only man who never makes mistakes is the man who never does anything."	Theodore Roosevelt
"If it can't be cured, it must be endured."	Salman Rushdie.
"When love and skill work together, expect a masterpiece."	John Ruskin
"Perfection is achieved, not when there is nothing more to add, but when there is nothing left to take away."	Antoine de Saint Exupery
"Life has taught us that love does not consist in gazing at each other, but in looking outward together	Antoine deSaint Exupery

in the same direction."	
"Hell is other people."	Jean-Paul Sartre
"It is wise to learn; it is God-like to create."	John Saxe
"Luck is what happens when preparation meets opportunity."	Lucius Annaeus Seneca
"Life is a play. It's not its length, but its performance that counts."	Lucius Annaeus Seneca
"Action is eloquence."	William Shakespeare
"All that glitters is not gold."	William Shakespeare
"Our bodies are our gardens to which our wills are gardeners."	William Shakespeare
"Great Britain and the United States are nations separated by a common language."	George Bernard Shaw
"The greatest of our evils and the worst of our crimes is poverty."	George Bernard Shaw
"Youth is a wonderful thing. What a crime to waste it on children!"	George Bernard Shaw
"Martyrdom ... is the only way in which a man can become famous without ability."	George Bernard Shaw
"We don't stop playing because we grow old; we grow old because we stop playing."	George Bernard Shaw
"Reasonable men adapt to the world. Unreasonable men adapt the world to themselves. That's why all progress depends on unreasonable men."	George Bernard Shaw
"Can a man who is warm understand one who is freezing?"	Alexander Solzhenitsyn
"Don't judge each day by the harvest you reap ... but by the seeds you plant!"	Robert Louis Stevenson
"Politics is perhaps the only profession for which no preparation is thought necessary."	Robert Louis Stevenson
"Vision is the art of seeing things invisible."	Jonathan Swift
"May you live every day of your life."	Jonathan Swift
"I am more afraid of an army of a hundred sheep led by a lion, than an army of a hundred lions led by a sheep."	Talleyrand
"Tis better to have loved and lost than never to have loved at all."	Alfred Lord Tennyson
"A good laugh is sunshine in a house."	William Thackery
"Love is real only when a person can sacrifice himself for another."	Leo Tolstoy
"It is better to keep your mouth closed and let people think you are a fool than to open it and remove all doubt."	Mark Twain
"Be careful about reading health books. You may die of a misprint."	Mark Twain
"Wrinkles should merely indicate where smiles have been."	Mark Twain
"The only thing in life achieved without effort is failure."	Unknown
"The speed of the leader determines the rate of the pack."	Unknown
"Many receive advice; only the wise profit from it."	Unknown
"Remember, no one can make you feel inferior, without your consent."	Unknown
"Obstacles are those frightful things you see when you take your eyes off your goals."	Unknown

"Genius is the ability to reduce the complicated to the simple."	Unknown
"The secret of happiness is not doing what one likes, but in liking what one does."	Unknown
"Only those who keep trying eventually win."	Unknown
"Getting something done is an accomplishment; getting something done right is an achievement."	Unknown
"Do not let what you cannot do interfere with what you can do."	Unknown
"The best time to do something worthwhile is between yesterday and tomorrow."	Unknown
"Conscience is a man's compass."	Vincent Van Gogh
"The progress of rivers to the ocean is not so rapid as that of man to error."	Voltaire
"Anything that is too stupid to be spoken in sung."	Voltaire
"God is a comedian playing to an audience too afraid to laugh."	Voltaire
"The greatest consolation in life is to say what one thinks."	Voltaire
"Doubt is not an agreeable condition, but certainty is an absurd one."	Voltaire
"The secret of being a bore is to tell everything."	Voltaire
"The only way to get rid of a temptation is to yield to it."	Oscar Wilde
"Some cause happiness wherever they go; other whenever they go.	Oscar Wilde
"My own business always bores me to death; I prefer other people's."	Oscar Wilde
"Experience is the name so many people give to their mistakes."	Oscar Wilde
"Wisdom is knowing how little we know."	Oscar Wilde
"To live is the rarest thing in the world. Most people exist, that's all."	Oscar Wilde
"The old believe everything, the middle-aged suspect everything, the young know everything."	Oscar Wilde
"No man is rich enough to buy back his past."	Oscar Wilde
"There are only two tragedies in life: one is not getting what one wants, and the other is getting it."	Oscar Wilde
"True friends stab you in the front."	Oscar Wilde
"Fashion is a form of ugliness so intolerable that we have to alter it every six months."	Oscar Wilde
"All cruel people describe themselves as paragons of frankness."	Tennessee Williams
"Education is not the filling of a pail, but rather the lighting of a fire."	William Butler Yeats
"The artist is nothing without the gift, but the gift is nothing without work."	Emile Zola

TENSES

When to use it?

* intentions, plans (75%, sure)
e.g. I'm going to call you tomorrow.

* 'I see proof'
e.g. Look. It's going to rain. (the sky is dark)

* impersonal statements
e.g. Liverpool are going to win the Cup.

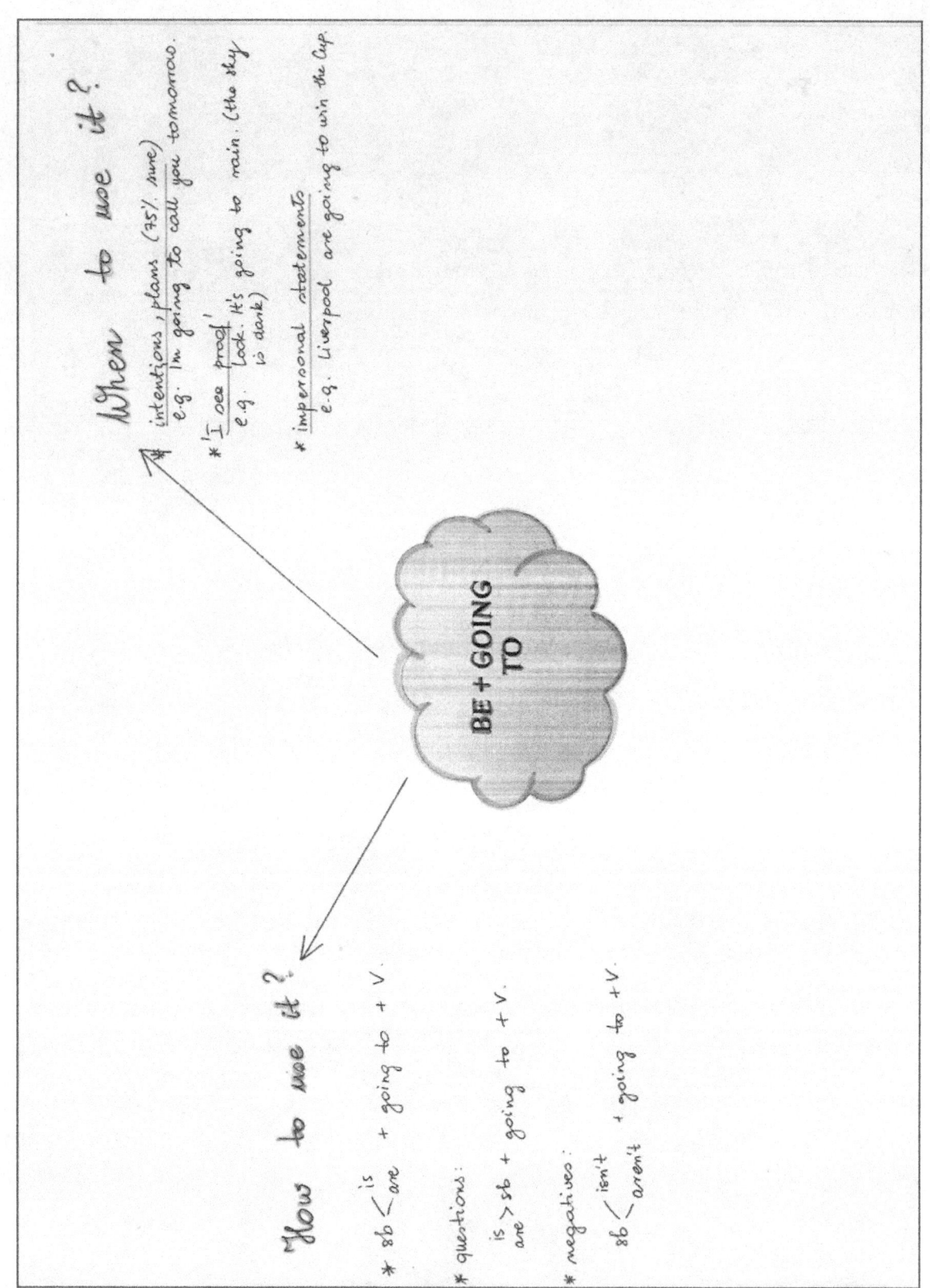

BE + GOING TO

How to use it?

* sb < is / are + going to + V.

* questions:
is > sb + going to + V.
are

* negatives:
is < isn't + going to + V.
are < aren't

When to use it?

* decision is made at the moment of speaking
  e.g. OK. I'll see you at 7 tonight.

* predictions with 'I believe', 'I expect', 'I hope', 'I think', etc.
  e.g. I think it'll be a nice day.

* offers, willingness
  e.g. Hop on. I'll give you a lift.

* requests
  e.g. Will you do me a favour?

* promises
  e.g. I will always love you.

* threats
  e.g. I will kill you.

* facts about the future
  e.g. National Day will fall on Monday this year.

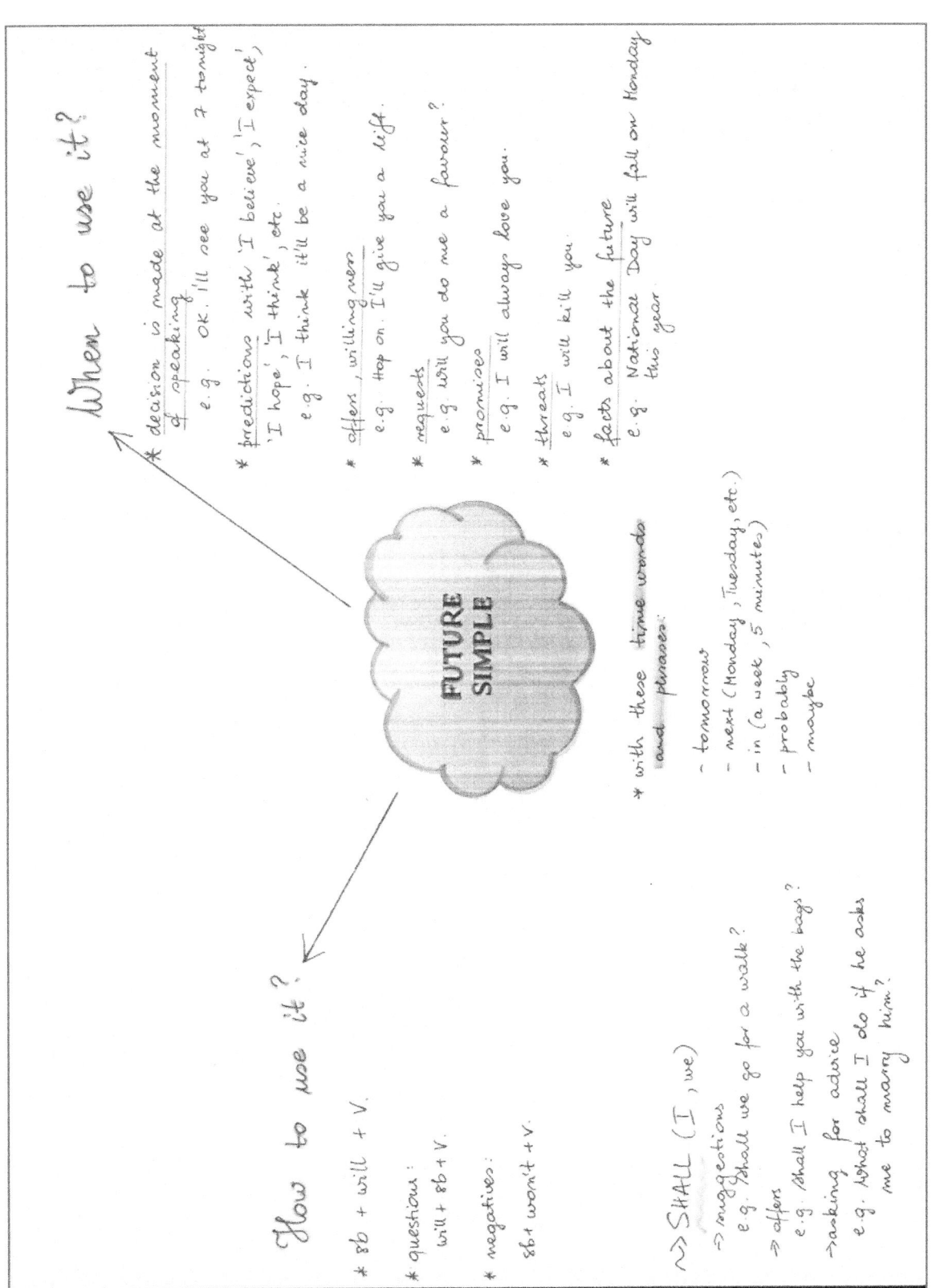

FUTURE SIMPLE

* with these time words and phrases:
  - tomorrow
  - next (Monday, Tuesday, etc.)
  - in (a week, 5 minutes)
  - probably
  - maybe

How to use it?

* sb + will + V.

* questions:
  will + sb + V.

* negatives:
  sb + won't + V.

↝ SHALL (I, we)
  → suggestions
    e.g. Shall we go for a walk?
  → offers
    e.g. Shall I help you with the bags?
  → asking for advice
    e.g. What shall I do if he asks me to marry him?

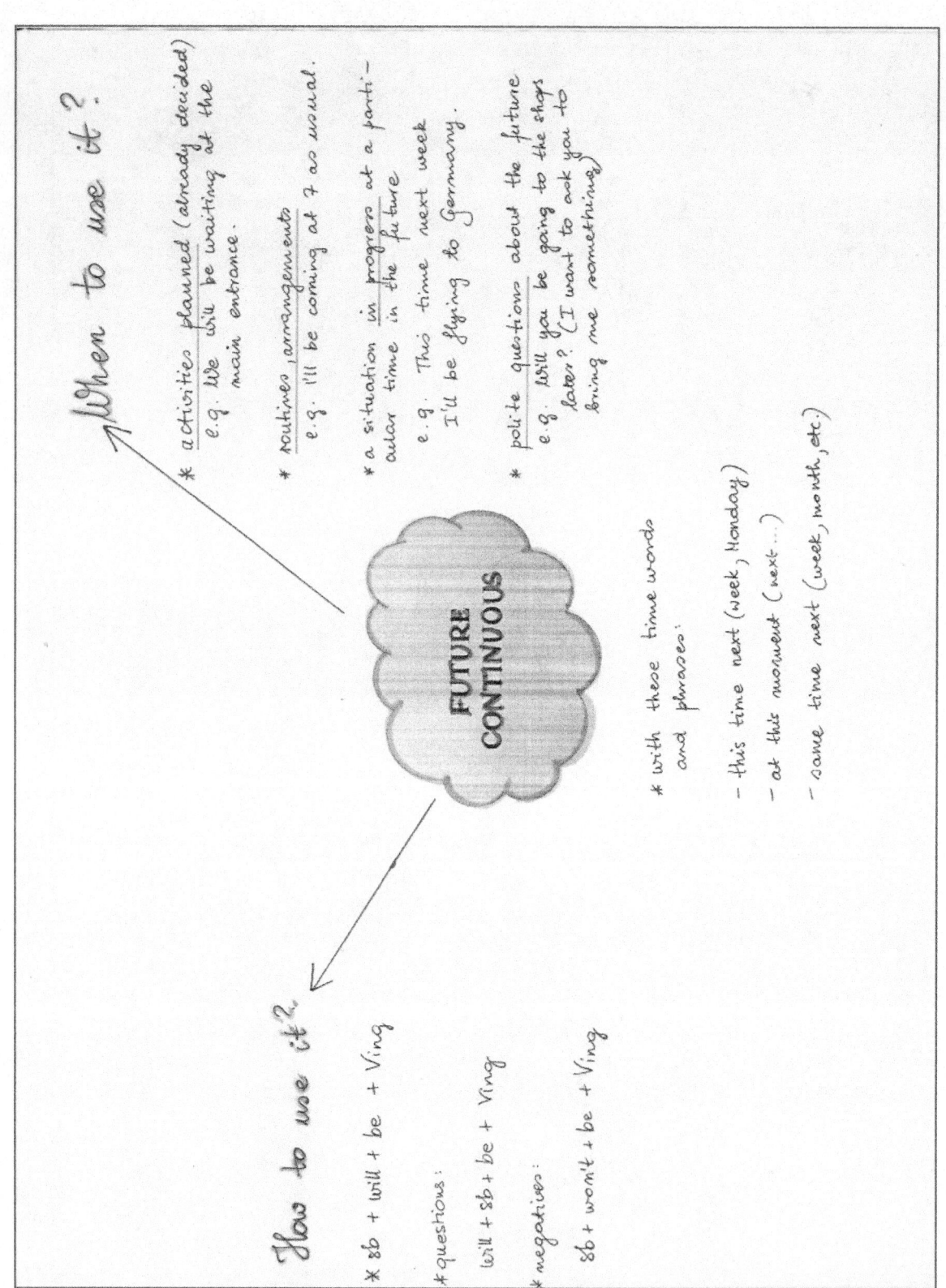

When to use it?

* activities planned (already decided)
e.g. We will be waiting at the
main entrance.

* routines, arrangements
e.g. I'll be coming at 7 as usual.

* a situation in progress at a particular time in the future
e.g. This time next week
I'll be flying to Germany.

* polite questions about the future
e.g. Will you be going to the shops
later? (I want to ask you to
bring me something)

FUTURE CONTINUOUS

How to use it?

* sb + will + be + Ving

* questions:
Will + sb + be + Ving

* negatives:
sb + won't + be + Ving

* with these time words
and phrases:

– this time next (week, Monday)
– at this moment (next ...)
– same time next (week, month, etc.)

410

When to use it?

* sth will be done (finished) at a time in the future
  e.g. I'll have finished this book by next Tuesday.

* we look back at from a future point
  e.g. By the end of the month, I'll have been working for this company for a year.

* to express an assumption
  e.g. You won't have heard the news, of course. (= I assume you haven't heard the news)

FUTURE PERFECT

How to use it?

* sb + will + have + past participle
  (reg = started
  (irr = known)

* questions:
  will + sb + have + past participle

* negatives:
  sb + won't + have + past participle

* with these time words and phrases:
  - by...
  - before
  - when
  - in... time

When to use it?

* completed action in the future,
  with the emphasis on duration
  e.g. This time next year, I will
  have been living here for 6
  years.

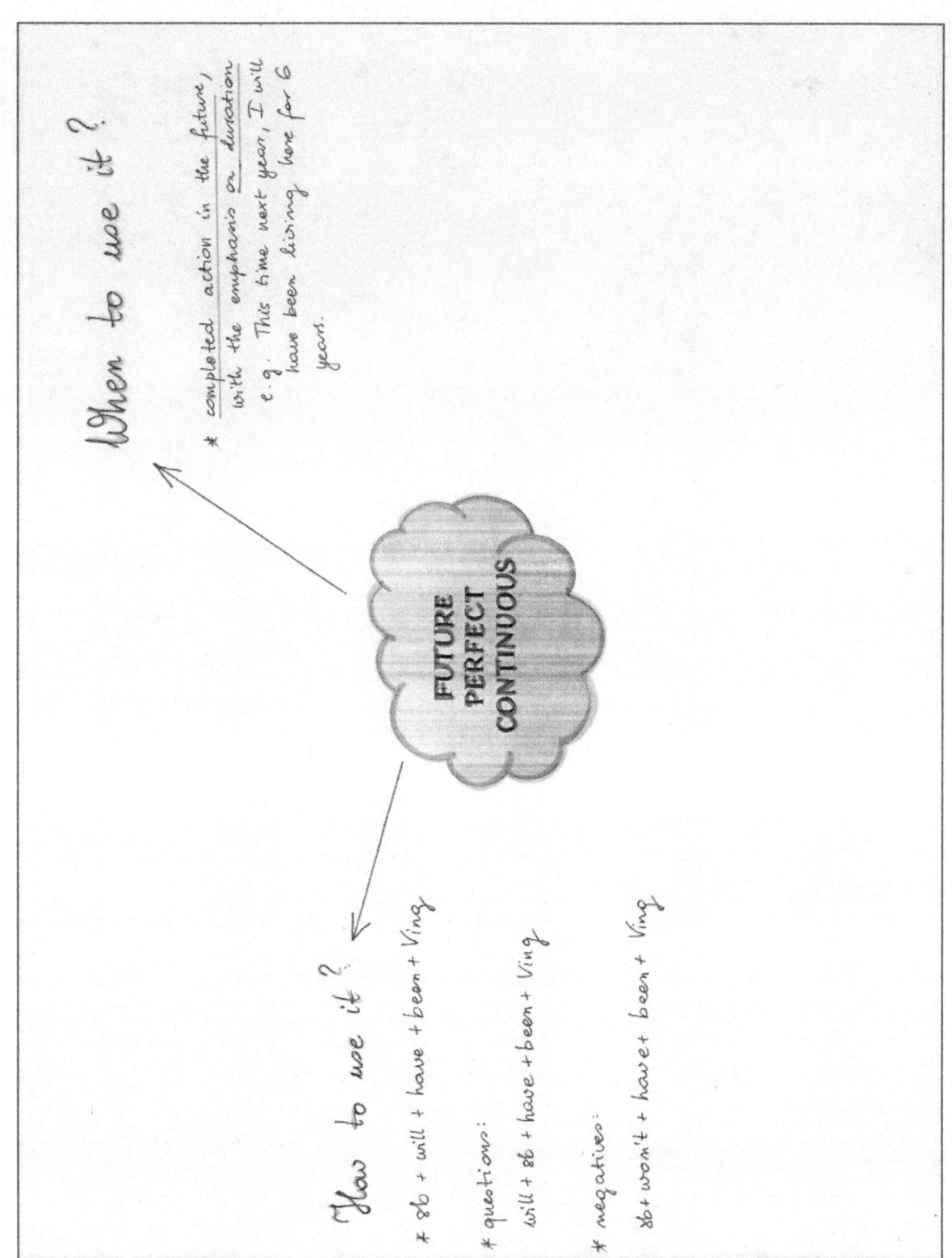

FUTURE PERFECT CONTINUOUS

How to use it?

* sb + will + have + been + Ving

* questions:
  will + sb + have + been + Ving

* negatives:
  sb + won't + have + been + Ving

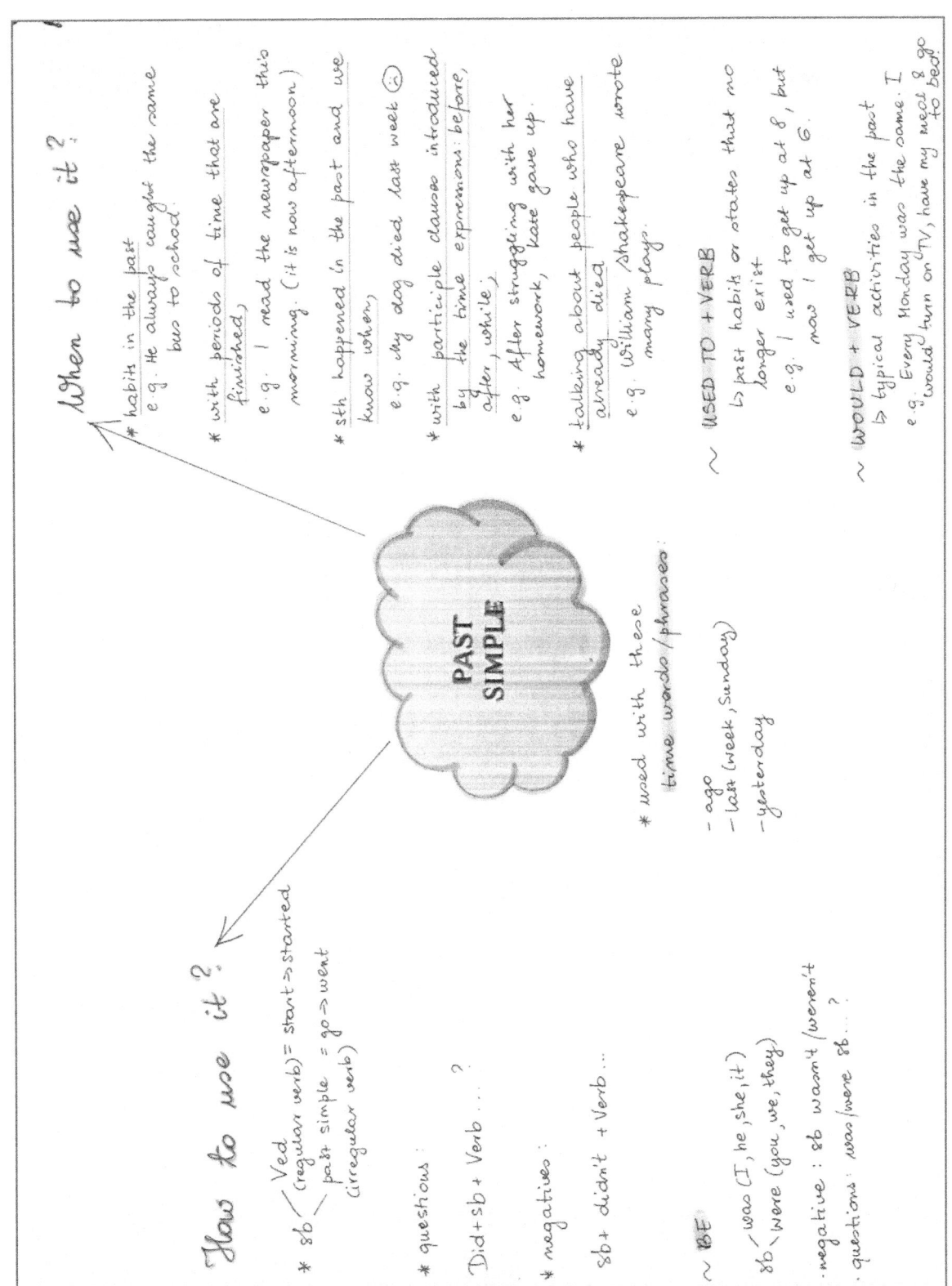

When to use it?

* habits in the past
  e.g. He always caught the same bus to school.

* with periods of time that are finished
  e.g. I read the newspaper this morning. (it is now afternoon)

* sth happened in the past and we know when
  e.g. My dog died last week ☹

* with participle clauses introduced by the time expressions: before, after, while;
  e.g. After struggling with her homework, Kate gave up.

* talking about people who have already died
  e.g. William Shakespeare wrote many plays.

~ USED TO + VERB
  ↳ past habits or states that no longer exist
  e.g. I used to get up at 8, but now I get up at 6.

~ WOULD + VERB
  ↳ typical activities in the past
  e.g. Every Monday was the same. I would turn on TV, have my meal & go to bed.

PAST SIMPLE

How to use it?

* sb < Ved (regular verb) = start → started
       past simple = go → went (irregular verb)

* questions:
  Did + sb + Verb .....?

* negatives:
  sb + didn't + Verb...

~ BE
  sb < was (I, he, she, it)
       were (you, we, they)
  . negative: sb wasn't/weren't .....?
  . questions: was/were sb .....?

* used with these time words/phrases:
  - ago
  - last (week, Sunday)
  - yesterday

413

When to use it?

* action in progress in the past
  e.g I was watching TV at 8 o'clock
  last night.

* to give background information
  e.g. It was raining heavily and
  I was wondering what to eat

* together with Past Simple to say
  that something happened
  in the middle of something else
  e.g. I was sleeping when you
  called.

* with 'think', 'hope', 'wonder'
  to give a polite or uncertain
  meaning
  e.g. I was hoping you would
  join me at the café tonight

* changing states
  e.g. The car was getting worse
  all the time.

* to criticize repeated actions
  e.g. When I was at school, I was
  always losing things.

* unfulfilled past events (sth that
  didn't happen)
  e.g. I was thinking of going
  to Italy this year, but I haven't
  decided.

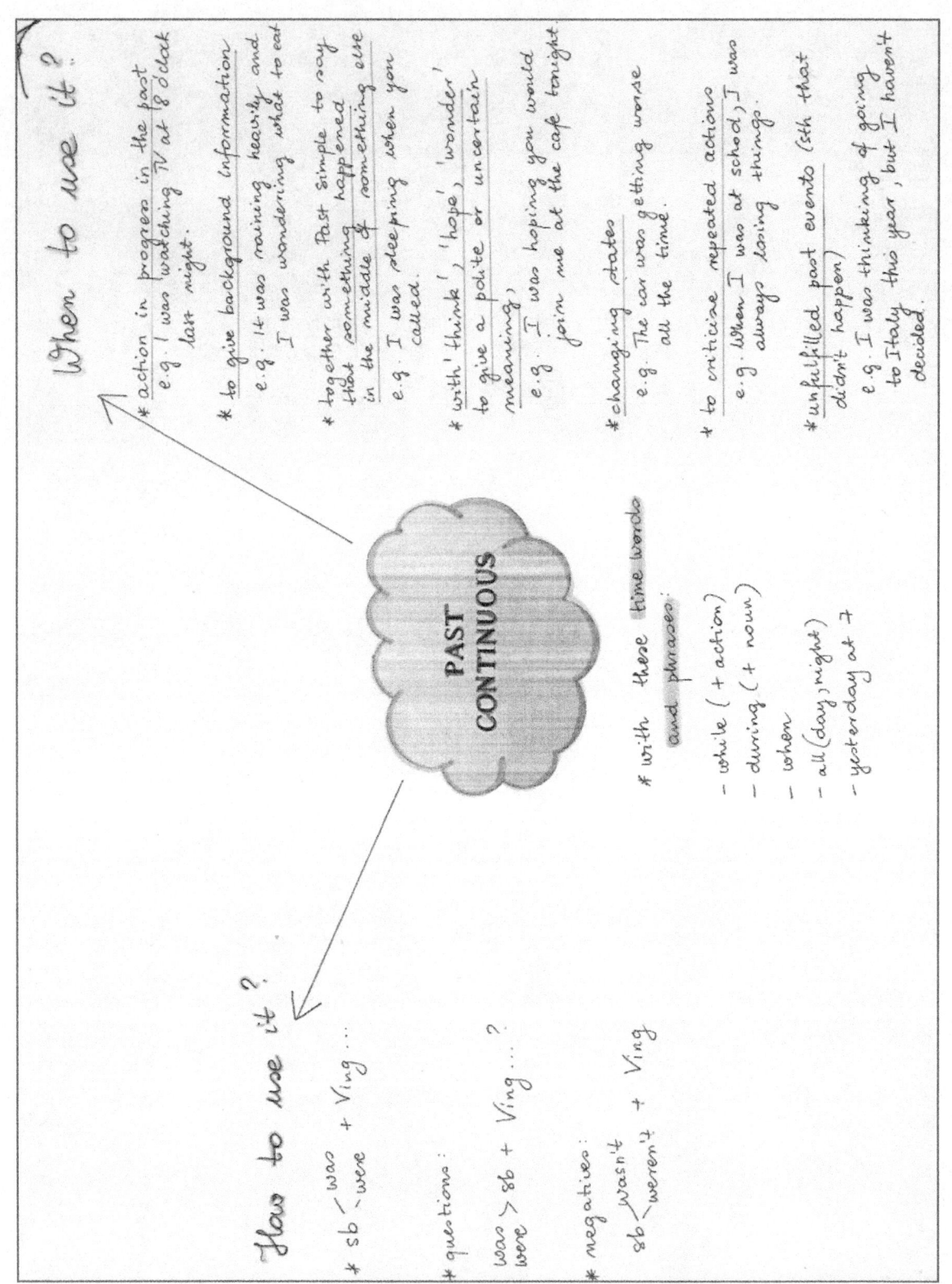

PAST CONTINUOUS

with these time words
and phrases:

- while (+ action)
- during (+ noun)
- when
- all (day, night)
- yesterday at +

How to use it?

* sb - was + Ving....
     - were

questions:
was > sb + Ving....?
were

* negatives:
sb - wasn't + Ving
   - weren't

414

How to use it?

* sb + V.

he
she ⟩ + Vs/Ves
it

* questions:

Do + sb + V.....?
Does + he/she/it + V.....?

* negatives:

sb + don't + V.
he/she/it + doesn't + V.

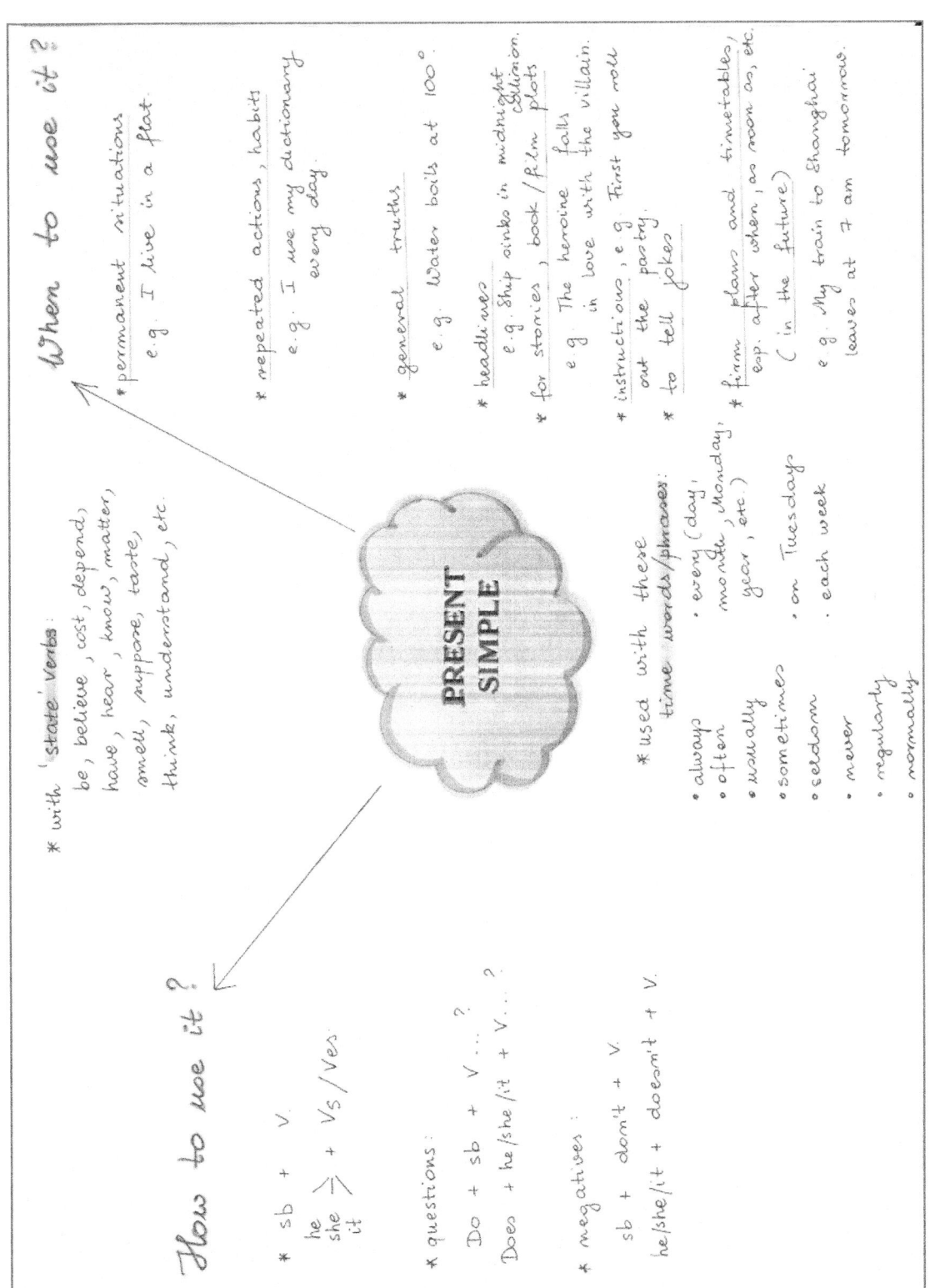

PRESENT SIMPLE

* used with these time words/phrases:

○ always
○ often   ○ every (day, month, monday, year, etc.)
○ usually
○ sometimes   ○ on Tuesdays
○ seldom
            ○ each week
○ never
○ regularly
○ normally

When to use it?

* permanent situations
  e.g. I live in a flat.

* repeated actions, habits
  e.g. I use my dictionary every day.

* general truths
  e.g. Water boils at 100°.

* headlines
  e.g. Ship sinks in midnight collision.

* for stories, book/film plots
  e.g. The heroine falls in love with the villain.

* instructions, e.g. First you roll out the pastry.
  to tell jokes

* firm plans and timetables/esp. after when, as soon as, etc.
  (in the future)
  e.g. My train to Shanghai leaves at 7 am tomorrow.

* with 'state verbs':
  be, believe, cost, depend, have, hear, know, matter, smell, suppose, taste, think, understand, etc.

415

When to use it?

* to talk about a **past event** which happened before **another past event**
  e.g. When I had done my shopping, I went back home.
  (past before past)

* in indirect speech when reporting the Past Simple or Present Perfect
  e.g. 'I have found the answer'
  →becomes: 'She told us she had found the answer.'

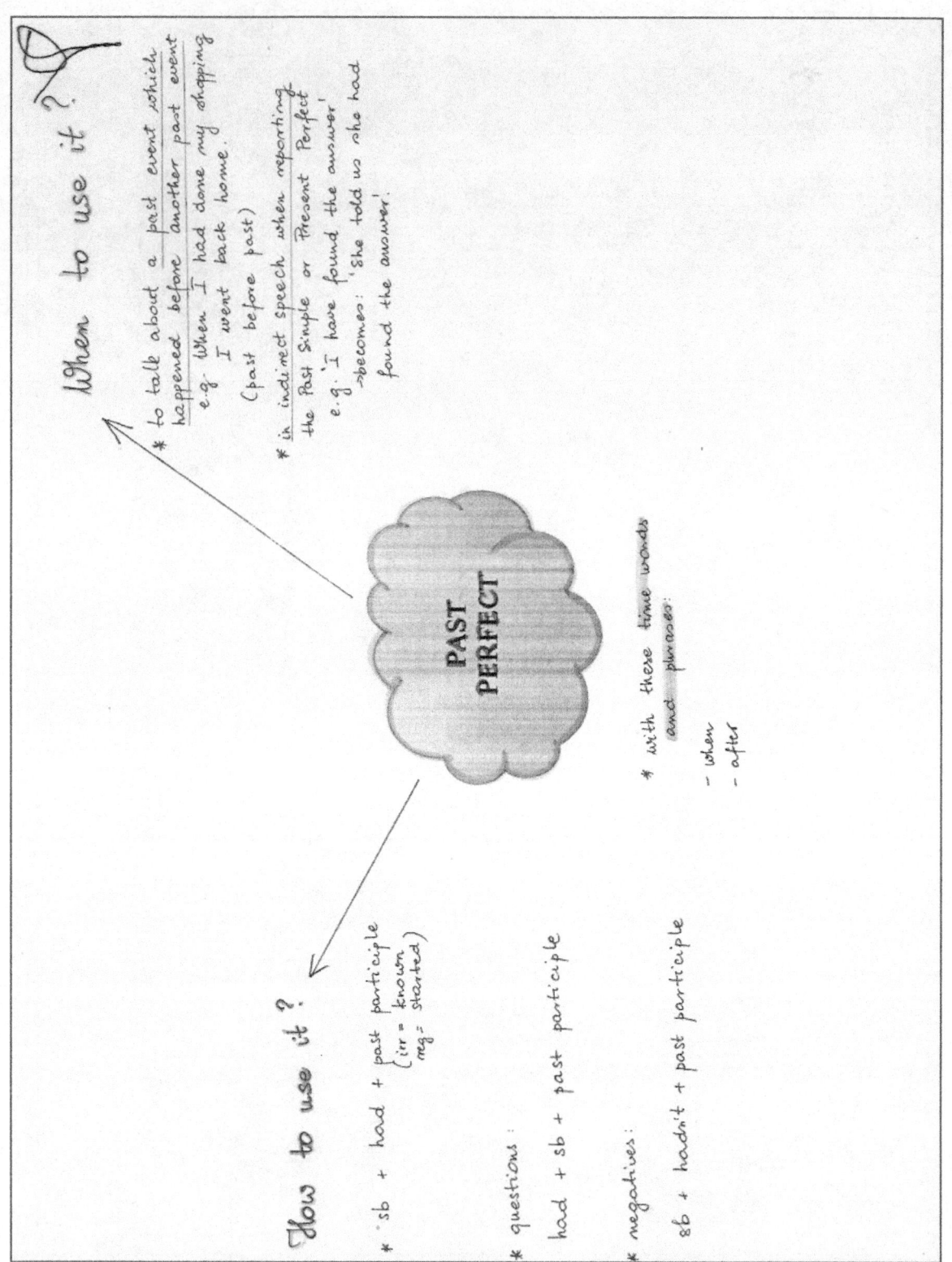

PAST PERFECT

How to use it?

* sb + had + past participle
  (irr = known
  reg = started)

* questions:
  had + sb + past participle

* negatives:
  sb + hadn't + past participle

* with these time words and phrases:
  - when
  - after

416

PRESENT CONTINUOUS

When to use it?

* temporary situations
  e.g. I'm studying at Hangzhou No 4 High School

* something is changing, developing
  e.g. The weather's getting warmer these days.

* actions happening at the moment of speaking (action in progress)
  e.g. You're walking too fast. I can't keep up.

* annoying habits with 'always'
  e.g. You're always borrowing money.

* plans for 100% in the future
  e.g. I'm having dinner with Tom tomorrow at 6 pm.

How to use it?

* sb + is / are + Ving

* questions:
  Is / Are + sb + Ving....?

* negatives:
  sb + isn't / aren't + Ving

* with 'state' verbs, but active meaning
  have : We are having a gripping talk.
  be : You are being crazy.
  think : What are you thinking about?
  taste : My mum is tasting the soup now.
  feel : I'm feeling groggy.
  appear : My favourite singer is appearing in tz this week.

* used with these time words/phrases:
  - now
  - at the moment
  - currently
  - at present
  - nowadays
  - today
  - tonight
  - presently
  - this (year, term, etc.)
  - these days
  - next (Friday, weekend)
  - constantly

When to use it?

* sth had been in progress up to the time in the past we are talking about

e.g. They had been climbing for 5 hours before they reached the top of the mountain.

~ the same contrast as between Past Simple & Past Continuous

~> the emphasis is on the duration

PAST PERFECT CONTINUOUS

How to use it?

* sb + had + been + Ving

* questions:
   had + sb + been + Ving

* negatives:
   sb + hadn't + been + Ving

* with these time words and phrases:

   – when
   – after

When to use it?

* action started in the past and continue up to the moment of speaking
  - e.g. I've been waiting for 2 hours.

* emphasis is on the duration
  - e.g. I've been doing my homework for hours.

* action is incomplete
  - e.g. I've been reading 'Hamlet' (= I haven't finished it yet.)

* with questions starting with 'How long...'
  - e.g. How long have you been studying English?

* with verbs: 'wait', 'sit', 'lie', 'stay'
  - e.g. I've been sitting here for ages.

PRESENT PERFECT CONTINUOUS

* used with these time phrases and words:
  - already   - for(+ period)
  - yet   - since (+ point)
  - still
  - never
  - ever
  - so far
  - lately

How to use it?

* sb < has (he, she, it) / have > + been + Ving

* questions:
  has > sb + been + Ving
  have

* negatives:
  sb + hasn't / haven't + been + Ving

When to use it?

* to report predictions in the past
  e.g. I thought it would be
  a tough test.

* to describe typical activities in
  the past
  e.g. Every evening Tom would
  turn on the radio, cook
  dinner and relax.

* repeated actions, not states
  e.g. Every month he would
  buy his wife a bunch
  of roses.

WOULD

How to use it?

* sb + would + V.

* questions:
  would + sb + V.

* negatives:
  sb + wouldn't + V.

420

PRESENT PERFECT

When to use it?

* action/state in the past which has a connection with the present:
  - e.g. They have bought a new car.
    (they can now use it)

* we see the result now
  - e.g. You've spilt the coffee all over my notebook.

* with periods of time that have not finished yet
  - e.g. We've built 20 new houses this year. (it is still this year)

* action/state in the past, but we don't know when it happened.
  - e.g. We've missed the turning.

* recent events
  - e.g. I've left my wallet in the car.

* after: 'It's / This is the first/second ... time ...'
  - e.g. This is the first time I have eaten Thai food.

* life experiences
  - e.g. I haven't travelled a lot.

How to use it?

* sb + have + past participle
  - has → he, she, it
    - started
    - known

* questions:
  - has + sb + past participle
  - have

* negatives:
  - sb + hasn't + past participle
    - haven't

* with time words/phrases:
  - rarely
  - seldom
  - already
  - before
  - ever
  - never
  - recently
  - still
  - yet
  - for (period of time)
  - since (point)
  - lately
  - so far
  - all my life

Printed in Dunstable, United Kingdom